THE ROUGH GUIDE TO

Bolivia

written and researched by

Brendon Griffin, Shafik Meghji and James Read

ROUGH GUIDES

roughguides.com

Contents

INTRODUCTION   4

Where to go   5   Things not to miss   12

When to go   10

BASICS   22

Getting there   23   National parks and reserves   36

Getting around   24   Health   36

Accommodation   28   Crime and personal safety   40

Food and drink   30   Culture and etiquette   42

Fiestas   33   Travel essentials   43

Outdoor activities   34

THE GUIDE   50

1 La Paz   50   5 Santa Cruz and the Eastern
                                             Lowlands   228
2 Lago Titicaca, the cordilleras and
   the Yungas   94   6 The Amazon   268

3 The southern Altiplano   136

4 Sucre, Cochabamba and the
   central valleys   190

CONTEXTS   302

History   303   Books   327

Wildlife and ecology   320   Spanish   329

Music and dance   322

SMALL PRINT & INDEX   334

OPPOSITE ALPACA PREVIOUS PAGE BUS HEADING TOWARDS SORATA

Introduction to
Bolivia

Stretching from the majestic icebound peaks and bleak high-altitude deserts of the Andes to the exuberant rainforests and vast savannahs of the Amazon basin, Bolivia embraces an astonishing range of landscapes and climates. This mystical terrain boasts scores of breathtaking attractions including stark otherworldly salt pans, ancient Inca trails and towering volcanic peaks. Landlocked at the remote heart of South America, Bolivia rewards the adventurous travellers and encompasses everything that outsiders find most exotic and mysterious about the continent.

The country's cultural diversity and ethnic make-up are equally fascinating. Three centuries of colonial rule have left their mark on the nation's language, religion and architecture, but this is essentially little more than a veneer overlying **indigenous cultural traditions** that stretch back long before the arrival of the Spanish. Though superficially embracing the Catholic religion, many Bolivians are equally at home making offerings to the mountain gods or performing other strange rites, such as blessing vehicles with libations of alcohol. And although Spanish is the language of government and business, the streets buzz with the cadences of Aymara, Quechua and more than thirty other **indigenous languages**.

Geographically, Bolivia is dominated by the **Andes**, which march through the west in two parallel chains, each studded with snowcapped peaks; between them stretch the barren, windswept expanses of the **Altiplano**. Reached via a series of lush valleys, the country's lowlands range from dense Amazonian rainforest to vast plains of dry thornbrush and scrub. The **geographical extremes** are fascinating to explore, but can take their toll on travellers. This varied topography supports an extraordinary diversity of **flora and fauna** from condors to pink freshwater dolphins– Parque Nacional Amboró, for example, has over 830 species of bird, more than the US and Canada combined. The country's underdevelopment has in some ways been a blessing for the environment, allowing vast **wilderness areas** to survive in a near-pristine condition.

ABOVE SALAR DE UYUNI **RIGHT** INDIGENOUS BOLIVIAN WOMAN

Though it covers an area the size of France and Spain combined, Bolivia is home to just under ten million people, who are concentrated in a handful of cities founded by the **Spanish**. Some of these, such as Potosí and Sucre, were once amongst the most important settlements in the Americas, but are now half-forgotten backwaters, basking in the memory of past glories and graced by some of the continent's finest colonial architecture. Others, like La Paz and Santa Cruz, have grown enormously, and are now bustling **commercial centres**.

Despite these attractions, Bolivia remains one of South America's least-visited countries. Some blame Queen Victoria, who after a diplomatic incident is said to have crossed the name from a map and declared that "Bolivia does not exist". Among those who have heard a little about Bolivia, meanwhile, it has a reputation for **cocaine trafficking** and **political instability**. These clichéd images have some basis in reality, though the 2006 election of Evo Morales has reduced the instability to a certain extent, and Bolivia remains one of the continent's **safest** countries for travellers. And for those who make it here, the fact that Bolivia – one of the continent's **least expensive** countries – is still not yet on the major tourist routes means you're unlikely to find yourself sharing the experience with hordes of other foreign visitors.

Where to go

Most visitors spend a few days in the fascinating city of **La Paz**, Bolivia's de facto capital (Sucre is its official capital), which combines a dramatic high-altitude setting with a compelling blend of traditional indigenous and modern urban cultures. La Paz is also close

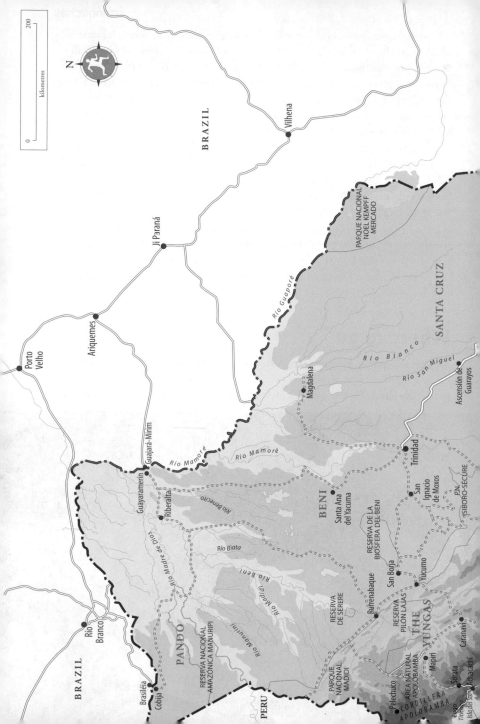

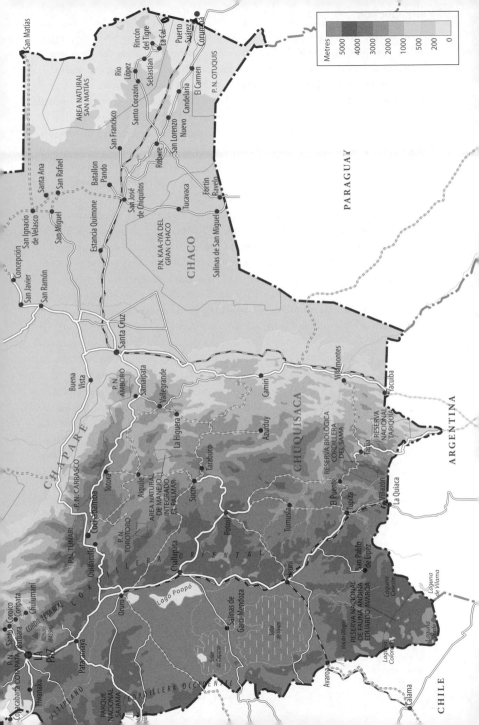

to magical **Lago Titicaca**, the massive azure lake that straddles the Peruvian border, and is a good base for trekking, climbing or mountain biking in the magnificent **Cordillera Real**.

Just north of La Paz the Andes plunge precipitously down into the Amazon basin through the deep, lush valleys of the **Yungas**. The Yungas towns of **Coroico** and **Chulumani** are perfect places to relax, while Coroico also makes a good place to break the overland journey from La Paz to the Bolivian **Amazon**. The best base for visiting the Amazon is the town of **Rurrenabaque**, close to the near-pristine rainforests of **Parque Nacional Madidi** and the wildlife-rich **Río Yacuma**. More adventurous travellers can head east across the wild savannahs of the Llanos de Moxos via the **Reserva de la Bíosfera del Beni** to the regional capital **Trinidad**, the start of exciting trips north along the Río Mamoré towards Brazil or south towards Cochabamba.

South of La Paz, the bleak **southern Altiplano** – stretching between the eastern and western chains of the Andes – is home to some of Bolivia's foremost attractions. The dour mining city of **Oruro** springs to life during its Carnaval, one of South America's most enjoyable fiestas, and the legendary silver mining city of **Potosí** offers a treasure-trove of colonial architecture and the opportunity to visit the Cerro Rico mines.

Further south, Uyuni is the jumping-off point for expeditions into the astonishing landscapes of the **Salar de Uyuni** and the **Reserva de Fauna Andina Eduardo Avaroa**, a remote region of high-altitude deserts and half-frozen, mineral-stained lakes, populated by flamingos. Further south lie the cactus-strewn badlands and canyons around **Tupiza** and the isolated but welcoming city of **Tarija**.

FACT FILE

• They look similar at a glance but alpacas have shorter legs, necks and snouts than llamas, and also have a fluffier fleece.

• Named after Simón Bolívar, Bolivia won its independence in 1825, after nearly three centuries as a Spanish colony.

• In 2001 the highest football match in the world was played on the top of the 6542m Sajama volcano.

• A bridge stretching from Potosí to Spain could reputedly have been built with the silver extracted from the Cerro Rico mines during the colonial period.

• Since independence, Bolivia has lost almost half its territory, including its Pacific coast, which was captured by Chile in 1879. Despite being landlocked, the country still has a navy.

To the north of Potosí, Bolivia's official capital, **Sucre**, boasts fine colonial architecture, but the city is very different in character: charming and refined, it is set in a warm Andean valley in the midst of a region noted for its textiles. Further north, the city of **Cochabamba** has less obvious appeal, but offers a spring-like climate and a friendly welcome. Not far from here are the rainforests and coca fields of the **Chapare region**, but for most travellers Cochabamba is just somewhere to break the journey between La Paz and **Santa Cruz**, the country's eastern capital. Completely different in character to the highland cities, Santa Cruz is a brash, modern and lively tropical metropolis. Though it has few attractions itself, the city is a good base for exploring the **Eastern Lowlands**, including the rainforests of **Parque Nacional Amboró** and the idyllic town of **Samaipata**. Scattered across the lowlands east of Santa Cruz, the immaculately restored **Jesuit missions of Chiquitos** provide one of Bolivia's most

unusual attractions, while a train line heads east to the Brazilian border and the wildlife-rich wetlands of the **Pantanal**. Santa Cruz is also the jumping-off point for trips to the remote and spectacular **Parque Nacional Noel Kempff Mercado**.

When to go

Generally speaking, climate varies much more as a result of altitude and topography than it does between different seasons. Nevertheless, there are clear-cut seasonal differences. **Winter** (*invierno*) runs between May and October: this is the **dry season**, and in many ways the best time to visit, though it's also the high season for tourism, so some prices will be higher and attractions busier. In the **highlands** it's noticeably colder at night, particularly in June and July. The days are slightly shorter, but usually sunny, and the skies crystal clear, making this the best time of year for trekking and climbing. Winter is also the best time for visiting the hot and humid **lowlands**, when temperatures are generally slightly (but pleasantly) lower, although the dry season is less pronounced and rain remains a possibility all year round. A few times a year, usually between July and August, the country is swept by **cold fronts** coming up from Patagonia, known as *surazos*, which can send temperatures plunging even in the Amazon. Towards the end of the dry season in late August and September, farmers set fire to cleared forest areas across much of Bolivia, which can obscure views and cause respiratory problems.

Summer (*verano*) is the **rainy season**, which runs roughly from November to March and is much more pronounced in the lowlands; in the Amazon, road transport becomes pretty much impossible, as huge areas are flooded and everything turns to mud – though, conversely, river transport becomes more frequent. Heat, humidity and mosquitoes are also much worse. In the highlands, particularly the Altiplano, it rains much less and travel is not as restricted, though delays and road closures still occur, while trekking trails get muddier and clouds often obscure views, particularly in the high mountains, where route-finding can become impossible. Despite this, the rainy season is also a very beautiful time in the Andes, as the parched Altiplano and mountainsides are briefly transformed into lush grassland and wild flowers proliferate.

COCA: SACRED LEAF OF THE ANDES

Nothing is more emblematic of Bolivia than **coca**, the controversial leaf that has been cultivated for thousands of years in the Andean foothills. To ordinary Bolivians, coca is at once a useful stimulant to combat hunger and tiredness, a medicine for altitude sickness and a key religious and cultural sacrament with magical powers used in rituals and offerings. To the outside world, however, it is infamous as the raw material for the manufacture of **cocaine** (as well as, reputedly, still a key ingredient of Coca-Cola).

Thousands of farmers depend on coca for their livelihoods, and President Evo Morales – who remains head of the biggest coca-growing union – has repeatedly stressed that the leaf is an intrinsic part of indigenous Andean culture. Although Morales has promised a policy of "zero cocaine but not zero coca", Bolivia remains the world's third-largest producer of the drug, and cocaine use within the country has risen dramatically in recent years. In 2011 the country renounced a **UN anti-drug convention** because it classified the coca leaf as an illegal drug.

Author picks

Despite enduring floods, several street protests, vehicle breakdowns and innumerable mosquito bites, Rough Guides authors covered every corner of Bolivia for this new edition, from the enchanting Isla del Sol to the untamed rainforests of the Amazon region. Aside from the major sights, here are their personal picks…

Sacred drink of the Incas No visit to Bolivia is complete without a glass or two of thick, tart and mildly alcoholic *chicha* – the Cochabamba Valley is particularly famous for it. p.219

Most extreme experience Once a source of fabled wealth, the Cerro Rico mines now offer a chance to see first-hand the almost medieval working conditions that miners still endure. p.162

Most spectacular flight The spectacular La Paz–Rurrenabaque flight whisks you from snow-capped mountains to verdant Amazonian rainforests. p.276

Tastiest local dish It may not be particularly sophisticated, but after a tough day on the road, sometimes only a *pique a lo macho* (a heaped plate of fried beef strips, sausages, chips or potatoes, onions, tomatoes and chillies) will do. p.32

Killer views The views of La Paz that open up as you crest the rim of the Altiplano and begin to descend into the city will take your breath away. p.52.

Off the tourist trail The stunningly remote Parque Nacional Noel Kempff Mercado boasts dramatic scenery that inspired Sir Arthur Conan Doyle's *The Lost World*. p.262

Best ice cream *Villa Bonita*'s idyllic garden café in Coroico serves Bolivia's finest *helado*, specializing in unusual flavours like lavender and *hierba buena* (a type of mint). p.127

Our author recommendations don't end here. We've flagged up our favourite places – a perfectly sited hotel, an atmospheric café, a special restaurant – throughout the guide, highlighted with the ★ symbol.

18

things not to miss

It's not possible to see everything that Bolivia has to offer in one trip – and we don't suggest you try. What follows, in no particular order, is a selective taste of the country's highlights: outstanding scenery, lively festivals, ancient sites and colonial architecture. Each one has a page reference to take you straight into the guide, where you can find out more.

2

1 PARQUE NACIONAL MADIDI
Page 281
Covering nearly nineteen thousand square kilometres, this park is home to some of the most diverse plant and animal life in South America.

2 SALAR DE UYUNI
Page 169
A vast, perfectly flat expanse of dazzling white surrounded by high mountain peaks, the Salar de Uyuni is the world's biggest salt lake and, perhaps, Bolivia's most extraordinary attraction.

3 TIWANAKU
Page 89
One of the cradles of Andean civilization, and once the centre of a massive empire, Tiwanaku is among South America's most intriguing archeological sites.

3

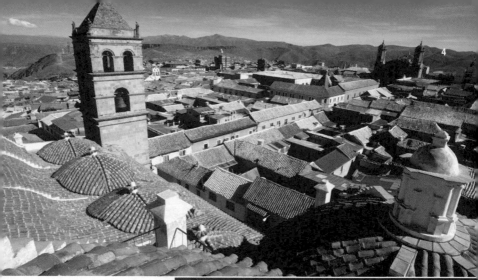

4 POTOSÍ
Page 150

The highest city in the world, the legendary silver-mining centre of Potosí boasts some of the finest Spanish colonial architecture on the continent.

5 PINK RIVER DOLPHINS
Page 282

Frolicking pink freshwater dolphins are a fairly common sight in the rivers of the Bolivian Amazon. You can even swim alongside them.

6 FOLK MUSIC AND DANCE
Page 322

Far more than just panpipes, Bolivian folk music and dance is as vibrant and varied as the country itself.

7 ORURO CARNAVAL
Page 143

One of South America's most colourful fiestas, during which thousands of costumed dancers parade through the streets and revellers indulge in heavy drinking and indiscriminate water fighting.

8 LA PAZ
Page 52

Nestled in a deep canyon at an altitude of over 3500m, Bolivia's de facto capital is the highest in the world, and a fascinating melting-pot of modern urban and traditional Aymara cultures.

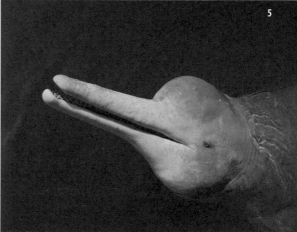

9

10

11

9 RESERVA DE FAUNA ANDINA EDUARDO AVAROA
Page 171
This starkly beautiful reserve is a haven for rare Andean wildlife.

10 MERCADO DE HECHICERIA
Page 61
La Paz's Witches' Market offers a fascinating insight into the secretive world of Aymara mysticism and herbal medicine.

11 BIKING DOWN THE WORLD'S MOST DANGEROUS ROAD
Page 124
The perilous highway from La Paz to Coroico is among the world's most spectacular, plunging from the Andes to the lush upper Amazon.

12 SALTEÑAS
Page 31
Pastry parcels filled with a rich stew of meat and vegetables, *salteñas* are an ideal mid-morning snack.

13 INCA TRAILS
Page 128
The Choro, Takesi and Yunga Cruz trails – the three so-called "Inca trails" – descend from the icebound peaks of the Cordillera Real to the subtropical Yungas.

12

13

14 ANDEAN TEXTILES
Page 85

The traditional weavings of indigenous highland communities are among the finest expressions of Andean culture.

15 THE JESUIT MISSIONS OF CHIQUITOS
Page 252

The Jesuit mission churches offer a splash of incongruous splendour and historical intrigue in the wilderness.

16 ISLA DEL SOL
Page 106

Isla del Sol is the spiritual centre of the Andean world, revered as the place where the sun and moon were created.

17 SUCRE
Page 195

Known as the White City, Bolivia's capital is a jewel of colonial architecture and a lively university city that combines serene dignity with a provincial charm.

18 MOUNTAIN CLIMBING
Page 35

With six peaks over 6000m Bolivia is a paradise for experienced mountaineers. Novices can arrange a guided climb up 6090m Huayna Potosí.

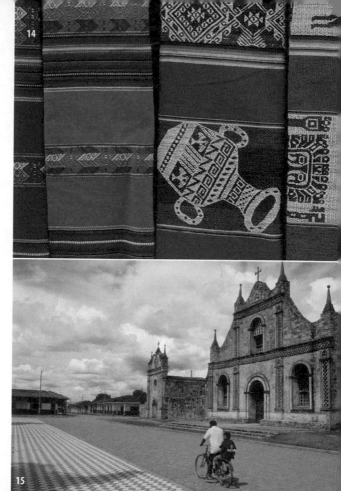

14

15

16

Itineraries

The following itineraries feature a mix of popular and off-the-beaten-path attractions, taking you right across the country, from Inca trails through Andean scenery to boat trips down wildlife-rich Amazonian waterways. Given the distances involved, you may not be able to complete the full lists. But even doing a partial itinerary – or mixing and matching elements from different ones – will give you a wonderful insight into Bolivia's stunning diversity.

THE GRAND TOUR

This four- to five-week trip takes in dramatic Andean landscapes, colonial cities and former Jesuit missions, colourful fiestas, ancient sites and Amazonian rainforests.

❶ La Paz The world's highest de facto capital city is also one of its most compelling, a riot of indigenous colour, vertiginous markets and street protests. See p.52

❷ Tiwanaku Though a mere fraction of this iconic pre-Columbian, pre-Incan city has been excavated, its mysterious, monumental slabs of sandstone are a must-see. See p.89

❸ Lago Titicaca A vast, striking blue expanse standing at 3810m, the lake is dotted with sacred islands and surrounded by snow-capped mountains. See p.98

❹ Salar de Uyuni and the Reserva de Fauna Andina Eduardo Avaroa Best visited together, the world's largest salt lake and this stunning high-altitude reserve have a desolate, otherworldly beauty. See p.169

❺ Potosí The highest city on earth has a tragic history, stunningly preserved colonial architecture and a legendary silver mine. See p.150

❻ Sucre Bolivia's most appealing city has a welcoming atmosphere, atmospheric whitewashed buildings, leafy plazas, and a year-round spring-like climate. See p.195

❼ The Jesuit missions of Chiquitos These Jesuit-founded towns in remote eastern Bolivia boast a series of stunning churches and a fascinating history. See p.252

❽ Rurrenabaque and the Amazon Perfectly sited on the Río Beni, buzzing Rurrenabaque has the biodiverse wonders of the Amazon on its doorstep. See p.274

NATURE AND WILDLIFE

For travellers who want to explore the country's stunning natural diversity, this three-and-a-half-week tour takes in the country's key national parks and protected areas.

❶ Yungas, Cordillera Real and Cordillera Apolobamba This Andean region is home to several excellent treks along pre-Columbian trails. See p.123

❷ Salar de Uyuni and Reserva de Fauna Andina Eduardo Avaroa Blindingly white lakes of salt, volcanic peaks and colonies of flamingos are just a few of the attractions at these two protected areas. See p.169

❸ Cordillera de Chichas A stark landscape of cactus-strewn badlands and canyons, evocative of the Wild West. See p.178

❹ Parque Nacional Amboró This park is home to over 830 different types of birds – the highest number of any protected area in the world – including the cock-of-the-rock. See p.241

⑤ Parque Nacional Noel Kempff Mercado
Remote, inaccessible and truly spectacular, this national park is a lost world of diverse ecosystems and abundant animal and bird life. **See p.262**

⑥ Parque Nacional Madidi Perhaps Bolivia's most famous national park, Madidi is readily accessible and amazingly biodiverse –the flora and fauna includes pink river dolphins. **See p.281**

INDIGENOUS CULTURE AND SPANISH COLONIALISM

This two-week tour allows you to explore Bolivia's cultural, artistic and musical diversity, as well as its distinct Spanish colonial heritage.

❶ Mercado de Hechicería, La Paz The outlandish Witches' Market offers a fascinating window onto the arcane world of Aymara folk medicine, with a bizarre array of wares. **See p.64**

❷ Peña A late-night showcase for traditional Andean music, performed on instruments such as charango, zampoña and quena, *peñas* have long been a La Paz institution. **See p.85**

❸ Tiwanaku The ancient ruins of Tiwanaku offer a tantalizing insight into the mysterious civilization that once had its centre in today's Aymara heartlands. **See p.89**

❹ Isla del Sol and Isla de la Luna, Lake Titicaca These sacred islands, considered the birthplace of the sun and the moon, were once among the most important religious sites in the Andean world. **See p.106 and 111**

❺ Casa Real de la Moneda, Potosí The country's former royal mint, now its finest museum, has an outstanding collection of colonial religious art. **See p.154**

❻ Sucre An evocative cluster of churches, monasteries and mansions, as well as a fascinating museum showcasing indigenous textiles. **See p.195**

❼ San Ignacio de Moxos This Amazonian former mission town has as rich a musical heritage as it does a religious one, with an archive of antique scores and a thriving Baroque music school. **See p.284**

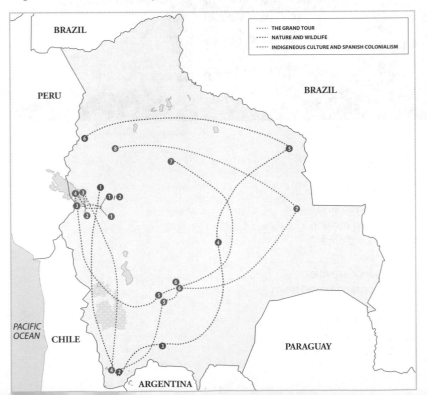

SUNDAY MARKET IN TARABUCO

Basics

23 Getting there
24 Getting around
28 Accommodation
30 Food and drink
33 Fiestas
34 Outdoor activities
36 National parks and reserves
36 Health
40 Crime and personal safety
42 Culture and etiquette
43 Travel essentials

Getting there

There are relatively few flights to Bolivia. At present, the only direct services to the country depart from Miami in the US, Madrid in Spain and from neighbouring South American countries – the most frequent connections are from São Paulo in Brazil, Buenos Aires in Argentina and Lima in Peru. In Bolivia itself the main international airports are in Santa Cruz and in the capital La Paz. The only alternative to flying is to make your way to South America and travel overland.

Airfares to Bolivia reflect the lack of competition, and are comparatively high. Prices depend on the season: high season runs from July to August and during Christmas and Easter; fares drop during the shoulder seasons (May–June & Sept–Oct) and even more during low season (Jan–April & Nov to late Dec).

Flights from the US and Canada

If you are travelling to Bolivia **from the US**, there are direct flights **from Miami** with American Airlines (Ⓦaa.com) and the Bolivian airline AeroSur (Ⓦwww .aerosur.com) to La Paz and Santa Cruz. Both routes take approximately seven hours and usually cost $800–950 return. Note that AeroSur flights, both international and domestic, are often delayed and standards on board are variable to say the least. There are regular daily flights to Miami from all major US cities. Alternatively, it's possible to fly from other US cities to another South American city (such as São Paulo, Buenos Aires or Lima) with an airline like Delta (Ⓦdelta.com) and then transfer onto a flight to Bolivia; travelling via this route costs around $1100 return. Passengers **from Canada** will have to fly via the US and connect with a flight to South America from there.

Flights from the UK and Ireland

There are no direct flights from Britain or Ireland to Bolivia. The most direct routes go **via Madrid, Miami**, **Buenos Aires** or **São Paulo**, each of which is connected by daily flights from London; British Airways (Ⓦbritishairways.com) flies to each of these destinations, and there are numerous other options for both Miami and Madrid; a return journey costs from around £1000. The most convenient services are the twice-weekly Aerosur (Ⓦwww.aerosur.com) flights between Madrid and

Santa Cruz, from where there are connections throughout Bolivia. However, this route is notorious for delays and poor service. The most convenient routings **from Ireland** all entail flying through London. Another option is Air Europa (Ⓦaireuropa.com), which has flights from London via Madrid to Buenos Aires and Lima, from where you can take a connecting flight.

Flights from Australia and New Zealand

The fastest way to reach South America **from Australasia** is to fly with either Qantas (Ⓦqantas .com) or Aerolineas Argentina (Ⓦaerolineas.com) from Sydney or Auckland **to Buenos Aires**, in Argentina, from where there are onward services to La Paz and Santa Cruz on Aerosur. The journey costs around Aus$2000 return. It is also possible to fly to **Santiago** in Chile via Tahiti and Easter Island with Qantas and LAN (Ⓦlan.com), but this route is significantly longer and involves lengthy stopovers. Alternatively, you can fly **via the US** from both Australia and New Zealand with an airline like Qantas or Air New Zealand (Ⓦairnewzealand.com).

Travelling overland from neighbouring countries

You can enter Bolivia **by land** on regular bus services from all five of the countries with which it shares a border – **Peru**, **Brazil**, **Chile**, **Argentina** and **Paraguay** – which makes the country easy to include in a wider South American trip.

Crossing the Peruvian border

The most widely used route – and also the easiest – is from **Puno** in Peru on the west shore of Lago Titicaca, via the **Kasani** border crossing near Copacabana or **Desaguadero**, south of the lake (see p.101); both crossings are an easy bus ride (around 4hr) away from La Paz.

A BETTER KIND OF TRAVEL

At Rough Guides we are passionately committed to travel. We feel that travelling is the best way to understand the world we live in and the people we share it with – plus tourism has brought a great deal of benefit to developing economies around the world over the last few decades. But the growth in tourism has also damaged some places irreparably, and climate change is exacerbated by most forms of transport, especially flying. All Rough Guides' trips are carbon-offset, and every year we donate money to a variety of charities devoted to combating the effects of climate change.

Crossing the Brazilian border

From Brazil, the main entrance point is at **Quijarro** (see p.265), in the far east of Bolivia close to the Brazilian city of **Corumbá**, which is the main base for visiting the Pantanal region and also well connected to the rest of the country. From Quijarro you can travel to **Santa Cruz** by train (13hr 30min–18hr 35min). There's another minor land crossing from Brazil in the far east of Bolivia at **San Matías**, a day's bus journey from the town of San Ignacio in Chiquitania (see p.259). You can also enter Bolivia from Brazil at several points along the northern border in Amazonia, most notably from **Brasiléia to Cobija** (see p.299) and **Guajarámerim to Guayaramerin**.

Crossing the Chilean border

From Chile there are three main routes, all of them passing through spectacular Andean scenery. You can travel to La Paz by bus along the well-paved road from Arica on the Pacific Coast via the border crossing of **Tambo Quemado** (see p.142); take the weekly train from **Calama** in Chile to **Uyuni** via Avaroa (see p.167); or cross the border at **Laguna Verde** in the far south of the Reserva Eduardo Avaroa on a jeep tour organized from the Chilean town of **San Pedro de Atacama**, a route which will bring you to Uyuni (see p.167).

Crossing the Argentinian border

From Argentina there are two straightforward crossings: from **La Quiaca** in Argentina to Villazón in the southern Altiplano (see p.181), from where there are road and rail connections north to Tupiza, Uyuni and Oruro; and from **Pocitos** in Argentina to Yacuiba in the Chaco (see p.267), from where you can travel by road and rail north to Santa Cruz or by road west to Tarija. There's also a minor crossing at **Bermejo**, south of Tarija (see p.184).

Crossing the Paraguayan border

In the dry season (May–Sept) you can enter Bolivia on the arduous bus journey from Asunción in the south of Paraguay to Santa Cruz (roughly 1000km/24hr).

AGENTS AND OPERATORS

Adventure Life ☎ 1-8003446118, Ⓦ adventure-life.com. Small, personal organization with a community focus. Trips include a nine-day tour taking in the Oruro Carnaval.

Andean Treks ☎ 1-8006838148, Ⓦ andeantreks.com. Camping and trekking tours to Bolivia that also take in Peru or Chile.

Audley Travel ☎ 01993838650, Ⓦ audleytravel.com. Classy tailor-made trips including two- and three-week tours of Bolivia, visiting La Paz, Potosí, Sucre, Santa Cruz and the Salar de Uyuni.

ebookers UK ☎ 0800082 3000, Ⓦ ebookers.com, Republic of Ireland ☎ 01488 3507, Ⓦ ebookers.ie. Low fares on an extensive selection of scheduled flights and package deals.

Explore Bolivia ☎ 8777088810, Ⓦ explorebolivia.com. Bolivian travel experts with an extensive range of activity and nature trips – including whitewater rafting on the Río Tuichi, kayaking and mountain biking – and an emphasis on visiting remote places.

North South Travel UK ☎ 01245608291, Ⓦ northsouthtravel .co.uk. Friendly, competitive travel agency that offers discounted fares worldwide. Profits are used to support projects in the developing world, especially the promotion of sustainable tourism.

On the Go Tours ☎ 0207311 1113, Ⓦ onthegotours.com. Runs an eleven-day tour that takes in La Paz, Sucre, Potosí and the Salar de Uyuni.

STA Travel US ☎ 18007814040, UK ☎ 08712300040, Australia ☎ 134 STA, New Zealand ☎ 0800474 400, SA ☎ 0861781 781, Ⓦ statravel.com. Worldwide specialists in independent travel. Also offers good discounts for students and under-26s.

Trailfinders UK ☎ 0845058 5858, Republic of Ireland ☎ 01677 7888, Australia ☎ 1300780 212, Ⓦ trailfinders.com. One of the best-informed and most efficient agents for independent travellers.

Getting around

Bolivia's topography, size and lack of basic infrastructure means that getting around is often a challenge. The majority of Bolivia's road network is unpaved, and most main roads are in a poor condition. However, travelling through the country's varied and stunning landscapes is also one of the most enjoyable aspects of a visit to Bolivia, and the pleasure of many places lies as much in the getting there as in the destination itself.

Most Bolivians travel by **bus**, as these go pretty much everywhere and are extremely good value. When there are no buses, they often travel on **camiones** (lorries), which are slower, much less comfortable and only slightly cheaper, but often go to places no other transport reaches. The much-reduced **train** network covers only a small fraction of the country, but offers a generally more comfortable and sedate (though not necessarily faster or more reliable) service. In parts of the Amazon lowlands **river boats** are still the main means of getting around.

Though few Bolivians can afford it, **air travel** is a great way of saving a day or two of arduous cross-country travel, and most of the major cities are served by regular internal flights. The approximate journey times and frequencies of all services are given in each chapter, but these should be treated with caution to say the least: the idea of a fixed timetable would strike most Bolivians as rather ridiculous. Buying or hiring a **car** is a possibility, but given the state of the roads in many areas and the long distances between towns, it's an adventurous way to travel and doesn't guarantee you'll reach your destination any faster.

By bus

Bolivia's **buses** (also known as *flotas*) are run by a variety of private companies and ply all the main routes in the country, moving passengers at low cost over great distances despite often appalling road conditions.

Cities and larger towns have **bus terminals** – known as *terminales terrestres* or *terminales de buses* – from which buses to most (but often not all) destinations leave. Departing passengers usually have to pay a small fee (Bs1–3) for the use of the terminal.

The terminals often have some kind of **information office**, but even so the number of different companies operating the same route can make it difficult at times to work out departure times and frequencies. If in doubt, taxi drivers usually have a good grasp of the timing of buses to different destinations and where they depart from. For less frequently used routes it's worth buying a **ticket** in advance, but there's no need on busier routes. Buses on many longer-distance routes travel only at night so Bolivian travellers can visit other cities without paying for accommodation.

The major long-distance intercity routes are served by more modern and comfortable buses, often equipped with reclining seats and TVs. Some routes are also served by comparatively luxurious overnight **sleeper-buses** (*bus-camas*), which have extra leg-room and seats that recline horizontally. These cost about fifty percent more, but are well worth it.

Most buses, however, are much older and in poor condition. **Breakdowns** are frequent, but fortunately many drivers are masters of mechanical improvisation. Other than sleeper-buses and some smarter long-distance services, Bolivian buses stop anywhere for anyone, even if they're only travelling a few kilometres, until every available crack of space has been filled.

Because of the poor condition of most roads and many vehicles, you should always be prepared for major **delays**; in the rainy season, buses can arrive days rather than hours late. Most buses stop for regular meal breaks, and food and drink sellers offer their wares at the roadside at every opportunity, but it's worth carrying some food and drink with you. When travelling in the highlands or overnight, you should have **warm clothing** and a blanket or sleeping bag to hand, as it can get bitterly cold, and heated buses are virtually unheard of. If you can, avoid sitting at the back of the bus, as on bumpy roads this is where you'll get bounced around the most.

By plane

Flying in Bolivia is a good way of avoiding exhausting overland journeys and saving time; it's

---

KEEP YOUR BAG SAFE

Unless it's small enough to keep with you inside the bus, your **luggage** will be put on the roof, at the back or in a locked compartment underneath the vehicle. This is usually pretty safe, but it's still worth keeping an eye out at each stop to make sure your bag isn't carried off, whether by accident or design.

With better-organized companies you may be given a **ticket** with which to reclaim your luggage at the end of the journey. Some travellers like to chain their bags to the roof, and you shouldn't be shy about climbing up to check yours if you're feeling nervous about its security. Even if it's under a tarpaulin on the roof or in a **luggage compartment**, it's a good idea to cover your luggage with a **nylon sack** (which you can pick up in any market) to protect it from the elements and the prying fingers of other travellers.

also relatively inexpensive, with most internal flights costing Bs350–700 ($50–100), and offers splendid bird's-eye views of the high Andes or the endless green expanse of the Amazon. **La Paz**, **Santa Cruz**, **Sucre** and **Cochabamba** are all connected by daily flights, and there are also frequent services to **Tarija**, **Trinidad** and a number of remote towns in the **Amazon** and the **Eastern Lowlands**.

The main carriers are currently **AeroSur** (ⓦwww .aerosur.com) and the **state-owned Boliviana de Aviacion** (ⓦboa.bo). A smaller operator, **Amazonas** (ⓦamaszonas.com), operates flights from La Paz, Cochabamba and Santa Cruz to the main towns in the Bolivian Amazon.

The Bolivian air force also operates passenger services under its commercial arm, **Transportes Aereo Militar** (TAM; ⓦtam.bo). TAM is often somewhat cheaper than the other airlines, and flies to some out-of-the-way places not served by the others, as well as between most of the main cities. The busier routes should be booked at least several days in advance, and it's important to **reconfirm** a couple of days before departure, as overbooking is not uncommon. Flights are often cancelled or delayed, and sometimes even leave earlier than scheduled, especially in the Amazon, where the weather can be a problem. **Baggage allowance** on internal flights is usually 15kg, with an additional charge payable on any excess.

Some particularly remote regions, such as the Parque Nacional Noel Kempff Mercado, are also served by **light aircraft**, such as five-seater Cessnas, which are an expensive but exciting way to travel.

By taxi, moto-taxi and micro

Taxis can be found anywhere at any time in almost any town and offer a cheap and safe way to get around. In Bolivia, anyone can turn their car into a taxi just by sticking a sign in the window, and many people in cities work as part-time taxi drivers to supplement their incomes. There are also **radio-taxis**, which are marked as such and can be called by phone; they tend to cost a little more and, in theory at least, are a safer way to travel.

Fares tend to be fixed in each city or town. A trip within any city centre will rarely cost more than Bs15, though there's a tendency to overcharge foreigners, so it's best to agree a price before you set off. Often, fares are charged per passenger rather than for the vehicle as a whole, and it's not unusual to share a taxi with strangers heading in the same general direction. You can also hire taxis by the day; with a little bargaining

this can actually be an inexpensive way of seeing a lot in a short time.

Moto-taxis are motorcycles used as taxis, and are most frequently found in remote cities and towns in the lowlands. In cities like Trinidad, they're by far the most common form of transport. Travelling this way is cheap, fast and only slightly frightening.

Micros are small minibuses that have almost completely replaced larger buses as the main form of urban public transport in Bolivia. A trip in a micro costs a couple of bolivianos or less, and they run with great frequency along fixed routes with their major destinations written on placards on the windscreen and shouted out by the driver's assistant. With extra seats fitted in their already small interiors, they're pretty cramped; if you need extra leg room, try to sit in the front seat next to the driver. Large estate cars – referred to as **trufis** or **colectivos** – are sometimes used in place of micros.

By lorry

The heavy-goods **lorries** (*camiones*) are the other mainstay of Bolivian land transport, and sometimes the only option in remote or little-visited regions. Most carry passengers to supplement their income from carrying goods. Lorries are, however, more uncomfortable, slower and generally more dangerous than buses, and stop more frequently. Still, travelling by lorry is a quintessential Bolivian experience.; passengers usually sit in the cab alongside the driver, or on the back.

The best place to find a lorry is around any town's market areas or at the police checkpoints (*trancas*) at the edge of town; most also stop for passengers who flag them down at the side of the road. This is the closest you'll get to **hitching** in Bolivia, and you will always be expected to pay something for the ride; private cars are few and far between outside towns and rarely pick up hitchers, and in any case hitching a lift in them is risky. For shorter journeys in remote areas, smaller pick-up trucks, known as **camionetas**, also carry passengers.

By train

Once a proud symbol of the country's tin-fuelled march to modernity, Bolivia's **railway** network, like the mining industry that spawned it, is now a shadow of its former self. The **Ferrocarril Andino** (or Occidental) (ⓦwww.fca.com.bo) runs passenger trains from Oruro south across the Altiplano via Uyuni and Tupiza to Villazón on the Argentine border. From Uyuni, another line, served by a weekly passenger train, runs southeast to Calama in Chile. The scenery on both these Altiplano routes is magnificent. The company also runs a slow if picturesque service between Sucre and Potosí.

The **Ferrocarril Oriental** (🌐 ferroviariaoriental .com) has two lines from Santa Cruz: one east to the Brazilian border at Quijarro; the other south to Yacuiba in the Chaco on the Argentine border. The former is known as the "Train of Death", not because it's dangerous but because it's such a boring ride.

By boat

Although Bolivia is a landlocked country, there are still several regions – particularly Lago Titicaca and the Amazon – where water is still the best way if getting around. Several high-end tour agencies run **hydrofoil** and **catamaran** cruises on Lago Titicaca, and smaller passenger launches run between Copacabana and the Isla del Sol.

River boats were for a long time the only means of transport in the Bolivian **Amazon**, but their use has declined rapidly with the expansion of the road network in the region. There are still plenty of river trips you can make, though, and travelling by boat is the ideal way to experience the rainforest. There are two main forms of river transport. **Dugout canoes** powered by outboard motors are the only real way to get deep enough into the jungle to see the wildlife. Tour agencies use these to take groups into protected areas like the Parque Nacional Madidi and irregular passenger services operate along some rivers. Alternatively, you can hire a canoe and its boatman for a few days – this means searching around the riverbank and negotiating, and the high fuel consumption of outboard motors means it won't be cheap.

The second (and much more economic) form of river transport are the larger **cargo boats** that ply the two main water routes not yet supplanted by roads: the **Río Mamoré**, between Trinidad and Guayaramerin on the Brazilian frontier, and the **Río Ichilo**, between Trinidad and Puerto Villaroel in the Chapare. Though generally far from comfortable, these slow-moving vessels allow passengers to hitch hammocks above the deck for a small fee and are a great way to see the Amazon if you're not in a hurry.

By car

If you're short on time or want to get to some really out-of-the-way destinations, **renting a car** is a possibility, but few travellers ever do. It's usually easier and not much more expensive to hire a taxi to drive you around for a day or longer.

Outside towns, most roads are unpaved and in very poor condition, so **four-wheel drive** (4WD) is essential. **Petrol** (gasoline) stations are few and far between and breakdown services even scarcer, so you should fill your tank whenever you can, carry

ROAD DISTANCE CHART

	Cochabamba	La Paz	Oruro	Potosí	Rurre	S Cruz	Sucre	Tarija	Trinidad	Uyuni
Cochabamba	x	383	210	520	809	473	366	888	985	739
La Paz	383	x	229	539	426	858	701	907	602	552
Oruro	210	229	x	310	736	683	472	678	812	323
Potosí	530	539	310	x	1046	774	162	368	1112	200
Rurrenabaque	809	426	736	1046	x	930	1208	1414	380	1059
Santa Cruz	473	858	683	774	930	x	612	703	550	1212
Sucre	366	701	472	162	1208	612	x	530	1162	362
Tarija	888	907	678	368	1414	703	530	x	1253	625
Trinidad	985	602	812	1112	380	550	1162	1253	x	1135
Uyuni	739	552	323	200	1059	1212	362	625	1135	x

ADDRESSES

Addresses are usually written with just the street name (and often only the surname if the street is named after a person), followed by the number – for example, "Paredes 704" rather than "Calle Max Paredes 704". Often, however, numbers are not used, and the nearest intersection is given instead – for example, "Illampu con Comercio". Note also that street numbers in Bolivia do not always run consecutively: number 6 could easily be between numbers 2 and 4.

extra fuel, and take food, drink and warm clothing in case you get stuck. Always carry your passport, driving licence and the vehicle's registration documents, as **police checks** are frequent, and any infringement will usually result in an on-the-spot fine, whether official or not. Small **tolls** are also charged on most roads. Speed limits are irregularly posted, but the speed is usually dictated by the state of the road. Most Bolivians regularly ignore traffic lights and don't indicate when turning, and some drive at night without lights. Vehicles drive on the right, though this rule is obviated on some mountain roads when the vehicle going uphill drives on the right and has priority.

Virtually none of the major international **car rental companies** is represented in Bolivia, but you'll find local rental companies in all the major cities. Rental **costs** vary but are generally a bit less than in Europe and the US at around Bs210–350 ($30–50) per day; 4WDs cost about double. You'll need to be over 25, and leave a major credit card or large cash deposit as security; most rental agencies can arrange insurance, though you should read the small print carefully first.

In several lowland towns, such as Trinidad, Guayaramerin and Riberalta, it's also possible to hire **mopeds** and **motorbikes** by the hour (Bs20-40) or by the day, leaving your passport as a deposit – a good way of heading off into the back country for a day.

By bicycle

Outside La Paz, **bicycles** are rarely available to rent, and those that are aren't usually suitable for extended riding. For proper touring, you'll need to bring your own bike from home; airlines are usually happy to carry them if they're packed in bike boxes with the pedals removed. Given the state of the roads, a mountain bike is better than a conventional

touring bike. Bring a comprehensive tool kit and a selection of essential spare parts.

The roads of the Bolivian Andes are ideal for **downhill mountain biking**, and the country is home to some of the world's best downhill rides. Several agencies in La Paz lead guided mountain bike trips (see p.73) and biking "the world's most dangerous road", in Coroico, is a popular activity (see p.124).

By organized tour

Although relatively expensive, **organized tours** offer a quick and effortless way to see some of Bolivia's popular attractions; they're also a good way of visiting remote sites that are otherwise difficult to reach. In addition, many adventure tour companies both in Bolivia and abroad offer excellent and increasingly exciting itineraries, ranging from mountain climbing, trekking, mountain biking and wildlife safaris to less strenuous city tours and countryside excursions. Tours tend to cost around Bs350–490 ($50–70) per person per day, depending on the nature of the trip, the degree of comfort and the number of people going along.

Most **tour agencies** are based in La Paz (see p.73), where you can arrange almost any trip in the country, but for the more popular wilderness excursions it's easier and cheaper to arrange things with local operators: in Uyuni for the Salar de Uyuni and Reserva Eduardo Avaroa, for example, and in Rurrenabaque for the Pampas del Yacuma and Parque Nacional Madidi. Relevant agencies are listed in the guide under each destination.

Accommodation

Accommodation in Bolivia is generally very good value, though standards in all price brackets are variable. In the larger cities you'll find a broad range of places to stay, including top-end hotels charging well over Bs700 ($100) a night. In smaller towns, however, there's not much choice, particularly in the mid- and upper price ranges, though there are usually plenty of decent budget places.

Room rates generally represent excellent value for money. In areas popular with tourists, rates rise slightly during the **high season** (July-August) and prices in any town can double or treble during a major fiesta. In addition, room rates in resort towns popular with Bolivians increase at the weekend.

These are also the only circumstances in which **reserving** a room in advance is necessary. Prices also vary by region: accommodation in big cities tends to cost more (notably in Santa Cruz), whereas smaller towns that see a lot of budget travellers – Coroico, Copacabana, Rurrenabaque – tend to have a good range of inexpensive places to stay.

Accommodation names – *hotel, hostal, residencial* and *alojamiento* – mean relatively little in Bolivia. Virtually all high end accommodation will call itself a **hotel**, but then many basic places do so as well. Smaller and cheaper hotels – also known as **hostales**, **alojamientos** or **residenciales** – tend to offer basic rooms with shared bathrooms only, but they still vary widely in price, cleanliness and comfort. **Cabañas** are self-contained cabins or bungalows, sometimes with their own kitchenettes, usually found away from big cities. Note that a **motel** is not an inexpensive roadside hotel, but a place where unmarried couples go to have sex, while a **pension** is a cheap place to eat, rather than somewhere to stay.

Hotels

There's no standard or widely used **rating system** for hotels, so other than the information given in this book, the only way to tell whether a place is suitable or not is to have a look around. It's usually worth asking to see a few different rooms and choosing one you like rather than just accepting the first you're offered. There's usually some flexibility in all price ranges, so a little haggling is always worth a try, especially when the hotel seems fairly empty, or if you're in a group: the phrase "*Tiene un cuarto más barato?*" ("Do you have a cheaper room?") is useful. The cheapest places often charge per person, but otherwise **single rooms** tend to

5 HOTELS NOT TO MISS
El Consulado La Paz. See p.76
Hostal La Cúpula Copacabana. See p.102
Hostal Sol y Luna Coroico. See p.126
Parador Santa Maria La Real Sucre.
    See p.205
La Víspera Samaipata. See p.245

cost as much as or only slightly less than double rooms. Rooms with double beds (*cama matrimonial*) usually cost less than those with two beds.

Even in the coldest highland cities **heating** is generally only found in the more expensive hotels. In the lowlands, heat rather than cold is often a problem. All but the cheapest rooms are equipped with a fan, and many places offer the option of air-conditioning. In the lowlands, you should also check whether the windows of your room are screened against mosquitoes or if the bed is equipped with a net.

All but the cheapest places have **hot water**, but the reliability and effectiveness of water-heating systems varies considerably. Many hotels have a **strong box** where you can lock up your valuables – though you should count cash carefully before handing it in, and ask for a receipt. Many places will also store **luggage** for you, often free of charge.

Hostels

The number of hostels in **Bolivia** is slowly increasing, and many of them are affiliated with Hostelling International (Ⓦ hihostels.com). Relatively few have dorms or traditional hostel facilities like communal kitchens, offering instead simple and inexpensive rooms, normally with a choice of either shared or private bathroom.

ACCOMMODATION PRICES

Unless otherwise indicated, the accommodation prices in this book are based on the price of a **double room in high season**.

The **cheapest** hotels tend to be found around bus terminals. At their most basic they offer nothing more than bare, box-like rooms with a bed and shared bathroom, and can be far from clean, though for around Bs70–140 you should expect a clean and reasonably comfortable double room. Many budget places offer a choice between private and shared bathroom, and some also include breakfast in their rates, though this is by no means universal.

Mid-range accommodation (Bs140 and upwards for a double room) should offer greater comfort, pleasant decor, reliable hot water, towels and soap and extras like television. For Bs210–350 or so you'll find some very pleasant hotels indeed, though you'll need to choose carefully – more expensive doesn't necessarily mean better. At the **top end** of the scale (Bs350 and upwards) there are some beautiful old colonial mansions which have been converted into delightful hotels, as well as more staid modern places aimed primarily at business travellers.

Camping

Few travellers bother **camping** in Bolivia, unless they're exploring the country's wilderness areas. Outside cities and towns, however, you can camp almost everywhere, usually for free. Be aware, though, that in the highlands it gets extremely cold at night, while in the lowlands, mosquitoes can be a real problem if your tent isn't screened. In the rainforest, a hammock combined with a fitted mosquito net and a tarpaulin to keep off the rain allows you to camp out pretty much anywhere.

When looking for a **place to camp**, it's usually okay to set up your tent in fields beyond the outskirts of settlements, but you should ask permission from the nearest house first. In wilderness areas where there's no one around to ask, you can camp freely. On the more popular trekking routes you may be asked for a small fee of a dollar or two by local villagers. Though **attacks** on trekkers are rare, you're obviously vulnerable if camping out alone: it's best to camp with at least one other person, and women shouldn't camp unless accompanied by men.

In some **national parks** and other protected wilderness areas you'll find rustic shelters – *albergues* or *refugios* – where you can stay for a small fee, often in the *campamentos* used by the park guards. Rudimentary cooking facilities and running water are usually available.

Specialist **camping equipment** is expensive and difficult to come by in Bolivia, being sold only in a few shops in La Paz and Santa Cruz, so you should bring all you need from home. If you do need to buy stuff, it's often best to look for travellers wanting to get rid of equipment they no longer need – check out the notice boards in popular budget hotels in La Paz.

Food and drink

You won't find much in the way of sophisticated cuisine in Bolivia, though options are improving all the time. Moreover, in most places it's easy to get a decent and filling meal, and there are some interesting national and local specialities. The style of food varies considerably between Bolivia's three main geographical regions: the Altiplano, the highland valleys and the tropical lowlands. Though the differences are fading, each region has comidas típicas (traditional dishes), which include some of the highlights of Bolivian cuisine.

Restaurants

All larger towns in Bolivia have a fair selection of **restaurants** (spelt the same way as in English, without the extra "e" at the end used in most Spanish-speaking countries). Almost all offer a set lunch, or **almuerzo**, consisting of a substantial soup (*sopa*) and a main course (*segundo*), usually made up of rice, potatoes, some form of meat or chicken, and a little bit of salad. Sometimes all this will be preceded by a small savoury appetizer and followed by a sweet dessert. Coffee, teas or a soft drink may also be included. Usually costing between Bs15–25, these set lunches are enormously filling and great value for money. Many restaurants also offer a similarly economical set dinner (**cena**) in the evening. In addition, most have a range of a la carte main dishes (*platos extras*) available throughout the day – these are usually substantial meat dishes like steak, and rarely cost more than Bs40. In smaller towns the choice is much more limited, and often the simple set almuerzo and cena will be the only meal on offer.

Ordinary restaurants rarely offer much in the way of **vegetarian food**; in out-of-the-way places, vegetarians may find themselves eating rather a lot of egg-based dishes. The situation changes a great deal in popular travellers' haunts, where international food is more and more common, and salads and vegetarian dishes are widely available. Although as a landlocked country Bolivia is obviously not the place to come for seafood, **fish** features regularly on menus. Lago Titicaca produces an abundant harvest of succulent *trucha* (trout) and *pejerrey* (kingfish), while native fish are abundant in the rivers of the lowlands: the tastiest is the juicy white fish known as *surubí*.

Most cities have at least one **Chinese restaurant** (or *chifa*), and **pizzerias** are also fairly widespread. Also reliable are Bolivia's cheap spit-roast **chicken restaurants** known as *pollos spiedo, pollos broaster* or *pollos a la brasa*.

Few restaurants open much before 8am for **breakfast** (*desayuno*) – Bolivians tend either to make do with a hot drink and a bread roll or, if they want something more substantial, to head to the market for soup or rice and meat. In touristy places, though, you'll find continental and American breakfasts, along with fruit juices and travellers' favourites like banana pancakes.

In smarter restaurants, you may find yourself paying Bs50 or more for a main course, but for this you should expect a pretty good meal, and even in the best restaurants in La Paz or Santa Cruz few dishes cost more than about Bs70. **Tipping** is not generally expected, but is always welcome. No additional tax is charged on meals, but there is often a cover charge in restaurants with live music performances, known as **peñas**.

Markets

Wherever you are in Bolivia, the cheapest place to eat is invariably the **market**. Here you'll find rows of stalls selling juices, soups, snacks and meals that can satisfy most appetites for less than Bs10. Markets, which open for business much earlier than most restaurants and cafés, are also often the best places to try out regional specialities. From around 6am you can find stalls selling coffee and tea with bread, sandwiches and pastries, and – more popular with the locals – *api*, a hot, sweet, thick maize drink flavoured with cloves and cinnamon and served with deep-fried pancakes known as *buñuelos*. Markets are also the place to go to stock up for a trek, a **picnic**, or if you just feel the urge to prepare your own food.

The standard of **hygiene** at market stalls is often not the highest, however, and you should probably avoid eating at them until your stomach has adjusted to local bacteria. In general, food cooked in front of your eyes is probably safe; food that's been left sitting around for a while may not be.

Snacks

The most popular snack throughout Bolivia is the **salteña**, a pasty filled with a spicy, juicy stew of meat or chicken with chopped vegetables, olives and hard-boiled egg. Named after the city of Salta in Argentina, *salteñas* are sold from street stalls and eaten in the mid-morning accompanied by a cold drink and a spoonful or two of chilli sauce if desired. The best *salteñas* are found in Sucre, where they're also sold in specialist cafés called *salteñerias*, which open only in the mid-morning and serve nothing else. *Salteñas potosinas*, made in Potosí, are less juicy (making them easier to eat in the mines) and are more likely to be meat-free.

Similar to *salteñas*, but deep-fried and with a higher potato content, are **tucumanas**, also named after a city (Tucumán) in Argentina. Also commonly available are **empanadas**, simpler pasties filled with meat, chicken or cheese and either baked or fried. Another snack typical of Santa Cruz is the **cuñape**, a tasty pastry made from cheese and yuca flour. Familiar international snacks are also common in Bolivia, including **hamburgers** (*hamburguesas*) and **hot dogs** (*choripan*).

WHERE TO EAT LIKE THE LOCALS

La Coca La Paz. See p.80
Kota Kahuaña Copacabana. See p.103
Paso del Los Abuelos Sucre. See p.205.
Casa de Campo Cochabamba. See p.216
Casa del Camba Santa Cruz. See p.239

Comida típica

In the **Altiplano**, traditional Aymara cuisine is dominated by the **potato**, often served alongside rice as one of two or three different carbohydrates on the same plate. The Andes are the original home of the potato, and over two hundred different varieties are grown in Bolivia. As well as being boiled, baked, mashed and fried, they are also freeze-dried using ancient techniques involving repeated exposure to sunshine and frost. Known as *chuño* and *tunta*, these dehydrated potatoes have an unusual texture and a distinctive, nutty flavour that takes some getting used to. They're often boiled and served instead of (or as well as) fresh potatoes, but they're best appreciated in the many different **soups** that are a feature of Altiplano cuisine. These are thick, hearty affairs laden with potatoes, vegetables and whatever meat is to hand – one of the most typical and widely available is *chairo*, typical of La Paz. Another standard soup ingredient is **quinoa**, a native Andean grain that has a distinctively nutty flavour and a remarkably high nutritional value.

The most common meat in the Altiplano is **mutton**, closely followed by llama, which is lean and tasty. Llama meat is often eaten in a dried form known as *charque* (the origin of the English word jerky). Other Altiplano mainstays include *sajta*, a spicy dish of chicken cooked with dried yellow chilli, potatoes, *tunta*, onions and parsley; and the *plato paceño*, a mixed plate of meat, cheese, potatoes, broad beans and maize which is typical of La Paz. If you like your food with a kick, all these dishes can be doused in **llajua** – a hot sauce made from tomatoes, small chilli peppers (*locotos*) and herbs.

The *comida típica* of the **valley regions** around Sucre, Cochabamba and Tarija shares many ingredients with the traditional cuisines of the Altiplano, but combines them with a wider range of fresh fruit and vegetables and tends to be spicier. Maize features strongly, either ground into a flour and used as the basis for thick soups known as *laguas*, or boiled on the cob and served with fresh white cheese – a classic combination known as *choclo con queso*. Meat and chicken are often cooked in spicy sauces known as *picantes*. Pork also features strongly: deliciously deepfried as *chicharrón*, roasted as *lechón* or made into *chorizos chuquisaceños* (spicy sausages originating from Sucre). A popular valley mainstay served throughout Bolivia is *pique a lo macho*, a massive plate of chopped beef and sausage, potatoes (or chips), onions, tomatoes and chillies.

In the **tropical lowlands** of the Amazon and Santa Cruz, **plantain** and **yucca** (similar to a yam) generally take the place of potatoes alongside rice as the mainstay sources of carbohydrate. One classic breakfast staple is *masaco*: mashed plantain or yucca mixed with shredded *charque* and fried. The lowlands are cattle-ranching regions, so good-quality, relatively inexpensive **beef** features strongly. This is usually barbecued or fried as steak, or cooked on skewers in massive kebabs (*pacumutus*). Another classic lowland dish is *locro de gallina*, a rich chicken soup. **Game** or bushmeat is also common in the lowlands: *jochi* (agouti), *tatú* (armadillo), *saino* (peccary) and *venado* (venison) all frequently appear on menus, though for conservation reasons it is better not to eat them.

Drinks

Known as **refrescos**, fizzy drinks are found all over Bolivia, including international brands like Coca-Cola and a wide range of nationally produced beverages. Bottled processed **fruit juice** from the Cochabamba region, sold under the name "Jugos del Valle", is a good alternative. The word *refresco* is also used to denote home-made soft drinks, usually fruit-based, served from street stalls. **Mineral water**, both sparkling (*agua mineral con gas*) and still (*sin gas*), is fairly widely available, as is less expensive purified water labelled "Naturagua" – a good thing, as it's best not to drink the tap water. Make sure the seals on all bottles are intact when you buy them.

The delicious variety of tropical fruits grown in Bolivia is available as **juices** (*jugos*) from market stalls, and freshly squeezed orange and grapefruit juice is also sold on the streets from handcarts. **Tea** (*té*) and **coffee** (*café*) are available almost everywhere, though the latter is rarely prepared to the strength favoured by most Europeans, and sometimes comes with sugar already added – a shame, as Bolivia produces some excellent coffee. **Café con leche** is a big glass of hot milk flavoured with coffee. Many Bolivians prefer herbal teas, known as **mates**; *mate de coca* is the best known. **Hot chocolate** is usually very good too.

CHICHA COCHABAMBINA

No visit to the Cochabamba is complete without a taste of **chicha Cochabambina**, a thick, mildly alcoholic beer made of fermented maize which is available throughout the region wherever you see a white flag or bunch of flowers raised on a pole outside a house. Considered sacred by the Incas, its tart, yeasty flavour is definitely an acquired taste, and it can play havoc with the digestion.

Alcoholic drinks

Locally produced **alcoholic drinks** are widely available, and drinking is a serious pastime. Drinking with locals can be great fun, but shouldn't be entered into lightly, as slipping away after a couple is easier said than done. Remember, too, that until you become acclimatized, high altitude magnifies both the effects of alcohol and the resulting hangover.

Beer (*cerveza*) is available in shops, restaurants and bars almost everywhere, and Bolivians consume it in large quantities, especially at fiestas. All the major cities have their own breweries, producing German lager-style beers of reasonable quality with a strength of around five percent. Most beer still comes in returnable bottles, though cans are becoming more widespread; a large 750ml bottle costs about Bs15. Paceña, produced in La Paz, is the most popular and widely available, followed by Huari, made by the same company but with a slightly saltier taste. Taquiña from Cochabamba is also good, while Potosina, from Potosí, has a stronger malt flavour; Ducal from Santa Cruz and Sureña from Sucre are less well thought of. Most breweries also produce a dark, rather sweet, stout-like beer known as **malta**. On some beer labels you'll see the word **tropicalizada** – this means it has been produced in the highlands but is more highly pressurized for consumption at lower altitudes where the air pressure is higher: if opened at altitude it will spray all over the place. More expensive **imported beers** are available only in larger cities.

Although not widely consumed, Bolivia also produces a growing variety of **wines** (*vinos*). Production is centred in the Tarija valley, home to the highest vineyards in the world, and quality is improving all the time – the best labels are Concepción, Kohlberg and Aranjuez. Imported wines from Chile and Argentina are also widely available and often cheaper, as they're frequently smuggled across the border to avoid tax and duty.

When Bolivians really want to get drunk they turn to spirits, in particular a white grape brandy called **singani,** produced in the Tarija valley. The more expensive high-grade *singanis* are very good, but most are pretty rough. It's usually drunk mixed with Sprite or Seven-Up, a fast-acting combination known as **Chufflay**. Those who can't afford *singani* (which includes most campesinos and miners) turn to virtually pure industrial **alcohol potable**, sold in large metal cans. Consumed at rural fiestas and used to make offerings to mountain spirits and other supernatural beings, this is fearsome stuff, and you drink it at your peril.

Fiestas

Bolivia enjoys a huge number of national, regional and local fiestas. These are taken very seriously, often involving lengthy preparations and substantial expense; the largest feature thousands of costumed dancers, massed brass bands and plenty of food and drink. You should definitely try to catch a fiesta at some point during your visit, as they are amongst the most vibrant and colourful spectacles Bolivia has to offer, and at the heart of the country's culture.

Most national fiestas mark famous events in Bolivia's post-conquest history and the standard festivals of the **Catholic Church**, but many of the latter coincide with far older **indigenous celebrations** related to the sun, stars and agricultural cycle. Carnaval time (late Feb or early March) is marked by fiestas and celebrations throughout the country (the most famous being in Oruro), and involves copious eating and drinking, and indiscriminate water-fighting.

In addition to the major national and regional celebrations, almost every town and village has its own annual **local fiesta** (some have several), usually to honour a patron saint. These celebrations can be much more fun to visit than major events in larger towns and cities, and often stretch out over a whole week, with religious processions, masked and costumed folkloric dances, traditional music and eating and drinking. In indigenous communities these fiestas are often important ritual events associated with religious beliefs and agricultural cycles – it's believed that if they're not celebrated with due extravagance, the Catholic saints or

mountain gods (or both) may be displeased, and the fortunes of the community will suffer as a result. Fiestas also play an important role in maintaining social cohesion, and are usually financed under a system known as *prestes*, whereby wealthier members of the community spend large amounts of money on food, drink and musicians, gaining enhanced status and respect in return.

The occasional visitor will usually be warmly welcomed to local fiestas, but these are often fairly private affairs, and crowds of camera-wielding tourists may provoke a hostile reaction – **sensitivity** is the key.

CALENDAR OF MAJOR FIESTAS AND PUBLIC HOLIDAYS

January 1 New Year's Day (public holiday).

January 6 Reyes Magos. The arrival of the Three Kings is celebrated with processions in various towns in the Beni.

January 24 Feria de Alasitas in La Paz. Large areas of the city are taken over by market stalls selling miniature items used as offerings to Ekeko, the household god of abundance (see p.66).

February 2 Fiesta de la Virgen de la Candelaria in Copacabana.

February 10 Public holiday in Oruro department.

February/March Carnaval. Celebrated throughout the country in the week before Lent. The Oruro Carnaval (see p.143) is the most famous, but Santa Cruz and Tarija also stage massive fiestas.

March 12 Pujjlay. Thousands of indigenous revellers descend on the town of Tarabuco, near Sucre, to celebrate a local victory over Spanish troops during the Independence War.

March/April Semana Santa (Easter) is celebrated with religious processions throughout Bolivia. Good Friday is a public holiday.

April 15 Public holiday in Tarija department.

May 1 Labour Day (public holiday).

May 3 Día de la Cruz. *Tinku* ritual combats (see p.165) are staged in some communities in the northern Potosí region.

May 25 Public holiday in Chuquisaca department.

May/June Corpus Christi (public holiday). La Paz stages the Señor del Gran Poder (see p.58), its biggest and most colourful folkloric dance parade.

June 21–22 The winter solstice and Aymara New Year are celebrated with overnight vigils and religious ceremonies at Tiwanaku, Copacabana, Samaipata and other ancient sites throughout the country.

June 24 San Juan. Christian version of the winter solstice and Aymara New Year, marked with bonfires and fireworks around Bolivia.

June Santísima Trinidad. Major religious fiesta in Trinidad in honour of the Holy Trinity.

July 16 Virgen del Carmen. Processions and dances in honour of the Virgen del Carmen, the patron saint of many towns and villages across Bolivia. Public holiday in La Paz department.

July 31 San Ignacio de Moos hosts the largest and most colourful folkloric fiesta in the Bolivian Amazon.

August 6 Independence Day (public holiday). Parades and parties throughout the country.

August 15 Virgen de Urkupiña. Pilgrims descend on the market town of Quillacollo, just outside Cochabamba, for the region's biggest religious fiesta.

August 24 San Bartolomé (also known as Ch'utillos). Potosí's biggest annual fiesta, a three-day celebration with pre-Christian roots, marked by folkloric dances and religious processions.

September 14 Public holiday in Cochabamba department.

October 1 Public holiday in Pando department.

November 1–2 All Saints and Day of the Dead (public holiday). Remembrance parties are held in cemeteries throughout the highlands, with the decorated skulls of dead relatives often on display.

November 10 Public holiday in Potosí department.

November 18 Public holiday in Beni department.

December 25 Christmas Day (public holiday). Christmas (or Navidad) is celebrated throughout the country, and there are particularly colourful festivities in San Ignacio de Moxos and Tarija.

Outdoor activities

Dominated by dramatic Andean scenery and home to some of South America's most pristine wilderness areas, Bolivia should be one of the world's top destinations for outdoor enthusiasts. As yet, though, its enormous potential is only just starting to be tapped – which for many travellers will only add to its appeal.

For climbers, trekkers and mountain bikers, Bolivia's possibilities are virtually limitless. The best season for all these activities is between May and September, during the **southern-hemisphere winter** (the most pleasant and reliable weather is between June and August). During the **rainy season** between December and March or April, rain turns paths and roads to mud, and streams to impassable torrents, while cloud covers the high passes and blocks many of the best views.

Trekking

Whether you want to stroll for half a day or take a hardcore hike for two weeks over high passes and down into remote Amazonian valleys, Bolivia is a paradise for **trekking**. The most popular trekking region is the **Cordillera Real**, which is blessed with spectacular high Andean scenery and is easily accessible from La Paz. The mountains here are crisscrossed by paths and mule trains used by local people that make excellent trekking routes –

the best of these are ancient stone-paved highways built by the Incas and earlier Andean societies. Starting near La Paz, three of Bolivia's most popular treks – the **Choro** (see p.128), **Takesi** (see p.130) and **Yunga Cruz** (see p.134) – follow these Inca trails across the Cordillera Real before plunging down into the humid tropical valleys of the Yungas. Another good base for exploring the Cordillera Real is the town of **Sorata**, north of La Paz, where many good trekking routes begin.

Isla del Sol and the shores of **Lago Titicaca** are also excellent for hiking, combining awesome scenery with gentle gradients. People looking for more seclusion should head for the remote and beautiful **Cordillera Apolobamba**, which is traversed by one of Bolivia's finest trekking routes, the **Trans-Apolobamba Trek** (see p.116). Elsewhere, the mountains around **Sucre** offer further excellent trekking possibilities, while the **Reserva Biológica del Sama**, near Tarija, is also home to a beautiful Inca trail (see p.188).

Equipment and guides

You should always be **well equipped** when walking, even if it's just a half-day hike. Weather can change quickly in the mountains and it gets very cold at night. You'll need strong hiking boots; warm layers; a waterproof top layer; a hat and gloves; an adequate first-aid kit (see p.39); a water bottle and water purifiers; sunscreen, a sun hat and sunglasses. For **camping** out you'll need a decent tent; a sleeping bag that keeps you warm in temperatures as low as -5°C; an insulated sleeping mat; and a cooking stove (ideally a multi-fuel stove).

The easiest way to go trekking is on an **organized trip**, which takes all the hassle out of route-finding and means you don't need to supply your own equipment. You'll also have all your meals cooked for you and transport to and from trailheads arranged. If you pay a little more, you can also have your gear carried for you by a **porter** or pack animal. Trekking this way costs around Bs210–420 ($30–60) per person per day.

Things are much cheaper if you have all your own equipment, organize the logistics yourself, and just hire a **guide** (around Bs140 a day). In rural towns and villages you can usually find local campesinos who know all the trails and will act as a guide for a relatively small fee (on treks of more than one day you'll also need to provide them with food and possibly a tent). If you're hiring **pack animals** (such as mules, donkeys or llamas), then the mule handlers double up as guides. As well as making sure you don't get lost, a local guide can help avoid any possible misunderstandings with the communities you pass through – it's also a good way to ensure local people see a little economic benefit from tourism.

If you plan to go trekking over longer distances without a guide, you should be competent at route-finding and map-reading, carry a **compass** and/or GPS, and equip yourself with the relevant topographical **maps**, where available. Most areas are covered by 1:50,000-scale maps produced by the Bolivian military and available in La Paz (see p.86). Really, though, it's much better to trek with a guide. Getting lost in remote mountain or forested regions is easy and can be very dangerous, and rescue services are pretty much non-existent. In addition, you should always let someone in town know your plans before you head off on a long walk. It's especially important **not to trek alone** – if you sprain an ankle, it could be the last anyone ever sees of you.

Climbing

With hundreds of peaks over 5000m and a dozen over 6000m, Bolivia has plenty of types of **mountain climbing**, and many new routes still to explore. As with trekking, the most popular region is the dramatic **Cordillera Real**, which is blessed with numerous high peaks, easy access from La Paz and fairly stable weather conditions during the dry season. In addition, the volcanic peaks of the **Cordillera Occidental**, particularly Sajama (see p.141), offer some excellent climbs, while the more remote **Cordillera Apolobamba** and **Cordillera Quimsa Cruz** also offer a wealth of possibilities. Several of the higher peaks are well within the reach of climbers with only limited experience, while **Huayna Potosí** (6090m), in the Cordillera Real, is one of the few 6000m-plus peaks in South America that can be climbed by people with no mountaineering experience at all.

Though some **equipment** is available for hire in La Paz, you should really bring your own equipment from home if you're planning on doing any serious independent climbing. You should also take care to acclimatize properly and be aware of the dangers of altitude sickness (see p.38) and extreme cold. A number of agencies in La Paz (see p.73) offer guided ascents of the most popular peaks: check carefully that the guide is qualified and the equipment reliable – if in doubt, go with a more reputable and expensive agency. You can get good advice and find fully qualified mountaineering

guides through the **Club Andino Boliviano** (☎022312875), in La Paz at Mexico 1638, just up from Plaza Estudiante.

Mountain biking

Bolivia is home to some of the finest **mountain bike** routes in the world, and travelling by bike is one of the best ways to experience the Andes. Numerous tour companies in La Paz (see p.73) have set up **downhill mountain biking** trips. These involve being driven up to a high pass, put on a bike, and then riding downhill at your own pace, accompanied by a guide and followed by a support vehicle. This is not an activity where you should try to save money by going with a cheap operator – look for a company with experienced guides, well-maintained and high-quality bikes and adequate safety equipment; Gravity Assisted Mountain Biking (see p.73) has the best reputation.

Easily the most popular route is down the road from **La Paz to Coroico** in the Yungas (see p.124), a stunning 3500m descent which many travellers rate as one of the highlights of South America, never mind Bolivia. You don't need any previous mountain-biking experience to do this ride, which is easy to organize as a day-trip from La Paz. Other popular routes include **Chacaltaya** (see p.88) to La Paz, and down the **Zongo valley** into the Yungas from Chacaltaya, while hard-core mountain bikers can try their luck on the **Takesi Trail** (see p.130). As with trekking and climbing, though, the possibilities are pretty much endless, especially if you have your own bike.

For advice on new routes or mountain biking in general, contact Bolivia mountain-bike pioneer and guru Alistair Matthew, of Gravity Assisted Mountain Biking – he can also help organize specialist guided tours.

Rafting and kayaking

The many rivers rushing down from the Andes into the Upper Amazon valleys offer massive potential for **kayaking** and **whitewater rafting,** though these activities are not as developed as they could be. The most easily accessible and popular river is the **Río Coroico**, in the Yungas, which offers rapids from grade II to IV (and sometimes higher) and is accessible on day-trips from Coroico. The most challenging trip is down the **Río Tuichi**, which runs from the high Andes down into the rainforest of the Parque Nacional Madidi (see p.281).

National parks and reserves

Bolivia's system of protected areas currently covers around fifteen percent of the country. These national parks (parques nacionales), national reserves (reservas nacionales) and "natural areas" (areas naturales de manejo integrado) encompass the full range of different terrains and ecosystems in Bolivia, from the tropical forests of the Amazon lowlands to the frozen peaks and high-altitude Andean deserts. They include many of Bolivia's most outstanding scenic attractions, but their principal aim is to protect native flora and fauna, and there are relatively few facilities for tourism. Though in some parks you can find basic accommodation, in general visiting these areas involves a wilderness expedition, which is usually possible only with the help of a tour operator.

The country's national parks and reserves are administered by the **Servicio Nacional de Areas Protegidas** (SERNAP), which has a head office in La Paz (☎022426272, ⊛www.sernap.gob.bo), though it offers little in the way of practical information. In cases where you need **permission** to visit a park or reserve, you can do so in the local or regional SERNAP offices. Details about permission and entrance fees for individual parks and reserves are given in the guide. Protected areas range in size from the vast 34,411-square-kilometre **Parque Nacional Kaa-Iya del Gran Chaco**, the largest in South America, to the relatively small 164-square-kilometre **Parque Nacional Toro Toro**.

Many of Bolivia's protected areas were established only relatively recently in response to pressure and incentives from international conservation groups. Some, including the Parque Nacional Madidi, were set up through **debt-for-nature swaps**, whereby international groups bought up large amounts of the country's international debt at discounted rates, then cancelled the debts in return for Bolivia agreeing to establish protected areas and invest money in their conservation. Parque Nacional Noel Kempff Mercado was expanded as part of a pioneer **carbon-trading scheme**, under which US energy corporations finance the protection of forest areas in Bolivia in return for being allowed to claim credits for the carbon dioxide the forests absorb from the atmosphere when meeting their own emissions targets.

Despite such schemes, many national parks and other protected areas are under intense pressure from **landless peasants**, mostly migrants from the highlands looking for new areas of forest to clear and cultivate. Small teams of park guards with almost no resources struggle to protect thousands of square kilometres of wilderness from incursions by hunters, logging and mining companies, cattle ranchers and peasant colonizers, who are often better organized, financed and equipped. In addition, though many Bolivians are aware of the enormous value of their remaining wilderness areas and support conservation measures, there is also widespread opposition to the **national parks system**. Peasant federations in particular view the protected areas as a form of imperialism whereby natural resources that are rightfully theirs are handed over to international conservation groups intent, they believe, on stealing Bolivia's biodiversity and patenting any scientifically valuable species discovered.

Health

Bolivia is one of the poorest countries in the Americas, and the public health system is extremely limited. Generally speaking, the larger the city or town, the better the medical care available is likely to be. In La Paz and Santa Cruz, English-speaking doctors trained overseas are fairly easy to find. Standards decrease rapidly the further you go from the cities, and in rural areas medical facilities are poor to non-existent. If you have a choice, private hospitals and clinics are better staffed and equipped than public ones. Make sure you have adequate health insurance before you leave home, as costs can mount rapidly, and remember to obtain itemized receipts of your treatment so that you can recover your costs.

You'll find **pharmacies** (farmacias) in most Bolivian towns; in larger places they operate a rota system, with at least one staying open 24 hours a day. These sell a wide range of familiar drugs and medicines without prescription (many, for example, sell the morning-after pill), so for minor ailments you can usually buy what you need over the counter. For any serious illness, you should go to a doctor or hospital; these are detailed throughout the guide in the relevant city listings. Many Bolivians are too poor to afford modern medical attention, and most make frequent recourse to traditional **herbalists**, known as *curanderos* – the most famous are the Kallawayas from the Cordillera Apolobamba (see p.114). In addition, the market of every town has a section selling curative plants, herbs and charms for the most common ailments.

Although Bolivia is home to some very unpleasant **tropical diseases**, you shouldn't get too paranoid about contracting them: most are rare and pose more of a threat to poor locals with limited access to healthcare and clean water. Most serious illnesses can be avoided if you take the necessary precautions and make sure you have the right **vaccinations** before you go.

If you're planning a long trip it's worth consulting your doctor before you leave, as well as having a **dental check-up** before you go. Take an adequate supply of any prescription medicines you normally use and, if you wear glasses or contact lenses, carry a spare pair and a copy of your prescription.

It's currently recommended that visitors to Bolivia have **immunizations** for hepatitis A, typhoid and yellow fever. Advice can change, however, so check with your doctor or a travel clinic at least two months before travelling so that there's time to have any courses of injections you might need. You should also make sure your polio and tetanus vaccinations and boosters are up to date. In the case of **yellow fever**, make sure you get an international vaccination certificate: you may have to show this when entering an infected area or arriving in the Bolivian Amazon from Brazil or Peru, and a certificate is always required when travelling overland to Brazil from Bolivia. If you don't have the certificate, you'll have to have an inoculation there and then.

Water and food

Though the **tap water** in some cities and towns is chlorinated, it's best to avoid drinking it entirely while in Bolivia. **Bottled water**, both mineral and purified, is sold throughout the country, though rarely consumed by Bolivians themselves: check the seals on all bottles are intact, as refilling is not unknown. Soft drinks, tea and coffee are also perfectly safe to drink, and more widely available.

There are several ways of **purifying water** while travelling, whether your source is tap water or a spring or stream. Boiling water for at least ten minutes is effective, though at high altitude water boils at below 100˚C, so you should let it boil for twice as long. Chemical purification with **iodine** (*yodo*) tablets or tincture (available in camping shops at home and at pharmacies in Bolivia) is easier, and generally effective, though not all microbes are eliminated and the resulting taste leaves much to be desired (although you can buy neutralizing powder that improves the taste somewhat, and a squeeze of lemon is also effective). Note that pregnant women, babies and people with thyroid complaints shouldn't use iodine. Portable **water filters** give the most complete treatment, but are fiddly, expensive and relatively heavy to carry.

Almost any kind of **food** served in any kind of restaurant can make you sick – even if the food is clean, the waiters' hands may not be – but you can reduce your chances of contracting a stomach bug by avoiding certain things. Be wary of anything bought from street stalls, and avoid salads, unpasteurized milk and cheese, undercooked or reheated fish or chicken and anything that's been left lying around where flies can get at it.

Diarrhoea and dysentery

However careful you are, the chances are that sooner or later you'll suffer a bout of **diarrhoea**, sometimes accompanied by vomiting and stomach cramps. This is usually caused by contaminated food or water, and there's not much you can do about it except drink plenty of liquid (but not alcohol or caffeine). Herbal teas like coca and camomile (*manzanilla*) can help with stomach cramps, and you should also replace **salts** either by taking oral rehydration salts or by mixing a teaspoon of salt and eight of sugar in a litre of purified water. "Blocking" drugs like loperamide (Imodium, Lomotil) are useful if you have to keep travelling when suffering from diarrhoea, but they only alleviate the symptoms temporarily and can actually make things worse if you have dysentery. Once you're holding down liquid, eat bland food like rice, soup and crackers, but avoid spicy, fatty and fried food, dairy products, raw fruit and alcohol until you've recovered.

You should seek **medical advice** if your diarrhoea contains blood; if it continues for more than five days; if it's accompanied by a high fever (over 39˚C); if abdominal pain becomes constant; or if the symptoms continue for more than five days. If your diarrhoea contains blood or mucus, the cause may be either amoebic dysentery, bacterial dysentery or giardia. With a fever, it could be caused by **bacterial dysentery**, which may clear up without treatment. If it doesn't, a course of antibiotics such as ciprofloxacin, tetracycline or ampicillin (consider taking a course of one of these with you if you're going off the beaten track for a while) should do the trick, though they will reduce your natural resistance to future bouts.

Similar symptoms to bacterial dysentery persisting or recurring over a period of weeks could indicate **amoebic dysentery**, which can have serious long-term effects such as liver damage. This can be treated with a course of metronidazole (Flagyl) or tinidazole (Fasigyn), antibiotics that should not be taken with alcohol. Sudden, watery and bad-smelling diarrhoea, accompanied by rotten-egg belches and flatulence, is probably giardia, which is also treated with metronidazole or tinidazole. You should only take these drugs without consultation if there's no possibility of seeing a doctor. The only sure way to tell what is causing your diarrhoea is to have a stool test, which can be arranged by doctors in most towns.

The sun

The sun can be strong in Bolivia, and serious **sunburn** and **sunstroke** are real risks. This is particularly true at high altitudes (where the temperature is not that hot but the thin air amplifies the harm done by ultraviolet rays), or when travelling by boat on rivers or lakes (where cool breezes disguise the effects of the sun as it is reflected off the water). Exposure to the sun can also increase your chances of developing skin cancer. Long sleeves and trousers protect your skin from the sun and reduce fluid loss, and you should use a wide-brimmed hat, decent sunglasses to protect your eyes and a high-factor sunscreen (fifteen or above) on all exposed skin. Sunblock and suntan lotion are available in pharmacies in the main cities, but they're generally expensive, so it's better to bring a supply with you from home. Sunscreen lip-balm is also worth using. Drink plenty of liquid, particularly if you're exercising, to prevent **dehydration**, and consider adding extra salt to your food to compensate for the effects of excessive sweating.

Altitude sickness

Altitude sickness – known as **soroche** in Bolivia – is a serious and potentially life-threatening illness caused by reduced atmospheric pressure and correspondingly lower oxygen levels at high altitudes. It can affect anyone who normally lives at low altitude and ascends **above 2500m**, and thus is a danger across much of Bolivia, including most major cities. You're most likely to be affected if you fly into La Paz from near sea level – the airport is at over 4000m, and almost everyone feels at least a touch of breathlessness.

Mild symptoms can include headache, insomnia, breathlessness, nausea, dizziness, loss of appetite, tiredness, rapid heartbeat and vomiting. The best way to avoid this is to ascend slowly, if at all possible, and allow yourself time to acclimatize. Avoiding alcohol and physical exertion and drinking plenty of liquid also help. Bolivians swear by **coca tea** (*mate de coca*) as a remedy, and this is available throughout the country; the prescription drug acetazolamide (Diamox) can also help with acclimatization. Normal advice is to ascend no more than 300m a day once over 3000m, so far as possible.

The symptoms of serious altitude sickness, also known as **acute mountain sickness**, are usually experienced only over 4000m. In this condition, fluid can build up in the lungs or brain, causing high-altitude pulmonary or cerebral oedema; left untreated, severely affected sufferers can lapse into unconsciousness and die within hours. Symptoms include loss of balance, confusion, intense headache, difficulty breathing and coughing up frothy, bloodstained sputum. Prompt and rapid descent is the only treatment, and you should seek immediate medical help.

Malaria and other insect-borne diseases

Malaria is fairly common in lowland regions of Bolivia, particularly the Amazon, and you should take anti-malaria tablets if you'll be going anywhere below 2500m – the altitude limit of the mosquito that spreads the disease (though it's uncommon over 1500m). Consult your doctor several weeks before you leave home to see which treatment is most suitable for you. Prophylactic treatment usually consists of chloroquine (Avloclor or Nivaquine) combined with proguanil (Paludrine); mefloquine (Lariam) is an alternative, particularly as chloroquine-resistant strains of malaria exist in Bolivia, but some nasty side effects have been reported. With both treatments, it's crucial that you keep taking the tablets for **four weeks** after leaving malarial areas. Malaria symptoms include fever, joint pains, loss of appetite and vomiting; if you suspect you've caught the disease, see a doctor and get a blood test.

The best way to avoid malaria, yellow fever and other diseases spread by **mosquitoes** is not to get bitten in the first place. Try to wear long sleeves, trousers and socks, and sleep in a screened room or under mosquito netting, preferably treated with a repellent chemical. It's also a good idea to put repellent on your skin: make sure it has at least 35 percent DEET content. It's best to bring this with

A TRAVELLER'S FIRST-AID KIT

The following list covers some of the items you might want to carry with you, especially if you're going trekking or travelling in remote rural and wilderness areas.

- Antiseptic cream
- Anti-fungal powder
- Insect repellent
- Sticking plasters
- Anti-blister moleskin (Compeed)
- Lint
- Sealed bandages and surgical tape

- A course of ciprofloxacin and tinidazole
- Imodium diarrhoea medicine
- Oral rehydration salts
- Paracetamol or aspirin
- Water-sterilization tablets or iodine tincture
- Sunscreen, lip salve, sunglasses
- Multivitamins

you from home, as it's hard to come by, expensive and usually of poor quality in Bolivia.

Another insect-borne danger is American trypanosomiasis, or **Chagas' disease**. This is spread by the bite of the *vinchuca*, also known as the assassin bug, a small flying beetle found mainly in thatched roofs and adobe walls in rural areas of the Cochabamba, Chuquisaca and Tarija departments up to elevations of about 3000m. The disease is fatal, though usually only after a number of years, and in some rural areas up to ninety percent of the human population are thought to be infected. The bite is usually painful and infection can be detected by a blood test; though the disease does respond to some drug treatments, the best defence is to try to avoid being bitten – if you do have to sleep under a thatched roof in affected regions, use a mosquito net.

Leishmaniasis is a gruesome protozoan disease spread by the bite of the sandfly, common throughout the Bolivian lowlands. The bites enlarge and ulcerate, causing large lesions that over months or years can spread to other parts of the body and eat the cartilage around the nose and mouth. Treatment involves a course of injections, available in some Bolivian hospitals; the only prevention is to avoid getting bitten. Less serious but still unpleasant is the **human botfly**, or *boro*, which lays its eggs on damp clothes or on the proboscis of a mosquito, which then transfers them to human flesh. When the eggs hatch, the larvae burrow under the skin, producing a painful lump as they grow. To remove them, cover with oil or Vaseline to cut off the air supply, then squeeze the larvae out.

Other health issues

Bolivia is home to a wide range of **venomous snakes** (*viboras*), some of which can be lethal. Most are more concerned with getting away from you than attacking, and, even if they do strike, there's a

good chance they won't inject any venom. Wearing boots, watching where you step and put your hands, and making a lot of noise when walking through vegetation all reduce the chances of getting bitten. In the event of a snakebite, keep the victim still and get medical help as quickly as possible. If possible, kill the snake for identification. **Stings and bites** from other creatures such as spiders and scorpions are uncommon but can be very painful or even fatal. It's a good idea to shake out your shoes and clothes before putting them on, and to check your bedclothes and under lavatory seats.

Rabies still exists in Bolivia and people do die from it. If you'll be spending time in remote areas or in contact with animals, it's worth having the vaccine, though all this does is buy you extra time to seek medical treatment. If you do get bitten by a dog, vampire bat or other wild animal, thoroughly clean the wound with soap and water followed by alcohol or iodine and seek urgent medical attention. The only treatment is a series of injections in the stomach, which must be administered as soon as possible; these are available in most Bolivian hospitals.

MEDICAL RESOURCES FOR TRAVELLERS

UK AND IRELAND

Hospital for Tropical Diseases Travel Clinic ☎ 0845155 5000 or 0207388 9600, ⓦ thehtd.org.
MASTA (Medical Advisory Service for Travellers Abroad) ☎ 0870606 2782, check ⓦ masta-travel-health.com for the nearest clinic.
Tropical Medical Bureau Republic of Ireland ☎ 1850487 674, ⓦ tmb.ie.

US AND CANADA

CDC ☎ 18773948747, ⓦ cdc.gov/travel. Official US government travel health site.
International Society of Travel Medicine ☎ 17707367060, ⓦ istm.org. Has a full list of travel health clinics.
Canadian Society for International Health ⓦ csih.org. Extensive list of travel health centres.

AUSTRALIA, NZ AND SOUTH AFRICA
Travellers' Medical and Vaccination Centre ☎ 1300658
844, ⓦ tmvc.com.au. Lists travel clinics in Australia, New Zealand and South Africa.

Crime and personal safety

Despite being among the poorest countries in the region, Bolivia has far lower levels of theft and violent crime than in neighbouring Peru and Brazil, though in recent years crime levels have risen. This is to the dismay of most ordinary Bolivians, who are shocked and outraged by stories of theft or assault, and in general the threat of crime is no greater in Bolivian cities than in North America or Europe.

The difference is that whereas back home you blend in and can spot potential danger signs much more easily, in Bolivia you stand out like a sore thumb – an extremely wealthy sore thumb, moreover, at least in the eyes of most Bolivians. There's no need to be paranoid, though: the vast majority of crime against tourists is **opportunistic theft**, and violence is rare. By using common sense, keeping alert and taking some simple precautions, you can greatly reduce the chances of becoming a victim and help ensure you join the vast majority of foreign visitors who visit the country without experiencing any trouble at all.

Theft

Petty theft is the most common crime that tourists face, and more often than not it's simply the result of carelessness. If you really don't want to lose something, don't bring it with you in the first place: wearing jewellery or expensive watches is asking for trouble.

Precautions

It's important to make sure you have adequate **travel insurance** (see p.44), and check what the insurance company's requirements are in the event that you need to make a claim – almost all will need a police report of any theft. To reduce the problems of a potential theft, make a careful note of airline ticket numbers, hotline phone numbers if you need to cancel a credit card, travellers' cheque numbers (always keep the receipt separately) and insurance details; in addition, copy the important pages of your **passport** and **travel documents** (or scan them and save them on a USB stick or email them to yourself) and keep all these details separate from your valuables. You should also keep an emergency stash of **cash** hidden somewhere about your person. If you're staying in Bolivia for a while, consider registering with your embassy: this can save lots of time if you have to replace a lost or stolen passport.

Always carry your valuables – passport, money, travellers' cheques, credit cards, airline tickets – out of sight and under your clothing next to your skin; and keep them on you at all times. **Money belts** are good for this, but you can also get secure holders that hang under your shirt or from a loop on your belt under your trousers; a false pocket sewn inside your clothing, a leg pouch or a belt with a secret zip for cash are even more difficult for thieves to find. It's also a good idea to keep your petty cash separate from your main stash of valuables, so your hidden money belt is not revealed every time you spend a few bolivianos.

Better hotels will have a **safe** (*caja fuerte*) at reception where you can deposit your valuables if you trust the staff – this is usually safe, though it's better to leave stuff in a tamper-proof holder or a signed and sealed envelope, get an itemized receipt for what you leave, and count cash carefully before and after. Never leave cameras or other valuables lying around in your hotel room, and be cautious if sharing a room with people you don't know well - other travellers can be thieves too. Officially, you're supposed to carry your **passport** with you at all times, but if asked by the police for ID it's usually sufficient to show them a photocopy of your passport and explain that the original is in your hotel.

You are at your most vulnerable, and have the most to lose, when you're on the move or arriving in a new town and have all your luggage with you. **Bus stations** are a favourite hunting ground of thieves the world over, and Bolivia is no exception: try not to arrive after dark, keep a close eye and hand on your bags, and consider taking a taxi from the bus terminal to your hotel as a security precaution. As well as transport terminals, markets, city centres, fiestas and other crowded public places where tourists congregate are favoured by pickpockets and thieves. If you're carrying a daypack or small bag, keep it in front of you where you can see it to avoid having it slashed; when you stop and sit down, loop a strap around your leg to make it more difficult for someone to grab.

Violent cime

Mugging and **violent robbery** are much less common, but do occur, usually at night, so try to avoid having to walk down empty streets in the early hours, particularly on your own. ATMs are an obvious target for robbers, so don't use them at night, if possible. If the robbers are armed, it's better not to resist.

Some travellers have been targeted for what's known as **express kidnapping.** This involves armed men, sometimes disguised as police, entering the taxi or minibus the victims are travelling in (usually with the complicity of the driver) and taking them to a secret location where they are forced to reveal their ATM credit card PIN and are held for several days while the account is drained. In two instances the kidnapped travellers were murdered, though most of the gang responsible have since been arrested. Most cases occurred on the La Paz–Copacabana route. As such, it's best to stick to larger buses with plenty of other travellers on board when travelling on that route, and to be particularly careful when arriving after dark in the cemetery district of La Paz.

Though usually safer than walking, **taxis** carry an element of risk. If travelling alone, don't sit in the front seat, lock passenger doors to stop people jumping in beside you, and be wary of cabs driving away with your bags – if your luggage is in the boot, wait for the driver to get out first. Radio taxis called by phone are safer than unmarked cabs, and you can always refuse to share a cab with strangers if it makes you uncomfortable.

Robbery is rare in **rural areas**, though campsites are sometimes targeted on some of the more popular trekking routes – keep all your possessions inside your tent at night, avoid camping near villages where possible, and always get local advice before setting off.

Scams

As well as opportunistic thefts, there are several **scams** used by teams of professional thieves that you should be aware of. One classic technique is distraction: your bag or clothing is mysteriously sprayed with mustard or the like, a friendly passer-by points this out and helps you clean it – while their accomplice picks your pocket or makes off with your coat or bag.

Another involves something valuable – cash, a credit card – being dropped at your feet. A passer-by spots it and asks you to check your wallet to see if it is yours, or offers to share it with you. The story ends with your own money disappearing by sleight of hand, or you being accused of theft, so walk away as quickly as possible and ignore anything dropped at your feet.

A third scam, usually used at **bus terminals**, involves thieves posing as plainclothes police officers, complete with fake documents, asking to see your money to check for counterfeit notes or something similar. Often, an accomplice (usually a taxi driver) will already have engaged you in conversation and will vouch for this being normal procedure. It isn't. If approached by people claiming to be **undercover police**, don't get in a car with them or show them your documents or valuables, and insist on the presence of a uniformed officer – you can call one yourself on ☎110.

The police

With any luck, most of your contact with the police will be at **frontiers and road checkpoints**. Sometimes, particularly near borders and in remote regions, you may have to register with them, so carry your **passport** with you at all times (though a photocopy may be enough if you're not travelling far). Generally the police rarely trouble tourists, but in any dealings with them it's important to be polite and respectful, as they can make problems for you if you're not. Anyone claiming to be an **undercover policeman** is probably a thief or confidence trickster (see opposite); don't get in a car with them or show them your documents or valuables, and insist on the presence of a **uniformed officer**.

If you are the victim of theft, you'll probably need to go to the police to make a report (*denuncia*) and get a **written report** for insurance purposes – this is rarely a problem, though it may take some time. In La Paz you should go to the **tourist police** if you are the victim of any crime – their office (open 24hr; ☎022225016) is at Edificio Olimpia 1314, Plaza Tejada Sorzano, opposite the stadium in Miraflores.

Occasionally, the police may search your bags. If they do, watch carefully, and ideally get a witness to watch with you, to make sure nothing is planted or stolen – a rare but not impossible occurrence. Possession of (let alone trafficking in) **drugs** is a serious offence in Bolivia, usually leading to a long jail sentence. There are a fair number of foreigners languishing in Bolivian jails on drugs charges, and many wait a long time before they come to trial. It's not unusual to be offered an opportunity to **bribe** a policeman (or any other official, for that matter), even if you've done nothing wrong. Often they're just trying it on, and there's no need to pay. But in some circumstances it can work to the advantage of both parties. In South America bribery is an age-old custom, and paying a bribe is certainly preferable to going to jail. Finally, bear in mind that all police are armed, and may well shoot you if you run away.

Political demonstrations

Political unrest is a constant in Bolivia, and demonstrations are a regular event in La Paz and the other major cities. Though usually peaceful and interesting to watch, these sometimes turn violent, so keep your distance and make sure you can get out of the area fast if things turn nasty.

Road blockades are also a feature of Bolivian political life, particularly in the Altiplano, where radical Aymara peasants often block the roads between La Paz and Peru. Generally, this is an inconvenience that travellers have to put up with, and you should follow events in the media if you're worried you may get cut off. If you get caught up in the blockades, keep your head down and get out of the area, and don't try running the blockades unless you really have to. Tempers can run high, with blockade-breaking buses sometimes getting stoned or torched.

The Chapare

The election of the coca-growers leader, Evo Morales, as president in 2006 did much to defuse the sometimes **violent confrontation** between the security forces and peasants in the **Chapare** in Cochabamba department, Bolivia's main cocaine-producing region. But away from the towns on the main road from Cochabamba to Santa Cruz this is still a dangerous area. Be wary of going off the beaten track in this region, as you may be mistaken for a drug trafficker or undercover drug-enforcement agent.

Culture and etiquette

Particularly in the highlands, Bolivia is quite a formal country, and old-fashioned values of politeness and courtesy are still widespread. It's normal to greet everyone you talk to with a formal "good morning/afternoon/evening" ("*buenos dias, buenas tardes/noches*") before starting conversation; indeed, failure to do so can be taken as rude. In smaller towns and villages, you'll find even strangers exchange greetings as they pass on the street. "Please" ("*por favor*") and "thank you" ("*gracias*") are also very important. Bolivians in positions of authority expect to be treated with due respect, and can make things difficult for you if you fail to show it. Generally, it's best to call people *señor* or *señora*, especially if they are older than you, and to use a formal title such as doctor or mayor when addressing someone who has one (or affects to, as many Bolivians do).

Many Bolivians are generous, but apt to take offence if you don't accept what they have offered you, particularly when it comes to food and drink. As for **alcohol**, escaping a drinking session after just one or two is difficult to achieve – it can be better to just slip away rather than announce that you've had enough.

Race is a very sensitive issue in Bolivia, both politically and on a day-to-day basis. Indigenous people should never be referred to as *Indios* (Indians) as this is considered racist and deeply offensive. *Indigena* is much better, but most refer to themselves by their specific ethnic or linguistic group – Aymara, Quechua, etc. **Religion** – both Christian and indigenous – is also a serious matter, and you should always ask permission before intruding on ceremonies, and act with due respect and sensitivity inside churches and at fiestas or ritual events. Similarly, always ask permission before taking anyone's **photo**, as some Bolivians find this offensive, or expect to be paid.

Attitudes to what constitutes **appropriate clothing** vary sharply between the highlands and the tropical lowlands. Bolivians everywhere are used to foreigners wearing shorts, but in the conservative highlands it's not the done thing to show off too much flesh. In remote villages in particular this can cause real offence. In the hot and humid lowlands, on the other hand, it's acceptable to strip down to a bare minimum of shorts and sleeveless vest. Santa Cruz is particularly liberal in this respect.

The **sexism and machismo** characteristic of Latin America is arguably less prevalent in Bolivia than in many other countries, but it can still present an annoyance for foreign women, particularly those travelling alone or accompanied only by other women. Generally speaking, everyday sexual harassment is less of a problem in high-altitude cities like La Paz, where indigenous cultures predominate, and worse in lower, warmer cities like **Santa Cruz**, where Latino culture has more of a hold. Harassment usually takes the form of whistling and lewd cat-calling in the street: most Bolivian women just walk on and ignore this, and you'll probably find it easiest to do likewise.

Many women find this problem increases in February and March in the run-up to **Carnaval**, when the usually good-natured custom of water fighting is used by some men as an excuse to harass women with water bombs. **Sexual assault** and rape are not common in Bolivia, but there have been a number of incidents reported by female travellers. It's best to exercise at least the same degree of caution as you would at home.

Most Bolivians do not have a very liberal attitude to **homosexuality**: though legal, it is frowned upon and kept under wraps. Though gay travellers are unlikely to suffer any direct abuse, it's best to be discreet and avoid public displays of affection. Larger cities have a handful of gay bars, but these tend to be fairly clandestine to avoid harassment.

Travel essentials

Costs

Bolivia is **one of the least expensive** countries in South America, and considerably cheaper than neighbouring Chile, Brazil and Argentina. Imported goods are expensive, but food, accommodation and transport are all relatively cheap, and travellers on a tight budget should be able to get around on Bs140/$20/£12/€14 per day, staying in basic hotels and eating set meals in local restaurants. For about Bs280 Bs280/$40/£25/€28 per day you can enjoy more comfortable hotels and good food, take taxis when necessary and go on the occasional guided tour. Spend more than Bs490 ($70) per day and you can have a very comfortable trip.

Things are a bit more expensive in larger cities, especially **Santa Cruz**, and in isolated regions where goods have to be brought in over long distances. Goods and services aimed specifically at foreign tourists tend to be more expensive, and there is sometimes a tendency to slightly overcharge foreigners – if in doubt, always agree a price in advance before accepting a service. Prices in shops and restaurants tend to be fixed, but there is some room for **bargaining** in markets, when looking for a hotel room or buying a bus ticket – try asking for a reduction (*rebaja*). There's a limit to this, though. Bolivians don't generally enjoy bargaining for its own sake, and there are few sights more ridiculous than a wealthy gringo haggling vociferously

for a tiny discount on an already inexpensive item being sold by a very poor market trader.

Disabled travellers

Very little provision is made in Bolivia for the disabled. Public transport, hotels and public places such as museums are seldom equipped with ramps, widened doorways or disabled toilets, and pavements, where they exist at all, are often narrow and covered with dangerous potholes and other obstructions.

Electricity

The electricity supply in most of Bolivia is 220V/50Hz; in La Paz, however, there are both 110V and 220V supplies, often in the same house, so check carefully before plugging in equipment. Plugs are two-pronged with round pins, but US-style flat-pinned plugs can also usually be used.

Entry requirements

Most visitors to Bolivia do not need a visa, although the situation does change periodically, so always check with your local embassy or consulate a few weeks before travelling. **US citizens** require a visa (Bs945/$135); this is available on entry, where it must be paid for in cash, or from a Bolivian embassy or consulate.

On arrival, all travellers are issued with a **tourist card** (*tarjeta de turismo*) valid for up to ninety days' stay for citizens of most EU countries, and up to thirty days for citizens of Australia, Canada and New Zealand; your passport will also be stamped. Make sure you ask for the full ninety days if you need it and are eligible, as border officials sometimes give only thirty days, particularly at remote border crossings. A thirty-day tourist card can be extended to ninety days at the **migraciones** (immigration offices) in La Paz, Santa Cruz and other major cities; this is free for most nationalities, but costs extra (around Bs175) for Canadians, Australians and New Zealanders; the process usually takes 24 hours.

Border officials may ask for evidence that you have enough money to support yourself during your stay, so be prepared to show a credit card or a wad of travellers' cheques; keep cash out of sight, as officials have been known to angle for bribes. Tourist cards, as well as entry and exit stamps, are **free of charge**.

If you want to **stay on** in Bolivia beyond the ninety-day limit, it's best to leave the country overland and return the next day, when you'll be issued with a new tourist card. If you lose your tourist card, go to a *migración* office to get a new one before you try to leave the country – this involves a lengthy bureaucratic procedure, so it's best not to lose your card in the first place. If you overstay, you'll be charged a **small fine** for each extra day, payable at a *migración* before you try to leave the country. If you're leaving Bolivia by a particularly remote border crossing, you may need to get an exit stamp **in advance** from the *migración* in the nearest major town. **Under-18s** travelling to Bolivia without their parents need written parental consent authorized by a Bolivian embassy.

Officially you must carry your **passport** with you at all times in Bolivia, but away from border areas it's enough in practice to carry a photocopy of the main page and your tourist card and entry stamps to show police or other officials when necessary.

Insurance

It's essential to take out an insurance policy before travelling to cover against theft, loss, illness or injury. A **typical policy** usually provides cover for the loss of baggage, tickets and – up to a certain limit – cash or cheques, as well as cancellation or curtailment of your journey. Most of them exclude so-called **dangerous sports** unless an extra premium is paid: in Bolivia this can mean white-water rafting, trekking and mountaineering, though probably not kayaking or jeep safaris.

Many policies can be chopped and changed to exclude coverage you don't need – for example, sickness and accident benefits can often be excluded or included at will. If you do take **medical coverage**, check whether benefits will be paid as treatment proceeds or only after you return home, and whether there is a 24-hour medical emergency number. When securing **baggage cover**, make sure that the per-article limit – typically under £500 – will cover your most valuable possession. If you need to make a claim,

you should keep receipts for medicines and medical treatment; in the event you have anything stolen, you must obtain an official statement (*denuncia*) from the police.

The internet

Like almost everywhere else in the world, Bolivia has seen a huge growth in internet use in recent years and, because few Bolivians have their own computers, this has meant an explosion of **internet cafés**, especially in places where there are large student populations. Internet cafés tend to charge about Bs3–5 an hour, and sometimes more in remote areas where competition is thin on the ground. The speed of machines and servers usually isn't very fast, especially outside the main cities.

Some of the better-equipped internet cafés also offer net phone or **Skype** services, which allow you to make calls via the internet for the same price as if you were just surfing the net – by far the cheapest way of calling home.

Increasing numbers of hotels, cafés, restaurants and bars in the more touristy areas offer free **wi-fi** access.

Laundry

In cities and larger towns you'll find **laundries** (*lavanderías*) where you can have your clothes machine-washed for around Bs10-15 per kilo; top end hotels can arrange this for you. Otherwise, most hotels can find someone to wash your clothes **by hand** if you ask. Some budget hotels have facilities for hand-washing your own clothes.

Living and working in Bolivia

Official requirements to gain **residency** in Bolivia are complicated and time-consuming, so most travellers who want to stay in the country for longer periods do so informally, leaving Bolivia every ninety days to come back in on a new tourist card.

BOLIVIAN EMBASSIES AND CONSULATES

Australia Suite 602, 90 Pitt St, Sydney, NSW 2000 ☎029247 4235, ⒻF029086 8199.
Canada Suite 416, 130 Albert St, Ottawa, Ontario KIP SG4 ☎613236-5730, ⒻF6132368237.

UK 106 Eaton Square, London SW1W 9AD ☎0207235 4248, ⒻF0207235 1286.
US Embassy 3014 Massachusetts Ave NW, Washington, DC 20008 ☎202483-4410.

There are several options available to people looking to work or study in Bolivia. Several cities have **language schools** where you can study Spanish, Quechua or Aymara, and those with initiative and enthusiasm shouldn't have much trouble finding **voluntary work** with one of the large number of NGOs operating in Bolivia. **Paid work** is more difficult to come by, and getting formal permission to work even more so, but opportunities do exist, particularly for those with valuable skills to offer.

Studying Spanish

Bolivia is a good place to **study Spanish**. Bolivian pronunciation is slow and clear, making the language easier to pick up, and tuition costs are lower than in neighbouring countries. Spending one or several weeks on an intensive course is a good way of immersing yourself in Bolivian culture and getting to know a particular city in more detail, and can provide a good reason for living in Bolivia for a while without being a tourist.

La Paz, Sucre and Cochabamba are the most popular places for studying Spanish – **language schools** are detailed in the listings section for each of these cities in the guide. You'll also find individual Spanish language teachers offering their services on a one-to-one basis in these cities and in smaller towns around Bolivia. These can be very good, though it's worth trying a lesson or two before you commit to a long course with a particular teacher. More adventurous linguists can also study **Quechua** (in Cochabamba) or **Aymara** (in La Paz).

Volunteering

There are ever-increasing opportunities for volunteering in Bolivia, though most require you to pay for your own food and accommodation and to stay for at least a month. Unless you're willing to pay the (often high) fees charged by agencies that match volunteers with charities, the best way to find volunteering work is by **word of mouth**. Ask around in cities like La Paz, Sucre and Cochabamba and you're likely to find something worthwhile to do if you're prepared to work for free, especially if you have useful skills to offer. Also try contacting

local NGOs – and international ones working in Bolivia – directly. You'll need a reasonable level of **Spanish** if you want to do any kind of volunteer work with local communities. A useful website with information on free and low-cost volunteering opportunities throughout South America is ⓦvolunteersouthamerica.net.

One place that does take volunteers on a regular basis is the **Parque Machía Inti Wara Yassi** animal refuge in Villa Tunari in the Chapare region, east of Cochabamba (see p.225). Volunteers do everything from maintaining trails and looking after rescued animals to cleaning toilets and showing school children around the park. Conservation-centred tour operator **Madidi Travel**, on Calle Comercio in Rurrenabaque (☎03 8922153, ⓦmadidi-travel.com), also welcomes volunteers to help out with both their Rurrenabaque office and private rainforest reserve; jungle-based volunteers get room and board.

Paid work

Unless you have arranged something in advance with an international company or non-government organization, your chances of finding paid work in Bolivia are slim. The best bet is **teaching English** in La Paz, Cochabamba or Santa Cruz, though pay is low unless you get work with the British Council or a similar international agency – this is best arranged in advance. Obviously, work as a teacher is easier to find if you have a formal TEFL qualification. Even if you do find paid employment, getting an official work permit is a costly and long-drawn-out bureaucratic nightmare – contact the *migración* in La Paz or any other major city for details.

Mail

Letters and postcards sent by airmail (*por avión*) to Europe and North America tend to take between one and two weeks to arrive; the rest of the world outside the Americas and Europe takes longer. Letters cost about Bs10–15 to Europe, the US, Canada, Australia or New Zealand. For a small extra charge, you can send letters **certified** (*certificado*), which is more reliable, but even then it's not a good idea to send anything you can't afford to lose.

Parcels up to 2kg can be airmailed from major post offices; this costs about Bs100 per kilo to Europe and about half that to North America; the contents must be checked by a customs officer in a post office before being sealed. There's no point sending anything from small town post offices, as you'll almost certainly reach the nearest city or large town before your letter or package does. If you have to send anything particularly important or urgent internationally, it's worth splashing out and using one of the internationally recognized **courier services**: FedEx and DHL have offices in major cities.

If you wish to **receive mail** in Bolivia, you can do so through the **poste restante** service available in most post offices – it's best to use those in major towns or cities. Have mail sent to "Lista de Correos, Correo Central, the town concerned, Bolivia", and make sure your surname is written in capitals and as obviously as possible, as your post will be filed under whatever the clerk thinks your surname is; if you suspect something sent to you has gone astray, ask them to check under your first name too. Mail is usually held for about three months, and you'll need your passport to collect it.

Maps

No two maps of Bolivia are identical, and none is absolutely accurate. Most errors are made in the mapping of **dirt roads and tracks**: some maps mark them incorrectly as proper roads; some miss them out altogether; and many mark roads quite clearly in areas where they have never existed except in the dreams of planners.

It's worth buying a good map of Bolivia from a **specialist map outlet** in your home country before you go, as they can be difficult to find in Bolivia

itself. That said, you can usually pick up a reasonably good national **road map**, entitled *Bolivia Highlights*, from the municipal tourist office in La Paz (see p.73), and from bookshops and tour agencies in La Paz and other major cities. The best **general map** of Bolivia is the *Travel Map of Bolivia* (1:2,200,000), produced by the US company O'Brien Cartographics, which you should be able to find at any good map outlet in your home country. Most good map outlets also sell sectional maps of South America that cover Bolivia reasonably well.

If you're planning to do any **trekking** or **climbing** in the Cordillera Real, O'Brien Cartographics produce an excellent map of that range which you should try to get hold of before you travel. In addition, the Bolivian Instituto Geográfico Militar, or IGM produces maps at a scale of 1:50,000 and 1:250,000 that cover about three-quarters of the country. These are very useful for trekkers or anyone planning to explore more remote areas and can be bought from the Instituto Geográfico Militar in La Paz (see p.86). They also sell some good smaller-scale maps covering the whole country.

The media

Newspapers and magazines

Newspapers are sold in the street and from shops and kiosks in all major towns and cities. In La Paz, the main quality **dailies** are *La Prensa*, which has good foreign coverage, the politically conservative *El Diario*, and the less reliable *La Razón*. The main provincial cities all have their own newspapers, which have a strongly regional outlook: *Los Tiempos* in Cochabamba is particularly good. The best of the Santa Cruz papers is *El Deber*, though its regional outlook is so strong you could be forgiven for

AVERAGE MONTHLY TEMPERATURES AND RAINFALL

	Jan	Feb	Mar	Apr	May	Jun	Jul	Aug	Sep	Oct	Nov	Dec
La Paz												
Max °C/°F	17/63	17/63	18/64	18/64	18/64	17/63	17/63	17/63	18/64	9/66	19/66	18/64
Min °C/°F	6/43	6/43	6/43	4/39	3/37	1/34	1/34	2/36	3/37	4/39	6/43	6/43
Rainfall (mm)	114	107	66	33	13	8	10	13	28	41	48	94
Santa Cruz												
Max °C/°F	34/93	25/77	28/82	33/91	30/86	31/88	19/66	32/90	31/88	27/81	27/81	28/82
Min °C/°F	24/75	23/73	25/77	24/75	19/66	23/73	16/61	20/68	23/73	20/68	17/63	23/73
Rainfall (mm)	282	180	89	78	136	1	16	16	1	65	296	203
Sucre												
Max °C/°F	18/64	22/72	19/66	19/66	20/68	17/63	20/68	25/77	25/77	23/73	23/73	14/57
Min °C/°F	11/52	12/45	8/46	8/46	5/41	5/41	3/37	4/39	7/45	10/50	7/45	11/52
Rainfall (mm)	238	91	86	32	0	0	0	5	8	68	34	175

thinking La Paz was a minor province of some faraway country, so little attention does it pay to events in the de facto capital. Most Bolivian newspapers now have their own **websites**. For serious analysis of political, social and economic developments, Bolivians turn to the weekly news magazine *Pulso*; the fortnightly *Juguete Rabioso* is also good.

International newspapers and magazines are quite hard to come by, though *Time*, *Newsweek* and *The Economist* are sold in city centres and expensive hotels in La Paz and Santa Cruz.

Radio

Radio is the most democratic of Bolivia's media, and the only one that adequately reflects the country's cultural diversity, with many of the country's hundreds of different stations broadcasting in **indigenous languages**. The leading national news radio station is Radio Fides, which is owned by the Catholic Church and broadcast on different FM frequencies in all the major cities. Other than the internet, carrying a short-wave radio is about the best way of keeping in touch with events back home and in the rest of the world. You can pick up the BBC World Service in English in most of Bolivia (though not in La Paz, where the surrounding mountains block the signal – check Ⓦbbc.co.uk/worldservice for frequencies), as well as other international broadcasters.

Television

Bolivians watch a growing amount of television, although many homes are still without a set. There are seven state and numerous private **terrestrial channels**, mostly serving up an uninspired cocktail of football, news and imported soap operas. Better hotels offer cable or satellite TV, which in bigger cities means up to eighty channels and often include the likes of CNN and BBC World, though in smaller cities local cable networks offer a far more limited selection.

Money

The Bolivian currency is the **peso boliviano** (Bs), referred to as both the peso and (more commonly) the **boliviano**. Thanks to the weakness of the Bolivian economy the boliviano remains extremely vulnerable to devaluation, and many businesses in Bolivia effectively operate in US dollars. Tour operators and many hotels quote their prices in US dollars rather than bolivianos, accepting payment in either currency. Otherwise, it's usual to pay for everything in bolivianos – indeed most places won't accept anything else.

Notes come in denominations of 200, 100, 50, 20, 10 and 5 bolivianos; coins in denominations of 1 and 2 bolivianos (these look very similar), and of 5, 10, 20 and 50 centavos. At the time of writing the exchange rates were roughly:

£1 = Bs11
$1 = Bs7
€1 = Bs10

You can check current exchange rates in any Bolivian newspaper or online at Ⓦxe.com/ucc.

Credit cards, travellers' cheques and cash

The best way to carry money in Bolivia is to have your funds in several different formats – a credit card (or cards), some travellers' cheques and some cash dollars hidden away for emergencies – so that if one lets you down you can turn to another. The easiest way to access funds is using plastic. Banks in all major cities and larger towns are connected to the nationwide Enlace network of **ATM**s, from which you can withdraw cash in US dollars or bolivianos using a credit or debit card – Enlace machines accept both Visa and Mastercard. Other than in the most expensive shops and restaurants (and in some hotels and tour agencies), credit and debit cards can rarely be used to pay for services directly – where they are, Visa is the most widely accepted, followed by Mastercard; American Express cards are rarely used.

Outside cities and larger towns, debit and credit cards and **travellers' cheques** are pretty much useless, so it's important to carry plenty of **cash** with you when you head to rural areas. US dollars can be changed into bolivianos at banks and by street money-changers almost everywhere in the country, and are a good way of carrying emergency back-up funds – even if there are no official money-changers around, you can usually find someone to change dollars at a reasonable rate by asking around in shops or hotels.

Small change is in chronic short supply in Bolivia and people are often reluctant to accept larger-denomination bills, so it's best to break them at every opportunity – in big shops, hotels and bus company offices. You should also be wary of forged notes – dollars and bolivianos – particularly if changing money on the streets.

Opening hours and public holidays

Shops, businesses and public offices in Bolivia generally open Monday to Saturday from around 8.30am or 9.30am. They mostly close for a **long**

lunch break between about noon and 2pm (even longer in some regions), and then open again until around 5.30pm to 7pm. Some offices, however, have adopted a newer system, known as *hora corrida*, whereby they work straight though from 8.30am to 4pm without closing for lunch.

Banks' opening hours are generally Monday to Friday from 8.30am to noon and 2.30pm to 5pm, and on Saturdays in the morning. **Public museums** usually open on Sundays for at least half the day, and close instead on Mondays. All these times are approximate, though: Bolivians aren't noted for their punctuality, and public offices in particular often open later and close earlier than they are supposed to; conversely, private businesses, particularly those connected with tourism, often work longer hours and open on Sundays. If you're arranging to meet a Bolivian, make it somewhere you don't mind waiting around, as they're unlikely to turn up on time. Note that during **public holidays** and **local fiestas** pretty much everything closes down.

Phones

Bolivia's phone system is now fairly efficient. The Bolivian national telephone company, **ENTEL**, has offices in all cities and most towns where you can make local, national and international calls. ENTEL offices are usually open daily from around 8am to 8pm, sometimes longer. Local calls are very cheap, and long-distance national calls are moderately priced, but international calls are relatively expensive, though costs are coming down. You can also use a **cardphone**, which are found on the streets of most towns. The cost of either method is the same. You can buy a phone card (*tarjeta telefonica*) at ENTEL offices and in shops and street stalls throughout Bolivia. Phone calls to North America and Europe cost around Bs1 per minute, and a little more to Australia and New Zealand.

You'll also find a small number of **coin-operated phones** in most towns. Most departments also have their own **regional telephone cooperatives** that have their own networks of cardphones. These are sometimes cheaper for local calls, though no good for international or national long-distance calls. Many shops and kiosks also have phones from which you can make short local calls for a small fee.

Mobile phones

Mobile phones are widely used in large towns and cities, and coverage is improving in rural areas. If you want to use one while in Bolivia, the easiest

TELEPHONE CODES AND USEFUL NUMBERS

TO PHONE ABROAD FROM BOLIVIA

Dial the international access code (00) + country code (see below) + area code (minus initial zero) + subscriber number

Australia	☎00 61	New Zealand	☎00 64
Canada	☎00 1	UK	☎00 44
Ireland	☎00 353	USA	☎00 1

TO PHONE BOLIVIA FROM ABROAD

Dial the international access code (00) followed by the Bolivian country code (☎591) and the relevant area code (see below), followed by the seven-digit landline number. If you are calling a mobile phone (which have eight-digit numbers) from either overseas or from within Bolivia, omit the area code.

REGIONAL AREA CODES

La Paz, Oruro and Potosí	☎2	Chuquisaca and Tarija	☎4
Beni, Pando and Santa Cruz	☎3		

COLLECT CALL AND CHARGE CARD ACCESS NUMBERS

BT Direct (UK and Ireland)	☎0800 0044	USA Sprint	☎0800 3333
USA MCI	☎0800 2222	USA AT&T	☎0800 112
Canada Direct	☎0800 0102		

USEFUL NUMBERS IN BOLIVIA

Directory enquiries	☎118	Emergency services	☎110
Operator	☎101	Changed-number information	☎104

USEFUL WEBSITES

Australian Department of Foreign Affairs Ⓦ dfat.gov.au, Ⓦ smartraveller.gov.au.

BoliviaBella Ⓦ boliviabella.com. Useful bilingual site; particularly good on Santa Cruz and the Eastern Lowlands.

Boliviaweb Ⓦ boliviaweb.com. Good general site with links to many other Bolivia-related web pages and general background information.

British Foreign and Commonwealth Office Ⓦ fco.gov.uk. Constantly updated advice for travellers on the safety situation in Bolivia (and some 130 other countries).

Canadian Department of Foreign Affairs Ⓦ dfait-maeci.gc.ca.

Chiquitania Ⓦ chiquitania.com. Excellent site on the Jesuit Missions circuit and the surrounding region.

Irish Department of Foreign Affairs Ⓦ foreignaffairs.gov.ie.

Latin America Network Information Centre Ⓦ lanic.utexas.edu/la/sa/bolivia. An excellent resource for Spanish speakers, with links to a massive range of Bolivia-related sites divided into themes including art, culture and environment.

New Zealand Ministry of Foreign Affairs Ⓦ safetravel.govt.nz.

South American Explorers Club Ⓦ saexplorers.org. Site of the long-established non-profit travel organization, with useful travel advice and information on Bolivia.

US State Department Travel Advisories Ⓦ travel.state.gov. Reliable source of travel alerts and warnings.

---

option is to bring your own phone from home and buy a Bolivian **SIM card** ("chip") from one of the several mobile network operators – such as Viva, Tigo or the ubiquitous ENTEL – which you can then top up with credit. Annoyingly, foreigners can only – officially at least – buy SIM cards from bigger branches of the mobile companies, which tend to be in the larger towns or cities; take your passport. SIMs are often free if you buy credit (from Bs15) at the same time.

Collect calls and charge cards

If your home phone operator has an arrangement with ENTEL, you can phone home collect using a **telephone charge card**. This enables you to make calls from most public and private phones in Bolivia by dialling an international operator. The calls are charged to your own account back home. It's worth having one of these cards, if only for emergencies. To get a card and PIN, and to find out rates, contact your domestic operator before you leave (see opposite).

Photography

The light in Bolivia is very bright, particularly at **high altitudes**, so use fast (100 ASA) film and a UV polarizing filter. In the highlands, the best times to take photos are early in the morning and late in the afternoon, when the sunlight is not too harsh. Under the **forest canopy** in the lowlands, on the other hand, light is poor, so you need to use slow film. Taking photos of people without permission can offend, particularly in rural areas. It's best to ask

politely (*"Puedo sacar una fotito?"* – "Can I take a little photo?"); most people react favourably to this approach, though some may refuse outright or ask for a small fee.

Time

Bolivia is four hours behind Greenwich Mean Time, an hour ahead of US Eastern Standard Time.

Tourist information

Bolivia has no national tourist offices. Although you can sometimes get limited tourist information from some of the country's embassies, you'll probably find that **tour companies** who run trips to Bolivia are a better bet. The internet is another good source of information, and a growing number of websites offer everything on the country from hard facts to trivia and travellers' tales.

Most major Bolivian cities have a **regional tourism office**, either run by the city municipality or by the departmental prefecture. Some are fairly helpful, handing out free leaflets and doing their best to answer questions (though rarely in English). Others offer a much more limited service, though you should at least be able to get a plan of the city from them. Local Bolivian **tour operators** are generally a good source of information, and many are happy to answer queries, often in English, though obviously their main aim is to sell you one of their tours. Finally, the best source of information is often **word of mouth** from fellow travellers.

La Paz

56 The colonial city centre

62 Plaza San Francisco and the market district

66 Avenida 16 de Julio and around

69 Zona Sur

69 El Alto

70 Arrival and departure

71 Getting around

73 Information and tours

74 Accommodation

78 Eating

82 Drinking and nightlife

84 Entertainment

85 Shopping

86 Directory

87 Around La Paz

VIEW OVER LA PAZ FROM EL ALTO

1

La Paz

Few cities in the world have as spectacular a setting as La Paz. Glimpsed for the first time as your bus or taxi crawls over the lip of the narrow canyon in which the city sits hunched, it's a sight that will leave your lungs gasping for oxygen they can't have. At over 3500m above sea level, amid a hollow gouged into the Altiplano, it's a scene of stunning contrasts: a central cluster of church spires and office blocks dwarfed by the magnificent icebound peak of Mount Illimani rising imperiously to the southeast. On either side, the steep valley slopes are covered by the ramshackle homes of the city's poorer inhabitants, clinging precariously to even the harshest gradients.

With a population of around 835,000, **La Paz** is the political and commercial hub of Bolivia and the capital in all but name (technically, that honour belongs to Sucre). Though protected to some extent from the tides of globalization by its isolation and singular cultural make-up, La Paz feels very much part of the twenty-first century, its manic bustle and offbeat, cosmopolitan feel luring travellers back time and again. Founded as a centre of Spanish power in the Andes, La Paz has always had a dual identity, with two very distinct societies – the indigenous and the European – coexisting in the same geographical space. Hi-tech international banks and government offices rub shoulders with vibrant street markets selling all manner of ritual paraphernalia for appeasing the spirits and mountain gods that still play a central role in the lives of the indigenous **Aymara**.

The Aymara, in fact, make up not only the majority of the city's population, but also that of **El Alto** (see p.69), La Paz's militant, red-brick alter ego, which continues to outstrip it in terms of rural migrant-boosted population, and often media coverage. For them, working life in La Paz is conducted largely on the streets, and at times the whole place can feel like one massive, sprawling market. Though you'd imagine the exigencies of life at high altitude would make the pace of life quite slow, in reality it's often more frantic than Buenos Aires or Rio, not least during the winter **Fiesta del Gran Poder** (see p.58), when young and old alike dance in riotous celebration of the sacred and the profane.

Horrendous congestion and belching-black pollution notwithstanding, most visitors find La Paz's compelling street life and tremendous cultural energy warrant spending at least a few days here, even if conventional tourist attractions are limited to a scattering of **colonial palaces, plazas** and **churches** in the centre of town. The city's **museums**, while perhaps not fully doing justice to Bolivia's fascinating history and culture, are nevertheless much improved from only a decade ago, and likewise warrant at least a day or two's browsing. The absence of green areas, meanwhile, is more than redeemed by the sight of Illimani, tantalisingly glimpsed through breaks in the urban sprawl.

Altitude sickness p.55
La Fiesta del Gran Poder p.58
La Chola Paceña p.60
Feria de Alasitas: the Festival of Abundance p.66
San Pedro Prison p.68
Street crime p.71
Tours from La Paz p.72

La Paz street food p.78
Top 5 breakfast bites p.79
Top 5 live music venues p.81
Thank God it's (bachelor) Friday p.82
The sacred geography of Tiwanaku and the Aymara New Year p.89
Sukakullos p.90

Highlights

❶ Fiesta del Gran Poder La Paz's biggest religious fiesta, during which thousands of extravagantly costumed Aymara dancers parade through the streets. **See p.58**

❷ Plaza San Francisco This lively square is the unofficial city centre for La Paz's indigenous communities, and also home to the city's most beautiful colonial church. **See p.62**

❸ Calles Sagárnaga and Linares La Paz's "gringo alleys" are the best place to buy clothes, weavings, instruments and other handicrafts from all over Bolivia. **See p.64**

❹ Mercado de Hechicería This most colourful and compelling of La Paz's innumerable street markets sells all manner of Aymara ritual paraphernalia and herbal cures. **See p.64**

❺ Feria de Alasitas In the last week of January the streets fill with colourful stalls selling miniature items that are bought and sold to bring prosperity. **See p.66**

❻ Tiwanaku Just an hour away from La Paz, the ancient ruined city of Tiwanaku is one of the most monumental and intriguing archeological sites in South America. **See p.89**

HIGHLIGHTS ARE MARKED ON THE MAPS ON P.54 & 57

1

Brief history

La Ciudad de Nuestra Señora de la Paz – **"The City of Our Lady of Peace"** – was founded on October 20, 1548 on the orders of Pedro de la Gasca, the supreme representative of the Spanish Emperor in Peru, to commemorate the end of almost ten years of bitter civil war between rival Spanish factions fighting over the combined territories of Alto and Bajo Peru. Sited in the Choqueyapu valley, the city developed an economy based on commerce rather than mining.

The seventeenth and eighteenth centuries

The merchants of La Paz grew rich through the trade in **coca** from the Yungas to the mines of Potosí, and the city also prospered as a waystation on the route between the mines and the coast, and between Lima and Buenos Aires. By 1665 some five hundred Spaniards were living in La Paz, with a much larger indigenous population housed on the other side of the fledgling city across the **Río Choqueyapu**. In 1781 an indigenous army led by **Tupac Katari** twice laid siege to La Paz (see p.309), though the city survived and held out until it was relieved by the army sent from **Buenos Aires** that finally crushed the rebellion.

Independence

By the time Bolivia's independence from Spain was finally secured in 1825 (see p.310), La Paz was the biggest city in the country, with a population of forty thousand. Though **Sucre** remained the capital, La Paz was increasingly the focus of the new republic's turbulent political life. In 1899 the growing rivalry between the two cities was resolved in a short but bloody **civil war** that left La Paz as the seat of government, home to the president and the congress, and the capital in all but name.

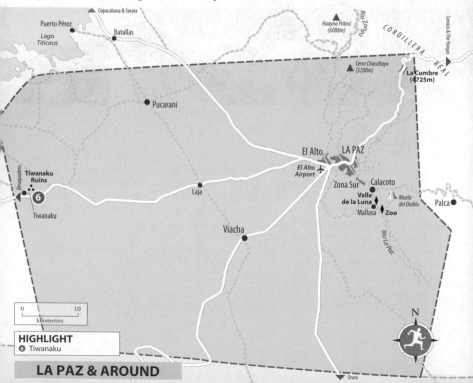

HIGHLIGHT
6 Tiwanaku

LA PAZ & AROUND

1

The twentieth century

The first half of the twentieth century saw La Paz's population grow to over three hundred thousand. In 1952 La Paz was the scene of the fierce street fighting that ushered in the **revolution** led by the MNR, or Movimiento Nacionalista Revolucionario (see p.314). The sweeping changes that followed further fuelled the city's growth as the Aymara population of the Altiplano, released from servitude by the Agrarian reform (see p.315), migrated en masse to the metropolis. This migration from the countryside profoundly changed the character of La Paz, quadrupling its population to over a million and transforming it into a predominantly Aymara city, albeit still ruled by a wealthy European-descended minority.

The twenty-first century

While this ethnic and geographical gulf is hardly without precedent in Latin America, age-old tensions reached a boiling point over the first half of the decade, with violent civil disturbances toppling a series of neo-liberal presidents. Plans to export natural gas via a Chilean pipeline prompted the first "**gas war**" in 2003 (see p.319). Further unrest over the unresolved gas issue erupted in May and June 2005 with hundreds of thousands of indigenous protestors massing in La Paz, effectively cutting off the city and effecting the resignation of then-president **Carlos Mesa**.

The reign of Evo Morales

With the 2005 election of Bolivia's first (and it's looking increasingly likely, most enduring) indigenous president, **Evo Morales**, the Aymara finally achieved real political power and the traditional campesinos vs the state ferment was superseded, to some extent, by a wider geo-political cultural spat between the radical Altiplano and the right-wing lowland departments of Beni, Pando, Santa Cruz and Tarija. Yet while much of the violence and unrest has taken place far from the capital, **demonstrations** by discontented miners, pensioners, fuel protestors, hunger strikers in the main Post Office and indeed anyone at all who feels hard done by, underlines the fact that La Paz, in its strategic relation to El Alto and the Highland Aymara communities, remains a vital crucible for popular protest.

ALTITUDE SICKNESS

The main problem you're likely to face when you arrive in La Paz is the **altitude**: the city stands at over 3500m above sea level, and the airport in El Alto is even higher, at over 4000m. If you're flying in or arriving by bus from lower elevations you may suffer from **altitude sickness**, also known as **soroche**, a debilitating and potentially dangerous condition caused by the reduced oxygen levels found at high elevations. Mild symptoms can include breathlessness and lethargy, sleeplessness, headaches and nausea, though for most people these fade within a few days as the body adjusts to the rarefied air. On arrival at high altitude you should take things very slowly and get straight to a hotel where you can leave your luggage and rest. It's also best to avoid smoking and alcohol, and to drink plenty of liquids, particularly **maté de coca**, an infusion of coca leaves that any local will tell you is the ideal remedy. Alternatively, all chemists stock *soroche* pills; they're high in caffeine, however, so don't take them at night unless you fancy even less sleep than the altitude already dictates.

In its more serious forms, altitude sickness can be dangerous or even **life-threatening**. If you think you may have the symptoms of high-altitude pulmonary or cerebral oedema (see p.38) you should seek immediate medical advice. The best place for this is the High Altitude Pathology Institute, Clinica IPPA, Av Saavedra 2302 (☎02 2245394, ⍟altitudeclinic.com).

1

Orientation

La Paz's geography makes it a difficult place to get lost in: if you do become disoriented, just head downhill and you'll eventually hit the city's main commercial thoroughfare, the broad avenue known locally as the **Prado** (or El Prado). Lined with trees – a rarity in La Paz – and with a central promenade full of pleasant gardens and benches, the Prado is one of the city's few flat and spacious areas, and a popular place for strolling and socializing. The street runs southeast along the course of the **Río Choqueyapu**, whose heavily polluted waters are now entombed in concrete beneath the streets.

To the east of the Prado, the **colonial city centre** is still the main commercial and government district, dominated by banks, ministries and the men in grey suits who run them. It also houses most of the city's museums and surviving colonial churches. To the west of the Prado, meanwhile, the main **indigenous neighbourhoods** sweep up the steep slopes of the valley. This is also where much of the budget accommodation and other tourist services are found, centred above all on **calles Sagárnaga** and **Linares**.

Heading southeast down the Prado, the street's official name changes from Avenida Mariscal Santa Cruz to Avenida 16 de Julio as it passes the suburbs of **San Pedro** to the west and Miraflores to the east. The Prado ends on Plaza del Estudiante, south of which is the pleasant middle-class suburb of **Sopocachi**. Many of the city's wealthiest residents likewise now live in the suburbs that have sprung up down the valley in the **Zona Sur**, about 5km from the city centre.

The colonial city centre

The well-ordered streets of the colonial city centre still preserve the neat grid pattern laid out by the city founders in accordance with Spanish laws governing the foundation of settlements in the Indies. At its centre stands the **Plaza Murillo**, home to both the Palacio Presidential and the parliament building, the Palacio Legislativo. A fair number of colonial buildings still survive, though most are in a poor state of repair, their crumbling facades and dilapidated balconies obscured by tangled phone lines and electricity cables. The exceptions to this are concentrated on and around the Plaza Murillo and nearby **calle Jaén**, both of which are also home to several **museums**.

Plaza Murillo

Though it remains the epicentre of Bolivia's political life, the **Plaza Murillo** – the main square of the colonial city centre – has an endearingly provincial feel, busy with people feeding pigeons and eating ice cream, and filled with smartly dressed families on weekends. On a sunny day it's a wonderful place to rest your feet, warm yourself up and retreat from the chaos all around, especially in winter when the city's otherwise shadowy streets are at their chilliest. Known as the Plaza de Armas during the colonial era, the square was renamed after independence in honour of the independence martyr Pedro Domingo Murillo, who was hanged here in 1810 after leading a failed rebellion against the colonial authorities, one of several bloody scenes the square has witnessed during Bolivia's turbulent political past. A statue of Murillo now stands at the centre of the plaza.

La Catedral

Plaza Murillo • Mon–Fri 8am–noon & 4–8pm, Sat & Sun 8am–noon • Free

On the south side of the plaza stand two great symbols of political and spiritual power in Bolivia, the Catedral and the Palacio Presidential. With its twin bell towers and

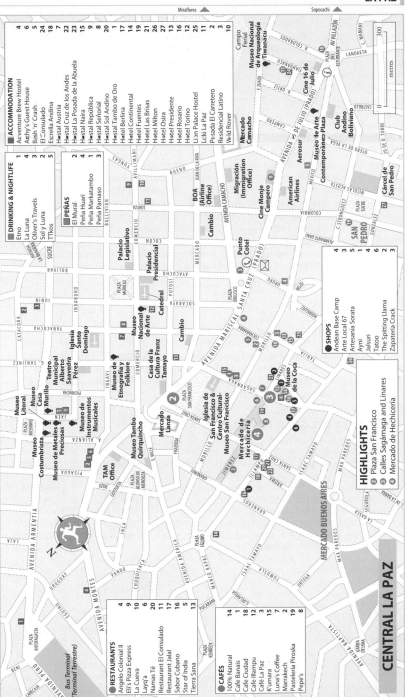

CENTRAL LA PAZ

● ACCOMMODATION
Acventure Brew Hostel	4
Arthy's Guest House	6
Bash 'n' Crash	5
El Consulado	24
Escrella Andina	18
Hostal Austria	7
Hostal Cruz de los Andes	22
Hostal La Posada de la Abuela	23
Hostal Naira	15
Hostal República	9
Hostal Señorial	8
Hostal Sol Andino	20
Hostal Tambo de Oro	1
Hotel Berlina	17
Hotel Continental	14
Hotel Fuentes	19
Hotel Las Brisas	21
Hotel Milton	26
Hotel Osira	27
Hotel Presidente	13
Hotel Rosario	16
Hotel Torino	12
Lçki La Paz	25
Lin Palace Hostel	11
Pesada El Carretero	2
Residencial Latino	3
Wild Rover	10

■ DRINKING & NIGHTLIFE
Etno	4
La Luna	3
Oliver's Travels	1
Sol y Luna	2
TTkos	5

■ PEÑAS
El Mural	2
Peña Huari	4
Peña Markatambo	1
Peña Parnaso	3

● RESTAURANTS
Angelo Colonial II	4
Eli's Pizza Express	9
La Cueva	6
Layq'a	10
Namas Té	20
Restaurant El Consulado	11
Restaurant Jalal	17
Sabor Cubano	16
Star of India	5
Tierra Sana	13

● CAFÉS
100% Natural	14
Cafe Banais	1
Cafe Ciudad	18
Cafe Illampu	12
Café La Paz	3
Kumara	15
Luna's Coffee	7
Marrakech	2
Pastelería Piroska	19
Pepe's	8

● SHOPS
Andean Base Camp	4
Arte Local 67	1
Artesania Sorata	5
Ayni	4
Jalsuri	6
Tatoo	7
The Spitting Llama	2
Zapateria Crack	3

HIGHLIGHTS
2 Plaza San Francisco
3 Calles Sagárnaga and Linares
4 Mercado de Hechicería

1

broad but rather plain Neoclassical facade, the **Catedral** is remarkable more for the time it took to complete (almost a century) than for its aesthetic value. The cool, vaulted interior is relatively unadorned, in contrast to La Paz's many Baroque churches; its most unusual feature is a stained-glass window depicting former presidents Mariscal Andrés de Santa Cruz and General José de Ballivián and their families receiving blessings from on high, a surprisingly explicit expression of the historic conflation in Bolivia of church, military and state.

Palacio Presidencial
South side of Plaza Murillo

Next door to the Catedral stands the elegant Neoclassical **Palacio Presidencial**, its ceremonial guards in red nineteenth-century uniforms from the War of the Pacific discreetly backed up by military policemen with more modern equipment. As the day-to-day office of the president, the palace isn't open to the public, but the guards may let you have a look at the central courtyard when the president is not in residence. Completed in 1852, the palace is generally known as the **Palacio Quemado** – the "Burnt Palace" – after it was badly damaged by fire in 1875 during one of the more violent of Bolivia's many revolutionary episodes. In front of the Catedral stands a bust of former president Gualberto Villaroel, himself thrown from a palace window by a mob and hanged from a lamppost as recently as 1946.

Palacio Legislativo
East side of Plaza Murillo

The **Palacio Legislativo** is the seat of the Bolivian parliament, built in a similar Neoclassical style to the Catedral in the early twentieth century on the site previously occupied by the Jesuit headquarters until their expulsion from the Spanish Empire in 1767. Even this hasn't been immune to the worst effects of Bolivia's tumultuous political climate, with a miner infamously blowing himself up inside the building in 2004, in protest at the lack of retirement provision.

LA FIESTA DEL GRAN PODER

The defining cultural and social event of the year in La Paz is undoubtedly **La Fiesta del Gran Poder**, a dramatic religious fiesta held during late May or early June in homage to a miraculous image of Christ known as **Nuestro Señor del Gran Poder** (Our Lord of Great Power). The origins of the Gran Poder are surprisingly recent. It started little over half a century ago as a local celebration amongst Aymara migrants living and working in the market district around Avenida Buenos Aires, but since the beginning of the 1980s it has grown into an enormous festival that has taken over the centre of the city and is enjoyed by Paceños of all different classes. In part, this expansion has followed the growing wealth and influence of the Aymara merchants, but it also reflects a growing acceptance of **Aymara culture** and folklore amongst the city's white and mestizo residents.

Tens of thousands of costumed dancers belonging to over a hundred different folkloric fraternities take part in the **entrada** – the procession that marks the start of the fiesta – parading through the centre of La Paz to the cacophonous accompaniment of massed brass bands. The various dances performed during the *entrada* represent different themes from Aymara folklore and **Catholic traditions** from all over the department of La Paz and further afield. The sight of grown adults dressed in outrageous costumes drinking and dancing their way through the city may seem an odd form of religious devotion, but the participants and spectators see no contradiction in combining the sincere expression of religious belief with a riotous party – indeed the act of dancing nonstop for several hours at high altitude in a heavy costume can be seen as an exhausting form of devotional sacrifice, while the Señor del Gran Poder would doubtless be disappointed if the celebration of his fiesta were not accompanied by sufficient revelry.

Museo Nacional de Arte

Southwest corner of Plaza Murillo • Mon–Fri 9.30am–12.30pm & 3–7pm, Sat 10am–5.30pm, Sun 10am–1.30pm • Bs10 • ⓦ mna.org.bo

The Palacio de Los Condes de Arana is one of La Paz's finest surviving colonial palaces; it would be difficult to think of a more magnificent setting for Bolivia's premier art gallery, the **Museo Nacional de Arte**, well worth visiting for its comprehensive collection of works by major Bolivian painters. Completed in 1775, when La Paz was at the peak of its colonial prosperity, the palace is a pre-eminent example of Baroque architecture, with a grand portico opening onto a central patio overlooked by three floors of arched walkways, all elaborately carved from pink granite in a Rococo style with stylized shells, flowers and feathers.

Colonial art

The emphasis of the museum's art collection is firmly on colonial religious art. Among the highlights are several works by **Melchor Pérez de Holguín**, the great master of Andean colonial painting, and a magnificent eighteenth-century picture by an anonymous La Paz artist of an Archangel Arquebusero, an iconic image of an angel carrying a primitive firearm, which neatly encapsulates the spiritual and military contradictions of the Spanish conquest. Perhaps the most fascinating of the museum's colonial works, however, is the small, anonymous canvas, *Virgin Mountain* (1720), donated by Madrid's Reina Sofía gallery, and based on a design attributed to **Francisco Tito Yupanqui**. The piece, one of the finest extant examples of mestizo-Baroque, depicts Potosí's Cerro Rico with the Virgin Mary inlaid ghost-like at its summit, flanked by the Pillars of Hercules and looming over tiny, stick-like representations of Inca Huayna Capac and Diego Huallpa (see p.305). Dense in allegory and syncretism, it conflates the purity of the Virgin with the purity of Cerro Rico's silver and Pachamama – the Andean earth goddess herself.

Modern art

There's a whole room dedicated to the elegant torsos of Bolivian sculptress **Marina Nuñez del Prado** yet the most compelling among the museum's modern pieces are arguably the works of **Cecilio Gúzmán de Rojas**, a leading figure in the Indigenismo movement of the early 20th century. His stylized depictions of the Andean feminine face are hugely compelling, strong and almost cat-like in their grace and power. His most striking work is probably the wall-sized *Mujeres Andinas*, an aquiline huddle of women under a blazing sky alive with animist spirits.

Museo de Etnografía y Folklore

Corner of Ingavi and Gerardo Sanjinez • Mon–Fri 9am–noon & 3–6.30pm, Sat 9am–4pm, Sun till 12.30pm • Bs15 • ⓦ www.musef.org.bo

Set inside an elegant colonial mansion on calle Ingavi is the small but rewarding **Museo de Etnografía y Folklore**, housed in a seventeenth-century mansion built for the Marques de Villaverde, whose coat of arms looks down on the central patio from an exquisite mestizo-Baroque portico, complete with floral designs, parrots and feline figures. The mansion's street facade boasts the only surviving example of the elegant carved wooden balconies that were common in colonial La Paz, and there's a branch of the ubiquitous *Angelo Colonial* café chain attached.

Inside, the museum has an exhibition on the history of **Andean ceramics**, with a horde of largely anthropomorphic pieces from the Chimú, Chancay and Tiwanaku cultures, as well as strange ritual *muñecas* (dolls), Inca *kerus* (ceremonial wooden cups), some lovely colonial painted vases and a room dedicated to *Arte Plumario*, or feather art. Conferring honour and respect on their wearers and serving as a kind of spiritual cleanser and conduit, the feathers on display here are much more than simply cast-off plumage: the brilliant designs of the Moxos plains are clearly reflections of the tropical

1

sun, while the Altiplano incarnations are conspicuous for their height; the Cabezade Phusipia headdress resembles a veritable flower garden in the sky.

If these aren't surreal enough for you, the darkened **mask room** should suffice, a by turns grotesque, outrageous, hilarious and never less than fascinating combination of the familiar and the more obscure, including a Nazca death mask, lesser seen Chaco carnival masks and the sinister *Aaqui Aaqui* from Charazani, a malformed doctor/lawyer parody.

The real feather in the museum's cap, however, has to be its exhaustive **textile room**, going way back into the pre-Columbian era with tattered fragments from the Chimú, Tiwanaku, Paracas, Nazca, Chancay and Inca cultures, much of it – in stark contrast to the more familiar linear patterns favoured from the colonial era onwards – featuring geometric designs and zoomorphic figures.

Calle Jaén

Three blocks northwest of Plaza Murillo lies the enchanting **Calle Jaén**, the best-preserved colonial street in La Paz and home to no fewer than five **municipal museums**. A narrow cobbled street lined with whitewashed houses adorned with elegant wooden balconies, red-tiled roofs and carved stone doorways opening onto quiet courtyards, calle Jaén could almost be in a small town in Andalucia or Extremadura, so strong is the Spanish feel.

Museo Costumbrista Juan de Vargas

At the top of Jaén; the entrance is around the corner on Sucre • Tues–Fri 9.30am–12.30pm & 3–7pm, Sat & Sun 9am–1pm • Except for the Museo de Instrumentos Musicales de Bolivia (see opposite) all the municipal museums are accessed on a single ticket, only sold at the Museo, Costumbrista Juan de Vargas; Bs4 • ☎ 02 2280758

Set inside a renovated colonial mansion, **Museo Costumbrista Juan de Vargas** gives a

---

LA CHOLA PACEÑA

One of the most striking images in La Paz is that of the ubiquitous **cholas paceñas**, the Aymara and mestiza women dressed in voluminous skirts and bowler hats, who dominate much of the day-to-day business in the city's endless markets. The word *chola* (*cholo* for men) was originally a derogatory term used to refer to indigenous women who moved to the city and adopted the lifestyle of urban mestizos, but now refers more to women who were born in La Paz (*paceñas*) and are proud of their urban indigenous identity.

The distinctive dress of the *chola* is derived from seventeenth-century Spanish costumes, which indigenous women were obliged to copy under colonial rule. The crucial element of the outfit is the **pollera**, a layered skirt made from lengths of material up to 5m long, which are wrapped around the waist and reinforced with numerous petticoats to emphasize the width of the wearer's hips. These skirts can make women appear almost as wide as they are tall, and represent a glorious celebration of a very distinct ideal of female beauty. The *pollera* is worn in combination with knee-high boots, an elaborate lacy blouse, a shawl wrapped around the shoulders and a felt bowler or derby hat. The **bowler hats** became common attire in the 1930s, though the origins of this fashion are somewhat mysterious. Some say the style was adopted from the hats worn by gringo mining and railway engineers, others that the trend was started by a businessman who erroneously imported a job lot of bowler hats from Europe and struck on the idea of marketing them as women's headgear.

The *chola* costume was originally confined to the wealthier mestiza women of La Paz, but has since become widespread amongst Aymara migrants in the city and across the Altiplano. The acceptability of the *chola* as one of the central icons of La Paz and an expression of pride in indigenous culture was confirmed in 1989, when **Remedios Loza** became the first woman to take a seat in the Bolivian Congress dressed in full *chola* regalia. In the decades since, not least since Evo Morales came to power in 2005, the colourfully attired *chola* has become almost as familiar a political fixture as the traditional drab-suited gent.

good introduction to the folkloric customs of the Altiplano, in particular the traditional dances and processions that form a central part of the region's religious fiestas. Though it can't match the collection in the Museo de Etnografía y Folklore (see p.59), the small cluster of **elaborate costumes** and **grotesque masks** is well worth a look, particularly the monstrous Danzante mask, whose wearer used to be expected to dance until he literally dropped dead, thereby ensuring a drought- and disease-free year for his community.

There is also a series of richly detailed **ceramic dioramas** of historical scenes, ranging from the founding of La Paz and the city's *tambos* (see p.62) to a poignant depiction of trains departing for the Chaco war. On the ground floor, meanwhile, there are diverting histories of both Bolivian radio and journalism – with assorted gramophones, radiograms, Voice of America microphones and even some dusty BBC Latin American Service vinyl – and the iconic Chola Paceña (see opposite).

Museo del Litoral Boliviano

Jaén 789 • Tues–Fri 9.30am–12.30pm & 3–7pm, Sat & Sun 9am–1pm • Except for the Museo de Instrumentos Musicales de Bolivia (see below), all the municipal museums are accessed on a single ticket, only sold at the Museo Costumbrista Juan de Vargas; Bs4

The **Museo Litoral** is dedicated to one of Bolivia's national obsessions: the loss of its coastline to Chile during the nineteenth century War of the Pacific (see p.311). Unless you share that obsession, however, the collection of old uniforms, photos of the lost ports and maps justifying Bolivia's claim to the coast is not very inspiring.

Museo de Metales Preciosos

Jaén 777 • Tues–Fri 9.30am–12.30pm & 3–7pm, Sat & Sun 9am–1pm • Except for the Museo de Instrumentos Musicales de Bolivia (see below), all the municipal museums are accessed on a single ticket, only sold at the Museo Costumbrista Juan de Vargas; Bs4

Next door to the Museo Litoral, the **Museo de Metales Preciosos** has a small but impressive hoard of Inca and Tiwanaku gold and silver ornaments, housed in a steel vault. The delicate skill evident in the work – everything from gold-encrusted stone pipes and thimble-like cups to gold disc-embroidered ponchos and funerary masks – makes it obvious why these indigenous artisans were so quickly enrolled into producing religious artwork by the Spanish.

Museo Casa de Murillo

Jaén 790 • Tues–Fri 9.30am–12.30pm & 3–7pm, Sat & Sun 9am–1pm • Except for the Museo de Instrumentos Musicales de Bolivia (see below), all the municipal museums are accessed on a single ticket, only sold at the Museo Costumbrista Juan de Vargas; Bs4

Inside the sumptuous mansion which was once the home of the venerated independence martyr after whom it's now named, the **Museo Casa de Murillo** houses an eclectic collection ranging from colonial religious art, furniture, ceremonial *keru* cups, and portraits of former presidents, to artefacts used in witchcraft and miniatures from past Alasitas fiestas (see p.66).

Museo de Instrumentos Musicales de Bolivia

Jaén 711 • Daily 9.30am–6.30pm • Bs5 • ☎ 02 2408177

Set around yet another pretty colonial courtyard on Jaén, the delightful **Museo de Instrumentos Musicales de Bolivia** is home to an astonishing variety of handmade musical instruments from all over Bolivia, some of which you can play with in-house lessons at competitive rates (Bs50/hour, for charango, *guitarra*, *zampoña* or quena; enquire at reception). A labyrinth of rooms kicks off with a collection of pre-Columbian pipes, nose flutes, wood and stone *oscarinas* and music-related ceramics. This is followed by a plethora of the **stringed instruments** – guitars, violins, mandolins and charangos – which were introduced by the Spanish, and eagerly seized upon by an indigenous population who quickly combined these two elements to create the distinctive Andean music of today.

1

Most interesting, however, are the **percussion and wind rooms**, cramming in maracas, bells and shells; toucan beaks; strange little leather trumpets; and wonderful palm-leaf *bajones* from San Ignacio de Moxos. Further chambers feature an array of Bolivian-invented instruments (many of them created by the museum's famous, charango-playing founder, Ernesto Cavour) including a chamber pot *tambor*, a saxophone-like quena and, for real Spinal Tap-esque overload, a five-necked charango. A collection of old concert posters, articles, scores and vinyl complete the tour.

Museo Tambo Quirquincho

Plaza Alonso de Mendoza • Tues–Fri 9.30am–12.30pm & 3–7pm, Sat & Sun 9am–1pm • Bs1

Just north of Plaza San Francisco is Plaza Alonso de Mendoza, on the southern side of which sits the **Museo Tambo Quirquincho**; like the Calle Jaén museums, this is run by the municipality, though it's far more friendly and helpful. Unfortunately, the place seems to have been divested of its former treasures and left to crumble quietly, home only to a collection of 60s/70s art. More interesting, perhaps, even if it is falling into disrepair, is the museum's setting: inside a restored eighteenth-century *tambo*, a compound that served during the colonial era both as accommodation and marketplace for rural Aymaras. The ornate mestizo-Baroque arches around the main courtyard were recovered from the ruins of the Conceptionist nunnery on Calle Genaro Sanjines after it was torn down to build a cinema.

Plaza San Francisco and the market district

At the north end of the Prado, **Plaza San Francisco** is the gateway to the main Aymara neighbourhoods of La Paz, which climb up the slopes of the valley to the west. Founded in the colonial era as the *parroquias de Indios* – the Indian parishes – these neighbourhoods were where the Aymara population from the surrounding country-side was encouraged to settle, living around churches built as part of the effort to convert them to Christianity; less idealistically, this separate indigenous quarter was also designed as a pool of cheap labour, neatly separated from the Spanish city by the Río Choqueyapu. Today the area retains a very strong Aymara identity and its narrow, winding and at times almost vertical streets are filled with the bustling markets that make it one of the most vibrant and distinctive parts of the city: nowhere more so than in the **Mercado de Hechicería** – without doubt one of the most extraordinary sights in La Paz.

Plaza San Francisco

Though the frenetic traffic running alongside detracts from its charm, the **Plaza San Francisco** (being completely redeveloped at the time of writing) is the focal point for the city's Aymara population and one of the liveliest plazas in La Paz, busy with people enjoying snacks and juices or crowding around the many comedians, story-tellers, magicians and sellers of miracle cures who come here to ply their trade. It's also the usual focus of the city's frequent **political protests**, and if you're in La Paz for more than a few days you're likely to witness a march by striking teachers, unemployed miners, indebted small traders or whichever social or political group has taken to the streets that week. Such protests are usually colourful pieces of political theatre, but they can sometimes provoke heavy-handed responses from the authorities, and clashes between police and demonstrators involving the fairly unrestrained use of tear gas are not uncommon.

Iglesia de San Francisco
West side of Plaza San Francisco • Free

The **Iglesia de San Francisco** is the most beautiful colonial church in La Paz. First built in 1549 as the headquarters of the Franciscans' campaign to Christianize Alto Peru, the original structure collapsed under a heavy snowfall early in the seventeenth century. Most of what you see today was built between 1750 and 1784, financed by donations from mine owners. The richly decorated facade is a classic example of the mestizo-Baroque style, showing clear indigenous influence, with carved anthropomorphic figures reminiscent of pre-Columbian sculpture as well as more common birds and intertwined floral designs. Above the main door is a statue of St Francis himself, facing towards the old city with his arms held aloft. Inside, the walls of the church are lined with extravagantly carved altarpieces where abundant gold leaf and smiling angels frame gruesome depictions of the crucifixion or images of individual saints that are the principal objects of veneration for those who come here to pray; San Judas Tadeo, the patron saint of the poor and miserable, is particularly popular amongst indigenous supplicants. To really experience the enormity of the place from on high (and to access the bell tower) it's well worth paying for a ticket to the excellent Centro Cultural – Museo San Francisco (see below).

Centro Cultural – Museo San Francisco
Entrance adjacent to Iglesia de San Francisco • Mon–Sat 9am–6pm • Bs20

Torched in the uprising of Tupac Katari in 1781 (see p.309), and subsequently used as, variously, a customs office, a barracks and a school, the elegant brick cloisters of the once resident Franciscans finally opened to the public in July 2005 as the **Centro Cultural – Museo San Francisco**, after a million-dollar restoration project. A sometimes unfocused yet always interesting exhibition of religious art, furniture, old photos and documents, it offers a revealing window into the lives of the Franciscans who once lived, ate, prayed and slept here, not to mention a must-see trip into the lesser visited extremities of the Iglesia de San Francisco itself. There's also an exquisite little museum café (open to non-visitors, and also accessed from Plaza San Francisco), *Profumó di Caffé* (Mon–Sat 9am–7.30pm), serving quality coffee and cakes.

The cloisters

While the bits and pieces of handsome **antique furniture** are possibly worth the price of the museum entry alone, perhaps the single most revealing item is the **photo** (dated July 1933) of a group of cloaked, beatific-looking monks with a dandy, jackbooted army officer resplendent at its centre. The Franciscans' military links are also fascinatingly revealed vis-à-vis their role in the Chaco War. More peaceful are the gorgeous, naturalistic **murals** uncovered in the cellars during the restoration, some in their entirety, depicting birds and trees, and others only in tantalizing patches.

The choir

Though it's not immediately clear, and easy to miss, your ticket also gives access to the Iglesia de San Francisco's **choir** in the loft at the upper eastern end of the nave (on the right after you climb the stairs from the museum entrance). Much more compelling than the cedar-wood stalls or the exhibits themselves (antique garments, chalices, reliquaries and the like), is the new perspective of the church from the choir's edge, verily a balcony seat to die for. You'll also get thrillingly close to the interior of the domes themselves and their magnificently worked stone.

Look out for the narrow door leading to the even narrower stone staircase up to the **roof**. Come near closing time and you'll be able to wander alone among the ageing bronze behemoths in the bell tower, with the weathered pantiles of the domes spread out below and a monks-eye view of La Paz in its chaotic entirety.

1

Calle Sagárnaga

To the south of Plaza San Francisco lies **Calle Sagárnaga**, La Paz's main tourist street (along with Linares, which bisects it), which is more crowded than it's ever been with hotels, tour agencies, restaurants, handicraft shops and stalls, with more seemingly opening every week. Often referred to as "Gringo Alley", the street has in fact always catered to travellers: in the colonial era, this was where wayfarers en route between Potosí and the Peruvian coast would be put up, and several of the buildings now occupied by hotels were actually built for that purpose in the eighteenth century.

Mercado de Hechicería

Linares and Jiménez • Daily, hours vary—Stalls open as early as 6am and close as late as 8pm in summer

The **Mercado de Hechicería**, or Witches' Market, provides a fascinating window on the usually secretive world of **Aymara mysticism** and **herbal medicine**. The stalls here are heavily laden with a colourful cornucopia of ritual and medicinal items, ranging from herbal cures for minor ailments like rheumatism or stomach pain, to incense, coloured sweets, protective talismans and dried llama foetuses. These items are combined in packages known as *mesas* or *pagos* and burned or buried as offerings to placate the various tutelary spirits and magical beings that are believed to hold sway over all aspects of daily life. There's no clear border between the medicinal and magical here: the *Yatiris* and *Kallawayas* – **indigenous traditional healers** – who are the market's main customers adopt a holistic approach in which a herbal cure for a specific symptom is usually combined with magical efforts to address the imbalances in the supernatural world that may be responsible for the ailment.

To get some insight into the uses and meaning of it all, it's worth chatting with the stallholders and perhaps making a purchase or two. Spending a few bolivianos on, say, a magic charm to protect you during your travels will certainly make the stallholders more talkative and amenable to having their photos taken, and could even prove to be a wise investment.

Museo de la Coca

Linares 906 • Daily 10am–7pm • Bs10 • Ⓦ cocamuseum.com

Tucked away inside an atmospheric little courtyard a block south of Sagárnaga on Linares, is the excellent **Museo de la Coca**, dedicated to the small green leaf that is both the central religious and cultural sacrament of the Andes and the raw material for the manufacture of cocaine. Crammed into a couple of small rooms, the museum gives a good overview of the history, chemistry, cultivation and uses of this most controversial of plants, imaginatively illustrated and explained in English and Spanish. There are excellent photos showing the cultivation and processing of coca in the Chapare – along with military attempts to eradicate it – and of its manifold uses.

A good selection of the packaging from some of the many modern **medicines** derived from coca, meanwhile, underlines its continuing industrial uses, despite the rhetoric of the war on drugs. One of the more surprising revelations is that, despite US anti-drugs rhetoric, the world's most popular soft drink still contains coca extract – according to the museum, in 1995 the Coca-Cola corporation imported over two hundred tons of the leaf.

Mercado Buenos Aires

Max Paredes and Avenida Buenos Aires • Daily, hours vary—stalls open as early as 6am and close as late as 8pm, with some food stalls open later

A few blocks to the northwest of Sagárnaga and Linares is **Mercado Buenos Aires**, also known as the **Huyustus**, an old indigenous name for the district. Centred on the

FROM TOP PLAZA MURILLO (P.56); LUCHA LIBRE DE CHOLITAS (P.70) >

1

> ### FERIA DE ALASITAS: THE FESTIVAL OF ABUNDANCE
>
> One of Bolivia's most unusual fiestas is the **Feria de Alasitas**, held in La Paz in the last week of January, when large areas of the city are taken over by market stalls selling all manner of miniature items. At the centre of the festivities is a diminutive figure of a mustachioed man with rosy cheeks and a broad smile, dressed in a tiny suit and hat and laden with foodstuffs and material possessions. This is the **Ekeko**, the household god of abundance. A common sight in Paceño homes, the Ekeko is a demanding god who must be kept happy with regular supplies of alcohol, cigarettes and **miniature gifts**. In return, he watches over the household, ensuring happiness and prosperity and returning in kind any gift he receives. At the fair each year, people buy objects they desire in miniature to give to the Ekeko, thereby ensuring that the real thing will be theirs before the year is out. Originally, gifts to the Ekeko would have been farm animals and foodstuffs, but in the modern urban context of La Paz, miniature cars, houses, electrical goods, wads of dollar bills and even airline tickets and university degrees are preferred to more traditional items.

intersection of Max Paredes with Avenida Buenos Aires, this is where La Paz's **Aymara majority** conduct their daily business, a vast open-air market sprawling over some thirty city blocks where anything and everything is bought and sold.

Street after street is lined with stalls piled high with all manner of goods: sacks of sweet-smelling coca leaf and great mounds of brightly coloured tropical fruit from the Yungas; enormous heaps of potatoes from the Altiplano; piles of smelly, silver-scaled fish from Lago Titicaca; stacks of stereos and televisions smuggled across the border; endless racks laden with the latest imitation designer clothes. Behind almost every stall sits or stands an Aymara woman in a bowler hat, calling out her wares or counting out small change from the deep pockets of her apron, often with a baby strapped to her back or sleeping in a bundle nearby, oblivious to the cacophonous din of the market all around.

Other stallholders sell the inexpensive drinks, meals and snacks that keep the market traders going through the day, ladling soup from steaming cauldrons, blending juices on wheeled trolleys, or hawking spicy *salteñas* from portable trays.

Avenida Buenos Aires and Calle Max Paredes

Highlights of the market include the numerous workshops above Avenida **Buenos Aires** where the elaborate masks and costumes for dancers in the city's main fiestas are made, and the shops and stalls along **Calle Max Paredes** selling the bowler hats, knee-length laced boots and endless petticoats favoured by Aymara women.

Though they are cheap and plentiful, the quality of the goods available in the street is not particularly high, and it's not really a place to come looking for souvenirs. Like most markets, it's also a favourite haunt of thieves and pickpockets, and the area is best avoided completely after dark.

Avenida 16 de Julio and around

In its southern reaches, a kilometre or so south of Plaza San Francisco, the busy, tree-lined Prado becomes Avenida 16 de Julio and passes between the suburb of **San Pedro** to the east and the more modern neighbourhood of **Miraflores** further to the west, before coming to an abrupt end at Plaza del Estudiante. Directly south of here lies the middle-class suburb of **Sopocachi**, the city's most pleasant residential area and home to many of its higher end restaurants and nightlife spots – the centre is around the parallel avenues 6 de Agosto and 20 de Octubre.

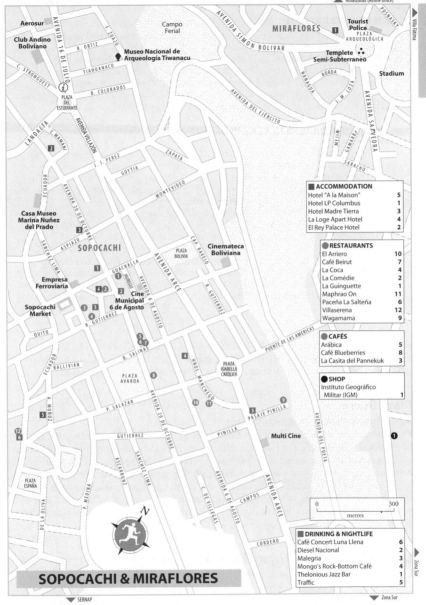

SOPOCACHI & MIRAFLORES

ACCOMMODATION

Hotel "A la Maison"	5
Hotel LP Columbus	1
Hotel Madre Tierra	3
La Loge Apart Hotel	4
El Rey Palace Hotel	2

RESTAURANTS

El Arriero	10
Café Beirut	7
La Coca	4
La Comédie	2
La Guinguette	1
Maphrao On	11
Paceña La Salteña	6
Villaserena	12
Wagamama	9

CAFÉS

Arábica	5
Café Blueberries	8
La Casita del Pannekuk	3

SHOP

| Instituto Geográfico Militar (IGM) | 1 |

DRINKING & NIGHTLIFE

Café Concert Luna Llena	6
Diesel Nacional	2
Malegria	3
Mongo's Rock-Bottom Café	4
Thelonious Jazz Bar	1
Traffic	5

Museo de Arte Contemporáneo Plaza

Av 16 de Julio 1698 • Daily 9am–9pm • Bs15 • ☎ 02 2335905

The **Museo de Arte Contemporáneo Plaza** is a decent showcase of both homegrown and international talent housed in a stunning nineteenth-century mansion. Amid the Gustave Eiffel stained glass and gilded staircases hang works which span the last six decades and the whole artistic spectrum, from vibrant indigenous oil paintings and a

1

SAN PEDRO PRISON

On the southeast side of Plaza Sucre rises the formidable bulk of **San Pedro Prison** (Cárcel de San Pedro), for years one of Bolivia's most infamous tourist "attractions". Critically overcrowded, structurally precarious, rife with tuberculosis and increasingly a scene of desperate protest, it nevertheless exerts a morbid fascination for the stream of foreigners who continue to find their way in despite it being officially **illegal** to do so, despite the obvious personal danger (no one will help you if trouble arises) and despite the negative effects it can have on the prisoners and their families when authorities periodically decide to clamp down.

Those whose curiosity gets the better of them will find what seems to so endlessly fascinate Europeans: a self-governed microcosm of Bolivian society, with **shops**, **restaurants** and **billiard halls**; prisoners with money can live quite well here. Comfortable cells in the nicer areas change hands for thousands of dollars, and many inmates have cell phones and satellite televisions. Like the city on the other side of the walls, the prison is divided into rich and poor neighbourhoods, with the most luxurious area reserved for big-time drug traffickers, white-collar criminals and corrupt politicians: the most high-profile resident in recent years has been the ex-Prefect of Pando, **Leopoldo Fernàndez** (see p.298).

Those without any income, however, sleep in the corridors and struggle to survive on the meagre official rations. **Family visitors** come and go regularly, and some children live inside with their fathers; when the riots erupt, it's the families who are often caught in the midst of it. If you're intent on a tour against all advice, it's worth thinking long and hard about the consequences it may have for both yourself and these families, even as you may feel your entry fee is financially assisting them. With the presence of guards minimal and **cocaine** widely available, moreover, some gringos are foolhardy enough to try taking some out with them; you can be assured that this is the best way to make your stay considerably longer than you intended.

glut of Che Guevara images, to the balletic poise of American Richard Hallier's sculptures and the powerful *Minero Crucificado* by Cochabama-born Hans Hoffman (*not* the famous abstract expressionist), strikingly wrought from soldered iron.

Plaza Sucre

Two blocks southwest of the Prado along Colombia, San Pedro

Plaza Sucre (also known as Plaza San Pedro) lies at the centre of **San Pedro**, one of the city's oldest suburbs. On the face of it, the square is peaceful enough, with well-tended gardens surrounding a statue of Bolivia's first president, the Venezuelan **General Antonio José de Sucre**, and home to portrait photographers with ancient box cameras. Yet looming over the plaza's southeastern edge are the pockmarked adobe walls of San Pedro Prison (see above), where a rash of recent protests has seen the teargas flying as police battle with disgruntled prisoners. The place – and in fact the whole San Pedro area – is best avoided entirely come nightfall.

Museo Nacional de Arqueología Tiwanaku

Tiahuanacu 93, two blocks from Av 16 de Julio • Mon–Fri 9am–12.30pm & 3–7pm, Sat 9am–noon • Bs10 • ☎ 02 2311621

Shortly before the Prado (Av 16 de Julio) ends at Plaza del Estudiante, a left turn down some steps and two blocks along Tiahuanacu brings you to the **Museo Nacional de Arqueología Tiwanacu**. Set inside a bizarre neo-Tiwanaku building that was originally home to the naturalized Bolivian archeologist Arthur Posnansky, who led some of the first serious excavations at Tiwanaku (see p.89), the museum has a reasonable collection of textiles, ceramics and stone sculptures from the Inca and Tiwanaku cultures, though the exhibits are poorly explained. Among the more eye-catching items is a collection of post-conquest Inca drinking cups, known as *kerus*, painted and carved with human faces, one of which is clearly chewing coca. Also interesting is a selection of drug paraphernalia from the Tiwanaku era, including long wooden tubes used for snorting powerful hallucinogens. Note that the museum was undergoing renovations at the time of writing and opening times and/or the exhibits themselves may be subject to change.

Zona Sur

From Plaza del Estudiante at the southern end of the Prado, Avenida Villazon heads southeast through Sopochachi, turning into Avenida Arce and then winding down into the **Zona Sur**, a fifteen-minute taxi ride away, where the suburbs of **Calacoto**, **San Miguel** and **Cota Cota** are home to a growing number of La Paz's wealthier residents, including politicians, senior military officers and most of the foreign business and diplomatic community. Almost 500m lower in altitude, the Zona Sur has a noticeably warmer climate, with luxury boutiques and villas ringed by harsh badlands. If you're passing through on the way to the Muela del Diablo (see p.88) or the Valle de la Luna (see p.87), it's worth stopping for a drink in one of the many cafés just to get an impression of how the city's elite live.

El Alto

At the opposite extreme in every sense from the Zona Sur is **El Alto**, the huge urban sprawl that has grown up over the last few decades around the airport, on the rim of the Altiplano overlooking La Paz. At over 4000m above sea level and some 5km from the city centre, El Alto enjoys beautiful views along the length of the snow-capped Cordillera Real, and the views of La Paz from the rim of the Altiplano are spectacular, even if they contrast sharply with the physical ugliness of the city itself. Populated largely by Aymara migrants from the surrounding Altiplano, when it was officially recognized as a separate municipality from La Paz in 1986, El Alto instantly became the fourth biggest, poorest and fastest growing city in Bolivia. With a bigger population than La Paz, and rapidly approaching one million (sixty percent of whom are under 25 years old), the place resembles a vast, impoverished yet dynamic suburb, its endless stretches of tin-roofed adobe shacks and often half-finished red-brick buildings broken only by the strangely minaret-like spires of churches and an increasing number of shops and businesses, industrial warehouses and endless lines of scruffy garages. Much of the population has no access to running water or electricity, employment is scarce and freezing night-time temperatures make it a desperately harsh place to live. Alteños nevertheless take pride in their urban-rural identity, their collective struggle against adversity and the challenges of urban life in what they refer to as the biggest indigenous city in the Americas, and denigrate La Paz, where many of them work, as *la hoyada* – "the hole".

Feria de El Alto

Thurs & Sun early morning to mid-afternoon

If you do want to spend some time in this harsh but fascinating environment, it's worth going up to see it's staggeringly huge **market**, the Feria de El Alto, known locally as *La Dieciseis* (The Sixteenth), which is held in the streets around the **Plaza 16 de Julio** in La Ceja, the main downtown district of El Alto. Selling everything from the latest knock-off gadgetry and plastic Chinese tat to cars and, sadly, live animals, it's a major part of what makes El Alto tick. It's also a pickpocket's paradise, so make sure your cash is out of temptation's way.

1

Lucha libre de cholitas

Multifuncional de la Ceja, Av Naciones Unidas • Sun 4–7pm • Bs80 with a package from Andean Secrets on Gonzales and Almirante Grau, San Pedro • Ⓦ cholitaswrestling.com

El Alto is probably the last place you'd expect to find Mexican-style wrestling, yet – as ever – Bolivia turns your expectations upside down, quite literally, as bowler-hatted *cholitas* aim flying pigtailed kicks at each other and a motley array of male and female masked baddies, while a mixed local/gringo crowd lap it up. It might not be in the best of tastes, but it's put El Alto firmly on the tourist map.

ARRIVAL AND DEPARTURE   LA PAZ

As the de facto capital of Bolivia it's no surprise that La Paz is the country's major transport hub, and many travellers use it as a base to which they return to collect or drop off luggage and equipment and rest up between forays into the country's many different geographical and climatic regions. Arriving here by **bus** or **plane** is a relatively painless experience: traffic problems notwithstanding, the city's small size makes it fairly easy to find your way around and there are inexpensive taxis and still cheaper public transport, though the latter isn't always easy to travel on with big bags.

BY PLANE

Given the great distances involved and the generally poor condition of the country's roads, the best way to travel in or out of La Paz is by plane – indeed, during the wet season this is sometimes the only way to reach certain destinations. International, and pretty much all domestic flights, arrive at and depart from El Alto airport on the rim of the Altiplano, about 10km away from – and almost 500m above – La Paz. At over 4000m above sea level, this is the highest international airport in the world, and it can feel as if planes have to climb rather than descend when they come in to land. Despite being an international airport serving Bolivia's de facto capital, the terminal has a very provincial feel. Basics has more information on international flight routes (see p.23).

INFORMATION

The airport's rather limited facilities include a 24hr information desk (☎02 2810122), a couple of banks where you can change US dollars and travellers' cheques (though not at the best rates), and an ATM where you can make cash withdrawals on Visa or MasterCard. There's also a café and restaurant, plus ENTEL/internet facilities and a few newsstands and souvenir shops.

TO/FROM TOWN

The easiest way into town from here is by taxi (30min; Bs60). Alternatively, an airport shuttle minibus (micro) runs down into the city along the length of the Prado to Plaza Isabella La Católica (Mon–Sat every 10–20min 6am–8pm, Sun every 30min; Bs3.50). If you're heading out to the airport, wait on the Prado and flag down any minibus marked "aeropuerto".

DOMESTIC AIRLINES

AeroSur (Av 16 de Julio 1616 ☎02 2313233, Ⓦ www .aerosur.com) is the main domestic operator, with frequent flights from La Paz to all Bolivia's main cities. Their website is routinely torture to navigate, however, and you might want to opt for the limited schedule of the generally cheaper, state-run BOA, (☎02 2117993, Ⓦ boa.bo) instead. Amazonas, at Av Saavedra 1649, Miraflores (☎02 2220848, Ⓦ amazonas.com) are your best bet for Rurrenabaque, while Aerocon, on Av Arce 2809 (☎02 2150093, Ⓦ aerocon .bo) cover the northern Amazon, as does – much more affordably – military airline TAM, on Av Montes 738 (☎268 1111, Ⓦ www.tam.bo). You can buy tickets for all these airlines from their own offices or, for a small commission, through any of the travel agents in La Paz. For TAM flights, it's easiest to book through a travel agent.

Destinations Cobija (5 daily; 1hr 40min; AC/AS/TAM/BOA); Cochabamba (14 daily; 45min; AC/AS/AM/TAM/BOA); Guayaramerín (4 daily; 1hr; AC/TAM); Puerto Suárez (3 weekly; 2hr; TAM); Riberalta (6 daily; 1hr; AC/TAM); Rurrenabaque (15 daily; 40min; AC/AM/TAM); Santa Cruz (14 daily; 1hr 30min; AC/AM/AS/TAM); Sucre (5 daily; 1hr; AC/AM/AS/TAM); Tarija (2 daily; 1hr 20min; AM/AS/TAM); Trinidad (10 daily; 1hr; AC/AM/TAM); Yacuiba (2 weekly; 1hr 30min; TAM).

BY BUS

There are three spots in the city where buses arrive to and depart from: they are the Terminal Terrestre, the cemetery district and Villa Fatima.

TERMINAL TERRESTRE

Most international and long-distance inter-departmental buses arrive at, and depart from, the Terminal Terrestre on Plaza Antofagasta, about 1km northeast of Plaza San Francisco. If you're heading to Uyuni you're better off taking the direct nightly service operated by Todo Turismo, Av Uruguay 102, Edificio Paula (☎02 2119418, Ⓦ todoturismo .bo) with departures from their office opposite the bus terminal; they even have toilets on board, which is unheard of in most Bolivian transport. From the terminal, it's a short taxi ride or a 20min walk down Av Montes to the main

STREET CRIME

Travellers arriving at the **main bus terminal** are occasionally targeted by thieves posing as plain-clothes police officers, complete with fake documents. One popular scam involves them asking to inspect your money for counterfeit notes, or your bags for drugs, then robbing you (they often work in tandem with someone pretending to be a tourist, who will befriend you before they approach and vouch for the legitimacy of their request). If approached by people claiming to be **undercover police** don't get in a car with them or show them your documents or valuables, and insist on the presence of an olive-green **uniformed officer** – you can call one yourself on ☎ 110. Scams of all kinds increasingly involve **taxi drivers**, so on arrival it's better not to share a taxi with strangers. Worse still, travellers and even ordinary Paceños have been assaulted, kidnapped (while the perpetrators empty their bank account at the nearest ATM), and occasionally even killed by rogue taxi and micro drivers. While the situation has improved in recent years, the police advise taking down the licence plate number and colour of any vehicle you travel in, and go so far as to warn against accepting any **food** or drink from your fellow travellers in case it contains sedatives. See p.72 for further info on taxi security.

accommodation areas in the city centre. The terminal has snack bars, luggage storage, a post office, telephones and an excellent information office (Mon–Fri 6am–10pm, Sat 8am–4pm, Sun noon–10pm; ☎02 2285858 or 2286061). Departing passengers have to pay Bs2 to use the terminal – tickets are sold from the kiosk marked "Boletería" in the centre of the station.

Destinations Cochabamba (hourly; 7–8hr); Oruro (every 30min; 3hr 30min); Potosí (2 daily; 11hr); Santa Cruz (15–20 daily; 16–18hr); Sucre (2 daily; 15hr); Tarija (2 daily; 24hr); and Arica, Chile (2 daily; 8hr).

CEMETERY DISTRICT

Buses and micros to the Lago Titicaca region, Charazani, Copacabana, Sorata and Tiwanaku, arrive and depart from outside various offices in the streets around the cemetery district high up on the west side of the city. Buses and micros to Copacabana leave from several different offices on Aliaga, just off Av Baptista opposite the cemetery itself. If you want to continue into Peru, it's very easy to do so from Copacabana, where there are frequent cross-border micros; you can also book a more expensive tourist micro direct to Puno in Peru through any tour agency in La Paz. Buses and micros to Tiwanaku and the Peruvian border at Desaguadero leave from offices stretched out along Eyzaguirre between Aliaga and Asín in the cemetery district. Buses to Sorata depart from offices a block further east on Bustillos, and those to both Charazani and Pelechuco in the Cordillera Apolobamba leave from Reyes Cardona, another block further along. Plenty of micros (marked *Cementario*) ply the route between the city centre and the cemetery, but it's a pretty chaotic and dangerous part of town, so it's a good idea to take a taxi (around Bs12), especially if you have heavy luggage.

Destinations Charazani (1–2 daily; 10hr); Copacabana (every 30min; 3hr 30min); Desaguadero (every 30min; 1hr 30min); Pelechuco (4 weekly; 13hr); Sorata (hourly; 4hr 30min); Tiwanaku (every 30min; 1h r30min).

VILLA FÁTIMA

Buses from Coroico and Chulumani in the Yungas, and from Rurrenabaque and the Beni, arrive at, and depart from the Villa Fátima district, 2km from the centre in the far northeast of the city; the different bus companies all have offices around the intersection of Av de las Americas and Yanacachi. Buses and micros for Coroico leave from the latter; Flota Yungueña has the best reputation. Those going to Chulumani leave from offices a block further up the same street and around the corner on San Borja. Buses to Rurrenabaque, Guayaramerín and Riberalta, and elsewhere in the Beni and on to Cobija in the Pando, depart from the offices of several different companies further along Av de las Américas and just off it to the left on Virgen del Carmen. For long-haul routes to the Beni and Pando, it's well worth coming up here and buying a ticket in advance. Again, plenty of micros head down to the city centre from here, east along J. J. Perez or south on Av 6 de Agosto, but a taxi (around Bs12) is quicker, easier and more secure.

Destinations Chulumani (hourly; 4hr 30min); Cobija (1 weekly; 48hr); Coroico (every 30min; 4hr 30min); Guayaramerín (1 daily; 32hr); Riberalta (1 daily; 30–40hr); Rurrenabaque (1 daily; 20hr).

GETTING AROUND

You'll probably spend most of your time in the city centre, which is compact and easily **walkable** – it takes less than 30min to get from one end of the Prado to the other on foot, and the traffic is so congested that walking is often the

1

quickest way to get around, though at this altitude the steeper streets can be pretty exhausting to climb. That said, **taxis** are plentiful and relatively good value, and the city's **public transport** network, though slow and hopelessly chaotic, is very cheap.

BY TAXI

Radio taxis To reduce your chances of being robbed, assaulted or worse, it's advisable to only ever take a Radio taxi: they're marked as such, usually with a telephone number painted on the side. When you enter the cab, the driver is obliged by law to call their office and inform them of your destination; drivers also often – but not always – have photo ID on display. They charge a flat rate of Bs10–12 for anywhere in the city centre regardless of the number of passengers, which makes them good value for more than one person. Bear in mind that Radio taxis are obliged to provide an exclusive service, and are not allowed to pick up other passengers en route; protest vehemently if they try to do so. Fares increase for longer journeys, especially if they involve a steep climb which consumes more fuel; a taxi to the Zona Sur should cost about Bs20. It's also a good idea to come equipped with a pocketful of small change as drivers rarely have any.

Long-distance taxis For trips outside the city, Trans Diplomático (☏ 02 2224343) offers a 24hr long-distance taxi service; you can usually pick one up outside the *Radisson Plaza* hotel on Av Arce.

BY MICROS

Privately owned minibuses known as micros run along all the city's main thoroughfares and are one of the main causes of the ever worsening traffic congestion. They're also pretty cramped, and usually entail a lot of getting out and in to accommodate your fellow passengers, a move you'll quickly master with the grace of a ballerina should you spend any amount of time in them. Destinations are written on signs inside the windscreen and bellowed incessantly by the driver's assistants, who hang from the open doors in the hope of coaxing just one more passenger into the already packed vehicle. The micros you'll most likely want to use are those that run up and down the Prado between the bus terminal and Plaza San Francisco in the north and Av 6 de Agosto in Sopocachi, to the south. To go anywhere else in the city, it's usually enough to wait by any major intersection until you hear the name of your destination shouted out; alternatively, ask a driver's assistant where to catch the relevant micro. Fares are usually fixed at around Bs2 for journeys in the city centre.

BY TRUFI

The city's third main form of transport is trufis – large estate cars that are used as collective taxis and follow fixed routes, mostly between Plaza del Estudiante and the wealthy suburbs of the Zona Sur (Bs3). They're designated by route numbers and, like micros, have their principal destinations written on a sign inside the windscreen. Like micros, trufis charge a flat fare of about Bs2 in the city centre. In common with micros, they also charge extra if your luggage fills a space that might otherwise be occupied by another passenger.

TOURS FROM LA PAZ

La Paz is home to an ever expanding plethora of **tour operators** (see opposite) offering everything from half- or one-day tours in and around the city, to expeditions to remote parts of the country lasting several weeks; the sheer number and variety – especially on calles **Sagárnaga**, **Illampu** and around – is literally mind boggling, and a fair number of them are not officially registered with the authorities. While this doesn't matter quite so much with the the standard day-trips offered by almost every company (including a **city tour**, usually combined with a visit to either the Valle de la Luna and Muela del Diablo, plus Tiwanaku or Chacaltaya, and costing from Bs70–350/person, you should take greater care when considering a **mountain biking** trip down the "world's most dangerous road" to Coroico, or any of the longer **mountaineering expeditions** and treks in the Cordillera Real.

GUIDES AND PRICES

With an average-sized group of four to six people, prices start at around Bs280/person/day, usually including food and accommodation, though be sure to check this. Whatever you do, don't buy tours from pirate operators approaching you in the street and if you do buy a more expensive climbing tour, make sure the name of the guide is on your receipt; you can then check their credentials on the **guide association website** ☒ agmtb.org. Cheaper companies may send a couple of *aspirantes* (part-qualified guides) alongside a fully qualified one, while the worst operators might send you out with a young, inexperienced guide in their late teens; avoid the latter at all costs; people can and do die.

INFORMATION AND TOURS

TOURIST INFORMATION

Plaza Estudiante at the end of the Prado (Mon–Fri 8.30am–noon & 2.30–7pm; ☎ 02 2371044). This is a small tourist information office that has plenty of information on La Paz and the surrounding area, but not much on destinations further afield. The staff are very friendly and helpful and there's usually someone who speaks a little English, plus they offer a free map of the city and have flyers for most of the main tour agencies. There is also a very helpful kiosk in the bus terminal–especially handy at weekends (see p.70).

SERNAP (Servicio Nacional de Áreas Protegidas) Francisco Bedregal 2904, Sopocachi ☎ 02 2426268, ⓦ www.sernap.gob.bo; map p.67. Though primarily an administrative nerve centre for Bolivia's numerous protected areas, this office can also provide information and maps.

TOUR OPERATORS

America Tours Ground floor office 9, Edificio Avenida, Av 16 de Julio 1490 ☎ 02 2374204, ⓦ america-ecotours .com. Veteran operator with a track record in conservation and sustainable tourism; they're the main booking agent for Albergue Ecologico Chalalán (see p.277) in Parque Nacional Madidi, and are a good place to book internal flights, as well as trips to the Pampas del Yacuma and the Salar de Uyuni if you want the limited security of booking in advance.

Andean Summits Muñoz Cornejo 1009 and Sotomayor, Sopocachi ☎ 02 2422106, ⓦ andean summits.com. Professional and much respected adventure tour operator with an excellent reputation that runs "off the beaten track" mountaineering and trekking expeditions throughout Bolivia, led by experienced and highly qualified English-speaking guides.

Climbing South America Linares 940 ☎ 02 2971543 or 7910 3534, ⓦ climbingsouthamerica.com. Sharing the same colonial space as *Café Illampu* and run by affable Australian Jeff Sandifort, this professional and dedicated company offers trips to all the Bolivian peaks, as well as those further afield such as Aconcagua in Argentina, along with pioneering two-week treks from the Cordillera Apolobamba to Rurrenabaque.

Deep Rainforest Corner of Murillo and Sagárnaga, inside Shopping Dorian ☎ 02 2150385, ⓦ deep -rainforest.com. The original boat-to-Rurrenabaque operator, and an attractive alternative to flying if you have the time and cash. The boat tours last three days and two nights, spending a half-day on the road to Caranavi, from where you take the 230km/two-and-a-half day river trip to Rurrenabaque. They also offer a "no noise" rafting alternative, slightly more expensive at five days and four nights.

Gravity Assisted Mountain Biking Av 16 de Julio 149, Edificio Avenida, ground-floor office 10, ☎ 02 2313849,

ⓦ gravitybolivia.com. The original, and still widely regarded as the best, downhill mountain-bike operator in Bolivia, with a sterling safety record, high-spec equipment and highly experienced and trained, rope rescue and first aid-certified guides. As well as the media-saturated Death Road jaunt (which now finishes up at the gorgeous La Senda Verde animal refuge (see p.128), there are other, more tantalizing trips, including a ride to the supposedly haunted, Chaco POW built El Castillo del Loro and, for the experienced, hardcore single-track expeditions around both Sorata and La Paz.

Huayna Potosí Travel Agency Sagárnaga 398 ☎ 02 2317324, ⓦ huayna-potosi.com. Friendly and long-established agency run by the inimitable Dr Hugo Berrios, specializing in climbing and trekking expeditions in the Cordillera Real. While most operators use the public *refugios*, Hugo accommodates expedition members in several of his own privately owned ones, including one at 5400m. He also offers ice-climbing courses at beginner, intermediate and advanced levels.

Kanoo Tours Illampu 832 ☎ 02 2460003, ⓦ kanootours.com. Operating from shiny, modern premises on Illampu, this English-owned place has established itself as one of the principal backpacker-oriented agencies in La Paz, selling all the usual tours including the Salar de Uyuni, mountain biking to Coroico, pampas trekking, etc. Additional offices in both the *Loki* and *Adventure Brew* hostels.

La Paz On Foot Prolongación Posnanski 400, Miraflores ☎ 02 2248350, ⓦ lapazonfoot.com. Conservation-minded, culturally orientated company with strong community links and an academically astute staff numbering biologists, archeologists, anthropologists and ecologists. Alongside city tours, their impressive portfolio includes trips to the Lago Titicaca village of Santiago de Okola, an organic Yungas coffee farm and butterfly sanctuary, and treks in the Apolobamba range.

Luna Tours Sagárnaga 380 ☎ 02 2310940, ⓦ lunatours.com.bo. The most high profile of the Coroico mountain biking newcomers, with a café (see p.79) and a separate office. They're wholly Bolivian owned, use Bolivian guides (all with at least eight years experience) and bikes are apparently equipped with the best parts available in the world.

Motorcycle Tours Bolivia Av Florida 609, Mallasa ☎ 02 2745572, ⓦ motorcycletoursbolivia.com. Bolivia's sole legal motorbike tour agency, with a sizeable fleet of machines and a choice of either guided trips (Salar de Uyuni, Yungas gold mining route via Mapiri and Guanay, etc) or a self-determined itinerary; they'll supply a support vehicle. Alternatively, you can simply rent a bike for the day for Bs525 ($75).

1

Topas Adventure Travel Bolivia Carlos Bravo 299 ⓣ02 2111082 or 73088333, ⓦtopas.bo. Operating since 1973 and now Danish-Bolivian owned and run, this veteran operator is housed in the basement of *El Consulado* boutique hotel (p.76)/restaurant (p.81), with knowledgeable and enthusiastic English-speaking staff and guides specializing in the Cordillera Apolobamba and the Choro, Takesi and Yunga Cruz trails.

Travel Tracks Sagárnaga 213, inside the Chuquiago Gallery ⓣ02 2316934, ⓦtravel-tracks.com. Another relatively new, often recommended operation run by lovely Dutch expat Ayla, specializing in two/three-day trips to the mountain of Huayna Potosí with a hands-on approach (check the photo on the flyer) and certified guides (one guide per two climbers), and also organizing Choro Trail and Salar de Uyuni tours.

ACCOMMODATION

There's been an explosion in the La Paz accommodation scene in recent years, even if prices have likewise risen steeply and there now seems to be a real dearth of rooms at lower mid-range. **Budget** accommodation – from around Bs50 – tends to be pretty spartan and chilly; ask for a room that gets some sunlight, as this makes a big difference in temperature. Heating is only available in the **top-range hotels**, though most places have 24hr hot water; it's worth checking to make sure it's not merely lukewarm - if it is you'll freeze.

CITY CENTRE

The bulk of the city's gringo-oriented accommodation is split between the busy market district west of Plaza San Francisco and the more sedate colonial centre to the east, where you'll find most of the best budget options, and where a few crumbling colonial bargains are still to be had. It's worth bearing in mind that the steep gradients of the city's streets mean that what appears a short walk back to your hotel on the map can in fact be an exhausting climb, particularly if you haven't yet adjusted to the altitude.

BUDGET

Adventure Brew Hostel Av Montes 533, next to Impuestos Internos (the inland revenue), opposite the petrol station on the corner of Pando ⓣ02 2461614, ⓦtheadventurebrewhostel.com; map p.57. At the time of writing, La Paz's original backpackers hostel was in the midst of big changes, with the main premises envisaged as a new B&B operation and the dorms being housed in what is shaping up to be a lordly colonial renovation just up the road. Accommodation will be grouped around a handsome courtyard over several floors, topped by a "sky bar" with a toughened-glass floor. Staff are incredibly friendly and the hostel itself still very popular so it's probably best to book online in advance. Dorms Bs55; doubles Bs210

Bash'n'Crash Av Montes 689 ⓣ02 2280934, ⓦbashandcrashbackpackers.com; map p.57. A new party hostel with a much more cosmopolitan mix of travellers than the competition. The owners are young, Bolivian, enthusiastic and welcoming, and accommodation consists largely of dorm beds, along with a few private rooms, while the communal areas retain enough cosy colonial charm (if a little too much tobacco smoke) to take the chill off the coldest of La Paz nights. Don't miss the antique table football table and the downstairs peña/disco (see p.85). Dorms Bs35; double Bs70

★ **Hostal Austria** Yanacocha 531, on the left at the top of the stairs ⓣ02 2408540, ⓔhotelaustria@acelerate.com; map p.57. With its lofty ceilings and maze of period wood and glass corridors, this place oozes history. The rooms are real period pieces, with undersized doors and an unintentionally shabby chic-cum-1960s minimalist feel. The only downside is the complete lack of private bathrooms and the rather dodgy gas-powered showers. Nevertheless, a must for retro fans and a real bargain for anyone else. Bs70

Hostal Señorial Yanacocha 540 ⓣ02 2406042; map p.57. Directly opposite *Hostal Austria* (see above) and equally steeped in period style, this place is as close as anything you'll find in La Paz to actually living in a rambling, ageing colonial house. Ceilings are so ridiculously high you wonder how on earth they applied the (original) cornicing, rooms are tranquil and clean, and there's a huge communal kitchen. If you're a light sleeper, however, beware the incessant, quarter hourly clang of the nearby Iglesia Santo Domingo bell. Bs85

Hostal Tambo de Oro Av Armentia 367 ⓣ02 2281565 or 02 2281050, ⓔhostal_tambodeoro@hotmail.com; map p.57. A veritable labyrinth of dark, hardwood corridors snaking between dowdy rooms (some of which are en suite) with semi-carpeted walls, varnished wooden ceilings and an antique, sequestered feel. Rooms at the front can also be incredibly noisy, although there's no denying its convenience for the bus terminal if *Arthy's* (see opposite) is full. Bs120

Lion Palace Hostel Linares 1017 ⓣ02 2900454, ⓦlionpalacehostel.com; map p.57. Opened in early 2011, this is one of the newer budget places in La Paz, a mini riot of Neoclassical-pillared, mock-colonial kitsch complete with plaster lion heads and a lurid blue and orange colour scheme. The parquet floors are already looking slightly tattered and some walls could do with a lick of paint but it's comfortable and clean enough, and decent value for the price. Bs110

Loki La Paz Loayza 420 ☎02 2119024, ⍵lokihostel .com; map p.57. The raucous La Paz branch of this Peru-based chain is located in a dandy pink, red velvet-draped townhouse formerly hosting the *Hotel Viena, and* it's probably worth staying here for the gilt-trimmed showpiece bar alone, located in the old *Viena* ballroom and the focus of the hostel's no-curfew, party-hard philosophy. Rooms are clean and comfortable with duvets, there's a small, soon-to-be-extended roof terrace and the twenty-something clientele are doubtless glad of a breakfast that's served till the uniquely generous hour of 1pm. Dorms Bs40; doubles Bs130

Posada El Carretero Catacora 1056, between Yanacocha and Junín ☎02 2285271, ✉elcarretero posada@gmail.com; map p.57. Blessed with the warmest, most welcoming and eccentric *dueña* in all Bolivia (the diminutive Sandra), this 50-year-old La Paz institution probably merits UNESCO heritage status. Basic, jovial and rambunctious, with shared bathrooms (also a few private), kitchen and laundry facilities, and decorated with decades of multilingual graffiti, it's akin to lodging in a funky – if surprisingly clean – squat. No surprise that it recently featured in a film about Yossi Ginsberg's infamous jungle disappearance; (see p.276). Bs70

Wild Rover Comercio 1476 ☎02 2116903, ⍵wildroverhostel.com; map p.57. La Paz's other big gringo party hostel, centred on a pleasantly open air, canary yellow-painted courtyard and an in-house bar that keeps the Guinness flowing till well into the wee hours. They claim they have "the comfiest beds in South America"; given the firm emphasis on living large, however, chances are you won't spend much time in them. Dorms Bs44; double Bs160

MODERATE

Arthy's Guesthouse Av Montes 693 ☎02 2281439, ⍵arthyshouse.tripod.com; map p.57. The best non-hostel option in the evirons of the bus terminal, this peaceful, welcoming, pot-planted retreat offers clean, whitewashed, carpeted rooms with bedside lamps, as well as a TV room and communal kitchen. Bs160

Estrella Andina Illampu 716 ☎02 2456421, ✉juapame_2000@hotmail.com; map p.57. Bright, fun and incredibly friendly, this place has recently expanded its reach, both upwards with an Illimani-eye-view roof terrace and sideways with the adjacent Hostal Sol Andino (see opposite). Decor wise, Andean naïf murals still fill every inch of plaster, with walls – and even doors – cannily painted as picture book windows to lend an impression of space; garish, but it almost works. The rooms themselves are clean and just as colourful, willing sweet dreams with wall-to-wall fantasies of a fume-free Bolivia. Heating, free wi-fi and buffet breakfast included. Bs240

Hostal Cruz de los Andes Aroma 216 ☎02 2451401, ✉cruzdelosandes@hotmail.com; map p.57. Another part of the growing *Estrella Andina* empire, this place has the requisite indigenous art and similarly furnished rooms, as well as an elegant wrought-iron stairwell and a sociable pool room. Prices are pitched somewhere between *Estrella Andina* and *Hostal Sol Andino* (see below) with wi-fi, heating and breakfast included. Bs190

★ **Hostal La Posada de la Abuela** Linares 947 ☎02 2332205, ⍵hostalposadaabuela.com; map p.57. Housed in a tastefully restored colonial mansion, rooms are furnished in fresh pine and wrought iron and built around a leafy *artesanía* courtyard also housing The Spitting Llama bookshop (see p.86). Front-facing rooms 202–205 are especially inviting, with balconies looking onto Calle Linares below, and the glowing recommendations in the guest book speak for themselves. Breakfast is included, as is internet, wi-fi and a ten percent discount for stays of more than two nights. Bs250

★ **Hostal Naira** Sagárnaga 161 ☎02 2355645, ⍵hostalnaira.com; map p.57. Though some paint is beginning to flake from the high, corniced ceilings, *Naira's* rooms remain as elegant and spotlessly clean as any in La Paz, making beguiling use of light and glass, and all set around a capacious colonial courtyard. As with most of the area's colonial conversions, it's the street-front rooms that really dazzle, with period shutters and svelte, gorgeously tiled balconies. Bs280

Hostal República Comercio 1455 ☎02 2202742 or 022203448, ⍵hostalrepublica.com; map p.57. The former home of Bolivian president Jose M Pando, this renovated pile is set around two cobbled courtyards, where the downstairs rooms tend to the fairly poky and noisy, and are in need of a facelift, as well as comfortable pillows. The upper rooms are brighter, however, and there's a modern five-person villa with a secluded garden and chairs at the back. Wi-fi is available and non-inclusive breakfasts are served in the adjacent café. Best of all, though, they sell hot water bottles (Bs28) which you can fill with hot water from the café. Villa Bs698 ($97); doubles Bs260 ($37)

Hostal Sol Andino Aroma 6 ☎02 2456421, ✉solandinohostal@gmail.com; map p.57. If the bright primary colours and Andean fantasy-scapes of *Estrella Andina* (see opposite) take your fancy, but the price doesn't, *Hostal Sol Andino* might be the answer. It's basically an extension of *Andina* with similar decor and furnishings for a significantly cheaper price, as well as free wi-fi; the entrance is round the corner on Aroma. Bs180

Hotel Berlina Illampu 761 ☎02 2461928, map p.57. Another relative newcomer in the increasingly crowded mid-range Illampu/Linares market, this place shows uncommon restraint on the mural front, indulging in mock-classical columns and in-room cornicing instead. The carpeted rooms are a blessing for winter nights. Bs220

1

Hotel Continental Ilampu 626 ☎02 2451176, ⓦhotelcontinentalbolivia.com; map p.57. A friendly HI affiliate that wears its 1970s colours proudly. Wood panelling and great old Bolivian tourist-board posters lend character, and although rooms can be on the dowdy and noisy side, the lovely old top-floor, four-person apartments (complete with period kitchen, living room and old canvases) are great value, even for small groups. Apartments Bs280; doubles Bs140

Hotel Fuentes Linares 988 ☎02 2334145, ⓦhotelfuentesbolivia.com; map p.57. While still decent value for the price, the family-owned *Fuentes'* four floors of bright, modern, pastel-yellow rooms are now looking slightly frayed at the edges and could do with a paint job, as well as proper sound (and smell)-proofing between some of the adjacent bathrooms. Ask for a room on one of the upper floors for some great views of the city's canyon-like skyline. There's a laundry service and free internet, though the meagre inclusive breakfast is served in a somewhat claustrophobic dining room; give the coffee a miss. Bs190

Hotel Las Brisas Illampu 742 ☎02 2463691; map p.57. Another busy mid-range Illampu newcomer, *not* run by *Estrella Andina* (see p.75) but clearly taking some pointers from them in the wall mural department, not to mention the smudged ochre paintwork. Quasi-rustic furniture warms the place up further, as does the welcome central heating. Breakfast is included, and there's free internet with wi-fi. Bs213

Hotel Milton Illampu 1126 ☎02 2353511 or 02 2368003, ⓦhotelmiltonbolivia.com; map p.57. *Milton's* interior has to be seen to be believed, a monument to late 70s excess, with maroon, studded-leather walls, vintage flower boxes and garish wipe-off wallpaper untouched since the place opened. It likewise probably deserves cultural landmark status and presumably it's the preserved-in-lurid-aspic style you're paying for, because otherwise it's way overpriced, if clean and comfortable enough. Stunning views from the east facing rooms as well, and very amiable staff. Breakfast included. Bs180

Hotel Torino Socabaya 457 ☎02 2406003, ⓦhoteltorino.com.bo; map p.57. With more than 90 years as a hotel under its creaking colonial belt this place really has seen and done it all. Something of a gringo mecca in the pre-mega hostel days, its appeal is latterly limited to those favouring antiquity over comfort. While the entry up a small flight of magnificent flagstones and a vaulted portico isn't matched in the shadowy maze of basic, lived-in rooms, the historic atmosphere really is tangible, further thickened by flickering lightbulbs. Yet the down sides can be numerous – the sometimes surly staff, whiffy drains, unreliable hot water and ridiculously useless towels. Bs140

Residencial Latino Junín 857 ☎02 2285463, ⓦresidenciallatino.com; map p.57. Renovated in early 2010, this veteran colonial place now makes for an excellent alternative to the nearby *Hostal República* (see p.75), with a wealth of clean, mildew-free, pastel-painted rooms facing onto a bright enclosed courtyard. The whole place feels incredibly spacious, with a black and orange colour scheme and faux-colonial lamps throughout. Breakfast included. Bs180

EXPENSIVE

Hotel Osira Av 20 de Octubre 1494, Plaza San Pedro ☎02 2492247, ⓦhotelosira.com; map p.57. Formerly *Max Inn*, this has been re-modelled into a very pleasant mid-range hotel with a colonial-lite theme (cod-medieval doors, gilt-framed religious art, etc), wonderfully sunny rooms and a great buffet breakfast; the cumulative effect of which is almost enough to make you forget you're within teargas distance of the notorious San Pedro prison. There's also wi-fi, parking and a stylish bar/restaurant with live music. Bs385 ($55)

Hotel Presidente Potosí 920 ☎02 2406666, ⓦhotelpresidente-bo.com; map p.57. That Ricky Martin once bedded down here is the *Presidente's* abiding claim to fame, and though the place is still frequented by visiting Latin American singers and celebs, it's debateable whether it's shagpile-tastically retro or simply shagged-out. Either way, it's worth a look for the lavish 1970s vintage of its reception alone – all swaggering chandeliers and mirrored ceilings, a jet set parallel to *Hotel Milton* (see opposite). The heated rooms are less ostentatious but still comfortable, nevertheless. Bs1120 ($160)

★**Hotel Rosario** Av Illampu 704 ☎02 2451658, ⓦhotelrosario.com/la-paz; map p.57. An older, well-heeled clientele potters around the *Rosario's* warren of elegant heated rooms and eccentric little corridors, all crammed in around a series of cobbled, pot-planted courtyards. A fair-trade shop and a great, sun-blushed rooftop café (with free internet) round out the experience, while the famous restaurant serves up such deluxe-native dishes as trout with Beni almonds and beef with Yungas pepper sauce. Bespoke breakfast buffet included. Bs500 ($70)

EL PRADO, SAN PEDRO, MIRAFLORES AND SOPOCACHI

La Paz's more luxurious hotels are located just off the Prado and also further south in the prosperous suburb of Sopocachi, home to most of the city's more fashionable bars and restaurants, and a pleasant place to stroll around in the evening. There are also a couple of places to stay in San Pedro and Miraflores, relatively less frenzied suburbs on either side of the main thoroughfare.

★**El Consulado** Bravo 299 ☎02 2117706, ⓦcafeelconsulado.com; map p.57. The majordomo of the city's colonial conversions, this boutique hotel near the Prado – the one-time Consulate of Panama – has a limited number of rooms, but what rooms they are, stylishly faithful to the original decor and fittings in a way the competition hasn't quite managed. Period wallpaper and chequered tiles, antique baths and feather duvets impart an organic sense of luxury you won't find elsewhere. You'd do well to avail yourself of the restaurant (see p.81), and there's also *artesanía* for sale, free wi-fi, a gourmet breakfast and the highly respected Topas Travel (see p.74) in the basement. Bs560 ($80)

★ **Hotel "A la Maison"** Pasaje Muñoz Cornejo 15, Sopocachi ☎02 2413704, ⓦalamaison-lapaz.com; map p.67. The name of this place translates as "like being at home", and it certainly lives up to that, if, in fact, you can find it in the first place. Cloistered within a cul-de-sac and almost entirely anonymous (no sign), it's essentially a house with a very low-key yet amenable staff and a jumble of spotlessly clean, discreet and spacious apartments, accessed by a beautifully tiled stairwell and idiosyncratically decorated with rustic furniture, hemp curtains, abstract art and faded French novels. Kitchens are more basic but supplied with butter, jam, fruit juice and fresh bread every morning. The views are superlative and wi-fi is available. A delightful alternative to a Sopocachi hotel, though do yourself a favour and take a taxi. Bs455 ($65)

Hotel LP Columbus Av Illimani 1990, Miraflores ☎02 2242444, ⓦwww.lphoteles.com; map p.67. Though it's slightly out of the way in a noisy part of Miraflores, this is a great-value mid-range option with the feel and facilities of an executive level establishment (albeit no pool or sauna). Housed in a swanky modern building looming over a sunken mock-up of Tiwanaku's Templete Semi-Subterraneo, the blue and beige-carpeted rooms offer business-like comfort (with memory foam beds and even a pillow menu) and functionality. Also high-speed wi-fi, as well as inclusive breakfast and one of the best-value almuerzo buffets (Bs22) in the city. Bs420 ($60)

Hotel Madre Tierra Av 20 de Octubre 2080, Sopocachi ☎02 2419910, ⓦhotelmadretierra.com; map p.67. As one of the few hotels slap bang in the middle of the Sopocachi action, this relatively new tower block represents fair value for money, with clean, brick-walled rooms, a spacious dining room with wrought-iron chairs and stained glass, and a generally bright, functional ambience. Staff are pleasant, there's wi-fi and a buffet breakfast is included. Bs340

La Loge Apart Hotel Pasaje Medinacelli 2234, Sopocachi ☎02 2423561, ⓦlacomedie-lapaz.com; map p.67. A very blue stairwell accesses this cluster of chic, self-catering apartments from the people who brought you *La Comédie* restaurant (see p.81). Decor is more polished and minimalist than the similarly French-owned *Hotel A la Maison*, with a breakfast bar-style kitchen (also with fresh fruit juice, bread and jam), and all rooms come equipped with internet-ready computer. Bs480 ($70)

★ **El Rey Palace Hotel** Av 20 de Octubre 1947, Sopocachi ☎02 2418541; map p.67, ⓦhotelreypalace .com. One of the most accommodating top-range options in La Paz, with stained glass, big, comfortable and newly refurbished rooms with feather duvets and polished dark wood furniture. Staff couldn't be more helpful and there's always great music tootling away in the background, while the dining room is endearingly plush and the kitchen big on quinoa and healthy food in general; if you have special dietary requirements, there's even a nutritionist on hand. Moreoever, should La Paz be in the grip of a blockade during your stay, they apparently have ways of getting you out... Bs595 ($85)

ZONA SUR

If you'd rather restrict your appreciation of La Paz's frantic charm to measured doses, or you simply want to minimize the adverse effects of altitude, the Zona Sur is a more oxygenated option. Akin to downtown Phoenix or Tucson, with an upfront and spectacular Wild West backdrop, palm tree-lined boulevards and a climate to match, it feels very much removed from the rest of the city.

Camino Real (Suites) Av Ballivián 369 and corner of C 10, Calacoto ☎02 2792323, ⓦcaminoreal.com .bo. A conspicuously modern, sun-glinting skyscraper that looks much taller than its eight floors suggest. Arranged in vertigo-inducing circles with lots of greenery above an imposing black marble reception, it's home to state-of-the-art executive rooms with great canyon views. Extras include pool, sauna, wi-fi, 24hr business centre, an inclusive American buffet breakfast and even entrance to the local golf club. If you're on a budget don't miss the regular weekend special with basic doubles slashed to a mere Bs525 ($75). Bs1365 ($255)

Casa Grande Hotel Av Ballivián and corner of C 17, Calacoto ☎02 2795511, ⓦcasa-grande.com.bo. Self-consciously stylish boutique hotel sporting a design midway between warehouse minimalism and retro comfort. The reception is all modernist leather sofas, glass and perforated steel, while the carpeted rooms are more dated if still inviting, equipped with kitchen, wi-fi and a daily newspaper. If you don't fancy cooking there's the colourful *Mezzo Café*, with a menu of trendy snacks. Breakfast included. Bs1106 ($158)

Hotel Calacoto C 13 No. 8009 and corner of Sánchez Bustamente ☎02 2774600, ⓦhotelcalacoto .com. Hidden away down a leafy, mercifully serene side street, this hacienda conversion has dispensed with much of its former quirky charm in favour of more blandly modern decor, though it's still a decent deal for the location and a fraction of the price of its skyscraping neighbours. There's a choice of rooms or self-catering apartments plus all the usual fringe benefits like wi-fi and inclusive breakfast, and they also offer horseriding in the surrounding badlands. Their trump card, however, is still the genteel garden. Doubles Bs476 ($68); apartments Bs596 ($85)

Hotel Oberland El Agrario 3118, Mallasa ☎02 2745040, ⊕h-oberland.com. Clean, calm, Swiss-owned complex in the environs of Valle de la Luna, with an environmental bias, and an "eco spa" with a dome-covered pool maintained at an inviting 35 degrees. The en-suite rooms and three-person apartments are modern-rustic, with beamed ceilings, rugged views and the occasional brick fireplace, while the well-manicured garden is the scene of regular BBQs and occasional embassy bashes. Wi-fi and buffet breakfast included. Apartments Bs630 ($90); doubles Bs392 ($56)

EATING

La Paz has an excellent range of **restaurants**, **cafés** and **street stalls** to suit pretty much all tastes and budgets. Few places open for breakfast much before 8am, and Paceños treat lunch as the main meal of the day, eating lightly in the evening. Most restaurants serve **set lunch menus** known as almuerzos (typically noon–2pm), which are generally extremely filling and great value. The city also has an increasingly cosmopolitan range of European-style restaurants, both in **Sopocachi**, and also on trendy **Calle Tarija**, just off the end of Linares. In stark contrast to neighbouring Argentina, restaurants begin serving dinner at around 7pm. As a general rule, the more gringo-friendly places will open later and fill up later, although it's difficult to find a formal sit- down meal anywhere after 11pm.

CAFÉS

100% Natural Sagárnaga 339; map p.57. Against a lime-green backdrop, orange-shirted staff serve a jungle's worth of fruit juice combinations including "secret house recipes" for flu, hangover and altitude sickness, though it's hard to beat the American, a mix of banana, papaya, coconut and strawberry. And if the altitude hasn't killed your appetite, don't miss the monster Bs22 breakfast. The only drawback is the relentless 1980s music. Daily 8.45am–10pm.

Arábica Av 20 de Octubre 2355 ☎02 2113293; map p.67. Engaging coffee-style bar/bistro converted from a house, and still retaining a front-room feel. While the breakfast menu could do with beefing up, the coffee itself is lavishly presented, and their lunches aren't bad value at Bs27. If the altitude is leaving you weak, go with their Popeye salad, a blend of spinach, hard-boiled egg, parmesan, asparagus, croutons and olive oil. Mon–Sat 7am–11.30pm.

★**Cafe Banaís** Sagárnaga 161 ☎02 2311214; map p.57. Adjacent to *Hostal Naira* (see p.75), this is one of the most reliable and enduring breakfast venues in La Paz, with smiling staff, hideaway booths, great chocolate milkshakes and mountainous bowls of fruit, yoghurt and muesli. Their coca tea crams in more leaves than water and even the hardback menus are tastefully designed. Daily 7am–10pm.

★**Café Blueberries** Av 20 de Octubre 2475, northeast side of Plaza Avaroa ☎02 2433402; map p.67. In a city where the coffee chain is king, this is a humble tea-drinker's haven, with an ambience as unhurried as the Miles Davis solos floating from its speakers. You can sip from exquisite pots of Ceylon, Darjeeling and Assam, and don't miss their sweetly astringent ginger brew. The pancakes are delicious, made with nutritious Andean blueberries, and their rich house yoghurt unlike anything you'll have tasted. There's also a garden backdrop and live jazz every Sat. Mon–Sat 8am–11.30pm, Sun 11am–9pm.

Cafe Ciudad Plaza del Estudiante ☎02 2441827; map p.57. Lively and long-established café that, incredibly for Bolivia, still manages to open 24hr a day, 365 days of the year. If you're staying in Sopocachi, it's great for a late-afternoon pit-stop when everywhere else is closed, and even though the coffee and food in general isn't amazing, their peerlessly fluffy omelettes (Bs20) are arguably the best in the city. There's also an upstairs terrace, annoyingly enough with only one table. Daily 24hr.

★**Cafe Illampu** Linares 940 ☎02 2971543; map p.57. Finally a La Paz branch of friendly Stefan's Sorata institution (see p.121), housed in one of the most elegant dining rooms on the whole of Linares. Once upon a time the *comedor* of the Linares family themselves, it's an edifying

LA PAZ STREET FOOD

For those whose stomachs have adjusted to basic local food, the cheapest places to eat are the city's **markets**, where you can get entire meals for less than Bs7, as well as hearty soups, snacks and large quantities of roast meat (though it's probably best to body-swerve the pork entirely). Try **Mercado Lanza**, just up from Plaza San Francisco, or **Mercado Camacho**, at the end of Avenida Camacho. **Street food** is another good low-cost option: the ubiquitous *salteñas* and *tucumanes* – delicious pastries filled with meat or chicken with vegetables – make excellent mid-morning snacks, especially if washed down by the freshly squeezed orange and grapefruit juice which is sold from wheeled stalls all over the city.

space – complete with original ceiling murals and chandeliers – to enjoy what Stefan describes as "the best breakfast in South America". He may just be right, what with his famous home-made white and wholemeal bread and jam, and organic yoghurt and eggs all the way from Sorata. His muesli is unarguably Swiss and the man himself couldn't be a more affable host. Mon–Sat 7.30am–8pm.

Café La Paz Av Camacho 1202, just beyond the corner with the Prado ☎02 2312266; map p.57. Though this august café isn't quite as atmospheric as it once was, the coffee is usually excellent, and the breakfasts cheaper than some of the nearby chains. The place is still pretty much a preserve of elderly gents, though, not least when there's a Barcelona vs Real Madrid match on the big screen. Daily 8am–midnight.

La Casita del Pannekuk Av Sanchez Lima 2235, Sopocachi ☎02 2910660; map p.67. La Paz, in general, doesn't really do homely, but "The Little House of Pancakes" is a textbook exception, shamelessly milking the Dutch theme with windmills, monochrome photos of Amsterdam and the requisite blue and white ceramics. Its motherly *dueña*, moreover, will make sure you're eating enough – not difficult when the honey-lathered, fruit-topped pancakes (3 for Bs15), crêpes and waffles are so delicious. Great French music as well. Mon–Fri 9am–noon & 5–9.30pm, Sat 5–9.30pm.

K'umara Tarija 263; map p.57. Another new Bolivian-owned start-up, this psychedelically-hued hutch-like hole-in-the-wall is perfect for a light, healthy breakfast. Mix and match your cereal from jars of organic Bolivian cereals such as quinoa and amaranto etc, with fresh fruit, natural yoghurt and strong coffee. The owners are young and enthusiastic, and there's some basic outdoor seating. 7am–1pm & 3–7pm.

Luna's Coffee Sagárnaga 289 ☎02 2311568; map p.57. The café arm of Luna Tours (see p.73), this is a friendly, engaging and always busy little place, serving moderately priced soups, sandwiches, omelettes and creamy-sweet milkshakes amid a handsomely shabby, crimson and vermillion colonial interior. The coca tea is prepared with fresh leaves rather than teabags – just as well, perhaps, for the pre-trip Death Road bikers enjoying their complimentary breakfast. Daily 7.30am–9.30pm.

Marrackech Jimenez 774 ☎7967 7205; map p.57. Service isn't the friendliest at La Paz's first bona fide Maghrebi tea house, but the place is authentic enough, with thimblefuls of mint tea rattling to loud North African rhythms. Food wise, along with Morroccan staples like *jarira* (a hearty soup of vegetables, chickpeas and lentils; Bs28) there's also such lesser spotted fare as *matbuja* (a conconction of tomatoes, mushrooms, garlic, onion, parsley and coriander) and Spanish tortilla. Daily noon to 10pm.

Pastelería Piroska Adjacent to Residencial Sucre, Plaza San Pedro; map p.57. This tiny bakery serves what

TOP 5 BREAKFAST BITES

Café Banaís see opposite
Café Blueberries see opposite
Café Illampu see opposite
La Casita del Pannekuk see below
K'umara see below

may be the finest apple pastries in the city, though they're only available Mon–Thurs. On Fri and Sat, they make way for the traditional *salteñas* and *tucumanes*. Mon–Sat 9am–7pm.

Pepe's Pasaje Jimenez 894, just off Linares between Sagárnaga and Santa Cruz ☎02 2450788; map p.57. Intimate and perennially popular little café near the heart of the Mercado de Hechicería with a gringo-centric menu and the most unassuming of *dueños*. The hefty, healthy *ensalada* with creamy avocado and rich, ripe tomato isn't to be missed, nor the Super Pepe's Juice, a thirst-thumping blend of strawberry, banana, papaya and orange. Weather permitting, there's a solitary outdoor table. Mon–Sat 8.30am–6.30pm.

RESTAURANTS

The least expensive restaurants are no-nonsense, hole-in-the-wall places catering to hungry workers and students. They're concentrated in the city's upper reaches, serving an often substantial set almuerzo for about Bs7. At mid-range restaurants you'll pay around Bs35–42 for an à la carte main course, but many of these places also serve a very good set almuerzo (often dubbed *almuerzo ejecutivo*) for Bs21–28 – not bad for five courses. Even in La Paz's poshest restaurants you'll rarely need to spend more than Bs140–175 per person (the *expensive* tag really is relative in Bolivia) to enjoy a really good meal; great value given the quality of food and service.

INEXPENSIVE

Cafe Beirut Belisario Salinas 380 ☎02 2444486; map p.67. Though this cavernous café/restaurant lacks pretty much any Middle Eastern atmosphere and the music – and much of the food – is in fact, inexplicably Mexican, their library-sized menu actually hides the moistest, tastiest falafel in the city. Look out also for their stuffed vine leaves and, if you have the stomach for it, the *kebbi*, a concoction of raw meat, wheat, lemon and spices. Daily 8am–11.30pm.

Eli's Pizza Express Av 16 de Julio 1800 ☎02 2318171; map p.57. Perennially popular, no-nonsense fast-food outlet with reasonably good pizza, a hefty slice of which makes for a great late-night snack at around Bs11. Outdoor tables on a Sun afternoon. Also branches on Plaza Avaroa and across the street in the Cine Monje Campero (see p.84). Daily 8.30am–11.30pm.

1

★ **Namas Té** Zoilo Flores 1334 ☎02 2481401, ⊛namastebolivia.com; map p.57. Run by Gonz Jove, an artist/sculptor responsible for several of the alfresco murals around La Paz, this colourful bohemian enclave offers the best value vegetarian (much of it vegan) almuerzos (Bs15) in the city, prepared with healthy doses of quinoa and a flair for traditional adaptations. The fruity desserts are likewise imaginative, and they do delicious takes on the usual sandwiches, burritos, tacos etc. There's also a lovely garden and weekend club nights hosted by Gonz's brother Paul aka Dj Pituko. Mon–Wed 8am–4pm, Thurs–Sat 8am–4pm & 7pm–1am.

Paceña La Salteña Av 20 de Octubre 2379 ☎02 2441993; map p.67. A La Paz institution with branches all over the city (also on Av Montenegro 1560 and Loayza 233), where a couple of perfectly pursed pastries won't set you back much more than Bs10. Note that the little bowl of chopped peppers that comes with your *salteñas* actually contains hot chilli peppers, even if they look suspiciously like the sweet variety. Mon–Fri 8am–2pm, Sat & Sun 8.15am–3pm.

Restaurant Jalal Sagárnaga 380 ☎7759 8088; map p.57. Jalal is housed in the same location, if not exactly the same room, as Lebanese specialist, Yussef, which closed in December 2010. Amenable owner Damian Yararí was the chef at the Clube de Unión Arabe in Zona Sur for twenty years, and he's kept on some of the old Yussef staff, serving up delicious tapas-like portions of falafel, hummous, *tabouleh*, *babaganoush* and other Middle Eastern classics for around Bs10 each. The decor and ambience still need a bit of work, but as a replacement for Yussef, it's well on its way. Mon–Sat 11am–11pm.

Sabor Cubano Sagárnaga 357 ☎02 2451797, ⊛saborcubanobolivia.com; map p.57. Cheap, tasty and filling food in satisfyingly tattered surroundings, with graffiti-choked walls and vintage Cuban sounds. Various permutations of rice, beans, avocado and yucca as well as standbys like *ropa vieja* (shredded beef, onion, wine and tomato) and the obligatory mojitos make this the best lazy evening option on Sagárnaga by far. Mon–Sat noon–midnight.

MODERATE

Anjelo Colonial II Av Mariscal Santa Cruz 1066 ☎02 2124979; map p.57. A rare gringo-oriented retreat from the ferocious traffic of the Prado, this is as convenient a place as any for that candlelit dinner. Rustic bench seating and a horde of antiques – from old maps and gramophones to gilt-framed portraits and a wonderful old cash till – make for second-hand atmosphere in abundance. The food, alas, doesn't quite match the fittings but you get what you pay for, with crêpes, omelettes and pasta dishes (though give the veggie lasagne a miss) in the Bs20–40 range. There's also a branch on Linares 922–924, off

Sagárnaga, more of a Western saloon-style affair, and several smaller branches around town including a lovely nook in the brick-vaulted cellars of the Museo Nacional De Arte, a great breakfast choice if you're lodged nearby. Daily 8am–11pm.

★ **La Coca** R. Gutiérrez 482 ☎02 2410892; map p.67. You won't find a more enthusiastic chef/restaurateur/host than the well-travelled Mirko Vargas, and this newly opened, pleasantly rustic bistro is his shrine to the wonders of pan-Andean, and specifically coca-inspired, cuisine: pizzas with coca flour, quinoa hamburgers, coca-infused crab, mouthwatering red quinoa soup and even coca ice ceam. While mains come in around Bs50, the almuerzo is outstanding value at only Bs22; get it while the price lasts. Takeaway planned. Daily 11am–midnight.

La Cueva Tarija, opposite Tierra Sana (see opposite) ☎02 2314523, ⊛4cornerslapaz.com; map p.57. Colourful, authentic-feeling Mexican with a sense of humour (check out the spicy Spiderman shrine), super-friendly management and a cosy orange glow. There's no menu as such; specials (look out for the pumpkin soup) are scrawled, Mexican-style, both on the board outside, and on another by the pint-sized bar, where it's easiest to place your order. Mon–Sat 11am–midnight, Sun 4pm–midnight; the bar stays open later.

La Guinguette Av 20 de Octubre and 339 Fernando Guachalla 399 ☎02 2421390; map p.67. Formerly *Café Montmartre* and *Le Bistrot*, this très arty bistro next door to the Alliance Francaise serves delectable French food and drink in an animated, candle-lit atmosphere, with a well-dressed clientele lapping up various permutations of duck and a heavenly French onion soup. Occasional live gypsy jazz. Mon–Fri noon–3pm & 7pm–midnight, Sat 1–4pm & 7pm–midnight (food served till 10.30pm max).

Layq'a On the first floor above the corner of Linares and Sagárnaga ☎02 2460903; map p.57. Convenient, if pricey and very touristy, place to try traditional Altiplano dishes, including huge llama steaks (Bs78) and *crema de chuño* – a delicious soup made from freeze-dried potatoes. The popular set almuerzo includes a salad bar, and don't miss the delectable peach, strawberry, papaya, yoghurt and vanilla milkshake. Daily 11am–3pm & 6.30–10pm.

★ **Star of India** Cochabamba 170 ☎02 2114409; map p.57. Though the decrepit, grey exterior suggests it might have closed down years ago, this is in fact an English-owned Indian restaurant, the first of its kind in La Paz. Amid a candlelit, wooden-beamed interior, draped with authentic Indian textiles, and lulled by a world music soundtrack and friendly staff, you may just pluck up the courage to attempt one of their fiendish vindaloos, though they also do the usual chicken *tikka masala*, *jalfrezi*, *rogan josh* etc, and all at very reasonable prices (from Bs45). A veggie list is topped by a hearty *saag paneer aloo* (Bs35); make sure you've worked up an appetite before attacking its Himalayan-sized mountain of fried cheese. There's even a bonafide Indian breakfast, but what really makes this place special is the astoundingly comprehensive list of Twinings tea, by the cup or pot (Bs14). Takeaway and delivery also available. Daily Mon–Sat 9am–11pm, Sun 4–11pm.

Tierra Sana Tarija 213 ☎ 02 2110115, ⓦ 4cornerslapaz .com; map.57. This new vegetarian restaurant is the latest joint effort between the various expats and Bolivians sprucing up Calle Tarija. Spare a thought for Belgian chef Luc Cueppers, who nightly dashes between various Tarija/ Murillo kitchens yet can still rustle up food as salivatory as the Brazilian peanut soup (Bs22). Other international options include a Cameroonian concoction of lentils, plantain and peppers, all served in a bright, fresh, self-consciously modern interior. The music isn't bad either, switching between 1960s pop, White Album Beatles and El Carratero-vintage Cuban roots. Daily 9am–10pm.

Villaserena Av Ecuador 2582 ☎ 02 2418151; map.67. The kitchen of this cultural complex – also housing Café Concert Luna Llena (see p.82), located in an impressively bohemian colonial conversion in Sopocachi, is commandeered by Catalan chef Juan Pablo Villalobos, whose unique take on new Andean-Spanish cuisine includes such fearless combinations as shrimp, lobster and llama with quinoa. The man also runs cookery courses for Bs700 ($100)/month. Mon–Fri 11am–3pm & 7–11pm, Sun noon–4pm.

EXPENSIVE

El Arriero Av 6 de Agosto 2535 ☎ 02 2310440; map p.67. Claiming "the best meat in the world", this Argentine steak house doesn't skimp on the calories, serving mammoth slabs of beef along with the obligatory chorizo, morcilla, tripe, and kidney. On Sun afternoons, especially, the sober wood-panelled walls and racks of Argentine wine set the scene for troupes of well-heeled Sopocachi families. There's also a sister branch in Calacoto on C 18 and Av Montenegro. Daily noon–3pm & 7–11pm.

Casa Nostra Av Ballivián 927, Zona Sur ☎ 02 2792417. Though the spartan interior and sliding doors lend it a quasi-oriental feel, this stylish trattoria prepares some of the most flavour-rich Italian cuisine in La Paz, more than justifying the trek from uptown. Mains – including a fiery, well-oiled rigatoni all' amatriciana and a buttery-rich red pesto – are worth every cent of their Bs53 price tag, while their Jugo de Cosa Nostra, a combination of fresh strawberry, lemon and pineapple, is even more mouth-watering than it sounds. Service is impeccable and there's also rich Tarijan wine by the glass. Mon–Sat noon–3pm & 7–11pm, Sun noon–4pm.

★ **La Comédie** Pasaje Medinacelli 2234 ☎ 02 2423561, ⓦ lacomedie-lapaz.com; map p.67. Indefatigably stylish and humorous (see if you can get your hands on one of their Bolivia 6–Argentina 0 commemorative posters), this Gallic institution is a favourite meeting place for La Paz's French community, who either linger by the bar or tuck into some of the city's most flawlessly conceived food. Amid an affable art and antique-arranged interior, you can watch the chefs beavering away behind a large plate glass window, whipping up several varieties of duck (Bs60) – potted, pâté-d and roasted – or lighter snacks such as tartodie (toasted French bread with cheese, tomato and anchovies). Veggies aren't completely neglected; the meat-free moussaka is to mourir for, as is the chocolate mousse. Needless to say, there's also a cellar of real French wine. Mon–Fri noon–3pm & 7–11pm, Sat & Sun 7– 11pm.

★ **Maphrao On** Hermanos Manchego 2586 ☎ 02 2434682; map p.67. Maphrao On was the first Asian restaurant in Bolivia when it opened in 2001, and it remains a difficult place to drag yourself away from, with bamboo furniture, great swathes of indoor vegetation, warm service, a great atmosphere and a soundtrack of nice, jazzy deep house; all things considered, it may just be the single most satisfying eating experience in La Paz. With the menu running the gamut of Indian, Chinese and South East Asian cuisine, you can savour the novelty of having a fiery Indian samosa starter and a creamy red Thai curry main. Or try the fish Haidarabad, cooked with cumin, sesame seeds, chilli and ginger (ninety percent of spices are imported from country of origin). Portions are substantial, so make sure there's enough space in your stomach before splashing out, and be sure to leave room for their orgasmic strawberry lemonade. Daily noon–4pm & 7pm–midnight.

★ **Restaurant El Consulado** Carlos Bravo 229 ☎ 02 2117706, ⓦ cafeelconsulado.com; map p.57. The rarest of finds in central La Paz, a real garden restaurant in the grounds of a stunning colonial conversion (see p.76), with seating both in a bright (heated) conservatory and – for those days when the air isn't too chilly – the garden itself. The prize-winning food is mouth-wateringly fresh and largely organic, with attentive service and obvious attention to detail; try the zingy-crisp minestrone soup, or a dish of "new Bolivian food" such as duck carpaccio smoked in coca leaves with quinoa and orange salad. Wash it down with a glass of

---

TOP 5 LIVE MUSIC VENUES

Café Concert Luna Llena see p.82
Casa de la Cultura Franz Tamayo/ Teatro Modesta Sanginés see p.84
Peña Markatambo see p.85
Teatro Municipal Alberto Saavedra Pérez see p.85
Thelonious Jazz Bar see p.84

1

their shocking pink hibiscus juice and don't miss the *mousse de cupuazú*, a spike of floral Amazonian flavour. Main dish prices nudge the Bs50 mark but are well worth it. Tues–Sun 8am–10pm.

Wagamama Pasaje Pinilla 2557, just off Av Arce ☎02 2434911; map p.67. Not part of the London-based Wagamama chain but a high-end, authentic and perennially popular Japanese restaurant in its own right, patronized by a wall-to-wall cross section of La Paz society. While the decor's a little tired and service can be slow (everything is prepared freshly from scratch), the varied menu includes sublime sushi and sashimi, and great tempura. Tues–Sat noon–2.30pm & 7–10pm, Sun noon–3pm.

DRINKING AND NIGHTLIFE

With more and more **gringo-friendly** nightlife springing up around Calles Linares, Tarija and Murillo, as well as the in-house hostel bars, it seems there aren't nearly so many travellers frequenting the designer haunts of **Sopocachi** as there once were. La Paz's **club** scene isn't the most cutting edge, moreover, with numbingly generic Latin pop, rock, salsa, *cumbia* and Eighties music commonplace. You'll find genuine Latin jazz/salsa, Brazilian, world, reggae, house, hip hop, techno, drum'n'bass and rock music if you look hard enough, however, and a forthcoming city-centre club from the loose grouping of restaurateurs and bar owners known as **4corners** (🖰4cornerslapaz.com) looks promising. For the lowdown on visiting international DJs, Spanish-readers should seek out the free magazine *beats*, while the free, English-language *Bolivian Express* (🖰bolivianexpress.org) usually has at least some coverage of La Paz nightlife in general.

Café Concert Luna Llena Av Ecuador 2582 ☎02 2418151; map p.67. Housed in an atmospherically renovated colonial pile, this cultural centre-cum-café-bar claims the cheapest beer in Sopocachi, including Saya and the quinoa-brewed Lipeña. The walls are routinely lined with works by some of La Paz's best young artists and photographers and, as well as literature and poetry readings, a busy live music programme runs the gamut from flamenco to heavy metal. Mon–Fri 9am–3am.

Diesel Nacional Av 20 de Octubre 2271, between Rosendo Gutiérrez and Fernando Guachalla ☎02 2423477; map p.67. Post-apocalyptic-style bar with aircraft engines dangling from the ceiling, a futuristic log brazier burning away in the centre (it tends to reek, however, so unless you're feeling the chill, try and sit elsewhere) and – delightfully incongruously – a drinks menu peppered with wry quotes from the likes of W.C. Fields and Compton McKenzie. Mon–Thurs 7pm–midnight, Fri & Sat till 2am.

Etno Jaén 722 ☎02 2280343; map p.57. The most self-consciously bohemian café-bar in town, tending towards the gothic, with spooky abstract photography and "Lady Bathory" and "Nosferatu" absinthe cocktails. Surprisingly enough, they also whip up arguably the city's best *café con leche*; be sure to taste their Amazonian whisky too. A nightly cultural programme keeps the art school clientele busy, with a little stage through the back where it all happens. Mon–Thurs 11am–3am, Fri & Sat 4pm–3am.

La Luna Oruro and Murillo; map p.57. Atmospheric, torn and frayed late-night drinking cave where you're almost always guaranteed great music (vintage Latin jazz, Seventies rock, blues etc), a comfy seat and a friendly welcome. A real tonic if you're suffering from cheesy Latin pop overkill and your backside's aching from too many functionally useless designer chairs. Daily 7pm till late.

Malegria Pasaje Medinacelli 2282 ☎02 2423700; map p.67. Tribal-themed nightclub with ethnic masks, stone walls and a middling music policy that runs between ska, Mexican and Argentinian rock, and the usual generic stuff. The real reason to come here is the live Thurs night Afro-Bolivian music, a veritable orgy of rhythm and colour. Thurs–Sat 10pm–3.30am.

THANK GOD IT'S (BACHELOR) FRIDAY

La Paz is generally fairly quiet on weekday evenings, but explodes into life on **Friday nights** – known as *viernes de solteros* (bachelor Fridays) – when much of the city's male population goes out drinking. In the city centre – and above all in the market district along Max Paredes and Avenida Buenos Aires – there are countless rough-and-ready **whiskerías** and **karaoke bars** where hard-drinking, almost exclusively male crowds gather to drown their sorrows in beer and *chufflay*, a lethal mix of *singani* and lemonade, while playing *cacho*, a popular dice game, or singing along to the latest Latin pop songs. Going out to these popular bars is certainly a very authentic Bolivian experience and can be great fun, but as a foreigner you should expect to attract a good deal of attention and be prepared to drink until you drop – refusing an invitation from a fellow drinker is considered rather rude. For women, such places are best avoided altogether.

1

Mongo's Rock-Bottom Café Hermanos Manchego 2444 ☎ 02 2440714; map.67. The granddaddy of La Paz's gringo hangouts, though there seem to be more locals than gringos here these days. A shame, as it's still a great place for an atmospheric early to mid-evening drink when the open fireplace is roaring (the logs smell heavenly), the candles haven't burned out and the DJ hasn't turned up the volume to ear-splitting level. Live Cuban music and free salsa lessons every Tues, and lunchtime opening planned for the near future. Daily 6pm–3.30am.

★ **Oliver's Travels** Corner of Murillo and Tarija ☎ 02 2311574, ⓦ 4cornerslapaz.com; map p.57. "Do you like cocaine?"; "Do you shy away from strangers?"; "Do you have a face like a bulldog chewing a wasp?"; this bar's cheeky job ads (these are the qualities that won't get you a job, by the way) exemplify its un-PC sense of humour, which also runs through the Scotsman, Englishmen, Irishman, Frenchman, etc jokes in the small print of their menu. Not to everyone's tastes, certainly, but if this sounds up your street, you'll doubtless have a grand old time, with honest to goodness pint glasses of beer (Saya, Paceña etc), superlative ginger and tomato curries (Bs40), live English Premiership and Champions League football, free wi-fi and classic British indie sounds. Daily 8am till late (or "until we get bored").

Sol y Luna Cochabamba with Murillo ☎ 02 2115328, ⓦ solyluna-lapaz.com; map p.57. Dutch-owned institution serving strong coffee and cold beer in a mellow, stone-walled, candlelit atmosphere, with huge windows perfect for watching La Paz's night-time street life hustle by. It's conveniently close to the main accommodation area and a good place to meet other travellers, with seating over several floors. Their food (in the Bs40 bracket) is excellent: try the Indonesian *gado gado*, a robust mix of tofu and vegetables in peanut sauce. If you're just here for a drink, there's a handsome selection to choose from, including offerings from Bolivia's domestic microbreweries; if it's in stock, don't miss the Hoegaarden-esque Chala from Ted's Cervecería. Likewise don't miss the annual riot of orange wigs that is the Queens Day party (30th April). Daily 10am–midnight.

★ **Thelonious Jazz Bar** Av 20 de Octubre 2172; map p.67. Venerable jazz venue with an intimate basement atmosphere, hosting excellent live jazz, Brazilian music and occasional Gypsy swing Wed–Sat. The cover charge (Wed & Thurs Bs20, Fri & Sat Bs25; no charge Mon & Tues) is tacked onto the end of your drinks bill rather than paid upfront, but is usually worth every centavo. The only downside is how chokingly smoky the place gets later in the evening; resign yourself to a morning-after laundry run. Mon–Sat 7pm–3.30am.

Traffic Av Arce 2549 ☎ 02 2118107; map p.67. Garishly designed bar-cum-restaurant-cum-club, with a chandelier-lit, brick-arched dining area, though it's more famous for its Fri/Sat night roster of big-name national – and occasionally international – DJs. Mon–Sat noon–2pm & 6pm–4am.

★ **TTkos** Mexico 1555 ☎ 7011 5660; map p.57. Hot, dark, sweaty and often packed subterranean bolthole with a jumping local crowd losing themselves in some of the best live music, DJs and club nights in La Paz, including live reggae (Tues), electronica (Wed) and world/Afro-beat (Thurs). Cover charge is a mere Bs10. Mon–Sat 10pm–4am.

ENTERTAINMENT

Appreciation of the **performing arts** in La Paz is limited to a small minority, but there are a few places where you can catch theatre, classical music concerts, ballet and even opera. **Film** is more popular, and though the emphasis tends to be on Hollywood action blockbusters (almost always in English with Spanish subtitles), La Paz, surprisingly perhaps, has two excellent **art house cinemas**. You can pick up *Jiwaki*, a free, pocket-sized monthly guide to public museums, galleries, cinema and theatre, at the artier cafés and bars, or check out the listings on municipal website, ⓦ lapaz.bo. The English-language *Bolivian Express* (ⓦ bolivianexpress.org) also has culture listings.

THEATRES AND CINEMAS

Casa de la Cultura Franz Tamayo/Teatro Modesta Sanginés Av Mariscal Santa Cruz, opposite Plaza San Francisco ☎ 02 2406877; map p.57. Hosts a wide range of cultural events including theatre, folk music, art exhibitions and film screenings. Most performances, recently including the likes of ace percussionist Alvaro Córdova, are, incredibly, free.

Cine 16 de Julio Av 16 de Julio 1897 just off Plaza del Estudiante ☎ 02 2441099; map p.57. Comfortable modern cinema showing the latest international releases.

Cine Monje Campero Av 16 de Julio 1495 ☎ 02 2333332; map p.57. Garishly painted Prado landmark showing standard Hollywood fare.

Cine Municipal 6 de Agosto Av 6 de Agosto 2284 ☎ 02 2442629; map p.67. Impressive municipally run cinema housed in a visually arresting Art Deco building and dedicated to national, Latin American and European film, often with a cultural/political/art house bent, and usually programmed by season.

Cinemateca Boliviana Zuazo and R. Gutiérrez ☎ 02 2444090, ⓦ cinematecaboliviana.org; map p.67. The best cinema in Bolivia, with a tastefully presented selection of Bolivian, Latin American and European releases past and present (as well as the odd Hollywood classic), and a fine upstairs café.

Multi Cine Av Arce 2631 ☎ 02 2124325; map p.67. US-style multi-screen complex in Sopocachi, showing the latest digitally enhanced animations and big-budget remakes.

Teatro Municipal Alberto Saavedra Pérez Genaro Sanjines and Indaburo ☎02 2406183; map p.57. Elegant Neoclassical building that is now the city's premier venue for theatre, folk, world and classical music, opera and ballet. Recent programmes have included Brecht's *Threepenny Opera*; a tribute to the late Mercedes Sosa; and top artists such as Bajofondo Tango Club collaborator Adriana Varela.

PEÑAS

For more traditional entertainment you should head to one of the folk music venues known as *peñas*, where you'll see Andean folk dancing accompanied by traditional Andean music involving drums, charangos, guitars, quenas (notched flutes) and the inevitable *zampoñas* (panpipes).

El Mural Av Montes 689; map p.57. Way off the regular *peña* tourist trail, this earthy, devilishly painted, mirror-balled venue is conveniently located below the new *Bash'n'Crash* hostel (see p.74) and residents get in free. Charges are Bs5 during the week and Bs20 on weekends, though that includes a free *singani* and orange juice. Once the charangos and open fire die down, the disco starts up. Shows 11.30pm & 1.30am.

Peña Huari Sagárnaga 339 ☎02 2316225; map p.57. The longest-established and most popular *peña* in town – hence the Bs105 cover charge – with a reasonably authentic folk music show and good, if pricey, traditional Altiplano food, including a list of llama dishes well into double figures. Shows daily 8pm.

Peña Markatambo Jaen 710 ☎02 2280041; map p.57. Perhaps the most authentic traditional music and dance show in La Paz, with an ideal setting in an old colonial mansion, though the food is mediocre. Bs35 cover charge. Shows Mon–Fri 10pm.

Peña Parnaso Sagárnaga 189 ☎02 2316827; map p.57. A very touristy *peña*, slap-bang in the middle of gringo alley. The food isn't bad (and they also have some vegetarian options), and reasonably compelling shows take place amid colonial cornicing, columns and a particularly tacky backdrop. Cover charge Bs80, though you can sometimes pick up flyers offering a free drink. Shows Mon–Sat 8.30pm.

SHOPPING

Given that the city can at times feel like one massive marketplace, it should come as no surprise that La Paz is a good place to go **shopping**. You'll find a wider range of **artesanía** (handicrafts) here than anywhere else in Bolivia, with goods from all over the country, which means you don't have to lug souvenirs back with you from Sucre or Potosí. Most of what's on sale is good quality, too, and prices aren't much higher than at the point of manufacture.

ARTESANÍA

The best places to shop for handicrafts and other souvenirs are Calle Sagárnaga, Calle Linares and the surrounding streets, where you'll find dozens of shops and stalls. Many of the different magic charms, bracelets and carved stone figures sold in the Mercado de Hechicería (see p.64) also make inexpensive souvenirs and outlandish gifts for people back home. Note that most of the fossils sold on the street are fake.

Prices The cost (though not necessarily the quality) of crafts is generally lower on the street stalls than in the shops and it's worth shopping around and comparing prices before you buy. There's room for a certain amount of bargaining, but don't expect prices to come down too much; haggling with someone far poorer than you over a dollar or two will make you look foolish and mean-spirited.

Textiles and clothing Some of the best offerings are the traditional textiles from all over the highlands, including beautiful handmade ponchos, woven belts, blankets and women's shawls that make very nice wall hangings. Be warned, though, that a well-made poncho with an intricate design can cost well over Bs700 ($100). For a more moderately priced and practical souvenir, you can't beat the llama and alpaca wool jumpers, socks and hats. You can pick up a hat for just Bs10 and a warm sweater for as little as Bs60 on the street stalls, though you can pay several times that for a finely made and professionally designed one in some of the shops.

Leather and jewellery Leather items are pretty good value – especially the hard-wearing and stylish belts and bags decorated with strips of traditional weaving. Silver jewellery is also abundant and very good value, though the silver content of the stuff sold on the streets isn't always as high as vendors claim it is.

Musical instruments There are several good musical instrument shops on Sagárnaga and Linares where you can pick up some beautiful handmade guitars, charangos and other stringed instruments, as well as cheaper quena flutes and *zampoñas* (panpipes), which make excellent gifts.

ARTESANÍA SHOPS

Artesanía Sorata Sagárnaga 363 ☎02 2485159; ⓦartesaniasorata.com; map p.57. Specializing in high quality, handmade alpaca garments since 1978, this company was operating on fair-trade principles well before the concept became commonplace, and currently runs various volunteer-run community programmes.

Ayni Illampu 704 ☎02 2457487, ⓦaynibolivia.com; map p.57. For almost a decade Ayni has flown the flag for

1

fair trade *artesanía* in La Paz, and is now a member of the World Fair Trade Organization. Look out especially for the "orange art", oven-dried orange peel made into exquisite keepsakes; not quite as intricate as the ones sold in Rurrenabaque (see p.280) but still a great buy. There's also a recently opened branch at Av Montenegro 911, in San Miguel, Zona Sur.

Jalsuri Sagárnaga 363, 2nd floor ☎02 2792359; ⓦjalsuri.org; map p.57. Sequestered on the far side of a courtyard off Sagarnaga and run by a non-profit foundation working with more than three thousand *artesanía* producers all over Bolivia (over eighty percent of whom are women, and many of whom are the wives of Potosí miners). Their eclectic range includes Pachamontera hats from Sucre, cactus wood from Tupiza, handsomely finished lamps from Chiquitanía and pricey replicas of gilt-edged colonial-era furniture.

BOOKS, MAPS AND OUTDOOR EQUIPMENT

⭐ **Andean Base Camp** Illampu 863 ☎02 2463782, Eandeanbasecamp@hotmail.com; map p.57. The number one company in La Paz for equipment rental, and the place where many of the operators come. The shop – tiny, usually full, with tents getting rolled and unrolled – gives the impression of a real grass roots passion for what they do, a bit like an old-school record store, and co-owner Christian Menn is an inexhaustible source of climbing-related info. They also stock some of the most up-to-date maps of both La Paz, the Cordillera Real and the Yungas as well as a healthy selection of used guidebooks. Mon–Sat 9am–7pm.

Instituto Geográfico Militar Av Saavedra 2303, Miraflores ☎02 2229786; map p.67. You can buy 1:50,000- and 1:250,000-scale topographical maps (as well as photocopies of those which aren't available) of most of Bolivia (some areas are yet to be surveyed) from the IGM, located in the military headquarters (Estado Mayor); you'll need your passport for identification. Mon–Fri 8.30am–12.30pm & 2.30–6.30pm.

Tatoo Illampu 828 ☎02 2451265, ⓦtatoo.ws; map p.57. Though the name is baffling, the interior blandly modern and the staff tending to the surly, the La Paz branch of this South American chain comes highly recommended and is one of the only places in the city you're guaranteed to get authentic brand name outdoor gear; they work with Marmot and Osprey among others. Mon–Sat 10am–7pm.

⭐ **The Spitting Llama** Linares 947, below Hostal La Posada de la Abuela (see p.75) ☎7039 8720, ⓦthespittingllama.com; map p.57. Excellent family-owned, community-tourism-minded bookstore with a formidable selection of used books and travel guides in English, German, Spanish, French and even Quechua and Aymara. There's also a smattering of new guides, as well as camping gear and a fascinating selection of maps. Staff are friendly and helpful and membership (Bs100) offers a twenty percent discount on gear and books. Daily 10.30am–7pm.

ANTIQUES AND MISCELLANY

⭐ **Arte Local 67** Linares 975; map p.57. If you've had your fill of *artesanía*, this is a great place to while away a spare hour, a rare Linares antique shop run by the lovely Judith Zeballos. Though the entrance – situated at the far end of Linares – isn't exactly prominent, it's well worth stepping inside for a fascinating selection of old music scores, antique books, postcards, old gramophones and even vintage Pujlley helmets from Potosí. Mon–Sat 10.30am–1pm & 3–7pm.

Zapatería Crack Next door to Arte Local 67; map p.57. If you have an interest in football memorabilia, it's worth stepping next door from Arte into this tiny, memorably named shoe shop specializing in football boots. Grizzled owner Don Julio has lined the walls of his tiny workplace with a fantastic selection of old photos, both of the national team and of various club teams, as well as a framed article on his good self, the one-time supplier of boots to no less than Pelé.

DIRECTORY

Banks and exchange There are plenty of banks with ATMs in the centre of town, especially on Av Camacho, and a growing number of freestanding ATMs line both the Prado and Calle Sagárnaga. The best places to change cash and travellers' cheques are the many cambios on Av Camacho and the Prado.

Car rental American, Av Camacho 1574 ☎02 2202933, ⓦamericanrentacarbolivia.com; Avis, Av Costanera and Pablo Guillén 24 ☎7729 9509, ⓦavis.com.bo; Barbol, Av Héroes, opposite El Alto airport ☎02 2820675; Budget, C 17 and Claudio Aliaga 8275, Calacoto ☎02 2775433.

Dentist Claudia Suarez Blancourt, Av Arce and corner of Pasaje Cordero, Edificio El Escorial, Ist Floor, Office No.105 ☎02 2433019. English spoken.

Doctor Clinica del Sur, Av Hernando Siles 3539, corner of C 7, Obrajes, Zona Sur, ⓦclinicadelsur.com.bo, has a 24hr emergency facility and is used by most embassy staff. Try Clinica Cemes, Av 6 de Agosto 2881, for less serious ailments. Basics has more information on severe altitude sickness (p.55).

Embassies and consulates Argentina, Aspiazu 497 ☎02 2417737; Australia, Av Arce, Edificio Montevideo ☎02 2971339, ⓦdfat.gov.au/missions/countries/bo.html;

Brazil, Av Arce, Edificio Multicentro ☎02 2166400, ⓦbrasil.org.bo; Canada, Victor Sanjinés 2678, Edificio Barcelona ☎02 2415141, ⓦcanadainternational.gc.ca/peru-perou/index.aspx; Chile, C 14 No. 8024, Calacoto ☎02 2797331; Ecuador, C 10 No. 8054, Calacoto ☎02 2784422; Ireland, Pasaje Gandarillas 2667, Sopocachi ☎02 2411873; Paraguay, Edificio Illimani II, Av 6 de Agosto ☎02 2433176; Peru, Fernando Guachalla 300 ☎02 2441250; UK, Av Arce 2732 ☎02 2433424, ⓦukinbolivia.fco.gov.uk/en; US, Av Arce 2780 ☎02 2168000, ⓦbolivia.usembassy.gov.

Emergencies Ambulance ☎118, police ☎110, tourist police ☎02 2225016.

Immigration For visa extensions go to the Oficina de Migración at Av Camacho 1433 ☎02 2203028 (Mon–Fri 8.30am–12.30pm & 4.30–6.30pm). It should be a same-day service, but don't count on it.

Internet In La Paz an internet café beckons at every other doorway; most charge about Bs1–3 an hour and are pretty much interchangeable.

Language schools The only accredited school which concentrates solely on Spanish as a second langauge is the Instituto de la Lengua Española, C 14 and Aviador 180, in the Achumani neighbourhood of the Zona Sur (☎02 2796074 , ⓦspanbol.com). If you're feeling linguistically adventurous, Instituto de Lengua y Cultura Aymara (ILCA), Casilla 2681 (☎02 2419650, ⓦilcanet.org), also offers Aymara and Quechua classes.

Laundry Most hotels have a laundry service, and there are plenty of *lavanderías* around town. Try Lavandería Maya, Sagárnaga 339, inside the same gallery as *Hostal Maya Inn*, or the friendly Finesse, Ilampu 853.

Pharmacies There's a 24hr, 365-day-a-year pharmacy on Av 16 de Julio 1473, near the Monje Campero cinema (☎02 2331838).

Photo equipment and film There are photo developing labs all over the city centre and along the Prado; try ABC, Av 16 Mariscal Santa Cruz. Tecnología Fotográfica, Ground Floor Office A, Edificio Renacer, Av 20 de Octubre 2255 (ⓦtecnologiafotografica.com), develops and digitizes slide and black-and-white film, repairs cameras (including digital) and sells a reasonable range of equipment.

Post office Correo Central, Av Mariscal Santa Cruz and Oruro (Mon–Fri 8am–8pm, Sat till 6pm, Sun 9am–noon). There's also an endearing little office in the far corner of the *Angelo Colonial* courtyard, Linares 922 (Mon–Fri 9am–noon & 3–7pm; Sat till 1pm, Sun till noon).

Telephones One of the cheapest places to make international calls is the small Punto Cotel on the Prado, opposite the main Post Office (walk right through past the first line of booths to the office at the back; Mon–Fri 8.30am–10.30pm, Sat & Sun till 8pm). Charges to the UK are only Bs1/minute. For directory enquiries call ☎104.

Tourist police Edificio Olimpia, Plaza Tejada Sorzano, opposite the stadium in Miraflores (24hr; ☎02 2225016). Come here to report thefts for insurance claims.

Around La Paz

Just south of the city the barren, moon-like landscapes of the **Valle de la Luna** and the **Muela del Diablo**, near the suburbs of **Mallasa** and **Calacoto** respectively, make for energetic day-trips if you want a little taste of the kind of dramatic mountain scenery that awaits you elsewhere in Bolivia; a gentler half-day can be had at Mallasa's zoo.

To the north of La Paz, the spectacular high Andean scenery of the Cordillera Real can be easily reached on a day-trip to **Chacaltaya**, even if the famous glacier and high-altitude skiing are now increasingly distant memories. Further east towards the Peruvian border lies the mysterious ruined city of **Tiwanaku**, Bolivia's most impressive archeological site.

Mallasa

From Calacoto, the southernmost suburb of the Zona Sur in La Paz, a road follows the course of the Río Choqueyapu about 5km southeast towards the suburb of **MALLASA**, in the surrounding environs of which you'll find both the **Valle de la Luna** and the **municipal zoo**.

Valle de la Luna

Daily 8am–5.30pm • Bs15 • Take micro #11 from the Prado or #231/#273 from Calle Mexico, and get off at the roundabout with the small obelisk, shortly after the road passes through two tunnels

The stretch of eerie, cactus-strewn badlands around Mallasa is known as the **Valle de la Luna**. Scarred by deep canyons and strange formations of clay and rock carved by

1

seasonal rains into pinnacles resembling church organ pipes, the valley is a popular excursion from the city and, at less than 3500m makes a pleasant area for a half-day walk, though if you're travelling in the Bolivian highlands for any length of time, you may find the scenery here rather tame by comparison. There's now an entry charge (as well as an *artesanía* shop and a subterranean information centre illuminating the valley's geology), payable at the kiosk on the left, on the road that switches back to the right from the roundabout; look out for the flags of the adjacent golf course, predictably dubbed the world's highest.

Zoo Municipal Vesty Pakos

Av Florida • Daily 10am–5.45pm • Bs3.50 • From the Valle de la Luna, pick up micro #11, #231 or #273 at the same place you got off; it's 1km further to the centre of Mallasa

Located at the end of the main road that runs through Mallasa and set in ample parkland shaded by eucalyptus groves, the city zoo is a great place to escape La Paz's concrete jungle, even if the stressed-looking big cats look like they'd rather be in a real one. The larger birds likewise look pretty miserable, though most of the animals have fairly spacious enclosures and overall it's a good place to familiarize yourself with Bolivian wildlife, including the rare Andean spectacled bear, pumas, jaguars, llamas, vicuñas and all manner of birds, some of them endangered.

La Muela del Diablo

Take micro #207 or #288 from the Plaza del Estudiante in La Paz to the village of Pedregal, a couple of kilometres beyond Zona Sur. From Pedregal, it's an hour's steep uphill walk to the foot of the Muela – the trail starts behind the cemetery and is easy to follow

Set amid more badlands east of Calacoto, the volcanic outcrop known as **La Muela del Diablo** – the Devil's Molar – makes another good half-day trip out of the city. The jagged rock formation is impressive rather than spectacular, especially if you've already travelled elsewhere in the high Andes, but the views back across the desert-like landscape towards La Paz are a dramatic reminder of just what an inhospitable and unlikely place this was to build a major city. You can climb the Muela, though this is not advisable without experience and some basic equipment. A further trail leads around the back of the peak, down and across the Río Choqueyapu via a hanging bridge and up to the zoo, a good half-day's hike in itself. Be sure to take sunscreen and plenty of water.

Chacaltaya

About 40km north of La Paz, **Chacaltaya** was, until recently, Bolivia's only developed ski slope and, at over 5000m above sea level, the highest in the world. The glacier has now melted completely, however, and with it the ski industry. For many observers, its demise remains one of the starkest examples of global warming in the Americas, and a portent of diminishing water supplies across the Andes. It's nevertheless still worth visiting for the magnificent scenery, even if you first need to be altitude acclimatized (and even then bring plenty of warm clothing, sunscreen and sunglasses). From up here the massive icebound peak of Illimani seems close enough to touch, while La Paz and El Alto, far below in the Altiplano, look minuscule by comparison. You can also see the crystalline waters of Lago Titicaca to the west, with the mountains of Peru rising behind, and on clear days the volcanic cone of Sajama, Bolivia's highest mountain, is visible far across the Altiplano to the southwest. If you make the short climb up the peak of **Mount Chacaltaya** behind the ski refuge, the views open up further – a truly breathtaking panorama.

ARRIVAL AND DEPARTURE CHACALTAYA

Tours There's no public transport to Chacaltaya, though many tour agencies in La Paz (see p.73) run trips for around Bs70 return, sometimes combined with the Valle de la Luna.

ACCOMMODATION

Refuge A well-insulated refuge offers overnight accommodation in a choice of dormitory or en-suite private rooms. For reservations contact Alfredo Martinez (☎7325 8841), former chief of Club Andino, the main organization that used to run ski trips to Chacaltaya. Bs30/person

EATING

Restaurant The ski refuge has a small restaurant where you can get basic meals and hot drinks: many consider coca tea essential at this altitude, though others favour the delicious hot chocolate with rum.

Tiwanaku

Daily 8am–5pm (last entry 4pm) • Bs80 • You can hire guides outside the museum for about Bs15/hour

Set on the Altiplano 71km west of La Paz, the ancient ruined city of **TIWANAKU** (also spelt **Tiahuanaco**) is one of the most monumental and intriguing archeological sites in South America. Founded some three millennia ago, Tiwanaku became the capital of a massive empire that lasted almost a thousand years, developing into a sophisticated urban **ceremonial complex** that at its peak was home to some fifty thousand people whose great pyramids and opulent palaces were painted in bright colours and inlaid with gold. The city was in many ways the cradle of Andean civilization, making an enormous cultural impact throughout the region and providing the fundamental inspiration for the better-known Inca empire. Though the city of Tiwanaku originally covered several square kilometres, only a fraction of the site has been excavated, and the main **ruins** occupy a fairly small area which can easily be visited in half a day – the only other major site that has been excavated is Puma Punku (see p.92), a pyramid complex a couple of kilometres to the north. The main ruins cover the area that was once the ceremonial centre of the city, a jumble of tumbled pyramids and ruined palaces and temples made from megalithic stone blocks. A couple of **museums** (see p.91) by the entrance house many of the smaller archeological finds. In view of recent bids to finance restoration here (see p.91), there's the possibility that the site

THE SACRED GEOGRAPHY OF TIWANAKU AND THE AYMARA NEW YEAR

For all its political and economic power, Tiwanaku's transcendental importance was undoubtedly **religious**. The first Spanish chroniclers to visit the site were told its name was "Taipicala", after the stone at the centre, where it was believed the universe was created and from whence the first humans set forth to colonize the world. The Incas themselves consciously sought to associate themselves with the spiritual legitimacy of Tiwanaku, claiming their own dynasty had been brought into existence at nearby Lago Titicaca.

The US anthropologist Johan Reinhard has sought to explain the spiritual importance of Tiwanaku in terms of **sacred geography**, a system of beliefs related to mountain worship and fertility cults, which is still prevalent in the Andes. The high mountain peaks are considered powerful deities, known as *achachilas* in Aymara, who control meteorological phenomena and the fertility of crops and animals.

The most spectacular manifestation of these beliefs is during the **Aymara New Year** on the June winter solstice, when hundreds of *yatiris* (traditional priests) from all over the region (as well as a sizeable contingent of gringos) congregate at Tiwanaku to watch the sun rise and celebrate with music, dancing, elaborate rituals and copious quantities of coca and alcohol. **Evo Morales** even sealed his election victory with a crowning ceremony here.

In terms of sacred geography, Tiwanaku's position could not be more propitious, set close to **Lago Titicaca** with a view east to **Illimani**, the most important **mountain god** in the Altiplano, and aligned with **Illampu** and **Sajama**, the second and third most important peaks. Though it can't be proved, it seems likely that the builders of Tiwanaku chose the site with these concepts in mind, even though it meant they had to transport stones weighing hundreds of tonnes from across the lake.

1

may close temporarily so it's worth checking with the tourist office in La Paz before heading out there.

Brief history

The Tiwanaku civilization was first established around 1200 BC, with an economy based on **potato cultivation** and **llama herding**. By 100 BC it had become an important urban centre, and an organized state with distinct classes of priests, warriors, artisans and aristocrats is thought to have emerged. By 400 AD this state controlled the whole Titicaca basin – an area of some 57,000 square kilometres extending out from the lake between Bolivia's Cordillera Real and Peru and Chile's Cordillera Occidental – and had begun extending its influence.

700–1000 AD

From around 700 AD Tiwanaku expanded rapidly to dominate an area comprising much of modern Bolivia, southern Peru, northeast Argentina and northern Chile. The key to this expansion was a remarkable agricultural system of raised fields, known as **sukakullo** (see below), which revolutionized food production along the shores of Lago Titicaca and freed vast amounts of labour for the construction of monumental temples and palaces. It also allowed trade with other societies, though as their power grew, direct control of other regions through conquest or colonization probably came to replace this. Tiwanaku's influence thus spread to encompass a vast area, crisscrossed with paved roads along which caravans of hundreds of llamas carried all kinds of produce to the centre of the empire.

Decline and abandonment

Some time after 1000 AD, Tiwanaku fell into a rapid and irreversible **decline**. The fields were abandoned, the population dispersed and, within a period of about fifty years, the empire disappeared, most likely due to climate change. Scientists studying ice cores from Andean glaciers have discovered that from about 1000 AD the region suffered a long-term decline in rainfall. Though the imperial storehouses could no doubt withstand a few lean years, this searing **drought** lasted for decades, even centuries. Unable to feed the hungry masses, Tiwanaku's civilization collapsed.

SUKAKULLOS

The most impressive achievement of the Tiwanaku civilization was undoubtedly the intensification of agriculture along the shores of Lago Titicaca using a system of raised fields known in Aymara as **sukakullo**. This system enabled the inhabitants of Tiwanaku to overcome the problems of drought, floods, frost and soil exhaustion. The Altiplano, the plain surrounding the ruins – which today provides a marginal living for just over seven thousand campesinos – was 1500 years ago producing harvests big enough to feed over one hundred thousand people.

The platforms stand over 1m high, with planting surfaces up to 200m long and 15m wide, and each is carefully structured, with a base of stones followed by a layer of clay to prevent **salination** by the slightly brackish waters of Lago Titicaca. Above this is a layer of gravel, followed by one of sandy soil and finally a coating of rich, organic topsoil. The raised fields run in parallel lines, with **water-filled ditches** running between them, providing irrigation during the dry season and preventing flooding when the level of the lake rose. By storing the heat of the sun during the day and releasing it at night, the water in the ditches also protected crops from frost, extending the growing season considerably. Whereas present-day farmers produce about three tons of potatoes per hectare, research suggests that the *sukakullo* produced astonishing yields of up to twenty tonnes a hectare. Experimental projects are now under way to help local **campesinos** reintroduce these techniques.

The colonial era to the twentieth century

Most of the **destruction** of the remains of Tiwanaku occurred relatively recently. When the Spanish first came here many of the buildings were still standing, but the presence of gold meant that they quickly set about tearing them down. Licences to loot the site were handed out by the Spanish crown in the same way as for mining, and many of the great stones were dragged away to build churches and houses. Still more were destroyed with **dynamite** at the beginning of the twentieth century to provide gravel for the foundations of the railway that passes nearby, while early archeological excavations varied little in nature from the looting of the Spaniards, stripping the site of its most beautiful statues to adorn the museums of Europe and the US. After years of neglect and deterioration due to dampness, moss and lichen, moreover, the Bolivian government recently appealed to **UNESCO** for financial help and decided to initiate criminal proceedings against officials in charge of a previous restoration.

The museums

Adjacent to the site entrance are two **museums**, access to both of which is included in the ticket price; it is projected that much of the aforementioned financial help will be invested in the restoration of their contents.

The **Museo Regional Arqueológico de Tiwanaku** houses some of the site's best carved stone idols and friezes, and there's a big collection of ceramics, themselves the main means used to distinguish between the different eras in Tiwanaku civilization. The earliest pottery, from between about 1000 and 300 BC – a period known as the Village Stage or Tiwanaku I – consists mainly of simple but well-made pots, decorated with geometric incisions and designs (including puma and bird motifs) painted in red, white and yellow on a chestnut-brown background. Ceramics from the period known as the Urban Stage – Tiwanaku II, from about the first century AD – show a clear advance in quality and design, with finely made pots richly painted with multiple colours and highly burnished. Through the periods III to IV, up to the end of the first millennium AD, the pots become ever more elaborate and iconographically distinctive, with highly stylized feline and serpentine figures. Some are decorated with distinctive human faces that make it easy to believe the local Aymara when they claim to be directly descended from the builders of Tiwanaku.

The **Museo Lítico**, a rather forlorn annexe, houses a solitary if huge exhibit, the 7.3m-high Bennett monolith, or Pachamama, relocated from Miraflores a decade ago.

Akapana

As you enter the ruins, the big mound on your right is **Akapana**, a great earth pyramid with seven terraced platforms faced with stone. This was the biggest structure in the complex, measuring about 180m by 140m, and some 18m tall, and is thought to have been the city's most important religious centre, constructed as an imitation of a sacred mountain. From the west it now looks more like a hill than a man-made feature, and in fact archeologists originally believed it had been built around a natural hill. You can still make out the pyramid's seven tiers, however, and some of the huge stone blocks are still in evidence on the east side, many of them carved with a step motif characteristic of Tiwanaku.

Kalasasaya

Next to Akapana, to the north, is **Kalasasaya**, a walled temple compound that's thought to have been the sacred centre of Tiwanaku, where the ruling god-emperors were buried. The stone walls of the complex are among the most impressive masonry still standing at the site, made with colossal megaliths weighing up to 150 tonnes interspersed with smaller blocks, and with carved stone drains that may also have been related to the ritual importance of water. The compound's re-erected monoliths, alas,

1

have suffered some of the most visible climatic damage in recent times. On the east side of the compound, a massive doorway is astronomically aligned so that the sun appears in its centre at the spring and autumn equinoxes.

The Puerta del Sol

Set into Kalasasaya's northeastern corner is the iconic **Puerta del Sol** – the Gateway of the Sun – an elaborately decorated portico carved from a single piece of rock weighing ten tonnes that has sadly been broken, probably when it was moved here from its original location, believed to have been Puma Punku. The **central figure** above the doorway is the best-known image of Tiwanaku, probably the supreme creator god known to the Aymara as Thunupa and to the Incas as Viracocha. The 24 rays emanating from his head have led some to think of him as a sun god, but there's not much evidence to suggest such a cult existed before the Incas: it's more likely that they're just a stylized representation of hair. From his arms hang severed heads, probably trophies of war. These are no mere metaphors: sixteen headless bodies were found during excavations in the Akapana pyramid, and human sacrifices involving decapitation are still occasionally reported around the shores of Lago Titicaca.

Putini and the Puerta de la Luna

Just west of Kalasasaya, ongoing excavations have revealed the remains of another extensive complex, known as **Putini**, which was probably a residential area for the city's ruling elite, or possibly a burial area. Several enormous stones cut with holes big enough to accommodate human bodies led early twentieth-century investigators, no doubt influenced by their contemporaries' fascination with Egyptology, to call it the "Palace of the Sarcophagi".

To the northwest, the **Puerta de la Luna** – the Gateway of the Moon – is another gateway cut from a single piece of stone, though smaller and without the elaborate decoration of the Puerta del Sol.

Templete Semi-Subterraneo

East of Kalasasaya, the **Templete Semi-Subterraneo** – the Semi-Subterranean Temple – is a sunken rectangular patio about 2m deep whose walls are studded with almost two hundred carved stone heads, which jut out like keystones. These are thought to represent the gods of different ethnic groups conquered and absorbed into the expanding empire – they may even have been idols taken from these peoples and held as symbolic hostages to represent their submission to the supremacy of Tiwanaku.

Puma Punku

Set apart from the main complex, some 3km to the south on the other side of the road and the abandoned railway, are the ruins of another major pyramid, **Puma Punko** – the Gateway of the Puma. Similar in style and function to Akapana, though slightly smaller, this pyramid is believed to have been built some two hundred years later, in around 700 AD. The skill and exactitude with which the massive stone blocks were carved is deeply impressive, particularly in a society without iron tools.

ARRIVAL AND DEPARTURE	TIWANAKU

By minibus Minibuses to Tiwanaku depart from the corner of Aliaga and Eyzaguirre in the cemetery district in La Paz (every 30min; 1hr 30min); on the way back they leave from the square in Tiwanaku town, just under 1km walk away down Av Ferrocarril, though you can flag them down as they pass the entrance to the ruins.

Tour operators Most tour agencies in La Paz run full-or half-day trips to the site (see p.73).

ACCOMMODATION AND EATING

Hotel Akapana Av Manco Kapac 20, just across from the site entrance ☎02 2895104, ⓦhotel-akapana .com. You can't miss the incongruous, quasi-temple-like exterior, though rooms are far more basic, if clean enough, with parquet floors and modern en-suite bathrooms. There's also a small library and garden, a decent restaurant, and, if you're feeling at all spiritually inadequate, they offer purification ceremonies every Thurs. Breakfast included. Bs80; Aymara New Year Bs200

Lago Titicaca, the cordilleras and the Yungas

98 Lago Titicaca

113 The Cordillera
Apolobamba

118 The Cordillera Real

123 The Yungas

Lago Titicaca, the cordilleras and the Yungas

Encompassing a wide variety of landscapes – including subtropical valleys, expansive plains and soaring Andean peaks – the beautiful high-altitude region surrounding La Paz can seem like a microcosm of the country as a whole, and is sometimes known as "Little Bolivia" because of it. Its focal point is the stunning, shimmering blue of Lago Titicaca, held sacred by the Incas and venerated to this day by local indigenous communities. The nearby Cordillera Real, Cordillera Apolobamba and the Yungas are dotted with tranquil towns, many with balmy temperatures and stunning views, which make them perfect places to relax or to escape the chill of the Altiplano. There are also innumerable options for exploring the diverse countryside on hiking, mountain-biking or climbing excursions. Moreover, with regular transport links to both La Paz and across the border to Peru, the area is easy to access and incorporate into a wider trip.

Lying some 75km northwest of La Paz, **Lago Titicaca** is a vast, high-altitude lake. Straddling the border with Peru it dominates the northern section of the Altiplano, the rolling, 3800m-high plateau that stretches between the eastern and western chains of the Andes – the c+ordilleras Oriental and Occidental – as they march south through Bolivia. The best base from which to explore the Bolivian side of the lake is **Copacabana**, which is home to the country's most revered religious image, as well as the jumping-off point for boat trips to Isla del Sol and Isla de la Luna, two idyllic islands dotted with Inca ruins.

Further north, on the Peruvian border, the isolated **Cordillera Apolobamba** (also part of the Cordillera Oriental) offers great trekking and climbing opportunities in a far more remote setting. South of here and just east of Lago Titicaca is the **Cordillera Real**, the highest and most spectacular section of the Cordillera Oriental within Bolivia. Stretching some 160km along the edge of the Altiplano, from **Mount Illimani** (6439m), southeast of La Paz, to the **Illampu massif** (6370m), which towers over the eastern side of Lago Titicaca, the Cordillera Real can easily be explored from La Paz or the town of **Sorata**, at the northwestern end of the range.

The Yungas' rugged, forest-covered mountains, rivers and warm, fertile valleys offer a stark contrast to the nearby Cordillera and arid Altiplano. With a new highway inaugurated in 2006, the old hair-raising route down to the Yungas from La Paz – dubbed the **most dangerous in the world** – is now largely the domain of mountain bikers. The most popular Yungas destination is **Coroico**, a resort town set amid

Luxury cruises on Lago Titicaca p.99
The Lady of the Lake p.101
Fiestas in Copacabana p.102
Isla del Sol and the Incas p.107
Hiking to Isla del Sol p.109
The secrets of the stars p.111
The Kallawayas: medicine men of the Andes p.114

Trekking and climbing in the Cordillera Real p.119.
Trekking from Sorata p.122
The world's most dangerous road p.124
Coroico's fiesta p.126
Hikes around Coroico p.128
Achachilas and Apus p.131
Afro-Bolivianos p.134

MOUNTAIN VIEW FROM COROICO

Highlights

❶ Copacabana Beautifully located on the shores of Lago Titicaca, this pretty town is also a major pilgrimage centre, and home to the Virgen de Copacabana, Bolivia's most revered religious image. **See p.100**

❷ Isla del Sol The spiritual centre of the Andean world, set amid the deep blue waters of Lago Titicaca and dotted with ancient ruins and traditional Aymara communities. **See p.106**

❸ Cordillera Apolobamba This remote and beautiful mountain range offers some of the best trekking in Bolivia, and is also home to the mysterious Kallawaya medicine men. **See p.114**

❹ Sorata Nestling in a deep valley at the heart of the Cordillera Real, the charming town of Sorata is the perfect base for trekking in the surrounding mountains. **See p.118**

❺ Coroico Scenically located in the lush subtropical valleys of the Yungas, this charming resort town offers the perfect antidote to the cold of the nearby Altiplano. **See p.123**

❻ Mountain biking to Coroico Descending over 3500m in a day, the mountain bike trip from La Paz down to Coroico is one of the world's most breathtaking rides. **See p.124**

❼ Inca trails Running from the high Andes down into the subtropical valleys of the Yungas, Bolivia's three "Inca" trails – the Choro (**See p.128**), Takesi (**See p.130**) and Yunga Cruz (**See p.134**)– are amongst the best trekking routes in the country.

HIGHLIGHTS ARE MARKED ON THE MAP ON P.98

beautiful scenery. Within easy striking distance of Coroico are the diverse ecosystems of **Parque Nacional Cotapata**, through which the rewarding **Choro Trail** passes. The **Takesi Trail**, which also follows a pre-Hispanic paved path, is one of the most popular treks in the region. **Chulumani**, a peaceful town, is less touristy than Coroico but boasts equally good views, while the **Yunga Cruz Trail** is the region's most scenic trek.

2 Lago Titicaca

An immense, sapphire-blue lake sitting astride the border with Peru at the northern end of the Altiplano, **LAGO TITICACA** is one of the classic images of Bolivia, and few scenes are more evocative of the country than the sight of a poncho-clad fisherman paddling across its azure waters against the backdrop of snowcapped mountains. Set at an altitude of 3810m, and measuring 190km by 80km, it's by far the biggest high-altitude body of water in the world – the remnant of an ancient inland sea formed as the Andes were thrust up from the ocean floor. The surrounding area is the heartland of the **Aymara**, whose language and culture have survived centuries of domination. The lake itself is rich in fish, and the water it contains stores the heat of the sun and then releases it overnight, raising average temperatures around its shores, making the region one of the most productive in the high Andes. Lago Titicaca is fed by a number of rivers that carry rainfall down from the Cordillera Real and across the Altiplano, though none of its waters ever reaches the sea, and almost ninety percent of the lake's water loss is through evaporation (the rest is drained by its only outlet, the Río Desaguadero). The water level in the lake fluctuates sharply with slight variations in rainfall; since 2000 levels have fallen to historic lows.

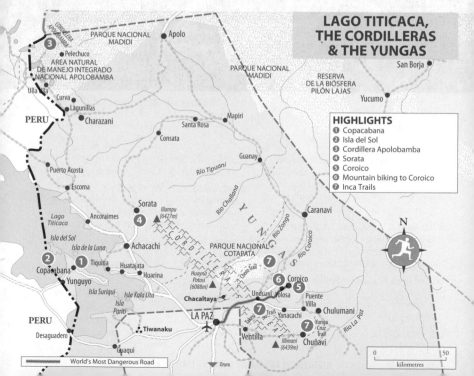

LAGO TITICACA, THE CORDILLERAS & THE YUNGAS

HIGHLIGHTS
1. Copacabana
2. Isla del Sol
3. Cordillera Apolobamba
4. Sorata
5. Coroico
6. Mountain biking to Coroico
7. Inca Trails

LUXURY CRUISES ON LAGO TITICACA

Several La Paz tour agencies offer **luxury cruises** on Lago Titicaca – they're also the only regular way to reach Peru from Bolivia by water. Trips with both Transturin and Crillon Tours cost from around Bs1050 ($150) per person per day; the price includes accommodation, food and transport, and most cruises last one to two days.

Crillon Tours Av Camacho 1223 (☏ 02 2337533, ⓦ titicaca.com) runs a similar service to Transturin, with faster hydrofoils from Huatajata. It offers accommodation at the classy *Inca Utama Hotel and Spa* in Huatajata and the exclusive *Posada del Inca Ecolodge* on Isla del Sol.

Transturin Alfredo Ascarrunz 2518 (☏ 02 2422222, ⓦ transturin.com), run sightseeing tours to Copacabana and Isla del Sol, plus trips to Puno in Peru, in luxurious catamarans from their dock at Chúa, a few kilometres west of Huatajata. The company also operates the comfortable *Hotel Titicaca* in Chúa.

Titicaca has always played a major role in Andean religious conceptions. As the biggest body of water in this arid region, it's considered a powerful female deity that controls climate and rainfall, and the Incas believed the creator god Viracocha rose from its waters, calling forth the sun and moon to light up the world. The Incas also claimed their own ancestors came into being here, and the remains of their shrines and temples can be seen on **Isla del Sol** and nearby **Isla de la Luna**, whose serene beauty and tranquillity is a highlight of any visit to the lake. Nor did Lago Titicaca lose its religious importance with the advent of Christianity: Bolivia's most important Catholic shrine is in **Copacabana**, the lakeside town closest to Isla del Sol.

GETTING AROUND
LAGO TITICACA

The main road to **Lago** Titicaca from La Paz runs northwest across the Altiplano, with the majestic Cordillera Real to the north. Just after the lake first comes into view, about 75km from La Paz, the road forks at the town of **Huarina**. One branch heads north towards Sorata in the Cordillera Real (see p.118) via the town of Achacachi, or along the remote east coast and up into the Cordillera Apolobamba (see p.113). The other branch continues west towards Copacabana, running along the north shore of the smaller section of the lake, known as **Wiñay Marka** or Lago Menor, which is joined to the main body of the lake by the narrow Tiquina straits. Just beyond Huarina on this road lies Huatajata (see p.112), a resort town popular with La Paz residents.

Copacabana

The pleasant little town of **COPACABANA** overlooks the deep blue waters of Lago Titicaca just a few kilometres from the Peruvian border. The town is an untidy collection of red-tiled houses and modern concrete buildings nestled between two steep hills. As well as being a good base from which to explore the Bolivian side of the lake, the town is the most important Catholic pilgrimage site in the country, being home to Bolivia's most revered image, the **Virgen de Copacabana**. Several times annually the town is overwhelmed by religious devotees who come to pay homage to the Virgin in colourful religious **fiestas**, while the rest of the year sees a steady stream of pilgrims seeking the Virgin's blessing. Copacabana is also the base for visits to **Isla del Sol** and **Isla de la Luna**, Titicaca's two sacred islands, while a series of mysterious **Inca ruins** lie within easy walking distance.

The beach
Pedal boats/kayaks Bs20–30/hr; motor launches Bs70–80/hr with boatman

Though without the attractions of its more famous namesake in Brazil (which was named in honour of the shrine here), Copacabana **beach** is a pleasant place for a stroll. There are numerous, almost identical food stalls serving beer and trout, and you can rent pedal boats, kayaks and motor launches, as well as catch boats to Isla del Sol.

2

COPACABANA

0 ────── 200
metres

● SHOP
The Spitting Llama

Cerro Calvario

Kusijata & Yampupata

Bullring

PLAZA DE TOROS

AVAROA

BALLIVIAN

COCHABAMBA

MICHEL PEREZ

1 ● 2 3

AVENIDA GENERAL JAUREGUI 4

3 DE MAYO

BOLIVAR

OURO

MICHEL PEREZ

PANDO

AVAROA

Mercado

BAPTISTA

5

Boats to Isla del Sol

AVENIDA 6 DE AGOSTO

9 4 5

1

Buses to La Paz & Kasani

PLAZA SUCRE

★

2

@ 6 i 7

6

Prodem

PLAZA 2 DE FEBRERO

JOSE MEJIA

LA PAZ

J. PEREZ

Lago Titicaca

AVENIDA COSTANERA

8

BUSCH

9

AVENIDA 16 DE JULIO

10

BOLIVAR

PANDO

Catedral

M. MANUEL MEJIA

ENTEL

N

R. PAREDES

11 7

POTOSI

12

Intinkala

MURILLO

● EATING & DRINKING
El Condor and
  the Eagle Cafe   6
La Cúpula   1
Kota Kahuaña   7
Mankha Uta   3
Nemos   5
La Posta   4
Sujma Wasi   2

AVENIDA FELIX TEJADA

La Paz

13

Kasani & Peru

Horca del Inca

■ ACCOMMODATION
La Aldea del Inca   4   Hostal Las Olas   1
Ecolodge Copacabana   13   Hostal Leyenda   8
Hostal Center   7   Hotel Ambassador   5
Hostal Colonial   Hotel Gloria   10
  Del Lago   6   Hotel Mirador   9
Hostal Emperador   12   Hotel Rosario del Lago   11
Hostal La Cúpula   2   Hotel Utama   3

La Catedral

Plaza 2 de Febrero, six blocks east of the waterfront • Museum opening times are erratic, ask one of the attendants • Bs8

Copacabana's imposing **Catedral** looks out over Plaza 2 de Febrero. Known as the "Moorish Cathedral", it shows clear *mudéjar* influences, with whitewashed stone walls and domes decorated with deep-blue *azulejo* tiles. Built between 1589 and 1669 by the Augustinian order (and funded partly by looted gold and silver offerings from local pre-Christian shrines) to house the miraculous Virgen de Copacabana, it has since been extensively modified.

Between the plaza and the cathedral is a broad walled **courtyard** with a minor chapel at each corner – a layout very similar to that of pre-conquest indigenous ceremonial centres. Inside the bright vaulted interior a door beside the massive gold altarpiece leads upstairs to a small chapel housing the **Virgen de Copacabana** herself. A slight image with an Andean face, the Virgin wears lavish robes embroidered with gold and silver thread, and is crowned with a golden halo; at her feet is a wide silver crescent moon – a traditional Andean symbol of female divinity. Encased in glass, the statue is only taken out during fiestas: locals believe moving her at any other time could trigger catastrophic floods. A small **museum** inside the compound has a collection of colonial religious art and sculpture, but is only open to groups of four or more. To the left of the Cathedral is the **Capilla de Velas**, a side chapel where supplicants come to light candles.

Plaza 2 de Febrero

Outside the cathedral, **Plaza 2 de Febrero** is often occupied by cars, buses and trucks decorated with colourful streamers and rosettes. These are blessed with holy water by a priest and doused liberally in beer and liquor in frequent rituals (generally daily around

10am and 2pm) known as **ch'alla**, which aim to ensure their future safety. At fiesta times, pilgrims bring models of desirable objects to be blessed, in the belief that doing so ensures that the real thing will be theirs within a year – a modern version of traditional requests for sufficient rain, bountiful harvests or successful fishing.

Cerro Calvario

A 30min walk along a trail that begins beside the church at the north end of Calle Bolívar

Cerro Calvario, the hill rising steeply above the north of town, is another interesting religious site. The summit is marked by a cross from where there are splendid views. It's popular with pilgrims throughout the year, but particularly during Easter, when thousands accompany the Virgen de Copacabana as she is carried up here in a candlelit procession. As well as the formal Christian crosses at the top of the hill, the summit is dotted with ramshackle stone altars where pilgrims light candles, burn offerings and pour alcoholic libations to ensure their prayers are heard.

2

ARRIVAL AND DEPARTURE   COPACABANA

By bus Public buses and micros to and from La Paz (roughly every half hour; 3hr 30min) depart and arrive from Plaza Sucre. The tourist buses plying this route, however, are more comfortable and only a little more expensive; most tour agencies sell tickets. Although there is talk of starting up a direct service to Sorata, at the time of writing the only way to reach the town without travelling via La Paz was to take a La Paz-bound bus as far as Huarina, where you can flag down a micro (3hr; every 30min).

CROSSING THE PERUVIAN BORDER

VIA KASANI

Micros to the border at Kasani (every 30min or so; 15min) leave from Plaza Sucre. At Kasani, get your exit stamp at passport control (8.30am–7.30pm) and then walk across the border. On the Peruvian side, micros and taxis wait to take passengers to the town of Yunguyo (10min), from where regular buses head to Puno and on to Cusco and Arequipa; there are also places to stay if you arrive too late to move on. Alternatively, catch one of the daily tourist buses from La Paz to Puno via Copacabana; tickets are available from travel agencies in Copacabana.

VIA DESAGUADERO

You can also cross into Peru at Desaguadero, on Lago Titicaca's southern side. This scenic route is served by micros (every 30min; 3hr) from La Paz; they leave from Calle Eyzaguirre between Calle Aliaga and Calle Asin in the cemetery district. Get your exit stamp at the frontier from passport control (8.30am–8.30pm), then walk across the bridge and get an entry stamp at the Peruvian *migración*. The scruffy Peruvian border town of Desaguadero has basic accommodation, but it's better to move on immediately by bus to Puno (hourly; 3–4hr).

THE LADY OF THE LAKE

The speed with which the **Virgen de Copacabana** emerged as the most revered religious image in the Altiplano after the Spanish conquest suggests that her cult was simply a continuation of previous, pre-Christian religious traditions associated with Lago Titicaca. Immediately after the conquest the **Inca temples** around the lake were looted by Spanish treasure-seekers, and their shrines and idols destroyed. These included, at Copacabana, a large female idol with a fish's tail – probably a representation of the lake as a goddess. The town was refounded in 1573 as the parish of Santa Ana de Copacabana, but a series of devastating early frosts ensued, convincing locals of the need for a new supernatural protector. Santa Ana was abandoned and the town rededicated in honour of the **Virgen de la Candelaria**, one of the most popular representations of the Virgin Mary during the Spanish conquest of the Americas.

A locally born man, **Francisco Inca Yupanqui**, grandson of the Inca Huayna Capac (himself the father of Atahualpa, whose capture by the Spanish led to the fall of the Inca empire), began fashioning an image of the Virgin. After his first crude efforts were rejected by the Spanish priests he went to Potosí to study sculpture, eventually returning with the figure that graces the church today, the **Virgen de Copacabana**, who was immediately credited with a series of miracles. The town quickly became the most important Catholic pilgrimage destination in the southern Andes, and after independence, the Virgin was also proclaimed the religious patron of Bolivia.

FIESTAS IN COPACABANA

Copacabana's main religious fiestas are the **Fiesta de la Virgen de la Candelaria** (Feb 2) and the **Coronación de la Virgen de Copacabana** (Aug 5), which attract thousands of pilgrims from across Bolivia and southern Peru. The Virgin's statue is paraded around town accompanied by brass bands and dance troupes and several days of festivities culminate in bullfights in the ring on the town's northern outskirts. **Semana Santa** (Easter) is more solemn. Many pilgrims walk to Copacabana from as far away as La Paz in penance, and thousands more take part in a candlelit nocturnal procession up Cerro Calvario, where they pray for the forgiveness of their sins and success in the coming years. Far more mysterious, distinctly non-Christian ceremonies are staged on the night of June 21 to celebrate the winter solstice and **Aymara New Year**, when small crowds led by traditional Aymara religious leaders gather to perform ceremonies at the Horca del Inca and Intinkala, two ancient shrines on the outskirts of town.

INFORMATION

Tourist information There's a rudimentary tourist information office just off Plaza Sucre on 16 de Julio (Wed–Sun 8am–noon & 2–6pm; ☎7191 5544), but the tour agencies are better placed to answer your questions.

ACCOMMODATION

Copacabana has an enormous number of places to stay. Most are simple *alojamientos* and *residenciales* catering for *pilgrims*, but recent years have seen a surge in smarter mid-range and top end hotels aimed at tourists. Rooms fill up fast, and prices double or triple during the main *fiestas*. All include breakfast unless stated otherwise.

La Aldea del Inca San Antonio ☎02 8622452, ☻aldeadelinca.com. Off a steep and unpromisingly rubbish-strewn street, this hotel has been designed to look like a traditional Incan village. The en-suite rooms though are refreshingly modern with bright furnishings and TV/DVD players. There's a cobbled courtyard, and a garden overlooking the lake, plus a coffee shop and laundry service. Bs224

Ecolodge Copacabana Av Costanera ☎02 8622500, ☻ecocopacabana.com. A 1.5km journey from the town centre along the beach road takes you to this peaceful lodge, which has adobe cabins (sleeping up to three people) with thatched roofs, solar heating and private bathrooms. There are also a couple of suites with kitchenettes (sleeping up to five people) – plus a restaurant and pleasant gardens. Cabins Bs240; suites Bs270

Hostal Center Av 6 de Agosto ☎02 8622230, ☻titicacabolivia.com. Overlooking Plaza Sucre, this is probably the best of Copacabana's bargain-basement traveller haunts. Run by the owner of *La Posta*, it has three floors of clean, modern, functional rooms with private hot-water bathrooms and TVs. No breakfast. Bs60

Hostal Colonial Del Lago Av 6 de Agosto and Av 16 de Julio ☎02 8622270, ☻titicacabolivia.com. On the edge of Plaza Sucre, this late 1990s landmark is ageing fairly well. The rooms are clean and bright, although views from the huge windows are blocked by a red-brick monstrosity and noise can be an issue. There's a lovely patio, internet café and tour agency on site. Bs175

Hostal Emperador Murillo 235 ☎7125 8184. Budget option with an enduring popularity that's difficult to fathom, especially given the awful colour scheme and a dilapidated sign that suggests it closed down years ago. Inside you'll find clean, simple rooms (with or without bathrooms) around a bare courtyard; those at the back are slightly better. There's a rudimentary kitchen and laundry facilities, but no breakfast. Bs40

★ **Hostal La Cúpula** Michel Pérez 1–3 ☎02 8622029, ☻hotelcupula.com. A delightful European-owned neo-Moorish-style hotel perched on a hillside with superlative views. Whitewashed arches lend an Andalucian air of seclusion that extends to the bamboo-furnished rooms (with heaters, comfy beds and shared or private bathrooms) and the hammock-slung gardens. There's a kitchen, laundry service, TV lounge, library, book exchange and a superb restaurant. Staff are extremely helpful and well-informed, and there are nice touches like hot water bottles. No breakfast. Bs140

Hostal Las Olas Michel Pérez ☎02 8622112, ☻hostallasolas.com. Just beyond *La Cúpula*, and under the same management, this wonderful lodge has a handful of sumptuous suites featuring stained glass windows, pine floors and eucalyptus wood stairs - and beautiful views. There's also a hot tub, log fire, hammocks and friendly service. No breakfast. Bs196

Hostal Leyenda Av Costanera and Busch ☎7350 8898, ✉ismaeltouroperador@hotmail.com. A unique mix of faux-colonial extravagance and elaborate neo-native trimmings, this eye-catching hotel in an enviable beachfront position won't be for everyone. If you're charmed by the presence of a full-sized traditional reed boat, dome-shaped fireplace and assorted other knick-knacks in your room, however, it's a good deal, particularly as you also get a private bathroom and TV. Bs80

Hotel Ambassador Jáuregui and Plaza Sucre 02 8622216. The faded grand dame of Copacabana hostelry, offering a warren of frilly rooms. Some are a bit dark and fusty but the whitewashed charm, old photos and net-curtained windows make up for it. Look out for the kitschy shrine hogging the courtyard. Bs110

Hotel Gloria Av 16 de Julio 02 8622094, hotelgloria.com.bo. This grand hotel has comfortable, if overpriced and dated en suites overlooking the lake. Its bay-windowed dining room, however, is the most elegant in town, with breathtaking views. There's also a games room (billiards, table football and ping pong), acres of garden and topiary animals out front. Bs395 ($56)

Hotel Mirador Av Busch and Costanera 02 8622289, titicacabolivia.com. Pastel yellow rooms framing an azure lake make this dusky pink seafront behemoth an attractive, good-value choice. The architectural style is determinedly quasi-colonial even if the imposing columns and wooden-railed staircases lend a strangely subcontinental feel. Staff, however, can be surly. Bs100

Hotel Rosario del Lago Rigoberto Paredes and Av Costanera 02 8622141, hotelrosario.com/lago. Plush sister hotel to its namesake in La Paz, set near the waterfront in a modern colonial-style building. All of the compact but very comfortable en-suite rooms have excellent lake views, heaters, safes, TVs and colourful bed covers and cushions; the spiral staircase-accessed, beam-ceilinged suite is well worth a splurge. Service is unfailingly polite, and there's a renowned restaurant, luxurious terrace and small museum. Suite BS995 ($142); doubles BS 630 ($90)

Hotel Utama Michel Pérez and San Antonio 02 28622013, utamacopacabana44@hotmail.com. Fairly unpromising in both its brick exterior and barn-like interior, this is nevertheless a friendly enough place, as the international flag-filled lobby testifies. Rooms come with chintzy bedspreads and murals, armchairs and – from the top corner rooms, 208 especially – fantastic lake views. Bs80

EATING AND DRINKING

There's no shortage of restaurants in Copacabana, most of them catering to **pilgrims**. Concentrated on Avenida 6 de Agosto and Jáuregui, all offer unexciting set almuerzos and cenas, or big plates of the delicious **Titicaca trout** (*trucha*). You can find more varied and expensive fare at the smarter restaurants aimed at tourists; some also double as bars. Most restaurants open daily from morning to evening, though some close early on **Sundays**; exceptions are noted in the reviews themselves. The **market** just off Plaza 2 de Febrero on Calle La Paz is a good place for cheap meals, and there are also numerous simple **foodstalls** on the waterfront serving fresh trout.

El Condor and the Eagle Café Av 6 de Agosto, just off Plaza Sucre. A sophisticated café serving excellent organic coffee, teas and hot chocolate (all Bs9–20), home-made dishes like baked beans on soda bread (Bs15), and cakes and muffins. There are books for sale, water bottle refills (Bs2/litre) and a useful compendium of travellers' tips to flick through. The only downside is the somewhat trying list of rules and regulations (which include orders not to talk too loudly).

★ **La Cúpula** Inside hotel of the same name 02 8622029. This luminous domed dining room overlooking the lake has probably the best food in town, with good breakfasts, creative main courses (including numerous vegetarian options, and superlative *trucha*), and tempting desserts. The highlights, however, are the decadent fondues. Mains Bs28–49, fondues Bs80–110. Closed Tues lunchtime.

Kota Kahuaña Inside Hotel Rosario del Lago 02 8622141. Huge windows with superb views are the backdrop for some of Copacabana's most adventurous cuisine. Highlights include trout with garlic, white wine and orange; llama with quinoa and bacon; and seafood paella. On weekends, when the weather's fine, there's a lunchtime barbecue on the terrace. Mains Bs30–90.

Mankha Uta Av 6 de Agosto, near the beach. Friendly, glass-fronted bar-restaurant with an emphasis on live music. The four set meals (including one for vegetarians; Bs23–28) are good value, though service is glacially slow. It also sells packed lunches, and has a small book exchange, a collection of DVDs to watch and board games to play.

Nemos Av 6 de Agosto, next to La Posta. This popular Anglo-Bolivian-run bar is a cool, low-lit space, with great sounds and drinks – both of the alcoholic variety, and coffees and hot chocolates. Drinks Bs10–25.

La Posta Av 6 de Agosto and Cabo Zapana. Partly Argentine-owned with a vague tango theme and sometimes a Carlos Gardel soundtrack, this joint is usually crammed with Argentine travellers, especially if there's a football match on TV. The pizzas (from Bs30) are the town's best.

Sujma Wasi Jáuregui 127 02 8622091. Charming cobbled courtyard with textile-topped stone tables, one block from Plaza Sucre. Veggie options are plentiful, as are the assiduously described breakfasts. Should you run out of high-factor sunscreen you can retreat to the rustic little bar, which doubles as a *peña* at weekends. Mains Bs25–50.

DIRECTORY

Banks and exchange There's no international ATM in town but Prodem (daily except Mon) on Av 6 de Agosto can usually service Visa and Mastercard transactions at a hefty charge of five percent. The Casa de Cambio Copacabana, at the eastern end of Av 6 de Agosto, changes dollars and travellers' cheques.

Books ★ The Spitting Llama (📞 02 2599073, 🌐 thespittingllama.com), Av 6 de Agosto, sells, exchanges and loans books (and travel and camping equipment). It also stores luggage (Bs3/day/item) and recycles plastic bottles and used batteries. *El Condor and the Eagle Café* also has a small selection of, predominantly spiritual, books. *La Cúpula* restaurant has a good book exchange.

Internet Punto Entel on Av 6 de Agosto offers slow access (Bs10/hr), international phone calls, pool tables, a book exchange and DVDs to watch.

Post office The post office is on Plaza 2 de Febrero, though if you're heading to La Paz you're better off posting letters when you get there.

Telephones ENTEL, Murillo, one block south of Plaza 2 de Febrero.

Around Copacabana

Although many were systematically destroyed by the Spanish, the Copacabana peninsula is still scattered with enigmatic Inca ruins and strange carved stones, three of which – the **Horca del Inca**, **Intinkala** and **Kusijata** – are within easy walking distance of town. You can also make a pleasant four- to five-hour hike following the route taken by Inca pilgrims to **Yampupata** at the tip of the peninsula, from where you can take a boat across to Isla del Sol. Further afield, the village of **Santiago de Okola** is home to an interesting community-run tourism project.

Horca del Inca

Daily 9am–6pm • Bs5; ticket also valid for Intinkala and Kusijata • Walk south to the end of Calle Murillo, then follow the dirt path uphill

High on Cerro Sancollani, the hill rising above Copacabana to the south, stands the **Horca del Inca**, a structure formed by two vertical crags of rock, their bases buried in the ground and topped by a stone lintel, creating a gateway. The name means "Gallows of the Incas", but this structure was almost certainly used by Inca astronomer-priests to observe the sun, since a small hole carved in another rock crag about 20m to the northeast casts a well-defined point of light onto the centre of the lintel on the morning of June 22, the date of the winter solstice and Aymara New Year.

Intinkala

Just southeast of town, opposite the cemetery 300m along the road to La Paz; take the path on the left • Daily 9am–6pm • Bs5; ticket also valid for Horca del Inca and Kusijata

A collection of large boulders carved with niches, steps, channels and abstract designs, **Intinkala** means "Seat of the Sun" in Aymara, and it's likely this site was a religious shrine used for astronomical observations. The biggest boulder is carved with a groove shaped like a serpent, which was likely used to channel offerings of *chicha* (maize beer) or sacrificial blood – it's believed throughout the Andes that large rocks like these are the home of powerful spirits. Along with the Horca del Inca, Intinkala hosts a small gathering of Aymara *yatiris* (traditional priests) to celebrate the winter solstice on the night of June 21–22.

Kusijata

3km northeast of Copacabana • Opening hours are very irregular: there's usually someone here at the weekend, but otherwise you may need to ask around nearby houses for the key • Bs5; ticket also valid for Horca del Inca and Intinkala • A return taxi costs Bs30 • Follow Calle Junín past the bullring, then cut across the football pitch; the track climbs towards a eucalyptus grove on the hillside (30–40min on foot)

Kusijata is a small network of well-made Inca agricultural terraces and stone irrigation canals, one of which feeds a pool known as the **Baño del Inca** – possibly a ritual bath. There's also a rather dilapidated museum with a small collection of local Inca ceramics. Even if you can't get into the museum, the pleasant walk out along the lakeside makes the trip worthwhile.

Santiago de Okola

Northeast of Copacabana • ☎ 02 2118442 or 7154 3918, ⓦ santiagodeokola.com • 1hr 30min by motorboat from Isla del Sol or a 2hr 30min drive from La Paz

The traditional fishing and farming village of **SANTIAGO DE OKOLA**, on the shore of Lake Titicaca, is home to a successful community tourism project, which gives travellers the opportunity to experience local life. There is a range of activities on offer including homestays, community tours, mountain biking, weaving workshops, guided walks to discover the area's medicinal plants, star-gazing trips and hikes up Lurisani (Sleeping Dragon), the rocky outcrop overlooking the village.

Isla del Sol

Just off the northern tip of the Copacabana peninsula, about 12km northwest of Copacabana, **ISLA DEL SOL** (Island of the Sun) has been attracting visitors for hundreds of years. In the sixteenth century the island, 9km long by 6km wide at its broadest point, was one of the most important religious sites in the Andean world, revered as the place where the sun and moon were created and the Inca dynasty was born, and covered with shrines and temples that attracted thousands of pilgrims. After the Spanish conquest the island was looted, and the cut stones from its temples plundered to build churches on the mainland. But five centuries later it's still easy to see why it was (and is) considered sacred. Surrounded by the azure Lago Titicaca, with the imperious peaks of the Cordillera Real rising above the shore on the mainland to the east, it's a place of great natural beauty and tranquillity.

Isla del Sol is the largest of the forty or so islands in Lago Titicaca and home to several thousand Aymara campesinos. The three main settlements, **Yumani**, **Challa** and **Challapampa**, are all on the east coast. Scattered with enigmatic ancient ruins and populated by traditional Aymara communities, it's an excellent place to spend some time hiking and contemplating the magnificent scenery.

Challapampa

The island's northernmost settlement, **CHALLAPAMPA** was founded by the Incas as a service centre for the nearby ceremonial complexes. Set on a narrow spit of land

ISLA DEL SOL & ISLA DE LA LUNA

ISLA DEL SOL AND THE INCAS

The remains of ritual offerings found by archeologists show that Isla del Sol was an important local religious shrine long before the arrival of the Incas. When the island came under Tiwanaku control around 500 AD, larger ritual complexes were built and pilgrimages to the island began. Under **Inca rule**, though, the island was transformed into a pan-Andean pilgrimage destination visited annually by thousands of people from across the empire. The Incas believed the creator god **Viracocha** rose from the waters of Lago Titicaca and called forth the sun and moon from a rock on the island. They also claimed the founding fathers of their own dynasty – **Manco Capac** and **Mama Ocllo** – were brought into being here by Viracocha before travelling north to establish the city of Cusco and spread civilization throughout the Andes. In fact, it's very unlikely the Incas originated on the shores of the lake. This dynastic myth was probably an attempt to add legitimacy to the Inca regime by associating them with Lago Titicaca and the birthplace of the sun – from which the Inca rulers claimed to be directly descended – as well as providing a link with the pre-existing Tiwanaku civilization that was based on the shores of the lake.

After conquering the region in the mid-fifteenth century, the Incas invested heavily in building roads, agricultural terraces, shrines and temples on Isla del Sol, and establishing the town of **Copacabana** as a stop-off point for pilgrims. The entire Copacabana peninsula, as well as the sacred islands, was cleared of its indigenous Lupaqa and Colla population and turned into a **restricted sacred area**, its original populace being replaced by loyal settlers from elsewhere in the empire, who maintained the places of worship, attended to the needs of the astronomer priests and visiting pilgrims, and cultivated maize for use in elaborate religious rituals. A **wall** was built across the neck of the peninsula at Yunguyo, with gates where guards controlled access to Copacabana (nearly five centuries later the **peninsula** is still separated from the rest of the mainland by the border between Peru and Bolivia, which follows almost exactly the same line). Pilgrims entering Copacabana would abstain from salt, meat and chilli and spend several days praying at the complex of shrines here before walking round to the tip of the peninsula at Yampupata, from where they would cross over the water to Isla del Sol.

Part of the island's religious importance was no doubt related to the fertility of its fields. Insulated by the waters of the lake, Isla del Sol enjoys slightly higher average temperatures than the mainland, as a result of which its terraced slopes produce more and better maize than anywhere else in the region. **Maize** was a sacred crop for the Incas anyway, but that grown on Isla del Sol was especially important. Though most was used to make *chicha* (maize beer) for use in rituals on the island, grains of maize from the Isla del Sol were distributed across the **Inca empire**, carried by returning pilgrims who believed that a single grain placed in their stores would ensure bountiful harvests for ever more.

between two large bays on the east coast of the island, the village has a small museum, and several places to stay. A short walk from the village lie several fascinating **Inca sites**. Free local guides meet boats and can show you around the area, though many travellers find this quite a slow process.

The museum

Daily 9am–5.30pm • Bs10; includes admission to the Kasapata, the Santuario and La Chincana; keep hold of the ticket, as there are a couple of checkpoints

The village's **museum** has artefacts found both on the island and at sites off the coast, where offerings were dropped into the water, and tales of lost underwater cities persist to this day. The collection includes bronze idols, Inca and Tiwanaku pottery, and miniature human and llama figures delicately carved from spondylus shells.

Kasapata

Daily 9am–5.30pm • Ticket for Challampa museum includes admission (see above); Bs10

From Challapampa it's a twenty-minute walk northwest along a steep but easy-to-follow path to the ruins of a substantial Inca site called **Kasapata**, which was probably a *tambo* (waystation) for pilgrims. It's mostly rubble now, but to the left of the path a large building still stands with five characteristically Incan trapezoidal doorways, while to the north is a large carved stone block that probably had ritual importance.

The Santuario

Daily 9am–5.30pm • Ticket for Challapampa museum includes admission (see p.107); Bs10

Another twenty minutes further along the path beyond Kasapata is the **Santuario**, a ruined Inca complex built around a sacred rock. The **entrance** to the Santuario is marked by the remnants of a low wall. About 100m beyond the entrance you can make out the rectangular foundations of a series of buildings that housed the priests and servants who attended the temple complex.

Inside the Santuario a path crosses a bare rock marked by two depressions shaped like **giant footprints** – dubbed the "Huellas del Sol" ("Footprints of the Sun") – before reaching the centre of the sanctuary. Here stands **Titikala**, the sacred rock from which the Incas believed the sun and moon first rose and after which Lago Titicaca was named, though there's little in the appearance of this large outcrop of weather-beaten pink sandstone to suggest what an important religious site it once was. During Inca times gold, silver, coca, shells, birds' feathers and sacrificial animals (and the occasional human) were brought here as offerings to the **sun god**, Inti, while the rock itself would have been covered in fine cloth and silver and gold plates; in the open space on its southern side was a large stone basin where sacred libations of *chicha* were poured and an **altar** where sacrifices were made.

The rock was the focal point of a ceremonial complex staffed by hundreds of priests and servants, and at certain times of year thousands of pilgrims, including the Inca himself, would come here to take part in elaborate rituals involving music, dance and sacrifices. Most pilgrims would not even be allowed near the rock, but worshipped from outside the sanctuary wall; those who entered the inner sanctum did so only after passing through a series of doorways where they would undergo **cleansing rituals**. The winter and summer solstices were probably amongst the most important religious celebrations; on the ridge to the northwest of the rock the point where the sun sets on the June solstice was marked by structures whose foundations can still be made out today. The nearby table made from a massive cut stone slab has been put together with stones from other ruined buildings as a place for picnics.

La Chincana

Daily 9am–5.30pm • Ticket for Challapampa museum includes admission (see p.107); Bs10

About 200m beyond Titikala to the northwest is a rambling complex of ruined buildings looking out west across the lake to the Peruvian shore. Known as **La Chincana** (The Labyrinth), this series of interlinked rooms, plazas and passageways with numerous trapezoidal niches and doorways is thought to have been both the storehouse for sacred maize grown on the island and the living quarters for the *mamaconas*, the so-called "Virgins of the Sun", women specially chosen for their beauty and purity who attended the shrine, making *chicha* and weaving cloth for use in rituals. If you have the energy, it's worth walking ten to fifteen minutes up to the peak at the far northern tip of Isla del Sol for panoramic views.

Challa

Museum: daily 9am–5.30pm • Free

About an hour south of Challapampa on the coastal path you reach **Playa Challa**, a picturesque beach on a wide bay, and the *Qhumphuri Hostal and Restaurant* (see p.110). Shortly beyond here the path climbs over a headland then drops down to the village of **CHALLA**, which sits above another bay. The small **museum** near the waterfront has a collection of intriguing dance costumes, masks and musical instruments.

Yumani

Just before entering the town you have to pay a Bs5 entry fee

From Challa, it's about another two hours' walk southeast to **YUMANI**, the island's largest village and home to most of its accommodation. The spectacular views and modest Iglesia de San Antonio aside, Yumani's most characteristic sight is the **Escalera del Inca**, a stairway running steeply down to the lakeshore through a natural amphitheatre covered by some of the island's finest Inca agricultural terracing, irrigated by bubbling stone canals. The canals are fed by the **Fuente del Inca**, a three-spouted spring believed to have magic powers: drink from all three, the locals say, and you'll gain knowledge of the Spanish, Quechua and Aymara languages. At the bottom of the stairway by the beach are the remains of a minor Inca building.

Pilko Kaina

Daily 9am–5.30pm • Entry fee to Yumani village Bs5

A short walk from Yumani, around the coast to the south along a path raised on an Inca stone platform, brings you to **Pilko Kaina**, the island's best-preserved Inca site. Set on a cliff about 20m above the lake, the main structure is a large and fairly well-preserved two-storey stone building with classic Inca trapezoidal doorways facing east across the lake to the Isla de la Luna and the mountain peaks beyond – its original function remains obscure. Pilgrims travelling to the Titikala from the mainland would have passed through here after landing at the far southern tip of the island.

ARRIVAL AND DEPARTURE   ISLA DEL SOL

You can visit Isla del Sol on a half- or full-day trip from **Copacabana**, but it's really worth spending at least a night on the island if you can. Boats call at the settlement of **Yumani**, where most of the hotels are located, and the village of **Challapampa** at the northern end of the island. It is also possible to hike to **Yampupata** at the tip of the Copacabana peninsula and then take a boat from there (see below).

HIKING TO ISLA DEL SOL

Instead of taking a boat directly from Copacabana to Isla del Sol (see above), you can follow the trail formerly used by **Inca pilgrims** by hiking to the tip of the Copacabana peninsula at the village of **Yampupata**, the closest mainland point to the island, and then take a boat from there. The walk to Yampupata takes about four to five hours, following a very pleasant 17km trail along the shores of Lago Titicaca (for a route map, see p.106).

COPACABANA TO TITICACHI

Follow Calle Junín out of town to the bullring, then continue along the lakeside road round the shore to the north. The flat, marshy land beside the lake is worked using the ancient system of raised fields called *sukakullos* (see p.90), which use the warmth of water taken from the lake to protect crops from frost and boost production. After about an hour the road climbs into the hills overlooking the lake; after another hour you'll see a grotto-like cave on the hillside to your left; now occupied by a statue of the Virgin, it was doubtless also a pre-Christian shrine. The road then climbs gently to a pass before descending, reaching the lakeside hamlet of **Titicachi**, which stands on a horseshoe bay, after about 45 minutes.

SICUANI TO YAMPUPATA

Another half-hour's walk along the shore brings you to the village of **Sicuani**, where you can spend the night and get a basic meal at the simple *Alojamiento Inca Thaki* (no phone; rooms around Bs60). The owner, Señor Hilario Quispe, takes visitors out onto the lake or to Isla del Sol in a *totora* reed boat or zippier motorboat for around Bs80-110; he is also a mine of local information. From Sicuani it's another hour or so to the village of **Yampupata**, where you should be able to find a rowing or motorboat (Bs20-35/Bs90-120 one-way) to take you across to **Yumani** (see above) on Isla del Sol, or Isla de la Luna.

2

BOAT TOURS

Boat tours leave from the beach in Copacabana at around 8.30am (for a full day), with additional half-day boats at 1.30pm. Full-day tours (Bs20–25) generally call briefly at Yumani before docking at Challapampa (sometimes stopping at Challa en route). They then head back to Yumani before returning to Copacabana in the afternoon. Isla de la Luna may also be included if enough passengers want to visit it. Some boats also visit the Islas Flotantes (floating reed islands), though these are not on the same scale as those on the Peruvian side of the lake and many travellers are underwhelmed. If you want to hike across the island, you can get off at Challapampa, walk to Yumani and be picked up in the afternoon (3.30–4pm). Alternatively, you can buy a one-way ticket (Bs15) and pay the return fare

to any available boat when you want to come back. Half-day tours, which dock at Yumani, only give you a brief glimpse of the southern end of the island, and aren't worth doing unless you're really short of time.

Tour agencies Plenty of agencies sell tickets for two boat companies, Andes Amazonia and Titicaca Tours; the former tends to be a bit quicker. A couple of smaller operators also run irregular services. Unless things are really busy, you can usually just turn up in the morning to buy a ticket.

BOAT HIRE

If you want to halve the journey time and escape the crowds (the boats can be disturbingly crowded) there's the option of private hire (Bs210–700/$30–100); shop around in Copacabana, and agree the itinerary beforehand.

GETTING AROUND

On foot The best way to see the island is to walk its length from Challapampa in the north to Yumani in the south – a roughly 8km hike (allow 3hr–4hr 30min). Two paths head from the Santuario towards Yumani at the other end of the island. The first runs directly southeast to Yumani along the bare, uninhabited ridge that bisects the centre of the island, with good views of the coast on both sides. The second returns to Challapampa, from where it continues southeast along the sheltered east coast of the island,

passing scattered hamlets and neatly terraced hillsides where maize and potatoes grow. At the midpoint of both paths you have to pay a Bs15 fee. At Yumani, you can either catch a boat back to Copacabana, spend the night and return the next morning, or get a boat across to Isla de la Luna (see opposite) or the mainland at Yampupata (see p.109). You could also do the walk across Isla del Sol the other way around, starting in Yumani and heading north to Challapamp, or simply visit both locations by boat.

ACCOMMODATION AND EATING

CHALLAPAMPA

The beach area in Challapampa boasts a few basic restaurants with al fresco tables and inexpensive almuerzos.

Hostal Inca Uta In a courtyard close to the dock ☎ 7151 5246. This stone-walled *hostal* boasts the relative luxury of en-suite rooms, though it remains very basic and – for Challapampa at least – a little overpriced. Bs70

Hostal Pachamama Just beyond the museum. No phone. A friendly place, overlooking the beach, with claustrophobic ground-floor rooms but better, more spacious ones upstairs; both have shared bathrooms. There are also basic laundry facilities. Bs40

PLAYA CHALLA

Qhumphuri Hostel and Restaurant Playa Challa ☎ 7152 1188. This friendly, family-run lodge on a hilltop overlooking Playa Challa has reasonable en-suite rooms and a campfire on the terrace in the evenings. The restaurant also serves decent, though simple meals. Bs40

YUMANI

The tightly packed thatched houses (and hotels) are arranged in a labyrinthine street plan that's difficult to find your way around, particularly after dark (bring a torch). The easiest hotels to locate are the high end ecotourism projects developed by the big La Paz-based operators. Most of the

village's hotels and *hostals* have in-house restaurants serving pizza, pasta and trout; prices are higher than in Copacabana.

Ecolodge La Estancia On a hilltop just outside town ☎ 02 2442727, ⊛ ecolodge-laketiticaca.com. Run by Magri Turismo, these delightful adobe thatched-roof en-suite cottages are arranged on terraces and connected by cobbled paths. Each has solar electricity and fantastic lake views. Rates include dinner on arrival and breakfast the following morning. Book in advance. Bs560 ($80)

Hostal Imperio del Sol Near the church on the left-hand side of the steps ☎ 7196 1863. This modern peach-coloured *hostal* has clean, though still pretty basic, rooms with shared or private bathrooms, plus a restaurant, internet café and pet llama. Bs70

Hostal Inti Kala Right at the top of town ☎ 7194 4013, ⊜ javierintikala@hotmail.com. A handsome stone and wood construction with huge windows, winding balconies and a spacious terrace with incredible views, the currently expanding *Inti Kala* also has some of the most stylish private bathrooms on the island. Breakfast is included in the room rate. Bs180

Hostal Inti Wayra In view of the church ☎ 7194 2015. A decent choice with sizeable, balconied rooms and excellent east-facing lake views. Those of a spiritual bent can avail themselves of the meditation room, and there's also a decent restaurant. Bs100

Hostal Puerta del Sol At the top of the main street, on the left-hand side ☎ 7195 5181. The mustard-coloured *Puerta del Sol* has plain, clean rooms and fantastic views from its terrace. An inclusive breakfast is served in a rustic little dining room. Bs80

Palla Khasa Ecological Hotel 500m before Yumani (if coming from the north) ☎ 7321 1585, ✉ pallakhasa @gmail.com. In a quiet spot, this lovely hotel has cosy yellow-walled rooms with rugs and stunning views; some

also have private bathrooms. There's a good restaurant, and rates include breakfast. Bs160

Las Velas Turn right just before the steps down to the dock and follow the signs to the eucalyptus woods. Run by a former chef at a top Bolivian resort, *Las Velas* has a similar menu to the other restaurants in Yumani, but significantly higher standards: try the vegetable pizza or trout in wine sauce. Mains around Bs50.

Isla de la Luna

About 8km west of Isla del Sol, the far smaller **ISLA DE LA LUNA** (Island of the Moon) was another important religious site. Made up of a single ridge 3km long and just over 1km across at its widest point, the island has limited agricultural land and is home to a small community. For much of the twentieth century the island was used as a political prison - the Incas, however, saw it as a site of great spiritual importance. Known as Coati ("Queen Island"), it was associated with the moon, considered the female counterpart of the sun, and a powerful deity in her own right. Many pilgrims would continue here after their visit to the Santuario on Isla del Sol.

Iñak Uyu
Daily 9am–5.30pm • Bs10

Isla de la Luna's main site – and one of Bolivia's best-preserved Inca complexes – is a temple on the east coast known as **Iñak Uyu**. The "Court of Women" was probably a temple dedicated to the moon and staffed entirely by women; it takes about an hour to reach by boat from Yumani on Isla del Sol. From the beach a series of broad Inca agricultural terraces lead up to the temple complex, stone buildings facing inwards from three sides onto a broad central plaza. The facades of the buildings contain eleven massive external niches over 4m high and 1.5m deep, still covered in mud stucco, and decorated with smaller niches with a stepped diamond motif more characteristic of the Tiwanaku Inca architectural style – the Inca builders may have incorporated this design to please local sensibilities. Colonial-era materials including finely made textiles have been found buried here, suggesting that ritual offerings were still being made long after the fall of the Incas.

THE SECRETS OF THE STARS

Anyone who sees the night sky from the Altiplano can't fail to be impressed by the bright canopy of the southern sky. It's no surprise that the Incas were fascinated by the stars, using their comparatively **advanced astronomical understanding** to forecast agricultural cycles and future climatic events. What is surprising, however, is that five centuries later their astronomical knowledge is still being used by Quechua and Aymara campesinos in both Peru and Bolivia. In June of each year the campesinos observe the **Pleiades** – a group of stars sacred to the Incas. If the eleven-star cluster appears bright and clear in the pre-dawn sky, they anticipate early, abundant rains and a bountiful potato harvest. If the stars appear dim, however, they expect a poor harvest and delay planting to reduce the adverse effects of late and meagre rains. This practice was considered just a superstitious peasant tradition until 1999, when a team of US anthropologists and astronomers discovered that using this method the campesinos were accurately forecasting the arrival of **El Niño**, a periodic change in Pacific Ocean currents that occurs every two to seven years, triggering changes in global weather patterns, including drought in the Andes. The scientists found that in El Niño years, high-altitude clouds form, which are invisible to the naked eye but which are sufficient to decrease the brightness of the stars. Thus, by using a traditional folk technique, Andean campesinos accurately predict the onset of El Niño, a capability modern science achieved less than twenty years ago.

2

Tour boats from Copacabana to Isla del Sol sometimes call at Isla de la Luna if there's enough demand. Otherwise, you can charter a **private boat** from Copacabana (see p.110), Yampupata (see p.109) or Yumani on Isla del Sol (around Bs210).

ACCOMMODATION AND EATING

Although far fewer (and more basic) than the accommodation options on Isla del Sol, there is a handful of simple, **locally run lodges** dotted throughout the island; a double room costs around Bs50. There are also a few shops to buy food, though you should bring some with you too.

Huatajata and the islands of Wiñay Marka

Around 35km east of Copacabana lies **HUATAJATA**, a lakeside village popular with Paceños, who come here to eat fresh trout, drink cold beer and enjoy the views from the numerous restaurants on the shoreline. Just off the coast of Huatajata, on **WIÑAY MARKA**, are a trio of islands: one has an ongoing tradition of making reed boats, while the others have some ancient Aymara sites.

Isla Suriqui

About 45 minutes by motorboat from Huatajata, **Isla Suriqui** is home to a small fishing community that still uses traditional boats made from the totora reeds that grow all around the lake. In the 1970s the boatmakers of Suriqui helped Norwegian explorer Thor Heyerdahl design and build the *Ra II*, a large reed boat in which he sailed from Africa to the Caribbean in an attempt to prove transatlantic travel was possible using ancient technology. Partly as a result of this, Isla Suriqui is now rather over-touristed, but you can still get a glimpse of a lifestyle that has changed little in centuries.

Isla Pariti

Just to the south of Isla Suriqui, the smaller **Isla Pariti,** home to another small Aymara fishing community, was an important ceremonial destination during the Tiwanaku era. A cache of beautiful ceramics dating back to this period was discovered here in 2004, and many of the items are displayed at the island's museum (Bs20).

Isla Kala Uta

Close by to Isla Pariti and connected to the mainland by a narrow spit when the level of the lake is low, **Isla Kala Uta** has a series of stone tombs (*chullpas*) built by the Aymara-speaking tribes who dominated this area before the Inca conquest.

By boat From Huatajata the road continues 26km west to the Estrecho de Tiquina, the narrow stretch of water that joins Wiñay Marka with the main body of the lake, known as Lago Mayor, and separates the Copacabana peninsula from the rest of Bolivia. All vehicles heading to Copacabana cross the straits on barges; bus passengers have to cross on small launches (Bs1.50). This is one of the few places where you'll see the Bolivian Navy, and troops may ask to see your passport here. From San Pedro on the west side of the straits, it's another 40km or so to Copacabana.

GETTING AROUND

By boat Many of the restaurants in Huatajata hire out boats to the nearby islands of Suriqui, Pariti and Kala Uta. Motorboat hire costs 210–280; a sailboat costs less but takes considerably longer.

TOURS

Fremen Tours Edificio Handal, Av Mariscal Santa Cruz, La Paz ☎ 02 2444808, ⊕ andes-amazonia.com. This La Paz-based agency runs informative trips to the area that visit several islands on Wiñay Marka; an overnight stay can also be added on.

The Cordillera Apolobamba

North of Lago Titicaca, flush with the Peruvian border, is the **Cordillera Apolobamba**, the remote northern extension of the Cordillera Oriental. The splendour of the high mountain scenery in this isolated range equals or even exceeds that of the Cordillera Real, and the environment is more pristine. The region is protected by the **Area Natural de Manejo Integrado Nacional Apolobamba**, which covers nearly five hundred square kilometres. The range is still rich in wildlife only rarely seen elsewhere: condors, caracaras and other big birds are frequently seen; pumas and spectacled bears still roam the most isolated regions; and large herds of vicuña can be seen from the road which crosses the plain of **Ulla Ulla**, a high plateau that runs along the western side of the range.

During the colonial era the Cordillera Apolobamba was an important gold-mining centre, and the mining settlements established by the Spanish also served as bases for conquistadors and missionaries to launch expeditions down into the Amazon lowlands, though these were never brought under effective Spanish control. During the Great Rebellion of 1781 many of the colonial mines in the region were abandoned, and rumours persist of a mother lode of gold concealed in a long-abandoned mine, still waiting to be discovered. Tourist infrastructure is virtually nonexistent in this isolated region, but for the adventurous it offers perhaps Bolivia's best high-mountain trekking. The only real towns in the Cordillera Apolobamba are **Charazani** and **Pelechuco**, both of which can be reached by tough but spectacular bus journeys from La Paz. Between the two runs the fabulous four- or five-day **Trans-Apolobamba Trek** (see p.116).

Charazani

Perched at about 3200m on the side of a deep valley and about 260km by road from La Paz, **CHARAZANI** is the market centre for the Kallawaya communities, and the nearest town to the Trans-Apolobamba Trek, north across the heart of the Cordillera Apolobamba to Pelechuco (see p.115). Charazani itself dates back to colonial times, but the steep valley slopes all around are sculpted into pre-Hispanic terraces. A few crumbling colonial houses still survive, but most of the town's buildings are cheap, modern constructions. A couple of *pensiones* on the plaza serve simple meals.

The aguas termales
Daily 7am–9pm • Bs5

About ten minutes' walk east of town along the road to Curva and then down a steep path to the valley floor are the **aguas termales**, natural hot springs channelled into an open-air concrete swimming pool that offer an excellent way to soothe tired muscles after a long trek.

ARRIVAL AND DEPARTURE CHARAZANI

By bus Buses from La Paz (1–2 daily; 6–8hr) depart around 6am from Calle Reyes Cardona in the cemetery district; they return from the plaza. From Escoma on the remote northeastern shore of Lago Titicaca, a rough road heads north into the Cordillera Apolobamba, climbing to over 4500m. After about 50km it forks, one branch heads north along the western edge of the cordillera and the Peruvian frontier to Ulla Ulla and Pelechuco (see p.115), the other drops down to Charazani.

ACCOMMODATION

Hotel Akhamani A block south of the plaza; no phone. The best place to stay in town; the clean rooms have shared bathrooms and there is a small private en-suite apartment with its own kitchen. Staff can help organize mules and guides for the trek to Pelechuco. Apartment Bs100; doubles Bs60

Curva

Sitting at 3780m, **CURVA** is the centre of Kallawaya culture (see below) and the starting or ending point of the Trans-Apolobamba Trek (see p.116). Even if you're not planning to trek to Pelechuco, the walk up to Curva is very rewarding: the valley is beautiful, its steep sides sculpted by ancient terraces, and the path takes you through several Kallawaya farming villages.

Perched on a narrow ridge above the valley, with the snows of Akhamani, the sacred mountain of the Kallawayas, rising above, Curva itself is a deeply traditional community and the effective capital of Kallawaya culture. With thatched stone houses and cobbled streets it's a picturesque village, but people here are quite wary of outsiders, and if you're staying the night you're better off in Lagunillas.

ARRIVAL AND DEPARTURE

CURVA

By bus Every other day or so, one of the La Paz–Charazani buses continues to Curva.

On foot Alternatively you can walk up to Curva from Charazani in about four hours, following the footpath

that starts near the hot springs and cuts across the valley floor, before climbing up the other side to Curva (the road itself contours round and takes much longer to walk).

THE KALLAWAYAS: MEDICINE MEN OF THE ANDES

The Cordillera Apolobamba is home to Bolivia's smallest and most mysterious ethnic group: the **Kallawayas**. Inhabiting half a dozen villages in the Upper Charazani Valley, the Kallawayas are a secretive caste of traditional **herbal medicine practitioners**, thought to number just a few hundred, who are famous throughout the Andes for their healing powers – even more so since UNESCO declared their "Andean cosmovision" (ie the totality of their belief system, encompassing every aspect of life) a Masterpiece of the Oral and Intangible Heritage of Humanity in 2003. The enormous **ecological diversity** of the Cordillera Apolobamba means the Kallawayas have a vast natural pharmacy of plants to draw on, while the region's proximity to the tropical lowlands has also given them access to the vast medicinal resources of **Amazonian shamanism**. Individual Kallawayas may know the medical properties of over nine hundred different plant species, a knowledge that is passed from father to son. Some historical sources credit the Kallawayas with being the first to use the dried bark of the cinchona tree, the source of **quinine**, to prevent and cure malaria; taken to Europe by the Jesuits, quinine remains to this day the basis for most treatments of the disease. More recently, scientists have studied chemicals derived from herbs used by the Kallawayas as possible treatments for **HIV**.

For many centuries the Kallawayas have wandered through the Andes collecting herbs and bringing their specialist medical skills to local people. Individual healers roamed **huge distances**, often on foot, travelling to Peru, Chile, Argentina and as far as Panama during the construction of the canal, as well as the length and breadth of Bolivia. Most Kallawayas are also powerful **ritual specialists**, combining their skills as herbalists with the supposed ability to predict the future and diagnose illness by reading coca leaves. Although the main language spoken in their communities is Quechua, and many also speak some Aymara or Spanish, the Kallawaya medicine men famously speak a secret tongue known as **Machaj Juyay**, which is used only in healing rituals and other ceremonies. Some researchers believe Machaj Juyay is related to the secret language spoken in private by the **Inca ruling elite**. Certainly, the earliest post-conquest chroniclers linked the Kallawayas to the Incas. One wrote that the Kallawayas were brought to Cusco to act as herbalists and carry out important religious ceremonies and divination rituals for the Inca rulers; another claimed they had been charged with carrying the litter of the Inca himself. Other evidence suggests that the Kallawayas date back far into **Andean prehistory**: in 1970 archeologists uncovered a skeleton in the Charazani valley which had been buried with recognizable Kallawaya paraphernalia – this was carbon-dated to between 800 and 1000 BC, two thousand years before the rise of the Inca Empire.

These days the Kallawayas no longer wander as far and wide as they used to, and their numbers are thought to be dwindling, as fewer sons acquire their fathers' knowledge. However, a growing number are now resident in **La Paz**, where their skills remain in high demand.

Lagunillas

A fifteen-minute walk below Curva, **LAGUNILLAS** is a modern settlement beside a lake. Usually busy with ducks, *huallata* geese and other wildfowl, the lake is actually artificial, having been built as a reservoir to feed a series of pools nearby which are used to prepare freeze-dried potatoes known as *tunta*. The rangers at the *refugio* (see below) can help find guides and mules to take you on the trek to Pelechuco, and you should register with them before proceeding further into the mountains. Ask around here and you should be able to arrange a consultation with a **Kallawaya medicine man** (see box opposite).

2

ACCOMMODATION LAGUNILLAS

Refugios No phone, ⓦsernap.gob.bo. The protected areas agency SERNAP has a couple of community-run refugios for trekkers here, with warm dormitories, solar-heated showers and a kitchen, though no restaurant; you can also camp beside the lake. Dorms Bs20

The Ulla Ulla plateau

From the junction where the side road to Charazani branches off, the road running north along the Peruvian frontier towards Pelechuco (see below) climbs onto the **Ulla Ulla plateau**, which runs along the western side of the Cordillera Apolobamba. Covering some two thousand square kilometres at an average altitude of 4300m, Ulla Ulla's broad expanse of green pasture and marshland is set against a dramatic backdrop of snowcapped peaks.

The plateau has been a protected area since 1972, when the **Reserva Nacional de Fauna Ulla Ulla** was established to protect the highly endangered vicuña population. The vicuña population has since made an astonishing recovery, and just driving across the plateau you'll see dozens of the animals, plus many hundreds of alpacas and llamas, as well as a wide variety of birds including flamingos, ibises and *huallata* geese. Signs of human habitacion, by contrast, are few and far between. The biggest settlement is **Ulla Ulla village**, though it has no facilities of any kind. If you want to spend the night here and explore areas away from the road you'll need to camp. If you've got your own transport, there are some good natural **hot springs** an hour's drive or so further north of Ulla Ulla village, just off the road at **Putina**.

Pelechuco

Beyond Ulla Ulla the road climbs up from the plateau and over a 4860m pass between glittering glacial peaks before dropping down to the town of **PELECHUCO**, set in a deep valley that is often shrouded in cloud. This is the end of the road for vehicles but the starting (or ending) point of the **Trans-Apolobamba Trek** (see p.116). Pelechuco was founded by the Spanish in 1560 as a gold-mining outpost, and limited mining activity continues, though the town now serves mainly as a market centre.

Some colonial-era buildings survive, notably the simple adobe **church** with its stone bell tower, but the rough stone houses with thatched roofs are being replaced by ugly modern structures. The steep valley slopes around the town are still covered in dense cloudforest, including large numbers of the rare high-altitude queñua tree. On some of the hillsides above the town you can see stone look-out posts, known as *pucaras*, which were probably built in Inca or pre-Inca times to guard the approach to the pass against raiding tribes coming up the valley from the Amazon lowlands.

ARRIVAL AND DEPARTURE PELECHUCO

By bus Buses to Pelechuco from La Paz (10–13hrs) depart most days from the Tranca Rio Seco on the outskirts of El Alto; they return from the centre of town.

Hotel Llajtaymanta On the central plaza; ☎ 7195 3252. The basic but friendly *Hotel Llajtaymanta* has a handful of clean rooms with shared bathrooms; those at the back are more comfortable. There are simple meals available, and owner Reynaldo Vasquez can help you find mules and guides. <u>Bs40</u>

The Trans-Apolobamba Trek

The tough four- or five-day **Trans-Apolobamba Trek** between Pelechuco and Curva takes you through the heart of the Cordillera Apolobamba and some of the most magnificent high-Andean scenery in Bolivia. It also passes through the homeland of the Kallawayas (see box, p.114), and around the peak of their sacred mountain, Akhamani. Crossing several high passes, including one over 5100m, this is a hard trek, and shouldn't really be attempted without a guide. There are no reliable maps of the region (the last survey was conducted by the British Royal Geographical Society in 1911–13), and even if you have good directions it's easy to get lost, particularly if you're over 4000m up and the clouds close in.

Ilo-Ilo to the Sunchuli Pass

From **Pelechuco**, the route heads steeply out of town to the southeast, climbing to a high pass at 4800m (4–5hr). Beyond the pass, the path zigzags down a steep scree slope to the head of a glacial valley about 300m below (30min). You can camp here, or continue down the valley to the village of **Ilo-Ilo** (30min), where you can buy basic supplies. From Ilo-Ilo the path climbs southeast towards the 5100m **Sunchuli Pass**, passing through the small village of Piedra Grande. A mining road runs up to the pass, but you should take the more direct path that branches off it to the left after the village; in all, it's a five- to six-hour climb from Ilo-Ilo to the pass. Don't attempt to clear the pass after about 4pm as clouds can close in quickly, reducing visibility and making route-finding impossible. There's a good but cold camping site on a green meadow about ninety minutes before the pass, where you should overnight if you can't clear this part of the route before mid-afternoon.

The Sunchuli Pass to Incachani

On the other side of the pass, follow the mining road down for about fifteen minutes to the top of a green valley; there are good camping spots a little further down beside a stream in the valley. Otherwise, when the road contours round to the left, cut across to the right-hand side until you hit a narrow irrigation canal, then take the path running above it to the east. After about 45 minutes the path climbs over the shoulder of the mountain to the east, opening up fantastic views to the south of the last cloud-covered ridges of the Andes. The route then drops steeply down to the abandoned mining village of **Viscachani**, before contouring round to the south, past a lake and up over another ridge. Above the lake to the right rises the peak of **Akhamani** (5700m), the sacred mountain of the Kallawayas.

From the ridge you can see the next pass, marked by two stone *apachetas* to the southwest. From there, take the path down to the southeast, which soon descends a hair-raisingly steep switchback path known as *mil curvas* ("a thousand bends") carved out of a loose scree slope. This descends from 4650m to 4150m in just an hour or two, bringing you out beside a small stream, where you'll find **Incachani**, a collection of ancient (presumably Inca) ruined buildings at the top of a green valley-an excellent place to camp.

Incachani to Curva

From here the path climbs southwest to a 4700m pass below the peak of Akhamani, before dropping down and contouring southwest to another pass, again marked by stone *apachetas*. From here, the path heads south down a deep valley to **Jatun Pampa**, an alpaca-herding hamlet set on the grassy valley floor where you can camp. From

Jatun Pampa it's another two to three hours to Curva. Continue down and across the river then climb diagonally up to the left on the opposite slope. Descend again and cross another river, then pick up a path climbing to the left to another mountain spur. From here you can see **Curva** a short distance below to the left, and **Lagunillas** (see p.115) by the lake a little further down to the right.

INFORMATION AND TOURS | **THE TRANS-APOLOBAMBA TREK**

Food and equipment You can buy basic foodstuffs in Pelechuco and Charazani, but you'll need to bring all other equipment and supplies with you from La Paz.

Guides and mules Guides and mules (around Bs70–15/ day) can be organized in Curva (through the rangers at Lagunillas), Pelechuco and Charazani, or you can arrange to do the trek with a tour operator in La Paz (see p.73).

Route You can walk the trek either from Pelechuco south to Curva or vice versa, though it's best to start in Pelechuco, where guides and mules are easier to arrange, and finish in

Curva, close to Charazani, from where transport out is much more reliable – end your trek in Pelechuco and you could wait several days for the next bus.

Tours An interesting alternative to the Trans-Apolobamba is the Pacha Trek, a four-day trek organized by local communities that visits remote Apolobamban settlements and offers an insight into traditional life. Contact Millenarian Travel, Av Sánchez Lima 2193, La Paz (☏02 2414753, ☷boliviamilenaria.com) for more information.

The Cordillera Real

Stretching for about 160km along the northeastern edge of the Altiplano, the **Cordillera Real** (Royal Range) is the loftiest and most dramatic section of the Cordillera Oriental in Bolivia. With six peaks over 6000m high and many more over 5000m, it forms a jagged wall of soaring, ice-bound peaks that separates the Altiplano from the Amazon basin. Easily accessible from La Paz, the **mountains** are perfect for climbing and trekking. Populated by isolated Aymara communities, the cordillera is a largely pristine natural environment: the Andean condor is still a common sight, and other birds like eagles, caracaras and hawks are also frequently seen; though rarely spotted, pumas still prowl the upper reaches, while the elusive Andean spectacled bear roams the high **cloudforest** that fringes the mountains' upper eastern slopes.

Sorata

Some 55km north of Achacachi, enclosed in a deep, fertile valley at the foot of the mighty 6400m Illampu massif, **SORATA** has a beautiful setting. Hemmed in by steep mountain slopes and often shrouded in cloud, it has a Shangri-la feel – early Spanish explorers even compared the valley to the Garden of Eden. At an altitude of 2695m, it is significantly warmer than La Paz, but is still cool at night compared to the Yungas. Though there's little to do in Sorata, it's a pleasant place to hang out while preparing for or recovering from some hard trekking or climbing, as well as a good base for less strenuous walks in the surrounding countryside.

Brief history

During the colonial era Sorata was an important trade and gold-mining centre with a large Spanish population. In 1781, at the time of the **Great Rebellion**, it was successfully besieged by supporters of neo-Inca rebel Tupac Amaru, who dammed rivers above the town and then released a torrent that swept it away. Sorata later enjoyed considerable prosperity as one of the main routes into the Yungas from the Altiplano, generating fortunes for the German merchants who dominated the town in the nineteenth century. Sorata was back in the headlines in 2003, when local solidarity with the El Alto-centred "**gas war**" (see p.319) resulted in several deaths. Its popularity was understandably dented, and today it is still struggling to regain its former appeal. Many businesses (including restaurants) close on Tuesdays.

TREKKING AND CLIMBING IN THE CORDILLERA REAL

The Cordillera Real abounds in trekking and climbing possibilities, with a wide range of options of varying lengths and difficulty levels.

TREKKING

Many of the best and most popular treks start close to La Paz, including the three so-called "Inca trails" which cross the cordillera, connecting the Altiplano with the warm, forested valleys of the Yungas (see p.123). Two of these ancient paved routes – the **Choro Trail** (see p.128) and the **Takesi Trail** (see p.130) – are relatively easy to follow without a guide; the third, the **Yunga Cruz Trail** (see p.134), is more difficult. You can do all three of these treks, as well as many other more challenging routes, with any of the adventure tour agencies in La Paz (see p.73).

The other major base for trekking is the town of **Sorata** (see opposite), nestled in a valley at the north end of the range at the foot of the mighty Illampu massif. From here, numerous trekking routes take you high up among the glacial peaks, while others plunge down into the remote forested valleys of the Yungas. Hiring guides and equipment in Sorata is cheaper than going with a La Paz tour operator.

Further afield, the remote and beautiful **Cordillera Apolobamba** (see p.113), a separate range of the Cordillera Oriental north of Lago Titicaca with almost no tourist infrastructure, also offers excellent trekking possibilities for the more adventurous traveller.

Maps and equipment: Unless you're going on a fully organized trek you'll need all your own camping equipment. If you're an experienced hiker, able to communicate effectively with local campesinos in Spanish (though many locals speak only Aymara) and have maps, detailed directions and a compass or GPS, you can try doing some of these treks without a guide.

The books *Trekking in Bolivia: a Traveller's Guide*, by Yossi Brain, and *Peru and Bolivia: Backpacking and Trekking*, by Hilary Bradt, both have detailed descriptions of many of the trekking routes. Most of the routes are also covered in the excellent *Cordillera Real Recreation Map*, published in the US by O'Brien Cartographics, while the Instituto Geográfico Militar in La Paz (see p.86) sells larger-scale maps covering some of the routes.

Guides and mules: Whatever you do, don't go trekking in these mountains alone, as the consequences of a minor fall or a twisted ankle can quickly prove disastrous; it's much better to go with a local guide. Getting lost is easy and can be very dangerous – rescue services are pretty much nonexistent. Hiring a guide is a good way to ensure local people benefit economically from tourism and in addition they can help avoid any possible misunderstandings with the communities you pass through. You may also want to hire a mule to carry your pack, either for your entire trip or for that first gruelling ascent to a high pass.

CLIMBING

With so many high peaks, the Cordillera Real is obviously an excellent place for **mountain climbing**. While serious climbers should bring all their own equipment from home, inexperienced climbers can also scale some of these high peaks with help from specialist agencies in La Paz (see p.73). **Huayna Potosí** (6090m), near La Paz, is one of the few peaks in South America over 6000m that can be climbed by people with no mountaineering experience. Agencies will take you up it for around Bs1050 ($150), though you should check carefully that the guide they provide is qualified and experienced and the equipment adequate – if in doubt, go with a more reputable and expensive agency. To avoid the risk of a potentially fatal high altitude cerebral oedema (a severe form of altitude sickness), the mountain should also not be ascended in a single day.

Plaza General Enrique Peñaranda

The heart of town is the ample **Plaza General Enrique Peñaranda**, shaded by massive palm trees and with good views of Mount Illampu. Inside the municipal offices on the west side of the square is a one-room **museum** (Wed–Mon 8am–noon & 2–5pm; free), with a rather paltry collection of pre-Columbian pots from nearby burial sites and some ornate old dance costumes.

Casa Gunther

Northeast corner of Plaza General Enrique Peñaranda

The most interesting building in Sorata is the **Casa Gunther**, a massive, rambling nineteenth-century mansion that was once home to a family of powerful German rubber merchants (from whom it takes its name). It was turned into a hotel in the late 1960s, and now houses *Residencial Sorata* (see opposite).

ARRIVAL AND DEPARTURE   SORATA

By bus Buses and micros from La Paz (hourly; 3hr 30min-4hr) pull up in front of the offices of Trans Unificada Sorata and Trans Larecaja on Plaza Enrique Peñaranda. There is talk of starting direct services to Copacabana; until then, the only way to reach Copacabana without going via La Paz is to take a La Paz-bound bus and change at Huarina.

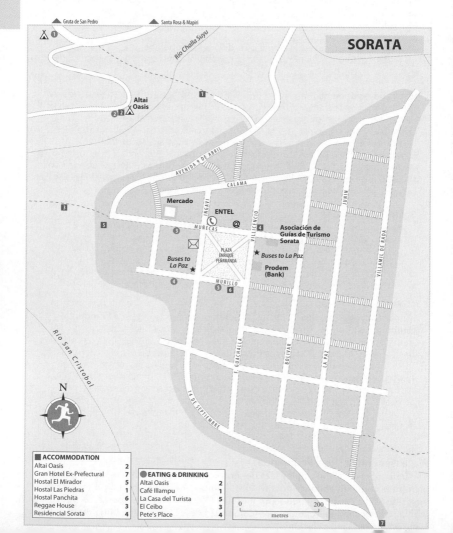

SORATA

ACCOMMODATION

Altai Oasis	2
Gran Hotel Ex-Prefectural	7
Hostal El Mirador	5
Hostal Las Piedras	1
Hostal Panchita	6
Reggae House	3
Residencial Sorata	4

EATING & DRINKING

Altai Oasis	2
Café Illampu	1
La Casa del Turista	5
El Ceibo	3
Pete's Place	4

INFORMATION AND TOURS

TOURIST INFORMATION

Sorata has no formal tourist office. The Asociación de Guías de Turismo Sorata and the manager of *Residencial Sorata* are experts on the region.

TOUR AGENCIES

Although based in La Paz at Linares 940, Andean Epics (☎ 7127 6685, ⓦ andeanepics.com) offers a wide range of mountain-biking trips in the countryside surrounding Sorata. Run by American expat – and local expert – Travis Yossarian Grey, the agency runs trips (Bs700–910/$100–130/day) on the area's high-altitude scree and Inca trails, as well as a five-day combined bike and raft expedition (Bs2520/$360) to Rurrenabaque, an annual mountain-biking downhill jamboree, the Doble Avalancha, every September, and Honda dirt-bike trips (Bs1505/$215 per day).

ACCOMMODATION

★ **Altai Oasis** Thirty minutes from town on foot via the road to the Gruta ☎ 7151 9856, ⓦ altaioasis .lobopages.com. Johny Resnikowski and partner Roxana have constructed a series of imaginative cabins, rooms and dorms among the wild anis, pine and eucalyptus on the folds of the riverbank. Accommodation includes a psychedelic log cabin (sleeping 3–4), a tree-house-like hideaway, a conical yurt-like construction, as well as more humble abodes; all have been conceived with real love and dedication. There are also camping spots, a dorm and a great eatery. Dorms Bs85, cabin Bs700 ($100), doubles Bs125, camping Bs30

Gran Hotel Ex-Prefectural Av Samuel Tejerina ☎ 02 2895003. Like a miniature, dilapidated version of the *Outlook Hotel* in *The Shining*, this place is an experience in itself. Built in the mid-1940s and long since gone to seed, it's not difficult to imagine ghosts stalking every endless, Gothic chandelier-lined corridor, peering through stained-glass windows. Rooms are musty but clean and come with comfy beds; some also have inspirational views. There's a bar, games room and an overgrown garden too. Bs140

Hostal El Mirador Muñecas 400 ☎ 02 2898503. This Hostelling International affiliate has a prime location and stunning views; the rooms – with shared or private bathrooms – don't match up sadly, but are clean enough and boast big windows. Some come with TVs, others with seat-less toilets and potentially lethal showers, so choose carefully. Bs120

★ **Hostal Las Piedras** Villa Elisa Calle 2, above the football field on the shortcut to the Gruta ☎ 7191 6341. Peaceful and homely, the German-run *Las Piedras* offers spotless, great-value, great-view rooms (with or without bathrooms) named after precious stones and styled with a creative dedication and attention to detail rare at budget level. Friendly owner Petra Huber is a mine of local information in German, English and Spanish, while her partner – owner of *Café Illampu* – supplies artisan breads, yoghurt, honey and marmalade for breakfast (included in room rates). Bs100

Hostal Panchita Plaza Enrique Peñaranda ☎ 02 2134242. A friendly place with simple rooms set around a small courtyard; those at the front have small balconies overlooking the plaza. Unfortunately the shared bathrooms are a bit grimy. There's a TV lounge and access to kitchen facilities. Bs70

Reggae House One block west of Hostal El Mirador ☎ 7199 4337. Popular with shoestring travellers, this Bolivian-run hang-out appears only half built. Still the Spartan dorms are inexpensive, the views from the rustic terrace are superb, and there's a small bar (named *Marley's*, inevitably enough), which has ad hoc live music sessions. Dorms Bs20

Residencial Sorata Plaza Enrique Peñaranda ☎ 02 2136672. Set in the rambling, nineteenth-century Casa Gunther, this hotel has a warren of ancient, dusky rooms with looming ceilings and metre-thick walls, while outside there is a series of overgrown, flower-filled courtyards. The older rooms have more charm, but the anonymous newer en-suite ones are more comfortable. Manager Louis Demers is a good source of information and there's a reasonable restaurant. Bs60

EATING AND DRINKING

Restaurant **opening times** are erratic: most places are open everyday except Tuesday, from around 9–10am to 9–10pm. Some restaurants have shorter opening hours during the rainy season (Nov to March), and a few close completely.

Altai Oasis In lodge of the same name ☎ 7151 9856. You can dine to the peal of wind chimes and distant rattle of campground bongos on *Altai's* idyllic outdoor deck. It's one of Sorata's best places to eat, with Eastern European dishes like goulash and *borsht*, numerous veggie options and a wide range of breakfast choices. Look out for the log-carved board games. Mains Bs25–50.

Café Illampu On the road to the Gruta San Pedro, a 30–40min walk out of town. Friendly open-air café on the mountainside looking back across to Sorata, serving beer, coffee, juices, good sandwiches (Bs15–20), snacks and delicious home-made bread, yoghurt and cakes in a laidback atmosphere. Closed Tues, as well as the low-season months of Feb and March.

La Casa del Turista Next to Hostal Panchita on the plaza. Skip past the array of pizzas and pastas, and plump

2

TREKKING FROM SORATA

As well as numerous half- and one-day hikes immediately around town the most popular of which is to the Gruta de San Pedro, (see below), some excellent longer treks start near Sorata. These take you through remote traditional communities and high Andean scenery, up among the glacial peaks of Mount Illampu or across the spine of the cordillera and down into the steamy tropical valleys of the Yungas.

Most local guides, porters and mule handlers in Sorata align themselves with the **Asociación de Guías de Turismo Sorata**, whose office is opposite *Residencial Sorata*, just off the plaza on Calle Sucre (☎02 2136672, ✉guiasturismosorata@hotmail.com). It can arrange guides for about Bs140 a day plus food and mules, which can carry up to 20kg and cost roughly Bs56 a day plus food for the handler. They also have a limited amount of camping equipment for rent. Most local guides know the routes up to the main base camps for climbing Illampu, though they're not qualified climbing guides; if you want a climbing guide you should hire one through a climbing agency in La Paz (see p.73).

THE GRUTA DE SAN PEDRO

The hike (4-6hr return trip) down the San Cristóbal valley to the **Gruta de San Pedro**, a large cave about 12km away, is one of the best short trails around Sorata. Follow Avenida 9 de Abril out of town past the football pitch, then take the left turn, signposted to the *gruta*, about fifteen minutes outside town, which leads you along the opposite side of the valley, past the *Café Illampu* (alternatively, cut straight across the valley from town). The road continues down the narrow ravine of the Río San Cristóbal, with good views of Illampu looming above. After about 11km you'll reach the small village of **San Pedro**; the Gruta de San Pedro is just above the road on the right, about 1km further on. The cave (daily 8am-5pm) is long, narrow and about 12m high, with plenty of bats – you can go about 150m inside before your way is blocked by an underground lake. A guardian will turn on the lights in the cave in return for the admission fee (Bs10).

THE LAGUNAS GLACIER AND CHILLATA TREK

One of the most popular high-altitude treks from Sorata is the four-day **Lagunas Glacier and Chillata Trek**. This takes you high up the western side of the Illampu massif to two lakes set at over 5000m.

THE ILLAMPU CIRCUIT

A longer, tougher and even more spectacular trek is the **Illampu Circuit** (6–7 days), which takes you round the Illampu massif past isolated settlements and over several passes between 4500m and 5045m, the highest of which, Abra Calzada, affords incredible views over Lago Titicaca. However, there have been violent robberies near Laguna San Francisco, towards the end of the circuit; many agencies have stopped operating the route: check the latest security situation before heading off, and always use knowledgeable local guides.

THE MAPIRI TRAIL

One of two long treks down into the tropical valleys of the Yungas, the **Mapiri Trail** (7–8 days) is a tough descent to the mining town of Mapiri, from where you can continue by motorized canoe and road to Coroico or down to Rurrenabaque. Built in the nineteenth century as a route for bringing quinine up from the Amazon lowlands, the trail runs through a beautiful and remote region of forest-covered mountains. It is frequently overgrown, so carry a machete; water is also scarce along much of the route.

THE CAMINO DE ORO

The **Camino de Oro** (Goldminers' Trail; 5–7 days) dates back to pre-Columbian times. It connects the Altiplano with the alluvial goldfields of the Yungas, and impressive remnants of Inca stonework can still be seen along its length, though the lower stretches pass through areas badly deforested by mining activity. The trail emerges at the gold-mining camps along the Río Tipuani, from where transport is available downriver to Guanay.

for one of the more interesting Mexican options: there are well-prepared tacos, enchiladas, quesadillas and nachos. The restaurant itself is cluttered with paintings, wall hangings and reed boats, and has a surprisingly well-stocked bar. Mains Bs15–28. Open daily.

El Ceibo Muñecas. This first-floor restaurant is probably the pick of the local joints, serving standard Bolivian fare at moderate prices (mains Bs15–30) in a rustic, low-lit dining room. The filling set *desayunos*, *almuerzos* and *cenas* are all good options. Open daily.

Pete's Place Esquivel 8, just off the southwest edge of the plaza. This keenly priced gringo favourite specializes in authentically spiced rarities like chicken and vegetable curries, as well as the full range of more familiar Bolivian meat and vegetarian options. The eponymous Pete is a good source of local info. Mains Bs15–50.

DIRECTORY

Banks and exchange There are no ATMs, though Prodem (daily except Mon), on Plaza Enrique Peñaranda, can give cash advances to credit card holders and changes money at its usual prohibitive rates.

Horseriding Staff at *Reggae House* organize horseriding trips (Bs105–140).

Internet access Slow access (Bs10/hr) is available at several internet cafés surrounding Plaza Enrique Peñaranda.

Laundry *Residencial Sorata* charges Bs10/kg.

Post office The post office is on Plaza Enrique Peñaranda.

Telephones ENTEL on Muñecas.

The Yungas

East of La Paz, the Cordillera Real drops precipitously into the Amazon lowlands, plunging through the **Yungas**, a region of rugged, forest-covered mountains and deep subtropical valleys. Blessed with fertile soils and watered by plentiful rains, the warm valleys of the Yungas produce abundant crops of coffee, tropical fruit and coca for the markets of La Paz and the rest of the Altiplano; indeed, long before the Spanish conquest the peoples of the Andes maintained agricultural colonies here to supply the Altiplano with coca and other subtropical products. Several of the sturdy stone roads that originally transported the leaves – and linked the Yungas outposts to the main population centres – today provide some of the most scenic, challenging hiking in the region.

Even if you don't hike, the journey down to the Yungas from the Altiplano is truly spectacular. The original road from **La Paz to Coroico** is widely considered the **most dangerous in the world**, hugging the forest-covered mountain slopes as it winds above fearsome precipices. It's also among the most scenic and dramatic, and – since the opening of a bypass – frequented predominantly by mountain bikers. While the road is still open, the vast majority of motorists use the bypass.

The most frequently visited Yungas town, **Coroico** itself is a tranquil place, with a warm climate and wonderful views that provide the perfect antidote to the bleak Altiplano. From Coroico, the road continues north towards Rurrenabaque and the Bolivian Amazon (covered in Chapter 6). Midway between Coroico and La Paz, **Parque Nacional Cotapata** is one of the few areas where the natural Yungas vegetation is still well preserved; the **Choro Trail**, one of a trio of so-called "Inca" trails (though they were probably earlier routes which were used and modified by Incas) in the region, passes through the pristine cloudforests of the park. Another of these trails, the **Takesi Trail**, also known as the Inca Trail (*Camino del Inca*), is one of the most popular treks in the Yungas. The quiet town of **Chulumani** is less frequently visited than Coroico, but has similarly good views, while the nearby **Yunga Cruz trail**, is more scenic than the two other "Inca" trails, and also poses a greater challenge.

Coroico

Peaceful **COROICO** is one of the most beautiful spots in the Yungas, perched on a steep mountain with panoramic views across the Andean foothills to the icy peaks of the Cordillera Real. Founded in the colonial era as a **gold-mining outpost**, the town is still an important market centre for the surrounding agricultural communities. At an altitude of

2

2

THE WORLD'S MOST DANGEROUS ROAD

Few highways have as intimidating a reputation as the original road linking La Paz with Coroico in the North Yungas. A rough, narrow track chiselled out of near-vertical mountainsides that descends more than 3500m over a distance of just 64km, it's still widely referred to as the **world's most dangerous road**, a title bestowed on it by the Inter-American Development Bank. Statistically, the sobriquet is difficult to dispute: dozens of vehicles went off the road each year, and with vertical drops of up to 1000m over the edge, annual fatalities reached into the hundreds.

Following the route in its entirety from Unduavi, the first 40km are the most perilous and spectacular of the entire route. At times the road is only 3m wide, looming over deep precipices. To make matters worse, the road is often swathed in **cloud**, and in places waterfalls crash down onto its surface. About 86km from La Paz, the road reaches Yolosa.

After years of construction, however, a new **multi-million-dollar bypass** around the most perilous stretch opened in 2006, following a route that looms high over the old road on the opposite side of the valley and which tunnels intermittently through the mountainside. While some of the concrete and supporting rods have fallen prey to the elements, it's still a huge improvement – at least space- and safety-wise – over the old route.

The 106km bypass has also slashed the journey time from La Paz to Coroico to about three hours by bus (2hr 15min by car); the old road took about four and a half hours. From Villa Fátima in La Paz, the road to the Yungas climbs northeast to **La Cumbre**, a 4800m pass over the Cordillera Real. From here it descends to the hamlet of **Unduavi**, where the road forks, one branch descending southeast towards Chulumani in the South Yungas (see p.131), the other heading down northeast towards Coroico and the Amazon lowlands.

The *nueva carretera* (new road) initially follows the original northeast fork before splitting off and climbing high above it, following a similar trajectory along the spine of the mountains before descending to join the original road north of **Yolosa**, a hamlet set at about 1200m. Here, a newly cobbled side road climbs up to Coroico, 11km away, while the main road continues 74km north to Caranavi and beyond to Rurrenabaque.

CYCLING DOWN

What the statistics don't tell you is that the old route – and to a certain extent the bypass as well – is among the most beautiful roads in the world. Starting amid the icebound peaks of the Cordillera Real, it plunges down through the clouds into the humid valleys of the Yungas, winding along deep, narrow gorges clad with dense cloudforest.

So spectacular is the descent that travelling the old Yungas road by **mountain bike** is one of Bolivia's most popular tourist attractions, an exhilarating 5–6hr ride that's easy to organize with tour companies in La Paz – Gravity Assisted Mountain Biking has one of the best reputations (see p.73). Local operator Cross Country Coroico, on Pacheco 2058 (☎7127 3015, ⓦmtbcoroico.co.cc), was one of the first to ply the route, and it also offers several less infamous but equally challenging rides, plus less taxing trips for beginners.

The re-routing of most traffic to the bypass means – in theory, at least – cycling the route is now **safer** than it's ever been, especially if you go with a reputable tour company with good guides and well-maintained bikes. Of course, the road is not entirely without risk, and people have been hurt and several even killed during the descent in the past, forced off the edge by traffic.

1760m, it enjoys a warm, pleasantly humid climate. While travellers might not need the same amount of time in Coroico they once did just to recover from reaching the town in the first place – whether making the journey down from the Altiplano by micro, following the old route by mountain bike or trekking the Choro Trail – Coroico is still worth visiting just for the sheer thrill of getting there. It also makes a great stopover if you're attempting the tough overland journey between La Paz and the **Amazon lowlands**.

Most visitors spend much of their time in Coroico lounging by a swimming pool and enjoying the fantastic views, but there are some pleasant walks through the surrounding countryside, plus increasing numbers of **adventure pursuits**. Coroico gets very busy at weekends and during Bolivian public holidays, when it's transformed by large numbers of Paceños on vacation; if you want to relax in peace, visit during the week. The mosquitoes here can be ferocious, so cover up and bring plenty of repellent.

ARRIVAL AND DEPARTURE COROICO

By bus Buses, micros and minivans to Coroico (2hr 15min–3hr 30min) depart from La Paz every half hour from the Villa Fatima district; they depart from and return to the bus station on the south side of town. Minivans are the quickest and most comfortable form of transport and cost only a little extra. It's worth buying a ticket in advance, especially at weekends, and travelling by day. If you want to go to Chulumani, you'll need to head back to Unduavi, where the roads to the north and south Yungas divide, and catch a through bus from La Paz to Chulumani. If you're heading into the Amazon, you can buy a

ticket on a through bus to Rurrenabaque (at least 15hr) from La Paz, from Trans Palmeras or Trans-Totai in the terminal; buses pass through Yolosita on the main road every day. The price includes a transfer from Coroico to Yolosita.

By boat For a more adventurous way to reach Rurrenabaque, Deep Rainforest, at the corner of Murillo and Sagarnaga in La Paz (☎02 2150385, ⓦ deep-rainforest.com) offers weekly dry-season (May–Oct) departures (3 days; Bs1260/$180) from Coroico via Guanay, where onward travel is via the Río Mapiri.

GETTING AROUND

On foot Coroico is a small town and almost everything is within easy walking distance of the plaza.

By taxi You can also usually find a taxi in the plaza to take you to the further flung hotels.

INFORMATION

Tourist information There is a tourist office staffed by local guides on the plaza (daily 8am–8pm; ☎7250 5402), which has a selection of flyers and maps, and can give

advice in Spanish. The bus station also has a tourist office, though it's only intermittently open. The website ⓦ coroi.co.cc is a useful resource as well.

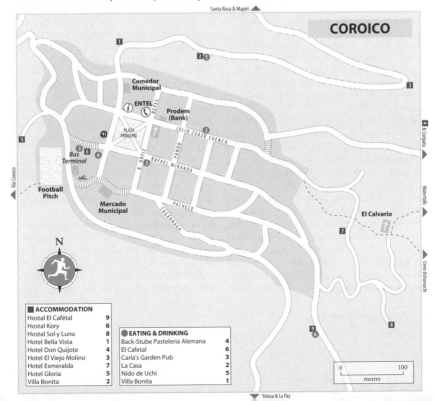

COROICO

Santa Rosa & Mapiri

Comedor Municipal

ENTEL

Prodem (Bank)

PLAZA PRINCIPAL

JULIO ZUAZO CUENCA

R. ORTIZ

PANDO

RAFAEL MIRANDA

Bus Terminal

Río Coroico

Football Pitch

Mercado Municipal

PACHECO

SAGARNAGA

El Calvario

N

Yolosa & La Paz

4 & Coripata

Waterfalls

Cerro Uchumachi

■ ACCOMMODATION	
Hostal El Cafétal	9
Hostal Kory	6
Hostal Sol y Luna	8
Hotel Bella Vista	1
Hotel Don Quijote	4
Hotel El Viejo Molino	3
Hotel Esmeralda	7
Hotel Gloria	5
Villa Bonita	2

● EATING & DRINKING	
Back-Stube Pasteleria Alemana	4
El Cafetal	6
Carla's Garden Pub	3
La Casa	2
Nido de Uchi	5
Villa Bonita	1

0   100
metres

2

TOURS

The gregarious guides at the tourist office offer a range of activities including hikes up nearby **Cerro Uchamachi** and down to the **Río Vagantes** in the valley below, and excursions to Afro-Yungueño villages like **Tocaña** and **Mururata**. It's also possible to go rafting, kayaking and inner-tubing near Coroico – ask at the tourist office for details.

Fly Over Coroico No office; telephone only ☎ 6069 6300, ⓦ energyparagliding.com. Offers tandem paraglider flights (Bs483/$69 for 15min).

El Vagante Just off the plaza on Cuenca ☎ 02 2413065, ⓦ elvagante.com. Organizes a range of activities, including canyoning trips (Bs420/$60).

Zipline Bolivia Contact via Carla's Garden Pub in Coroico ☎ 02 2313849, ⓦ ziplinebolivia.com. A Kiwi-Bolivian-run outfit with 1555m of ziplines near Yolosa, sessions cost around Bs210 ($30).

ACCOMMODATION

Coroico has an impressive range of places to stay, aimed primarily at visitors from La Paz. At weekends and on **public holidays** (especially in the high season) everywhere gets very full and prices go up, so it's worth booking in advance. Even if you're on a tight budget, it's worth spending a little more to stay somewhere with a **swimming pool**. The following all include breakfast unless stated otherwise.

Hostal El Cafétal Near the hospital, a 10min walk southeast of the centre ☎ 7193 3979, ⓦ elcafetal .co.cc. This French-run institution offers accommodation in bamboo-furnished en-suite rooms with splendid views and a gratifyingly earthy aroma. The cheaper "backpacker" rooms are smaller and have shared bathrooms. There's also a pool with a few forlorn-looking deckchairs, plus a good restaurant. Breakfast costs extra. Bs80

Hostal Kory P. Linares ☎ 7156 4050. A good-value choice with a huge pool (open to non-guests for Bs10) and clean, parquet-floored en-suite rooms with incredible views. There are also some cheaper options with shared bathrooms, plus a restaurant, communal kitchen and laundry service. Bs140

★ **Hostal Sol y Luna** Just under 1km outside town uphill on Julio Zuazo Cuenca, beyond the *Hotel Esmeralda* ☎ 7156 1626, ⓦ solyluna-bolivia.com. A veritable enchanted forest of a retreat, *Sol y Luna* has to be one of the most charming hideaways in Bolivia. There is a collection of delightful rustic cabins (sleeping 2–3) and apartments (sleeping 2), most situated in discreet seclusion at the end of winding, subtropical paths. The whitewash and thatch of the older, Spanish-style cottages contrasts with newer, more environmentally integrated additions like the attractive *Jajata* cabin, and an amazing treehouse. If you're after a specific choice (check the website), it's advisable to book in advance. There are also several simple, inexpensive rooms, a hot tub, camping space (Bs20/person), and a restaurant and bamboo meditation hall. Yoga (Bs20) and massages (Bs80) are on offer too, and breakfast costs extra. A taxi from town costs about Bs15. Cabins Bs200; doubles and apartments Bs100

Hotel Bella Vista Heroes Del Chaco, two blocks north of the plaza ☎ 02 2136059, ⓔ coroicohotelbellavista @hotmail.com. This stylish, Bolivian-owned place has faux-colonial decor, towering ceilings and a contemporary twist. Each of the en-suite rooms come with TVs and inspirational views, though the paint's peeling a bit. There's a large mural in reception depicting the oppression and emancipation of black slaves, with the Bible placed pointedly at its centre. There are bikes for hire and a laundry service. Bs250

Hotel Don Quijote About 1km outside town on the road to Coripata ☎ 02 2136007, ⓦ hoteldonquijote .net. This long, stable-like bungalow hotel has dark but cool net-curtained rooms with private bathrooms, as well as a restaurant, bar, spacious swimming pool, ping pong and billiards tables, and uninterrupted views of the horizon. It is popular with Bolivian weekenders and foreign tour groups alike. Bs200

Hotel El Viejo Molino 1km from town on the road to Caranavi ☎ 02 2895506, ⓦ hotelviejomolino.com. Isolated on the far northeastern fringe of town, the perfectly perched "Old Mill" has an air of exclusivity about it. Although the rooms are slightly musty, they're very comfortable and moreover the hotel also has a

COROICO'S FIESTA

Around October 20 each year, Coroico celebrates its biggest annual **fiesta** with several days of drinking, processions and costumed dances. The fiesta commemorates the day in 1811 when the statue of the Virgin in the church – brought here from Barcelona in 1680, when Coroico was founded – supposedly summoned a ghost army to drive off a force of indigenous rebels that were besieging the town.

lovely large pool, restaurant with wraparound vistas and a sauna. **Bs420 ($60)**

Hotel Esmeralda 400m above town up Julio Zuazo Cuenca ☎02 2136017, ⊛hotelesmeralda.com. This large hotel has great views, an attractive garden and pool, and a reasonable restaurant. There's a wide range of dorms and rooms; the best of the latter have private bathrooms and bamboo balconies with stunning vistas. There's also table football, internet access and a book exchange, and breakfast is included. If their free transfer service isn't there to pick you up from the plaza or bus terminal, they'll refund your taxi fare. Dorms **Bs75**; doubles **Bs180**

Hotel Gloria Linares ☎02 2407070. A slightly dilapidated colonial-style building with an edge-of-town

location. The en-suite rooms are bright and pleasant, though a little small, and come with TVs; make sure you get one facing the valley rather than the car park. There is also a lounge with panoramic views, a modest pool and a restaurant. **Bs300 ($43)**

Villa Bonita 100m past *Hotel Bella Vista* on the road to Caranavi, ☎7191 8298, ✉Villa_Bonita05@yahoo.com. Amid the laidback, familial environs of their raspberry-coloured home and leafy garden – site of a great café also – (see below)–friendly Bolivian-Swiss couple Ninfa and Gianni have three lovely, wooden-shuttered rooms and a four-berth cabin. Ninfa offers free yoga classes at 4pm on Mon; gifts of fruit or vegetables are appreciated. Cabin **Bs260**; doubles **Bs100**

EATING AND DRINKING

There's a good variety of places to eat, including several European-owned places, as well as a number of interchangeable restaurants around the plaza serving gringo fare. The best-value places are in the **Mercado Municipal**, a block south of the plaza on Sagárnaga; there's also a cheap **Comedor Municipal** and assorted nocturnal food stalls on Héroes Del Chaco, just north of the plaza and at the convent of the Madres Clarisas, diagonally opposite *Carla's Garden Pub*, the nuns sell home-made cakes, biscuits and wine; just ring the bell to be let in. Nightlife can get quite lively at weekends in the high season, and many of the restaurants double up as bars.

Back-Stube Pasteleria Alemana Just off the Plaza Principal. German café-bakery serving excellent breakfasts, home-made cakes, salads, sandwiches and main meals (Bs30–50): for a hearty feed, try the *saurbraten* (a thick beef stew served with noodle-style dumplings). It has a wonderful terrace affording yet more amazing views, and plays a 1960s/70s soundtrack. Open Wed–Fri 10am–2.30pm & 6.30–10pm, Sat–Sun 9am–10pm.

El Cafetal In the hostal of the same name. Great-value French-run restaurant with panoramic views and delicious food (Bs20–50), including trout lasagne, steak in Roquefort sauce, crêpes, soufflés and curries. All that's missing is the French wine, although Tarija supplies a fine substitute. Wed–Mon 8.30am-4pm & 6.30–9.30pm.

Carla's Garden Pub 50m down the steps beyond Hostal Kory. This relaxed spot with views down the valley is a great spot for a sundowner – choose from draught beers (around Bs15) or well-mixed cocktails. The only problem is struggling back up the steps to the plaza at the end of the night. Mon–Sat 6pm–midnight.

La Casa Julio Zuazo Cuenca, two blocks east of the plaza, ☎7328 1035. Akin to a continental sitting room, complete with cuckoo clock and cheesy European jigsaw scenes, this German-run restaurant serves authentic fondues for a minimum of two people, including a chocolate version, as well as dishes like raclette and goulash (Bs30–50). Daily from 6pm.

Nido de Uchi On the plaza. A fine spot to sample locally produced fair-trade coffee (Bs4–15), *Nido de Uchi* also has breakfast options (Bs10–28), sandwiches, cakes, pancakes and ice cream sundaes. It doubles up as an internet café. Open daily.

★ **Villa Bonita** In the garden of the hotel of the same name. This idyllic garden café has just a handful of chairs, delightful service and a concise menu with wonderful breakfasts (Bs10–19), pastas, salads, sandwiches and pancakes. The highlights, however, are the mouthwatering home-made ice creams and sorbets (Bs4/scoop) flavoured with local ingredients like *hierba buena* (a type of mint), lavender and passion fruit: the sundaes (Bs15–29) should not be missed. Daily 8.30am–5.30pm.

DIRECTORY

Banks and exchange Prodem (closed Mon), on the north side of the plaza, changes dollars and gives five percent advances on Visa cards. *Hotel Esmeralda* changes travellers' cheques, and *La Casa* will change euros.

Horseriding Guided horseriding trips (Bs50/hr) are offered by El Relincho (☎7192 3814), about a ten min walk beyond *Hotel Esmeralda* on the road to the *Hostal Sol y Luna*.

Hospital A 10min walk southeast of town along Pacheco.

Internet access Try Unete on the plaza (Bs5/hr).

Language lessons The amiable and ubiquitous Siria Leon Domínguez (☎7195 5431, ✉siria_leon@yahoo .com) and Chilean expat Claudia Alvarez (☎7190 7301, ✉claudiaalvar@yahoo.com) offer private Spanish lessons (Bs28–40/hr).

Laundry *Hotel Bella Vista* has a service open to both guests and non guests (Bs20/kg).

2

HIKES AROUND COROICO

Coroico is surrounded by lush subtropical hills and valleys that offer numerous possibilities for hiking. Although you can do some hikes on your own, it is often safer – and easier – to go with a guide; they are available from the tourist information office on the main plaza (see p.125).

TO CERRO UCHUMACHI AND THE WATERFALLS

In recent years there have been several robberies and rapes on both the Uchumachi and waterfalls hikes. Travellers are strongly advised to seek local advice before setting out and certainly not to attempt either hike alone.

The hike up **Cerro Uchumachi**, the hill rising above Coroico, takes about two hours there and back. To reach the summit, continue uphill beyond the *Hotel Esmeralda* along a path marked by the Stations of the Cross, which leads to the El Calvario chapel. From here a path climbs to the summit, marked by three wooden crosses; there are excellent views.

To reach the waterfalls (*cascadas*), from the chapel, follow the path to your left (if you're facing uphill) around the hillside; the trip takes three to four hours return.

TO PUENTE MURURATA

A difficult to follow but rewarding hike follows the path that heads down into the valley to the **Río Coroico** from beside the football pitch. After about an hour's walk downhill the path hits the main road to Caranavi; turn right and you'll soon reach **Puente Mururata**, a bridge over the stream of the same name, upstream of which there are some pools where you can swim. From the other side of Puente Mururata a path climbs to the left of the road to the peaceful Afro-Yungueño village of **Tocaña**, about a twenty-minute walk away.

THE KORI HUAYKU TRAIL

This new trail (around 8–9hr return) starts from Coroico Viejo, near the settlement of Yolosa. Guides can take you through coca fields to the Kori Río Huayku, from where you follow an old Inca trail. There are opportunities to swim and spot monkeys and other wildlife.

La Senda Verde Just outside Yolosa ☎ 7010 5222, Ⓦ sendaverde.com. If you fancy staying in the area, *La Senda Verde* has accommodation in lovely cabins and a treehouse, and also offers a restaurant, pool and animal refuge. Bs200

Post office The post office is on the plaza, though it's only open irregularly (closed all day Mon); you're better off sending letters when you get back to La Paz.

Telephone office The ENTEL office is on the north side of the Plaza.

Parque Nacional Cotapata

Around 20km north of La Paz, some four hundred square kilometres of the north face of the Cordillera Real are protected by **PARQUE NACIONAL COTAPATA** (otherwise known as Parque Nacional y Area Natural de Manejo Integrado Cotapata). Ranging in elevation from 1000m to 6000m, Cotapata encompasses many of the astonishing range of different ecosystems and climatic zones formed as the Andes plunge down into the valleys of the upper Amazon Basin. Within a remarkably short distance high mountain peaks, snowfields and *puna* grasslands give way to dense cloudforest, which in turn blends into the humid montane forest that covers the lower slopes of the Andes in a thick green blanket. The **cloudforest** – also known as the *ceja de selva* or "jungle's eyebrows" – is particularly striking, made up of low, gnarled trees and home to many unique bird species, and elusive pumas and spectacled bears.

The Choro Trail

The only way to visit Cotapata properly is by walking through the park along the pre-Hispanic **Choro Trail**. Running almost entirely downhill, the 70km trail is easy to follow and can be walked in three to four days. If you have your own camping equipment, a compass and (ideally) a map, it's relatively simple to do without a guide.

La Cumbre to Chukura

The trail starts near **La Cumbre**, the high pass 22km north of La Paz. From the lakes just before La Cumbre, head north-northwest to another pass, **Abra Chukura** (4860m), which is marked by a stone cairn (*apacheta*). This 45-minute walk is the only part of the route that is difficult to follow – if in doubt stick to the rough track winding up to the pass. From the *apacheta*, a well-paved stone path plunges down the left side of the deep valley of the Río Phajchiri, passing the ruins of an Inca waystation, or *tambo*, after an hour or so. After two to three hours you'll reach the small village of **Chukura**.

Chukura to Challapampa and Chairo

Below Chukura the cloudforest begins, the vegetation gradually thickening as you descend. After another hour you reach **Challapampa**, a small village with a shop and a camping spot by the stream. Three hours down the valley, at the village of Choro, the path crosses over the river on a bridge and climbs east along the right-hand side of a deep, densely forested valley – the track is still largely paved and is supported by a well-preserved stone platform in places. Note that several travellers have reported robberies in this area. The next available water and camping spot is another two hours or so away where a stream crosses the path; about three hours beyond that you reach **Sandillani**. From here it's another two hours down the valley to the end of the trail at the village of **Chairo**.

ARRIVAL AND DEPARTURE   PARQUE NACIONAL COTAPATA

By bus To reach the Choro Trail, take any bus heading to the Yungas from Villa Fátima in La Paz and get off at La Cumbre. Departing from Chairo, it's about 11km to the main road and another 4km to Yolosa (see p.124). There's regular transport from here on to Coroico and back to La Paz. If you're lucky you'll find a *camioneta* from Chairo to Yolosa, though it's more likely you'll either have to walk or hire a taxi to take you there (about Bs280).

TOURS

Tours Most trekking agencies in La Paz run tours along the Choro Trail – as does the community-run Urpuma Ecoturismo project (☎ 7195 1006, ⓦ ecoturismo.com.bo).

ACCOMMODATION AND EATING

There is a shop selling soft drinks, beer and food in **Challapampa**. There's a good camping spot by the stream here, though locals will expect you to pay a small fee. There's also a campsite a further three hours down the valley, just before the village of **Choro**, then two hours away where a stream crosses the path. You can also camp at **Sandillani**, in the beautifully tended garden of a venerable Japanese man; there's also a small shop here. Finally, there's camping and supplies in **Chairo**.

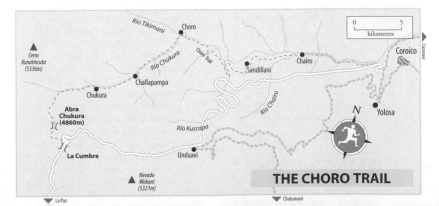

THE CHORO TRAIL

Urpuma Ecoturismo Lodge Sandillani ☎ 7195 1006, ⓦ ecoturismo.com.bo. The best place to stay on the trek is this community-run lodge, which has stone and mud cabins housing dorms and private rooms with traditional furnishings and hot showers. There's a restaurant, and rates include breakfast. Dorms Bs80; doubles Bs196

The Takesi Trail

One of Bolivia's best and most popular treks, the **Takesi Trail** (2–3 days) is a fantastic 40km hike starting near La Paz that crosses the Cordillera Real and plunges down into the steamy forested valleys of the Yungas, emerging at the village of **Yanacachi**, west of Chulumani on the road from La Paz. Also known as the Camino del Inca (the Inca Trail) the Takesi is one of the finest remaining **pre-Columbian** paved roads in Bolivia, and passes through an amazing variety of scenery. Relatively easy to follow and not too strenuous, it's ideal for less experienced trekkers and can be done without a guide.

Ventilla to Estancia Takesi

The Takesi Trail starts at **Ventilla**, a small village set at an altitude of 3200m some 20km east of La Paz. From Ventilla, turn left off the main road and follow the clearly signposted track that winds up the valley northeast to the village of **Choquequta**, ninety minutes away. Here you can usually hire mules for the ascent to the pass or the entire length of the trek. Follow the track uphill for another ninety minutes until you reach a crumbling wall with a map of the route painted on it. Turn off the road to the right along a broad path which winds steeply uphill, with fine pre-Columbian paving soon evident along its length. After ninety minutes or so you reach the highest point on the trail, a 4600m pass marked by a stone *apacheta* from where there are fantastic views of the looming glacial peak of Mururata (5868m) to the east. From here the trail continues about ninety minutes northeast down a broad valley, through llama pastures to the herding hamlet of **Estancia Takesi**, passing an abundance of good camping spots along the way.

THE TAKESI & YUNGA CRUZ TRAILS

To Kakapi and Chojila

Below Estancia Takesi, the path crosses the Río Takesi onto its right bank, where it winds along steep slopes high above a thundering gorge. The air gets warmer and more humid by the minute as the trail drops below 3000m, and the sides of the valley are soon covered in lush vegetation. After two to three hours you'll reach the village of **Kakapi**, after which the path, now heading east, again crosses a river. Continue uphill for half an hour to **Chojila**, a small and friendly settlement with a campsite (see opposite). It's still over three hours from here to Yanacachi, so if you're not in a hurry, it's the perfect place to stay overnight.

ACHACHILAS AND APUS

To locals, the high mountain peaks are more than just breathtaking natural phenomena. Known as *achachilas* in Aymara and *apus* in Quechua, they're also considered living beings inhabited by powerful spirits. As controllers of weather and the source of vital irrigation water, these mountain gods must be appeased with constant offerings and worship, since if angered they're liable to send hailstorms, frost or drought to destroy crops. At almost every high pass you'll see stone cairns known as **apachetas**. As well as marking the pass on the horizon to make it easier for travellers to find, these *apachetas* are also shrines to the mountain gods. Travellers carry stones up to the pass to add to the *apacheta*, thereby securing the good will of the *achachilas* and leaving the burden of their worries behind. Offerings of coca and alcohol are also made at these shrines, which vary in size and form from jumbled heaps of rocks to neatly built piles topped by a cross, depending on the importance of the route and the relative power and visibility of the nearby peaks.

Chojila to Yanacachi

From Chojila, descend for 45 minutes until you reach a concrete bridge; cross it and turn to the right. After a while, you'll reach an aqueduct, which leads straight to a road. Be careful if you're following the aqueduct in the dark – there are holes in the concrete slabs underfoot. When you reach the road, follow it around the bend and take the left, uphill fork. Soon, the road passes an unpleasant sulphur mining settlement known as the **Chojlla mining camp**. Unless you get a lift from a passing vehicle, you'll have to follow the road for another two hours to get to the tranquil village of **Yanacachi**, just off the La Paz–Chulumani road.

ARRIVAL AND DEPARTURE   THE TAKESI TRAIL

By micro Several micros to Ventilla depart from the corner of Luis Lara and Rodriguez in La Paz (7am–noon; 3hr); they return at similar times; alternatively you can walk to the main road in about an hour, and then flag down buses (hourly) travelling in either direction between Chulumani and La Paz.
By taxi A taxi from La Paz to Yanacachi costs Bs350 ($50).

ACCOMMODATION AND EATING

Meals and food Basic meals and food supplies are available in the main villages, though it's advisable to carry at least some of your own supplies.
Camping In Chojila, enterprising locals have terraced some ground to create a campsite with gorgeous views over the lush subtropical valleys below. Yanacachi has several basic *alojamientos* and places to eat.

Chulumani

From Unduavi on the road from La Paz to the Yungas, a side road heads east towards the provincial capital of **CHULUMANI**, providing a dramatic ride as it plunges down from the high Andes into the lush vegetation of the Yungas. Chulumani is far less touristy than Coroico, though its setting – at an elevation of 1640m, on a steep hillside overlooking a broad river valley – is equally scenic. With its palm-shaded plaza and steep, dusty, narrow cobbled streets, lined with scruffy houses with red-tiled roofs, Chulumani is a typical Yungas town, and makes a perfect base for exploring the surrounding countryside. In the 1950s, however, it was notorious as a hideout for fugitive Nazi war criminals, including Klaus Barbie, the "Butcher of Lyon", who reputedly once sold fruit juices on the plaza.

ARRIVAL AND INFORMATION   CHULUMANI

By bus There are regular services to and from La Paz (roughly hourly; 4hr–4hr 30min).
Tourist information The best source of information is Javier Sarabia, owner of the *Country House*, who can advise on hikes from Chulumani; he also runs guided excursions and camping trips, and can arrange bicycle and motorbike rental.

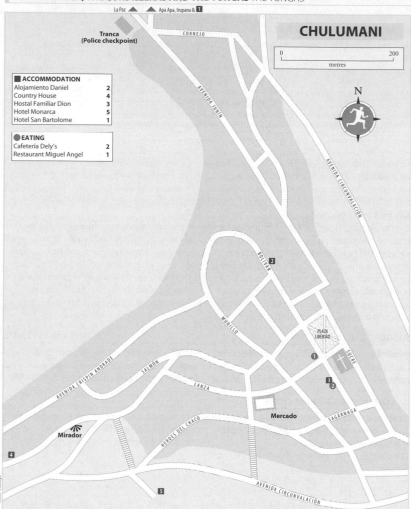

La Paz ▲ ▲ Apa Apa, Irupana & **1**

Tranca
(Police checkpoint)

CORNEJO

CHULUMANI

0   200
metres

N

■ **ACCOMMODATION**
Alojamiento Daniel   2
Country House   4
Hostal Familiar Dion   3
Hotel Monarca   5
Hotel San Bartolome   1

● **EATING**
Cafetería Dely's   2
Restaurant Miguel Angel   1

AVENIDA JUNIN

AVENIDA CIRCUNVALACION

BOLÍVAR   **2**

MURILLO

PLAZA
LIBERTAD

AVENIDA CRISPIN ANDRADE

SALMÓN

1

SUCRE

LANZA

3
2

Mercado

SAGARNAGA

Mirador
HEROES DEL CHACO

4

Ocabaya

5

AVENIDA CIRCUNVALACIÓN

ACCOMMODATION

Alojamiento Daniel Uphill from the plaza on Bolívar ☎ 02 2136359. Simple but clean rooms with rough-hewn pink walls and a choice of shared or private bathrooms; those upstairs have balconies and great views. Staff are friendly too. **Bs35**

★ **Country House** 1km southeast of town beyond the Mirador ☎ 7322 9014. This bohemian guesthouse is Chulumani's best option. It has funky rooms set around an eccentric garden with a psychedelic swimming pool. Walls and shelves are crammed with old wine bottles, magazines, books, art, textiles, insect specimens and random newspaper articles. Helpful English-speaking owner Javier Sarabia is a mine of

information, serves tasty food (which costs extra) and organizes excursions. **Bs100**

Hostal Familiar Dion Southwest of the plaza; entry through the adjoining Cafetería Dely's ☎ 02 2136070. Run by genial middle-aged sisters, this homely *hostal* consists of well-scrubbed, unassuming rooms – with shared or private bathrooms – ringing a flowery courtyard. Rates include breakfast. **Bs60**

Hotel Monarca Below the town on Av Circumvalación ☎ 02 2136121. Although the front gate is evocative of Alcatraz, this dated holiday camp-style hotel is friendly enough. The parquet-floored, net-curtained chalets are en suite, have fans and look out onto a huge pool that's seen better days. There's also a bar and a decent restaurant. Breakfast included. **Bs90**

Hotel San Bartolome 2km from town on the Irupana road ☎ 7251 4779. This out-of-town retreat has ten cosy bird's-eye-view cabins (sleeping up to six people) with 1970s furniture, plus ten bungalow-style rooms styled in similar retro fashion. The place also boasts Chulumani's nicest pool, a mini golf course, and billiards and ping pong tables. Breakfast included. **Bs210**

EATING

The selection of places to eat in Chulumani is disappointing, and the better places are usually open only at **weekends**. There is a decent restaurant in the *Monarca*, though finding it open is another matter; even if you're a guest, it will usually require some notice. **Stalls** at the market offer simple meals.

Cafetería Dely's Just south of the plaza. For a sandwich, burger or juice, head to *Cafetería Dely's*, where in a spotlessly clean interior you can watch your food being prepared while you wait. Snacks Bs10–20. Low season opening times are erratic.

Restaurant Miguel Angel On the plaza. The prominent *Miguel Angel* is probably the pick of the (admittedly underwhelming) restaurants surrounding the plaza, serving reasonable almuerzos (Bs15–20).

Around Chulumani

The main attraction of Chulumani is the opportunity to explore the peaceful hamlets, **splendid scenery** and exuberant tropical vegetation of the surrounding countryside. Many of the steep mountain slopes have been sculpted over centuries into neat terraces covered in coca bushes, while the fertile valley floor is a patchwork of coffee and orange groves filled with flowers and hummingbirds. The best day-trip is to the **Bosque Ecológico Apa Apa**, but almost any path leading out of town makes for a good hike: try following the path that climbs up the ridge behind the town.

From Chulumani, a road runs northeast, past the Bosque Ecológico Apa Apa, before curving south to reach the picturesque colonial village of **Irupana**, 15km away on the other side of the valley. From here you can visit **Pasto Grande**, an area of extensive but largely overgrown Inca agricultural terracing a couple of hours' walk away. Further afield you can reach the coca-growing centre of **Coripata**, about 35km north of Chulumani, by heading back along the road to La Paz as far as the turn-off at Puente Villa, where you can pick up through traffic; basic food and accommodation is available here.

Bosque Ecológico Apa Apa

9km from Chulumani on the road leading northeast to Irupana, then another 2km up the marked turn-off to the left • No fixed opening times – call ahead to organize a visit • Tours Bs55–60 per person for a group of at least five • ☎ 02 2136106, 📧 apapayungas@hotmail.com

Comprising five square kilometres of the dense and humid montane forest that once covered most of the Yungas, the **Bosque Ecológico Apa Apa** is a private nature reserve whose dense vegetation stands in stark contrast to the deforested slopes of the surrounding mountainsides. The kindly Bolivian-American family who own the reserve run **tours** (3–4hr) led by informative English-speaking guides. You're likely to see a great variety of bird life including hummingbirds and parrots; if you're lucky you may even spot deer or monkeys, while pumas and spectacled bears inhabit the higher reaches.

ARRIVAL AND DEPARTURE   AROUND CHULUMANI

Irupana Served by frequent micros from Chulumani and La Paz.

Coripata Occasional *camionetas* travel 30km along a very rough road to Coroico. There are no regular buses between Coripata and Chulumani; a taxi costs around Bs150.

Bosque Ecológico Apa Apa The owners will pick you up from Chulumani if you contact them in advance; otherwise, you'll need to walk or take a taxi; try Delfin Murillo Rios (around Bs35; ☎ 7255 4386).

2

AFRO-BOLIVIANOS

Isolated in a handful of villages in the Yungas valleys is perhaps Bolivia's most forgotten ethnic group: the **Afro-Bolivianos**. Numbering about eight thousand, the Afro-Bolivianos are descendants of African slaves brought to the Andes by the Spanish during the colonial era to work in the Potosí mines. When silver-mining declined they were moved to the Yungas to work on coca and other plantations – their higher natural **resistance to malaria** meant they were more resilient workers than Aymara migrants from the Altiplano. Though slavery was officially abolished with **independence from Spain** in 1825, Bolivia's black population remained in bondage to landowners until the early 1950s. Most subsequently remained in the Yungas to cultivate coca, fruit and coffee.

The Afro-Bolivianos have been heavily influenced by their indigenous neighbours: most speak Aymara as well as Spanish, and many Afro-Bolivian women dress in the bowler hats and pollera skirts favoured by the Aymara. But they also maintain a distinctive cultural identity. The most powerful reminder of their African roots is found in their **music and dance**, such as the intricate and compelling drum-driven rhythms of musical styles like the *saya*. Incorporated into dances like the *Morenada*, seen at the Oruro Carnaval and fiestas throughout the Andes, these rhythms are also reminders of the cultural influence this small group has had on mainstream Bolivian society, despite a tendency by the authorities to ignore their existence.

ACCOMMODATION AND EATING

Bosque Ecológico Apa Apa 9km from Chulumani on the road leading northeast to Irupana, then another 2km up the marked turn-off to the left. There are clean, comfortable rooms (breakfast included) in the family's delightful old hacienda at the centre of a working farm. Guests can use the lovely pool, while the café serves delicious home-made ice cream. There's also a bucolic, fully equipped, but expensive, campsite, with hot showers and cooking facilities. Camping Bs70/tent plus Bs20/person; doubles Bs100

The Yunga Cruz Trail

Connecting Chuñavi, at the foot of the mighty Mount Illimani, with Chulumani in the Yungas (see p.131), the three to four-day **Yunga Cruz Trail** (see map p.130) is at once the toughest, most scenic and most pristine of the three Inca trails that link the Altiplano with the tropical valleys. Instead of following a river, like most Bolivian trails, the path leads along the spine of a giant ridge nearly all the way, giving trekkers a condor's-eye view of the dramatic landscape. Water is scarce and the weather unpredictable, with heavy rain a possibility even during the dry season: carry at least two one-litre water bottles per person and take waterproof clothing. Route-finding is fairly difficult, so ideally go with a guide, and take a machete, as stretches of the trail may be overgrown.

Chuñavi to Cerro Yunga Cruz

The trail starts in **Chuñavi**, a small village on the northeast slopes of Mount Illimani, six hours by road from La Paz. From here a path with Inca stonework heads east to a small lake about ninety minutes away, before curving left along a broad ridge with plenty of decent places to camp, but no good source of water. The path then continues for about two hours along the ridge and around the side of the 4378m **Cerro Khala Ciudad** (Stone City Mountain) – look out for the condors that nest amidst its soaring towers. After a sharp turn to the right, the Inca stonework suddenly stops and Illimani disappears from view. Look out for the faded white arrow painted on the rock and turn uphill – after a few big steps, you should be climbing an impressive stone staircase. Another two hours further on, the path curves to the right, leading along the top of a broad green valley. Half an hour later, a stream crosses the path. Fill up with enough water for the night and continue for another hour until you reach a soggy campsite, just below the summit of **Cerro Yunga Cruz**, the last place to pitch a tent for several hours.

Cerro Yunga Cruz to Chulumani

Soon after leaving the campsite, the trail is crossed by a stream which is the last reliable water source before Chulumani. From here, the trail descends some 2000m through dense cloudforest. After two hours, the trail splits in two; take the right fork. Half an hour later, you'll reach a clearing. Go to the end of it, then turn right, leaving the peak of Cerro Duraznuni behind you to the left. **Chulumani** should be visible in the distance to the northeast, perched on the edge of the ridge across the valley on your left. From here it's another three to four hours to the main road just southeast of Chulumani, past deforested hillsides patchworked with bright-green coca plantations.

2

ARRIVAL AND DEPARTURE   **THE YUNGA CRUZ TRAIL**

By micro A micro to Chuñavi leaves most days at around 7am from Calle Burgoa in La Paz's San Pedro neighbourhood. See the Chulumani section (p.131) for information on the return journey.

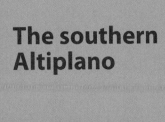

The southern Altiplano

140 Parque Nacional Sajama

142 Oruro

149 Around Oruro

150 Potosí

161 Around Potosí

165 Uyuni

168 The far southwest

174 Tupiza

178 Cordillera de Chichas

180 Villazón and the Argentine border

181 Tarija

186 Around Tarija

EL ÁRBOL DE PIEDRA

The southern Altiplano

South of La Paz, the southern Altiplano – the high plateau between the eastern and western chains of the Andes – stretches 800km to the Chilean and Argentine borders. It was formed millions of years ago by sediments washed down from the mountains into the deep valley between the cordilleras Oriental and Occidental as they were pushed up from the sea bed. Set at an average altitude of around 3700m, this starkly beautiful, barren landscape has arid steppes stretching to the horizon, where snowcapped mountains shimmer under deep-blue skies. With scant rainfall and infertile soils it supports only a sparse rural population. Since the Spanish conquest, the Altiplano's prime importance has lain in its rich mineral deposits; its silver deposits have largely run out but tin and lithium deposits remain.

3

The unavoidable transport nexus of the region is the rather grim tin-mining city of **Oruro**, 230km south of La Paz. West of Oruro, a chain of snowcapped volcanic peaks – the Cordillera Occidental – marks the border with Chile and the edge of the Altiplano. One of these peaks, **Volcán Sajama**, is Bolivia's tallest mountain and centre of a national park. Some 310km further southeast of Oruro is the legendary silver-mining city of **Potosí**, marooned at 4100m above sea level.

From **Uyuni**, 323km south of Oruro, you can venture into the dazzling white **Salar de Uyuni**, the world's biggest salt lake and one of Bolivia's best-known attractions. Beyond the Salar in far southwestern Bolivia is the **Reserva de Fauna Andina Eduardo Avaroa**, a remote region of high-altitude deserts, surreal rock formations, volcanic peaks and mineral-stained lakes that supports great populations of flamingos and vicuñas. Southeast of Uyuni the Altiplano changes character. The town of **Tupiza** is surrounded by arid red mountains and cactus-strewn badlands. Different again is **Tarija**, in the far south, a welcoming city in a fertile valley known as the Andalucia of Bolivia.

The whole region is bitterly **cold** at night, particularly from May to July. Even during the day temperatures can fall sharply, though you'll also need to protect yourself from the fierce, high-altitude sunshine.

GETTING AROUND   THE SOUTHERN ALTIPLANO

In addition to the harshness of the natural environment, travel around the region is painfully **slow**, given that few of the roads south of Oruro are paved, although the **trains** which run between Oruro and Villazón on the Argentine border offer a faster and more comfortable alternative.

Scaling Sajama's peaks p.141
Dancing with the Devil: the Oruro
  Carnaval p.143
The King of Tin: Simón Patiño
  p.146
The unique Chipaya community
  p.149
Fiestas in Potosí p.150
Double meanings: the churches of
Potosí p.156

Cerro Rico Tours p.162
Sympathy for the Devil: El Tío p.164
Tinku: ritual combat in the Andes p.165
Tours of the Salar and the Reserva
  Eduardo Avaroa p.173
Organized tours from Tupiza p.177
The last days of Butch Cassidy and the
  Sundance Kid p.179
Fiestas in Tarija p.181
Tarija's wines p.187

IGLESIA Y CONVENTO DE SAN FRANCISCO, POTOSÍ

Highlights

❶ Oruro Carnaval One of South America's most colourful folkloric fiestas, the Oruro Carnaval features thousands of dancers in extravagant devil costumes. **See p.143**

❷ Casa Real de la Moneda The monumental former royal mint in Potosí houses Bolivia's best museum and numerous stunning examples of colonial religious art. **See p.154**

❸ Churches of Potosí The highest city in the world boasts exceptional Spanish colonial-era architecture and some of the most outstanding churches in the Americas. **See p.156**

❹ Cerro Rico A journey into the labyrinthine Cerro Rico mines offers the chance to witness working conditions of incredible harshness, as well as the bizarre customs and beliefs that help the miners survive them. **See p.162**

❺ Salar de Uyuni Perhaps Bolivia's most extraordinary landscape, featuring the world's biggest salt lake – a vast expanse of dazzling white surrounded by mountains. **See p.169**

❻ Reserva de Fauna Andina Eduardo Avaroa This remote and spectacular region of icebound volcanic peaks and mineral-stained lakes is home to a surprising array of wildlife, including flamingos and vicuñas. **See p.171**

❼ Tarija Enjoy wine from the world's highest vineyards in the self-styled Andalucia of Bolivia, a charming colonial city in a warm Andean valley. **See p.181**

HIGHLIGHTS ARE MARKED ON THE MAP ON P.140

Parque Nacional Sajama

Southwest of La Paz, the road to Chile passes through some of the Altiplano's starkest scenery, a desert plain virtually devoid of vegetation presided over by the perfect snowcapped cone of **Volcán Sajama**. At 6542m, Sajama is Bolivia's highest mountain, and the first in a chain of icebound volcanic peaks known as the Cordillera Occidental that straddle the Chilean border and mark the edge of the Altiplano – although Sajama stands alone, separated from the rest of the range. Sajama is also the centre of Bolivia's oldest national park, the **PARQUE NACIONAL SAJAMA**, established in 1939 to protect the local population of **vicuñas**, a wild relative of the llama that had been

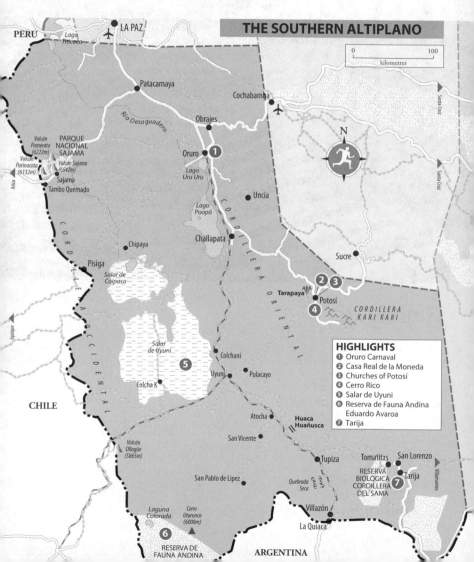

THE SOUTHERN ALTIPLANO

HIGHLIGHTS
1. Oruro Carnaval
2. Casa Real de la Moneda
3. Churches of Potosí
4. Cerro Rico
5. Salar de Uyuni
6. Reserva de Fauna Andina Eduardo Avaroa
7. Tarija

SCALING SAJAMA'S PEAKS

Mountain climbing is only allowed between April and October, when the ice on the mountain is sufficiently frozen. To climb Sajama or any of the surrounding peaks you must first register with the park administration in Sajama village (see below). They can help arrange guides, mules and porters, but you'll need to bring your own equipment and supplies. **Volcán Parinacota**, to the west of the park on the Chilean border, is also a technically simple climb and, as you can drive to the base camp, is particularly popular with climbers eager to conquer a 6000m peak.

hunted to the verge of extinction for its wool. The animals have since made a dramatic recovery, and large herds can be found grazing 25km or so north of the village at the area known as Patoca.

The park covers roughly one thousand square kilometres, encompassing the entire mountain and a large area of the surrounding desert, where pumas, Andean deer and rheas are also found – though rarely seen. Sajama's slopes also support the world's highest forest, a patch of **queñua** trees that survive up to 5200m. The records don't stop there: in 2001 the highest football match in the world was played in the crater at the top of Sajama.

Most visitors are **climbers**, drawn by the chance to ascend a peak of over 6000m that requires relatively little technical expertise. However, the mountain's lower slopes make for excellent **hiking**, and there are bubbling geysers and hot springs to be explored in the plain below. West of the park on the Chilean border, the two volcanic peaks of **Parinacota** (6132m) and **Pomerata** (6222m) provide a stunning backdrop. Known as the *payachatas* ("twins"), and considered the female consorts of Sajama, these mountains can also be scaled.

Sajama and around

The park's administrative centre is the village of **SAJAMA** at the foot of the volcano. Here you can find food, accommodation, guides, jeep hire and information. The routes to attractions close to the village are marked with signposts and are reasonably easy to follow. One of the best hikes (3–4hr each way) is up to the **Sajama base camp**, a well-marked trek that offers fantastic views. The **highest forest in the world** is about thirty minutes' walk up from Sajama village, though it's not overly impressive.

The geyser field

The **geyser field** roughly 8km west of the village in the foothills of the *payachatas* is a good excursion. An easy walk (around 1hr 30min) along a well-defined trail, the geyser field is made up of 87 different pools of boiling water. The mixture of mineral salts and algae that thrive in the warm waters creates bizarre colours, including blood reds, shiny greens and sulphurous yellows. On no account should you bathe in any of the geysers, as temperatures can change rapidly.

Aguas termales

Bs60

There are some **aguas termales** (hot springs) about 4km north of the village if you do fancy a soak, again along an easy-to-follow trail. The natural hot water is fed into an open-air pool, making it a fantastic place to relax and ease you're aching limbs while enjoying the scenery.

ARRIVAL AND DEPARTURE	SAJAMA AND AROUND

By bus Take a morning Oruro-bound bus from La Paz to the town of Patacamaya (every 30 min; 1hr 30min), from

where a micro travels to Sajama village (1 daily, usually around 1pm; 3hr 30min). Alternatively catch a bus from La

Paz headed for Arica, Chile (2 daily; 3hr 30min–4hr), and alight at the turn-off to Sajama on the main road. Jeeps (around Bs70) usually wait at the turn-off to collect passengers arriving from La Paz and take them to the village 12km away. Alternatively, you could walk to Sajama village in two-and-a-half to three hours from the turn-off.

CROSSING THE CHILEAN BORDER

Via Tambo Quemado Crossing into Chile is straightforward: the Chilean border is 9km west of the turn-off to Sajama at Tambo Quemado. There's a *migración* where you get your exit stamp and a couple of restaurants. If you're coming from La Paz the bus will take you all the way through to Arica on Chile's Pacific coast, though you may want to stop off at the Parque Nacional Lauca, which encompasses similar scenery to the Parque Nacional Sajama. If you're heading to Chile from Sajama, you can get to the border on the 6.30am micro to Patacamaya, which comes to Tambo Quemado to pick up passengers, then walk across the frontier and pick up transport on the Chilean side.

GETTING AROUND

By jeep You can rent a jeep with driver from the park office if you want transport to any of the park's attractions or back to the main road to catch a bus; most trips cost around Bs70–100 per vehicle.

INFORMATION

Tourist information Upon arrival in Sajama village you must register at the park office (daily 8am–noon & 2.30–7pm; ☎02 5135526) and pay the Bs30 entrance fee. The park rangers can answer most questions about the reserve and they can arrange porters, mules and guides (each around Bs100/day) for mountain climbers.

ACCOMMODATION AND EATING

The park rangers (see "Information") can arrange accommodation in **homestays** (Bs30–60/person) in the village: these are generally cold, bare rooms with outside toilets. If you want to **camp** at Sajama base camp – or elsewhere in the park – you need to be prepared for very low temperatures. Several places in Sajama serve simple and inexpensive set breakfasts, almuerzo and cenas, though it's best to order a few hours in advance. There are a few **shops** selling basic foodstuffs.

Albergue Tomarapi Tomarapi village, 12km from Sajama village ☎02 2414735. A significant step up in comfort, the community-run *Albergue Tomarapi* has pleasant cabins with heaters, private bathrooms and hot water, as well as a good restaurant. Staff can organize guides and excursions. Bs560 ($80)

Oruro

Huddled on the bleak Altiplano some 230km south of La Paz, **ORURO** was Bolivia's economic powerhouse for much of the twentieth century, centre of the country's richest **tin-mining** region. Mines established in the nearby mountains in the late nineteenth century turned Oruro into a thriving industrial city. After the fall of world tin prices in 1985, however, Oruro's fortunes plummeted, and though it's still the biggest city in the Altiplano after La Paz and El Alto, years of economic decline have turned it into a shadow of its former self.

Situated 3709m above sea level and swept by bitter Altiplano winds, Oruro is a cold and rather sombre place. This dour demeanour is deceptive, however, as every year Oruro explodes into life when it celebrates its **Carnaval** (see box opposite). At other times, however, there's little reason to stop here, though given its importance as a transport hub you're almost certain to pass through at some stage.

Although a few buildings dating from Oruro's heyday still survive, the city is dominated by the unappealing, functional architecture you'd expect to find in a mining town at the wrong end of half a century of decline. Architecture aside, the **Museo Antropológico Eduardo López Rivas** is one of Bolivia's better provincial museums. The **Santuario del Socavón**, focus of the Carnaval, which sits on top of an abandoned mineshaft now occupied by the **Museo Etnográfico Minero**, is also worth checking out.

DANCING WITH THE DEVIL: THE ORURO CARNAVAL

A moveable feast celebrated in late February or early March, the **Oruro Carnaval** is Bolivia's most spectacular fiesta. During the week-long party thousands of costumed dancers parade through Oruro in a vibrant and bizarre celebration of the sacred and profane that combines Christian beliefs with Andean folklore – as well as heavy drinking and chaotic water-fighting.

On the first Sunday of November the Santuario del Socavón church hosts a special Mass, and rehearsals are then held every subsequent Sunday until Carnaval itself. The Carnaval's main event is the **Entrada** on the Saturday before Ash Wednesday, a massive procession of costumed dancers accompanied by brass bands. The parade is led by floats festooned with offerings for the Virgen del Socavón (see p.145), in whose honour the Carnaval is held. Behind them comes the Carnaval's central feature, the **Diablada** (Dance of the Devils), led by two dancers representing Lucifer and St Michael, followed by hundreds of devil dan`cers, and massed brass bands.

On one hand, the Diablada is a morality play in which the Archangel Michael triumphs over the Devil of Christian belief. But the dance is also a celebration of the devil as an incarnation of **Huari**, the pre-Columbian god of the underworld – closely related to El Tío – (see p.164)–who owns the mineral wealth of the mines and is a jealous patron of the miners dancing in his honour.

Behind the Diablada follows a bewildering variety of other costumed dance troupes, each with its own folk history and mythology. The procession continues well into Sunday morning, and dancing and drinking takes place for much of the following week. On Ash Wednesday, townsfolk visit a series of rocks on the outskirts of Oruro to make offerings to what are claimed to be the petrified remains of the fearsome beasts defeated by the Virgin to save the town. Finally, on Thursday, the troupes conduct their **despedida fiestas**, saying their farewells until the following year.

CARNAVAL PRACTICALITIES

The main procession route is lined with benches that are rented out (Bs80–350/day) by the shop or house in front of which they stand or the tourist offices. Gringos are popular targets for water-bomb attacks, so be prepared to get soaked – and to strike back.

Brief history

Originally named the Villa Imperial de Don Felipe de Austria in honour of the reigning Spanish king, Felipe III, Oruro was **founded** on November 1, 1606, a decade after the discovery of rich **silver** deposits in the nearby Cerro Pie de Gallo. Though its mines never rivalled Potosí's, Oruro grew quickly, and by the 1670s was the second biggest city in Alto Peru, with a population of about eighty thousand.

It was the biggest Spanish city to be captured during the **Great Rebellion** of 1780–81, when the city's mestizos and criollos joined the indigenous uprising led by Tupac Amaru, massacring the Spanish-born population. This multi-class alliance did not last long: the rebel army raised from the *ayllus* of the surrounding Altiplano soon turned on the criollo instigators of the uprising, looting and burning their houses and killing their leader, Sebastián Pagador, before meeting the same fate themselves at the hands of the royalist army when it eventually retook the city.

Oruro changed hands several times during the **Independence War** (1809–24), and its economy was severely disrupted. The city gradually recovered as silver production grew again, aided by foreign capital, improved industrial technology and the completion of a railway linking Oruro with the Pacific coast in 1892. The railway meant Oruro was perfectly placed to exploit the growing world demand for **tin**, which was found in great abundance in the surrounding mountains.

The three Bolivian mining entrepreneurs who controlled most of the **mines** of Oruro – Aramayo, Hochschild and Patiño – soon came to dominate the national political scene, but their treatment of the miners sowed the seeds of their downfall. The radical FSTMB mineworkers' union that emerged from Oruro's mining camps played a key

ORURO

0 — 200 metres

3

ACCOMMODATION

Flores Plaza Hotel	1
Gran Sucre Hotel	5
Hotel Bernal	2
Hotel Hidalgo	4
Hotel Repostero	6
International Park Hotel	3

EATING & DRINKING

Bar Huari	1
Club Social Arabe	2
Confitería Center	3
El Fogón	4
Govinda	5
Nayjama	7
Suigeneris	6

role in the 1952 revolution that led to the nationalization of the mines. However, when the price of tin crashed in 1985, the mining industry collapsed; with it went the power of the miners' union and Oruro's economic fortunes. Most of the mines were closed and thousands lost their jobs; although some (gold and tin) mines have opened since, Oruro has never really recovered.

Plaza 10 de Febrero

In the city centre sits the **Plaza 10 de Febrero**, named after the date the people of Oruro joined the Great Rebellion of 1781. It has a statue of Aniceto Arce, the president who oversaw the construction of the vital first railway link between Oruro and the coast in 1892. Nearby are a few buildings hinting at past prosperity, most notably the **Palais Concert Theatre** on the southeast corner and the grandiose **post office** a block north on Avenida Montes.

Casa de Cultura Simón I. Patiño

Northwest of Plaza 10 de Febrero on Soria Galvarro • Mon–Fri 8–11.30am & 2.30–6pm • Bs10

The **Casa de Cultura Simón I. Patiño** is the city's best reminder of the great wealth the Oruro mines once produced. This elegant Neoclassical palace was built as a town house for the eponymous tin baron (see box, p.146) in the early years of the twentieth century, though by the time it was completed he no longer lived in Bolivia. Many rooms have been maintained in their original state: set around a beautifully tiled, glass-roofed central patio are the astonishingly opulent living quarters, with Venetian crystal chandeliers, Louis XV furniture and Persian carpets.

Faro de Conchupata

Entrance on the corner of calles La Plata and Montecinos • Free

Three blocks up Soria Galvarro from the Casa Cultura, a left turn takes you up a steep hill to the **Faro de Conchupata**, a lighthouse monument built to commemorate the first raising of the current Bolivian national flag, which took place on this site in 1851. The lighthouse serves no practical purpose but – municipal budget permitting – still lights up every evening. There are good views from its base.

Avenida La Paz

Most of the city's Carnaval costumes and masks are made in workshops on **Avenida La Paz**, which runs northwards parallel to Soria Galvarro, and it's worth strolling along the street to have a look at the beautiful craftsmanship. As well as being very expensive, most of the masks are too bulky and delicate to make good souvenirs, though some shops sell affordable pocket-sized copies.

Santuario del Socavón

Five blocks east of the Plaza 10 de Febrero at the foot of the Pie de Gallo mountain • Daily 9–11.15am & 3.15–5.30pm • Free

The **Santuario del Socavón** (Sanctuary of the Mineshaft) is home to the image of the Virgen del Socavón, the patron saint of miners, in whose honour the Carnaval celebrations are staged. The sanctuary was first built around 1781 to shelter the image, and was expanded and rebuilt in the 1990s. It's now a rather haphazard construction, with a modern concrete shell, a stone nineteenth-century belltower, and an elegant sixteenth-century portico. Inside, the high, arched ceiling is painted with bright frescoes of the Virgen del Socavón defending Oruro from various supernatural menaces.

3

THE KING OF TIN: SIMÓN PATIÑO

Few individuals played a greater role in shaping modern Bolivia than tin baron **Simón Patiño**, who rose from humble mestizo origins to become one of the world's richest men, popularly known as the "Rockefeller of the Andes" and the "King of Tin". Born in 1860 to a poor family in the Cochabamba valley, Patiño moved to Oruro in 1894 to work in a mining supply store. A year later he bought his first share in the nearby **La Salvadora mine**, and in 1897 bought out his partner to control what turned out to be one of the biggest deposits of **high-grade tin** in the world. Legend has it that at first he and his wife Albina dug out the precious ore with their own hands, carried it downhill in wheelbarrows and then across country by llama train. But in 1900 Patiño struck one of the richest veins of ore ever found in Bolivia, which was to make his fortune.

By 1905, La Salvadora was the **country's most productive mine**, operated by foreign technicians with high-tech equipment. Patiño used the wealth it generated to buy up the surrounding mines and link them to the main railway line to the coast. Within fifteen years he controlled **about half of Bolivia's tin output**, was the country's most important private banker, and enjoyed an income far greater than the government, which he effectively controlled. This wealth came at the expense of the thousands of miners he employed. However, these miners suffered low pay, appalling working conditions and **severe oppression**.

Patiño also expanded his empire internationally, buying up mining interests and foundries in Asia, Africa, Germany, the USA and Britain. This corporation controlled the entire production process for about a quarter of the world's tin and played an important role in **setting international prices**. Rumoured to have Nazi sympathies, he was said to have helped finance Franco's victory in the Spanish Civil War. By the early 1920s his fortune was estimated at **$100 million**, making him one of the five richest men in the world. Despite this, Patiño never really overcame the prejudices of Bolivia's white elite, and from 1924 onwards lived permanently abroad. In 1925 he moved his corporate base to the USA, but spent most of his time in London, Paris and the French Riviera. He died in Buenos Aires in 1947 and thus never lived to see the nationalization of his Bolivian mine holdings.

The Virgen del Socavón

Painstakingly restored, the image of the **Virgen del Socavón** stands behind the altar, painted on an adobe wall. A simple picture of the Virgin Mary in a blue robe being crowned by two cherubs, the image is said to have appeared miraculously in the late eighteenth century inside the abandoned mineshaft upon which the church is built. This mineshaft was used as a hideout by **Chiru-Chiru**, a bandit with a reputation for stealing from the rich and giving to the poor. As he lay mortally wounded in the mine after a shoot-out with the authorities, Chiru-Chiru repented before a vision of the Virgin; after his death, her image was discovered painted on the wall beside his body. Chiru-Chiru's deathbed scene is depicted in one of the stained-glass windows of the church.

Museo Etnográfico Minero

Underneath the Santuario del Socavón • Daily 9–11.15am & 3.15–5.30pm • Bs10

The abandoned mineshaft beneath the church houses the **Museo Etnográfico Minero**, which looks at the history of mining from the miners' perspective. Guided tours (in Spanish) take you into the mine via a flight of steps at the back of the church. On your way down, you'll see a lifesized statue of Chiru-Chiru. At the bottom of the shaft the mine gallery is lined with an interesting collection of **mining equipment**. At one end of the shaft stand two statues of **El Tío**, the devil-like figure worshipped by Bolivian miners (see p.164). A section upstairs is filled with Carnaval paraphernalia.

Plaza del Folklor

Directly in front of the Santuario del Socavón sits the **Plaza del Folklor**, a broad, paved square where the climax of the Carnaval procession takes place. At the south end of the square stands a modern **statue** commemorating the revolutionary role played by mineworkers in Bolivia's political history.

Museo Antropológico Eduardo López Rivas

On Av España in the city's southern outskirts • Mon–Fri 8am–noon & 2–6pm, Sat & Sun 10am–6pm • Bs5 • Take a taxi (Bs10–15) or micro #7, #101 or #102 heading south from Plaza 10 de Febrero

The **Museo Antropológico Eduardo López Rivas** has an extensive collection of artefacts, ranging from ancient stone axes and arrowheads to Carnaval masks and costumes. Sadly, though, most of the displays are poorly explained, with little background information. Many exhibits are from the **Aymara** or **Colla** kingdoms that dominated the Altiplano between the fall of Tiwanaku and the Inca conquest of the region in the fifteenth century. Another section of the museum is dedicated to the **Chipayas**, or Urus, the ethnic group which was probably the first to inhabit the Altiplano, but is now confined to a small territory around the Salar de Coipasa, west of Oruro.

Museo de Mineralogía

A few kilometres southwest of the city on Calle Universidad • Mon–Fri 9am–noon & 2.30–6pm • Bs10 • Take a taxi (Bs10–15) or any micro marked "Ciudad Universitaria" from outside the train station

The **Museo de Mineralogía** has one of South America's biggest collections of minerals – about four thousand different pieces. Of most interest to those with a specialist interest in geology or mineralogy, the bewildering variety of shapes and colours is still impressive.

ARRIVAL AND DEPARTURE   ORURO

By train Oruro is still at the centre of what's left of Bolivia's railway network. Trains (ⓦwww.fca.com.bo) south to Villazón (15hr 35min–17hr 15min) via Uyuni (6hr 50min– 7hr 20min) and Tupiza (12hr 30min–13hr 35min) depart four times a week from the train station, just east of the centre on Av Galvarro and Aldana. The *Expreso del Sur* (Tues & Fri) is quicker and more comfortable than the cheaper *Wara Wara del Sur* (Wed & Sun).
By bus All buses heading south or west from La Paz pass through Oruro. Most long-distance buses pull in at the

Terminal Terrestre, ten blocks northeast of the centre on Villarroel. A taxi into town should cost Bs6; alternatively take any micro heading south along Av 6 de Agosto. There are frequent buses to Cochabamba (hourly; 6hr), La Paz (roughly every 30min; 3hr 30min) and Santa Cruz (hourly; 12hr), and less regular services to Iquique, Chile (daily; 8hr), Potosí (8hr), Sucre (11hr), Uyuni (7–9hr) and Villazón (15hr). Buses passing through from Tarija en route to La Paz will drop you off on Av Ejército on the eastern outskirts of the city.

INFORMATION

Tourist information There are information offices at the bus station (daily 24hr), opposite the train station (Sat & Sun 8am–noon & 2.30–6pm) and in the old theatre on

Plaza 10 de Febrero (Mon–Fri 8am–noon & 2.30–6pm; ☎02 5250144); opening times at each should be taken with a pinch of salt.

ACCOMMODATION

There's a decent range of places to stay, though everything fills up during **Carnaval** (in late Feb or early March), when prices go up by as much as five times, and most places only rent rooms for a minimum of three nights. It's best to book well in advance, though even if you arrive the day before you should be able to find a place to sleep in a **private home** – ask at one of the tourist offices.

Flores Plaza Hotel Av A. Mier 735 ☎02 5252561, ⓦfloresplazahotel.com. This modern hotel overlooking the main plaza couldn't be more central. The rooms are

clean and functional: all have en-suite bathrooms and TVs; those at the top also have great views. There's also a restaurant, bar and disco. Breakfast included. **Bs290**

Gran Sucre Hotel Sucre 510 ☎ 02 5276800, ✆ hotebol .com.bo. Characterful hotel harking back to Oruro's heyday, with elegant wood-panelled corridors and a glass-roofed ballroom (where the included breakfast is now served). The rooms are cosy with floral furnishings, private bathrooms, TVs and phones. There's also an internet café. **Bs310**

Hotel Bernal Av Brasil 701, opposite the bus terminal ☎ 02 5279468. Rooms are dilapidated but good value, with abundant hot water in the private or shared baths; choose one of the quieter ones at the back. There's internet access and helpful, English-speaking staff. **Bs70**

Hotel Hidalgo Av 6 de Octubre 1616 ☎ 02 5257516, ✉ hotelhidalgo@hotmail.com. Modern but gloomy place offering decent carpeted rooms with private baths and slightly claustrophobic ones without; both types have TVs and rates include breakfast. **Bs140**

Hotel Repostero Sucre 370 ☎ 02 5258001. This once elegant nineteenth-century building is now crumbling and rather rundown. The renovated rooms, however, overlook a sunny courtyard, and have comfortable beds, private bathrooms and TVs; there are also some considerably less comfortable older rooms. Breakfast included. **Bs160**

International Park Hotel Rajka Bakovick ☎ 02 5276277. Directly above the bus terminal this hotel is slowly going to seed but remains convenient if you're just overnighting in Oruro. The rooms have heaters and TV, and there's a so-so restaurant (breakfast included). **Bs250**

EATING AND DRINKING

Most restaurants don't open until mid-morning (and are closed on Sun), so for an early breakfast, head to the **Mercado Campero**. On Friday and Saturday nights restaurants and bars stay open late, while on **Calle 6 de Octubre**, stalls serve local speciality *rostro asado*, roasted sheep's head; several restaurants serve more palatable roast-lamb dishes like *mecheado* and *brazuelo*.

Bar Huari Junín and Galvarro. Once Oruro's most fashionable drinking joint, *Bar Huari* is now sadly run-down, though it still preserves a certain charm and is lively at weekends. Bolivia's national cocktail, the *chufflay* (*singani* and 7 Up), was reputedly invented here by British mining engineers. Beer Bs12–15.

Club Social Arabe Junín. Although the dining room still features Middle Eastern paintings, the odd Islamic plaque and heavy gilt mirrors, there's barely a trace of the Arabian peninsula on the menu. Still it's a friendly place with a good-value set lunch (Bs13) and live music on weekends.

Confitería Center Plaza 10 de Febrero and Meier. Mellow bar-café attracting an older crowd with good coffee, juices and snacks, giving way to beers and spirits in the evening. Snacks around Bs10.

El Fogón San Felipe and Brasil. A convenient restaurant near the bus terminal, specializing in pork dishes like *lechón* (roast pork) and *chicharrón* (deep-fried pork) and *charque* (dried llama meat, similar to jerky), all accompanied by *wa'tya* (potatoes cooked in a traditional earth oven). Mains Bs25–45.

Govinda Junín. This Hare Krishna-run vegetarian restaurant is decorated with paintings of Hindu gods, and classical Indian music plays gently in the background. The short menu features a few Indian dishes like samosas (Bs6), plus pastas, pizzas, soya burgers and fresh juices. Set lunches Bs10–16. Closed Sun.

Nayjama Pagador and Aldana. Oruro's best restaurant serves vast portions of tasty dishes like roast lamb, fresh *pejerry* (kingfish) and *surubí* (catfish), and a mixed grill known as "*El Intendente*" (Bs80) after the visiting government official who devised it. The *criadillos* (Bs50) – prairie oysters (bull's testicles) – are not for the faint-hearted. Mains Bs35–80. Closes early on Sun.

Suigeneris 6 de Octubre. This hip, low-lit joint is a good spot day or night. Earlier on it brews a fine cup of coffee (Bs6–15), and offers a predominantly fast-food menu. Later on local bands and musicians frequently take to the small stage at the front.

DIRECTORY

Banks and exchange The Banco de Crédito, at Montes and Bolívar, and Banco Union, at Mier and La Plata, change cash and travellers' cheques and have ATMs.

Hospital Hospital General (☎ 02 5277408), 6 de Octubre and San Felipe.

Internet El Planerario (Bs3/hr) on the corner of Galvarino and Bolivar.

Laundry Lavandería, Washington and Cochabamba (Bs10/kg).

Post office Half a block north of the Plaza 10 de Febrero on Pddte Montes.

Telephone office ENTEL, on Plaza Manuel Castro de Padilla.

Travel agencies Charlie Tours (☎ 02 5252979, ✉ charlietours@yahoo.com), Leon 501, runs tours both in and around Oruro, and further afield.

Around Oruro

There are a handful of worthwhile excursions around Oruro. If you're in need of some relaxation, head to the **thermal baths** at Obrajes, 25km away. **Lago Uru Uru**, meanwhile, is home to hundreds of flamingos during the rainy season. South of Oruro is **Lago Poopó**, Bolivia's second largest lake, while to the southwest is a road leading to the **Chilean border**.

Aguas termales

About 25km northeast of Oruro • Daily 7am–6pm • Bs10 • Micros heading to Obrajes leave every half-hour or so from the corner of Av 6 de Agosto and Caro

The **aguas termales** (thermal baths) at Obrajes are a good place to soak away the chill of the Altiplano. Fed by hot springs with reputedly curative powers, there are also more expensive private baths for rent, as well as places to buy drinks and snacks, and an overpriced restaurant.

Lago Uru Uru and the Chilean border

Roughly 12km southeast of Oruru, **Lago Uru Uru** is a shallow, brackish lake fed by the Río Desaguadero, which drains the overflow from Lago Titicaca to the north. During the rainy season (between Jan and March, or later if it has been a wet year) you may see hundreds of flamingos in the shallow waters of the lake. The marshy fringes of the lake have long been home to small communities of **Urus**, the oldest ethnic group of the Altiplano.

From Lago Uru Uru a rough road heads southwest to the **Chilean border** at Pisiga, 228km from Oruro, though relatively few travellers use this route. It cuts across the northern fringes of the lake along a colonial-era raised causeway, the **Puente Español**, a thirty-minute drive from Oruro. From the start of the causeway, a short walk around the lakeshore to the northwest takes you to **Chusaqueri**, a virtually abandoned farming hamlet overlooked by about a dozen pre-Columbian tombs known as **chullpas**. These 2m-high adobe structures sit on solid stone platforms, with narrow doorways and roofs tiled with flat stones.

Lago Poopó

Heading south from Oruro you pass the shallow, brackish waters of **Lago Poopó**. Flamingos are sometimes spotted here, though mining pollution has greatly reduced their numbers. At Challapata, an important market centre, the road forks: one branch continues south to **Uyuni** (see p.165); the other climbs into the mountains to the southeast, passing through a series of high plains, then dropping into a deep valley before climbing again to reach **Potosí** (see p.150), 201km from Challapata.

THE UNIQUE CHIPAYA COMMUNITY

About 180km southwest of Oruro, the remote village of Chipaya is home to the **Chipayas**, an ethnic group culturally and linguistically distinct from both the Aymara and Quechua. Now confined to a small territory in this desolate region, the Chipayas are thought to have descended from the **Urus** (see above). Driven into the unforgiving environment of this remote corner of the Altiplano over several centuries under population pressure from the Aymara, the Chipayas eke out a marginal living by growing quinoa, fishing and catching aquatic birds. Despite their desperate poverty, the Chipayas have maintained their unique language, culture and religious beliefs, and many of the village's buildings are still distinctive **circular huts** with doors made from cactus and roofs thatched with aquatic reeds. If you're interested in observing something of the Chipayas's daily life, contact **Charlie Tours** (see opposite).

Potosí

I am rich Potosí, treasure of the world, king of the mountains, envy of kings.

Legend on Potosí's coat of arms

On a desolate, windswept plain amid barren mountains at almost 4100m above sea level, **POTOSÍ** is the highest city in the world, and at once the most fascinating and tragic place in Bolivia. It owes its existence to **Cerro Rico** (Rich Mountain), which rises imperiously above the city to the south. Cerro Rico was the richest source of silver the world had ever seen: its mines turned Potosí into the richest jewel in the Spanish emperors' crown, and one of the world's wealthiest and largest cities. In the early seventeenth century its population was 160,000, far bigger than contemporary Madrid, and equal in size to London. The expression "*eso vale un Potosí*" ("this is worth a Potosí") was used in colloquial Spanish to describe anything priceless. However, this wealth was achieved at the expense of the lives of millions of indigenous forced labourers and African slaves.

Today, Potosí, a UNESCO World Heritage Site, is a treasure-trove of **colonial art and architecture**; it has more than two thousand colonial buildings, many of which have been restored. Hundreds of town houses and mansions remain, complete with red-tiled roofs and decorative balconies. Even more striking are the 25 or so **churches**: the most exuberant of these is **San Lorenzo de Carangas**. The city's most outstanding monument, however, is the **Casa Real de la Moneda**, the colonial royal mint, which has some stunning pieces of colonial religious art. Potosí's **tragic history** weighs heavily though, and is evident in the sense of sadness that seems to haunt its narrow streets and the appalling conditions still endured by miners at Cerro Rico.

A brief history of silver in Potosí

Legend has it the **Incas** were on the point of mining Cerro Rico in 1462 when a supernatural voice warned them that the gods were saving the silver for others who would come from afar. Inca Huayna Capac subsequently declared the mountain sacrosanct, naming it *Ppotojsi* (Quechua for "thunder" or "burst"). The silver was

---

FIESTAS IN POTOSÍ

Potosí is known as the "*ciudad de los costumbres*" ("the city of customs") because of the importance its inhabitants attach to traditional religious rituals and celebrations, which combine Catholic and traditional Andean beliefs.

The Circumcision of Christ (Jan 1). Procession and folkloric dances in the San Benito neighbourhood.

Día de los Compadres (Feb, two weeks before Carnaval). Miners carry the crosses (*Tata Ckacchas*) that stand at the entrances to the mines down from Cerro Rico accompanied by brass bands, dancers and dynamite explosions.

Carnaval (Feb/March). Celebrated with waterfights and costumed dances, and also the occasion for *ch'alla* – the blessing of cars, buildings and other property with ritual libations of alcohol, streamers and llama or sheep blood.

San Juan de Dios (March 8). Procession of the image of San Juan de Dios which is kept in San Lorenzo de Carangas, accompanied by folkloric dances.

Semana Santa (April). Easter is marked by a series of Masses and processions, and a special meal of seven meat-free dishes.

Pentecostés (May or June). Llama sacrifices – accompanied by eating, drinking, coca-chewing, music and dance – are performed in the mines on the seventh Sun after Easter in honour of Pachamama, the earth goddess.

San Bartolomé or **Ch'utillos** (Aug 24–26). Potosí's biggest fiesta centres on the re-enactment of an ancient legend by unmarried young men (Ch'utillos) mounted on horseback and dressed in their finest traditional costumes. Accompanied by dancers and musicians, the Ch'utillos ride to the Cueva del Diablo (Devil's Cave) near La Puerta village, where an evil spirit was reputedly exorcized by priests using a San Bartolomé statue.

Señor de la Vera Cruz (Sept 14). Procession celebrating Potosí's patron saint, whose statue is housed in Iglesia de San Francisco.

apparently rediscovered in 1545 by llama herder **Diego Huallpa**. Caught out after dark on Cerro Rico, he started a fire to keep warm, only to see a trickle of molten silver run out from the blaze. News of this reached the Spaniards, and a **silver rush** was soon under way. Over the next twenty years Potosí became the richest single source of silver in the world.

This growth was based on the extraction of surface deposits with high ore contents, which were easily processed. As these ran out and shaft mining developed, the purity of the ore declined and production costs rose. Labour also became increasingly scarce, thanks to the appalling conditions in the mines. This crisis was overcome by **Viceroy Francisco de Toledo**, who arrived in Potosí in 1572 and orchestrated the construction of a massive system of dams, artificial lakes and aqueducts to power the water wheels that crushed the ore for processing. Toledo also introduced the newly discovered amalgam process for refining silver using mercury, established the first royal mint and regulated property rights. Most importantly, he tackled the labour shortage by adapting the Inca system of mandatory labour service, the **mita**. This provided an annual workforce of about 13,500 *mitayos* at almost no cost to the mine owners.

These reforms greatly boosted silver production, and Potosí boomed for almost a century. By the beginning of the seventeenth century Potosí's population was 160,000 and the city boasted dozens of magnificent **churches**, as well as theatres, gambling-houses, brothels and dancehalls. The silver also had a global impact, funding Spain's wars and fuelling economic growth throughout Europe.

The human cost

For the **indigenous workers** and **imported African slaves** who produced this wealth, however, the consequences were catastrophic. Staying deep underground for up to a week at a time and forced to meet ever more outrageous quotas, they died at a terrible rate; outside, the highly toxic **mercury** used in processing the silver posed an equal threat to workers in the large foundries. One sixteenth-century writer described the mines as a ravening beast that swallowed men alive. Estimates of the total number who died over three centuries of colonial mining in Potosí run as high as nine million, making the mines a central factor in the demographic collapse that swept the Andes under Spanish rule.

The end of the boom

From about 1650, silver production – and Potosí – entered a century-long decline, though the city remained rich enough to be hotly disputed during the **Independence War**. However, by the time independence was won in 1825, Potosí's population was just nine thousand. From the end of the nineteenth century the city came to increasingly rely on **tin mining** – another metal found in abundance in Cerro Rico, but previously ignored. However, when the price of tin collapsed in 1985, the state-owned mines closed down or were privatized. Though cooperative miners continue to scrape a living by working Cerro Rico's tired old veins for tin and other metals, Potosí never recovered from the decline of silver production, much less the tin crash.

Plaza 10 de Noviembre

The centre of the city is the **Plaza 10 de Noviembre**, a pleasant square shaded by trees, with a fountain and a mini Statue of Liberty, erected in 1926 to commemorate Bolivian independence. The square was formerly surrounded by the city's principal church, the *cabildo* (town hall) and the first royal mint, though sadly none of these has survived. On the square's north side, the site of the original church is now occupied by the Neoclassical **catedral**, completed in 1836. Inside are striking wooden images of Christ carved in the sixteenth century by renowned sculptor Gaspar de la Cueva, who was responsible for many of the city's other religious statues; its museum was closed for research at the time of research but should re-open within the next couple years.

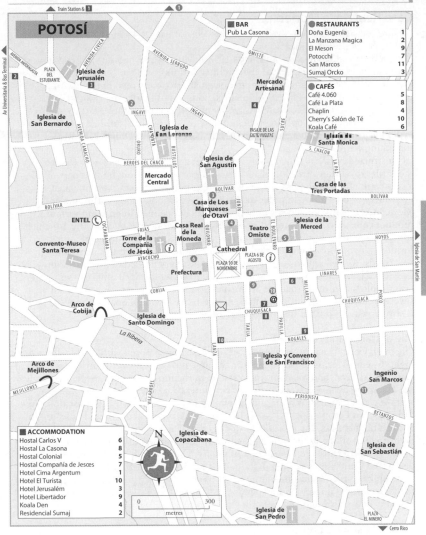

POTOSÍ

■ BAR

Pub La Casona	1

● RESTAURANTS

Doña Eugenia	1
La Manzana Magica	2
El Meson	9
Potocchi	7
San Marcos	11
Sumaj Orcko	3

● CAFÉS

Café 4.060	5
Café La Plata	8
Chaplin	4
Cherry's Salón de Té	10
Koala Café	6

■ ACCOMMODATION

Hostal Carlos V	6
Hostal La Casona	8
Hostal Colonial	5
Hostal Compañía de Jesœs	7
Hotel Cima Argentum	1
Hotel El Turista	10
Hotel Jerusalém	3
Hotel Libertador	9
Koala Den	4
Residencial Sumaj	2

3

The site of the *cabildo* is now occupied by the departmental **Prefectura**, a nineteenth-century administrative building whose simple carved stone portico is all that remains of the colonial town hall; the site of the first Casa Real de la Moneda (Royal Mint) is occupied by the late nineteenth-century **Palacio de Justicia**.

Plaza 6 de Agosto

On its eastern side, Plaza 10 de Noviembre adjoins another open space, the **Plaza 6 de Agosto**. At its centre is a column commemorating the 1824 Battle of Ayacucho, which secured Bolivian independence. On the north side is the **Teatro Omiste**, a former church, hospital and convent completed in 1753, with a recessed mestizo-Baroque facade; it was converted into a theatre in 1850. Along the east side of the plaza runs **El Boulevard**, a bustling pedestrianized street.

Casa Real de la Moneda

Calle Ayacucho, half a block west of the Plaza 10 de Noviembre • Tues–Sat 9–10.30am & 2.30–5.30pm, Sun 9–10.30am • Guided tours Bs20 (1hr 30min–2hr), camera Bs20, video Bs40

The unmissable **Casa Real de la Moneda** (Royal Mint) is one of South America's most outstanding examples of colonial civil architecture and home to Bolivia's best museum. The vast, eclectic collection includes the original machinery used in the minting process; some of Bolivia's finest colonial religious art; militaria; archeological artefacts; and a huge collection of coins. Visits are by **guided tour** only: these start soon after the morning and afternoon opening times and are conducted in Spanish, English or French depending on demand. It can be very cold inside the complex, so wear something warm.

Constructed between 1759 and 1773 for over a million *pesos de oro* to replace the earlier royal mint, La Moneda is a formidable construction, built as part of a concerted effort by the Spanish crown to reform the economic and financial machinery of the empire in order to increase its revenues. Along with Lima and Mexico City, Potosí was one of only three cities in Spanish America authorized to produce **coins**. Occupying an entire city block, La Moneda is enclosed by 1m-thick stone walls with only a few barred windows, giving it the appearance of a fortress. Inside is a two-storey complex of about two hundred rooms off five internal courtyards. As well as housing all the **heavy machinery** needed to produce coins La Moneda also housed troops, workers, slaves and senior royal officials, who were responsible for ensuring that the Spanish crown received its ten-percent cut of all silver produced in Cerro Rico's mines. A vital nerve centre of Spanish imperial power, it also served as a **prison**, treasury, and stronghold in times of strife.

The entrance and courtyard

The main Calle Ayacucho entrance is an ornate Baroque portal with double doors 4m high: the coat of arms above them, bear the lion and castle of the Spanish kingdoms of Castille and Léon, and the door knockers are in the form of the double-headed eagle of the Habsburg dynasty. Overlooking the first interior courtyard is a large plaster mask of a smiling face crowned by a garland of leaves and grapes. Known as **El Mascarón**, this caricature has become one of Potosí's best-known symbols, though neither its origin nor meaning is clear. The most likely story is that it was made by Eugenio Mulón, a Frenchman working in the mint in the mid-nineteenth century – it's variously thought to represent Bacchus, the Roman god of plenty; Diego Huallpa, the llama herder who discovered Cerro Rico's silver; a parody of either President Belzu or of the mint's director; or a veiled caricature of avarice. It has also been suggested that the mysterious mask was created during the Independence War to cover a royal coat of arms in mockery of Spanish rule.

Colonial religious art

The guided tour typically begins in a room full of **colonial paintings**, including a series depicting eighteenth-century battles between Spain and the Turks. There are also portraits of the Spanish emperor, Carlos III, and several leading mine owners. The next room is dedicated to paintings of the Virgin Mary, many of them by unnamed indigenous artists in the mestizo-Baroque style. Of these, the most outstanding is the **Virgen del Cerro**, one of the most important paintings ever produced in Bolivia. Painted in the eighteenth century by an anonymous (presumably indigenous) artist, it depicts the Virgin Mary in the form of Cerro Rico, fusing the Catholic Mother of God with Pachamama, the Andean earth goddess. From the heavens above the Virgin-mountain, the Father, Son and Holy Ghost reach down to place a crown on her he-ad. On the ground below is an earthly spiritual hierarchy of pope, archbishop and priest (bottom left), and the temporal hierarchy of emperor, town councillor and knight of Santiago (bottom right). In the sky, either side of the Virgin, are the sun and the moon, central figures in Inca religion. The mountain slopes too are richly detailed. Diego Huallpa sits by the fire that first revealed the existence of silver; miners are at work; a lordly Spaniard arrives, preceded by a priest on horseback; and at the foot of the mountain stands the Inca Huayna Capac, his presence a subtle reminder, perhaps, of the people to whom these lands once belonged.

The paintings of Melchor Pérez de Holguín

The second room on the tour is filled with paintings by **Melchor Pérez de Holguín**, who was perhaps the finest exponent of the Andean Baroque style. Known as *La Brocha de Oro* – the Golden Brush – Holguín was the outstanding painter of the Potosí School. His religious paintings found their way into all the major churches and convents of the city as well as further afield, and his style was widely imitated. The paintings here form the single biggest collection of his work, and range from his earliest efforts to the series of portraits of the Evangelists he produced shortly before his death in about 1730.

Coins and minting machinery

The third part of the tour returns to the ground floor and the massive halls in which silver was processed and coins minted. The **Numismatic Room** is filled with coins minted in Potosí. The earliest silver coins – known as *macuquinas* – were crudely made using hammers and primitive die stamps. Later coins, produced with more advanced machinery, have regular edges and clearer detail. More interesting are the massive wooden **laminadoras**, or rolling mills, used to press the silver into thin sheets from which the coins were punched. These huge, intricate and perfectly preserved machines – once powered by mules or African slaves – are the only examples of Spanish engineering of their type and era still in existence.

The smelting rooms

The tour concludes in the **smelting rooms**, where the silver was melted down before rolling – one of these has been preserved, complete with furnaces and crucibles. Other smelting rooms now house a haphazard collection of carved retables from some of Potosí's churches, plus other displays including a collection of arms and uniforms, archeological and geological finds, and silverwork.

La Torre de la Compañia de Jesús

Calle Ayacucho • Mon–Fri 8am–noon & 2–6pm, Sat 9am–noon & 2–6pm • Bs10

A block west along Calle Ayacucho from the Casa Real de la Moneda stands the bell tower of **La Torre de la Compañia de Jesús**, which is all that remains of a Jesuit church originally founded in 1581. Completed in 1707, the grandiose tower is one of Bolivia's finest eighteenth-century religious monuments and a sublime example of the mestizo-Baroque style. Climb to the top of the tower for panoramic **views** of the city and Cerro Rico. To get in, go up the stairs inside the tourist office building, whose sloping mirror-glass front reflects the tower perfectly from behind.

Convento-Museo Santa Teresa

At the western end of Calle Ayacucho • Mon–Sat 9am–12.30pm & 3–6.30pm, Sun 9am–noon & 3–6pm • Guided tours Bs21 (up to 2hr), camera Bs10

The **Convento-Museo Santa Teresa** is a beautiful colonial church and convent worth visiting both for its fine collection of colonial religious painting and sculpture, and for a somewhat disturbing insight into the bizarre lifestyle of nuns in the colonial era. Visits are by guided tour only, so get here at least an hour before closing. Built between 1686 and 1691 by the order of Carmelitas Descalzadas, the convent thrived on donations from rich mine owners, and once sprawled over several city blocks. It's now

DOUBLE MEANINGS: THE CHURCHES OF POTOSÍ

With beautifully carved porticos and interiors dripping with gold leaf, Potosí's churches are amongst the finest examples of the **mestizo-Baroque style**, in which Christian European and pre-Christian Andean symbolism are combined. The churches were built partly as a straightforward expression of religious faith, but gratitude for the wealth of Potosí also played a role: whereas Catholic churches almost always face west, those of Potosí look south towards Cerro Rico. They were also part of a determined effort to **convert** the indigenous population: with hundreds of thousands of indigenous people from different ethnic groups spending time in the city as workers under the **mita** system, Potosí offered a perfect opportunity for inculcating the Catholic faith. As well as the many churches and convents built for their own use, the Spaniards built fourteen parish churches for exclusive use by the indigenous *mitayos*.

In time, Christianity gained widespread acceptance amongst the indigenous population, at least on the surface. But as responsibility for building and decorating Potosí's churches passed to indigenous and mestizo craftsmen and artists, a very distinct religious vision began to emerge. From the second half of the sixteenth century the religious art and architecture of Potosí began to incorporate more and more **indigenous religious motifs** in a style that became known as mestizo-Baroque. The sun, moon and stars – central objects in traditional Andean religion – appear alongside images of Christ and the saints, with the Virgin Mary represented in **triangular form** like a mountain, clearly conflated with the Andean earth goddess Pachamama.

These developments did not pass unnoticed by the Spanish authorities, but allowing a little Andean religious imagery into the decoration of churches may have seemed a small price to pay for getting the indigenous population to accept Christianity, albeit superficially.

Despite their beauty, however, these churches were the product of **slave labour**, and they could scarcely conceal the contradiction between the avowed Christian beliefs of the Spanish mine owners who funded them and the brutal reality of the mining regime these same men controlled. It was said that though God ruled in Potosí's 34 churches, the Devil laughed in his six thousand mines.

greatly reduced in size, and much of what is left has been converted into the museum, though some areas are still reserved for the small surviving community of nuns – after the tour you can buy some of their delicious home-made sweets.

During the **colonial era**, young women who entered the convent as nuns renounced the material world in order to dedicate themselves to matters spiritual. These women were mostly drawn from the families of wealthy Spanish aristocrats and mine owners, who paid handsomely in return. Once inside, girls submitted to a rigid regime of prayer, work and abstinence.

The convent's simple but elegant pink stone **facade** is the oldest example of mestizo-Baroque architecture in Potosí, dating back to 1691. Inside is a peaceful complex of courtyards, gardens and cloisters, and an exhaustive collection of colonial religious art. There are more than two hundred beautifully preserved **paintings**, including outstanding works by Melchor Pérez de Holguín and Gaspar Miguel de Berrio. The convent **church** also features a lavish carved wooden Baroque retable, along with a beautiful panelled wooden roof painted in *mudéjar* style.

Arco de Cobija

Heading south from the Convento-Museo Santa Teresa and following the street down and round to the left brings you to the **Arco de Cobija** on Calle Cobija, a colonial stone gateway that once marked the entrance to the Spanish city centre from the Indian parishes to the south. Unlike the Spanish side of the city, the Indian parishes have a much more disordered layout, with narrow, cobbled streets winding between crumbling colonial and nineteenth-century houses.

Iglesia de Santo Domingo

Calle Cobija • Free

Unexceptional by Potosí's standards, the **Iglesia de Santo Domingo** dates back to 1620, but was extensively remodelled in the nineteenth century in Neoclassical style. It's rarely open to the public, but if you manage to get in before or after the Sunday-morning service, check out the carved wooden statue of the Virgen del Rosario, which was brought over from Spain in the sixteenth century and used as a model by Tupac Yupanqui when he carved the Virgen de Copacabana in 1582 (see p.100).

Calle Chuquisaca

On and around Calle Chuquisaca, a block south of Plaza 10 de Noviembre, are some of Potosí's best preserved and most luxurious **colonial town houses**, their carved stone doorways decorated with the coats of arms of the Spanish noblemen who owned them. Many are painted in pastel shades – such as pale blue or lemon yellow – or the rich ochre colour made with natural pigments from the red earth of Cerro Rico.

3

Iglesia y Convento de San Francisco

Calle Tarija • Mon–Fri 9am–noon & 2–5pm, Sat 9.30am–noon • Bs15

A couple of blocks south of Chuquisaca is the **Iglesia y Convento de San Francisco**, once a church and convent and now a museum, worth visiting for the views from its roof, as well as for its collection of colonial religious art. The original church, the first to be built in Potosí, was created when the Franciscan monastery was founded in 1547, but demolished in 1707 and replaced by the bulky structure you see today.

The main point of interest inside is the reputedly miraculous statue of the **Señor de la Vera Cruz**, the patron saint of Potosí, which stands behind the altar. According to legend, this statue of a crucified Christ appeared in front of the church one morning in 1550 and was adopted by the Franciscans. Christ's beard is made of real human hair and is said to need regular trimming, while the cross is also thought to grow a little each year – some believe the world will end when it reaches the floor of the church. Among the paintings on display are two big canvases by Holguín, one a luridly detailed Day of Judgement. The climb up onto the roof of the church is well worth it for the panoramic **views**. You can also visit the **crypts**, where the skulls of the monks and wealthy citizens buried here lie in heaps.

Ingenio San Marcos

Calle La Paz • Mon–Sat 2.30–6.30pm • Bs5

The **Ingenio San Marcos** is the only colonial-era silver foundry to have survived in a reasonable state of preservation and is now a museum. You can see the raised stone canal that carried water from the lakes and reservoirs in the mountains above the city – the water was used to power the huge waterwheel and heavy stone hammers that crushed the ore for processing – as well as the nineteenth-century furnaces used to cook the mineral ore. More machinery from the age of steel and steam is on display inside the old Republican-era plant. This also houses the *San Marcos* **restaurant** (see p.161).

Iglesia de la Merced

Calle Hoyos • Mon–Fri 11am–12.30pm & 2–6pm, Sat 11am–12.30pm • Free

A block east of Plaza 6 de Agosto along Calle Hoyos, stands the attractive **Iglesia de la Merced**, completed in 1687 alongside a Mercedarian monastery dating back to 1555. It has a two-level carved stone facade featuring the coat of arms of the Mercedarian order and there are great views from the rooftop café.

Iglesia de San Martín

Calle Hoyos • Free

The **Iglesia de San Martín** is an adobe church with a simple stone portico and a beautiful interior. It was built in 1592 as the parish church for *mita* labourers from the Lupaca tribe. Inside, the walls are covered in paintings, including individual portraits of all the archangels; behind the altar stands a fabulous wooden retable.

Along Calle Bolívar

Two blocks north of Plaza 10 de Noviembre, **Calle Bolívar** is a narrow street bustling with commercial activity, which runs past the **Mercado Central**. A short walk east of the market is the **Casa de las Tres Portadas**, an eighteenth-century colonial house with wooden balconies and three highly ornate doorways decorated with varied designs including the sun and moon, angels, floral patterns and gargoyle-like faces.

Casa de los Marqueses de Otavi

Calle Bolívar • Mon–Fri 8am–noon; open to the public but this is a working bank • Free

A colonial mansion (now occupied by the Banco Nacional de Bolivia) with a strikingly carved mestizo-Baroque stone facade – unusual in a non-religious building – the **Casa de los Marqueses de Otavi** features two lions with near-human faces holding aloft a coat of arms, flanked by the sun and moon.

El Pasaje de las Siete Vueltas

If you turn right down Calle Junín from Calle Bolívar, and then right again, you'll reach the narrow, twisting alley known as **El Pasaje de las Siete Vueltas** ("Seven-turn Passage"), the only remnant in the Spanish city centre of the disorderly street plan that existed before Viceroy Toledo ordered it to be relaid.

Iglesia de San Agustín

Bolívar and Junín • Free

The seventeenth-century **Iglesia de San Agustín** was the church used by Potosí's substantial Basque community in the colonial era. Only the simple but elegant Renaissance portico survives from the original structure, and the bare interior is rarely open.

Iglesia de San Lorenzo de Carangas

Bustillos and Heroes del Chaco • Free

Behind the Mercado Central stands the spectacular **Iglesia de San Lorenzo de Carangas**, whose splendid carved stone portal is perhaps the defining example of the mestizo-Baroque architectural style in Potosí. One of Potosí's oldest churches, it was built in the mid-sixteenth century and initially called La Anunciación and used only by the Spanish. The church was renamed a few decades later when it became the parish church for *mitayos* belonging to the Carangas tribe.

The richly decorated **doorway** was created in the eighteenth century, when the church was thoroughly remodelled. It features fantastically intricate floral patterns intertwined with twisting grape-laden vines and angels' faces, while the inner arch on either side of the door is supported by bizarre carved figures of bare-breasted women. Stranger still are the mermaids who strum guitars above the doorway: they are thought to represent creatures who figure in legends of the powerful mountain god Thunupa.

Iglesia de San Bernardo

On the south side of the Plaza del Estudiante • Free

From the Mercado Central, Calle Oruro runs northwest to the university and the Plaza del Estudiante, which is flanked by two colonial churches. The bulky **Iglesia de San Bernardo** was built from uncut stone blocks and completed in 1731. It now houses the workshops used in the ongoing restoration of Potosí's historic buildings, and though it's not officially open to the public, you can usually have a peep inside.

Iglesia de Jerusalén

On the north side of the Plaza del Estudiante • Mon–Fri 8.30am–noon & 3–6pm, Sat 9am–noon • Free

The small, late seventeenth-century **Iglesia de Jerusalén** has been converted into a museum featuring yet more colonial religious art. Highlights include an extravagant mestizo-Baroque retable covered in gold leaf, and an ornate carved pulpit decorated with tiny pictures painted on bronze by Melchor Peréz de Holguín. The most unusual painting is a portrait of **Francisco de Aguirre**, a wealthy mine owner who turned his back on worldly goods to become a priest, and is now buried in the walls of the church.

ARRIVAL AND DEPARTURE

POTOSÍ **3**

By plane The nearest airport with scheduled flights is at Sucre (see p000), which is easily accessible by bus.

By train There are trains to Sucre (8am Tues, Thurs & Sat; 6hr) from the station on Av Sevilla and Av Villazón, 1.5km northwest of the city centre; it is a pleasant trip, though much slower then travelling by road.

By bus Services to La Paz (hourly; 8–10hr), Oruro (6–7 daily; 5–8hr) and Sucre (every 30min; 3hr) arrive and depart at the Terminal de Buses on Av Universitario, on the way out of town towards Oruro; it has a small information office (daily 7am–noon & 2–8pm; ☎ 02 6227354). A taxi to

the centre costs Bs4–6. There are overnight buses to Cochabamba (8hr), Tarija (2hr), Tupiza (8hr) and Villazón (12hr). Uyuni buses (6–8hr) pull in here or at the various bus company offices on the corner of Av Universitario and Sevilla, two blocks up; most depart around 10am. There is a Bs2 departure tax for all buses. A new terminal has been mooted for some time.

By taxi Quick collective taxis for Sucre (2hr 30min) depart from behind the bus terminal as soon as they have at least four passengers; to save a wait, organize through your hotel.

GETTING AROUND

By micro You can also reach the city centre from the bus terminal by catching micro "A" heading up Avenida Universitario, which will take you to Plaza 10 de Noviembre.

On foot It is a steep walk (20–30min) up to the city centre

from the bus terminal – not much fun at this altitude. If you're arriving from the Sucre or Tarija valleys, take things easy for the first day or so until you get used to the higher altitude.

INFORMATION AND TOURS

TOURIST INFORMATION

The fairly helpful Oficina de Turismo Municipal (Mon–Fri 8am–noon & 2–6pm, Sat 9am–noon & 2–6pm; ☎ 02 6227404) is in the modern mirrored building through the arch of Torre de la Compañía on Calle Ayacucho.

TOUR OPERATORS

Most tour operators offer half-day trips to the Cerro Rico mines (see p.162) and city tours. Some also organize hikes in the Cordillera Kari Kari (see p.164). You can arrange Salar de Uyuni tours here, though this is more expensive than doing so in Uyuni.

Hidalgo Tours Bolívar and Junín ☎ 02 6229512, ⓦ hidalgotours.net. High-end operator offering mine, city and Salar trips.

Koala Tours Ayacucho 5 ☎ 02 6222092, ⓦ koalabolivia .com. Experienced, reliable operator with English-speaking mine guides. They also run hiking trips (Bs175/day) around the Kari Kari lakes, mountain biking and Macha Tinku tours (see p.165).

Sumaj Tours Oruro 143, inside Hotel Jerusalén ☎ 02 6224633, ✉ hoteljer@entelnet.bo. Friendly, well-organized company running mine and city tours, and other excursions.

ACCOMMODATION

Night-time temperatures often dip below zero, so the main consideration when choosing where to stay is **warmth**. Most of the smarter places have heating; if your hotel does not, try at least to find a room that gets some sun during the day, and ask for extra **blankets**. It's worth booking in advance if you want to stay in one of the mid- or top-end hotels, especially between June and August.

3

Hostal Carlos V Linares 42 ☎02 6231010. Charming hotel offering cosy, tasteful rooms with shared facilities and more spacious ones with private bathrooms, flatscreen TVs and huge beds. There's a communal kitchen, internet and wi-fi access, a TV and DVD lounge, laundry service and tiny pub with home-brewed beer. Breakfast included. Bs140

★ **Hostal La Casona** Chuquisaca 460 ☎02 6230523, ✉casona@boliviahostels.com. This well-run hostel is an excellent choice for anyone travelling on a tight budget. There are private rooms (with either shared or en-suite bathrooms – the latter have flatscreen TVs too) and a dorm, as well as a sociable buzz, wi-fi and internet access, a TV and DVD room, laundry service and book exchange. Breakfast included. Dorms Bs35; doubles Bs80

Hostal Colonial Hoyos 8 ☎02 6224265. Beautifully restored colonial mansion with a centrally heated modern interior and compact, well-furnished rooms set around two peaceful tiled courtyards with fountains and cacti. Breakfast included. Bs360 ($51)

Hostal Compañía de Jesœs Chuquisaca 445 ☎/☏02 6223173. Right in the centre of town, this economical hotel has a range of clean rooms, hot showers and a welcoming atmosphere. It's not the warmest place, however, so ask for extra blankets. Breakfast included. Bs100

Hotel Cima Argentum Villazon 239 ☎02 6229538, ✇hca-potosi.com. Top-end choice, a 15min (uphill) walk from the centre, with a sunny central atrium presided over by an eye-catching copper eagle. The rooms are very comfortable, if not the most stylish: each one has radiators, a fridge, TV, safe and modern bathroom. Service is sharp, and rates include breakfast and wi-fi access. Bs350 ($50)

Hotel El Turista Lanza 19 ☎02 6222492, ✉hotelturista10nov@hotmail.com. This friendly old hotel has an orange exterior, 1960s-era leather sofas and flights of rickety stairs. The rooms are slightly musty but comfortable and come with private bath, heaters, TVs and wi-fi access. For excellent views of Cerro Rico, ask for room 33 or 34 at the top of the building. Breakfast available. Bs200

Hotel Jerusalém Oruro 143 ☎02 6224633, ✉hoteljer@entelnet.bo. An unappealing exterior conceals a warm, peaceful interior with well-decorated rooms (though bathrooms could do with a spruce up) around a bright, communal balcony adorned with plants and deckchairs. Staff are helpful, and there's abundant hot water and wi-fi access. Breakfast included. Bs250

Hotel Libertador Millares 58 ☎02 6227877. Smart, modern hotel with central heating and bright rooms with private baths, flatscreen TVs and phones. Apart from a sun terrace with good views of Cerro Rico, though, it could be anywhere in the world. Breakfast included. Bs350 ($50)

Koala Den Junin 56 ☎02 6226467, ✇koalabolivia .com. Run by the tour agency of the same name (see p.159), and located just off a quaint street, this friendly hostel has clean dorms and private rooms, hot showers, a TV/DVD lounge, book exchange, laundry service, bike rental and free internet and wi-fi. It also has a smaller annexe nearby. Dorms Bs35; doubles Bs100

Residencial Sumaj F. Gumiel 12, just off Plaza Simón Bolívar ☎02 6223336. Away from the centre towards the bus terminal, this Hostelling International-affiliated is a decent choice for those travelling on a shoestring. It offers dark, boxy rooms with shared bath (and limited hot water) around a central patio; those on the second floor are a bit better. TVs cost Bs10 extra. Bs60

EATING, DRINKING AND NIGHTLIFE

Potosí has a growing variety of places to eat, with more and more cafés and restaurants offering vegetarian food and travellers' favourites. Don't miss out, however, on the tasty **local cuisine**, particularly the thick, warming soups and meat dishes cooked in spicy sauces. Most restaurants open daily except Sunday from 8–10am to around 10pm; cafés have similar opening times, though tend to close in the early evenings. The **Mercado Central** on Calle Bolívar is the best place to eat if you're on a **budget**, with coffee, pastries and *apí* – a hot thick maize drink flavoured with cloves and cinnamon – served up from early in the morning. The *salteñas* and *empanadas* sold by **street vendors** throughout the city also make tasty snacks. Outside the main fiestas, **nightlife** is fairly tame, though a few restaurants and cafés double as **bars**, which tend to come to life on Friday and Saturday nights, and several places host **live folk music** performances.

RESTAURANTS

Doña Eugenia Opposite the cemetery just off Chayanta. This inexpensive restaurant on the outskirts of the city is just about the only place that serves regional speciality *kala phurka*, a thick, spicy maize soup served in earthenware bowls into which a hot stone is plunged just before serving, so it stays piping hot and bubbles like a volcano as you eat it. Mains Bs15–40. Daily except Wed for breakfast and lunch.

La Manzana Magica Oruro 239. Welcoming vegetarian joint serving hearty breakfasts, good-value set almuerzos and a variety of salads, omelettes and snacks (all Bs10–25) including multiple takes on the veggie burger. Closed Sun evening.

★ **El Meson** Corner Tarija and Linares. One of the smartest restaurants in town with a French-flavoured menu featuring excellent steaks (including a fine chateaubriand), llama and trout, all served up by black and white-suited waiters. The decor is similarly sophisticated with exposed beams and brickwork, wooden floors and medieval-style chandeliers. Mains Bs35–40. Closed Sun.

Potocchi Millares 13. Small restaurant serving reasonable traditional Bolivian and international food (Bs20–35) – it's worth visiting for the live folk music shows it hosts several nights a week, when there's a small cover charge. Daily.

San Marcos Inside the Ingenio San Marcos museum (see p.157). Excellent restaurant with glass tables mounted on restored pieces of nineteenth-century industrial machinery and an inventive menu featuring llama carpaccio, ceviche and garlic prawns; the rainbow trout and salmon dishes are well worth trying too. You can also have a look round the museum while you're here. Mains Bs25–65. Daily for lunch and dinner.

Sumaj Orcko Quijjaro 46. Inexpensive restaurant-bar serving large portions of hearty local cuisine and good-value set almuerzos. Regional specialities include *picante de viscacha* – a large Andean rabbit-like animal cooked in a spicy sauce – and *perdiz* – a partridge-like game bird. Mains Bs20–40. Mon–Sat for breakfast, lunch and dinner; Sun breakfast and lunch only.

Café La Plata Plaza 10 de Noviembre. Slick café-bar overlooking the plaza with good coffees (Bs7–20), cakes and pastries (including *churros*) for the daytime, as well as beer (from Bs12) and wine in the evening. There's a rack of magazines and numerous board games to keep you occupied. Mon 1.30–11pm, Tues–Sat 10.30am–11pm.

Chaplin Matos and Quijjaro. Friendly place attracting a young local crowd with a wide range of inexpensive snacks (Bs5–20), including burgers and *empanadas*, plus juices and decent coffee. Daily except Sun

Cherry's Salón de Té Padilla 8. Appealing tearoom with orange walls, faux wrought iron furnishings and plastic flowers. The economical menu features breakfasts (Bs12–18), sandwiches and burgers (Bs6–13), cakes (Bs3.50–6) and ice cream sundaes (Bs15–16), as well as a few more substantial meals. Daily.

Koala Café Ayacucho 5. Mellow travellers' café opposite the Casa Real de la Moneda serving a mix of local and international dishes; if you're hungry, try the five-course set lunch/dinner (Bs40). The walls are covered with travel articles about Bolivia, and there's 15min free internet access for every diner.

CAFÉS

★ **Café 4.060** Hoyos 1. This contemporary café-bar has a slick, low-lit interior and an array of drinks: the coffee (Bs7–27) is organic and has been grown at an altitude exceeding 4060m in the Yungas, and there's a lengthy cocktail, wine and beer list. The food (mains Bs25–76) is good quality, but a little pricey. Mon–Sat 4pm–midnight.

BARS

Pub La Casona Frias 41. The liveliest nightspot in town, housed in an eighteenth-century mansion whose inside walls are decorated with contemporary graffiti. The atmosphere is friendly, with ice-cold beer and good food (Bs20–50) including excellent trout. Live music on Fri nights. Mon–Sat 6pm–12.30am.

SHOPPING

Unsurprisingly, Potosí is home to a fair number of **silversmiths**, though they tend to produce traditional religious ornaments and household items rather than fashionable jewellery. There are several silverwork shops on Bolívar and Sucre, but be careful when buying silver from street stalls as purity is often low. A wide variety of beautiful **textiles** (*tejidos*) can also be picked up: they're hand-woven by different indigenous groups in the region; the most famous weaving communities include Potolo, Chayanta and Calcha. Textiles are sold from shops on Sucre and in the **Mercado Artesanal** on the corner of Sucre and Omiste, where you can also find a good range of hand-crafted **musical instruments**. There's also a cooperative shop selling weavings from Calcha beside the Ingenio San Marcos on La Paz.

DIRECTORY

Banks and exchange The Banco Nacional de Bolivia on Bolívar changes cash and travellers' cheques. There are numerous ATMs, including the Banco de Crédito, on Bolívar and Sucre.

Internet There are plenty of cyber cafés: try the nameless

place near *Cherry's* cafe on Padilla (Bs2/hr).

Laundry Lavarap, corner of Quijjaro and Matos (Bs10/kg).

Post office Correo Central, a block south of Plaza 10 de Noviembre on Lanza and Chuquisaca.

Telephone office ENTEL, Av Camacho and Plaza Arce.

Around Potosí

There are several worthwhile excursions from Potosí, most notably to the **mines** of Cerro Rico. Immediately southeast of the city, the **Cordillera Kari Kari** is a good place for hiking amidst the lakes that provided water for the silver-processing *ingenios* (smelters). To the northwest, the natural **hot springs** at Tarapaya are a calming place to relax.

Cerro Rico

There are those who, having entered only out of curiosity to see that horrible labyrinth, have come out totally robbed of colour, grinding their teeth and unable to pronounce a word; they have not known even how to ponder it nor make reference to the horrors that are in there.

Bartolomé Arzans de Orsua, Historia de la Villa Imperial de Potosí, 1703

Immediately south of Potosí the near-perfect cone of **Cerro Rico** (Sumaj Orko in Quechua) rises above the city, its slopes stained startling hues of red and yellow by centuries of mining waste, and pockmarked with the entrances to thousands of mines. For many travellers a visit to one of the mines is a highlight of their trip to Potosí, an amazing and disturbing journey into the bowels of the earth. No less fascinating are the customs, rituals and beliefs that sustain the Quechua-speaking miners.

Most of the miners are reworking old silver mines for tin, lead and other less valuable metals, so the entrances to the shafts tend to be lined with stone facing dating back to the **colonial era**. As you descend deeper, though, the passageways become narrower and less well made. The miners work in shift teams who divide the profits of what they extract on an equal basis, though some of those working in the mines – particularly the children – are paid a fixed daily wage as employees. The miners are generally proud of their work, and are usually happy to talk about their lives with visitors. Many of the miners previously worked in large **state-run mines**; others are campesinos who come to work in the mines for short periods on a seasonal basis. Few earn more than a marginal living, though the dream of striking lucky sustains many in their labour. **Life expectancy** in the mines is about fifteen years, with most miners falling victim to the deadly lung disease **silicosis**. Cave-ins and other accidents claim the lives of many others.

Few miners eat when they are underground, relying for sustenance instead on coca leaves, harsh black-tobacco cigarettes and the occasional swig of neat cane alcohol.

CERRO RICO TOURS

Several agencies run regular **tours** to the mines (see p.159). These last half a day and cost around Bs100 per person, though some companies charge less, particularly outside the June to September high season. Most guides are former miners and know what they're talking about, though few speak more than limited English. Groups should be no bigger than eight, and you should be provided with rubber boots, a mining jacket or overalls, safety helmet and headlamp; it's worth bringing along a handkerchief to cover your mouth and some water.

Be warned, though, that this is an unpleasant and highly **dangerous** environment, where safety precautions are largely left to supernatural forces. The mines are dirty, wet, muddy and very **claustrophobic**. The air is fetid with dust and gases, including arsenic, and the chances of being hit by falling rocks or a speeding mine trolley are real. Many of the tunnels are narrow and have low ceilings, and temperatures can reach over 40°C, so walking and crawling through the mines would be exhausting even if the entrances weren't situated at over **4000m above sea level**. From every group, one or two usually head for the exit within ten minutes of entering the mine – if you don't like it, your guide will lead you out. Once inside, tours generally involve walking, crawling and clambering through often dirty and narrow tunnels deep underground for two or three hours – you should be reasonably fit and altitude-acclimatized; don't visit if you have heart or respiratory difficulties or are claustrophobic. Some people also question the ethics of making a tourist attraction of a workplace where conditions are so appalling. That said, however, most people who do visit the mines find the experience one of the most unforgettable in Bolivia.

Tours of the mines begin with a visit to the **miners' market** around Plaza El Calvario, where you can buy coca, dynamite, black-tobacco cigarettes, pure cane alcohol and fizzy drinks – take a selection of these as **gifts** for the miners you'll be visiting. Thousands of miners still work in Cerro Rico (including a high proportion of children), divided between around 27 different mining cooperatives. The most commonly visited mines include Candelaria, Santa Rita, Santa Rosita and Rosario.

SYMPATHY FOR THE DEVIL: EL TÍO

In every mine, usually in an alcove just beyond the point from which the last ray of sunlight can be seen, you'll find a statue of a sinister horned and bearded figure complete with erect phallus and leering smile. Known as **El Tío** (the Uncle) this demonic character is considered to be the king of the underworld, to whom sacrifices must be made and homage paid if miners are to stay safe and find rich deposits. El Tío is given regular **libations** of alcohol and offerings of coca and lit cigarettes, particularly on Fridays. At certain times of the year, **blood sacrifices** are also made to El Tío, with llamas being slaughtered outside the mine entrance to assuage a thirst for blood that might otherwise be satisfied only by the death of a miner. Though El Tío is clearly related to **pre-Columbian mountain deities** and is never referred to as the Devil by name, there's little doubt that he owes much to **Christian belief**. When the first *mitayos* heard Spanish priests describe heaven and hell, they can only have concluded that the mines were hell itself. If that was so, then they were working in the Devil's domain, and it was to him that they had to look for succour. To this day most miners are Christians when above ground, taking part in fiestas and worshipping Christ and the Virgin. But once inside the mines, it is to the owner of the minerals and the king of the underworld that they pray.

3

Today, as in the colonial era, **coca** is considered an essential requirement without which work in the mines would be impossible. Miners spend a good hour chewing coca before entering the shaft to begin work, and all agree that it helps them endure the heat, exhaustion and backbreaking labour. Coca, tobacco and alcohol are also taken in as offerings to **El Tío** – the supernatural being who is believed to own the mine's silver and other metals (see above).

Cordillera Kari Kari

To reach the lakes by foot, walk up to Plaza Sucre along Calle Chuquisaca, then follow the road to the southeast that turns into a track leading up into the mountains

The **Cordillera Kari Kari** is home to a network of artificial lakes, dams, aqueducts and dykes that Viceroy Toledo ordered to be built in the late sixteenth century to ensure a supply of water to the foundries in Potosí. By contemporary standards, the artificial lakes represented a monumental feat of construction, employing twenty thousand indigenous forced labourers and taking the best part of half a century to complete. During peak silver production there were 32 lakes, but only a few now survive to supply the city's water. In 1625 the retaining wall supporting Laguna San Sebastián burst, killing thousands of people.

Set amid arid red-brown mountains, the lakes are easily reached from the city and make a good place for **hiking**, albeit at altitudes of up to 5000m. If you're planning to stay overnight you'll need your own food and camping gear, and you'll have to be prepared for sub-zero temperatures. Alternatively, you can go on an organized trip (see p.159). The first lake, about 5km from the city centre, is **Laguna San Sebastián**, which is supported by a massive retaining wall, built by hand in the sixteenth century. From here you can head across the ridge to the northeast to **Laguna San Idelfonso**, about 1.5km away, or continue south along the remains of an abandoned aqueduct towards lagunas **Pisco Cocha** and **Chalaviri**. Keep sight of Cerro Rico and you shouldn't have any problems finding your way back to Potosí.

Tarapaya hot springs

Bs5 • Take a micro to Tarapaya (roughly every half-hour from Av Universitaria) and ask to be dropped off just after the bridge before Tarapaya, from where it's a ten-minute walk up the track that climbs to the left. Return taxi trip (with waiting time) Bs70

The *aguas termales* (hot springs) at **Tarapaya**, 25km northwest of Potosí, can be visited as a half-day trip. Known as **El Ojo del Inca** ("The Eye of the Inca"), the natural hot springs bubble up into a perfectly circular pool about 50m in diameter and are believed to have curative powers. As with all hot springs you should check the temperature before jumping in. Locals also strongly advise against swimming out into the centre of the pool, where they say occasional whirlpools can suck unwary bathers to their doom – best be careful and stay close to the edge. There are further, less appealing hot springs beyond Tarapaya in the resort village of **Miraflores**.

Uyuni

Set on the bleak southern Altiplano 212km southwest of Potosí, the town of **UYUNI** has little to recommend except its usefulness as a jumping-off point for journeys into the beautiful and remote landscapes of the surrounding region. Founded in 1889 at the junction of the railways that enter Bolivia from Chile and Argentina, in its heyday Uyuni was Bolivia's main gateway to the outside world, a symbol of modernity and industrial progress. Today, by contrast, its streets are lined with a collection of shabby houses and semi-abandoned railway yards.

At 3668m above sea level and with no shelter from the wind, Uyuni is a bitterly cold town that has little to distract you for more than an hour or two. The effective centre of town is the nineteenth-century **clocktower** at the intersection of Arce and Potosí. On Avenida Ferroviaria in front of the station are several monuments to the golden age of steam: keep an eye out for the **statue** of a railway worker, spanner in hand, and the well-maintained **steam locomotive**, made in West Yorkshire in the early twentieth century.

Given the decline in the fortunes of Bolivia's railways, it is surprising Uyuni hasn't become a ghost town like many of the mining settlements whose ore exports once passed through it. That it hasn't is due to the ever-growing number of travellers who

---

TINKU: RITUAL COMBAT IN THE ANDES

The **Tinku** is a form of ritual hand-to-hand combat that still takes place on certain feast days in some small rural towns in the northern areas of Potosí department. During the *Tinku*, young men from two rival communities (*ayllus*) take turns to engage in bloody one-on-one **fist fights** in the midst of a drunken and raucous fiesta. The young fighters wear **leather helmets** modelled on those worn by the Spanish conquistadors, and leather breastplates for protection. They bind their fists with woven belts, sometimes adding a stone in the palm of their hand to add extra force to their blows.

The **two-or three-day fiestas** start with the arrival of the young men from their home villages, marching and playing long panpipes known as *suqusu*. The clashes take place in a charged atmosphere of music, dancing and drunkenness. Local people and sometimes the police oversee proceedings, but as the fiesta goes on things often escalate beyond their control, with pitched battles between rival *ayllus*, and it's rare for a year to go by without someone being killed. That said, **bloodshed** is perhaps the most important part of the ritual: as well as serving as a warlike rite of passage for young men, the *Tinku* acts as a **fertility rite** during which blood must be shed on both sides to satisfy the earth goddess, **Pachamama**, and ensure a bountiful harvest. The *Tinku* is also an important way of reaffirming indigenous cultural identity, and can help defuse all too real conflicts between communities that can otherwise erupt into more serious violence. **Unmarried young women** also sometimes fight in the *Tinku*, though their aim is usually to pull hair and rip clothes rather than draw blood.

The best-known *Tinku* takes place in the community of **Macha**, 120km north of Potosí, in the first week of May, but there are several others in small villages in the region at other times of the year – including Torotoro (see p.222). Several **tour companies** in Potosí (see p.159) take groups along each year. Be warned, though, that these violent and alcoholic spectacles often get out of hand and it's easy for an outsider to unwittingly provoke trouble. If you do visit, go with a Bolivian guide who knows the area, stay clear of the crowds, don't take photographs without permission and generally exercise maximum cultural sensitivity.

Salar de Uyuni

ACCOMMODATION

Los Girasoles	2
Hostal Marith	3
Hotel Avenida	7
Hotel Jardins de Uyuni	5
Hotel Kory Wasy	4
La Magia de Uyuni	1
La Petite Porte	8
Toñito Hotel	6

EATING & DRINKING

16 de Julio	2
Arco Iris	4
Extreme Fun Pub	1
La Loco	3
Minuteman Pizza	5

UYUNI

come here to visit the spectacular scenery of the **Salar de Uyuni** and the **Reserva de Fauna Andina Eduardo Avaroa**.

Museo Municipal

Av Arce, near the corner with Colón • Mon–Fri 8am–noon & 2–6pm • Bs5

Half a block north of the town's clocktower on the left-hand side of Arce, is the small **Museo Municipal**, whose random collection of skulls, mummies, postcards and other archeological finds from the region offers a reasonable way of passing twenty minutes.

Cementerio de Trenes

A fifteen-minute walk west down Avenida Ferroviaria and along the railway line takes you to the **Cementerio de Trenes** (Train Cemetery). Set on the desolate fringe of the Salar, with good views back towards the town, this graveyard of rusting steam locomotives, passenger carriages and freight wagons that used to carry ore from long-abandoned mines is a sombre monument to the past glory of the age of steam and steel.

ARRIVAL AND DEPARTURE   UYUNI

By plane There are no flights to Uyuni as yet, but airstrips are currently being built just outside town, and in San Cristobal, a two-and-a-half-hour drive away.

By train If you're heading north to Oruro (6hr 50min–7hr 20min) and beyond, or south to Tupiza (5hr 20min–5hr 45min) and Villazón (8hr 25min–9hr 15min), you should travel by train (@ www.fca.com.bo) if possible. The *Expreso del Sur* (2 weekly in each direction) is quicker and more

comfortable than the cheaper *Wara Wara del Sur* (2 weekly in each direction). The train station is on Av Ferroviaria, in the town centre.

By bus Buses from Potosí, Oruro and Tupiza pull up in front of the various bus company offices (an area optimistically described as "the terminal"), three blocks north of the train station along Avn Arce. There are several morning and evening buses to Potosí (6–8r);

services to Oruro (2–3 daily; 7–9hr) leave in the evening. Todo Turismo (☎02 6933337, ⓦtouringbolivia .com), on Cabrera, has easily the most comfortable services to La Paz (around 10hr) via Oruro; its buses have heaters and a meal service, though cost significantly more than the competition. Several buses (6–9hr) make the scenic but rough journey to Tupiza; you may have to changes buses midway at the town of Atocha; quicker and more comfortable jeeps sometimes run for part of the journey.

CROSSING THE CHILEAN BORDER

Via Avaroa There are two ways of crossing into Chile from Uyuni. A weekly passenger train (Mon 3am; 4hr 30min) travels from the town to the Bolivian border post of Avaroa, from where there are bus connections to Calama in Chile. If you're travelling this way you'll need to get an exit stamp at the *migración* office in Uyuni, on Potosí between Arce and Sucre.

Via Laguna Verde A more popular route into Chile is across the border at Laguna Verde in the far south of the Reserva Eduardo Avaroa. Most agencies will drop you off here at the end of the tour and arrange transport across the border into Chile and on to the town of San Pedro de Atacama; make sure this is included in the cost of your tour.

INFORMATION

Tourist information There is a small tourist office (Mon–Fri 8.30am–noon & 2–6pm) in the nineteenth-century clocktower on Potosí, though it's only really worth coming here if you want to complain about a tour agency – tourist police officers share the same office. The Reserva Eduardo Avaroa (Mon–Fri 8.30am–12.30pm & 2.30–6pm; ☎02 6932400) has an office on Colón near the junction with Avaroa; you can buy your entry ticket here. The tour agencies themselves, all situated within a few blocks of Av Arce, can be a good source of information, though obviously their main aim is to sell you a trip.

ACCOMMODATION

Although the majority of Uyuni's hotels are aimed at backpackers, there are several smarter options. Most places stay open late for **train passengers** arriving in the middle of the night. Hotels fill up between June and September, when it is worth booking in advance.

Los Girasoles Santa Cruz 155 ☎02 6933323, ⓔgirasoleshotel@hotmail.com. *"The Sunflowers"* is another comfortable mid-range choice featuring pleasant rooms with private bathrooms, heaters, TVs and plenty of space. Internet access, laundry service and bike rental are all available. Rates include breakfast. Bs480 ($69)

Hotel Avenida Av Ferroviaria 11 ☎02 6932078. The best budget option in town, with clean, functional rooms set around a sunny central courtyard brightened up with rows of flowers. It's diagonally opposite the train station, and big enough to ensure getting a room is rarely a problem. Bs60

Hotel Jardins de Uyuni Av Potosí 113 ☎02 6932989. Under renovation at the time of research, this smart hotel, a short walk from the centre, has attractive communal areas slung with hammocks, a small indoor pool and a very welcome sauna. The rooms don't quite match up to the rest of the hotel, but are still very comfortable. Bs500 ($71)

Hotel Kory Wasy Av Potosí 304 ☎02 6932670, ⓔkory_wasi@hotmail.com. This friendly place has compact, somewhat bare en-suite rooms set around a plastic-roofed central hallway. Some rooms are a bit gloomy, so ask to see a few before making your choice. Breakfast included. Bs160

La Magia de Uyuni Colón 432 ☎02 6932541, ⓦhostalmagiauyuni.com. Despite a much-needed revamp this hotel still emits a certain old-world charm, with wooden bannisters and doors, chairs fashioned from salt in the covered courtyard, and antique rifles on display in the restaurant. Rooms come with private bathrooms, TVs and rustic decor. Breakfast included. Bs280

Hostal Marith Potosí 61 ☎02 6932174. This Uyuni stalwart has a motley collection of rooms set around a central courtyard; they're clean but can get very chilly. Bs60

★ **La Petite Porte** Av Ferroviaria ☎7388 5960, ⓦhotel-lapetiteporte-uyuni.com. This delightful B&B, a ten-minute walk east of the train station, has just three super-stylish rooms with wooden floors, central heating and private bathrooms. Service is excellent, and breakfast is included. Advance reservations are a must. Bs560 ($80)

Toñito Hotel Av Ferroviaria 60 ☎02 6933186, ⓦbolivianexpeditions.com. Well-run hotel with "new" and "old" wings set around two communal lounges: rooms in both are bright and comfy with private bathrooms and big beds; the new ones are a little smarter and have heaters. Staff are friendly, and there's a good book exchange, wi-fi and laundry service. An excellent breakfast is included at the attached *Minuteman* pizzaria (see p.168). Bs400 ($57)

EATING AND DRINKING

Uyuni has a limited selection of places to eat, though there are a couple of gems. Many restaurants are centred on pedestrianized Plaza Arce, though the majority only offer mediocre gringo-oriented fare. Stalls in Potosí's **indoor market** are inexpensive, though hygiene isn't always a top priority.

16 de Julio Plaza Arce. Despite recent price rises, this glass-fronted restaurant remains a good choice for its hearty Bolivian staples such as beef and llama steaks, *pique a lo macho* (fried strips of beef with chips, tomatoes, onions and chillies), *silpancho* (thin breaded steak), and passable pizzas. Mains Bs22–50. Open daily.

Arco Iris Plaza Arce. Decent but rather expensive pizza and pasta in a cosy ambience with good background music. Despite the very slow service, it's popular with travellers, particularly in the evenings. Open daily from 4pm.

Extreme Fun Pub Av Potosí. Although it doesn't quite live up to its name, this first-floor bar has a sociable atmosphere, decent food (Bs30–50), a book exchange and a wide range of *tragos* (alcholic drinks) – as well as plenty of drinking games to go with them. Daily mid-afternoon–1am. Happy hour 7–9pm.

★ **La Loco** Av Potosí. This rustic French-run restaurant-bar has an open fire, candles protruding from empty liquor bottles, and a wall covered with travellers' scribblings. The Gallic touch is more in evidence on the desserts (Bs12–15) than on the mains (Bs30–48): on offer is a trio of crêpes plus a decadent chocolate and Brazil nut tart. Mon–Sat 4pm–2am. Happy hour 7–8pm.

★ **Minuteman Pizza** Av Ferroviaria 60. Inside the *Toñito Hotel*, this pizzeria serves a truly superb buffet breakfast (Bs50) featuring delights like English muffins, bagels and muesli. The pizzas (Bs35–100), sandwiches and desserts (Bs15) keep up the high standards, and there are nice touches like photocopied crossword puzzles to keep you occupied while you wait. If you drop off your old sunglasses here, *Minuteman* will donate them to salt workers in the Salar. Open daily for breakfast and dinner.

DIRECTORY

Banks and exchange The Banco de Crédito on Potosí between Arce and Bolívar changes dollars and has a fairly reliable ATM. Many tour agencies also change dollars and travellers' cheques (the latter for a hefty commission); some occasionally accept credit card payments.

Internet Macinternet (Bs5/hr) on Potosí is one of the better cyber cafés.

Shopping Street stalls along Potosí sell woollen jumpers, hats, gloves, socks and ponchos; the Thurs market is a particularly good hunting ground.

Telephone office The ENTEL office is just south of the clocktower on Av Arce.

The far southwest

Covering some nine thousand square kilometres of the Altiplano west of Uyuni, the **Salar de Uyuni** is the world's biggest salt lake, and one of Bolivia's most extraordinary attractions. Equally dramatic is the **Reserva de Fauna Andina Eduardo Avaroa**, a 7147-square-kilometre wildlife reserve covering the most southwestern corner of Bolivia and ranging between 4000m and 6000m in altitude. South of the Salar de Uyuni, en route to the Reserva Eduardo Avaroa, you also pass **Ollagüe**, Bolivia's only active volcano, followed by a series of ancient lava fields, several lakes populated by flamingos, and some surreal rocky outcrops.

Even compared to the rest of the Altiplano, the Reserva Eduardo Avaroa and, especially, the Salar de Uyuni can get extremely cold. Though by day the sun can take temperatures as high as 30°C, the high altitude and reflective surface of the Salar mean that little heat is retained, so night temperatures can drop below -25°C, and as far as -40°C when the **wind-chill factor** is included – one of the widest day-night temperature fluctuations anywhere in the world. Take a good sleeping bag to supplement the blankets that are usually available in the refuges, a warm hat, gloves, a windproof jacket and several layers of clothing including a fleece or woollen jumper and, ideally, thermal underwear. You should also take sun block and sunglasses to counter the fierce glare – snow blindness is a real possibility here.

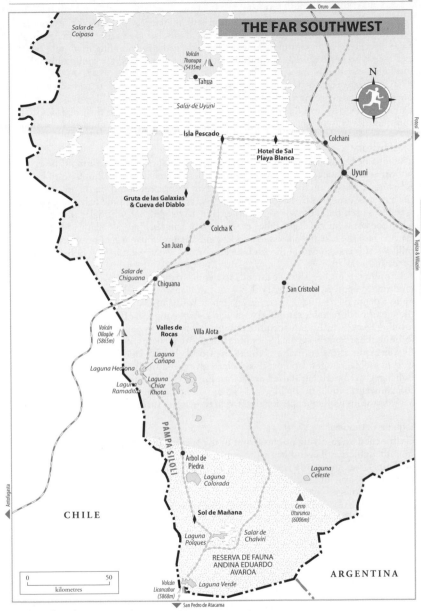

Salar de Uyuni

The **SALAR DE UYUNI** is not a lake in the conventional sense: though below the surface it is largely saturated by water, its uppermost layer consists of a thick, hard **crust of salt**, easily capable of supporting the weight of a car. Driving across this perfectly flat white expanse, with unbroken chains of snowcapped mountains lining the far horizon, it's easy to believe you're on another planet, so harsh and **inhospitable** is the terrain. When dry, the dazzling salt surface shines with such intense whiteness that it appears to be ice or snow, while by night the entire landscape is illuminated by the eerie white glow of moonlight reflected in the salt. When it's covered in water after rain (Dec to April), the Salar is turned into an enormous mirror that reflects the surrounding mountain peaks and the sky so perfectly that at times the horizon disappears and the mountains appear like islands floating in the sky.

No less strange are the tenacious **ecosystems** that survive around its arid and salty margins, including colonies of cacti and other hardy plants, rabbit-like viscachas and flamingos that nest here during the rainy season. Equally hardy are the isolated communities of Aymara and Quechua campesinos eking out a marginal existence here.

Brief history

The Salar de Uyuni occupies what was once the deepest part of an enormous lake, known as **Lago Tauca**, which covered the southern Altiplano until 12,000 years ago. Reaching depths of up to 70m, Lago Tauca existed for a thousand years and covered the area now occupied by Lago Poopó, the Salar de Coipasa and the Salar de Uyuni – and was itself the successor to an earlier lake, Lago Minchín. The Salar was formed when the last waters of Lago Tauca evaporated, leaving behind salt that had been leached into the lake from the surrounding mountains, where it had been deposited millions of years ago before the Andes were formed, when what is now Bolivia was beneath the ocean.

According to studies, the **salt** extends to depths of up to 120m, packed in layers sandwiched between sedimentary deposits. In the dry season, the surface of the Salar, up to a depth of 10–20cm, becomes extremely hard and dry. Beneath this crust, though, the salt remains saturated with water. As the top layer dries, it contracts, forming cracks which draw the underlying salt water up by capillary action, thereby forming the strange polygonal lines of raised salt that cover the Salar in the dry season. As well as salt, the Salar is also home to the world's largest deposit of **lithium** (a mineral used in mobile phones, laptops, iPods, electric cars and many other devices). The Bolivian government has started extraction projects – and international mining conglomerates would dearly like to do so too – but there are fears that mining could have disastrous consequences for the fragile ecosystems surrounding the Salar.

Legends of the Salar

For the campesinos living on the shores of the lake, explanations of the Salar's origin are rather different. Legend has it the mountain goddess **Yana Pollera** – the nearest peak to Uyuni – was amorously involved with both Thunupa, the volcano on the north shore of the Salar, and a second volcano named Q'osqo. When she gave birth to a child, the two male volcanoes fought bitterly over who was the father. Worried for the child's safety, Yana Pollera sent it far away to the west. Then, concerned that her child would not survive alone, she flooded the plain between them with her milk so it could feed. Eventually the milk turned to salt, and the lake – traditionally known as the **Salar de Thunupa** – came into being.

Colchani

Tours generally enter the Salar via **COLCHANI**, a salt-processing village on its eastern shores about 20km north of Uyuni. Here you can see how locals extract salt, scraping it off the ground into small mounds, which are then carried off for processing. Until relatively recently, communities like Colchani exploited the salt primarily to exchange with other indigenous communities. Every year dozens of pack llamas would set off carrying salt as far away as Tarija, returning with maize, coca and other goods not produced in the Altiplano, though such caravans are a rarity now. There's a small museum (Bs5) about salt in Colchani, as well as several places to buy souvenirs fashioned from salt. A few kilometres west is the **Hotel de Sal Playa Blanca**. It used to be possible to spend the night but this has been curtailed due to well-founded environmental concerns – indeed, there is talk of removing the hotel entirely; travellers are advised to boycott the hotel should their tour stop at it.

Isla de Pescado

Bs15

Tours then head 60km or so west across the Salar to the **Isla de Pescado** or Fish Island, one of several small islands in the Salar, more properly known by the traditional name of Inca Wasi ("Inca House" in Quechua). From its peak, a short sharp climb up from the shore on a well-marked trail, the views across the immense white expanse of the Salar are unforgettable. To the north is a series of snowcapped peaks, including the imperious Thunupa, the extinct volcano that is considered the region's most powerful *achachila*, or mountain god. To the west you can just make out a straight line like an old agricultural terrace running along the mountainside that rises from the shore: this is the ancient shoreline of Lago Tauca, 70m above the surface of the Salar. On the island itself, the rocks are covered in **fossilized algae.**

The island is also covered by **giant cacti**, some more than 10m tall and thought to be hundreds of years old; in January and February they produce bright white flowers that attract giant hummingbirds. The trunks of these giant cacti are about the only locally available source of wood, and you can see their distinctively pockmarked timber in doors and roofs all around the Salar.

In the rainy season this part of the Salar is sometimes too deeply flooded to be crossed by car. When it's dry enough, though, tours head straight down from Isla de Pescado via Colcha K and the island gets very busy with tours during the high season.

Ollagüe

Southwest of the Salar, on the border with Chile, the 5865m **Ollagüe** is Bolivia's only active volcano, and you can usually make out thin plumes of smoke rising from just below its peak – if you have an extra day available you can arrange with your tour operator to visit the summit. The track south runs through a series of ancient lava fields, where eroded red rock is interspersed with stretches of grey dust strewn with black volcanic rocks. It then passes a series of four brackish, blue-white lakes – Cañapa, Hedionda, Ramaditas and Chiar Khota – surrounded by snowy peaks. All four lakes support large colonies of **flamingos** and other water birds like ducks and wallata geese, and you're also likely to see herds of vicuña nearby.

The track then climbs still higher to over 4500m and across the **Pampa Siloli**, a high-altitude desert of volcanic ash and gravel scattered with rock outcrops that have been sandblasted into surreal shapes by the constant, howling winds. The strangest of these is the **Árbol de Piedra** (Stone Tree), a massive boulder 8m high that balances on a narrow stem. Amongst the rock outcrops you may catch a glimpse of a viscacha or an Andean fox.

Reserva de Fauna Andina Eduardo Avaroa

Bs150; payable at the park office by Laguna Colorada (see box, p.173)

From Colcha K, just south of the Salar de Uyuni, it's a 160km drive down to the entrance to the **RESERVA DE FAUNA ANDINA EDUARDO AVAROA**. En route you cross the edge of the smaller Salar de Chiguana, a railway line running from Uyuni to the Chilean border, and a forlorn military outpost where you may have to show your **passport**. The track then climbs above 4000m and passes a series of snow-frosted volcanoes straddling the border. It is not advisable – and, in any case, extremely difficult – to visit the reserve independently (see box, p.173).

Like the Salar de Uyuni, the desolate landscapes of the Reserva Eduardo Avaroa possess a surreal, otherworldly beauty. This is a land of **glacial salt lakes** whose icy waters are stained bright red or emerald green by microorganisms or mineral deposits; of snowcapped **volcanic peaks** and frozen, **high-altitude deserts**; of **rocky outcrops** scoured by the unremitting wind into strange, Dalí-esque formations.

There is a wide range of rare **Andean wildlife here**, including many species rarely seen elsewhere. The salt lakes support large colonies of all three South American species of flamingo, including the world's largest population of the rare James flamingo, one of the eighty different bird species found in the reserve. You're almost certain to see large herds of vicuñas grazing on the scant vegetation of the high, semi-desert grasslands. Viscachas and even the elusive Andean fox are also frequently spotted.

Laguna Colorada

Soon after entering the Reserva Eduardo Avaroa the main track drops down to the extraordinary blood-red waters of **Laguna Colorada**, the reserve's biggest lake. It owes its bizarre red colour, which changes in intensity during the day, to the natural pigments of the algae that live in its shallow, mineral-laden water. These algae are also a rich source of food for flamingos, all three species of which nest here in large numbers – the lake is thought to be the single biggest nesting site of the rare James flamingo in the world. The fringes of the lake are encrusted with bright white deposits of ice and borax, a mineral used in paint, acid and glass manufacture. The park office is here, as well as several basic huts and refuges where many tour groups spend the night. It gets bitterly cold, with temperatures often dropping below -20°C.

Sol de Mañana geyser and Laguna Polques

You need to set off before dawn the next morning in sub-zero temperatures to enjoy the full spectacle of the **Sol de Mañana geyser**. Set at an altitude of 5000m amid boiling pools of mud and sulphur, the geyser's high-pressure jet of steam shoots out from the earth to a great height, but diminishes in power later in the day. After the geyser the trail drops down to **Laguna Polques**, which has a series of **hot springs** on its southern shore. The deliciously warm waters are the perfect antidote to the high-altitude chill.

Laguna Verde

Thirty kilometres further on from Laguna Polques is **Laguna Verde**, a striking green lake set at over 4300m in the southeasternmost corner of the reserve – and, indeed, of Bolivia. Covering about seventeen square kilometres and divided into two sections by a narrow causeway, the lake owes its dramatic green hues to the arsenic and other minerals that are suspended in its waters – the lake's colour ranges from turquoise to deep emerald depending on how much the wind stirs up its sediments. Above the lake rises the perfect snow-covered cone of **Volcán Licancabur**, a 5868m dormant volcano straddling the border with Chile; on its peak are the ruins of an Inca ceremonial site.

There's a small **refuge** beside the lake, though most groups press on from here; some travellers return to Uyuni, others cross into Chile.

CROSSING THE CHILEAN BORDER — THE FAR SOUTHWEST

Via Laguna Verde You can cross into Chile at the border post 7km from Laguna Verde in the far south of the Reserva Eduardo Avaroa – it's usually possible to get an exit stamp here, though it's advisable to get one in advance in Uyuni. If you want to continue into Chile you should let the tour company you're travelling with know before leaving Uyuni, as they should be able to arrange onward transport to San Pedro de Atacama, 35km away, which otherwise may be hard to come by.

ACCOMMODATION

There are some wonderful places to stay around the **Salar de Uyuni** and the **Reserva Eduardo Avaroa**, including several hotels made from salt. It is illegal to build on the salt flats themselves, however, which is why **Hotel de Sal Playa Blanca** (see p.174) should be avoided. Another result of this regulation – and the desire to give guests a sense of isolation and tranquility – is that hotels in the region are spread out over a wide area.

TOURS OF THE SALAR AND THE RESERVA EDUARDO AVAROA

Given their remoteness, really the only way to visit the Salar de Uyuni and Reserva Eduardo Avaroa is on an **organized tour**. Even if you have your own 4WD complete with supplies and navigational aids, you should be very cautious; it's very easy to get lost, the hard crust on the surface can occasionally give way under the weight of vehicles and the consequences of a breakdown can be grave. Even with the best-maintained vehicles **mechanical failures** and breakdowns are not uncommon; drivers from different companies do, however, usually help each other out to make sure everyone gets back to Uyuni safely.

TOUR AGENCIES

Uyuni has dozens of **tour agencies**, all of which run combined trips to the Salar and the reserve. Some run one- or two-day excursions (around Bs175–420/$25–60 per person), but if you've come this far it would be crazy not to go for the full circuit. The most popular trip is a **three-day tour** taking in, among other sights, the Salar de Uyuni, Lagunas Colorada and Verde, and the Sol de Mañana geyser.

Choosing an agency can be a bit random: all offer almost **identical tours**, but all are prone to the same problems; late departures, dangerous drivers, insufficient food, inadequate accommodation and vehicle breakdowns. Agencies regularly swap drivers, guides and vehicles, and many travellers find that they booked with one company only to be put on a tour run by another. While the bigger, more expensive **La Paz-based operators** (see box, p.73) are generally reliable and have smaller groups, none of the locally based operators have a blemish-free record, and some have even been involved in fatal accidents. The best way to make a decision is by chatting with travellers who have just returned from a tour. You should also visit several companies, ask for written itineraries, check the vehicles and confirm how many other people will be in the jeep with you: six or fewer is preferable; seven or eight can be very uncomfortable. Despite all the hassles and potential pitfalls, however, these tours are well worth the trouble, and almost everyone who goes counts them among their best experiences in Bolivia.

COSTS

The standard three-day tour costs roughly Bs700–1050/$100–150 per person. You'll get charged more in **peak season** (June–Aug) and when the Salar is partly covered in water during the rainy season (Dec–April), since the salt water damages the vehicles – it can sometimes get so deep that parts of the Salar become impassable. Be wary of very cheap deals – the savings will be made at your expense. Even if you're travelling alone, you should be able to find a group easily in Uyuni. The cost includes food, accommodation, transport and Spanish-speaking guide (an English-speaking guide costs extra). You also have to pay a Bs150 fee to enter the **Reserva Eduardo Avaroa**, payable at the rangers' office at Laguna Colorada. Make sure you get a ticket when you pay; otherwise the money is unlikely to end up funding wildlife protection, as is intended.

ACCOMMODATION AND EATING

On the less expensive trips accommodation is in very basic **huts** or **refuges**. Food is usually little more than adequate, so it's worth taking along some extra supplies. On the more expensive trips, by contrast, there are some very comfortable hotels (see p.174) with equally good restaurants.

CUSTOMIZE YOUR SALAR TOUR

While the classic three-day trip is very rewarding, there is a lot of scope for creating your own tour. As well as reversing the three-day circuit (which allows you to see the Salar in glorious morning light on the final day) you can add in a connection to **San Pedro de Atacama** in Chile or **Tupiza** (see p.174). There are also some excellent hotels to stay at (see box, p.177). If you have the time and money, a four-day (or longer) trip gives you more time to explore, the chance to escape other tour groups, and the opportunity to build in extra activities: **volcano climbing** is increasing in popularity and several **hikes** are possible.

There are also other, less-touristed regions of the Salar to visit including, in the far south, the **Gruta de las Galaxias** and the **Cueva del Diablo**: the former is filled with petrified coral and algae, the latter has a pre-Inca cemetery. North of the Salar is another salt flat, the **Salar de Coipasa**. There are several other lakes to visit, including the beautiful **Laguna Celeste**, as well as the bizarre, haunting formations of the **Valles de Rocas** . The mining town of **San Cristóbal** also makes an interesting stop-off.

Luna Salada Hotel ☎ 7616 9888, ⓦ lunasaladahotel
.com. Located 30km from Uyuni and 7km from Colchani,
this slick hotel is contructed almost entirely from salt - from
the walls to the chairs to the beds (though thankfully not
the mattresses) – and also boasts a good restaurant.
Bs770 ($110)

Palacio de Sal ☎ 02 6229512, ⓦ palaciodesal.com
.bo. The "Palace of Salt", 25km from Uyuni, has
comfortable en suites, a restaurant-bar, and – somewhat
bizarrely – a nine-hole golf course (par 36; open May-
Nov). If you need a post-round pick-me-up, there's also a
spa with sauna, whirlpool, massages and salt-based
treatments. Bs945 ($135)

THE TAYKA PROJECT

The community-run sustainable-tourism Tayka project
(☎ 02 6932987 or ☎ 7202 0069, ⓦ taykahoteles.com) has
four excellent hotels in stunningly remote locations. All
have solar-power, hot water and good restaurants, and
staff can organize transport and activities.

Hotel de Piedra. The "Rock Hotel" is located at the
southern edge of the Salar, 170km northeast of the Chilean
city of Calama and close to some fascinating rock
formations and ancient remains. Although it has been
designed to look like a pre-Columbian village, the
atmospheric lodge has modern standards of comfort.
Bs665 ($95)

Hotel de Sal. Near the village of Tahua, 110km west of
Uyuni, Hotel de Sal sits in the foothills of the Thunupa
volcano. Constructed predominantly of salt, the hotel has
comfortable rooms with wooden floors, private baths and
colourful throws. Bs665 ($95)

Hotel de los Volcanes. The newest Tayka hotel, 230km
from Uyuni and 130km from Tupiza, close to the Chilean
border, looks out at the dramatic Uturunco volcano. The
terracotta-coloured lodge has homely rooms with wooden
fixtures and fittings. Bs770 ($110)

Hotel del Desierto. A 1hr 30min-drive from Laguna
Colarada and 220km from Uyuni this beautiful stone-
walled lodge is surrounded by spectacular otherworldly
terrain – at times it feels as if you are on the surface of
Mars. Bs770 ($110)

Tupiza

Some 200km southeast of Uyuni, the isolated town of **TUPIZA** nestles in a narrow,
fertile valley that cuts through the harsh desert landscape of the Cordillera de Chichas.
Sheltered from the bitter winds of the Altiplano by steep jagged mountains, the town
enjoys a comparatively warm climate, while its friendly and laidback inhabitants help
make it a popular stop for travellers passing through southern Bolivia. The real
attraction, though, is the **dramatic desert scenery** that surrounds Tupiza, a landscape of
red, eroded rock formations, cactus-strewn mountains and deep canyons that is ideal
for hiking, mountain biking, horseriding or just touring in a jeep – all of which are
easy to arrange in town.

Tupiza was founded in 1535 by the conquistador **Diego de Almagro**. For most of its
history the town's economy has been dominated by mining operations in the
surrounding mountains. In the late nineteenth and early twentieth centuries it was the
base of Carlos Aramayo, one of Bolivia's biggest mining barons, and the mine payrolls
were rich enough to attract the attentions of **Butch Cassidy** and the **Sundance Kid**
(see p.179), who are believed to have died some 100km to the northwest. Today, the
mineral deposits are largely exhausted, and Tupiza's economy depends more on its role
as a **market centre** for the agricultural communities of the surrounding region and,
increasingly, on tourism.

Plaza de Independencia

A pleasant place to hang out, Tupiza has few conventional tourist attractions. At the
centre of the main square, the **Plaza de Independencia**, stands a statue of José Avelino
Aramayo, founder of the once great Tupiza-based mining dynasty. As in most Bolivian
mining towns, the late nineteenth- and early twentieth-century civic architecture
around the square reflects a past age of prosperity now long gone. The unexceptional
Neoclassical church on the west side dates from 1897.

3

Tupiza museum

On Calle Sucre • Mon–Fri 8am–noon & 2–6pm• Bs10

There's a **museum** of sorts behind the town hall just south of the plaza, which has a limited collection of historic photographs and archeological finds. If you arrive during the official opening times to find it closed, you'll have to ask in the town hall for someone to let you in.

Statue of Christ

The hillside to the west of town is topped by a **statue of Christ**, from where there are good views over the town's tin rooftops and the narrow valley of the Río Tupiza; to reach the statue just walk a few minutes west of the plaza along Avaroa, then follow the Stations of the Cross up the hill.

El Cañon

There is a good walk (2hr return) up **El Cañon**, a deep, narrow canyon lined with spectacularly eroded rock pinnacles. Walk out of town to the west, past the church, and follow the road as it curves round behind the hill with the statue of Christ. From here, turn up the (usually) dry river bed that climbs into the mountains on your left – the canyon gets deeper and narrower as you climb.

ARRIVAL AND DEPARTURE

TUPIZA

By train The train station is three blocks east of the main plaza on Av Serrudo. You can travel north to Uyuni (5hr 20min–5hr 45min) and Oruro (12hr 35min–14hr 15min) and south to Villazón (2hr 55min–3hr) by train (ⓦ www .fca.com.bo), a far better option than the bus. The *Expreso del Sur* (2 weekly in each direction) is quicker and more comfortable than the cheaper *Wara Wara del Sur* (2 weekly in each direction).

By bus The terminal is on Av Araya, three blocks south and two blocks east of the main square, Plaza Independencia. Several buses leave every morning and evening for Potosí (8hr) and La Paz (15hr), and frequent services depart throughout the day for Villazón (2hr). A

couple of buses to Tarija (9hr) depart in the evening; if you want to travel this beautiful route by day, take an early-morning bus to Villazón and pick up a connection from there. Several buses make the rough journey to Uyuni (6-9hr) at around 10am; you may have to change buses at the town of Atocha halfway through the journey; there are sometimes quicker, more comfortable jeeps for part of the journey.

By taxi Taxis wait for arriving passengers at the train and bus stations, but everything is so close that you may as well walk. All routes out of Tupiza pass through some fairly spectacular landscapes, so try to travel in daylight.

INFORMATION

Tourist information There's no formal tourist information office, but the town's tour operators (see

below) can tell you all you need to know, though obviously with a view to selling you some kind of trip.

ACCOMMODATION

Hostal Valle Hermoso Av Pedro Araya ☎ 02 6942370, ⓦ bolivia.freehosting.net. Split between two main buildings and a smaller "backpacker" annexe, the Hostelling International-affiliated Valle Hermoso has a range of clean and sunny dorms and private rooms (with either shared or private bathrooms; most also have TVs).

There's a book exchange, laundry service, common rooms with TVs, a DVD library and a roof terrace. Dorms Bs20; doubles Bs100

Hotel La Torre Av Chichas and Chuquisaca ☎ 02 6942633, ✉ latorrehotel@yahoo.es. A fine alternative to the bigger operators, with a welcoming,

---

ORGANIZED TOURS FROM TUPIZA

Tupiza's **tour agencies** all offer broadly similar excursions into the desert landscapes around the town in 4WDs (Bs700/$100/day for a whole vehicle seating four to six) or on mountain bike, horseback or foot (Bs140–175/day), as well as longer trips to **San Vicente** (around $115/Bs805/vehicle), where Butch Cassidy and the Sundance Kid are thought to have died, and **Huaca Huañusca** (around Bs700/$100 per vehicle) where they committed their final robbery (see p.179). An increasingly popular excursion is the "triatlons", a day-trip that combines mountain biking, horseriding and a jeep ride.

Tupiza's agencies can also organize trips (around Bs1295/$185/person in a jeep seating four people for a four-day circuit) to the **Reserva de Fauna Andina Eduardo Avaroa** and the **Salar de Uyuni**, entering the reserve via the remote Sur Lípez region, heading north into the Salar and then either dropping you off in Uyuni or returning to Tupiza. This route is arguably more aesthetically pleasing than the traditional circuit leaving from Uyuni – though a rapid ascent to 5000m the second day can be a bit challenging.

La Torre Tours Inside *Hotel La Torre* ☎ 02 6942633, ⓦ latorretours-tupiza.com. Friendly, professionally run operation, with a range of tailored Salar tours and local excursions, plus trips to Sajama.

Tupiza Tours Inside *Hotel Mitru* ☎ 02 6943003, ⓦ tupizatours.com. The oldest and biggest tour operator in Tupiza, they have one of the better

reputations for Reserva and Salar tours. They also run a two-day jeep tour following the last steps of Butch and Sundance.

Valle Hermoso Tours In the *Hostal Valle Hermoso* ☎ 02 6942370, ⓦ vallehermosotours.com. Offers the same range of excursions as Tupiza Tours, as well as longer horseback camping trips.

3

family feel: there are pot plants galore, polished floors and a lovely roof terrace. Aside from a couple with shared facilities, all the rooms have private bathrooms and TVs. Rates include breakfast and kitchen access. Bs100

★ **Hotel Mitru** Av Chichas 187 ☎02 6943001, ⓦtupizatours.com. Tupiza's top hotel is divided into the older "Garden" and more modern "Cactus" sections: rooms in both are comfortable, spacious and not without style; the more expensive ones have private bathrooms, TVs and phones. There's a heated pool, central courtyard, book

exchange, wi-fi access and laundry service. Rates include breakfast. Bs90

Hotel Mitru Annexo Av Avaroa and Chichas ☎02 6943002. Just around the corner from its sister hotel, and with similar standards, Mitru Annexo has benefitted from a recent renovation. Rates include breakfast and use of *Hotel Mitru's* pool. The same management have also opened up a new budget facility, *El Refugio del Turista* on Santa Cruz, featuring basic rooms with shared bathrooms and no breakfast. *Hotel Mitru Annexo* Bs90; *El Refugio del Turista* Bs80

EATING

The cheapest place for food is at the **Mercado** (market), on the first floor of the corner of Chichas and Florida; try the tasty *tamales* (spicy meat covered with mashed corn and cooked in corn husks). There are also numerous, rather samey restaurants aimed at foreign travellers. Keep an eye out for local specialities like *asado de cordero* (roast lamb) and *cangrejitos* (soft-shelled freshwater crabs). Most restaurants open everyday from 8–10am to around 10pm, though some close early on Sundays.

Il Bambino Corner Florida and Santa Cruz. Eating at this first-floor restaurant feels a little like dining in someone's house, and appropriately the food has a homely touch: there are good breakfasts (from Bs16) and *salteñas* (meat-filled pastries) (Bs3) in the morning, decent almuerzos, and pizza, meat and chicken dishes in the evenings.

Los Helechos Inside Hotel Mitru Annexo. Popular travellers' hang-out serving all the gringo favourites (at gringo prices) including fruit salads, American breakfasts, pizza, pasta and chicken. Mains Bs20–50.

El Rinconcito Quilmes Suipacha. The best food in town, popular with locals for its filling set almuerzos (Bs12), excellent meat dishes (including delicious Argentine-style steaks), and special lamb roasts at the weekend. There's live music on Sun afternoons.

La Torre de Italiana Florida. As well as reasonable pizza and pasta (Bs25–95), this tourist-oriented restaurant has decent Mexican fare (Bs25–40), Spanish-style tortillas and a good range of coffees. Bring a book, as service takes an age.

DIRECTORY

Exchange Several cambios on Calle Avaroa will change travellers' cheques, as well as US dollars and Argentine pesos. *Hotel Mitru*, and the *Hostal Valle Hermoso* also change all of the above, and may also allow you to take cash out on your credit card (for a hefty charge).

Internet Viva near the market on Florida (Bs3/hr).
Post office The post office is just west of Plaza Independencia on Avaroa.
Telephone office The ENTEL office is on the corner of Avaroa and Av Aramayo, a block west of the plaza.

Cordillera de Chichas

Around Tupiza stretches the harsh but beautiful **CORDILLERA DE CHICAS**, a striking landscape of cactus-strewn badlands, deep gulches and canyons, and strangely shaped rock formations and pinnacles. The easiest way to see the cordillera is to take a jeep excursion with one of Tupiza's tour companies (see p.177), but travelling on foot, bike or horseback offers a much more relaxed way to explore the eerie desert landscapes and enjoy the tranquillity and ever-changing colours of the mountains, as well as giving you the chance to indulge any Wild West outlaw fantasies you may harbour. Bring plenty of water with you, particularly if travelling on foot, as the sun can be very intense and water is scarce. There are plenty of good spots to camp in the cordillera's secluded valleys, but avoid pitching your tent on river beds in case of flash floods after rain.

Quebrada de Palala

A few kilometres northwest of Tupiza along the road to Uyuni is the mouth of the **Quebrada de Palala**, a ravine formed by a tributary of the Río Tupiza. The river bed is dry for most of the year, and is used as a highway by vehicles heading to isolated mines to the northwest. If you journey 6km or so up the gorge you'll come to a series of red rock formations that have been eroded into massive fins. A few kilometres further on you'll reach a high saddle between two peaks known as **El Sillar**, around which stands a stone forest of tall pinnacles of eroded rock.

Quebrada de Palmira to the Canyon del Inca

A few kilometres southwest of Tupiza, the **Quebrada de Palmira** is another deep, cactus-strewn ravine gouged out of the red mountains by a seasonal river, with dramatic rock formations on either side. If you walk, ride or drive about 6km along the *quebrada* you'll reach the **Puerta del Diablo** ("Devil's Gate"), a gateway formed by two great vertical slabs. A few kilometres further along is the **Valle de Los Machos**, a stone forest of rock pinnacles eroded into distinctly phallic shapes. The ravine eventually peters out into a narrow canyon with steep blood-red walls, the **Canyon del Inca**.

3

THE LAST DAYS OF BUTCH CASSIDY AND THE SUNDANCE KID

The wilds of Bolivia have always attracted their fair share of renegades and desperadoes, but few have received as much posthumous attention as **Butch Cassidy and the Sundance Kid**. Made famous by the 1969 movie starring Paul Newman and Robert Redford, they belonged to a band of outlaws who robbed banks, trains and mines in the Rocky Mountains in the United States. In 1901, with the golden age of Wild West gunslingers coming to an end, a price on their heads and the ruthless Pinkerton Detective Agency (the predecessor of the FBI) hot on their trail, Butch and Sundance fled by ship to South America.

They settled in **Argentina** under assumed names, living on a ranch in the Cholilla Valley in Patagonia. But the Pinkerton Agency had not given up the hunt, and in 1905 the two outlaws went on the run after their names were linked with a bank robbery in Río Gallegos, in the far south of Argentina. They fled to **Chile**, apparently returning to Argentina to rob another bank, before showing up in **Bolivia** in 1906, where they found work at the Concordia Tin Mine – their duties, ironically, included guarding the payroll. A year later they made a trip to Santa Cruz, and Butch returned determined to start life again as a rancher in the Eastern Lowlands. Perhaps in need of capital to finance their retirement, in 1908 they quit their jobs and returned to their old ways, heading to **Tupiza**, where the wealth of the Aramayo mining company offered a tempting prize. Put off from robbing the town bank by the presence of Bolivian troops, on November 3 Butch and Sundance intercepted a convoy of mules carrying a mine payroll at **Huaca Huañusca** (see p.180), a mountain pass north of Tupiza. Finding only $90,000 rather than the half million they had expected, the outlaws fled south with the loot. With military patrols and posses of angry miners (whose pay had been stolen) scouring the countryside, and the Argentine and Chilean border guards alerted, the bandits stopped at the home of an English friend, mining engineer A. G. Francis.

Warned the authorities were on their trail, Butch and Sundance turned north, heading towards Uyuni. On November 6 they stopped for the night in **San Vicente** (see p.180), a remote mining village about 100km northwest of Tupiza. Unknown to them, however, a four-man military patrol was also spending the night in the village. Informed of the outlaws' presence, they attacked the room where Butch and Sundance were staying. After a brief shoot-out, all went quiet. In the morning, the two bandits were found dead, Butch having apparently shot his wounded partner before turning his gun on himself. The bodies were buried in an **unmarked grave** in the cemetery.

Or were they? In subsequent decades rumours suggested the two dead men were not Butch and Sundance. The two outlaws were reported to have returned to the US or Argentina having assumed new identities; one report even had them finally gunned down in Paris. In 1991 forensic anthropologists exhumed a body from the San Vicente cemetery, but were unable to settle the mystery surrounding the outlaws' fate.

Quebrada Seca

Ten kilometres to the south of Tupiza, **Quebrada Seca** is a deep and usually dry ravine with dramatic, eroded rock formations. Here, soft conglomerate rock has been worn by wind and seasonal rain into a series of spires, pinnacles and even arches, giving the sides of the valley the appearance of a Gothic cathedral.

La Angostura

A few kilometres east of Quebrada Seca, also about 10km south of town, the road and railway to Villazón pass through a narrow defile known as **La Angostura**, where the Río Tupiza has cut a deep gorge through a narrow opening – it's usually included in day-long jeep tours of the region around Tupiza, though it isn't worth making a special journey to see on its own.

San Vincente

Museum Bs10

Tupiza's tour agencies run several trips following the trail of the infamous US outlaws, **Butch Cassidy and the Sundance Kid**. Located some 100km northwest of Tupiza at an altitude of over 4300m, the bleak mining village of **San Vicente**, where Butch and Sundance are believed to have died in a shoot-out, is pretty much abandoned. There's a small museum, the adobe hut where the outlaws made their last stand, and the grave in the cemetery where they are thought to have been buried. Apart from that, however, there's little else to look at in this virtual ghost town. Note that although the trip takes 6–7 hours, you only spend an hour or so at the site.

Huaca Huañusca

There's very little to see at **HUACA HUAÑUSCA**, the mountain pass about 45km north of Tupiza where Butch and Sundance made their last robbery. There's not really much point visiting unless you have a real interest in the two dead outlaws. Having said that, quite a few travellers obviously do, and it's usually possible to get a group together for a tour within a day or two.

Villazón and the Argentine border

About 92km south of Tupiza, the ramshackle frontier town of **VILLAZÓN** is the main **border crossing** between Bolivia and Argentina. Set at an altitude of 3445m, it's a busy little place bustling with cross-border traffic. Most of the people crossing the border here are Bolivian migrants who live and work in Argentina. Unless you get stuck overnight, there's really no reason to linger here; it's better to push straight on into Argentina or to Tupiza or Tarija

ARRIVAL AND DEPARTURE

By train The train station is about 400m north of the bus terminal. The best way to travel north from Villazón is by train (🚋 fca.com.bo). There are services to Tupiza (2hr 45min–2hr 55min), Oruro (15hr 30min–17hr 10min and Uyuni (8hr 20min–9hr 45min). The *Expreso del Sur* (Wed & Sat) is quicker and more comfortable than the cheaper *Wara Wara del Sur* (Mon & Thurs).

By bus The bus terminal is just north of the central plaza on Av República de Argentina, the main road out of town. There are frequent buses to Tupiza (2hr) and several to Potosí (12hr). There are also less regular services to Oruro (15hr), overnight buses to Tarija (8hr), and services to Buenos Aires and other destinations in Argentina.

CROSSING THE ARGENTINE BORDER

Crossing the border couldn't be easier. Walk south from the plaza down to the frontier along Av Internacional and get an exit stamp at the Bolivian *migración* office (daily 24hr), then cross the bridge into Argentina, where immigration is open daily 7am–11pm. From the Argentine border town of La Quiaca there are regular buses to the city of Jujuy, from where there are connections to the rest of the country. Accommodation and food in La Quiaca are much better than in Villazón, but cost more.

ACCOMMODATION AND EATING

There are plenty of **food stalls** around the bus terminal and inside the **covered market** on the east side of the plaza, and a number of cheap fried-chicken restaurants on the way down to the border along Avenida Internacional.

Hotel Plaza On the main square ☎ 02 5963535. The best place to stay in Villazón is the clean and comfortable *Hotel Plaza*, which has simple rooms with shared baths and slightly more expensive ones with private baths and TVs. Bs80

Residencial Mirador ☎ 02 5962492. If you are on a really tight budget, head to Av Republica, which has a string of shoestring hotels including Residencial Mirador. Rooms are super basic but acceptable for a night. Bs50

DIRECTORY

Exchange Several cambios change dollars and Argentine pesos; some also change travellers' cheques, though only for a steep commission. If you're heading into Argentina, it's best to get rid of your Bolivian pesos before you cross the border.

Tarija

In the far south of the country, hemmed in by the high Altiplano to the west and the cactus-choked hills that drop down into the impenetrable forests of the Chaco to the east, isolated **TARIJA** feels a world away from the rest of Bolivia. Indeed, the country's two biggest cities, La Paz and Santa Cruz, are both 24 hours away by road. Set in a broad, fertile valley at an altitude of 1924m, Tarija lies at the centre of a rich agricultural region known as the Andalucia of Bolivia on account of its sunny climate, vineyard-filled valley and the arid mountain scenery that surrounds it. Indeed, so

FIESTAS IN TARIJA

Tarijeños are known throughout Bolivia for their love of music, dance and a good party. Though not as strongly influenced by pre-Christian beliefs as the festivals elsewhere in the Bolivian Andes, fiestas in Tarija are still deeply rooted in the agricultural cycle, as well as the calendar of Catholic saints' days. The distinctive Chapaco **folk music** features strongly at all the fiestas, played on unusual woodwind instruments like the *erque* and *quenilla*. This music is accompanied by poetic and often comic folk songs known as *coplas* – usually sung as duets. The best known of the region's folkloric **dances** is the *chuncho*, in which dancers wear brightly coloured robes, feathered headdresses and masks in ritual portrayal of the Chiriguano tribes of the Chaco.

Tarija's **Carnaval** celebrations in February or March are among the most colourful in Bolivia. On the Thursday before Carnaval, the Dia de Comadres is marked by an exchange of cakes and gifts, and a parade of all the women in the city. Carnaval itself is celebrated with a mass parade of folkloric dances and campesinos in elaborate traditional costumes, and several days of water-fighting, dancing, singing, drinking and eating. The fiesta ends with the ritual burial of the devil. The end of Carnaval coincides with the **Fiesta de la Uva** (Grape Festival) in La Concepción, 35km south of Tarija, where grape-growers show off their wares amid further celebrations.

On August 15 Tarijeños celebrate the fiesta of the **Virgen de la Asunción** with a mass pilgrimage to the village of Chaguaya, 70km south of the city. Tarija's patron saint is **San Roque**, whose fiesta is celebrated on the first weekend of September with a religious procession accompanied by troupes of *chuncho* dancers.

3

TARIJA

▲ San Lorenzo, Potosí, Villazón & Tupiza

▲ 8

Airport & Yacuiba ▲

N

0   metres   300

Mirador
San Juan

Stadium

PROMETA

Iglesia de
San Francisco

Viva
Tours

Banco de
Santa Cruz

BNB

Mercado
Central

Casa Dorada

Museo
Paleontologico

Catedral

ENTEL

PLAZA
SUCRE

PLAZA
LUISDE
FUENTES

PLAZA
URIONDO

Río Guadalquivir

Bus Terminal

Streets
POTOSI · ORURO · INGAVI · MADRID · AVENIDA BELGRANO · 15 DE ABRIL · LA PAZ · AVAROA · AVENIDA LAS AMERICAS · BOLIVAR · PADILLA · EJERCITO · O'CONNOR · JUNIN · ISAAC ATTIE · SANTA CRUZ · MADRID · DELGADILLO · MENDEZ · SUIPACHA · COLON · DANIEL CAMPOS · AVENIDA DOMINGO PAZ · SUCRE · VIRGINIO LEMA · A. DE CAPRIO · AVAROA · INGAVI · GRAL TRIGO · 15 DE ABRIL · JUAN MISAE SARACHO · CAMPERO · BALLIVIAN · RAMON ROJAS · MADRID · SEVILLA · F. MINGO · A. CORRADO

■ ACCOMMODATION
Gran Hotel Tarija	8
Hostal Carmen	5
Hostal Miraflores	3
Hostal Zeballos	2
Hostería España	1
Hotel del Sol	6
Hotel los Ceibos	7
Luz Palace Hotel	4
Victoria Plaza Hotel	9

● EATING & DRINKING
Cabaña Santa Cruz	10
Café Mokka	5
La Candela	7
Chifa New Hong Kong	9
Club Social Tarija	2
Mediterraneo	4
Nougat	3
Paparazzi	8
Taberna Gattopardo	1
El Tropero	6

striking are the similarities with southern Spain that Luis de Fuentes, the conquistador who founded the city, named the river on whose banks it sits the Guadalquivir, after the river that flows past Seville.

Laid out in a classic grid pattern, Tarija has few obvious sightseeing attractions – its appeal lies more in the easy charm of its citizens and the warm, balmy climate. Although the population has mushroomed to over one hundred thousand, the city remains provincial in the best sense of the word: small enough to get around on foot and culturally self-contained, but open to foreign influences and welcoming to outsiders. Moreover, Tarija's **Carnaval** is one of Bolivia's most enjoyable fiestas.

Brief history

Tarija was founded on July 4, 1574 as a Spanish frontier outpost on the far southeast edge of Alto Peru to guard against incursions by the indomitable **Chiriguano** tribes of the Chaco. The settlement thrived, exporting wine, cattle and grain to the mines of the Altiplano, but despite its prosperity, Tarija remained on the front line of missionary and military expeditions against the Chiriguanos – only after the final Chiriguano uprising was crushed in 1892 were outlying settlements finally freed from the threat of tribal raiders. The greatest moment in Tarija's history came during the **Independence War** on April 15, 1817, when a combined force of Argentine troops and Chapaco guerrilla riders led by a one-armed rebel named Eustaquio "Moto" Mendez defeated a Spanish army outside the city at the battle of **La Tablada**. After this victory Tarija enjoyed eight years of de facto independence before voting to join the newly proclaimed Republic of Bolivia rather than Argentina in 1825.

Tarija is famous for its **wine** production, and the valley's rich soils and fecund climate attracted many **Andalucian farmers** during the colonial period. The peasant culture they brought with them is still evident in the traditional costumes, folkloric dances, religious fiestas, love of food and wine, and languid, sing-song accents of the Tarijeños. Known as **Chapacos**, Tarijeños take considerable pride in their distinct cultural identity; closer culturally to northern Argentina, they think of themselves as a people apart from the rest of Bolivia, and though the region has provided two **presidents** in recent decades, it otherwise managed to avoid much of the upheaval of the past century.

Plaza Luis de Fuentes

Bounded by calles Madrid, Sucre, 15 de Abril and Trigo

The focal point of the city is the peaceful, palm-lined **Plaza Luis de Fuentes**, named after the city's founder, whose statue stands in the middle, dressed in full conquistador armour, flourishing his sword in front of him. Surrounding the plaza are several restaurants, cafés and ATMs.

La Catedral

A block west of Plaza Luis de Fuentes on Campero • Free

The dull modern **Catedral**'s only redeeming feature is its brightly coloured piece of stained glass depicting local peasants harvesting grapes. It stands on the site once occupied by the Jesuit college, which was founded in 1690 and provided an important base for missionary ventures down into the Chaco, before the order was expelled from the Spanish empire in 1767.

Iglesia de San Francisco

A block east of Plaza Luis de Fuentes on Madrid • Free

The simple **Iglesia de San Francisco**, founded in 1606, was Tarija's first church. The Franciscan college next door still houses a massive archive of historical documents from several centuries of Franciscan missionary endeavour, and there's also a small collection of colonial religious art inside, but you'll need to persuade one of the priests to show you around.

Museo Paleontológico

A block south of the plaza on the corner of Virginio Lema and Trigo • Mon–Fri 8am–noon & 3–6pm, Sat 9am–noon & 3–6pm • Free

The **Museo Paleontológico** has a fantastic collection of **fossils** from the Tarija valley. Most are of mammals from the Pleistocene era (between a million and 250,000 years ago), and many are from species similar to ones that still exist today, such as horses, bears and llamas. There is a complete skeleton of the extinct **Andean elephant** (mastadon), plus several skulls with tusks over 1.5m long. Also on display is an enormous skull of the **megatherium** (giant sloth), at 5m in length one of the biggest land mammals ever to exist, and said by scientists to be long extinct, though it's rumoured to live on in the depths of the Amazon rainforest. Stranger still is the fossilized skeleton of a **glyptodon**, an extinct mammal that looks like a distant relative of the armadillo. Upstairs there's a modest collection of archeological finds.

Casa Dorada

Corner of Ingavi and Trigo • Mon–Fri 8am–noon & 2.30–6.30pm • Free

The looming, garish and decidely kitsch "**Gold House**" dates back to 1903. Built in the Art Nouveau style for local businessman Moisés Navajas Ichazo and his wife Esperanza, it now functions as a museum and cultural centre. Inside much of the decor has been preserved: there are extravagant murals and frescos, crystal lamps in the dining room, and a music room with a grand piano.

Mirador San Juan

Northwest of the city centre

On a hilltop above the city, the **Mirador San Juan** is a pleasant park shaded by palm trees, with good views across Tarija and the mountains rising above the valley beyond. To get there, walk west along Avenida Domingo Paz then follow the Stations of the Cross up the hill to your right.

ARRIVAL AND DEPARTURE   TARIJA

By plane The airport (☎04 6642195) is a few kilometres east of the bus station along Av Las Américas. Departure taxes are Bs11 (domestic flights) and Bs175 (international services). A taxi into the centre costs around Bs25; there are also frequent micros. To return to the airport (or the bus terminal) catch a micro heading east along Av Domingo Paz, which runs alongside the market. There are regular flights to Santa Cruz, Cochabamba and La Paz, as well as less frequent international services to neighbouring countries.

By bus The bus terminal is ten blocks or so southeast of the city centre on Av Las Américas – roughly twenty minutes on foot. Alternatively, take a taxi (around Bs5) or one of the frequent micros that run along Av Las Américas. Buses depart for La Paz (4 daily; 24hr) via Oruro (20hr) at around 5pm and for Santa Cruz (2 daily; 24hr) via Villamontes (10–12hr) at around 4pm. There are also services to Potosí (5 daily; 12hr) and Yacuiba (6-8 daily; 10–12hr). Buses to Tupiza (2 daily; 9hr) and Villazon (1–2 daily; 8hr) depart in the morning.

CROSSING THE ARGENTINE BORDER

The closest border crossing into Argentina is at Bermejo (5–6 daily; 4hr), a town just over 200km south of Tarija.

GETTING AROUND

By micro Unusually for Bolivia, micro stops in Tarija are marked with the destination of the vehicles that stop at them, though other than travelling to the bus terminal or the airport, you're unlikely to need to use them.

By taxi Radio Taxi Tarija ☎04 6647700.

INFORMATION AND TOURS

TOURIST INFORMATION

Tarija's two main tourist information offices are friendly but of limited help; the Oficina Departmental de Turismo (Mon–Fri 8.30am–noon & 2.30–6.30pm; ☎04 6672633) is on the corner of Ingavi and Trigo; the Oficina Municipal de Turismo (Mon–Fri 8am–noon & 2.30–6.30pm; ☎04 6633581) is on the corner of Bolívar and Sucre. There is also an intermittently open tourist information booth at the bus station (☎04 6636508). Viva Tours and VTB Tours (see opposite) are better sources of information. For permission to visit the Reserva Biológica Cordillera del Sama (see p.188) and information on the region's other protected

areas, visit Prometa at Alejandro del Carpio and O'Connor (☎04 6633873, ⓦ prometa.org.bo).

TOUR OPERATORS

VTB Tours (☎04 6643372, ⓔvtb_hostalcarmen @hotmail.com), inside *Hostal Carmen* at Ingavi 784, and Viva Tours (☎04 6638325, ⓔauriventur@hotmail.com), at Bolivar 251, run enjoyable tours (from around Bs100) of the Tarija Valley's vineyards with experienced English-speaking guides. Both also take groups on the Inca Trail in the Reserva Cordillera del Sama (see p.188), while VTB runs palaeontology tours (see p.187).

ACCOMMODATION

Tarija has a good range of accommodation, almost all located in the city centre. Some of the mid-range hotels are particularly good value. Book ahead if you're visiting during **Carnaval**. All include breakfast unless stated.

3

Gran Hotel Tarija Sucre 762 ☎04 6642893. Aimed predominantly at business travellers, the rooms here are very comfortable – each has a/c, TV, safe and minibar – though somewhat lacking in character. There's also a restaurant-bar, sauna and wi-fi access. Bs210

★ **Hostal Carmen** Ingavi 784 ☎04 6643372, ⓔvtb_hostalcarmen@hotmail.com. This rightly popular hostal has well-decorated en-suite rooms with wooden floors and furniture, fans, TV and phones; there's also a small apartment with a kitchenette. Free wi-fi, filtered water, tea and coffee. Bs280

Hostal Miraflores Sucre 920 ☎04 6643355. Converted colonial house with a sunny central courtyard, efficient staff and a choice between decent rooms with TVs and private bathrooms, and tiny, spartan rooms without. No breakfast. Bs100

Hostal Zeballos Sucre 966 ☎04 6642068. Although the exterior could do with a fresh lick of paint, this *hostal* is still a decent option. It has plain, clean rooms with private bathrooms – as well as gloomy ones with shared facilities that are best avoided – and a patio overflowing with plants. There's also a laundry service. Bs100

Hosteria España Corrado 546 ☎04 6641690. This welcoming *hosteria* has small but clean rooms set around a flower-filled courtyard; the cheaper options with shared bathrooms, however, are

essentially windowless cells. Laundry facilities are available, but no breakfast. Private bathroom Bs120; shared bathroom Bs80

Hotel del Sol Sucre 782 ☎04 6665259, ⓔhoteldelsol @entelnet.bo. This stylish city-centre hotel, just across from the central market, is the best bet in its price range. The slick rooms have modern bathrooms and flatscreen TVs, and there's free internet access. Bs350 ($50)

Hotel los Ceibos Av Las Américas and Madrid ☎04 6634430, ⓦhotellosceibos.com. Luxurious hotel with warm, spacious and well-appointed rooms with TVs and wi-fi access: each one has a private balcony overlooking the large swimming pool. There's also a restaurant, bar and gym. Bs560 ($80)

Luz Palace Hotel Sucre 326 ☎04 6635700, Eluzpalac @cossett.com.bo. A lovely faintly Moorish-style courtyard is the focal point of this reliable business hotel. The en-suite rooms – with minibars, TVs and phones – are bright and comfortable rather than stylish. Rates have risen recently, but it remains a good choice. Bs450 ($64)

Victoria Plaza Hotel Madrid and Sucre ☎04 6642600. This grand, old-fashioned hotel overlooking the main plaza feels as if it is slowly fading away. The rooms, however, remain lavish and well equipped. There's a café-bar and internet access. Bs250

EATING AND DRINKING

Tarija's strong **Argentine** influence is particularly evident in its restaurants; good-quality grilled beef features strongly and is ideally accompanied by a glass of local wine. There are also some great spicy-sauced dishes to try, including *ranga-ranga* (tripe with potatoes, onions and yellow chilli), *saice* (meat in a red chilli sauce) or *chancao de pollo* (spicy chicken); the best place to sample these is in the **Mercado Central**. A particular local speciality is *sopa la poderosa*, a rich soup made with a bull's penis – considered, unsurprisingly, to be a powerful aphrodisiac. **Nightlife** involves sitting around outdoor tables with a bottle or two of wine until late at night. On the weekends, local youngsters congregate around **Plaza Sucre** to indulge in billiards, pizza and beer. Most restaurants and bars open daily except Sunday from 8–10am to around 10pm; exceptions are noted in the reviews themselves.

3

Cabaña Santa Cruz Av Las Americas, between Campero and Trigo. No frills local restaurant with a good-value almuerzo (Bs15–20) that includes a starter, salad, main meal and salad. Dishes might include *sopa de maní* (peanut soup) and grilled beef.

Café Mokka Plaza Sucre. In a great people-watching spot, this busy café has a lengthy menu featuring 22 types of coffee (Bs9–19) and Argentine-style *submarinos* (hot chocolate), as well as cocktails and beer. Food-wise the breakfast and snacks are good, but the mains are a bit overpriced.

La Candela Plaza Sucre. Cosy bar-café with a bohemian atmosphere – it attracts a lively young crowd who come here for wine and snacks (Bs10–30) in the evening.

Chifa New Hong Kong Sucre and Victor Paz. Complete with laughing Buddhas and fish tanks, the decor in this Chinese restaurant is more authentic than the food, but it still makes an enjoyable change. Main dishes big enough for two people go for about Bs25–35.

Club Social Tarija Plaza Luis de Fuentes. Good-value traditional almuerzos (around Bs15–20) in a rather staid atmosphere favoured by Tarija's business community and older citizens. Open Mon–Fri for lunch.

Mediterraneo Plaza Luis de Funtes. Pricey by local standards (mains Bs40–85), but with a classy dining room and an appealing menu with well-prepared fish (including trout and *surubi*), seafood and meat dishes (like house specialty *osso bucco*) with – as the name suggests – a Mediterranean touch. Daily for lunch and dinner.

Nougat Plaza Luis de Funtes. Sophisticated stone-walled café-bar serving tasty salads, sandwiches and wraps (all Bs16–30), pastas and steaks (Bs35–42), cakes and sundaes, plus local wines and cocktails.

Paparazzi Daniel Sossa and Ingavi. Near the cinema, a twenty-minute walk from the centre, *Paparazzi* has a good range of local and international dishes. On Fri there's live music and DJs from 9pm, and on Sun there's a lunchtime all-you-can-eat buffet (Bs45). Open daily.

★ **Taberna Gattopardo** Plaza Luis de Fuentes. Vintage typewriters, radios and rifles, jazz paintings and discreet booths give this stylish restaurant-bar plenty of character. The vast menu includes sandwiches, pizzas, pastas, grilled meat and chicken, and the odd Mexican dish, plus good coffee. Mains Bs24–56. Daily.

El Tropero Virginio Lema and Daniel Campos. This Argentine steakhouse is more authentic than the vast Coca-Cola mural that covers the exterior might suggest, serving excellent grilled beef and chicken, as well as a filling almuerzo. Mains Bs20–40.

DIRECTORY

Banks and exchange The Banco Nacional de Bolivia, opposite *Gran Hotel Tarija*, changes cash and travellers' cheques, and has an ATM. There are numerous other ATMs, including at the Banco de Santa Cruz on Trigo and Domingo Paz.

Consulate The Argentine consulate is on Ballivián and Bolívar ☎ 04 6644273.

Internet Try Ricky's (Bs3/hr) on Plaza Sucre.

Laundry La Esmeralda on Madrid between Campos and Colón.

Post office The Correo Central is on Lema and Sucre.

Telephone office ENTEL is on Lema and Daniel Campos.

Around Tarija

There are some worthwhile excursions in the warm and fertile **Tarija valley**, which is notable for its sleepy villages, easy pace of life and beautiful countryside. Just outside Tarija itself are rich **fossil deposits** that attract palaeontologists from all over the world, while further afield you can visit the bodegas and **vineyards** of the world's highest wine-producing region; the spring (Jan–April) is a great time to visit the latter, as this is when the vineyards come to fruit. Above the Tarija valley to the west, the **Reserva Biológica Cordillera del Sama** has striking high Andean scenery and an Inca trail that makes an excellent hike.

Tarija valley fossils

Free • VTB Tours Bs175

About 5km northeast of Tarija, the eroded gulches and badlands around the airport and the gas pipeline on the other side of the main road are a treasure-trove for **fossil** hunters. The sedimentary layers of volcanic ash, clay and sand here are full of well-preserved fossilized bones and teeth from Pleistocene megafauna like the mastodon

(Andean elephant) and megatherium (giant sloth), as well as distant ancestors of llamas, horses and other contemporary mammals. You can take a micro or taxi out here, but if you have a particular interest in fossils it's worth hiring a knowledgeable **guide**; VTB Tours (see p.185) run special trips in which you're allowed to excavate major fossils under supervision before handing them over to the museum.

Tarija valley vineyards

The **Tarija valley** and surrounding area is Bolivia's prime wine-producing region (see box below). At up to 2000m above sea level, these are the highest vineyards in the world; they are at their greenest and most beautiful during the February to March grape harvest. A visit to one or more of the **bodegas** (wineries) makes an excellent half-day excursion. You can see all the stages of the production process, as well as sample a few glasses at source. The closest bodega to Tarija is **Aranjuez**, on the southern outskirts of the city, while **Kohlberg** and **Casa Real** are in Santa Ana, a small village about 15km further southeast.

Concepción-Rugero bodega

Free • ☎ 04 6118008

Roughly 35km south of Tarija in the idyllic Valle La Concepción, which runs down into the Tarija valley from the west, the **Concepción-Rugero** bodega is easier to visit independently – and produces arguably the best wine in Bolivia. If you telephone in advance to make an appointment, staff are usually happy to show you around, though visits may not be possible during busy periods of the harvest.

Tomatitas

About 5km north of Tarija, the village of **TOMATITAS** is a popular weekend getaway for Tarijeños, who come here to swim in the natural river pools during the warmer, wetter summer months from November to April. You can also picnic in the fragrant eucalyptus woods beside the river, or eat in one of the village's many inexpensive **restaurants**, where you can sample traditional local specialities like *chicharron* (deep-fried pork) and *cangrejitos* (soft-shelled freshwater crabs).

San Lorenzo

Museum Daily 9am–noon & 2.30–6pm • Free

Ten kilometres north of Tomatitas, the peaceful farming village of **SAN LORENZO** has many colonial buildings including, on the corner of the plaza, the former home of the one-handed independence guerrilla hero, **Eustaquio "Moto" Méndez**, which has been preserved as a shrine-like museum. The leader of a guerrilla band that played a key role

---

TARIJA'S WINES

The first vines in the region were planted by Franciscan monks, who found the **soil** and **climate** of the Tarija valley ideal for producing wine. During the colonial era Tarija produced much of the wine consumed in Potosí, as well as large quantities of **singani**, a fierce, roughly 40° proof, white-grape brandy that is extremely popular throughout Bolivia. Today, Tarija's expanding wine industry produces well over two million litres of wine a year. Wine consumption within Bolivia is growing, and production techniques in the main bodegas have been modernized, with quality improving all the time. The main obstacle to further increases in production is the influx of contraband wine from Chile and Argentina, which is much cheaper than Bolivian wine, as no duty is paid on it.

in the Battle of La Tablada, which liberated Tarija from Spanish control in 1817, "Moto" Méndez is considered the consummate ideal of Tarijeño manhood. Inside, the colonial-era house has been left much as it was when he lived there, complete with rustic furniture and agricultural tools.

Reserva Biológica Cordillera del Sama

Starting about 5km west of Tarija, more than a thousand square kilometres of the Altiplano and the deep valleys that drop down into the Tarija valley are protected by the **RESERVA BIOLÓGICA CORDILLERA DEL SAMA**, which is home to many endangered species including vicuñas, Andean deer, pumas and a wide variety of birds. Established in 1991, the reserve is administered by conservation NGO Prometa (see p.185) who you should contact for permission to visit the region. Most of the reserve is composed of the high-altitude grasslands (*puna*) of the Cordillera de Sama, which rises above the Tarija valley to an altitude of over 4000m and marks the eastern edge of the Altiplano. The three brackish lakes here – the largest is the **Laguna Tajzara** – are home to many different water birds, including all three species of Andean flamingo.

The Inca Trail

From a high pass about two hours' walk (or a 4WD journey) due east of Pasajes – a village around two hours drive from Tarija on the road to Tupiza – a well-preserved **Inca Trail** drops down through spectacular scenery to the village of Los Pinos in the Tarija valley, making for an excellent hike. If you get an early start from Laguna Tajzara (or if you're lucky enough to get a lift up to the pass with Prometa), at a push you can walk this trail in a day and be back in Tarija the same evening. The trail itself is a good seven- or eight-hour hike, and from its end at the village of Los Pinos it's another 16km – about three hours – along a flat road to the village of San Andrés, where you can get transport back to Tarija. If you have camping equipment, it may be better to break the walk into two days. Alternatively, you can arrange to do the hike with a tour agency in Tarija (see p.185).

The first pass is marked by a large *apacheta* (stone cairn) visible from Pasajes below; once you've found it, the rest of the trail is easy to follow without a guide. From the pass, the trail zigzags down to the village of **Calderillas**, about two hours' walk away. From Calderillas, walk southeast for about thirty minutes to where two rivers meet and enter a narrow gorge. Cross over to the right bank of the river and follow the lower path that runs into the gorge along the river bank. After about 45 minutes the path climbs to the right and over a ridge, opening up spectacular views of the Tarija valley below – it's also an excellent spot to see condors. The path follows the ridge round and then zigzags down to the east to **Los Pinos**, about two hours' walk away.

ARRIVAL AND DEPARTURE
AROUND TARIJA

TARIJA VALLEY VINEYARDS

Generally you can only visit the Aranjuez, Kohlberg and Casa Real bodegas on an organized trip with Tarija-based agencies (around Bs100 for a half-day tour). To get to the Concepción-Rugero bodega take a micro marked "V" from the Plaza Sucre in Tarija. This will drop you in the village of Concepción, from where it's about a twenty-minute walk to the bodega along a track that heads out across a bridge to the right of the main road.

SAN LORENZO

Trufis to San Lorenzo depart from Av Domingo Paz in Tarija every 20min or so.

TOMATITAS

Micros "A" and "B" to Tomatitas depart from Av Domingo Paz in Tarija every 15–20min.

RESERVA BIOLÓGICA CORDILLERA DEL SAMA

The main road from Tarija to Tupiza passes through the reserve close by the lakes: take any Tupiza- or Villazón-bound bus and ask the driver to drop you at the village of Pasajes, about two hours' drive from Tarija. Pasajes is about 2km from Laguna Tajzara.

THE INCA TRAIL

Viva Tours and VTB Tours in Tarija can provide a guide and transport to the pass and back to Tarija from Los Pinos; an all-inclusive two-day trip costs from around (Bs700) $100; alternatively, you could arrange transport and a guide (or transport alone) independently for considerably less money (though significantly more hassle). From Los Pinos at the end of the trail, an easy-to-follow road runs 16km to San Andrés, from where there are frequent micros back to Tarija. If you arrive after dark when the last micro has gone, use the public telephone in a shop on the plaza to call a Radio taxi from Tarija to come and pick you up (around Bs70–100).

ACCOMMODATION

RESERVA BIOLÓGICA CORDILLERA DEL SAMA

Prometa Visitors' Centre Laguna Tajzara ☎04 6633873. Unless you are equipped to camp, the Prometa Visitors' Centre is the only place to stay in the reserve. It has simple rooms sleeping two to five people, hot water and a kitchen. Meals can be arranged if you contact Prometa two days in advance of your arrival. Bookings are essential. Doubles Bs200; five-person rooms Bs500 ($71)

3

Sucre, Cochabamba and the central valleys

195 Sucre

206 Around Sucre

209 Cochabamba

218 Around Cochabamba

222 Parque Nacional Torotoro

225 The Chapare

UNIVERSIDAD DE SAN FANCISCO XAVIER

Sucre, Cochabamba and the central valleys

East of the Altiplano, the Andes march gradually down towards the eastern lowlands in a series of rugged north–south mountain ranges, scarred with long narrow valleys formed by rivers draining to the east. Blessed with rich alluvial soils, and midway in climate and altitude between the cold of the Altiplano and the tropical heat of the lowlands, these central valleys have historically been among the most fertile and habitable areas in Bolivia. In the fifteenth century the Incas established substantial agricultural colonies in the region, which formed the easternmost frontier of their empire – to this day the majority of the rural population still speak Quechua, the language the Incas introduced. The Spanish were attracted by the same qualities, and the two main cities they founded, Sucre and Cochabamba, remain the most important in the region, though origins aside they could not be more different in character.

4

The administrative, political and religious centre of Bolivia during Spanish rule, and still officially the capital, **Sucre** is a masterpiece of immaculately preserved colonial architecture, full of elegant churches, mansions and museums. It's also the market centre for the deeply traditional Quechua-speaking communities of the surrounding mountains, whose fine weavings are sold at the regional market town of **Tarabuco**.

The charms of **Cochabamba**, on the other hand, are much more prosaic. A bustling trading hub for a rich agricultural hinterland, it has few conventional tourist attractions, and for most travellers is no more than a place to break a journey between La Paz and Santa Cruz in the eastern lowlands. Those who do spend some time here, however, find it to be one of Bolivia's friendliest cities, and the surrounding Cochabamba Valley's mixture of Inca ruins and lively rural market towns is worth exploring as well. It's also the jumping-off point for an adventurous journey south into the remote Northern Potosí province, where the diverse attractions of **Parque Nacional Torotoro** include labyrinthine limestone caves, deep canyons and waterfalls, dinosaur footprints and ancient ruins.

East of Cochabamba, meanwhile, the main road to Santa Cruz passes through the **Chapare**, a beautiful region of rushing rivers and dense tropical forests, where the last foothills of the Andes plunge down into the Amazon basin. The area has become notorious as the source of most of Bolivia's coca crop, which is used to make a large proportion of the world's cocaine supply, and conflicts continue between government drug-enforcement officers and local peasant farmers. As such, it's hardly an ideal area for travellers, though some areas remain safe to visit.

Fiestas in Sucre p.195

Jalq'a and Tarabuceño weavings p.201

Sucre's culinary delights p.205

The Tarabuceños: master weavers p.208

The Carnaval de Tarabuco p.209

Cochabamba and the Water War p.210

Cochabamba's street numbers p.214

Fiesta de la Virgen de Urkupiña p.220

Parque Machia p.225

RED-FRONTED MACAWS, PARQUE NACIONAL TOROTORO

Highlights

❶ Sucre Known as the White City, Bolivia's official capital combines delightful colonial-era architecture with the lively atmosphere of a university town. **See p.195**

❷ Museo de Arte Indigena Sucre's best museum is dedicated to the remarkable weavings of the indigenous groups from the surrounding region. **See p.201**

❸ Chicha The sacred drink of the Incas, this thick, tart and mildly alcoholic maize beer is for sale wherever you see a white flag on a pole in the Cochabamba Valley – though it's something of an acquired taste. **See p.209**

❹ Cochabamba A friendly and modern city, Cochabamba boasts a year-round sunny climate, some great restaurants and a buzzing nightlife scene. **See p.209**

❺ La Cancha Cochabamba's vast covered market is the throbbing heart of this commercial city, and of the Quechua-speaking communities of the surrounding valley. **See p.211**

❻ Parque Nacional Torotoro Set amid deep canyons and rushing waterfalls Bolivia's smallest national park is dotted with dinosaur footprints and pre-Inca ruins. **See p.222**

HIGHLIGHTS ARE MARKED ON THE MAP ON P.194

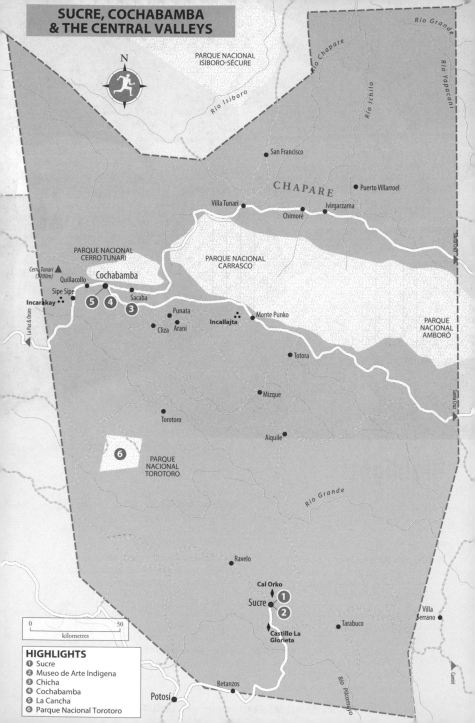

Sucre

In a broad highland valley on the Altiplano's eastern edge, about 162km north of Potosí, **SUCRE** is Bolivia's most refined and beautiful city. Known at various times as Chuquisaca, Charcas and La Ciudad de la Plata – and thus also as "The City of Four Names" – it has some of the finest Spanish colonial architecture in South America, and enjoys a spring-like climate all year round, thanks to its setting at an altitude of 2790m.

The centre of Spanish power in Alto Peru, Sucre was made **capital of Bolivia** after independence, a status it retains today, although all real power has long since passed to La Paz. The city exudes the sense of being frozen in time somewhere back in the late nineteenth century. Although the courtly manners and conservatism of the old aristocratic families who dominate Sucre can seem stuffy and pompous, it's nicely tempered by the youthful vitality the city enjoys as home of one of the Americas' oldest universities.

Laid out in a classic grid pattern, the city is an architectural jewel, with splendid churches, monasteries and mansions. The **historic centre**, a UNESCO World Heritage Site, is protected by strict building codes, and as a result most of it has been preserved as it was a century ago. Municipal regulations require all buildings to be whitewashed once a year, maintaining the characteristic that earned Sucre another of its many grandiose titles: "La Ciudad Blanca de Las Americas" – "The White City of the Americas".

Sucre is also the market centre for a mountainous rural hinterland inhabited by Quechua-speaking indigenous communities that are renowned for their beautiful **weavings**; their work can be seen at Sucre's stunning **Museo de Arte Indigena**, or on a day-trip to **Tarabuco**, a rural town about 60km to the southeast.

4

Brief history

Sucre was founded some time between 1538 and 1540 (the exact date is still hotly disputed by Bolivian historians) by the conquistador Pedro de Anzures during the second major Spanish incursion into the Andes south of Lago Titicaca. Initially named **Chuquisaca** (probably a Spanish corruption of the original indigenous name Choquechaca, meaning "Golden Bridge"), it was given the official title **Villa de la Plata** ("City of Silver") after significant quantities of silver were found nearby. The title proved prescient, as the massive silver deposits of Potosí were discovered soon after, and the city quickly emerged as the administrative headquarters for the mines and the centre of Spanish political, religious and military power in the region. In 1559 the **Audiencia de Charcas** – an independent court representing the Spanish crown, with judicial and executive power over an area comprising modern-day Bolivia, Argentina and part of Peru – was established here. The city became home to the first bishopric in Alto Peru in 1552, and in 1624 the **Universidad de San Francisco Xavier** – only the third university in all the Americas – was founded here to train the religious and administrative specialists needed to manage the vast conquered territories.

FIESTAS IN SUCRE

Sucre's main religious celebration is the **Fiesta de la Virgen de Guadeloupe**, held annually on September 8 and marked by a procession and folkloric dances. In the second half of September each year the city hosts an **International Cultural Festival**, with performances by local and international theatre and dance groups.

The anniversary of the 1809 "**Primer Grito Libertario de America**", the first declaration of independence in South America, is marked every May 25 with civic and military parades, and is a public holiday throughout the Department of Chuquisaca. The department's most famous annual fiesta, however, is the indigenous celebration of **Pujjlay** (see p.209), staged on the third Sunday of March in Tarabuco, 60km southeast of Sucre.

SUCRE

ACCOMMODATION

Alojamiento La Plata	4
Hostal Charcas	3
Hostal Colonial	6
Hostal Cruz de Popayan	7
Hostal de Su Merced	11
Hostal Recoleta del Sur	1
Hostal San Francisco	2
Hostal Sucre	9
Parador Santa Maria La Real	10
La Posada	8
Residencial Bolivia	5

RESTAURANTS

Los Balcones	6
El Huerto	1
Locot's Café Aventura	5
New Hong Kong	8
Pizzeria Napolitana	9
La Taverne	4
Tentaciones	3

SALTEÑERIAS

Paso del Los Abuelos	15
El Patio	2

CAFÉS & BARS

Amsterdam	7
Bibliocafé	13
Flavour	14
Florin	12
Joy Ride Café	11
El Mirador	16
Para Ti Café	10

LIVE MUSIC

Origenes Bolivianos	2
Casa de Cultura	1

Bus Terminal

Cochabamba

& Airport

Potosí & Train Station

Convento-Museo La Recoleta

& Tarabuco

ENTEL

Iglesia de Santa Teresa

Iglesia de San Lázaro

Museo de Arte Indigena

Museo-Convento Santa Clara

Banco de Santa Cruz

Iglesia de Santo Domingo

Iglesia de San Francisco

Banco Nacional de Bolivia

Museo de Etnografía Y Folklore

Mercado Central

Museo Universitario Charcas

Alcaldia Municipal

Punto ENTEL

Prefectura

Iglesia de San Miguel

Iglesia de Basilica Mayor

Museo Eclesiastico

Iglesia de la Merced

Casa de la Libertad

University

Iglesia de Santa Mónica

Facultad de Derecho

Catedral

Iglesia de San Felipe Neri

Corte Suprema de Justicia

Teatro Gran Mariscal

Hospital Santa Bárbara

Plaza de la Libertad

Parque Bolívar

Iglesia de San Agustín

PLAZA 25 DE MAYO

N

0   100   200   metres

The silver boom

The first half of the seventeenth century was La Plata's golden age, as the **wealth** from Potosí's mines funded the construction of lavish churches, monasteries, palaces and administrative buildings. Its power waned with the flow of silver, however, and in 1776 it was made subject to the rule of the new Spanish Virreinato de la Plata in Buenos Aires, reverting to the name of Chuquisaca to avoid confusion. The university retained its importance, and became a centre in developing the **liberal ideas** that led to the first qualified declaration of independence from Spain, which was made here on May 25, 1809.

Post independence

After independence in 1825 the city was made the **capital** of the Republic of Bolivia and renamed Sucre in honour of Antonio José de Sucre, the Venezuelan general who completed the defeat of the Spanish at the battle of Ayacucho and served as Bolivia's first president. Its economic importance continued to decline, however, and the seat of both congress and the presidency was moved to La Paz after the 1899 civil war between the two cities. In a very Bolivian compromise, Sucre remained the seat of the supreme court and was allowed to retain the title of official or **constitutional capital**, an honorary position it still holds today.

Plaza 25 de Mayo

The centre of Sucre is the spacious **Plaza 25 de Mayo**, shaded by tall palms and dotted with benches where people of all social classes pass the time of day chatting, reading newspapers or greeting passing acquaintances. In the middle of the plaza, flanked by bronze lions, stands a statue of **Mariscal Antonio José de Sucre**, the Venezuelan-born South American independence hero and first president of Bolivia whose name the city bears. The plaza is lined with elegant colonial and republican public and religious buildings, all painted an immaculate white that dazzles in the usually bright sunshine.

Casa de la Libertad

Plaza 25 de Mayo • Tues–Sat 9am–12.30pm & 2.30–6.30pm, Sun 9am–noon • Bs15

On the northwest side of the square is the Neoclassical **Casa de la Libertad**. Built in 1888 to replace a colonial *cabildo*, the Casa de la Libertad (then known as the Alcadia Municipal) was where the Bolivian **Act of Independence** was signed on August 6, 1825. The building now houses a small but interesting museum dedicated to the birth of the republic. Inside, the original signed document proclaiming a sovereign and independent state is on display in the assembly hall where the declaration was made; the same hall also housed the Bolivian congress from then until the seat of government was moved to La Paz in 1899. On the walls hang portraits of Sucre and Bolívar – the latter, by the Peruvian painter Gil de Castro, was described by the *Libertador* himself as being the best likeness ever made of him. Beside the Casa de la Libertad stands the simple but well-preserved colonial facade of the original seventeenth-century **Jesuit University**.

La Prefectura

Plaza 25 de Mayo

Around the corner from the Casa de la Libertad on the southwest side of Plaza 25 de Mayo stands the lavish Neoclassical facade of what was to have been the **presidential palace**, a glorious monument to hubris completed shortly before the seat of the presidency was moved to La Paz; it now houses the Prefectura (departmental government) de Chuquisaca.

4

La Catedral

Plaza 25 de Mayo • Mon–Sat 8–9am & Sun 9–11.30am for Mass; alternatively you can visit via the Museo Eclesiastico (see below) • Free

Next to the Prefectura, facing sideways onto the southwest side of the plaza, stands the **Catedral**, or Basilica Mayor. Built between 1551 and 1712 and extensively modified since, it combines a variety of architectural styles. The side door facing the plaza and main door looking onto Calle Ortiz are both highly decorative seventeenth-century stone porticos carved in the distinctive **mestizo-Baroque style**, while the square belltower with three balconies decorated with statues of the Apostles and Evangelists dates from the late eighteenth century; the clock in the tower, which still keeps perfect time, was made in London in 1772.

The decor in the lavish **Neoclassical interior** dates back to 1826, with soaring pillars painted in immaculate white and piped with gold, extravagant crystal chandeliers and massive silver candlesticks. A side chapel houses the jewel-encrusted image of the **Virgen de Guadeloupe**, the religious patron of Sucre. Painted in 1601 by Fray Diego de Ocaña, the image quickly developed cult status, and wealthy devotees began sticking gold, diamonds, emeralds and pearls to the picture as an expression of faith or in gratitude for wishes granted and miracles performed. These were arranged in a more orderly fashion when the image was laminated in gold in 1734, and though the popular saying that the value of the jewels would be enough to pay off Bolivia's international debt is probably an exaggeration (as well as a veiled critique of the wealth of the Church compared to the poverty of many Bolivians), the glittering opulence of the bejewelled Virgin is astonishing nonetheless.

Museo Eclesiastico

The entrance to the museum is beside the cathedral on Calle Ortiz • Mon–Sat 10am–noon & 3–5pm • Bs20

Although it is open in the mornings for Mass, the best way to see the cathedral – and the Virgin – is as part of a visit to the **Museo Eclesiastico**, which boasts a fine collection of colonial religious art. Visits are by **guided tour** only, so it's best to turn up shortly after opening, as otherwise you may have to wait a while for the next group to form; tours last about an hour. Among the paintings on display is a series of portraits of saints by the Cochabamba-born master of the mestizo-Baroque style, Melchor Pérez de Holguín, as well as several works in a much more European style by the sixteenth-century Italian-born Jesuit Bernardo Bitti, who studied under Raphael. There's also a substantial hoard of finely crafted silver and gold religious paraphernalia, much of it encrusted with gems, further evidence of the enormous wealth that flowed through Sucre (and the Church) during the silver-mining boom in Potosí.

Iglesia de San Felipe Neri

Two blocks southwest of Plaza 25 de Mayo on Calle Ortiz • Roof access Mon–Sat 2.30–6pm • Bs10

The formidable Neoclassical bulk of the **Iglesia de San Felipe Neri**, with its two tall bell towers was built in the last years of the nineteenth century. This is the only building in the city not painted white – its tall brick and stone walls have been left bare, as they have been throughout its existence. The church itself is rarely open to the public, but you can get up onto its roof to enjoy the splendid panoramic views across the city – access is via the adjoining former monastery, which boasts an elegant colonial courtyard surrounded by arched cloisters on two levels, and is now a school.

Iglesia de la Merced

Diagonally opposite the Iglesia de San Felipe Neri on the corner of calles Perez and Azurduy • Mon–Fri 10am–noon & 3–5pm • Bs5

The seventeenth-century **Iglesia de la Merced** has an unremarkable exterior, but its

interior boasts some extravagant Baroque altarpieces smothered in gold leaf, one of which is thought to be the oldest in Bolivia; the elaborately carved wooden pulpit and altar are also very beautiful. Climb the bell tower for stunning views over the city.

Museo Universitario Charcas

A block east of the Iglesia de la Merced on the corner of calles Dalence and Bolívar • Mon–Fri 8.30am–noon & 2.30–6pm, Sat 9am–noon & 3–6pm • Bs15

Housed in a delightful seventeenth-century mansion, the rambling but worthwhile **Museo Universitario Charcas** is really four museums in one. It combines the university's archeological, anthropological, colonial and modern art collections, all of which are set around a series of colonial patios and surrounded by arched cloisters. Visits are by guided tour (mainly in Spanish, though some guides speak a little English) only and last at least an hour.

The **modern art** collection is perhaps the least impressive of the four, comprising works by local artists in derivative styles ranging from surrealism and abstract expressionism to socialist realism, all applied to local subjects. The **colonial religious art** collection is much more substantial and includes some very fine works, though the subject matter – Christ, the Virgin, and assorted saints and bishops – is repetitive, to say the least. Highlights include a whole room full of pictures by the mestizo-Baroque master **Melchor Pérez de Holguín** and a finely detailed bird's-eye view of Potosí painted in 1758 by Gaspar Miguel de Berrio. There's also some beautiful colonial furniture on display, including decorative desks richly inlaid or delicately carved with images of flowers and animals. The **anthropology section** is a mishmash of indigenous costumes and artefacts from all over Bolivia: Andean musical instruments; woven vegetable-fibre clothes from the Amazon; lurid *diablada* masks from Oruro. The **archeology section** comprises an extensive collection of artefacts – pottery, tools, weapons, some metalwork, textile fragments – from all the major Andean civilizations.

Museo-Convento Santa Clara

Corner of Calvo and Bolívar • Mon–Fri 2–6pm, Sat 2–5.30pm • Bs15

If you still have an appetite for further colonial religious art after visiting the university and cathedral museums, it's worth making a trip to the **Museo-Convento Santa Clara**. This still-functioning nunnery has a range of fairly standard colonial religious pictures, most of them painted by anonymous indigenous artists in the seventeenth and eighteenth centuries, as well as some antique furniture and religious vestments; you can also see the church's Neoclassical interior, most notable for its seventeenth-century organ.

Convento-Museo La Recoleta

On the southeast side of Plaza Pedro de Anzares, a 20min uphill walk southeast of Plaza 25 de Mayo • Mon–Fri 9–11.30am & 2.30–5.30pm, Sat 3–5pm • Bs10

The **Convento-Museo La Recoleta**, a tranquil Franciscan monastery, houses an interesting little museum of colonial religious art and materials related to the missionary work of the Franciscan order in Bolivia. Visits are by guided tour only, so it's best to turn up shortly after the museum opens so that you don't have to wait long for a tour – if you do have to wait, the nearby *Café Mirador* (see p.206) is a good place to pass the time.

Founded in 1538, La Recoleta was for nearly three centuries the headquarters of Franciscan efforts to convert the indigenous peoples of Bolivia. Set around a series of delightful flower-filled colonial patios lined with arched cloisters, the museum is home to a substantial collection of **colonial religious paintings**. More interesting is the display of items relating to Franciscan missionary efforts, including bows and arrows, feather headdresses and plant-fibre clothing given to the missionaries by the different lowland tribes they contacted, and photographs of early twentieth-century missionaries.

Though it dates back to 1600, the **monastery church** was remodelled in rather anodyne style in the nineteenth century: the one noteworthy feature is the exquisite set of Baroque wooden choir stalls in the upper choir, beautifully carved in 1674 with gruesome images of a massacre of Franciscan missionaries in Nagasaki, Japan. Though it is now back in Franciscan hands, in the early nineteenth century the monastery was briefly requisitioned by the Bolivian authorities and used as a barracks; in the corridor outside the choir a plaque and portrait mark the spot where the Bolivian president Pedro Blanco was murdered during a successful coup in 1829, just five days after taking office. Beside the monastery stands the **Cedro Millenario**, a great, gnarled *cedro* tree over a thousand years old and 5m in diameter.

Museo de Arte Indigena

Three blocks southeast from Plaza 25 de Mayo on the corner of calles San Alberto and Potosí • Mon–Fri 8.30am–noon & 2.30–6pm, Sat 9.30am–noon & 2.30-6pm • Bs22 • ☎ 04 6453841, ⓦ asur.org.bo

In an elegant colonial building, the fascinating **Museo de Arte Indigena** is dedicated to the distinctive weavings of two local Quechua-speaking indigenous groups: the **Jalq'a**, who number about 26,000 and live in the mountains west of Sucre, and the **Tarabuceños** (see p.208), a more numerous group who live around the town of Tarabuco to the east. The museum is run by an NGO, ASUR (Antropologos del Sur Andino), which works with Jalq'a and Tarabuceño communities to revive traditional weaving designs and techniques that had been dying out. This renaissance of indigenous art has seen both the quality and market value of the weavings of both groups rise dramatically, turning the craft into a source of income for hundreds of desperately poor campesino families.

JALQ'A AND TARABUCEÑO WEAVINGS

The difference in style between the weavings of the Jalq'a and Tarabuceños could hardly be more dramatic, even though the two groups live only a short distance apart to the west and east of Sucre. **Tarabuceño ponchos** (*unkus*) are woven with bright stripes of orange, black, red, green and gold, while smaller items like the *chu'spa* coca bags and *chumpi* waist bands are decorated with finely detailed and usually symmetrical designs depicting scenes from everyday life: wild and domestic animals; trees and crops; people ploughing, harvesting or dancing at fiestas.

The **Jalq'a** designs, on the other hand, are entirely figurative, eschewing symmetry and abstract geometry. Woven into women's shawls known as *aqsus* and almost always only black and red in colour, they depict a kind of primordial chaos filled with strange beasts: animals with elongated bodies and multiple heads or eyes sprouting from their tails; birds with puma heads; toads with wings. The few human figures that do appear seem lost in this forest of supernatural animals. This is the **ukchu pacha**, a mythological underworld of extraordinary and untamed creatures, over which rules the *Sax'ra*, a horned devil-like figure with wings who appears in the centre of some of the weavings, part Andean demon and part god of fertility and abundance. Many of the designs are inspired by dreams, and new themes are constantly being incorporated, but though every piece is unique they all fall within a set of artistic norms that makes them instantly recognisable as Jalq'a – both to neighbouring ethnic groups and to international art collectors.

Examples of both weaving styles are available to buy in a shop attached to the museum, and though they're far from cheap (particularly the Jalq'a items – larger individual pieces can cost well over $100/Bs700) the money goes direct to the **indigenous artists** who made them, and the quality is exquisite.

Expertly laid out, with precise text explanations in Spanish, English, French and German, the museum introduces the different ethnic groups with maps and colour photos, then explains the weaving techniques and describes the different plants used to make natural dyes. There is often a Jalq'a or Tarabuceño woman weaving away in the courtyard as you wander around the museum, so you can see the creative process in action. The **archeological finds** on display demonstrate that many of the wood and bone weaving tools in use today are identical to those used in the Andes more than a thousand years ago, while some beautiful and well-preserved ancient **textile fragments** reveal an astonishing continuity of style, technique and aesthetic vision stretching back over many centuries. The central attractions, though, are the weavings themselves: brightly coloured, intricately detailed and laden with a complex symbolism, they're works of great creativity that express a distinctively Andean artistic vision. The textiles are displayed in chronological order, revealing the development and changing style over time. There are also examples of how they are worn in daily dress and in ritual costumes for fiestas.

Museo de Etnografía y Folklore

Two blocks northeast of the cathedral at España 74 • Mon–Fri 9.30am–12.30pm & 2.30–6.30pm, Sat 9.30am–12.30pm • Free

Popularly known as **Musef**, and housed in the colonial-era former Banco Nacional building, this museum showcases Bolivia's cultural diversity through a collection of anthropological and ethnological exhibits, which includes traditional musical instruments, and icons used in rites and ceremonies. The highlight, however, is the stunning ground-floor display of masks and headdresses, which features numerous elaborate examples from Carnaval celebrations.

Iglesia de San Francisco

A block northeast of Plaza 25 de Mayo beside the bustling public market, on the corner of Ravelo and Arce • Daily 7–9am & 4–7pm • Free

The **Iglesia de San Francisco** was built between 1540 and 1581 to minister to the growing indigenous population of the newly founded city, and remains the most popular church with Sucre's Quechua-speaking population – modern signs on the walls warning against the use of holy water in witchcraft and magic reveal that, centuries later, the priests here still face an uphill struggle against deeply entrenched pre-Christian practices. The entrance to the church is flanked by two square towers, one of which houses the **Campana de la Libertad**, the bell that sounded the call to arms at the start of the pro-independence uprising in 1809. The interior boasts splendid gilded Baroque altarpieces and an elaborate panelled *mudéjar* ceiling.

Iglesia de San Miguel

Half a block northwest of Plaza 25 de Mayo along Calle Arenales • Open early for Mass most mornings • Free

The modest whitewashed Baroque facade of the **Iglesia de San Miguel**, completed in 1621, conceals one of the most lavish church interiors in Sucre, with glorious carved Baroque altarpieces covered in **gold leaf** and an exquisite panelled *mudéjar* ceiling of intricate interlocking geometric shapes.

Iglesia de Santa Mónica

Half a block on from the Iglesia de San Miguel, on the corner of calles Arenales and Junín • Free

The **Iglesia de Santa Mónica**, founded in 1547, boasts an extravagant stone portico that is the finest example of the **mestizo-Baroque** style in Sucre, carved with palm trees and floral designs, spiralled columns, and pillars supported by human figures who look like pre-Columbian idols; sadly, the interior is closed to the public.

Universidad de San Francisco Xavier

Just southwest of the Iglesia Santa Mónica on Junín • Free

The main entrance to the **University** (or the Universidad Mayor Real y Pontificia de San Francisco Xavier, to give it its full title) is on Junín. The university was originally founded by the Jesuits in 1624, predating Harvard in the US, and was a major seat of learning throughout the colonial period as well as an important centre of liberal thought in the early nineteenth century. Crucial ideas developed here, particularly the so-called *Silogismo altoperuano* – the argument that the loyalty of the colonies was owed to the personage of the king and not to the Spanish government, and that sovereignty therefore reverted to the colonies once King Fernando VII was forced to abdicate by Napoleon – and played a key role in the declaration of independence from Spain in 1809. The university is still central to the city's social, cultural and economic life, and is worth visiting for a look inside the **Facultad de Derecho** at Junín 652, which has the biggest colonial courtyard in Sucre.

Plaza de la Libertad

Three blocks northwest of Plaza 25 de Mayo on Calle Arenales

The small **Plaza de la Libertad** is lined with palm trees and centred on an obelisk donated by the city of Buenos Aires to commemorate the 1809 Declaration of Independence. On the southwest side of the square stands the elegant Renaissance facade of the **Hospital Santa Bárbara**, built between 1554 and 1563 and still functioning as a health centre. Set back from the northwest side of the square is the grandiose facade of the **Teatro Gran Mariscal**, one of several buildings in this part of town built in French Neoclassical style at the start of the twentieth century.

Parque Símon Bolívar

One block northwest of the Teatro Gran Mariscal, just off Calle Kilometro 7

Kilometro 7 runs from the right-hand side of the Teatro Gran Mariscal to **Parque Símon Bolívar**, a peaceful park neatly laid out in a French style – there's even a model of the Eiffel Tower at its centre. Looking over the park from its south end stands the grandiose **Corte Suprema de Justicia**, completed in 1945 in opulent French Neoclassical style. This is the only branch of government still based in Sucre, and as such the only real justification for the city's continuing status as constitutional capital of Bolivia.

ARRIVAL AND DEPARTURE   SUCRE

By plane The airport (☎04 6454445) is about 8km northwest of the city; Micros I and F run from there into the centre of town along Av Siles (30–45min); alternatively, a taxi costs about Bs35. There are regular flights to La Paz and Santa Cruz, and less frequent services to Cochabamba and Tarija. The domestic departure tax is Bs11; for international flights it is Bs175.

By train A single-carriage service to Potosí (Mon, Wed & Fri 8am; 6hr) departs from the El Tejar station, 1km south of the centre on the road to Potosí. It's a pleasant journey, but considerably slower than travelling by road.

By bus All long-distance buses arrive at and depart from the bus terminal (☎04 6456732), about 3km northeast of the city centre on Av Ostria Gutiérrez. From here it's a short taxi ride (around Bs10) into central Sucre, or you can catch Micro A, which runs down to the Mercado

Central, a block north of the main Plaza 25 de Mayo. Numerous buses leave for Cochabamba (10–12hr) in the early evening and for Santa Cruz (14–16hr) from the late afternoon onwards; some of the latter travel via Samaipata. Frequent buses leave for Potosí (3hr) throughout the day, and there are several evening services to La Paz (15hr) and Oruro (11hr). When the road is passable, usually only in the dry season, buses also head via Camiri to Villamontes (20–25hr) and Yacuiba (21–26hr), an arduous but exceptionally scenic journey down from the Andes into the Chaco lowlands.

By taxi *Collectivo* taxis from Potosí will drop you off outside your hotel or anywhere else in the centre of town; heading in the opposite direction, they can be caught from the bus station or organized via your hotel. Regular taxis for journeys around town generally cost Bs5–10.

4

INFORMATION AND TOURS

TOURIST INFORMATION

The helpful main municipal tourist office is on the first floor of the Casa de Cultura (Mon–Fri 8.30am–noon & 2.30–6pm; ☎04 6435240), a block southeast of Plaza 25 de Mayo on Calle Argentina; there are also useful information booths at the airport and the bus terminal (Mon–Sat 8.30am–noon & 2.30–6pm). There's also a university-run tourist office at – appropriately enough – Estudiantes 49, Just off Plaza 25 de Mayo (Mon–Fri 8.30am–12.30pm & 2.30–6.30pm; ☎04 6452283); it is manned by enthusiastic students who sometimes act as guides.

TOUR OPERATORS

★ **Candelaria Tours** On Plaza Cochabamba, at the corner of Perez and Azurduy ☎04 6440340, ⓦ candelariatours.com. Runs excellent one- and two-day trips (Bs567–847/$81–121 person based on a group of two) to Candelaria village, which has a long-standing textile tradition. It's far less touristy than Tarabuco (see p.208), and you can stay at a delightful hacienda.

Volunteering opportunities and numerous other tours are also on offer.

Joy Ride Bolivia Corner of Audiencia and Ortíz ☎04 6425544, ⓦjoyridebol.com. Dutch-run company next to the *Joy Ride Café*, which organizes mountain biking (from Bs154), hiking (fromBs210), horseriding (from Bs280), climbing (from Bs210), paragliding (Bs595/$85) and motorbike trips (from Bs392/$56/), as well as city tours and other excursions.

Locot's Located in the café of the same name at Bolívar 465 ☎04 6915958. Like Joy Ride Bolivia, Locot's is a reliable operator offering a range of tours in and around Sucre, including hiking (Bs210) and horseriding (Bs280) excursions, as well as some more adrenalin-fuelled activities such as motorbiking, climbing and paragliding.

Off Road Bolivia Contact via Florin (see p.206) or ☎7033 8123, ⓦoffroadbolivia.com. Runs guided quad, ATV (all-terrain vehicle) and motorbike tours through the countryside surrounding Sucre. A three-hour beginners trip costs from Bs196 ($49), while a six-hour "Xtreme" ride is Bs596 ($149).

ACCOMMODATION

Sucre has a good range of accommodation, most of it located in the heart of the old city centre. There are some particularly beautiful places set inside converted **colonial mansions**, which represent very good value in the middle and upper price ranges: if you're on a tight budget but like to splash out every so often, this is the place to do it. All rates include **breakfast** unless stated otherwise.

BUDGET

Alojamiento La Plata Ravelo 32 ☎04 6452102. If you're on a really tight budget, these bare, cell-like rooms with shared bathrooms set around a sunny courtyard are acceptable for a night or two. No breakfast. Bs60

Hostal Charcas Ravelo 62 ☎04 6453972, ⓔhostalcharcas@yahoo.com. Welcoming and efficient establishment with abundant hot water and helpful, welcoming staff. The rooms are scrupulously clean but rather cramped, and those with private bathrooms lack ventilation. Breakfast costs extra. Bs80

Hostal Cruz de Popayan Loa 881 ☎04 6440889, ⓦhotelcruz.com. This popular *hostal* is based in a restored seventeenth-century townhouse. Although the rooms are a bit scruffy, most are en suite and come with TVs and free wi-fi access. There is also a six-bed dorm. Dorms Bs40; doubles Bs140

Hostal San Francisco Arce 191 ☎04 6452117. Modern, colonial-style building with three floors of rooms set around a delightful courtyard. The rooms don't quite match up with the courtyard, but are still very good value: they have plenty of space, flowery bed covers, private bathrooms and TVs. Breakfast costs extra. Bs120

Residencial Bolivia San Alberto 42 ☎04 6454346. This friendly *residencial* has spacious rooms with shared or private bathrooms and TVs; there are some duds, so ask to

be shown a few first. They are set around a courtyard with plenty of plants and a questionable mauve and peach colour scheme. Bs100

MODERATE

Hostal Colonial Plaza 25 de Mayo 3 ☎04 6440309, ⓦhostalcolonial-bo.com. Excellent location on the plaza, though somewhat lacking in character. Rooms are adequate, if a bit musty and gloomy, and only the somewhat overpriced suites (#117 and #118) have views over the plaza. Bs280 ($40)

Hostal Recoleta del Sur Ravelo 205 ☎04 6454789, ⓔmairusta34@hotmail.com. This reliable mid-range choice has comfortable, carpeted, en-suite rooms with TVs in a converted colonial house with a glass-roofed patio. Bs180

Hostal Sucre Bustillos 113 ☎04 6451411, ⓦhostalsucre.com.bo. This hotel features period decor and two charming flower-filled courtyards. The rooms themselves are a little dated, but come with private bathrooms and TVs. Internet access is available. Bs200

EXPENSIVE

Hostal de Su Merced Azurduy 16 ☎04 6442706, ⓦdesumerced.com. Immaculately restored and converted eighteenth-century house that has a wonderful

SUCRE'S CULINARY DELIGHTS

The **salteñas** (meat-filled pasties) in Sucre are rightly considered Bolivia's best, and locals consume them with a passion – they're available from stalls and handcarts throughout the city, and from specialist *salteñerias*, which open only from mid-morning to noon and serve almost nothing else. Another local specialty is **chorizos chuquisaqueños**, spicy pork sausages sold in the market and in restaurants. Sucre is also famous throughout Bolivia for the quality and variety of its **chocolates**, which you'll find on sale at specialist shops on Calle Arenales, just off the plaza; Para Ti at #7 is the pick of the bunch, and has a delightful café (see p.206).

rooftop sun terrace with panoramic views of the city. Rooms combine opulent antique furniture with a full range of modern comforts. The multilingual staff are welcoming and attentive. Bs390 ($56)

★ **Parador Santa Maria La Real** Bolivar 625 ☎04 6439592, ⍵parador.com.bo. Sucre's best hotel is a joy: a painstakingly-renovated colonial building housing elegant rooms with period furnishings, arched ceilings and sinks fashioned from old Singer sewing machine stands. There's

also a roof terrace, and a jacuzzi with vistas over the city. Free internet and wi-fi access. Bs560 ($80)

La Posada Audiencia 92 ☎04 6460101, ⍵hotellaposada.com.bo. This top-end hotel boasts beautiful gardens, a superb restaurant and very professional service. The rooms, meanwhile, have exposed wooden beams, whitewashed walls and all the modern comforts you would expect. Bs360 ($51)

EATING, DRINKING AND NIGHTLIFE

Sucre has a good variety of restaurants (a disproportionate number of which are run by Dutch expats) where you can get everything from the spicy local cuisine to authentic international dishes. If you're on a budget, the **Mercado Central**, at the junction of calles Ravelo and Arce, has inexpensive meals. Several restaurants host frequent performances of **Andean folk music**, and some double as late-night drinking spots.

RESTAURANTS

Los Balcones Plaza 25 de Mayo. The main meals at this smart first-floor restaurant are overpriced, but the four-course set almuerzo (Bs40) – featuring meat-heavy dishes and a well-stocked salad bar –is worth checking out, particularly if you can nab one of the tables on the balcony overlooking the plaza. Live folk music on Fri nights. Daily for lunch and dinner.

El Huerto Ladislao Cabrera 86. Ask a local for the best restaurant in town, and the chances are they'll direct you here. The menu features excellent meat, chicken and fish dishes (Bs25–60) cooked to both traditional Bolivian and international recipes and served in a beautiful garden. It is some distance north of the city centre, but well worth the taxi fare (around Bs10). Thurs–Sun for dinner and Mon–Wed for lunch.

Locot's Café Aventura Bolívar 465. Popular travellers' restaurant-bar serving good breakfasts and Bolivian, Mexican and Italian dishes (mains Bs20–50) in an attractive space. The building reputedly once served as the stables for one of Bolivia's most notorious presidents, Mariano Melgarejo – infamous for trading a valuable swath of Bolivian territory to Brazil for a white horse. Daily 7am–late; happy hour Thurs–Sat 10–11pm.

New Hong Kong San Alberto 242. The obligatory photos of the Great Wall, red lanterns and paper fans are all present and correct at this *chifa*, as well as a menu of tasty fried rice, noodles and Cantonese stir-fry dishes. Mains

Bs25–50, almuerzos Bs30–35. Mon–Sat for lunch and dinner.

Pizzeria Napolitana Plaza 25 de Mayo 30. Sucre's longest-established Italian restaurant serves reasonable pizza and pasta, home-made ice cream, strong coffee and six different set lunches (Bs30). Open daily except Tues.

★ **La Taverne** Arce 35. The Alliance Française's restaurant, tucked away in a tranquil little courtyard, has a mix of French standards and international dishes from as far away as India and Thailand (mains Bs32–42). All are well prepared, and presented with flair. There's a good value four-course lunch (Bs45) too. Mon–Sat 9am–11pm.

Tentaciones Arenales 11. New restaurant with amiable staff, relaxed vibe and an inviting menu featuring home-made pastas (Bs32–40), fondue (Bs120 for four people), cheese and cured meat boards (don't miss the Bolivian-made Serrano ham), gourmet coffee and Bolivian wines. Daily 8am–10.30pm.

SALTEÑERIAS

Paso del Los Abuelos Bustillos 216. Smart *salteñeria* where Sucre's wealthier citizens go for their mid-morning snacks: at Bs6 each, the *salteñas* are relatively expensive, but worth every cent. Mon–Sat for breakfast and lunch.

El Patio San Alberto 18. Popular *salteñeria* serving rich, juicy *salteñas* (Bs3–5) in a beautiful colonial patio filled with bougainvillea and other flowering plants. Mon–Fri mornings only.

CAFÉS AND BARS

Many of Sucre's cafés also double up as bars in the evenings; there's a lively student scene and many places stay open into the early hours, especially at weekends.

Amsterdam Bolivar 426. Funky, wood-panelled bar decorated with modern art and photos of the Dutch capital. The beer (from Bs11) is nice and cold, and there's a good range of spirits and wines, plus sandwiches (Bs16–18) and snacks. Wi-fi access, a book exchange and frequent live music performances complete the package. Daily 3pm–late; happy hour 9–10pm.

Bibliocafé N. Ortiz 50. Bohemian bar-café, split between two adjacent sites, attracting a mix of locals and travellers from early evening until late at night with its mellow music and intimate atmosphere. Also serves decent food (almuerzos Bs25–35), and there are live bands at weekends. Closed Mon.

Flavour Bustillos 117. Snug and welcoming café with great coffee, sandwiches (from Bs8), cakes, cookies and brownies. If you're feeling homesick, it also stocks a selection of hard-to-find goodies - from pesto to peanut butter - and it has a book exchange. Mon–Sat 10am–7.30pm.

Florin Bolivar 567 ☎04 6451313. This lively Dutch-run place has an authentic pub-feel with a huge central bar, prominent photos of Holland's football team, excellent beer (including several from a local microbrewery), and a daily happy hour (9.30–10.30pm). The menu has dishes from all over the world, including a full English breakfast, baked Camembert and Pad Thai (mains Bs20–50). Mon–Thurs 7.30am–2am, Fri–Sat 7.30am–3am, Sun 7.30am–midnight.

★ **Joy Ride Café** Ortíz 14, ⊚joyridebol.com. Part of a Dutch-run mini empire (there's also a travel agency and a shop), this bar-restaurant serves local and international dishes (Bs35–65), as well as cocktails and ice-cold beer (from Bs14). There are film screenings, pool tables, a heated patio, book exchange and internet and wi-fi access. It gets pretty lively on Fri and Sat nights too. Mon-Fri 7am–late, Sat–Sun 9am–late.

El Mirador Plaza Anzures. Grab a deck chair in the lush garden of this outdoor café and enjoy the fantastic views over the city. There are snacks, light meals and treats like crêpes and tiramisu, along with beer, juices and excellent iced cappuccinos. Profits help fund a museum and educational project for local children. Drinks Bs5–20, snacks Bs10–30. Daily 9am-8pm.

★ **Para Ti Café** Audiencia 68. Sucre's finest chocolatier also has a tiny café (there are just three tables) and a short menu of delicious hot chocolates, and chocolate-flavoured milkshakes, coffees and liqueurs. There's also home-made cakes and – of course – a vast array of chocolates and sweets to choose from. Daily.

LIVE MUSIC

Origenes Bolivianos Azurduy 473 ☎04 6457091, ⊚origenesbolivianos.com. Puts on entertaining folkloric dance and music shows; buy tickets (Bs120 with dinner) from the *Flavour* café (see above) or a tour agency. Tues–Sun 8.30pm.

Casa de Cultura Calle Argentina, a block from the plaza. Home of the city's main tourist office and the public library, the Casa de Cultura often hosts folk music performances, as well as small exhibitions of local arts and crafts, and other events.

DIRECTORY

Banks and exchange Casa de Cambios Ambar, San Alberto 7 and El Arca, España 134, both change travellers' cheques and cash at reasonable rates. There are also plenty of ATMs around town, including at the Banco de Santa Cruz and Banco Nacional de Bolivia, opposite each other near the corner of San Alberto and España.

Car rental Auto Cambio Chuquisaca, Av Mendoza 1106 ☎04 6460984.

Hospital Hospital Santa Bárbara, Plaza de la Libertad ☎04 6451900.

Immigration Bustillo 284 ☎04 6453647.

Internet There are innumerable internet cafés, most charging around Bs3/hr: try Punto ENTEL on the plaza.

Language courses Academia Latinoamericana de Español, Dalence 109 and Ortiz (☎04 6439613, ⊚latinoschools .com), is the most prominent of the numerous Spanish schools in Sucre. It offers private or group lessons, and can arrange homestays and voluntary placements.

Laundry Lavarap (Bs6/kg), Bolívar, next to *Hotel Parador Santa Maria La Real*.

Post office Correo Central, Junín and Ayacucho.

Telephone office The main ENTEL office is at España 271, and there are smaller Punto ENTEL offices on the northeast side of Plaza 25 de Mayo and on the corner of Ravelo and Junín.

Around Sucre

The green hills and pleasant climate surrounding Sucre make this an area well worth setting aside time to explore. While the dinosaur tracks at **Cal Orko** and the market at **Tarabuco** are the most popular day-trips – and the latter will give you some sense of countryside by way of a bus window – forays by foot, mountain bike or horse will give you a much more intimate view (see p.204).

Cal Orko dinosaur footprints

Parque Cretácico Mon–Fri 9am–5pm, Sat & Sun 10am–5pm • Bs30; the footprints are free to view through the gate

Five kilometres outside Sucre on the Cochabamba road, the low mountain of **CAL ORKO** is home to the world's biggest-known collection of **dinosaur footprints**, which were discovered in 1994 by workers at a local cement works and limestone quarry. Approximately five thousand prints from at least 150 different types of dinosaur can be seen here, covering an area of around thirty thousand square metres of near-vertical rock face, an astonishing profusion given that the second-biggest known site, in Germany, contains just 240 prints from two types of dinosaur. The prints were laid down between 65 and 85 million years ago on a flat bed of mud or sand covered by shallow water, and were then covered by a protective layer of ash from a **volcanic explosion**. Further layers of ash, silt and other sediments followed, the prints became fossilized, and about 25 million years ago the Andes began to rise, eventually bringing them to where they stand today.

The prints are scattered across a long plane of greyish rock about 100m high and set at an incline of about seventy degrees, and they look at first like so many pockmarks. Study them for a while, though, and you'll see the clear footprints of many different sizes running in long lines across the surface, and the astonishing fact that you're looking at the trails of animals who lived some seventy million years ago in the Cretaceous era begins to sink in. It's thought the site may have been the scene of a chase and kill by predators, who were followed by various scavengers. The largest prints are about 1m in diameter – these are thought to have belonged to an **apatosaurus** (commonly, though erroneously, referred to as a brontosaurus). The longest single track (and by far the longest in the world) stretches for over half a kilometre and was laid down by a **baby tyrannosaurus rex** known to researchers as Johnny Walker. The cement plant is still operating, and new prints are constantly being revealed, but ongoing quarrying and natural erosion threaten to destroy the tracks so far uncovered. The site has been declared a national monument, but no serious conservation measures are yet in place, though there are plans to preserve them with silicon injections into the rock face.

Unfortunately, it is no longer possible to approach the tracks to a distance of closer than several hundred metres. Upon arrival you can either gaze upon the tracks through a chain-link gate or pay an additional fee to enter the thoroughly underwhelming **Parque Cretácico**, which has a slightly better positioned viewing platform. The entrance fee includes a guided tour of the park, but your best bet is really to skip the tour, which spends the majority of its time focusing on plaster replicas, and proceed directly to the viewing platform overlooking Cal Orko.

Castillo La Glorieta

Daily 8.30am–noon & 2–6pm • Bs10

About 6km outside Sucre on the road south to Potosí is the bizarre shell of the **Castillo La Glorieta**, a must for lovers of kitsch. Built over seven years from 1890 as a home for mining baron Francisco Argandoña and his wife Clotilda, La Glorieta is probably the most ridiculous construction in Bolivia. The extravagant **pink sandstone structure** combines a surreal mishmash of different architectural styles, including a minaret, a Gothic clocktower and a Byzantine onion dome, while life-size stucco horses' heads running the length of the roof add a sublime Dalí-esque touch. The once-lavish interior still boasts elaborate Neoclassical stucco ceilings, Venetian stained glass and fireplaces of pink Veronese marble, as well as portraits of Francisco and Clotilda in full princely regalia meeting Pope Leo XIII, who pronounced them "Principes de la Glorieta" ("the Princes of Glorieta") during their visit to Europe in 1898 in recognition for their work looking after orphans.

Tarabuco

By far the most popular excursion from Sucre is to the small rural town of **TARABUCO**, set amid crumpled brown mountains about 60km southeast of the city. The town itself is an unremarkable collection of red-tiled adobe houses and cobbled streets leading to a small plaza with a modern church, but its real claim to fame is its **Sunday market**, which acts as a focus for the indigenous communities of the surrounding mountains, the so-called **Tarabuceños** (see below), who come to sell the beautiful **weavings** for which they're famous throughout Bolivia. The market is a bit of a tourist trap – there are usually several busloads of foreign tourists in attendance – but it's still principally geared towards the indigenous campesinos of the surrounding region, and the stalls selling weavings and other handicrafts to tourists are far outnumbered by those selling basic supplies such as dried foodstuffs, agricultural tools, sandals made from tyres, big bundles of coca and pure cane alcohol. If you walk a few blocks away from the centre of town you can still see campesinos engaging in **trueque**, a traditional Andean system of non-monetary trade in which agricultural products from different ecological zones are exchanged according to standard ratios – potatoes for maize, dried llama meat for oranges, and so on.

You can pick up some nice **souvenirs** at the market, though it's best to have some idea of quality and price before you arrive (have a look at things on sale on the streets of Sucre). Small items like decorative *chuspa* coca-bags make good mementoes; larger items like ponchos and shawls cost a lot more. Be prepared to bargain, but not too hard: many of the sellers are poor campesinos who may be desperate to sell something so they can buy essential goods to take home to their families. **Photographing people**

THE TARABUCEÑOS: MASTER WEAVERS

Though they wear the same traditional costume, speak the same language (Quechua) and share many cultural traditions, strictly speaking it's not correct to refer to the **Tarabuceños** as an ethnic group: the name was simply given by the colonial authorities to all the indigenous communities living around Tarabuco. When the Spanish first arrived, the region had only recently been conquered by the Incas and marked the very limit of their domain. To secure the frontier and defend against raids by the indomitable Chiriguano tribes to the east, the Incas settled the area with different ethnic groups brought from elsewhere in the empire. All these indigenous communities speak **Quechua**, the lingua franca of the Inca empire, and at some point after the Spanish conquest they also adopted the distinctive costumes that give a semblance of unity today, but they have no collective name for themselves nor any tradition of collective political organization that suggests a common origin.

These distinctive **traditional costumes** make the Tarabuceños difficult to miss: the men wear leather hats, known as *monteros* and shaped like the steel helmets worn by the Spanish conquistadors, along with woollen ponchos woven with bright, horizontal stripes of red, yellow, orange and green on a brown background, and three-quarter-length white trousers. In addition, they often use finely woven accessories like *chumpi* belts and *chuspa* coca-bags. Though generally more muted in colour, the traditional costumes worn by the women, particularly the woollen shawls known as *llijlas* or *aqsus*, are also decorated with beautiful and **complex designs**, and the ceremonial hats and headdresses they wear on special occasions match the *monteros* of the men in their unusual shape and design: black pillboxes with a flap covering the neck decorated with sequins and bright woollen pom-poms, or boat-shaped sombreros embroidered with silver thread. More even than their costumes, however, it is Tarabuceño **weavings** (see p.201) that draw travellers to Tarabuco, and selling them has become a major source of income for the Tarabuceños, who otherwise depend on agriculture for their livelihoods and live in great poverty.

THE CARNAVAL DE TARABUCO

Every year on the third Sunday of March, Tarabuco celebrates **Pujllay** (or the Carnaval de Tarabuco), one of the best-known indigenous fiestas in Bolivia. Pujllay commemorates the **battle of Jumbate** on March 12, 1816, during the Independence War, when the Tarabuceños ambushed a battalion of marauding Spanish troops, slaughtering all but the drummer boy and eating their hearts in ritual revenge for abuses committed by the Spanish. During the fiesta, all the surrounding Tarabuceño communities come to town dressed in their finest **ceremonial costumes**, joined by thousands of tourists. Following a Mass to commemorate the battle, the participants stage folkloric dances and parades whilst knocking back copious amounts of *chicha* (fermented maize beer), beer and pure cane alcohol. The climax of the celebration takes place around a **ritual altar** known as a *pukara*, raised in honour of the Tarabuceños who died in the battle and formed from a kind of wooden ladder decorated with fruit, vegetables, flowers, bread, bottles of *chicha* and other agricultural produce. Drinking and dancing continues through the night: if you want to sleep, you're better off returning to Sucre.

without permission is considered rude and can provoke an angry reaction: ask first, and be prepared to pay a few bolivianos for the privilege. If you want a less touristy experience, try one of Candelaria Tours' trips (se p.204) to Candelaria village.

ARRIVAL AND DEPARTURE

AROUND SUCRE

CAL ORKO

By truck Transport to the dinosaur tracks is provided by two companies, Dino-Truck (☎04 6451863) and Sauro Movil (☎04 6436469), which leave Sucre daily around 9.30am, noon and 2.30pm from outside the cathedral. There's no need to buy tickets (Bs10 return) in advance as they lay on extra transport when numbers are high.

CASTILLO LA GLORIETA

By micro Take micro #4 from the corner of calles Ravelo and Arce in Sucre, a thirty-minute trip. A taxi costs around Bs50.

TARABUCO

By bus/truck Buses and trucks to Tarabuco (2hr) leave on Sun morning (and most weekdays) from Plaza Huallparimachi in the east of Sucre, returning in the afternoon.

By tourist bus It is much more convenient and only slightly more expensive to go on one of the tourist buses organized by hotels and tour agencies in Sucre, which will pick you up outside the Mercado Central on Calle Ravelo in the morning and bring you back in the afternoon – *Hostal Charcas* organizes a service every Sun around 8.30am (Bs35).

ACCOMMODATION AND EATING

TARABUCO

Several restaurants on the plaza serve basic meals and drinks, though on Sundays it's more fun to do as the locals do and eat soup or *chicharrón* (deep-fried pork) from the market stalls.

HI Cej-Tarabuco ☎04 6440471. One block back from the central plaza, this Hostelling International-affiliated hostel has clean and simple dorms and private rooms; the latter have either shared or private facilities. There's also a café and TV lounge. Dorms Bs32; doubles Bs60.

Cochabamba

At the geographical centre of Bolivia, midway between the Altiplano and the eastern lowlands, **COCHABAMBA** is the commercial hub of the country's richest agricultural region, the Cochabamba Valley. With a population of more than six hundred thousand, it's a modern, unpretentious and outward-looking commercial city. Named the "City of Eternal Spring", it enjoys a year-round sunny climate that is matched by the warmth and openness of its population. Although most travellers who visit are just passing through, those who spend time here find Cochabamba to be Bolivia's most welcoming city. It is also a good base for exploring the attractions of the surrounding valley – chief among these, in the eyes of the locals at least, is **chicha**, a thick, lightly alcoholic maize beer.

COCHABAMBA AND THE WATER WAR

Referred to by its inhabitants as "La Llacta", the Quechua equivalent of the Spanish word *pueblo*, meaning at once city and people or nation, Cochabamba is the centre of a vigorous **regional identity**, and throughout Bolivian history has enjoyed a reputation for political independence and rebelliousness, a tradition that continues to this day. In 2000 the city's water system was privatized and sold to a consortium of international companies which immediately doubled or even tripled water rates. In response, Cochabamba erupted in a series of spontaneous protests that became known as **La Guerra del Agua** – "the Water War". Thousands of citizens from all social classes took to the streets to demand rates be lowered, blocking roads in and out of the city. The Banzer government responded in familiar fashion: a state of siege was declared, protest organizers were arrested, **armed troops** were sent in and plainclothes snipers opened fire on protesters, killing one and injuring many others. Despite this oppression, the demonstrations continued, and the water consortium eventually backed down – a popular victory that was welcomed by anti-globalization campaigners around the world. The excellent 2010 film *Tambien la lluvia ("Even the Rain")*, starring Gael Garcia Bernal, is set during the Water War.

For all its charm, Cochabamba has few conventional tourist attractions, and little remains of the original colonial city centre. The **Museo Archeológico** is worth a visit, as is the **Cristo de la Concordia**, the Christ statue that overlooks Cochabamba from the east. Otherwise, the most interesting areas are the massive, rambling **street markets** that stretch to the south of the centre, the commercial heart of this market city.

Brief history

The **Incas** were quick to spot the region's agricultural potential when they conquered it in the mid-fifteenth century, moving Quechua-speakers here to cultivate maize. Inca control of the area was ended by the **Spanish**, who founded the city of Cochabamba on January 1, 1574, originally naming it La Villa de Oropeza in honour of the Conde de Oropeza, father of the Viceroy Francisco Toledo, who ordered its settlement. Locals soon reverted to calling it by the indigenous place name Cochabamba, a combination of the Quechua words for lake and plain, though all but one of the shallow, swampy **lakes** that once stood here have now been filled in.

The Spanish established **haciendas** to produce grain for Potosí's silver mines, and so important was their agricultural work to the colonial economy that the valley's indigenous population was exempted from having to work in the mines under the *mita* system. When the mines went into decline towards the end of the colonial period and the early republican era, much of the hacienda land was rented out, and the region saw the emergence of a class of small but independent Quechua-speaking **peasant farmers**, very different in culture and outlook from the rather closed Aymara *ayllus* of the Altiplano. These peasant farmers played a central role in the emergence of Bolivia's radical peasant political organizations in the 1950s and 1960s and, as migrants to the Chapare, have assumed a key role in the coca-growers' movement of recent years.

Plaza 14 de Septiembre

The centre of Cochabamba is **Plaza 14 de Septiembre**, a peaceful and pleasant square with flower-filled ornamental gardens, a colonial stone fountain (which amazingly for Bolivia actually works) and benches shaded by tall palm trees. At its centre stands an obelisk topped by the statue of a condor – a monument to the Cochabambinos who died during the Independence War. The plaza is flanked by nineteenth-century buildings that extend over the pavement and are supported by pillars, forming arched arcades.

La Catedral Metropolitana

Plaza 14 de Septiembre • Mon–Fri 8am–noon & 5–7pm, Sat & Sun 8am–noon • Free

Sideways on to the south side of Plaza 14 de Septiembre stands the **Catedral Metropolitana**, founded in 1571 and the city's oldest church, though little of the original structure remains. The main entrance, facing out onto Calle Arce, is a fairly straightforward mestizo-Baroque portico decorated with spiralled columns, carvings of flowers and squat angels that look rather like pre-Columbian idols. The airy but unexceptional Neoclassical interior is brightly painted with floral designs and images of saints.

Museo Archeológico

Corner of calles Aguirre and Jordán • Mon–Fri 8.30am–5.30pm, Sat 8.30am–2.30pm • Bs10

A block south of Plaza 14 de Septiembre sits the interesting and extensive **Museo Archeológico**. The items on display are poorly explained, but as you peruse the collection a picture of the evolution of **pre-Hispanic culture** in the Cochabamba region gradually emerges, stretching from the Tiwanaku culture, through a number of regional groups to the Incas. Among the most interesting exhibits is a series of small **stone idols** (thought to represent Pachamama), along with bronze Inca axeheads, ceremonial knives, star-shaped stone maces and some well-preserved Tiwanaku woven skull caps made specially to fit skulls deformed by ritual trepanation. Also intriguing is the series of items used by early Catholic missionaries in their efforts to convert the indigenous peoples – these include sheepskins painted with bizarre hieroglyph-like ideographs, and clay discs encrusted with fragments of stone and pottery which were used like rosaries to remember sequences of prayer and other mysteries of the faith. There's also a small display of ethnographic material from the peoples of the **Amazon lowlands**.

4

Colina San Sebastián

West of the bus terminal on Avenida Aroma, about 600m south of Plaza 14 de Septiembre

A tree-lined pedestrian avenue leads up to the summit of the **Colina San Sebastián**, a low hill with good views over the city that was the scene of one of the most dramatic events in Cochabamba's history. During the Independence War, the city was quick to join the rebellion against Spanish rule, but in 1812, after its menfolk had gone off to fight elsewhere, the women of Cochabamba found themselves virtually defenceless against an advancing royalist army. Refusing calls to surrender, the women fortified the hill where, on May 27, they fought heroically until finally overwhelmed. Known as Las Heroinas de la Coronilla, these women are commemorated by a **monument** at the top of the hill, a cast-iron statue of Christ surrounded by images of women fighting or sheltering their children. In Bolivia, Mothers' Day is celebrated on May 27 in memory of the Heroinas de la Coronilla.

La Cancha

Nine blocks south of Plaza 14 de Septiembre

In the south of the city, an entire block between calles Tarata and Pulucayo on the east side of Avenida San Martín, is occupied by the massive covered street market known as **La Cancha** ("walled enclosure" in Quechua), where campesinos and merchants from throughout the region come to buy and sell their produce. Wandering through the market's sprawling labyrinth of stalls is the best way to get a feel for the vibrant commercial culture of the city and the surrounding area: the buzz of Quechua fills the air and the **traditional costumes** of different campesino groups are very much in evidence, in particular the straw sombreros and bright-coloured *pollera* skirts of the women of the Cochabamba Valley. This is effectively one massive clearing house for **agricultural produce**, and the range of foodstuffs on sale reflects the full diversity of

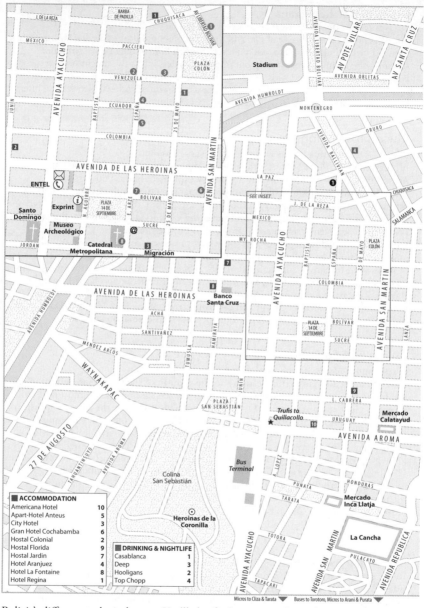

ACCOMMODATION
Americana Hotel	10
Apart-Hotel Anteus	5
City Hotel	3
Gran Hotel Cochabamba	6
Hostal Colonial	2
Hostal Florida	9
Hostal Jardín	7
Hotel Aranjuez	4
Hotel La Fontaine	8
Hotel Regina	1

DRINKING & NIGHTLIFE
Casablanca	1
Deep	3
Hooligans	2
Top Chopp	4

Bolivia's different ecological zones. You'll also find pretty much anything else poor Bolivians might need: sacks, rope, ironmongery, medicinal herbs, ritual items for making offerings to Pachamama and the mountain gods, and cheap manufactured goods. La Cancha has overflowed its original bounds, and now spreads across Avenida San Martín onto the disused railway, and northwest to occupy another entire block between Tarata and Punata, an area now known as the **Mercado Inca Llajta** ("Inca Town" in Quechua).

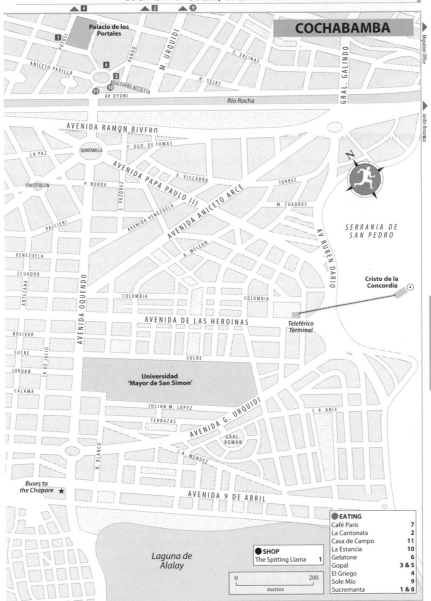

Palacio de los Portales

Almost 1km north of the city centre, with its entrance on Avenida Potosí • Palace Guided tours Tues–Fri 3.30–6pm, Sat 9.30–11am, Sun 11–11.30am • Bs10 • Garden Tues–Fri 3–6.30pm, Sat–Sun 9am–noon • Free

The **Palacio de los Portales** is the luxurious former house of the Cochabamba-born "King of Tin", **Simón Patiño** (see box, p.146). Built between 1915 and 1922 in a bizarre mix of architectural styles including **French Neoclassical** and *mudéjar*, the palace shows that the mining magnate possessed rather more money than artistic sense.

The interior is decorated with astonishing opulence: marble fireplaces and statues of Roman emperors and St Bernard dogs; walls covered in rich damask or panelled in fine wood; Venetian crystal chandeliers and Louis XV furniture. If anything, though, it's the magnificent **garden** that really impresses, laid out in perfect proportion by Japanese specialists and featuring a beautiful and rare ginkgo tree. Patiño never actually lived here, as by the time the palace was complete he was based permanently overseas, and the building now houses the Instituto Cultural Simón I. Patiño, a charity set up in his name to promote education and literacy.

Cristo de la Concordia

Above Avenida Ruben Dario • **Cristo de la Concordia** It's possible to climb inside the statue Sat & Sun 10am–6.30pm • Bs2 • Cable car Daily except Mon 10am–7pm • Bs6 return

About 1.5km east of the city centre, on the summit of the Serrania de San Pedro, stands the **Cristo de la Concordia**, a monumental statue of Christ with arms outstretched overlooking the city. The statue was modelled on the more famous Christ figure that looms over Río de Janeiro in Brazil but, as locals will proudly tell you, it's just that little bit taller, measuring over 34m (40m, if you include the pedestal), and is thus the tallest statue in South America. Towering high above the city and weighing over two thousand tons, by Bolivian standards it's a truly massive monument.

From a station at the eastern end of Avenida Las Heroínas, a modern **cable car** (*teleférico*) makes the five-minute journey up the Serrania de San Pedro to the statue (the alternatives are a hard slog up the steps at the end of Avenida Heroínas or a more expensive taxi ride). A visit to the foot of the Cristo is popular with locals, particularly at weekends, but it never gets too crowded and is usually fairly peaceful. The **views** of the city and surrounding valley from the base of the statue are splendid, and on weekends you can climb up the spiral staircase inside the hollow steel figure for an even better panorama. There's also a small **café**, and several stalls rent binoculars and telescopes.

ARRIVAL AND DEPARTURE

COCHABAMBA

By plane Jorge Wilsterman airport (☎ 04 4222846) is a few kilometres southwest of the city; a taxi into the centre costs Bs25–35; alternatively, take micro B, which goes up Av Ayacucho to Plaza 14 de Septiembre. There are several daily flights to La Paz and Santa Cruz, and less frequent services to Riberalta, Sucre, Tarija and Trinidad. In addition, there are international flights to Asunción in Paraguay, Buenos Aires in Argentina and São Paulo in Brazil. The departure taxes are Bs11 for domestic flights and Bs175 for international services.

By bus Most long-distance buses arrive at and depart from Cochabamba's bus terminal, in the south of the city on Av Ayacucho just south of Av Aroma. The terminal is modern and fairly well organized, with an information kiosk, post office, plenty of phone booths, a left-luggage store, a restaurant, and several ATMs. The area around the bus station can be rough, especially at night, so take care. A taxi to the city centre costs about Bs5. There are regular buses to La Paz (7–8hr) and Oruro (4–6hr), and a couple of weekly services to Vallegrande (10–12hr). Buses to Santa Cruz (10–12hr) leave either early in the morning or in the evening, and there are several overnight buses to Sucre (10–12hr). Services to the Chapare region (including Villa Tunari; 3hr–3hr 30min) depart when full from close to the junction of Av Oquendo and Av 9 de Abril, southeast of the city centre.

COCHABAMBA'S STREET NUMBERS

Cochabamba's **street numbers** are prefixed N, S, E or O – north, south, east or west – depending on whether they run north or south from Avenida Heroínas, or east or west from Avenida Ayacucho. The first two digits in the street number refer to the block in terms of how far it is from these two major intersections, the second two to the number of the building: thus España N-0349 is on España at no. 49, three blocks north of the intersection with Avenida Heroínas.

INFORMATION AND TOURS

TOURIST INFORMATION

The tourist office, located on the second storey of a building on the northwest corner of Plaza 14 de Septiembre (Mon–Fri 8am–noon & 2.30–6.30pm; ☎04 4258030), usually has free city maps and leaflets. There is also an information kiosk at the bus station (see opposite; officially daily 6am–10pm; ☎04 4220550).

TOUR OPERATORS

Respected Cochabamba tour operators include Turismo Santa Rita, Buenos Aires 866 (☎04 4280305, ⓦturismosantarita.com), and Collasuyo Tours, Ayacucho and Achá (☎04 4511747), both of which run trips to most of

the same regional destinations – city tours, Valle Alto, Incarakay and Incallajta, Torotoro and the Chapare.

Fremen agency Tumusla N-0245 ☎04 4259392, ⓦandes-amazonia.com. An excellent tour agency offering a wide range of tailor-made tours throughout Bolivia. In the Cochabamba region, they run trips down into the Chapare (where they own the *Hotel El Puente* in Villa Tunari – see p.227), as well as city tours and visits to the market towns of the Valle Alto, to the Parque Nacional Torotoro, and to the ruins at Incarakay and Incallajta. They also organize adventurous camping trips by motorized canoe into the Parque Nacional Isiboro-Sécure (see p.288), starting in the Chapare and ending in Trinidad.

ACCOMMODATION

Accommodation in Cochabamba is unexceptional and generally not aimed at tourists. The better places tend to be rather dull **business hotels**, though there are a few decent budget options; the flophouses around the bus station are best avoided. The only time accommodation can be difficult to find is in mid-August during the **Fiesta de la Virgen de Urkupiña** in nearby Quillacollo (see p.219): it's best to book in advance during this period.

Americana Hotel Arze S-0788 ☎04 4250552. Good-value high-rise hotel with attentive staff and comfortable, well-equipped en-suite rooms with TVs and good views. The area isn't the safest, however, so take care at night. Bs200

Apart-Hotel Anteus Potosí N-1365 ☎04 4245067, ⓦhotelanteus.com. Small, modern hotel located across the street from the Palacio de los Portales in a residential neighbourhood, an easy walk from Blrd Recoleta. The bright rooms have private bathrooms, TVs and kitchenettes. Bs288

City Hotel Jordan N-0341 ☎04 4222993, ✉cityhotel42@hotmail.com. Although a little frayed around the edges, this central hotel is a sound choice. Its en-suite rooms feature phones, TVs and faded decor – those at the back of the building are the best. Rates include breakfast. Bs200

Gran Hotel Cochabamba Plaza Ubaldo Anze E-0415 ☎04 4282551, ⓦgranhotelcochabamba.com. Luxurious Art Deco country club-style hotel with spacious, fully equipped rooms (with flatscreen TVs, minibars and safes) looking over a swimming pool and a palm-filled garden. There's also a classy restaurant and bar, and breakfast is included. Bs700 ($100)

Hostal Colonial Junín N-0134 ☎04 4221791, ✉hostal.colonial@hotmail.com. Very friendly, family-run place offering clean but slightly dilapidated en-suite rooms (with TVs) on two floors, overlooking a charming garden overflowing with lush tropical vegetation. Bs100

Hostal Florida 25 de Mayo S-0583 ☎04 4257911,

✉floridahostal@latinmail.com. Popular backpacker favourite located halfway between the bus terminal and the city centre. The clean rooms come with shared or private baths –and a bilingual copy of the New Testament – and are set around a sunny central courtyard. Bs160

Hostal Jardin Hamiraya N-0248 ☎04 4247844. Compact but reasonably comfortable rooms (with or without bathrooms) opening out onto a peaceful garden with outdoor seating. Rates include breakfast. Bs50

Hotel Aranjuez Buenos Aires E-0563 ☎04 4240158, ⓦaranjuezhotel.com. Located in the smart Recoleta neighbourhood, *Hotel Aranjuez* is a professionally-run place whose en suites – each with TV, minibar, phone and wi-fi access – are set around a bird-filled garden. There's also a restaurant-bar. Breakfast included Bs525 ($75)

Hotel La Fontaine Hamiraya N-0181 ☎04 4252838, ✉eduardoelc@yahoo.es. Small and comfortable business-traveller hotel offering nicely furnished modern rooms equipped with fridges, TVs and private bathrooms, and decorated with colonial religious paintings – but beware the hazardously low ceiling beams. Breakfast included. Bs200

Hotel Regina Reza with España ☎04 4257382, ⓦhotelreginabolivia.com. Good-value mid-range hotel with efficient and helpful staff, plus a bar and restaurant. The large, bright and comfortable en-suite rooms have TVs and kitchenettes, though could do with a redecoration. Breakfast included. Bs350 ($60)

EATING

The most affordable places to eat are Cochabamba's many **markets**, in particular the Mercado Calatayud, on San Martín and Aroma, which offers **local specialities** like *picante de pollo* (chicken in a spicy sauce), *silpancho* (a breaded beef schnitzel), and delicious *empanadas* and *salteñas*, which seem twice as big as elsewhere in Bolivia and are served with a choice of different sauces. *Cochabambinos* are generally adventurous eaters, and the choice of **restaurants** here is broad.

Café Paris España with Bolivar. Sophisticated French café with Parisian posters on the walls, wrought iron chairs and a stained-glass-covered bar. There's a concise menu of coffees (Bs5–19), sweet and savoury crêpes (Bs15–21), and snacks like croissants and quiches, plus free wi-fi. Daily.

La Cantonata España with Venezuela. Elegant and sophisticated restaurant serving good but slightly overpriced Italian food (mains Bs35-70) to Cochabamba's wealthiest residents. Closed Mon.

Casa de Campo Blvd Recoleta and Pando. An attractive, if tourist-orientated restaurant, serving classy versions of traditional dishes (mains Bs25–55) around a pleasing central courtyard. There are often peña-style programmes at the weekends. Daily.

La Estancia Blvd Recoleta and Pando. Excellent Argentine parilla (barbecue restaurant) serving generous portions of delicious grilled beef (go for the slightly more expensive Argentine cuts), chicken or fish accompanied by a massive salad bar. Mains Bs30–60. Daily for lunch and dinner.

Gelatone San Martín, near corner with Bolivar. This blue and white candy-striped heladería serves delicious Italian-style ice cream in a variety of forms – from tubs to cones (from Bs7), sundaes (Bs18–22) to affogatos (ice cream with hot coffee poured over it) – to eat in or take away. Daily.

Gopal España N-0250. Inexpensive Hare Krishna wholefood restaurant serving up inexpensive and tasty vegetarian meals, including a buffet lunch (Bs18) that features twenty different salads, as well as numerous other dishes. There's another branch at Rocha E-0375. Weekdays for lunch and dinner.

El Griego España and Venezuela. Inexpensive Greek restaurant serving tasty gyros accompanied by good Greek salads or not-so-Greek spaghetti. Mains Bs15–40. Closed Sun, evenings only.

Sole Mio América E-826. This Italian-run restaurant has decent, fairly thin-crust pizzas (Bs30–65), as well as a range of pastas, risottos and salads (Bs15–50). Sat–Sun lunch and dinner, Mon–Fri dinner only.

Sucremanta Arze S-0348. Popular restaurant specializing in traditional pork-based dishes from the Chuquisaca department (Sucre) including delicious chorizo sausages and fritanga, a thick, spicy stew. There's another branch on Av Ballivián. Mains Bs15–30. Weekday lunchtimes.

DRINKING AND NIGHTLIFE

Nightlife in Cochabamba is centred on three different districts, each catering to a distinct crowd. Wealthy Cochabambinos head to **Boulevard Recoleta**, just east of Plaza Quintanilla, north of the Río Rocha at the top of Avenida Oquendo, about 1km from Plaza 14 de Septiembre. This pedestrianized street is lined with classy restaurants and bars. More straightforward entertainment – inexpensive steakhouses, beer palaces with football on big-screen TVs and sound systems pumping out Latin pop music – can be found along **Avenida Ballivián** (also known as El Prado), just north of the city centre. Centred on the intersection of **España and Ecuador**, in the city centre, meanwhile, is a laidback bohemian scene of small bars and cafés popular with Cochabamba's large student population. Many restaurants stay open late at weekends and double as bars, and in all three areas places go in and out of fashion very quickly.

Casablanca 25 de Mayo and Ecuador. Popular with Cochabamba's sizeable population of young foreign volunteers and language school students, this Hollywood-themed bar serves cold beer and good cocktails. The first-floor balcony is great for people-watching, and classic films are sometimes screened.

Deep On the circle between Recoleta and Padilla. One of the most popular nightclubs in town, Deep features dance and Latin music and a crowd of upwardly mobile locals.

Hooligans On a lane off the Pando, just beyond Hotel Portales. More salubrious than its name suggests, this friendly bar is a popular pre-club spot. Later in the night, the crowd moves on to Mandarina Lounge, which is conveniently located next door.

Top Chopp Av Ballivián and Reza. Raucous place pumping out loud Latin dance music and serving cheap, cold beer and straightforward Bolivian food.

DIRECTORY

Banks and exchange There are plenty of ATMs, including at the Banco Nacional de Bolivia, Jordán and Aguirre. eFex, on Plaza 14 de Septiembre, changes US dollars.

Bookshops and camping equipment The Spitting Llama (📞 04 4894540, 🌐 thespittingllama.com) on España is an excellent multilingual bookstore and exchange. It also stocks camping and travel supplies, as does Bazar Aventura on Bolívar with San Martín.

Car rental J. Barron's, Sucre E-0727 📞 04 4222774.

Doctor Clínica Belga, Antezana N-0457 📞 04 4231404.

Immigration The migración office is a few kilometres' northeast of town near Puente Muyrurni.

Internet Internet cafés abound here: one of the best is Café Internet Conections (B3/hr) on Arze, just off the plaza.

Language classes Escuela Runawasi, Maurice Lefebvre N-0470, Villa Juan XXIII 📞 04 4248923, 🌐 runawasi.org, offers Spanish and Quechua lessons, plus homestays.

Laundry Superclean, 16 de Julio and Jordán, has a same-day service.

Post office Correo Central, Av Ayacucho and Av Heroínas.

Telephone office ENTEL's main office is at Av Ayacucho and Achá.

Around Cochabamba

East of Cochabamba stretches the densely-populated upper Cochabamba Valley, or **Valle Alto.** Set at an altitude of about 2600m, it is blessed with rich alluvial soils and a warm, spring-like climate. The valley's fields of maize and wheat are among the most fertile and productive in the country – not for nothing is it known as the breadbasket of Bolivia. This region is dominated by peasant farmers: though still Quechua-speaking, they're much more outward looking than the communities of the Altiplano, and played a key role in the emergence of radical peasant federations in Bolivia in the 1960s and 1970s.

Cliza, Punata and Arani

Cliza market: Sun• Punata market: Tues • Arani market: Thurs

The rural centres of **CLIZA** (40km from Cochabamba), **PUNATA** (45km) and **ARANI** (55km) all make interesting excursions, especially during their bustling weekly **agricultural markets**, when peasants from the surrounding districts come to buy supplies, sell produce, meet friends and drink *chicha*. The women wear the characteristic brightly coloured *pollera* skirts and white straw boaters of the Cochabamba Valley, and carry their goods on their backs in luridly striped shawls. The markets are rather prosaic compared to the more tourist-orientated market at Tarabuco (see p.208), and there's almost nothing in the way of handicrafts on sale, but it's still interesting to watch the energetic scenes, as people haggle over great piles of fruit and vegetables, live sheep and

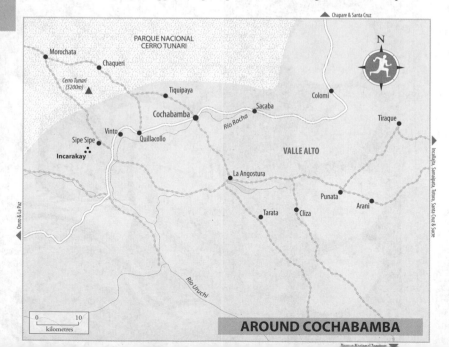

AROUND COCHABAMBA

cattle, and cheap manufactured clothes. The liveliest markets are in Arani and in Cliza; the market in Punata, 45km from Cochabamba, is smaller, but the town is famed as home to Bolivia's best *chicha*. With a tart, yeasty flavour *chicha* is definitely an acquired taste, and can play havoc with the digestion, but drinking a few glasses is the best way to get talking with the local campesinos.

Parque Nacional Cerro Tunari
Immediately north of Cochabamba • Free

Some three thousand square kilometres of the Cordillera Tunari – the mountain range that forms the northern boundary of the Cochabamba Valley – is protected by **Parque Nacional Cerro Tunari**. Named after the region's tallest peak, the 5200m Cerro Tunari, the park was set up primarily to protect the forested watershed that provides the irrigation water that is vital to the agriculture of the Cochabamba Valley, and to conserve rare high-altitude queñua forests, home to the Cochabamba mountain finch, which is found nowhere else in the world. Given its proximity to the city, the park's ecosystems are far from pristine; the lower slopes closest to Cochabamba in particular are affected by illegal building. It's easy to visit from the city, however, and is popular amongst Cochabambinos at weekends.

From the gate, a track climbs steeply up into the park; an hour or so's walk (or a short drive) will bring you to a series of picnic sites and children's playgrounds amid eucalyptus groves where Cochabambinos like to relax around a barbecue, enjoy the views and stroll or ride mountain bikes along the various tracks and trails. If you continue walking uphill for two to three hours you'll reach a series of small **lakes** from which the views are even more spectacular. If you make an early start and travel via Quillacollo (see below), it is also possible to visit the higher reaches of the park and the peak of Cerro Tunari itself, from where you can gaze down at Cochabamba and the valley and – on clear days – across to the shimmering peaks of the Cordillera Real far to the west. Condors are also a frequent sight.

Quillacollo

About 15km west of Cochabamba, and all but engulfed by the city's urban sprawl, is the bustling market town of **QUILLACOLLO**, the Cochabamba Valley's second-biggest settlement. It's a lively commercial centre and transport hub famous for its **Fiesta de la Virgen de Urkupiña** (see p.220), staged annually in August. Outside fiesta time, however, there's little to see other than the reputedly miraculous but rather ordinary-looking image of the Virgen de Urkupiña herself, inside the modest Neoclassical Iglesia de San Idelfonsino a few blocks south of the main plaza. The town is also well known for the spicy food and heady brews available in its raucous *chicherías* (traditional restaurants serving *chicha*).

Incarakay

Set high on the mountainside overlooking the Cochabamba Valley about 25km west of the city, the ruins of the Inca outpost of **Incarakay** make an excellent if rather strenuous day-trip from Cochabamba. The site itself is fairly small, a collection of a dozen or so buildings made of rough-cut stones with the trapezoidal internal niches and doorways and **earthquake-resistant** inward-leaning walls characteristic of Inca architecture. What really impresses, however, is the setting: perched on the mountainside at an altitude of 3200m, Incarakay enjoys fantastic views over Cochabamba to Cerro Tunari. From up here, the flat expanse of the Cochabamba Valley with its neatly irrigated green fields of maize seems a vision of order and fertility in contrast to the harsh, arid mountain ranges on either side.

It's not certain quite what purpose Incarakay served, but it seems likely it was some kind of **imperial administration centre**. The Incas invested great energy in the

4

THE FIESTA DE LA VIRGEN DE URKUPIÑA

Every year for three days around August 15, Quillacollo hosts the **Fiesta de la Virgen de Urkupiña**, which attracts up to half a million visitors and involves a massive parade of costumed dancers from all over Bolivia, as well as copious eating and drinking intertwined with sincere expressions of spiritual faith – many pilgrims walk to Quillacollo by night from Cochabamba as a sign of religious devotion. The fiesta dates back to the early nineteenth century, when a local Quechua-speaking shepherdess had repeated visions of the Virgin Mary on the nearby **Cerro Cota hill**. When the villagers of Quillacollo investigated, they saw a brief glimpse of the Virgin ascending to heaven, and later found a carved image of her hidden among the rocks. This was carried to the parish church of San Ildefonsino, and soon credited with numerous miracles. The name Urkupiña is derived from the Quechua for "on the mountain" – the shepherdess's cry when she pointed out the Virgin to the villagers.

As with most major Bolivian religious fiestas, however, there's little doubt that its true origins lie deep in the pre-Christian past. Significant pre-Hispanic burial sites have been uncovered in the centre of Quillacollo, and the town's name means **"mountain of the moon"** in Quechua – the Incas considered the moon to be a major female deity, and following the Spanish conquest it was often conflated with the Virgin Mary. As well as the procession and dances, a central feature of the fiesta is a visit to the rocky outcrop where the Virgin appeared, during which tourists and pilgrims alike hack lumps of rock from the **sacred mountain** to take home with them in the belief that this will ensure health and material prosperity. They also make libations of coca and alcohol and burn candles, offerings associated with the Andean earth goddess **Pachamama**. As in the fiesta of Alasitas in La Paz (see p.66), pilgrims buy miniature replicas of objects they wish to possess in the belief that by doing so the real thing will be theirs before the year is out.

The best way to visit the fiesta is as a **day-trip** from Cochabamba, though you'll need to get to Quillacollo early in the morning to ensure a good spot from which to watch the dances. Accommodation in Cochabamba can be hard to find during the fiesta.

Cochabamba Valley after they conquered the region in the mid-fifteenth century, bringing in agricultural settlers from other parts of the empire to cultivate the **maize** which fed the Inca armies, and this would seem a perfect site from which to calculate how much the imperial share of the harvest should amount to each year. On the return journey it's well worth stopping off in the town of Sipe Sipe to sample some **chicha**, the fermented maize beer that was sacred to the Incas and which is still produced and consumed in large quantities in the Cochabamba Valley, It is served from huge earthenware pots and drunk from gourds. You'll find it on sale in a number of private houses, marked by a white flag or bunch of flowers raised on a pole outside.

Incallajta

The other major Inca site in the Cochabamba region is **Incallajta**, a far more substantial complex about 143km east of the city, which was built as a military outpost to protect the valley from raids by the unconquered Chiriguano tribes of the eastern lowlands. There are good camping spots at the ruins and water is available, but you'll have to take all the food you need with you. Incallajta is 15km off the road to Sucre, just south of the point where it joins the old highland road between Cochabamba and Santa Cruz.

Totora

The road from Cochabamba to Sucre, 366km to the southeast, passes through a scenic region of rugged mountains and fertile valleys, but unfortunately all public transport between the two travels overnight, so unless you've got your own transport, you're unlikely to see much. The road also passes through what was once one of the prettiest colonial villages in Bolivia – **TOTORA**. Sadly, the village was devastated by a powerful earthquake that shook the region in 1998, but after a lengthy corruption-plagued reconstruction effort it has finally regained much of its original charm. The entirely, and generally faithfully, rebuilt central plaza offers a unique opportunity to experience the colonial plaza much the way it would have looked at the height of Spanish rule.

ARRIVAL AND DEPARTURE

CLIZA, PUNATA AND ARANI

Micros and trufis to Arani (every 15–20min; 45min) and Punata (every 30min; 40min) leave from the corner of Av Republica and Manuripi in the south of Cochabamba; those for *Cliza* (every 15–20min; 25min) leave from the corner of Av Barrientos and Manuripi.

PARQUE NACIONAL CERRO TUNARI

To reach the most accessible section of the park, immediately above Cochabamba, flag down trufi #103, which heads along Av Ayacucho to the park gate, about 7km north of the city centre. To get into the higher reaches of the park and climb the peak of Cerro Tunari itself, you'll need to take a micro very early in the morning to Quillacollo (see below) and then catch another micro from there towards the rural town of Morochata (1 daily at about 7am), which lies north of Quillacollo on the other side of the Tunari range and the national park. You alight from the micro at the hamlet of Chaqueri, about 25km from Quillacollo at an altitude of 4200m, from where a path leads to the summit; it's a fairly straightforward ascent (4–5hr), though you may need to ask locals for directions. Transport back to Quillacollo passes by Chaqueri in the afternoon, but given the timing you'll need to camp overnight if you're doing the ascent independently. Alternatively save yourself the hassle and go on an organized trip with a Cochabamba-based tour agency (see p.215), which will provide transport, a guide and accommodation.

QUILLACOLLO

Frequent micros run from Av Aroma in Cochabamba (every 10–15min; 25min).

AROUND COCHABAMBA

INCARAKAY

To reach the ruins, take a micro from Av Aroma in Cochabamba to Quillacollo (see above), then another from Plaza Bolívar in Quillacollo to Sipe Sipe (every 15–20min; 20min), a peaceful agricultural town about 8km east of Quillacollo. From Sipe Sipe it's a steep two- to three-hour climb up to Incarakay; the route is fairly easy to find on your own, though if in doubt you can always ask directions from the locals. From the southwest corner of the plaza in Sipe Sipe, follow the road that heads out of town towards the mountainside. About 1km from the plaza, the road crosses a stream and turns sharply to the left; about 160m further on, just past a gully, a path climbs from the right-hand side of the road up to the ruins. The path is indistinct, but if you keep climbing towards the southwest the ruins will eventually become visible above you.

INCALLAJTA

Unless you rent a 4WD, the easiest way to visit Incallajta is with a Cochabamba-based tour agency – a day-trip costs about Bs560–700 ($80–100) per person for a group of four people. Reaching Incallajta by public transport is very difficult: you'll have to catch a bus from Cochabamba heading to Totora as far as the turn-off at the village of Collpa, then walk 15km to the ruins and spend the night there before returning the next day.

TOTORA

While it is possible to get off one of the through buses in the middle of the night, it is much better to visit Totora on a day-trip from Cochabamba. Micros leave from the corner of Av 6 de Agosto and República between 1pm and 4pm (3hr). Shared taxis, which depart when full, shave an hour from the journey, and only cost a little more.

ACCOMMODATION

PARQUE NACIONAL CERRO TUNARI

If you want to scale Cerro Tunari independently, you will need to take your own camping gear, food and water supplies, as public transport timings do not allow you to do the ascent in one day.

QUILLACOLLO

Eco Hotel Spa Planeta de Luz 5km north of Quillacollo ☎04 4261234, ⌨planetadeluz.com. This Hostelling International-affiliated lodge, set amid expansive gardens, has a hippy vibe. There are options for most budgets – including clean dorms, smart private rooms and romantic cabins – as well as a pool, sauna, spa

treatments and restaurant specialising in vegetarian cuisine. Dorms Bs55; doubles and cabins Bs240

INCALLAJTA

There are good camping spots at the ruins, but you'll have to bring your own tent, plus all the food and water you will need for your trip.

TOTORA

Hostal Colonial Just uphill from the central plaza; no phone. If you want to spend the night here, the unmarked *Hostal Colonial* is one of a handful of basic but decent lodges in town. Bs30

4

Parque Nacional Torotoro

Some 130km south of Cochabamba, **PARQUE NACIONAL TOROTORO** protects a remote and sparsely inhabited stretch of the arid, scrubby landscape that is characteristic of the eastern foothills and valleys of the Andes. Covering just 164 square kilometres around the village of the same name, Torotoro is Bolivia's smallest national park, but what it lacks in size it makes up for with its powerful scenery and varied attractions. The park encompasses a high, **hanging valley** and deep eroded **canyons**, ringed by low mountains whose twisted geological formations are strewn with fossils, dinosaur footprints and labyrinthine limestone cave complexes. In addition, the park's woodland supports considerable wildlife – including flocks of parakeets and the rare and beautiful red-fronted macaw, found only in this particular region of Bolivia – while ancient rock paintings and pre-Inca ruins reveal a long-standing human presence. The main attractions are the limestone caves of **Umajallanta**, the beautiful, waterfall-filled **Torotoro Canyon**, and hiking expeditions to the pre-Inca ruined fortress of **Llama Chaqui**. Two days are generally enough to see the main attractions though it's worth taking longer if you want to explore the area more fully.

Brief history

Though reached from Cochabamba, Parque Nacional Torotoro actually lies within Northern Potosí department. Before the Spanish conquest this was the core territory of the **Charcas Confederation**, a powerful collection of different ethnic groups subject to Inca rule. Following the conquest, the different Quechua- and Aymara-speaking groups that made up the confederation retained their distinct identities, each as separate *ayllus* (extended kinship groups, similar to clans or tribes). The *ayllus* of Northern Potosí mostly live in the higher-altitude lands to the west of the region, where they grow potatoes and raise livestock, but they maintain islands of territory in the dry valleys such as Torotoro, where they cultivate maize, wheat and other lower-altitude crops. This system ensures each group has access to the produce of different altitudes, and represents a distinctly Andean form of organization that has long fascinated anthropologists.

Throughout the colonial era and long after independence, Northern Potosí was the focus of frequent **indigenous uprisings**. As recently as 1958, during the upheaval following the 1952 revolution, Torotoro village – which was formed in the late colonial period by mestizo migrants from Cochabamba – was ransacked by armed *ayllu* members, who seized the lands of the haciendas that had been established on their traditional valley territories.

Torotoro

The administrative centre of the park and the only base from which to explore it is the sleepy village of **TOROTORO**. Home to just a few hundred people, it stands beside the river of the same name at the top of a broad hanging valley at an altitude of about 2600m and is the place to find food, accommodation, guides and information (see p.215). Torotoro's main annual celebration is the **Fiesta de Tata Santiago**, held on July 25 each year, when the *ayllus* descend on the village to drink, dance and stage ritual Tinku fights (see p.165).

The dinosaur tracks of Cerro Huayllas

The park's clearest **dinosaur tracks** are on the lower slopes of Cerro Huayllas, the mountain just east of the village across the Río Torotoro (generally only a stream in the May–Sept dry season). To reach them, walk back along the road to Cochabamba and cross at the ford, turn right and walk upstream about 100m, then climb about 20m up the rocky slope to your left. The tracks were made by a quadruped herbivore that roamed the region in the Cretaceous era more than sixty million years ago – they comprise a trail of deep circular prints about 50cm in diameter imprinted in a sloping plane of grey rock and set about 1m apart. A little further upstream there's another trail of smaller (and much less distinct) prints left by a three-toed carnivore.

Along the Río Torotoro

Follow the Río Torotoro downstream from the Cerro Huayllas dinosaur tracks for about twenty minutes and you'll reach a stretch where the rushing rainy-season waters have carved great stone basins out of the soft bedrock – locals refer to this stretch as **Batea Cocha** (Beating Pool), as they look a bit like basins for pounding laundry. About 7m up the rock face on the left bank, protected by a low adobe wall, is a collection of ancient **rock paintings** (*pinturas rupestres*). Mostly abstract designs painted in red ochre, with several zigzags – including one that looks like a serpent and another that could be the sun or a star – the paintings are all less than 1m long and have been partly defaced, but they provide a focus for what is anyway a pleasant stroll down the river. A little further downstream there's a pretty **waterfall** that forms a good swimming hole; beyond that, the river plunges down into the deep Torotoro Canyon and you can walk no further, though you can access the canyon from further downstream (see below).

Torotoro Canyon

Just north of Torotoro village the Río Torotoro plunges through the deep **Torotoro Canyon**, probably the park's most beautiful section. Enclosed on either side by sheer, 200m-high cliffs covered with stunted trees and spiky bromeliads, the river creates a series of waterfalls as it tumbles over a jumble of massive boulders, forming pools that are ideal for swimming. The route down to the rock-strewn canyon floor is easy to find without a guide (though you shouldn't go alone in case you hurt yourself and can't get back).

To get down into the canyon, follow the road out of town towards Cochabamba for about 200m. Where the road turns sharply to the right, follow the track heading off to the left, and walk for about twenty minutes until you see some well-made stone steps dropping steeply down the side of the canyon to your left. The most picturesque stretch of the canyon is a few hundred metres downstream from where the steps reach the bottom, where a ten-metre-high waterfall known as **El Vergel** emerges from the side of the canyon on the right in several streams which cover the rock face in slimy-green water weeds.

Caverna de Umajallanta

The most extensive and easiest to visit of the park's many limestone cave systems is the **Caverna de Umajallanta**, where nearly 5km of underground passages have been explored. The cave makes a great day-trip from Torotoro and is one of the park's most popular attractions; on no account attempt to visit without a guide as it is easy to get lost once inside. Its entrance is about 8km northwest of Torotoro, a walk of ninety minutes to two hours across the rolling landscape with good views of the dramatic geology of the mountain ridges that surround the Torotoro valley – about halfway you'll pass a trail of **dinosaur footprints**.

The cave complex was formed by the waters of the **Río Umajallanta**, which disappears below the surface here and re-emerges as a waterfall high above the

Torotoro Canyon, 6km away to the east. It consists of a series of interconnected limestone caverns of varying sizes, one of which contains a lake fed by the river that is home to some blind white fish. Sadly, most of the stalactites and stalagmites have been broken off by visitors in the years before protective measures were established (they should grow back in a few centuries), but a visit to the cave is still very enjoyable, unless you're claustrophobic – trips involve clambering and crawling for a couple of hours through some very tight places up to 800m underground. Take a torch and drinking water and expect to get dirty. For serious cavers and speleologists there are a number of o ther caves in the area to explore – talk to staff at the park office.

Llama Chaqui

About 16km east of Torotoro stands **Llama Chaqui**, a ruined pre-Inca fortress that energetic hikers can visit (with a guide) in a long day-trip from the village. The walk to the ruins takes you over the mountains to the east of the Río Torotoro, with spectacular views across the deep valley of the Río Caine and the rugged brown mountains that march away to Cerro Tunari, the peak that rises above Cochabamba. The scenery is very beautiful, with steep rocky slopes and narrow hanging valleys patchworked with maize and barley fields set around the occasional isolated hamlet.

Set on a knife-edge ridge high above the **Río Caine**, Llama Chaqui itself is an excellent observation point and natural fortress, though other than the walled enclosure (still sometimes used as a cattle pen) little remains of the ancient settlement and the entire complex is heavily overgrown. Even so, you can still make out the foundations of individual houses, and the ground is scattered with pottery fragments and rough-cut stones.

ARRIVAL AND DEPARTURE   PARQUE NACIONAL TOROTORO

By bus Buses to Torotoro leave Cochabamba from the corner of Av 6 de Agosto and Av Republica at 5.45–6am (Wed, Thurs, Sat & Sun), and return from Torotoro at 6am (Mon, Tues, Fri and Sun). The bus ride lasts about seven hours in the dry season (May–Sept), a rough and dusty trip along unpaved roads and dry riverbeds – in the rainy season (Nov–March) it takes much longer and the route can sometimes become impassable.

INFORMATION

Tourist information On arrival, head to the tourist office on the main street of the village (officially daily 8am–noon & 2–5pm), where you'll need to pay the Bs20 park admission fee. The office has basic information about the park and can find you a local guide for around Bs70–100 a day – the village is so small that forming a group with other travellers is rarely a problem if you want to share the cost.

ACCOMMODATION

Hostal Las Hermanas ☎ 04 4135736. This simple, welcoming lodge is the best of the village's low-budget *alojamientos*. The rooms - with either shared or private bathrooms – are clean, basic and fine for a night or two. There's also good homecooking available. **Bs50**

Villa Etelvina ☎ 7073 7807, ⌨ villaetelvina.com. Easily the best place to stay in Torotoro, the well-run Villa Etelvina has comfortable en-suite bungalows sleeping four people, rooms with shared bathrooms and camping facilities; breakfast included. There's a restaurant, and staff can organize hikes, mountain biking and rapelling. Advance bookings are essential. Doubles **Bs160**; bungalows **Bs480**; camping/person **Bs40**

EATING

Torotoro doesn't have any real restaurants other than the one at Villa Etelvina, but some villagers prepare simple, inexpensive meals if you order a few hours in advance – just ask around to find out who's cooking. Otherwise, there are a few basic shops where you can buy simple provisions, though it's worth bringing some supplies with you from Cochabamba to supplement this rather meagre fare, particularly if you're planning a longer stay.

The Chapare

Northeast of Cochabamba, the main road to Santa Cruz crosses the last ridge of the Andes and drops down into the **CHAPARE**, a broad, rainforest-covered plain in the Upper Amazon Basin that has been heavily settled by peasant migrants from the highlands, who over the last few decades have turned the region into the main source in Bolivia of coca grown to manufacture **cocaine**. For the traveller, the ongoing conflict between cocaine producers and Bolivian government troops means that despite its great natural beauty the Chapare is not the place for expeditions far off the beaten track. For all the region's troubles, however, the towns along the main Cochabamba to Santa Cruz road are peaceful and safe to visit, though most are fairly unattractive. The exception is **Villa Tunari**, a one-time narco-traffickers' playground that is now at the centre of efforts to promote the Chapare as a tourist destination. The rainforests of the **Parque Nacional Carrasco** are within easy reach, and the town enjoys a beautiful setting and is a good place to relax. Otherwise, the main point of stopping in the Chapare is to make the exciting river trip from **Puerto Villarroel**, the region's main port, north to Trinidad in the Beni.

Villa Tunari

About 160km from Cochabamba, **VILLA TUNARI** is the biggest settlement in the Chapare and the centre of efforts to develop the region as a tourist destination. Set beside a broad sweep of the Río San Mateo, with the last forested foothills of the Andes rising behind, Villa Tunari is picturesque, and at an altitude of just 300m enjoys a warm, tropical climate. Its chances of becoming a successful resort or an ecotourism destination like Rurrenabaque, however, are limited so long as the current instability continues, and independent travel off the beaten track in the surrounding area remains inadvisable. This is a shame, as from **Puerto San Francisco**, an hour's drive north of Villa Tunari, you could rent a motorized canoe and boatman to take you down the ríos Chipiriri and Isiboro into the rainforests of the **Parque Nacional Isiboro-Sécure** (see p.288); though the Cochabamba-based tour agency Fremen runs trips along this route, doing so independently is not advisable at present.

The main Cochabamba-Santa Cruz road, which runs through the town, is lined with restaurants and hotels where in better days the movers and shakers of the **cocaine industry** would come to blow some of their massive earnings, but which now depend on weekenders from Cochabamba, foreign development workers and a small number of tourists. The main plaza is two blocks north of the road, opposite *Hotel Las Palmas*.

Parque Machia

Daily except Mon, 9am–5pm • Bs6, cameras Bs30

A 250m walk east along the main road in Villa Tunari and across the bridge over the Río Espirito Santo brings you to the entrance of the **Parque Machia**, a small, private ecological reserve that also serves as a refuge for Amazonian animals rescued from captivity. The park has 4km of trails running through the forest and some lookout points with beautiful views across the Río Chapare and the forest-covered mountains rising to the high peaks of the Andes behind. Along the trails you'll meet most of the semi-tame animal residents, which include several species of monkey, macaws and a puma, many of which roam free but still depend on humans for food. After heavy rains, the trails are sometimes closed for safety reasons.

Parque Nacional Carrasco

Daily 9am–5pm, last entry 3pm • Bs35–70, depending on size of group • ☎ 7937 1991

A few kilometres south of Villa Tunari on the other side of the Río San Mateo, some 6226 square kilometres of the forested northern slopes of the Andes are protected by

Parque Nacional Carrasco, which adjoins the Parque Nacional Amboró (see p.241) to the east. Plunging steeply down from high mountain peaks, the park encompasses a variety of ecosystems from high Andean grasslands and cloudforest to dense tropical rainforest, ranging in altitude from 4000m to just 300m. It also supports a great range of wildlife, including all the major Amazonian mammals, among them jaguars, tapirs and peccaries, and over seven hundred species of bird, including several which are endemic to the region. The park is seriously threatened by illegal logging, hunting and forest clearance for agriculture by settlers along both its northern and southern margins, but the mountainous forest-covered landscape is so impenetrable that the inner regions remain pristine.

One of the most popular excursions into the park is to see the **Cavernas del Repechón**, a group of natural caves that are home to a large population of *guacharós*, or **oil birds**. These large nocturnal fruit-eating birds are found in very few other places in South America. Visits to the cave are by guided tour only (included in the park entry fee), so arrive early to ensure you don't miss the park guards when they set off. From the park entrance, you will be taken across the tumultuous Río San Mateo on a primitive cable car. It's a thirty-minute walk through the rainforest to the caves, where you'll be able to see (and hear) the oil birds nesting (except in May and June, when they migrate to Venezuela). The birds only leave the caves at night to eat fruit, and navigate by echolocation, emitting a strange clicking sound. For longer trips into the park, contact Fremen Tours in Cochabamba.

Ivirgarzama

About 29km east from Chimoré along the Chapare road, the unappealing market centre of **IVIRGARZAMA** has little to distinguish it from other Chapare towns apart from the fact that it's from here that a side road leads north to Puerto Villarroel, from where you can travel by boat to Trinidad (see p.286) in the Beni. There are a couple of very basic *alojamientos*, but no reason to spend the night here.

From Ivirgarzama the main road continues east to Santa Cruz, 247km away, passing through **Buena Vista** (141km), the main entrance point to the Parque Nacional Amboró (see p.241).

Puerto Villarroel

From Ivirgarzama, a rough dirt road runs 26km north to **PUERTO VILLARROEL**, a small river port on the **Río Ichilo** from where regular cargo boats travel north to Trinidad (see p.286). This river route is the main transport link between Cochabamba department and the **Beni**, and was the only route between Trinidad and highland Bolivia until the road from Santa Cruz to Trinidad was completed in the 1970s. Puerto Villarroel is an untidy collection of tin-roofed houses, many of them raised above the muddy, unpaved streets to protect them from flooding when the river bursts its banks – a not infrequent occurrence in the November to March rainy season. Most activity takes place on the river bank, where there's a naval base, a series of oil storage tanks and a **rudimentary port** where ramshackle river boats line up to load and unload cargo.

ARRIVAL AND DEPARTURE | THE CHAPARE

VILLA TUNARI

By bus Regular buses and trufis (3hr–3hr 30min) to Villa Tunari leave from the intersection of Av Oquendo and Av 9 de Abril in Cochabamba. Heading back to Cochabamba from Villa Tunari, you can catch a bus or trufi from the office of Trans Tours 7 de Junio on the main road; alternatively flag down one of the services passing through town on their way to Cochabamba from elsewhere in the Chapare.

Through buses from Santa Cruz will drop you off at the police control *tranca* at the west end of town, and buses heading to Santa Cruz sometimes pick up passengers here if they have room, though most pass through in the middle of the night.

PARQUE NACIONAL CARRASCO

By taxi To visit the park you'll need to reach the settlement of Paracito, about 10km from Villa Tunari on a side road heading south off the main road just east of town – a taxi should cost about Bs40–60, and twice that if you want the driver to wait around for a few hours and take you back after your visit.

IVIRGARZAMA

By bus and trufi Buses to Ivirgarzama (every 2–3hr; 5–6hr) depart from the intersection of Av Oquendo and Av 9 de Abril in Cochabamba. If you are travelling from Villa Tunari to Ivirgarzama, you need to take a trufi to Shinaota (every 20–30min; 20min), then another one from Shinaota to Chimoré, and finally a third from Chimoré to Ivirgarzama. Trufis to Shinaota and buses to Cochabamba leave from one end of the main street, trufis to Puerto Villarroel (every 20–30min; 30min) from the other.

PUERTO VILLARROEL

By trufi Trufis to Ivirgarzama (every 20–30min; 30min)

arrive and depart from the small central plaza, where you'll find an ENTEL telephone office.

By boat To find a boat to take you downstream, ask around amongst the captains or in the Capitanía del Puerto (the naval port authority office). The river journey through the rainforest to Trinidad should cost around Bs175–280 including food and takes five to seven days, depending on the level of the river, the size and power of the boat, and how many stops it makes to load and unload cargo. In the dry season (May–Sept) river levels can drop so low that the trip downstream becomes impossible. During the rest of the year there are usually several departures to Trinidad each week, though you may have to wait around a day or two – boat captains generally let passengers sleep on board while waiting to load. You'll need your own hammock and mosquito nets (you can buy these in the markets in Cochabamba or Ivirgarzama), insect repellent and drinking water, and fruit and snacks to supplement the basic food supplied on board.

ACCOMMODATION

VILLA TUNARI

Hostal Los Cocos A block north of the main road, opposite the church ☎04 4136578. Economical choice with a football trophy-laden lobby, small pool and clean rooms with shared or private bathrooms; only the latter have fans. No breakfast. With shared bathroom Bs100; with en-suite bathroom Bs140

Hotel Las Palmas On the south side of the main road ☎04 4136501. A somewhat overpriced mid-range hotel offering a pool and comfortable but rather run-down en-suite rooms with fans and fridges; some also have river views. There's a good restaurant. Bs320

Hotel San Martín On the south side of the main road ☎04 4136512. Although it is a little scruffy, *Hotel San Martín* has reasonable, somewhat musty rooms with fans and private bathrooms, a pool, and a restaurant-bar with a billiards table and a dartboard. Breakfast included. Singles Bs130, doubles Bs180, triples Bs250.

★ **Hotel de Selva El Puente** About 4km east of town ☎04 4259392, ⊛andes-amazonia.com. Villa Tunari's best option is *Hotel El Puente*, operated by Fremen Tours (p.215), which has simple en-suite *cabañas* with fans set amid a patch of rainforest. There's a swimming pool,

fourteen delightful natural river pools (open to non-guests for Bs10) and a restaurant. A taxi from town costs Bs10–15. Breakfast included. Bs240

PARQUE MACHIA

Wara Yassi organization ☎04 4136572, ⊛intiwarayassi.org. The park and refuge are managed by the Inti Wara Yassi **Inti** organization, which relies largely on volunteers, many of them young foreign travellers who stop here for a month or two. Volunteers must stay for a minimum of fifteen days and can sleep in the Casa de Voluntarios dormitory. It is also possible for travellers to camp here. Volunteer dorms Bs100; camping/person Bs10

PUERTO VILLARROEL

Alojamiento La Pascana Just off the plaza. No phone. A bit quieter, though no more comfortable, than some of the other lodges in town, *La Pascana* has bare-bones, cleanish rooms with shared bathrooms. Bs50

Alojamiento Sucre Opposite La Pascana. No phone. This friendly place has a few spartan rooms off a big dancehall (which can get very noisy on the weekends). Bs50

EATING

VILLA TUNARI

Inexpensive food is available from stalls along the main road, though hygiene is not necessarily the top priority. Most hotels have restaurants open to non-guests.

San Silvestre On the main road. The town's best restaurant is a huge open-walled place with coconut trees and outdoor seating overlooking the river. The menu

features a good range of coffees and alcoholic drinks, plus pizzas, pastas and comida tipica, including local river fish like the delicious *surubí*. Mains Bs18–45.

PUERTO VILLARROEL

There are a few restaurants selling cheap set almuerzos and tasty fried river fish.

Mono Saavedra
Mariela Aguirrezábal
· Rosario - Arg. 2007·

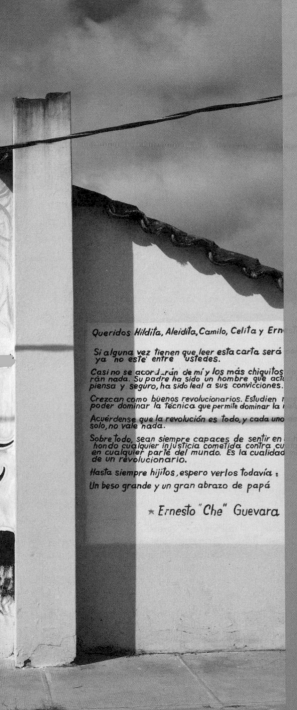

Queridos Hildita, Aleidita, Camilo, Celita y Ern...

Si alguna vez tienen que leer esta carta será
ya no esté entre ustedes.

Casi no se acordarán de mí y los más chiquitos
rán nada. Su padre ha sido un hombre que act...
piensa y seguro, ha sido leal a sus convicciones.

Crezcan como buenos revolucionarios. Estudien ...
poder dominar la Técnica que permite dominar la ...

Acuérdense que la revolución es todo, y cada uno
solo, no vale nada.

Sobre todo, sean siempre capaces de sentir en ...
hondo cualquier injusticia cometida contra cu...
en cualquier parte del mundo. Es la cualidad ...
de un revolucionario.

Hasta siempre hijitos, espero verlos todavía :

Un beso grande y un gran abrazo de papá

★ Ernesto "Che" Guevara

Santa Cruz and the Eastern Lowlands

232 Santa Cruz

240 Buena Vista

241 Parque Nacional Amboró

243 Samaipata

246 Around Samaipata

248 Vallegrande

250 La Higuera and around

252 Chiquitos: the Jesuit missions

262 Parque Nacional Noel Kempff Mercado

264 East from Santa Cruz

266 The Chaco

HOSPITAL SEÑOR DE MALTA, VALLEGRANDE

5

Santa Cruz and the Eastern Lowlands

Stretching from the last Andean foothills to Brazil, Paraguay and Argentina, Bolivia's Eastern Lowlands – the Llanos Orientales – form a vast and sparsely populated plain. The areas varied ecosystems range from Amazonian rainforest in the north, through broad savannahs and tropical dry forest in the centre, to the immense wetlands of the Pantanal in the far east and the arid Chaco to the south. Rich in natural resources, the region's economy has in recent years become the most important in the country, fuelled by oil and gas reserves, cattle-ranching and massive agricultural development. Its attractions are diverse, from the vibrant city of Santa Cruz to wildlife-rich Parque Nacional Amboró and the fascinating former Jesuit missions of Chiquitos.

At the centre of the Lowlands' economic boom is **Santa Cruz**, the lively tropical regional capital, which in just a few decades has been transformed from an isolated provincial backwater into a booming modern metropolis with a brash commercial outlook utterly distinct from the reserved cities of the Bolivian highlands. The city has few conventional tourist attractions, but is a crucial transport hub and the ideal base for exploring the surrounding area, where much of the beautiful natural environment survives, despite the ravages of deforestation and development.

About 40km west, the exceptionally biodiverse rainforests that cover the easternmost foothills of the Andes are protected by the **Parque Nacional Amboró**. The beautiful cloudforest that covers the upper regions of Amboró can be visited from **Samaipata**, an idyllic resort town and home to the intriguing pre-Inca archeological site El Fuerte. From Samaipata, you can also head further southwest through the Andean foothills to the town of **Vallegrande** and the hamlet of **La Higuera**, which witnessed the last desperate guerrilla campaign of Che Guevara, who was killed here in 1967.

East of Santa Cruz the railway to Brazil passes through the broad forested plains of **Chiquitos**, whose beautiful Jesuit mission churches played a crucial role in Spanish colonial history, when a handful of priests established a semi-autonomous theocratic state in the midst of the wilderness. In the remote far north of the region, accessible only by air or an extremely arduous overland journey, **Parque Nacional Noel Kempff Mercado** is perhaps the most beautiful and pristine of Bolivia's protected rainforest areas, combining dramatic scenery with unparalleled wildlife-spotting opportunities. Finally, south of Santa Cruz stretches the vast and inhospitable **Chaco**, an arid wilderness of dense thorn and scrub, reaching south to Argentina and Paraguay.

Evo-lution p.233
Mercado Los Pozos p.238
Community-based tourism
 projects p.240
Excursions from Samaipata p.246
Accommodation around
 Samaipata p.247
The life and death of Che Guevara p.250

The utopian kingdom of the Jesuits in
Chiquitos p.254
The Chiquitos musical renaissance p.255.
San Juancito p.257
The Mennonites p.261
Huanchaca Plateau p.262
The Pantanal p.264
The Guaraní people p.266

THE MISSION TOWN OF SANTA ANA

Highlights

❶ Santa Cruz nightlife Bolivia's eastern capital comes to life at night, and in many ways is closer in style and spirit to Brazil than to the rest of the country. **See p.239**

❷ Parque Nacional Amboró The country's most accessible rainforest boasts a spectacular abundance of birdlife, with more species than any protected area in the world. **See p.241**

❸ Samaipata Charming town set in an idyllic valley with excellent hiking nearby, as well as the mysterious pre-Hispanic ceremonial site of El Fuerte. **See p.243**

❹ The Che Guevara trail Admirers of the iconic Argentine revolutionary can retrace his final steps through the town of Vallegrande and the hamlet of La Higuera, where his ill-fated guerrilla campaign ended in capture and execution. **See p.250**

❺ The Jesuit Missions of Chiquitos Scattered across the sparsely populated forest region east of Santa Cruz, the immaculately restored mission churches of Chiquitos are a reminder of one of the most unusual episodes in Bolivia's colonial history. **See p.252**

❻ Parque Nacional Noel Kempff Mercado Bolivia's most remote and spectacular national park, with abundant wildlife, pristine Amazonian rainforest and magnificent waterfalls tumbling down from the plateau that inspired Sir Arthur Conan Doyle's The Lost World. **See p.262**

HIGHLIGHTS ARE MARKED ON THE MAP ON P.232

5

Santa Cruz

Set among the steamy, tropical lowlands just beyond the last Andean foothills, **SANTA CRUZ** is Bolivia's economic powerhouse. An isolated frontier town until the middle of the twentieth century, the city has since become the biggest in the country, a sprawling metropolis with a booming oil, gas, timber, cattle and agro-industry economy. This rapid growth – and the availability of land – has attracted a diverse range of immigrants

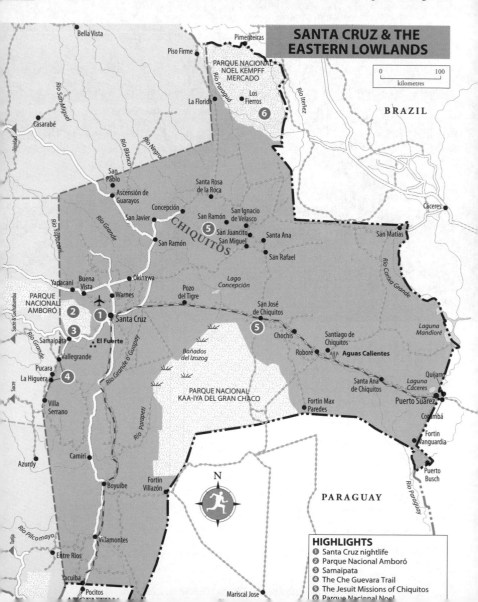

SANTA CRUZ & THE EASTERN LOWLANDS

0   100
kilometres

BRAZIL

PARAGUAY

HIGHLIGHTS
1 Santa Cruz nightlife
2 Parque Nacional Amboró
3 Samaipata
4 The Che Guevara Trail
5 The Jesuit Missions of Chiquitos
6 Parque Nacional Noel

> ## EVO-LUTION
>
> Santa Cruz is a **flash point** for tension between the country's eastern and western halves. The Chaco area in the south of the Santa Cruz region is rich in natural gas and oil and, as a result, Santa Cruz's economic output represents around 30–40% of the country's GDP. However, much of the wealth is filtered off to La Paz, which has caused a great deal of resentment. Santa Cruz has become the central focus for rallying calls for greater autonomy and even independence. In 2006, President Evo Morales put the **national gas industry** under state control in an effort to share the proceeds with the impoverished, indigenous majority, rather than continue to line the pockets of a privileged few. The terms of nationalization, however, seriously jeopardized agreements with the area's foreign investors. Morales' dramatic **land reform** policy (a proposed redistribution of two hundred thousand square kilometres of land) was also bitterly opposed by Santa Cruz landowners. Huge swathes of state-owned land have already been redistributed to help the nation's poor recover from historical injustice, and the government has also started to seize privately owned land that is unproductive, or was obtained illegally, and distribute that as well. In Santa Cruz, the **autonomia** movement is very evident, with T-shirts, graffiti and green-and-white regional flags all bearing witness to the anti-government feeling. Tensions seem unlikely to dissipate any time soon.

to Santa Cruz, including Japanese rice farmers, German-speaking Mennonites and, far poorer, indigenous migrants from the Andes.

Native **Cruceños**, however, still dominate the city. Known as **cambas**, they are culturally a world apart from the rest of Bolivia (they in turn refer with mild contempt to the highland immigrants as **collas** – the two terms being old Inca words for lowland and highland peoples respectively). Generally loud, brash and happy-go-lucky, their language, music and outlook are infused with a tropical ease and sensuality, which feels closer in spirit to Brazil or Colombia. Santa Cruz has few conventional tourist attractions, and some find its brash commercialism and pseudo-Americanism unappealing. However, others enjoy its dynamism and tropical insouciance.

The city continues to grow at a phenomenal rate, spreading inexorably in a mixture of ragged shantytowns, commercial developments and exclusive residential districts where oil executives, businessmen and made-good drug-traffickers relax in opulent mansions and drive around in imported 4WDs (known as "narcocruisers"). The old colonial **city centre**, however, is still dominated by whitewashed houses with tiled roofs that extend over the pavements, and when everything closes up in the middle of the day for an extended lunch break the city is suffused with a languid tropical indolence.

Brief history

Santa Cruz de la Sierra was founded in April 1561 by the conquistador **Nuflo de Chavez**, who had arrived in the region at the head of a large military expedition accompanied by thousands of indigenous Guaraní. The original city stood 260km east of its present location, close to San José de Chiquitos (see p.258). The new settlement proved precarious, however, surrounded by a hostile indigenous population and far from any other outpost of Spanish power. In 1594 it was moved to its present location, a more easily defended site on the west of the **Río Grande**, close to the last foothills of the **Andes**. For the next three and a half centuries Santa Cruz remained an isolated frontier outpost. Things began to change in the 1950s with the construction of a railway link to Brazil and a road to Cochabamba. Subsequently Santa Cruz became the main supplier of cotton, rice, sugar, soy and other tropical agricultural produce to the rest of Bolivia (and, increasingly, foreign markets as well).

The cocaine, oil and gas economy

Santa Cruz's economic boom really took off in the 1970s, when the city emerged as the centre of the Bolivian **cocaine industry**. Cocaine brought enormous wealth – as well as corruption – to the city, much of which was reinvested in land, agriculture,

5

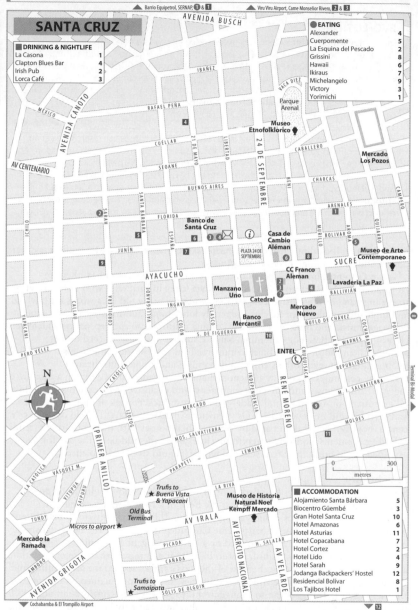

SANTA CRUZ

▲ Barrio Equipetrol, SERNAP, ❶ & ❶   ▼ Viru Viru Airport, Carne Monseñor Rivero, ❷ & ❸

AVENIDA BUSCH

■ DRINKING & NIGHTLIFE
La Casona   1
Clapton Blues Bar   4
Irish Pub   2
Lorca Café   3

● EATING
Alexander   4
Cuerpomente   5
La Esquina del Pescado 2
Grissini   8
Hawaii   6
Ikiraus   7
Michelangelo   9
Victory   3
Yorimichi   1

■ ACCOMMODATION
Alojamiento Santa Bárbara   5
Biocentro Güembé   3
Gran Hotel Santa Cruz   10
Hotel Amazonas   6
Hotel Asturias   11
Hotel Copacabana   7
Hotel Cortez   2
Hotel Lido   4
Hotel Sarah   9
Jodanga Backpackers' Hostel   12
Residencial Bolívar   8
Los Tajibos Hotel   1

0   300
metres

construction and other legitimate businesses. Growth was further fuelled by oil and gas revenues from the Chaco, and generous government subsidies to large landowners and agro-industrialists. The population of Santa Cruz leapt from around 42,000 in 1950 to well over one and a half million today. Since coming to power, however, President Evo Morales has come through with pledges to increase state control or even nationalize foreign-owned oil fields, refineries and utility companies to ensure that more revenue and jobs benefit Bolivia's poor. As Latin America's second-richest country in natural resources, this has caused shockwaves throughout the region – especially in Santa Cruz (see box, p.233).

Plaza 24 de Septiembre

At the centre of Santa Cruz is **Plaza 24 de Septiembre**, a spacious leafy square named after the day in 1810 when Santa Cruz declared independence and joined the struggle against Spanish rule. At its centre stands a statue of **Colonel Ignacio Warnes**, a pro-independence Argentine guerrilla leader who was military governor of Santa Cruz from 1813 to 1816. He massacred over a thousand indigenous Chiquitano prisoners captured fighting on the Spanish side, before being executed himself along with nine hundred others when a Spanish army recaptured Santa Cruz.

La Catedral

Plaza 24 de Septiembre • Catedral daily 7am–7pm; mirador daily 8am–noon & 3–7pm • Bs3

On the south side of the plaza stands the salmon-pink **Catedral** (or Basílica Mayor de San Lorenzo), a hulking brick structure with twin bell towers. The cathedral was built between 1845 and 1915 on the site of an original church dating back to 1605. The cool, vaulted interior boasts some fine silverwork around the altar. Just to the right of the main entrance, you can climb up to a **mirador** in the bell-tower with good city views.

Museo de Arte Sacro

La Catedral, Plaza 24 de Septiembre • Tues, Thurs & Sun 8.30am–noon & 2.30–6pm • Bs10

The city's best religious art, sculpture and silverware is tucked away in the **Museo de Arte Sacro**, whose entrance is just to the right of the cathedral's altar. There are some beautiful eighteenth-century mestizo-Baroque wood carvings of saints, including a magnificent **Santiago Matamoros** (St James the Moor-slayer), representing the patron saint of Spain. Other exhibits include some exquisite silverwork and a 7mm book – one of the world's smallest – in which the Lord's Prayer is written in various languages

Museo de Arte Contemporáneo

Corner of Sucre and Potosí • Mon–Fri 9am–noon & 3–8pm, Sat–Sun 3–7pm • Free

A former public school has been converted into the pleasant courtyard setting of the **Museo de Arte Contemporáneo**. Various peculiar and eccentric art displays can be found throughout the maze of small rooms, and there is usually someone at the door who is more than happy to help you try and make sense of them.

Museo Etnofolklórico

Inside Parque Arenal, a 10min walk northeast of the plaza • Daily 9am–noon & 3–6pm • Free

The **Museo Etnofolklórico** has a small but varied collection of artefacts from the region's different indigenous ethnic groups. Exhibits include photos and examples of traditional dress, including colourful costumes, wooden masks carved with animal faces and bright feather headdresses. Particularly striking are the brightly coloured robes and hoods of the "Gigantes" costumes from San Ignacio de Velasco – these are worn by dancers who use tall stilts and white facemasks to represent mythological giants.

Museo de Historia Natural Noel Kempff Mercado

Eight blocks south of the plaza on Av Irala, near the corner with Av Ejército Nacional • Mon–Fri 8am–noon & 3–6.30pm • Free • ⓦ museonoelkempff.org

The **Museo de Historia Natural Noel Kempff Mercado** houses an extensive collection of dead insects, stuffed birds and pickled snakes from Bolivia, all displayed with good

5

explanations in Spanish of their biology, habitat and lifecycle. Of particular interest is the display of dangerous insects, such as the *vinchuca* or **assassin bug** (see p.39. Look out also for the *vibora cuco*, a moth that bears a passing resemblance to a snake's head and which is widely (but incorrectly) considered extremely dangerous.

Biocentro Güembé

Kilómetro 7, Camino a Porongo/Zona Los Batos • Daily 8.30am–6.30pm • Adults Bs90, children Bs40, with a basic day package • ☎ 03 3700700, ⓦ biocentroguembe.com • It's a 30min taxi ride (Bs30–40) from the centre; it's best to look at the map on the website before visiting to better direct your taxi driver

Eight kilometres north of Santa Cruz's city centre, **Biocentro Güembé** is a luxurious 46-acre resort with an array of attractions including a huge **butterfly dome**, an **orchid park** and a series of picturesque **pools**. There are opportunities for trekking, horse-riding and swimming, a fine restaurant (almuerzo Bs80), and various accommodation options (see p.237). Though it may be too artificial for some, it is a place to be seen for wealthy Cruceños, who flock here at the weekends, and this in itself makes it an entertaining place to while away an afternoon.

ARRIVAL AND DEPARTURE   SANTA CRUZ

Santa Cruz is divided into concentric rings by successive ring roads – called **anillos** – beginning with the Primer Anillo, which encompasses the colonial city centre, and extending outwards to the ninth ring. Other than the main airport, most places of use and interest are within the first two *anillos*.

By plane The Aeropuerto El Trompillo, south of the centre in the Segundo Anillo, is sometimes used by military airline TAM and smaller carriers. The modern Aeropuerto Viru-Viru (☎ 03 3852400) is 17km north of the city centre, a Bs50 taxi ride away; alternatively, catch a micro (every 20min; 30min) to the old bus terminal, seven blocks southwest of the city centre. The departure tax is: Bs15 (domestic flights) and Bs175 (international flights).
Destinations Daily flights: Cochabamba; La Paz; Sucre; Trinidad. Less frequent services: Cobija; Guayaramerin; Riberalta; Puerto Suarez; Tarija. International departures: Asunció Buenos Aires; São Paulo; Miami.
By train The Terminal Bi-Modal – the bus and train terminal (☎ 03 3463388, ⓦ ferroviariaoriental.com) – is 2km east of the city centre at the end of Av Brasil. Services from here travel east to the Brazilian border at Quijjaro (13hr 30min–18hr 35min), via San José de Chiquitos (around 5–7hr) twelve times a week. There are three different trains: the *Regional* (the slowest and cheapest), the *Expresso Oriental* and the *Ferrobus* (the quickest, most comfortable and priciest). Getting a seat at intermediate stations can be a problem. There is also a weekly service (Thurs 3.30pm) south to the Argentine border at Yacuiba (16hr 25min) via Villamontes (13hr 25min). Unless you're taking the *Ferrobus*, you can expect delays. Buy tickets for all services in advance from the Terminal Bi-Modal; note that there's a departure tax of Bs3 for train passengers.
By bus Services arrive at and depart from the Terminal Bi-Modal (the combined bus and train terminal;

☎ 03 3463388), 2km east of the city centre at the end of Av Brasil. A taxi into the centre costs Bs10–15; alternatively take any micro heading east along Av Brasil and marked "Plaza 24 de Septiembre". For the major routes there's generally no need to buy tickets in advance, but for all other destinations try to get one the day before. Note that long-distance buses generally travel overnight. There's a departure tax of Bs3 for bus passengers.
Destinations Cochabamba (hourly; 10–12hr); Concepcion (around 8 daily; 6-7hr); La Paz (around 20 daily; 16-18hr); Trinidad (around 10-12 daily; 10–12hr). Less frequent services: Asunción; Paraguay (24hr); Buenos Aires, Argentina (34–36hr); Camiri (5–6hr); Oruro (12–14hr); San Ignacio (evening; 10–12hr); San Javier (morning and early evening; 4–5hr); Sucre (14–16hr); Tarija (24hr); Yacuiba (10–14hr); Vallegrande (6–7hr); Villamontes (8–12hr).
By trufi and micro The quickest, most comfortable way to reach Buena Vista and Samaipata is by trufi, collective taxis/minivans that depart when full (most people travel in the morning). For Buena Vista (1hr 30min–2hr), catch a trufi to the town of Yapacani from Calle Izozog La Riva, just north of the old bus terminal. To Samaipata (2hr 30min–3hr), trufis depart from two blocks south of the old bus terminal on Av Omar Chavez and Solis de Olguín.
By taxi Most journeys cost Bs10–15. Radio taxi companies include El Cristo (☎ 03 3622828) and Exclusivo (☎ 03 3572323).

INFORMATION AND TOURS

TOURIST INFORMATION

Inside the Prefectura building on the north side of Plaza 24 de Septiembre (Mon–Fri 8am–12.30pm and 2.30–8pm; ☎03 3368900). You can get a good free city map, and the staff will answer simple questions in Spanish. The SERNAP office (☎03 3352325, ⓦwww.sernap.gob.bo), on Calle 9 Oeste in Barrio Equipetrol, has limited information on the country's national parks; come here first if you are planning an independent visit to Noel Kempff Mercado.

TOUR AGENCIES

Many agencies run trips to Parque Nacional Amboró, the Jesuit Mission towns, Parque Nacional Noel Kempff Mercado and the Pantanal.

Amboro Tours Pari 161 ☎03 3390600, ⓦamborotours. com. Well-established Bolivian set-up with friendly staff.
Forest Tours Cuéllar 22 ☎03 3372042, ⓦforestbolivia .com. Professionally-run, good-value agency specializing in Amboró trips.
Fremen Calle Beni 79 ☎03 3338535, ⓦandes -amazonia.com. A professional Bolivia-wide organization offering all manner of trips, including river tours from Trinidad.
Ruta Verde 21 de Mayo 332 ☎03 3396470, ⓦrutaverdebolivia.com. Highly recommended agency run by a very helpful couple, Gijs and Maria, who have excellent local knowledge and speak Spanish, Dutch and English. A superb choice for Noel Kempff, the Pantanal and Amboró in particular.

ACCOMMODATION

Possibly because building and running **luxury hotels** is a good way of investing and laundering dirty money, there's an oversupply of top-end accommodation in Santa Cruz. However, most of it is located on the outskirts in the wealthy Barrio Equipetrol, about 5km northwest of the city centre. Most **mid-range** and **budget accommodation** by contrast is conveniently located in or around the old city centre. A fan or air conditioning is pretty much essential – all but the cheapest rooms have one or the other.

BUDGET

Alojamiento Santa Bárbara Santa Bárbara 181 ☎03 3321817. This no-frills budget option is strictly for shoestring travellers. It has tight, musty rooms with tiled floors and shared bathrooms (but no fans) around a small courtyard. Dorms Bs25; doubles Bs100
Hotel Amazonas Junín 214 ☎03 3334583. Rooms here vary widely, so choose carefully: some resemble darkened cells, but others are far nicer, with more space and light, and less of a tropical-damp feel. All have TVs and phones. Bs150
Hotel Sarah Sarah 85 ☎03 3322425, ⓔhotel.sarah @hotmail.com. A series of colourful, slightly kitsch murals on tropical themes give this hotel plenty of character. The en-suite rooms are on the small side, but well kept, and come with TVs. Bs160
★**Jodanga Backpackers' Hostel** El Fuerte 1380 ☎03 3396542, ⓦjodanga.com. Run by an extremely helpful Bolivian-Australian couple, this excellent Hostelling International-affiliated backpacker haven is a 20min walk from the plaza. It has private rooms (with shared or en-suite bathrooms) and six- to ten-bed dorms, plus a swimming pool, jacuzzi, TV/DVD room, communal kitchen, internet access and laundry service. Rates include breakfast. Dorms Bs70; doubles Bs170
Residencial Bolívar Sucre 131 ☎03 3342500, ⓔresidencial-bolivar@hotmail.com. This longstanding backpackers' haunt has helpful staff and small but clean rooms with fans and shared or private bathrooms around a cool, leafy patio with hammocks and several resident toucans. It's very popular, so reserve in advance. Breakfast included. Dorms Bs70; doubles Bs160

MID-RANGE AND LUXURY

Biocentro Güembé Kilómetro 7, Camino a Porongo/ Zona Los Batos ☎03 3700700, ⓦbiocentroguembe .com. If you fancy staying in a more verdant setting, Biocentro Güembé (see opposite) has a wide range of very comfortable, faux-rustic cabins, rooms and camping spots spread throughout its ample grounds. There are plenty of facilities on hand, and it's a particularly good option for families. Camping Bs200/person; cabins Bs781 ($112); doubles Bs660 ($94)
Gran Hotel Santa Cruz Moreno 269 ☎03 3348811, ⓦgranhotelsantacruz.com. Built in a grandiose style with lashings of marble, this is one of the few top-range hotels within easy walking distance of the plaza. It has spacious rooms and suites, as well as a pool, jacuzzi, sauna, gym, restaurant and bar. Breakfast included. Bs735 ($105)
Hotel Asturias Calle Moldes 154 ☎03 3339611, ⓔh_asturias@hotmail.com. Evocative of a 1970s-era US motel, this whitewashed mid-range hotel has dated, but comfortable en-suite rooms with a/c, minibars and TVs, as well as a decent-sized pool, and a restaurant. Breakfast included. It's a 15min walk to the plaza. Bs350 ($50)
Hotel Copacabana Junín 217 ☎03 3362770, ⓔhotelcopcacabanascz@hotmail.com. Functional Hostelling International-affiliated hotel with clean, comfortable but drab rooms with TV and fan (or more expensive a/c), set around a narrow central courtyard with a slightly prison-hall feel, despite the many plants. There's also a restaurant, and breakfast is included. Bs276

5

Hotel Cortez Cristobal Mendoza 280 ☎03 3331234, ⓦhotelcortez.com. This swish hotel in the Segundo Anillo, just round the corner from lively Calle Monseñor Rivero, has very comfortable – if not particularly stylish – rooms with private bathrooms, flatscreen TVs, phones, a/c and plenty of space; those at the front, however, suffer from road noise. There's also a pool and a restaurant-bar. Breakfast included. Bs547 ($78)

Hotel Lido 21 de Mayo 527 ☎03 3363555, ⓦlido-hotel.com. Stylish, modern and efficiently-run mid-range hotel. The spacious rooms have plush furnishings, TVs and a/c. There's also a restaurant, and rates include breakfast. (Bs350) ($50)

Los Tajibos Hotel Av San Martín 455 ☎03 3421000, ⓦlostajiboshotel.com. This large hotel in Barrio Equipetrol is the best in the city – Kofi Annan and former Brazilian president Lula have both stayed here. The contemporary-styled rooms lack a little character, but have all the facilities you'd expect; the "executive" rooms even have private jacuzzi baths. There are lovely gardens, a pool, spa, health centre and several excellent restaurants (notably *Jardin de Asia*) and bars. Standard rooms Bs1113 ($159); executive rooms Bs1337 ($191)

EATING

Santa Cruz has a wide range of restaurants, catering to all budgets. **International cuisine** and **vegetarian food** is widely available, though local *camba* (lowland) food can also be found, mostly good beef accompanied by rice and yucca or plantain. Most restaurants open Monday to Saturday for lunch and dinner, though on Sundays many only serve lunch. On Friday and Saturday nights, many stay open late and turn into bars. Cafés are generally the best bet for breakfast. With a few exceptions, the places listed here are in the **city centre**, though many popular restaurants are further afield on the **Segundo Anillo** ring road (Av Cristóbal de Mendoza) between calles Alemania and Beni, 1.5km to the north: particularly popular are the massive, open-air places serving huge plates of barbecued meat at weekends. European-style bars and restaurants are strung along **Calle Monseñor Rivero**, about seven blocks directly north of the plaza. As elsewhere in Bolivia, the markets are the best bets for cheap eats (see box below).

CITY CENTRE

Alexander Junín. This domestic coffee chain does a good impression of its more famous international counterparts, serving fine coffee (brewed from Bolivian-grown beans), breakfasts, snacks, cakes, pastries and a few light meals. Free wi-fi. There is another branch on the corner of Santa Fe and Monseñor Rivero. Coffee Bs8–30, breakfasts Bs27–36.

Cuerpomente Aroma 64. Busy vegetarian restaurant offering a varied self-service buffet priced by weight (good value at around Bs15–20/kg) as well as soups, juices and *empanadas*. The food is tasty and wholesome, though the overzealous healthy-living mantras posted on the wall are a bit off-putting.

La Esquina del Pescado Florida and Sara. Excellent, inexpensive and very popular fish restaurant in a shabby little corner building, serving big portions of delicious freshwater fish like *surubí, sabalo* and piranha fried, grilled or baked. There's tasty ceviche (Bs20–25), and the fish soup with yucca on the side (Bs10–12) is a meal in itself.

Grissini Corner Ñuflo de Chavéz and Cobija. Welcoming Italian restaurant in a quiet neighbourhood with a few outdoor tables on a small patio and an a/c dining room. The pizzas (Bs30–100) and pastas (Bs45–60) are authentic and generously proportioned, and there's an array of free nibbles to keep you going before your mains arrive.

Hawaii Sucre and Beni. An ice cream parlour-cum-café-cum-bar, *Hawaii* is a popular spot throughout the day for its array of sundaes (Bs20–25), fast food-style meals (around Bs35) and inexpensive *tragos* (alcoholic drinks) later on. Daily.

Ikiraus Corner Sucre and 24 de Septiembre. Also known as *La Pascana*, this garishly-coloured café – the

---

MERCADO LOS POZOS

In the northeast corner of the city centre, the **Mercado Los Pozos**, is arguably the best food market in Bolivia, with row upon row of stalls serving inexpensive and delicious local dishes like *locro de gallina* (chicken stew) and *sopa de maní* (peanut soup), while others sell an astonishing variety of tropical fruit juices and excellent *empanadas* and *salteñas*. There's also a whole subsection of Chinese foodstalls where you can get a tasty meal for less than Bs15. You might also like to spend a few hours at the **Mercado La Ramada**, Avenida Grigota and Calle Sutos, where pretty much everything you can think of is on sale across a sprawling mass of stalls. **Mercado Nuevo** is smaller but has the same hectic market bustle and is a conveniently short walk from the central plaza.

decor features splashes of pink, white, orange, green and yellow – on the plaza has cosy booths, buzzers on the tables to attract the waitresses and a menu of sundaes (Bs28–50), sweet and savoury snacks (Bs10–35), coffees and alcoholic drinks.

⭐ **Michelangelo** Chuquisaca 502. ☎ 03 3348403. One of the finest restaurants in Santa Cruz (it's worth reserving a table), offering superb Italian cuisine and immaculate service in an intimate atmosphere. Prices are a little steep (mains Bs50–100), but it is an excellent place for a treat. Mon–Fri lunch only, Sat dinner only.

Victory Junín and 21 de Mayo. On the first floor of the Galeria Casco Viejo shopping arcade, this popular bar-restaurant is a good place to relax and watch the world rush by on the busy streets below. It has decent breakfasts, sandwiches and burgers (Bs14–20), and a good selection of beers (from Bs13) and cocktails.

SEGUNDO ANILLO

Casa del Camba Av Cristóbal de Mendoza 569. The best of the many large, traditional Cruceño restaurants on this stretch of the Segundo Anillo, and a great place to enjoy a reasonably-priced *parillada* (mixed grill) or *pacumutu* (a kind of massive shish kebab) to the accompaniment of live traditional *camba* music. Mains Bs30–60. Daily 11am–1am.

DRINKING AND NIGHTLIFE

Makhassan Las Americas 7. There's also another branch on the corner of Monseñor Rivero and Fortin Arce. The chefs at this restaurant have cooked at some of the world's finest hotels and have created a menu featuring superlative Asian and European dishes that make use of excellent local ingredients. *Char Sui* pork, trout with hollandaise sauce and French cauliflower soup are just some of the delights on offer. Expect to pay about Bs150 a head, but it's worth splashing out.

⭐ **Yorimichi** Busch 548. On the border of the first and second anillos, a 20min walk from the plaza, is this superior Japanese restaurant. Although the plastic garden chairs feel a little out of place in an eatery of this class, the food is stunningly authentic, with the sushi, sashimi and tempura all highlights. Dishes cost Bs42–198.

CALLE MONSEÑOR RIVERO

Freddo Monseñor Rivero 245. This Santa Cruz outpost of the famous Argentine ice cream chain serves excellent – if pricey – *helado* (from Bs12). The various *dulce de leche* flavours are a fine place to start.

Taberna Terramar Monseñor Rivero 281. Charming Spanish restaurant with tasteful decor and comfy seats, offering traditional dishes like gazpacho, tortilla española and, of course, paella (Bs100–200 for two people).

Whether it's because of the humid climate (as visiting *collas* from the highlands assert), the beauty and hot-bloodedness of the Cruceñas (as locals insist), or the combination of large disposable incomes and abundant cocaine (as one may suspect), many Cruceños love nothing better than to stay up late, eating, drinking and dancing the night away. This comes to the fore during **Carnaval** (late Feb or early March), when the city stages a series of wild masked balls. Most of the flashier clubs are in the brashly exclusive **Barrio Equipetrol**, about 5km northwest of the centre, on a stretch of Avenida San Martín between the second and third anillos. Cover charges (Bs30–50 upwards) are standard, and doormen aren't afraid of turning away scruffy gringos.

CITY CENTRE

Nightlife within the city centre is relatively low-key and dispersed, but there's still a good range of **bars**, many with live music on the weekends.

La Casona Arenales 222 ☎ 03 3378495, ⊛ bistrolacasona.com. Smart bohemian bar-restaurant in a nineteenth-century building with a lovely patio, mellow music and a relaxed ambience. There's live jazz and blues on Thurs–Sat nights (cover charge around Bs15), as well as refined German, Italian and local dishes (mains Bs39–110) and a lengthy menu of beers, including some pricey imported options. There's also a small deli. Mon–Sat 11.30am–late.

Clapton Blues Bar Ballivián 159. As the name suggests, this is a dimly lit, smoke-filled blues bar that only gets going after about 11pm on Thurs–Sat nights,

when blues, rock, reggae and jazz bands perform. Closed Sun & Mon.

Irish Pub Plaza 24 de Septiembre. On the first floor of the Bolívar shopping centre, with tables overlooking the plaza, this joint has a fairly authentic Irish pub feel, and is a great place to enjoy a beer (Bs14–24), cocktail or coffee. It gets very lively in the evenings, especially at weekends. Food is also available, including relatively exotic delights like Irish stew (Bs38) and a full Irish breakfast (Bs27). Mon–Sat 9am–1.30am, Sun 4pm–1.30am.

⭐ **Lorca Café** René Moreno 20, first floor. This funky cafe-bar has a balcony overlooking the plaza, an interior filled with arty displays and live jazz, blues or folk music Thurs–Sun nights. There's also a tasty array of gringo-pleasing delights (Bs30–60), and sometimes more exotic dishes like cayman tails.

5

> ## COMMUNITY-BASED TOURISM PROJECTS
>
> The Santa-Cruz-based NGO **PROBIOMA**, 29 Calle 7 Este, Barrio Equipetrol (☎03 3431332, ⓦprobioma.org.bo) links tourists to communities without taking a cut of the money, unlike tour operators offering similar deals. The projects it promotes are managed and run locally, ensuring the money goes to help the community as a whole. The surrounding environment is also protected as tourism provides an economic alternative to damaging practices such as logging, or exhaustive farming techniques. One of the most successful of these sites is **Ecoalbergue de Volcanes** on the south side of Amboró, where you can camp or stay in one of the comfortable cabins. It is reached by an 8km trek along the Río Colorado from Bermejo, about 40km east of Samaipata on the Santa Cruz road. Situated to the north of Amboró, **Villa Amboró** and **Isama** are both great centres for hiking and observing wildlife. There is also a project in **El Chochís** (see p.264). A stay at one of these sites will cost about Bs350 ($50) a day, including food and expert guides.

DIRECTORY

Banks and exchange You can change foreign dollars, euros and travellers' cheques at Casa de Cambio Aleman, on the east side of Plaza 24 de Septiembre, and there are plenty of ATMs: try the Banco Mercantil, Av Moreno and Figueroa, or the Banco de Santa Cruz, just west of the plaza on Junín.

Bookshops Lewy Libros, Junín 229, has a limited stock of English-language books.

Cultural centres Centro Cultural Franco Aléman, Plaza 24 de Septiembre (☎03 3350142, ⓦccfrancoaleman.org): French-German complex with a multilingual library, café, and cultural centre with an extensive programme of events. Manzana 1, behind the cathedral on Calle Independencia (☎03 3395792, ⓦmanzanauno.org.bo): regular exhibitions from domestic and international artists.

Hospital Clinica Lourdes, Moreno and Pari (☎03 3325518), is a good place to go if you need a doctor. For emergencies, head to Hospital San Juan de Dios Cuéllar

with España (☎03 3332222), or Hospital Japonés, 3rd Anillo, close to junction with Conavi (☎03 3462031).

Internet Numerous cyber cafés (all around Bs4/hr) can be found on the first floor of Bolívar Shopping, the arcade on the east side of the plaza.

Laundry Lavandería La Paz, La Paz 42, offers a same-day service (Bs15/kg).

Outdoor equipment Caza y Pesca El Aventurero, at Arenales 150, has quality imported equipment.

Pharmacy Farmacia Gutierrez, just off Plaza 24 de Septiembre 21 de Mayo 76 (and Junín). Daily 9am–9pm.

Post office Correo Central, just northwest of Plaza 24 de Septiembre on Junín.

Spanish lessons Jodanga Backpackers' Hostel offers good value language classes (Bs50/hr guests, Bs70 non-guests), as does Residencial Bolívar.

Telephone office The main ENTEL office is on Warnes and Av Moreno.

Buena Vista

Some 100km northwest of Santa Cruz lies the peaceful little town of **BUENA VISTA**, the northern gateway to **Parque Nacional Amboró**. Raised slightly above the plains, the town is aptly named, enjoying good views of the densely-forested mountain slopes of Amboró. Buena Vista is a popular summer retreat for weekenders from Santa Cruz, though during the week it remains a sleepy place. The town was originally founded in 1694 as a **Jesuit mission**. Sadly, the eighteenth-century Jesuit church was demolished in the 1960s and replaced by the unattractive modern brick structure that stands today.

ARRIVAL AND DEPARTURE   BUENA VISTA

By trufi/micro Regular trufis and micros (1hr 30min–2hr) to and from Santa Cruz arrive and depart from the plaza.

By motorbike taxi Motorbike taxis are the easiest way to get to some of the more far-flung hotels; they congregate on the plaza.

INFORMATION

Tourist information There is no tourist office, but tour agencies on the plaza, as well as operators in Santa Cruz

and Samaipata, can organize excursions into Parque Nacional Amboró. There's a SERNAP office two blocks southwest of the plaza where you can buy an entry permit, though beyond that it is of limited help. Ⓦbuenavistabolivia.com is a useful website about the town.

ACCOMMODATION

Accommodation is limited, though **budget** options are on the increase. There are also a number of **luxury** country club-style places with air conditioning and swimming pools, several kilometres from town on the main Cochabamba–Santa Cruz road, but these are expensive and inconvenient if you want to visit Amboró.

Amboró Eco Resort 7km away along the Carretera Nacional to Santa Cruz Ⓣ03 3422372. Set in beautiful forest surroundings with a network of private trails, this smart resort has comfortable, spacious a/c rooms and a swimming pool with accompanying bar. Bs700 ($100)

Buenavista Hotel A 15min walk southwest of the plaza, near the football pitch Ⓣ03 9322104, Ⓔbuenavista.hotel@hotmail.com. Large complex with rows of cabins and rooms in a main building: all are en suite and have a/c and kitchenettes, though the decor could do with a freshen-up. There's a curvy pool, sauna, restaurant-bar and a terrace with great views. Doubles and cabins Bs150

Cabañas Quimorí About 400m outside town on the road south towards Huaytú Ⓣ03 9322081. Clean, well-appointed *cabañas* with private bathrooms set amid a spacious and secluded forest garden, with good views of Amboró. Bs100

La Casona On the plaza Ⓣ03 9322083. This whitewashed building, bang in the centre of town, is popular with shoestring travellers for its clean, no-frills rooms with fans and shared facilities. Bs50

Hotel Flora and Fauna 4km from town on the road south towards Huaytú, then another 1km up the marked drive off to the left Ⓣ7104 3706, Ⓔhotelfandf@hotmail.com. Owned by renowned British ornithologist Robin Clarke, this delightful place is ideal for nature lovers. Its simple but comfortable en-suite cabins with fans are set amidst well-preserved, wildlife-rich rainforest – there's a bird observation tower and expert guides can be arranged. Good food is on offer too. With breakfast Bs490 ($70); full board Bs840 ($120)

Residencial Nadia Just off the north corner of the plaza Ⓣ03 9322049. A reasonable budget choice, the family-run Residencial Nadia offers plain, if slightly overpriced digs with fans. Bs160

EATING AND DRINKING

There are several restaurants and cafés on the **plaza**, though the cheapest place to eat is the **market**, a block back from the plaza; this is also the place to buy food and supplies if you're heading into the Parque Nacional Amboró. Most restaurants open daily for lunch and dinner, though some close early on Sundays.

Paraba Azul Inside the plaza. This pleasant café has a huge thatched roof and a cheerful parrot motif. It's a good spot for a coffee or beer (Bs15) and a light meal or snack.

La Plaza Overlooking the plaza. Accomplished restaurant with a surprisingly diverse range of meat, fish and seafood dishes, pastas and pizzas, including a tasty surf and turf. Prices, however, are a little steep. Mains Bs50–105. Daily except Mon.

DIRECTORY

Internet Try Punto Viva, on the corner of the plaza (Bs4/hr).

Money There are no banks so bring cash with you.

Parque Nacional Amboró

Forty kilometres west of Santa Cruz, **PARQUE NACIONAL AMBORÓ** spans 4300 square kilometres of a great forest-covered spur of the Andes. Situated at the confluence of the Andes, the Amazon rainforest and the Northern Chaco, and ranging in altitude from 3300m to just 300m above sea level, Amboró's steep, densely forested slopes support an astonishing biodiversity. Over 830 different types of **bird** have been recorded here – the highest confirmed bird count for any protected area in the world – including rarities such as the cock-of-the-rock, red-fronted and military macaws and the blue-horned curassow or unicorn bird, which was once thought to have been extinct. There are also jaguars, giant anteaters, tapirs and several species of **monkey**. Its enormous array of plant and insect species,

5

meanwhile, is still largely unexplored. This biological wealth is all the more amazing given that Amboró is so close to Santa Cruz. You must be accompanied by a **guide** (roughly Bs150–200 per day) – best organized before setting out through a travel agency or hotel in Buena Vista or Samaipata – to enter the park.

Brief history

The national park, established in 1984, was expanded in 1990 to encompass some 6300 square kilometres. However, by this time the park's fringes were already under huge pressure from poor **peasant farmers**, who began clearing the forest for agriculture, as well as hunting and logging inside the park boundaries. In 1995, amid rising tension, the Bolivian government gave in to political pressure and reduced the park by two thousand square kilometres, creating a "Multiple-Use Zone" around its borders. This buffer zone is now largely deforested, and the peasant farmers are beginning to encroach on the remaining park area. The easiest parts of the park to reach are also the most likely to have been affected by this **encroachment**, though the pristine interior regions of the park are deliberately kept relatively inaccessible. Nonetheless, the park refuges are set amid splendid, largely intact rainforest, and the chances of spotting wildlife are fairly high. The park's higher-altitude southern section, which includes beautiful **cloudforests**, can only be visited from Samaipata.

The Buena Vista section

From Buena Vista, a rough road runs southeast along the borders of the Multiple-Use Zone (marked by the Río Surutú), passing through a series of settlements, the landscape around which is heavily deforested. However, on the west side of the river the steep, densely forested mountains of Amboró loom inviolate.

Some 20km from Buena Vista, the road reaches **Huaytú**, from where a rough track crosses the river and enters the park. It then leads 14km to **La Chonta**, a park guards' station. There are plenty of trails through the surrounding forest from here, and you can swim in the nearby **Río Saguayo**. About four hours' walk from here in the interior of the park is a site where the extremely rare blue-horned currasow can be seen, while a tough day's walk downstream along the Río Saguayo brings you to another park guards' station, Saguayo, from where it's another day or so on foot back to Buena Vista.

Continuing along the main track beyond Huaytú for a further 15km brings you to the settlement of **Santa Rosa**. From here, a rough 10km track crosses the river and heads to the park guards' refuge at **Macuñuco**, inside the Multiple-Use Zone. There are plenty of trails here, one of which leads to a delightful waterfall. A few kilometres before you reach Macuñuco on this track, you pass the village of **Villa Amboró**, where there's another basic **refuge** and a series of forest trails.

The Samaipata section

The southern border of the park lies just a dozen kilometres from Samaipata (see opposite) on the other side of the **mountain ridge** that rises to the north, and is easy to visit with one of the town's tour agencies (see p.244). This section is much higher in altitude than the areas close to Buena Vista, and is therefore ecologically very different, comprising beautiful cloudforest with gnarled trees covered in lichen and epiphytes. Most one-day trips to Amboró head to the hamlet of **La Yunga**, from where a short walk takes you into the **cloudforest**. Although you'll see large numbers of rare and strangely prehistoric-looking tree ferns up to 10m high, this region lies in the Multiple-Use Zone close to areas of human settlement, so the chances of seeing much in the way of wildlife are slim. To reach pristine cloudforest you'll need to trek further into the park and camp overnight.

ARRIVAL AND DEPARTURE

By micro A micro from the plaza in Buena Vista runs daily along the boundary of the park via Huaytú and Santa Rosa, returning the next day – times vary, so ask around in Buena Vista. Also check the return time with the driver so you don't get stuck on the way out. From the road you'll still have to cross the Río

PARQUE NACIONAL AMBORÓ

Saguayo (which can be impassable in the Nov–April rainy season) and walk over 10km to reach either La Chonta or Macuñuco.

By jeep A good alternative is to rent a jeep and driver to take you into the park and return later to collect you – you can arrange this through one of the tour operators.

TOURS

Tour operators You can only visit the park with a guide or official tour operator. Agencies in Buena Vista, Samaipata and Santa Cruz offer tours ranging from day-trips to twenty

days; prices start at around Bs150 per person per day. The park entry fee is Bs15.

ACCOMMODATION

Refuges Overnight trips in the park involve stays at one of several rustic refuges, or camping; the cost of this (and food) is generally included in the price of your tour. The

Santa Cruz-based NGO PROBIOMA also has a trio of comfortable community-run lodges around the park (see p.240).

Samaipata

Some 120km west of Santa Cruz on the old mountain road to Cochabamba, the peaceful little town of **SAMAIPATA** is a popular destination for Bolivians and foreign travellers alike. Nestled in an idyllic valley surrounded by rugged, forest-covered mountains, the town enjoys a cool, fresh climate compared to the sweltering eastern plains. Innumerable good walking trails run through the surrounding countryside, the beautiful cloudforests of the Parque Nacional Amboró are close by, and just outside town stands one of Bolivia's most intriguing archeological sites, **El Fuerte**. All this makes Samaipata the kind of place many travellers end up staying longer than they expected – indeed, many European residents have settled here permanently, setting up hotels, restaurants and tour agencies. The town's heart is the **Plaza Principal**, which lies at the centre of a small grid of tranquil, unpaved streets, lined with pretty whitewashed houses. Although generally peaceful, things can get busy with visiting Cruceños at weekends.

Museo Archeológico

A block north and two blocks east of the plaza on Bolívar • Mon–Sat 8.30am–noon & 2–6pm, Sun 8.30am–4pm • Bs5 or free with an El Fuerte entry ticket

The **Museo Archeológico** has a small collection of archeological finds from across Bolivia, including some beautiful Inca ceremonial *chicha*-drinking cups known as *kerus*; Inca stone axes and mace heads; and a range of pottery from various different cultures. Disappointingly, however, there's little on display related to El Fuerte.

Zoológico El Refugio

2km southeast of town on the road to San Juan • Daily 8am–6pm • Bs20

A pleasant walk from the plaza, the **Zoológico El Refugio** is a refuge for rescued animals, and has everything from cats and dogs to some very playful monkeys. You can also ride horses (Bs25/hr or Bs150/day), and there's a small café, camping space and volunteering opportunities if you would like to get involved.

ARRIVAL AND DEPARTURE

SAMAIPATA

By bus Services to Vallegrande (3hr 30min) or Sucre (around 12hr) can be flagged down on the main road

opposite the petrol station. Those for Vallegrande pass through 11.30am–12.30pm and 3.30–4.30pm, and

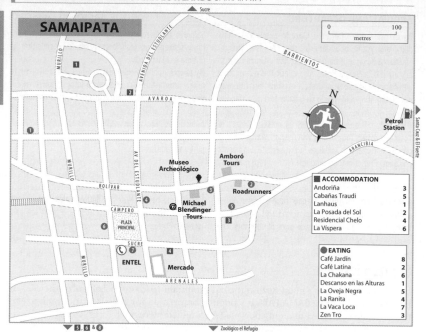

SAMAIPATA

Sucre

BARRIENTOS

0 — 100 metres

MURILLO

AVENIDA DEL ESTUDIANTE

AVAROA

N

Petrol Station

Santa Cruz & El Fuerte

ARANCIBIA

MURILLO

AV DEL ESTUDIANTE

BOLIVAR

Museo Archeológico

Amboró Tours

Roadrunners

CAMPERO

@ Michael Blendinger Tours

PLAZA PRINCIPAL

SUCRE

MURILLO

ENTEL

Mercado

ARENALES

Zoológico el Refugio

■ ACCOMMODATION

Andoriña	3
Cabañas Traudi	5
Lanhaus	1
La Posada del Sol	2
Residencial Chelo	4
La Víspera	6

● EATING

Café Jardín	8
Café Latina	2
La Chakana	6
Descanso en las Alturas	1
La Oveja Negra	5
La Ranita	4
La Vaca Loca	7
Zen Tro	3

always stop for passengers; those for Sucre pass through 6–7.30pm but are often full. You've a better chance of getting on one from Mairana, 16km west (a taxi costs around Bs50); alternatively, for a small fee one of the travel agencies will buy you a ticket in advance from Santa Cruz. The quickest way to get to Cochabamba is via Santa Cruz.

By micro Micros from Santa Cruz (3hr) arrive and depart from the plaza, but trufis (2hr 30min–3hr) are quicker, more comfortable and only a little more expensive. Coming from Santa Cruz, they stop at the plaza and can normally be persuaded to drop you at your hotel; heading back, they leave when full from both the plaza and the petrol station.

By taxi For trips around town and to surrounding attractions, taxis can be found at the office on the plaza.

INFORMATION AND TOURS

TOURIST INFORMATION

The best places to go for information are the tour agencies (see below). There's also a useful website: ⓦ samaipata.info.

TOUR AGENCIES

Samaipata's tour agencies make it easy to visit the surrounding area's less accessible attractions; most offer English-speaking guides. Prices vary according to the number of people going on the trip: generally, for small groups, you'll pay around Bs150–250/person/day. One of the most popular excursions is along the Ruta del Che, a two-day, one-night trip that traces the last steps of iconic revolutionary Che Guevara (see p.250).

Boliviajes Guesthouse La Víspera ⓣ 03 9446082, ⓦ lavispera.org. Long-established Dutch-run agency with expert local knowledge, specializing in trips to Amboró and the mountains south of Samaipata. Treks include a five-hour walk to El Fuerte, an eighteen-day trans-Amboró trek to Buena Vista and a lovely hike between Camiri and Sucre

that retraces Che's early movements in Bolivia. They also hire horses and rent camping equipment.

Don Gilberto Aguilera Sucre ⓣ 03 9446050 or ⓣ 7261 5523. Samaipata's most experienced trekking guide, Don Gilberto is the man to go with if you want an off-the-beaten-track adventure in the cloudforest north of Samaipata, or a trip on the Ruta del Che. If you speak Spanish, go with him.

Michael Blendinger Nature Tours Bolívar, opposite the museum ⓣ 03 9446227, ⓦ discoveringbolivia.com. Multilingual guides with a highly professional approach. Offering trips on the Ruta del Che as well as to Amboró and tailor-made trips further afield to places like Noel Kempff and the Pantanal.

Roadrunners Bolívar ⓣ 03 9446193, ⓔ theroad runners@hotmail.com. A very friendly, enthusiastic and efficient German-run agency leading frequent trips to Amboró, El Fuerte and La Pajcha. They also organize longer Che-themed trips that cover a wider area than the classic Ruta del Che excursion, and rent out bikes.

ACCOMMODATION

You are really spoilt for choice for accommodation in Samaipata. There are two categories: simple budget **alojamientos** in the centre of town and more expensive chalet-style **cabañas** on the outskirts of town. Everything fills up (and prices rise) at weekends and on public holidays, particularly between October and April. See also "Accommodation Around Samaipata" (p.247).

★ **Andoriña** Campero, east of the plaza. ✆ 03 9446333, ⊚ andorinasamaipata.com. Top-class, welcoming hostel with comfy mattresses, spacious and attractive communal areas, plus the best breakfast in Samaipata. Free hikes, slide shows, film screenings and photo exhibitions are just some of the perks. Dorms $\overline{Bs40}$; doubles $\overline{Bs90}$

Cabañas Traudi Outside town, 800m south of the plaza ✆ 03 9446094, ⊚ traudi.com. A wide range of quirky en-suite *cabañas* sleeping between two and eight people, with kitchens and fireplaces. They are set amid spacious grounds with a large pool (open to non-guests for Bs15), sauna and a talkative pet parrot. Doubles $\overline{Bs140}$.

Landhaus Murillo, 200m north of the plaza ✆ 03 9446033, ⊚ samaipata-landhaus.com. Neat and tidy rooms come with private bathrooms and TV at this well-run hotel, which also has cabins that sleep larger groups. There's also a small pool and garden area, book exchange and a restaurant. Doubles $\overline{Bs150}$; cabins $\overline{Bs200}$

La Posada del Sol Three blocks up from the plaza ✆ 03 9446218, ⊚ laposadadelsol.net. This professional, whitewashed hostel has great views and staff who go out of their way to ensure you make the most of your stay. Rooms are clean and spacious, and there's a tasty breakfast (which costs extra) with excellent espressos. Excursions, an extensive DVD collection and Spanish classes (Bs50/hr) are also on offer. Dorms $\overline{Bs50}$; doubles $\overline{Bs120}$

Residencial Chelo Half a block east of the plaza ✆ 03 9446014. Good-value little place with pleasant modern rooms (with private bathrooms and TVs) around a plant-filled courtyard. $\overline{Bs50}$

★ **La Víspera** Outside town, 1km south of the plaza ✆ 03 9446082, ⊚ lavispera.org. Outstanding Dutch-run rural idyll with fantastic views, a beautiful herb garden and fields with horses, dogs and cats. There's a range of rooms and cabins, each thoughtfully decorated, as well as a fully fitted campsite. Delightful owners Pieter and Margarita – true pioneers of tourism in Samaipata – are a wealth of information and enthusiasm. They also run the Boliviajes tour agency (see opposite) and a superb café-restaurant (see below). Camping $\overline{Bs30}$; doubles $\overline{Bs210}$

EATING

There is a varied range of restaurants and cafés in town, though some only open at weekends. At the **market**, a block south of the Plaza Principal, you can get inexpensive meals and picnic provisions; for the latter you can also try *La Ranita* (see below).

★ **Café Jardín** At La Víspera. If you're not staying here, don't miss out on a meal at the lodge's excellent outdoor bistro, which takes advantage of an extensive range of home-grown, organic produce (including a diverse herb garden). The menu features Mexican, Italian, Thai, Chinese and Indian dishes, wonderful teas and tempting deserts like rhubarb tart and authentic scones with cream and jam. Mains Bs30–45. Daily 8am–6pm; last orders 5pm.

★ **Café Latina** A block north and three blocks east of the plaza at Bolívar 3. Charming owners Lenny and Sylvain have created a sophisticated atmosphere with romantic lighting, modern artwork and an appealing wooden bar. The concise menu features high quality steaks, pastas, salads and desserts, and there's a good choice of beers and wines to wash them down. Mains Bs30–50. Mon–Fri dinner only, Sat–Sun lunch and dinner.

La Chakana Plaza Principal. Small European-run café serving good juices, breakfasts, snacks, more substantial meals (Bs22–55) and a good-value two-course menu del dia (Bs22). It has a small book exchange, a useful folder of tourist information and runs tours. Daily.

Descanso en las Alturas Two blocks north and three blocks west of the plaza. Friendly, family-run Argentine restaurant (also known as *Chancho Rengo*), offering decent pizzas with imaginative toppings (Bs25–80), and big, juicy *churrascos* (Bs38–40). Mon–Sat for lunch and dinner.

La Oveja Negra Calle Campero. A relaxing spot for a coffee, beer, glass of wine, slice of apple crumble cake or portion of *tiramisu*, La Oveja Negra ("The Black Sheep"), also has a book exchange, plenty of board games and a dart board to keep you occupied. Deserts Bs12–15, alcoholic drinks from Bs12. Daily except Tues 6pm–late.

La Ranita Av del Estudiante. Delightful French café-bakery producing some of the best croissants, pain au chocolats and breads in Bolivia, as well as fine coffees, teas and breakfasts (Bs16–40). The artwork on the walls and a selection of crafts and jewellery are for sale too. Thurs–Mon 8am–noon & 2–6.30pm.

La Vaca Loca Sucre, on the main plaza. This bovine-themed restaurant and ice cream parlour is a good spot throughout the day, with coffees, sandwiches, pancakes and main meals (dish of the day around Bs22). The highlight, however, is the sundaes (Bs15–25), including the Copa La Vaca Loca (Bs49), which features eight flavours and serves two. Wed–Sat noon–10pm.

Zen Tro Bolívar. Serene café-cum-cultural centre

5

EXCURSIONS FROM SAMAIPATA

There are numerous interesting places to explore around Samaipata. About 40km south of town on the road towards the village of Postrer Valle, a path leads 6km or so to **La Pajcha**, a beautiful triple-tiered waterfall that plunges 30m into a cool pool that is excellent for swimming. There's no public transport, so you'll either have to come by taxi (around Bs250 return with waiting time), or go on an organized trip. The nearby **Condor Hike** is also best with a guide. It offers a fantastic opportunity to observe these gigantic birds with wingspans of up to 3m at sometimes frighteningly close quarters. The hike takes roughly five hours and it's about a two-and-a-half-hour drive (each way) to the start of the Condor trail. Bus trips with local tour operators (see p.244) from Samaipata leave before 7am (Bs230–380/person). About 20km east of Samaipata, a set of three waterfalls, **Cascadas las Cuevas**, is a very accessible option for seeing a little more of the countryside when you're pushed for time (a taxi costs about Bs70 return, with waiting time). You can swim in the pools, which makes it very popular with local families.

---

specializing in tea (Bs10–20) – infusions include jasmine and mint green tea. Once you've quenched your thirst, the owners aim to soothe your body and soul with excellent massages, yoga sessions, reflexology, salsa and samba dance classes, film screenings and art exhibitions all on offer. Thurs–Sun 4–7pm.

DIRECTORY

Exchange There is no bank in Samaipata, but Cooperativa La Merced (daily except Sun), on Sucre, just off the plaza, changes dollars and sometimes offers cash withdrawals on credit cards.

Internet Café Internet Anyi has slow connections (Bs7/hr).

Laundry Michael Blendinger Tours charges Bs40/5kg. Amboro Tours and several hotels also offer services.

Shopping Along Sucre from the plaza, Carmen Luz Art has an array of artwork from local craftspeople on sale.

Telephones There's an ENTEL office on the plaza.

Around Samaipata

The fascinating site of **El Fuerte** is the key attraction in the surrounding countryside, but too many tourists see nothing else before they shuffle back to the bright lights of Santa Cruz. The opportunities to explore the surrounding countryside are immense in this beautiful region of rugged, forested mountains, divided by lush valleys whose lower slopes are covered by rich farmland, where hummingbirds, condors and flocks of green parakeets are a frequent sight. The low mountains surrounding Samaipata make for excellent hiking – just follow any of the paths or tracks leading out of town. You can also access the Samaipata section of nearby **Parque Nacional Amboró** (see p.241).

El Fuerte

Daily 9am–5pm • Bs50

About 9km east of Samaipata, the archeological complex known as **EL FUERTE** is amongst the most striking and enigmatic ancient sites in the Andes. At its centre lies a great sandstone rock carved with a fantastic variety of **abstract and figurative designs**, including animals and geometric shapes. The rock is surrounded by the remains of dozens of **Inca buildings**, but the carvings predate Inca occupation of the region by over two thousand years. The site's original indigenous name has been lost – the Spanish name El Fuerte, meaning "the fort", reveals more about the military obsession of the Spanish conquistadors than it does about the primary purpose of the site, which was clearly religious and ceremonial.

Brief history

It's thought the first carvings at El Fuerte were made before 1000 BC by an ancient lowland people who were perhaps driven from the region by the **Chiriguanos** – a collective name given to those from the eastern Chaco. The Chiriguanos arrived here in force in the fifteenth century after migrating across the Chaco from the lands east of the Río Paraguay. It is believed that they might also have considered this an important ceremonial centre. The **Incas** arrived here around the same time and occupied the site, which served as an administrative and military outpost at the easternmost fringes of their empire. They altered and embellished the rock itself, suggesting that they too considered it a sacred site – though, like the Spanish, they had a habit of appropriating the religious centres of conquered peoples as a means of reinforcing their domination. Archeological evidence shows the Inca occupation occurred in two distinct periods, suggesting the outpost may have been overrun and destroyed by Chiriguano raiders before being re-established. The site was then occupied by the **Spanish** and their indigenous allies in the 1570s during their border war with the Chiriguanos, and eventually abandoned when the town of Samaipata was founded in the early seventeenth century.

The site

On a hilltop at just under 2000m above sea level, with commanding views of the surrounding mountains and the valley below, **the rock** itself is a huge lump of reddish sandstone measuring 160m long and up to 40m wide. Its entire surface has been sculpted and carved with all manner of figurative and abstract designs, including pumas, serpents, birds, lines, steps and niches.

On the **western end** of the rock you can still make out two circular carvings, 2m in diameter, of pumas or jaguars, and one of a coiled serpent. Beyond this is a series of square indentations and a low Inca wall with numerous niches, behind which are two long, parallel slots running exactly west to east with zigzags down either side and in the centre: it's likely to have been used for ritual libations of *chicha* or blood.

A path runs along the **south side** of the rock, which is carved with stone steps, platforms, seats and niches of all shapes and sizes, including classic Inca trapezoids 2m high, all facing due south: these probably once held idols and the mummified bodies of long-dead Inca priests and officials. On your right as you walk round are the foundations of several Inca stone buildings that may have housed priests and other attendants, and the remains of a small sixteenth-century Spanish building. Walking round to the **north face** of the rock you'll find a low Inca wall, five massive north-facing niches cut out of the rock face and a good view of the surface of the rock, here carved with recesses and channels. **East of the rock** a path leads down to the ruins of a building with commanding views of the valley below, then on to the foundations of a classic Inca *cancha* (living compound), where archeologists have also found post holes from

---

ACCOMMODATION AROUND SAMAIPATA

If the idea of having a base in the breathtaking **countryside** around Samaipata sounds appealing, there are a couple of attractive options. In addition to those below, Michael Blendinger Tours (see p.244) also has a wide range of cabins to rent across the region.

Gingers Paradise No phone, ⓦgingersparadise .lobopages.com. A working organic farm, around 35km from Samaipata, where owners Cristobal and Sol offer hearty meals and a host of activities, including handicraft sessions, horseriding, swimming in nearby rivers and Quechua lessons. To find it, ask the bus driver to stop at Bermejo (about 76km from Santa Cruz on the road to Samaipata), cross the hanging bridge and walk about 250m up the path where you will see their multi-coloured house. Full board Bs100

El Refugio Los Volcanes ⓣ03 3372042, ⓦrefugiovolcanes.net. *Los Volcanes* is a pleasant lodge situated about 75km along the road to Samaipata from Santa Cruz in a deep valley with spectacular views of lush forests and sandstone cliffs. The comfortable double rooms have private bathrooms and solar power. It's a great place for observing wildlife – over two hundred bird species have been spotted from the lodge. Book in advance directly or via a Santa Cruz agency such as Ruta Verde. Full board including transport Bs2240 ($320); full board without transport Bs1400 ($200)

5

wooden houses and ceramic fragments suggesting an earlier, possibly Chiriguano occupation of the site.

From the rock's east end, a path runs downhill to the south, reaching a broad terrace. From here, the path continues 200m to **La Chinkana**, a deep well that has inspired improbable myths of underground tunnels leading to faraway Inca sites. Returning to the terrace and turning right brings you to the site's main complex of Inca buildings. Passing the foundations of several ruined buildings, you emerge on a broad plaza measuring about 100m by 150m and flanked on three sides by partially overgrown Inca ruins of which only low walls or foundations now remain.

ARRIVAL AND DEPARTURE

EL FUERTE

By taxi The easiest way to reach El Fuerte is by taking a taxi from Samaipata (about Bs40 one-way, or Bs70 return with an hour's waiting time) or going on a guided tour, many of which involve beautiful treks.

By foot You can walk to the ruins in about two hours

– follow the road out of Samaipata towards Santa Cruz for a few kilometres, then turn right up the marked side road that climbs to the site; note that it's an uphill slog on the way there, though significantly easier on the way back.

Vallegrande

Some 68km southwest of Samaipata on the old road from Santa Cruz to Cochabamba, a side road leads 53km south to **VALLEGRANDE**, a pleasant market town set in a broad valley at an altitude of just over 2000m. The town's main attraction is the erstwhile grave of **Ernesto "Che" Guevara**, which attracts a steady trickle of pilgrims.

Brief history

A peaceful backwater founded as a Spanish outpost in 1612, Vallegrande leapt briefly to the world's attention in 1967, when the arid region of low mountains and broken hills to the south of the town became the scene of a doomed guerrilla campaign led by hero of the Cuban revolution, **Ernesto "Che" Guevara** (see box, p.250). Vallegrande served as the headquarters of the Bolivian army's successful counter-insurgency campaign; after Che was captured and executed on October 9 in the hamlet of La Higuera, about 50km to the south, his body was flown here strapped to the skids of a helicopter and put on display in the town hospital.

What happened next remained a closely guarded secret for the next 28 years, until the Bolivian general Mario Vargas Salinas revealed that **Che's body** – minus his hands, which were amputated for identification purposes – had been buried by night in an unmarked pit near the **airstrip** on the edge of town, to prevent his grave from becoming a place of pilgrimage. After a year and a half of investigation, in 1997 his remains, along with those of several of his guerrilla comrades, were found by a team of Cuban and Argentine forensic scientists and flown to Cuba, where they were re-interred in a specially built mausoleum on the outskirts of the city of **Santa Clara**, the scene of his greatest victory in the Cuban revolutionary war.

Museo Municipal Ruta del Che Guevara

On the southwest side of Plaza 26 de Enero • Mon–Fri 8.30am–noon & 2–5pm • Bs10

The small **Museo Municipal Ruta del Che Guevara** has an upstairs room dedicated to Che, with plenty of photographs of him and his guerrilla comrades in camp; of Bolivian soldiers hunting them down; of their bullet-ridden corpses; and of the emotional ceremonies held in La Higuera to mark the thirtieth anniversary of Che's death. There's also an unexciting collection of local archeological finds downstairs. Next door there is an information office where you can hire a guide to take you to the town's various Che sights (Bs60).

Hospital Señor de Malta

Three blocks south of Plaza 26 de Enero on Señor de Malta • No fixed opening hours; generally visited on a guided tour from the Museo Municipal Ruta del Che Guevara (see opposite) • Free

At this hospital you can visit the **laundry room** where Che's body was put on gruesome display to the world's press, though there's little to see here today. At the time, word that he bore a striking resemblance to Jesus Christ spread quickly, and local women cut locks from his hair as good-luck charms.

Che's mausoleum

A 10min walk northeast of Plaza 26 de Enero or a short taxi ride away • No fixed opening times • The building and the graves of his comrades can only be visited on a guided tour (Bs60); guides can be hired from the office next door to the museum (see opposite)

Che's mausoleum is on the edge of the airstrip on the outskirts of town: 100m away behind the cemetery (and thus not on consecrated ground) you'll find the grave from which his remains and those of six other guerrillas were exhumed in 1997. The pit has been left open and is now covered with a red-tiled brick and concrete mausoleum filled with photos of Che. If you return to the fork in the road and walk up the right side you'll reach a house on the right with a swimming pool, behind which are four pits where the bodies of many of Che's mostly Cuban and Bolivian guerrilla comrades were buried after being killed in combat or executed after capture.

ARRIVAL AND DEPARTURE
VALLEGRANDE

By bus A couple of daily buses from Santa Cruz (6–7hr) via Samaipata (3hr 30min) arrive and depart from the offices of two different bus companies: Trans Vallegrande on Santa Cruz and Florida, two blocks southeast of Plaza 26 de Enero, and Trans Señor de los Milagros, a block further southeast on Florida.

By micro/trufi There are also more frequent micros and irregular trufis to Santa Cruz and Samaipata; they generally pass through the main square looking for passengers.
By taxi A taxi from Samaipata to La Higuera, via Vallegrande, costs from around Bs805 ($115) for a two-day, one-night trip.

ACCOMMODATION

Hostal Juanita Caballero 123 ☎03 9422231, @hostaljuanita@cotas.net. A welcoming place with a central courtyard and a (non-functioning) fountain, *Hostal Juanita* has comfortable rooms with private or shared bathrooms; some have TVs and fridges. Bs60
Hostal Vallegrande Santa Cruz 125 ☎03 9422281, @hostalvallegrande@bolinet.net.bo. Clean, simple rooms with either shared or private bathrooms are on offer here; the latter are well worth the extra Bs10 and come with TVs too. En-suite rooms Bs50; shared bathroom Bs40

Hotel Santa Cruz Near the market on Santa Cruz and Florida ☎03 9422518. Smarter than most of its competitors, *Hotel Santa Cruz* has decent rooms – all en-suite and with TVs – and rates include breakfast. Bs80
Seda Residencial Ganadera A block northeast of Plaza 26 de Enero at Bolívar 115 ☎03 9422176. An inexpensive choice, *Sede Residencial Ganadera* has reasonable rooms with private bathrooms and breakfast included. Bs50

EATING

Calle Chaco There are plenty of inexpensive places to eat on Calle Chaco near the covered market.
Churrasqueria El Gaucho Just off the plaza on Señor de Malta. If you're looking for a hearty feed, *Churrasqueria El Gaucho* serves massive slabs of Argentine-style steak with all the trimmings. Mains Bs25–50. Mon–Sat.

El Mirador Overlooking the town from the top of Escalante y Mendoza. With great views of the town, *El Mirador* also produces a good range of steaks, chicken and fish dishes, as well as a few pizzas and pastas. There's plenty of Che memorabilia on display too. Mains Bs25–49. Daily.

DIRECTORY

Exchange Several shops on Chaco change dollars, but not travellers' cheques.
Internet On the main plaza and Santa Cruz.

Telephones The ENTEL office is just off Plaza 26 de Enero on Bolívar.

THE LIFE AND DEATH OF CHE GUEVARA

Of all the romantics and adventurers to pass through Bolivia, none has matched the iconic status of **Che Guevara**, the Argentine-born hero of the Cuban revolution who was killed in the backwoods southwest of Santa Cruz while attempting to launch a continent-wide guerrilla war. Born in the Argentine town of Rosario to upper middle-class parents on May 14, 1928 (though his birth was registered a month later to conceal the fact that he was conceived before his parents were married), Ernesto Guevara de la Serna studied **medicine** at the University of Buenos Aires and qualified in 1953, but never practised as a doctor in his homeland: he preferred life on the road as a self-styled vagabond and adventurer, travelling virtually penniless throughout Latin America both during and after his studies, including a brief period in Bolivia during the revolutionary upheaval of the early 1950s.

A MEETING OF MINDS

By 1954 his travels brought him to **Guatemala**, where he witnessed the CIA-backed military overthrow of the progressive Arbenz regime, an event that confirmed both his growing commitment to revolutionary Marxism and his fervent opposition to US imperialism. It was also here that he was given the nickname **Che**, after his typically Argentine habit of peppering his speech with the Guaraní-derived word, used to mean "hey you" or "mate". From Guatemala he headed to Mexico City, where he met **Fidel Castro**, an exiled Cuban rebel planning to return to his country to launch a guerrilla campaign to overthrow the dictator Fulgencio Batista. Che was signed up as the expedition's doctor, but over the next two years of fighting, he proved himself amongst the most ruthless, determined, fearless, politically radical and tactically astute of the guerrilla commanders. By the time Fidel Castro took power in January 1959, Che was one of his closest associates. For several years he served **Cuba** as president of the National Bank, roving ambassador and Minister of Industry. His mixture of good looks, incendiary rhetoric and self-sacrifice made him appear the living embodiment of the revolutionary "New Man".

FROM CUBA TO THE CONGO

However, his radicalism and his continued insistence on promoting revolution in other countries proved a liability to Castro's Soviet allies, who feared being drawn into a war with the US and were suspicious of Che's Maoist leanings. Che saw the Cuban revolution as the first step in a continent-wide revolution against **US imperial control**, and believed the guerrilla strategy used in Cuba – whereby a small rural *foco* or nucleus of determined fighters could radicalize the peasantry and create the conditions for revolution, as detailed in his book *Guerra de Guerrillas* – was a scientific model that could be exported all over the world. In 1965 he formally resigned

La Higuera and around

LA HIGUERA, the hamlet where Che Guevara's dreams of leading a continent-wide revolution ended in defeat and death, lies about 50km south of Vallegrande, a three-hour drive along a very rough dirt road via the slightly larger village of Pucará. Set in a region of low, crumpled mountains covered in scrubby vegetation broken by occasional maize and potato fields, La Higuera is a tiny collection of simple adobe houses with tiled roofs. A handful of **monuments** commemorate the fallen guerrilla leader. The most recent is a large, well-made bronze bust of Che, erected in 1997 on the thirtieth anniversary of his death. The other is a small, roughly fashioned plaster bust that was destroyed three times by the Bolivian army over the years, and replaced each time by local sympathizers. The schoolhouse where Che was executed has been turned into a small museum. Many of Che's admirers visit, but unless you share their veneration of the charismatic revolutionary icon, there's little reason to come here.

If you ask around you'll probably find someone willing to guide you to the **Quebrada del Churo**, the ravine a few kilometres away where Che was captured. It is a beautiful, and poignant, two-hour hike. You may have to pay a small (Bs5–10) fee to pass through private land en route.

his Cuban citizenship, ministerial position and rank of *commandante*, left his family behind and set off to spread revolution. After an unsuccessful stint leading a Cuban guerrilla contingent supporting rebels in the **Congo**, he turned his attention to Bolivia, where he hoped to start a guerrilla conflagration that would spread into neighbouring countries (including his native Argentina) and draw the US into a "second Vietnam", culminating in a continent-wide revolution. Bolivia's rugged terrain, strategic position in the centre of the continent and proximity to Argentina made it an attractive location, though in fact the choice was to prove a fatal mistake – in all South America, Bolivia was the only country where **radical land reform** had already been carried out, and so the revolutionary potential of the peasantry was low.

ON THE RUN IN BOLIVIA

In 1966, Che set off to Bolivia with a few chosen Cuban companions and set up his base at Ñancahuasu, a farm on the fringes of the Chaco in the Andean foothills, 260km southwest of Santa Cruz. In hindsight, Che's Bolivian venture was doomed from the start. Opposed to Che's guerrilla strategy and anxious to run things on its own territory, the **Bolivian Communist Party** quickly withdrew its support. The few Bolivian recruits he did manage to enlist proved unreliable and squabbled with the Cubans, and the guerrillas' presence was betrayed by deserters even before initial preparations were complete. Unable to attract a single recruit from the local peasantry, Che's small band (they never numbered more than fifty) quickly found itself on the run, divided into two groups blundering through harsh terrain with little food or water while the Bolivian army, backed by US military trainers and CIA advisers, closed in from all sides. Without sufficient medicine, Che himself was crippled by asthma, and reduced to travelling by donkey. On September 26, 1967, Che's ragged fighters marched through the hamlet of **La Higuera**, straight into an army ambush in which three guerrillas were instantly killed. Che and the sixteen other survivors retreated into a canyon, the **Quebrada del Churo**, where they were quickly surrounded. On October 8 they were captured by a company of elite US-trained Bolivian Army Rangers. In the ensuing shoot-out, Che was hit in the calf; another bullet destroyed his carbine, and he was captured. Filthy and emaciated, he was taken to La Higuera and held in the schoolhouse for interrogation by Bolivian army officers and a Cuban-born CIA agent. The next day, the order to execute Che came through from the Bolivian high command. His dreams of a continent-wide revolution were ended by two bursts from a semi-automatic rifle fired by a sergeant who volunteered for the task. According to legend, Che's last words were: "Shoot, coward, you are only going to kill a man."

His body was flown to **Vallegrande** and displayed to the press before being secretly buried, as if his enemies feared him more in death than in life. In many ways, they were right to do so, as Che's example inspired thousands of young men and women across Latin America.

Museo Comunal La Higuera

No fixed opening times; if you ask around, you can normally find someone with a key • Bs10

This one-room **museum**, in the schoolroom in which Che was killed, has the atmosphere of a shrine. It features relics like Che's machete; the wooden chair where he sat for the last time; bullets, ammo clips and a rifle used by the other guerrillas or their military pursuers. There's also a map of the campaign; plenty of photos and newspaper cuttings; and lots of leaflets and pamphlets donated by Che sympathizers. A local guide is always available at the museum and will know a great deal about the failed guerrilla campaign. On October 8–9 each year there's a small gathering of revolutionaries and other sympathizers who come to commemorate Che's death.

ARRIVAL AND DEPARTURE   LA HIGUERA

By taxi A taxi from Vallegrande to La Higuera costs around Bs245 return; one from Samaipata costs from around Bs805 ($115) return. Most people, however, opt for a tour run by one of Samaipata's travel agencies (see p.244).

ACCOMMODATION AND EATING

There are a couple of accommodation options in La Higuera. Those listed below can also both provide meals. There's also a small **shop** selling basic provisions, though if you're self-catering its best to pick up supplies in **Pucará** en route.

5

La Casa del Telegrafista No phone, ⓦwww
.lacasadeltelegrafista.com. In an old telegraph building
that was used by Che's comrades, this French-run lodge has
very atmospheric, stone-walled rooms with high ceilings
(but no electricity) and shared bathrooms set around a
patio filled with cacti and plants, and strung with
hammocks and gaslights; the *Casa* also provides excellent

salads, sandwiches, omelettes and main meals (Bs15–35),
as well as tasty plates of locally produced cheese and
home-baked bread. Bs40

School No phone. For travellers after seriously low-cost
digs, La Higuera's school provides very basic, dorm-like
accommodation in buildings surrounding the playground.
There are toilets but no showers. Dorms Bs10

Chiquitos: the Jesuit missions

East of Santa Cruz stretches a vast, sparsely-populated plain covered in scrub and
fast-disappearing dry tropical forest, which gradually gives way to swamp as it
approaches the border with Brazil. Named **Chiquitos** by the Spanish (apparently
because the original indigenous inhabitants lived in houses with low doorways
– *chiquito* means small), in the eighteenth century this region was the scene of one
of the most extraordinary episodes in Spanish colonial history, as a handful of Jesuit
priests established flourishing **mission towns** where the region's previously hostile
indigenous inhabitants converted to Catholicism and settled in their thousands,
adopting European agricultural techniques and building some of South America's
most magnificent colonial churches. This theocratic socialist utopia ended in 1767,
when the Spanish crown expelled the **Jesuits**, allowing their indigenous charges to be
exploited by settlers from Santa Cruz, who seized the Chiquitanos' lands and took
many of them into forced servitude. Six of the ten Jesuit **mission churches** still
survive, however, and have been restored and declared UNESCO World Heritage
Sites – their incongruous splendour in the midst of the wilderness is one of Bolivia's
most remarkable sights.

San Javier

Some 220km northeast of Santa Cruz, **SAN JAVIER** (also known as San Xavier) is the
westernmost of the Chiquitos Jesuit mission towns and was the first to be established
in the region, having been founded in 1691. The town is now a quiet cattle-ranching
centre with no real attractions other than the mission church itself.

Iglesia de San Javier

On the main plaza • Daily 8am–7pm • Free

Completed in 1752 under the direction of **Martin Schmidt**, the formidable Swiss Jesuit
priest, musician and architect who was responsible for several Chiquitos mission
churches (which were immaculately restored between 1987 and 1993 under the
guidance of the equally dedicated Swiss Jesuit architect Hans Roth), the huge church
has a squat, sloping roof supported by huge spiralled wooden pillars, with a simple
Baroque plaster facade. Above the doorway a **Latin inscription** common to most Jesuit
mission churches in Bolivia reads *Domus Dei et Porta Coeli* (House of God and
Gateway to Heaven).

On the right side of the church as you face it a doorway leads into a cloistered
courtyard, which features a freestanding bell tower. Inside the church the
exquisite modern wooden **retablo** behind the altar features beautiful carved
scenes from the Bible and of the Jesuit missionaries at work in Chiquitos.
The IHS inside the flaming sun at the top of the retablo stands for "Jesus Saviour
of Man" in Latin: combined with three nails and a crucifix, this is the symbol of
the Jesuit order, and you'll see it painted and engraved on mission buildings
throughout Chiquitos.

5

THE UTOPIAN KINGDOM OF THE JESUITS IN CHIQUITOS

When the Spanish first arrived in what is now eastern Bolivia, the vast, forest-covered plains between the Río Grande and the Río Paraguay were densely populated by up to fifty different **indigenous groups**. To the Spaniards this was a strategically vital region, providing a link between the silver of the Andes, their settlements in Paraguay and the Río de la Plata. However, a century of constant military expeditions failed to subdue the indigenous population – known collectively as the **Chiquitanos**.

In exasperation, at the end of the seventeenth century the colonial authorities in Santa Cruz turned to the **Jesuits** to pacify the region and secure the empire's frontier. By this time the Jesuits had more than a century of experience in South America, and were quick to implement the missionary strategy that had proved successful elsewhere. Small groups of dedicated priests set out to convert the indigenous peoples and persuade them to settle in missions known as **reducciones**, places where they could be brought together and "reduced" to European "civilization", which included being converted to Catholicism. Though many missionaries met gruesome deaths at the hands of those they sought to convert, the different tribal groups of Chiquitania quickly flocked to join the new settlements, which offered them many advantages. After a century of war, many had anyway been seeking a peaceful accommodation with the colonial regime, and under the aegis of the Jesuits they were protected from the rapacious slave raids of the Spaniards in Santa Cruz and the Portuguese in Brazil, as well as from their own tribal enemies.

"CIVILIZING" THE CHIQUITANOS

Ten **missions** flourished under the Jesuit regime: European livestock and crops were successfully introduced; the Chiquitanos had limited autonomy under their own councils or *cabildos*, and were taught in their own languages (one of these, Chiquitano, was eventually adopted as the main language in all the missions); indigenous craftsmen were trained in European techniques and built magnificent churches; European musical instruments were introduced and quickly mastered by the Chiquitanos, establishing a **musical tradition** (see box, p.255) that survives to this day. The missions were not quite the autonomous socialist utopia Jesuit sympathizers have since tried to make out – many indigenous people were brought in by force, and the political and ideological control exercised by the fathers was pretty much absolute – but in general the missions provided a far more benign regime than anything else on offer under Spanish rule.

SPANISH DOMINANCE

In the end, though, for all their self-sufficiency and autonomy, the Jesuit missions were utterly dependent on the Spanish colonial authorities. When in 1767 political developments in far-off Europe led the **Spanish king** to order the Jesuits out of the Americas, the fathers meekly concurred, and the Chiquitanos were quickly subjected to **forced labour** and the seizure of their best lands by the settlers of Santa Cruz. Within a few decades the missions were a shadow of their former selves, and this decline has continued pretty much ever since, leaving only the beautiful mission **churches**, now restored to their full glory with European aid money, to testify to the missions' former prosperity.

Concepción

About 68km to the east, the former mission town of **CONCEPCIÓN** is slightly larger than San Javier, but otherwise very similar. The mission was founded in 1709 by **Father Lucas Caballero**, who was killed two years later by the Puyzocas tribe, which later settled here. At the town's centre is a broad **plaza** lined with single-storey whitewashed adobe houses with tiled roofs that extend over the pavement, a colonial architectural style introduced after the expulsion of the Jesuits. In the middle of the square stands a simple **wooden cross**, surrounded by four palm trees – originally a feature of all the mission compounds.

Concepción is the centre for efforts to reconstruct the Jesuit mission churches of Chiquitos, and the main **workshops** for woodcarving and painting are behind the church a block east of the plaza. The staff here are usually happy to show visitors around for free at 10.30am and 3.30pm from Monday to Friday.

Catedral de Concepción

On the east side of the plaza • Daily 8am–6pm • Bs15

The town's mission church, now the **Catedral de Concepción** is a massive barn-like structure with an overhanging roof supported by 121 colossal tree-trunk columns, and with a separate, similarly supported bell tower. Originally designed by **Father Martin Schmidt** and completed in 1756, it was the first Jesuit church in Chiquitos to be restored, and is the most extravagantly decorated of them all, with a lavishly painted facade decorated with golden Baroque floral designs, angels and two images of the Virgin Mary on either side of the door. The interior is smothered with **gold leaf**, a powerful reminder of the vast wealth the missions once possessed. Amid the beautifully carved altarpieces, confessionals and statues of saints, the most interesting detail is the modern **Via Crucis**, a depiction of the Easter story that runs around the top of the walls. Christ is shown living in present-day Chiquitos, surrounded by lush tropical forest inhabited by parrots and tortoises, and his betrayal and death are imbued with contemporary political and ecological metaphor.

Museo Misional

On the south side of the plaza • Mon–Sat 8am–noon & 2.30–6.30pm, Sun 10am–12.30pm • Bs6

An old colonial house that was the childhood home of the former military dictator and later elected president Hugo Banzer, now houses the **Museo Misional**, dedicated to the restoration of the mission churches of Chiquitos. On display are some good pictures of the different churches before, during and after reconstruction; examples of the crumbling original wooden pillars and statues which were replaced; and a **small workshop** where a local craftsman demonstrates the laborious task of restoring the original statues. There are also **photographs** of letters written and musical scores composed by Father Martin Schmidt that were discovered in the 1970s, and an irreverent totem pole-like statue of Hans Roth, the architect who led the

---

THE CHIQUITOS MUSICAL RENAISSANCE

Of all the European arts and crafts introduced to Chiquitos by the Jesuits in the eighteenth century, the one that gained most rapid acceptance among the indigenous tribes was **music**. Imported organs, trumpets, violins and other instruments were enthusiastically adopted by the Chiquitanos, who quickly learned to manufacture their own instruments, while the choirs and orchestras of the mission settlements were said by contemporaries to have matched anything in Spanish America at the time. **Father Martin Schmidt**, the Swiss Jesuit who designed the churches of San Javier, San Raphael and Concepción, was a keen composer who taught music and brought the first church organs to the region, while the missions also benefited from the presence of an Italian named **Domenico Zipoli**, who had been a well-known composer in Rome before coming to South America.

Like all the cultural accomplishments of the missions, their musical tradition all but disappeared in the centuries following the expulsion of the Jesuits, though its influence remained in the **folk music** of the Chiquitanos themselves. When the restoration of the mission churches began in the 1970s, however, researchers in Concepción discovered a substantial archive of liturgical and orchestral Renaissance Baroque musical scores, including works by Schmidt and other Jesuit composers. The rediscovery of this lost music inspired a musical revival in Chiquitos, and throughout the mission towns and outlying settlements you'll come across children and young adults playing violins and other instruments.

In 1996 this revival inspired a group of music lovers to organize the first **Chiquitos Missions Music Festival**, featuring performances of the music recovered from the lost archives. Since then, the festival has grown into a major biennial event (in even numbered years), attracting dozens of orchestras and musical groups from around the world, and involving performances in all the mission towns of Chiquitos as well as in Santa Cruz. For further information, visit ⓦfestivalesapac.com.

5

reconstruction effort for 27 years until his death in 1999. The museum **shop** sells beautiful miniature carved wooden angels and other souvenirs made by local craftsmen, as well as CDs of Baroque music; there are several other handicrafts shops around the plaza.

San Ignacio de Velasco

178km east of Concepción, **SAN IGNACIO DE VELASCO** was founded in 1748, just nineteen years before the expulsion of the Jesuits from South America, but quickly grew to become one of the largest and most developed of the mission towns. Now the largest settlement in Chiquitos, it acts as a bustling **market centre** for an extensive frontier hinterland of large cattle ranches and isolated indigenous Chiquitano communities. At its centre lies the broad **Plaza 31 de Julio**, which is graced by numerous massive swollen-bellied toboroche trees, whose tangled branches blossom into brilliant pink and white in June and July. The town's wide, unpaved streets fan out from the plaza, and are lined with low houses whose tiled roofs extend over the pavement, supported by wooden beams.

Catedral de San Ignacio

Main plaza • Daily 4–6pm • Free

The **Catedral de San Ignacio** stands on the north side of the plaza. The town's magnificent original church collapsed in 1948 – the attempt to rebuild it in the style of the original is spoiled by the ugly modern concrete bell tower but otherwise well executed, though the painted facade decorated with statues of saints, each accompanied by an animal, is if anything too neat and symmetrical. The **interior** still houses many of the original statues of saints and magnificent carved Baroque altarpieces that graced the old mission church.

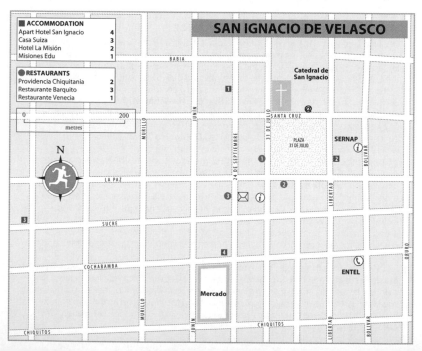

SAN IGNACIO DE VELASCO

ACCOMMODATION
Apart Hotel San Ignacio 4
Casa Suiza 3
Hotel La Misión 2
Misiones Edu 1

RESTAURANTS
Providencia Chiquitania 2
Restaurante Barquito 3
Restaurante Venecia 1

Catedral de San Ignacio

PLAZA 31 DE JULIO

SERNAP

ENTEL

Mercado

Laguna Guapamó

A short distance behind the church to the north, on the outskirts of town, the streets run down to **Laguna Guapamó**, an artificial lake created by the Jesuits to provide water and fish for the mission, where locals like to come swimming and fishing on sultry afternoons; note that the lake is home to piranhas.

San Miguel

Set amid scrubby forest broken by patches of cattle pasture, **SAN MIGUEL** is a sleepy collection of whitewashed houses about 40km south of San Ignacio on the main road to San José de Chiquitos. Its humble structures make the first sight of the splendid **Iglesia de San Miguel** even more astounding: set on a small rise overlooking the central plaza and dominating the town, the restored church is perhaps the most beautiful of the mission churches. Founded in 1721 and built in the same barn-like style as most of the others, the church facade is beautifully painted with Baroque floral designs, with pictures of St Peter and St Paul on either side of the main door.

To get inside, enter the walled **cloister** to the right – part of the original mission compound or Jesuit college, which is now used by the parish priest: go under the freestanding white adobe bell tower and ask in the parish offices for someone to let you in – you are likely to have to ask around for someone with a key. Inside, the soaring roof is supported by massive tree trunks carved in spirals, while the walls are lined with metre-high wooden statues of angels. The main **altarpiece** is smothered in gold leaf, with alcoves filled by statues of angels and saints including (in the centre) the Archangel Michael, in a golden helmet and shield, holding a three-pronged sword aloft as he tramples the devil underfoot.

San Rafael

The second Jesuit mission in Chiquitos when it was founded in 1696, the town of **SAN RAFAEL** sits 35km southeast of San Miguel, and boasts the biggest of all the region's Jesuit churches, the **Iglesia de San Rafael**. A cavernous structure with a free-standing bell tower supported by four spiralled wooden pillars, it was built under the direction of Martin Schmidt between 1747 and 1749. The magnificent interior features beautiful frescoes of angels, and some beautifully carved statues of saints in the alcoves of the golden altarpiece.

Santa Ana

About 20km north of San Rafael on a different road back to San Ignacio, the village of **SANTA ANA** is home to perhaps the least architecturally imposing of the mission churches of Chiquitos. Occupying one side of a large grassy plaza where donkeys graze

---

SAN JUANCITO

For those tired of the mission circuit's unsociably timed buses and lusting for a bit of an adventure, the community tourism project at **San Juancito** is the perfect fix. Situated about 20km from San Ignacio, the forty family-strong community is rustic (no running water or electricity) but provides a fascinating window into life in rural Santa Cruz and Chiquitano culture. You can learn traditional *artesanía*, see coffee growing and even help out in the fields. There are also opportunities for horseriding, hiking and fishing. The basic rooms (dorms Bs15/person) are comfortable and prices include three meals of wholesome home-cooking. Take one of the Santa Cruz buses and ask to be dropped off at San Juancito (about 20min along the road), or go by taxi (about Bs40) or motorbike taxi (about Bs15). See ⓦzorpia.com/sanjuancito, for more details.

and schoolchildren play football, the **Iglesia de Santa Ana** has not yet been fully restored and as such retains an intimate, rustic charm more in keeping with the sleepy atmosphere of its surroundings than the grandiose edifices of San Rafael or Concepción. There's some speculation as to whether this is the original Jesuit church at all – built entirely of wood, it has none of the usual IHS signs and may have been rebuilt shortly after the order was expelled in 1767.

San José de Chiquitos and around

About 130km south of San Rafael, the dusty town of **SAN JOSÉ DE CHIQUITOS** is home to a distinctive mission church, and also stands on the railway line that runs east from Santa Cruz to Puerto Suarez, Quijarro and the Brazilian border. Despite this (for Chiquitos) abundance of **transport connections**, like the other mission towns San José has a torpid feel and is now nothing more than a dreary frontier market town and supply centre for the surrounding cattle ranches and Mennonite colonies.

The mission complex

Main plaza • Daily 7am–noon & 2.30–7pm • Free

The mission of San José was founded in 1696, close to the original site of the city of Santa Cruz de la Sierra. Its **mission complex** was built in the last decades before the Jesuits' expulsion in 1767. Occupying one side of the central plaza, it's utterly distinct from the other churches of Chiquitos, being closer in design to those of the Paraguayan missions, with an elegant Baroque stone facade. The complex consists of four buildings linked by a 3m-high wall that forms a defensive compound. From right to left, these four buildings are the **Casa de los Muertos**, were bodies where once stored before being buried; the **church** itself; the four-tiered stone **bell tower** that would also have served as a lookout post; and the **Jesuit college**. That these elegant structures have survived for over two and a half centuries is all the more impressive given the fact that they were built by indigenous masons with no previous experience of stonework. Behind this facade, however, the main body of the church is built of wood, with a roof supported by tree-trunk pillars: this may have been completed by the Chiquitanos after the Jesuits had departed. The interior itself is in a poor state of repair but is currently undergoing restoration, and there are beautiful but dilapidated religious statues and other ornaments.

Santa Cruz La Vieja

Other than the church there's nothing to see in San José, though if you've got an afternoon to kill you could walk down to the site of **Santa Cruz La Vieja**, the original site of the city of Santa Cruz, founded by conquistador Nuflo de Chavez in 1561 but abandoned in 1594 in the face of persistent indigenous attack and moved to its current site 260km to the west. From the plaza, turn right as you face the church and head south out of town for about 4km and you'll reach a sign to the **Parque Nacional Histórico Santa Cruz La Vieja**, a grandiose title for what is in fact simply a series of overgrown mounds set amid dense scrub and giant cactus trees.

ARRIVAL AND DEPARTURE   **CHIQUITOS: THE JESUIT MISSIONS**

The missions can be visited in a five- to seven-day loop by road and rail from Santa Cruz. From the city a rough road runs northeast to **San Javier** and **Concepción**, then continues to **San Ignacio** (from where the churches of San Miguel, San Rafael and Santa Ana can all be visited by taxi in a day). From San Ignacio, the road heads south to San José de Chiquitos, the easternmost of the surviving missions, which is on the railway line between Santa Cruz and the Brazilian border at Quijarro. **Buses** connect all these mission towns as far as San José, from where you can get the **train** back to Santa Cruz or continue east to the Brazilian border. Alternatively, you could travel the loop counter-clockwise, starting from San José and returning to Santa Cruz by road via the other mission towns – indeed, transport links are slightly more convenient going in this direction.

SAN JAVIER

By bus There are several bus services (around 7 daily; 4–5hr) between Santa Cruz and San Javier; in addition, all buses between Santa Cruz and Concepción (1hr) also stop off in San Javier to pick up or drop off passengers. If you just want to visit the church you could easily come here on the first bus in the morning from Concepción or Santa Cruz, spend an hour or two looking around, and then catch another bus onwards.

CONCEPCIÓN

By bus Buses from most companies arrive a block north of the plaza; Flota Jenecherú services arrive two blocks south of the plaza on Lucas Cabellero. For the Flota Jenecherú service, you can buy a ticket in advance from the company's office on Lucas Cabellero. There are several buses to Santa Cruz (around 8 daily; 6–7hr) that travel via San Javier (1hr). To reach San Ignacio de Velasco, you need to catch a through bus (3 daily, departing between 5.30pm and 8pm; 6–7hr) from Santa Cruz, which passes through roughly between 11.30pm and 3am. Buses from San Ignacio de Velasco often arrive in the early hours of the morning – if you are coming from there, consider booking a room in advance.

SAN IGNACIO DE VELASCO

By plane Military airline TAM (ⓦ tam.bo) sometimes operates flights between San Ignacio and Santa Cruz. The airstrip in San Ignacio de Velasco is around five blocks south of the main plaza.

By bus San Ignacio has no bus terminal, so buses arrive and depart from the offices of the various different bus companies, most of which are located in the market area, a block east and one to three blocks south of the plaza. Services to Santa Cruz (3 daily; 10–12hr) via Concepción (6–7hr) or San Javier (9–11hr) generally travel by night. There is usually a daily bus to San José de Chiquitos (5–6hr) too; schedules tend to change frequently, so check the departure times when you arrive. Several buses leave daily for San Matías (10–12hr) on the Brazilian border. If you're heading to the Parque Nacional Noel Kempff Mercado, there is

usually a weekly bus (12–14hr) to La Florida; check departure days at the SERNAP office at Bolívar 87 (ⓣ 03 3932747).

SAN MIGUEL, SAN RAFAEL AND SANTA ANA

San Miguel is about 40km south of San Ignacio on the main road to San José de Chiquitos, and San Rafael is another 35km or so further southeast on the same road. From San Rafael another road runs back to San Ignacio via Santa Ana, 20km away. None of the churches have fixed opening times, but even if you find them closed, you can usually find someone to let you in.

By micro A couple of micros travel each day between San Ignacio and San Miguel (1hr), San Rafael (1hr 30min) and Santa Ana (1hr), though visiting by taxi saves you a great deal of time.

By taxi San Miguel, Santa Ana and San Rafael can be visited together in a one-day trip from San Ignacio de Velasco. A taxi should cost around Bs200; you can find them on San Ignacio's main plaza.

SAN JOSÉ DE CHIQUITOS

By train The train station (ⓦ ferroviariaoriental.com) is two blocks north and four blocks east of the plaza. Trains to Santa Cruz (around 5–7hr) pass through late at night; trains heading towards Quijarro (around 8–12hr) near the Brazilian border call in slightly earlier. There are a dozen services weekly in each direction; the Ferrobus is the quickest and most comfortable option. Buy tickets in advance from the train station.

By bus Buses along the bumpy – but passable, even in rainy season – road to San Ignacio arrive and depart from the offices of the two bus companies that serve the route: Trans Carreton, a block east of the plaza; and Trans Universal, four blocks north of the plaza beyond the petrol station on the road out of town. The once-daily buses to San Ignacio (5–6hr) tend to leave early in the morning, but you should check the latest timetables when you arrive. There is also usually a service or two to Santa Cruz (16–17hr), though the train is a far better option.

INFORMATION

An excellent website with detailed practical and contextual information on the **mission circuit** is ⓦ chiquitania.com; ⓦ mancochiquitana.org can also be useful.

CONCEPCIÓN

Tourist information There is an intermittently open tourist office on Moreno, near the church (officially Mon–Fri 9am–noon & 3–5pm; ⓣ 03 9643057).

SAN IGNACIO DE VELASCO

Tourist information There's a small tourist office in the Casa de Cultura, just off the main plaza (Mon–Fri 9am–noon & 3–5pm; ⓣ 03 9622056). SERNAP has an office at Bolívar 87 (Mon–Fri 9am–noon & 2.30–4pm; ⓣ 03 3932747) – call in here if you're planning to visit Parque Nacional Noel Kempff Mercado.

5

ACCOMMODATION

SAN JAVIER

Alojamiento San Javier On the main road ☎ 03 9635038. This relaxed, friendly place does the basics well: there are clean, comfortable rooms with or without private bathrooms, plus a garden and a TV lounge. **Bs70**

Hotel Momoqui Av Santa Cruz, not far from the plaza ☎ 03 9635121. This modern mid-range hotel has pleasant, if not especially stylish en-suite rooms with a/c and fridges. There's also an appealing pool in a neatly-tended garden, and an Italian restaurant. Tours can be arranged here. Rates include breakfast. **Bs250**

CONCEPCIÓN

Alojamiento Tarija A block north of the plaza, opposite the Linea 131 del Este office ☎ 03 9643020. One of the better options for shoestring travellers, *Alojamiento Tarija* offers cleanish, sparsely furnished rooms with shared or private bathrooms. **Bs60**

Apart Hotel Las Misiones Just off the plaza to the north on Lucas Caballero ☎ 03 9643021. A comfortable choice, *Apart Hotel Las Misiones* offers well-furnished a/c rooms with cool tiled floors around a flower-filled garden that features a pool. Breakfast included. **Bs200**

Gran Hotel Concepción On the west side of the plaza ☎ 03 9643031, ⓦ granhotelconcepcion.com. At the top of the range is the incongruously luxurious *Gran Hotel Concepción*, which has immaculate rooms around a beautiful courtyard garden with a swimming pool, hammocks, sun loungers and an outdoor restaurant. Breakfast included. **Bs315**

Hotel Colonial Half a block north of the plaza on Subteniente Roca Lado ☎ 03 9643050. The friendly *Hotel Colonial* offers clean modern rooms with private bathrooms (and a choice of a/c or fans) and hammocks strung outside in the shade. Breakfast included. **Bs150**

SAN IGNACIO DE VELASCO

Apart Hotel San Ignacio Cochabamba and 24 de Septiembre ☎ 03 9622157, ⓦ aparthotel-sanignacio .com. A very smart hotel with a beautifully kept garden and swimming pool. Its spacious en-suite rooms have TVs and a/c. Breakfast included. **Bs245**

★ **Casa Suiza** A block south and six blocks west of the plaza on Sucre ☎ 7630 6798. This charming guesthouse has a welcoming, homely feel. The simple but clean rooms

come with good beds and shared bathrooms (with excellent showers). The owners also run a *lecheria*, and breakfast includes what must be the best yogurt in Bolivia. There's also a fairly extensive book exchange. Full and half board options available. **Bs100**

Hotel La Misión Plaza 31 de Julio ☎ 03 9622333, ⓦ hotel-lamision.com. This opulent neo-colonial style modern hotel features carved wooden pillars outside and a cool courtyard with a fountain and small swimming pool within. The en-suite rooms (with a/c, TVs and phones) are suitably swish, and there's a good, if pricey restaurant. **Bs420 ($60)**

Misiones Edu Just along from the church in the direction of the lake ☎ 7604 0395. With immaculately clean, tastefully-decorated rooms and a peaceful garden, this is the best budget option in San Ignacio. **Bs35**

SAN MIGUEL

La Pascana On Sucre, just off the main plaza ☎ 03 9624211. This *alojamiento* has a collection of no frills, somewhat bare rooms with shared bathrooms, as well as a restaurant. **Bs100**

SAN RAFAEL

Hotel Lorena Just off the main plaza ☎ 03 9624015. The plain and simple rooms (with shared bathrooms) here are fine for a night, though there's little in the way of creature comforts. **Bs60**

SANTA ANA

Alojamiento Santa Ana Close to the main plaza, no phone. There are currently only two places to stay in Santa Ana, and both are very basic. *Alojamiento Santa Ana* is marginally the most comfortable. **Bs60**

SAN JOSÉ DE CHIQUITOS

Hotel Denisse Four blocks east of the plaza on Géricke ☎ 03 9722230. An economical choice located just a short walk from the plaza. The spick-and-span en-suite rooms come with a/c or fans. **Bs100**

Hotel Turobo On the west side of the plaza opposite the church ☎ 03 9372037. The clean and comfortable *Hotel Turobo* is the best bet in town, offering both simple rooms with fans and more expensive options with private bathrooms and a/c. **Bs100**

EATING

Most restaurants are open Monday to Saturday for lunch and dinner; getting a decent meal on Sundays, however, can be tricky – hotels are generally the best places to try.

SAN JAVIER

El Ganadero On the main plaza. This centrally located restaurant serves the best steaks in town, as well as a few

milanesas (thin breaded steaks) and chicken dishes, and a set lunch. Mains Bs20–40.

THE MENNONITES

San José's most unlikely sight is the bizarre spectacle of tall white people with flaxen hair and ruddy cheeks – the men dressed in denim dungarees and straw hats, the women in full-length dresses and headscarves – walking around town or driving horse-drawn buggies. These are the **Mennonites**, members of a radical Protestant sect founded in the Netherlands by Menno Simmons in the sixteenth century. For the next four centuries the Mennonites found themselves driven from country to country as they attempted to escape religious persecution and conscription, and to find land on which to pursue their dreams of an agrarian utopia. After migrating to Germany, they moved in succession to Russia, the US and Canada, Mexico and Belize, until finally arriving in Bolivia and Paraguay in the twentieth century, attracted by the availability of cheap land and guarantees of religious freedom. Perhaps twenty thousand Mennonites now live in communities across the **Eastern Lowlands**, farming and raising cattle in self-contained agricultural communities.

The central tenets of the Mennonites are the refusal to take oaths or bear arms (they are exempt from military service in Bolivia); the baptism only of believers (ie only of people who willingly adopt the faith, which excludes infants); simplicity of dress and personal habits; and an unwillingness to marry outside the faith. They also to varying degrees reject most **modern technology**, including cars and computers, though faced with the difficult agricultural conditions of Chiquitos, many Bolivian Mennonites allow the use of tractors – though not, bizarrely, of rubber tyres, so their wheels are covered with steel spikes. Though some speak Spanish, and a few of the older ones who grew up in North America also have some English, among themselves they speak **Plattdeutsch**, an archaic German dialect. If you can bridge the language barrier, many Mennonite men are happy to talk about their lives.

However, there seems to be some level of distrust between the Mennonites and the locals, possibly based on the Mennonite buying up of land in the area. The irony is that, two and a half centuries after the **Jesuits** were expelled, religiously inspired utopian dreams are still being pursued in the plains of Chiquitos, albeit by white Protestants instead of indigenous Catholics. This isn't, however, an irony that would have been appreciated by the Jesuits themselves – their order was set up precisely to combat Protestant sects like the Mennonites.

CONCEPCIÓN

Alpina On the southwest corner of the plaza. A good place to escape the heat, this ice cream parlour offers decent sundaes (Bs10–20), as well as coffee, cold drinks and snacks.

Buen Gusto On the north side of the plaza. One of the town's top restaurants, Buen Gusto specializes in traditional Bolivian cuisine, serving hearty soups, stews and chicken and beef main courses (Bs20–40) in a shaded courtyard filled with plants and local crafts.

Club Social Ñuflo de Chavez On the west side of the plaza. Another good choice, with views of the church, *Club Social Ñuflo de Chavez* has a range of sizeable set lunches and dinners (around Bs20–25) – the steaks are particularly good.

ASCENSIÓN DE GURAYOS

As you head towards the main plaza from the bus station there are various cafés and restaurants serving fried chicken and *milanesas*.

SAN IGNACIO DE VELASCO

Providencia Chiquitania On the southwest corner of the plaza. Serves good coffee and fresh juices (Bs10–15), snacks like burgers, *empanadas* and *sonso* (fried balls

of cheese and manioc flour) and mains like steak and *milanesas*.

Restaurante Barquito A block west of the plaza on 24 de Septiembre. If you're seriously hungry, head to *Barquito*, which offers a tasty, economical and plentiful Brazilian-style buffet (Bs15–20). Unsurprisingly barbecued beef features heavily.

Restaurante Venecia On the southwest side of the plaza. Ideally located for looking out onto the attractive plaza, *Venecia* serves filling set almuerzos and main courses (Bs20–40) like steak, chicken and *pique a lo macho* (strips of beef with onions, tomatoes, chips and a spicy sauce).

SAN MIGUEL, SAN RAFAEL AND SANTA ANA

Eating out options are decidedly limited in all three towns: in San Miguel, *La Pascana* serves traditional, filling meals; in San Rafael, there is a clutch of simple restaurants just off the plaza; and in Santa Ana, try *Club Social* near the plaza.

SAN JOSÉ DE CHIQUITOS

El Cubanito On the plaza adjacent to Hotel Turobo. A reliable choice, *El Cubanito* serves wholesome Bolivian fare (Bs20–40) in a simple but pleasant dining room.

5

Pizzeria Romanazzi Bolívar. A surprisingly accomplished restaurant, *Romanazzi* serves excellent and authentic pizzas, as well as a few pasta dishes. Mains Bs20–50.

DIRECTORY

SAN IGNACIO DE VELASCO

Banks and exchange San Ignacio is the only mission town with an ATM (on the plaza); it also has a couple of banks and a few currency exchanges, mostly located on or around the plaza.

Parque Nacional Noel Kempff Mercado

Occupying 16,000 square kilometres of the far northeast on the Brazil border, **PARQUE NACIONAL NOEL KEMPFF MERCADO** is the country's most isolated, pristine and spectacular national park, and one of the most remote wilderness regions in South America. Encompassing several different ecosystems including Amazon rainforest, savannah, and scrubby Brazilian *cerrado*, the UNESCO World Heritage Site supports an astonishing range of **wildlife**, including over 630 species of birds, eleven species of monkey, all the major Amazonian mammals, pink freshwater dolphins and the highly endangered giant river otter. Moreover, your chances of seeing these animals are much higher here than elsewhere in Bolivia.

Established in 1979 as the **Parque Nacional Huanchaca**, the park was renamed (and expanded) in 1988 in honour of the pioneering Bolivian biologist and conservationist Noel Kempff Mercado, who was murdered by drug traffickers after stumbling across a secret cocaine laboratory on the Huanchaca plateau. The park was expanded again in 1997 under a pioneering "carbon credit" scheme, whereby two US energy corporations and the oil giant BP paid around $10 million to buy out loggers operating in an adjacent forest area of 6340 square kilometres, which was then added to the park.

The park's remote location means it is expensive and difficult to visit: even the organized tours can be pretty tough going. The park's southern border is over 200km from the nearest town, **San Ignacio de Velasco**, itself another 400km from Santa Cruz. It is also extremely difficult – and often impossible – to visit the park during the rainy season (Nov–May), when the mosquitoes and other insects are also particularly ferocious.

Camp Los Fierros

Currently the only camp open in the reserve, **Camp Los Fierros** lies at the southern end of the park, within easy hiking distance of the Huanchaca plateau. It is also close to numerous trails that lead through the surrounding rainforest and savannahs and have excellent wildlife-spotting possibilities. The most popular excursion is to **El Encanto**, a narrow but spectacular waterfall that plunges 80m off the sheer sides of the plateau. The waterfall is a one-day walk from the camp, and there's a basic shelter close by where you can camp out if you have your own equipment, but otherwise you're better off hiring the park guards' pick-up truck to take you there and back in a day. Other day hikes lead up onto the plateau and to the **Laguna Chaplín**, which is home to abundant aquatic bird life.

HUANCHACA PLATEAU

The park's most remarkable natural feature is the **Huanchaca plateau** (or the Caparú Plateau), a vast sandstone *meseta* (plateau) rising 500m above the surrounding rainforest to an elevated plain of grasslands and dry *cerrado* woodlands, from where spectacular waterfalls plunge down the sheer escarpment into the park's rivers. This isolated plateau covers over seven thousand square kilometres, just under half the park, and inspired Sir Arthur Conan Doyle's novel *The Lost World* – at least according to Colonel Percy Harrison Faucett, the legendary British explorer who was the first European to see the plateau when he came here in 1910 while demarcating Bolivia's borders, and who later described the landscape to Conan Doyle in London.

Camp Flor de Oro

Based in a former ranch that once belonged to one of the suspected drug traffickers implicated in the murder of Noel Kempff Mercado, **Camp Flor de Oro** has a beautiful setting on the banks of the Río Iténez, which marks the border with Brazil. It was closed at the time of research but may well reopen in the future; check the latest situation with travel operators in Santa Cruz. Flor de Oro's key attraction is the opportunity to visit the **Ahlfeld and Arco Iris waterfalls**, which tumble down from the Huanchaca plateau. Reaching them involves a four-hour motorboat trip down the Río Iténez and up the smaller Río Paucana to **Campamento Ahlfeld**, a trip that is only possible during the rainy season (Nov–May). The Ahlfeld waterfall, twenty minutes' walk from the camp, is a stunning multiple waterfall, 40m high and twice as wide.

The Arco Iris waterfall

It's a lengthy but rewarding hike (4–5hr return) to the **Arco Iris waterfall** from Campamento Ahlfeld, including a steep climb up the escarpment onto the top of the Huanchaca plateau. The vegetation on the plateau is very different from the rainforest below, consisting of dry and thorny scrub and low forest *cerrado*. Utterly unaltered by human action and surrounded by a seemingly endless sea of rainforest below, it's easy to see why this landscape inspired Arthur Conan Doyle's fantasy of a lost world inhabited by strange prehistoric beasts. Viewed from above, the Arco Iris waterfall is an overwhelming sight: a vertical cascade plunging 100m down through virgin rainforest and throwing up great clouds of spray that refract the sunlight, creating the innumerable rainbows that give the falls their name.

ARRIVAL AND DEPARTURE

PARQUE NOEL KEMPFF MERCADO

ORGANIZED TOURS

Only a few hundred people visit the park each year, and almost all of those arrive by chartered light aircraft from Santa Cruz; a spectacular flight that can be arranged by several Santa Cruz-based tour agencies (see p.237). A return flight to Camp Los Fierros (or Flor de Oro, if it has reopened) costs several hundred dollars per person. A typical five-day all-inclusive package to the park, travelling by plane, costs about Bs6650 ($950) per person based on a group of four. If you substitute the flights for a gruelling overland journey, the price is roughly halved.

TRAVELLING INDEPENDENTLY

Considering the difficulties, taking an organized tour is highly advised. Independent travellers who have attempted the trip on a strict budget often turn back as arriving by public transport is extremely arduous and sometimes impossible. If

you are still undaunted, however, head to San Ignacio de Velasco, from where there is usually a weekly bus (at least 12–14hr) to La Florida on the western edge of the park. There are some basic huts (around Bs50/hut) at La Florida where you could stop for a few nights; bring your own bedding. Once in La Florida, it's still another 35km to Camp Los Fierros along a rainforest track; if you're attempting this route, its highly advised that you arrange for the rangers at Los Fierros to pick you up and take you back again, including an excursion to the El Encanto waterfall; this costs around Bs1050 ($150); contact them via SERNAP's offices in Santa Cruz or San Ignacio de Velasco (see p.259). Alternatively you may be able to hire a pick-up truck in San Ignacio or La Florida to take you all the way; it is also possible to hire local guides in La Florida. If Camp Flor de Oro camp has reopened, it can be reached on a circuitous route via the Brazilian town of Pimenteiras taking at least two to three days.

INFORMATION

Tourist information If you want to visit the park independently, you must inform SERNAP in Santa Cruz (see p.237) or San Ignacio de Velasco, Bolivar 87 (☎03 3932747) first. The Santa Cruz-based tour operators,

particularly the recommended Ruta Verde (see p.237), are a better source of information. There's no official entry fee, but local communities sometimes charge around Bs70–100 per vehicle.

ACCOMMODATION

Cabins and camping Accommodation in Camp Los Fierros is in very basic cabins with dorms sleeping two to four with foam mattresses and shared bathrooms. You can also camp here if you have your own equipment. Independent travellers should

bring all their food and drinking water with them, as there are no facilities. Camp Flor de Oro is currently closed, but Ruta Verde (see p.237) is looking into setting up accommodation with the local community in this area. Cabins **Bs150**

5

East from Santa Cruz

From **Santa Cruz**, the railway line runs some 680km east to the **Brazilian border** across a seemingly endless expanse of forest and tangled scrub, gradually giving way to the vast swamplands of the **Pantanal** as the border draws near. Settlements along the line remain few and far between, and the region's main towns are both close to the Brazilian border: **Puerto Suárez**, a half-forgotten lakeside outpost that was once the focus of Bolivian dreams of access to the Atlantic via the Río Paraguay, and the dismal border trading settlement of **Quijarro**, the train's last stop before the frontier.

Chochis

Between San José de Chiquitos and the town of Roboré, an immense mass of red rock marks the community of **CHOCHIS**, about 360km east of Santa Cruz. At the foot of this spectacular rock tower is the **Santuario de Chochis** – a beautifully quaint church established by the survivors of a disaster that rocked the area in 1979. After twenty days of torrential rain, on January 15, 1979 a volcanic eruption caused the railway bridge to collapse, killing many passengers on a passing train. It is well worth the climb to take the path that goes some way up the *cerro*, as the views stretch right across the strange moon-like landscape.

Puerto Suárez

Just before reaching the Brazilian border at Quijarro, the railway line passes through the older and more agreeable **PUERTO SUÁREZ**, situated on the shores of Lago Cáceres, which is linked to the mighty Río Paraguay. Founded in 1875, the town has long been the focus of Bolivia's ambitions to gain access to the Atlantic Ocean via the Paraguay and Paraná rivers, but Lago Cáceres has always been too shallow to take anything other than small boats. Puerto Suárez has yet to really tap into the growing number of tourists who visit the region to visit the wildlife-rich wetlands of the Pantanal (see box below). This is a shame, as it's a peaceful and dignified place, beautifully set on a bluff overlooking the calm blue waters of the lake, and with the city of Corumbá in Brazil visible in the distance.

THE PANTANAL

Much of Bolivia's far east along the Brazilian border is covered by the **Pantanal**, the vast flood plain on either side of the Río Paraguay that forms the world's biggest freshwater wetland system. Stretching over two hundred thousend square kilometres is a mosaic of ecosystems, including swamps, lakes, seasonally flooded grasslands and different kinds of forest, most of which is turned into an immense inland freshwater sea during the rainy season (Nov–March). This largely pristine wilderness supports possibly the densest concentration of **wildlife** in the Americas, including a vast array of birds, reptiles like anacondas and caymans, and mammals including swamp deer, giant otters, jaguars, capybaras and tapirs, all of which can be seen with greater frequency here than anywhere in the Amazon.

About eighty percent of the Pantanal lies in Brazil, but the fifteen or so percent within Bolivia's borders (the rest is in **Paraguay**) is arguably more pristine and virtually uninhabited. In theory it is also better protected – north and south of Puerto Suárez, huge areas of the Pantanal are covered by the **Area Natural San Matías** and the **Parque Nacional Otuquis**, which together cover almost forty thousend square kilometres. The flipside is that it can be difficult to visit: facilities few and far between, and it's generally cheaper to organize expeditions into the Pantanal from Corumbá in Brazil.

Several Bolivian **tour operators** offer a Pantanal package, however, including Ruta Verde in Santa Cruz (see p.237) and Michael Bledinger in Samaipata (see p.244). Hotels in Puerto Suárez and Quijarro also arrange excursions. Alternatively, more simply, you can hire a fisherman in Puerto Suárez to take you out across **Lago Cáceres**.

Quijarro

5

The last stop on the railway line in Bolivia is **QUIJARRO**, a fairly dismal collection of shacks and dosshouses surrounding the station – if you're heading on to Brazil, you're better off pushing on to the border at Arroyo Concepción, 2km away. However, there are a couple of decent hotels in and around town, which can also organize Pantanal trips.

ARRIVAL AND DEPARTURE

EL CHOCHIS

By train The *Tren Regional* (6 weekly), which runs between Santa Cruz and Quijarro, stops at the station at Chochis.

PUERTO SUAREZ

By plane Military airline TAM (⊛tam.bo) has several weekly flights to and from Santa Cruz; Aerosur (⊛www .aerosur.com) sometimes has services too. The airport is 6km outside town.

By train The train station is a couple of kilometres from Puerto Suárez; you can walk into town or take a taxi (Bs10). See the Quijarro section below for schedule information.

By bus Several daily buses from Quijarro to Santa Cruz

EAST FROM SANTA CRUZ

(15–24hr) pass through Puerto Suárez. However, the same journey is quicker and much more comfortable by train

QUIJARRO

By train There are twelve trains (check ⊛ferroviariaoriental.com for the latest schedules) each week to Santa Cruz (officially 13hr 30min–18hr 35min, though delays are common); the Ferrobus is the quickest and most comfortable service, though also the most expensive. The train station is by the main square; buy tickets as far in advance as possible.

By bus Several daily buses travel from Quijarro to Santa Cruz (15–24hr), but the train is a far better option.

CROSSING THE BRAZILIAN BORDER

Via Arroyo Concepción Collective taxis run when full to the Brazilian border at Arroyo Concepción from the train stations in Quijarro (around 2km) and Puerto Suárez (around 10km). To cross the border at Arroyo Concepción, get your passport stamped at the Bolivian *migración* office (daily 8am–noon & 2.30–5.30pm), then walk across into Brazil, where taxis, motorcycle taxis and regular buses wait to take passengers across the bridge over the Río Paraguay

and on into the city of Corumbá, where you'll need to get an entry stamp from the Federal Police office at the bus station. If you need a visa, the Brazilian consulate (Mon–Fri 8am–2pm) is two blocks southeast of the plaza on the waterfront in Puerto Suárez. You will also need a yellow fever certificate to enter Brazil. If you're arriving from Brazil, you should go straight to the train station to buy a ticket for a train heading east, as these can sell out quickly.

ACCOMMODATION

CHOCHIS

NGO PROBIOMA (see p.240) supports a community project that has cabins and camping facilities, provides excellent food and offers guide services. Book in advance.

PUERTO SUAREZ

Hotel Beby A few blocks northwest of the plaza along Av Bolívar ❶03 9762700. For those on a tighter budget, the basic *Hotel Beby* has acceptable box-like rooms with fans or a/c. Bs50

Hotel Sucre On the main plaza ❶03 9762069. The best place to stay is the *Hotel Sucre*, which offers small but comfortable a/c rooms around a pleasant courtyard garden. It also has a decent restaurant. Bs150

QUIJARRO

Hotel El Pantanal Around 2km outside town ❶03 9782020. The most luxurious option in the region has swanky a/c rooms, a pool, lush grounds, a sauna, a couple of restaurants and a bar-nightclub. Pricey Pantanal tours can be arranged too. Breakfast included. Bs623 ($89)

Tamengo Costa Rica 57, five blocks from the bus station ❶03 9783356. Hostelling International-affiliated, *Tamengo* has a real resort feel, with a pool, restaurant, bar and TV lounge. There are dorms and decent private rooms, and staff can organize good-value Pantanal trips, Spanish or Portuguese lessons, and volunteering placements. Dorms Bs60; doubles Bs240

EATING

PUERTO SUAREZ

El Mirador On the bluff overlooking the lake two blocks southeast of the plaza. This outdoor restaurant offers fresh river fish and even – if your conscience allows – *jacaré* (small caymans).

QUIJARRO

There's a series of insalubrious-looking eateries opposite the station but the *Tamengo* hotel has a much better restaurant. Most restaurants open daily for lunch and dinner, though many close early on Sundays.

5

The Chaco

South of the Santa Cruz–Quijarro railway line, the tropical dry forest gradually gives way to **the Chaco**, a vast and arid landscape of dense scrub and virtually impenetrable thornbrush stretching south to the Paraguayan border and far beyond. Inhabited only by isolated cattle ranchers and occasional communities of Guaraní and semi-nomadic Ayoreo, the Chaco is one of South America's last great wildernesses and supports plenty of wildlife – much of it now protected by the **Parque Nacional Kaa-Iya del Gran Chaco**, which covers over 34,000 square kilometres southeast of Santa Cruz adjacent to the Paraguayan border. However, there are few organized tourist facilities in the Chaco, and unless you hire your own 4WD, your view of the region will be limited to what you can see from the window of a bus or train. The region's main towns are **Villamontes**, the Bolivian Chaco's biggest settlement, and **Yacuiba**, on the Argentine border. Adventurous travellers can also take the strenuous trans-Chaco road, which heads east to the Paraguayan border at Fortín Villazón, and then onto the Paraguayan capital, **Asunción**.

Villamontes

A hot and dusty but welcoming frontier town with a mostly Guaraní population, **VILLAMONTES** was the scene of one of Bolivia's few military victories during the disastrous **Chaco War** (see p.314) with Paraguay. Today the town remains very much dominated by the Bolivian army.

Museo Historico Militar Heroes del Chaco
Plaza 15 de Abril • Tues–Sun 8am–noon & 2–6pm • Bs2

Housed in a large white mansion, the **Museo Historico Militar Heroes del Chaco** is full of military paraphernalia and the garden is filled with trenches, dugouts, bunkers and artillery pieces. Inside, there are photos of the terrible conditions endured by troops on both sides in the Chaco War, in which around 65,000 Bolivian soldiers were killed (out of a population of roughly two million).

Yacuiba

The modern border town of **YACUIBA** lies about 90km south of Villamontes by road and rail, and most travellers just pass through en route to or from Argentina. Yacuiba

---

THE GUARANÍ PEOPLE

The western Bolivian Chaco is home to the **Guaraní** people – known historically as the Chiriguanos – the largest indigenous group in the Bolivian lowlands, with a population of about 75, 000. The Guaraní originally migrated across the Chaco from east of the Río Paraguay in search of a mythical "Land Without Evil", occupying the southwestern fringes of the **Andes** in the fifteenth and sixteenth centuries just as the Inca empire was expanding into the same region. Despite this, the Guaraní successfully resisted conquest by the Incas, and subsequently proved among the fiercest and most tenacious indigenous opponents of the **Spanish**. Not until well into the Republican era were they completely subjugated, when the last great Guaraní uprising was brutally crushed in 1892, after which their remaining lands were seized by the Bolivian state and divided into large private ranches defended by **army forts**. In recent decades, the Guaraní have been struggling to regain control of their ancestral territories using **land reform** and indigenous rights legislation, and in spite of obstructive bureaucracy have now recovered large areas, where they farm maize, cotton, peanuts and other crops. Despite this, hundreds if not thousands of Guaraní still work on large **cattle ranches** under conditions of debt servitude that are little different from slavery.

sprang up following the construction of the railway and oil pipeline to **Argentina** in the 1960s, and retains a distinctly Argentine flavour, dominated by restaurants and duty-free shops. There's no reason to linger unless you arrive at night and have to wait for transport out.

ARRIVAL AND DEPARTURE

VILLAMONTES

By train The train station is two blocks north of the bus terminal on the same street. There are weekly trains to Yacuiba (Fri 5.03am; 2hr 50min) and Santa Cruz (Fri 7.48pm; 13hr 25min). Check the latest information at ⓦ ferroviariaoriental.com.

By bus The centre of Villamontes is the broad Plaza 6 de Agosto, from where the town's main street, Av Mendez, runs north eight blocks to the small bus terminal, where several daily buses to Tarija (10–12hr) and Santa Cruz (8–12hr) arrive and depart.

By micro/trufi Micros and trufis to Yacuiba (1hr 30min) arrive at and depart from Av Mendez, three blocks north of the plaza.

YACUIBA

By train The train station is two blocks south and a block west of the main plaza. There is a weekly train north to

THE CHACO

Santa Cruz (Fri 5pm; 16hr 25min) via Villamontes (2hr 50min). Check the latest information at ⓦ ferroviariaoriental.com.

By bus The bus terminal, from where there are morning and evening departures to Tarija (10–12hr) and Santa Cruz (10–14hr), lies about 1km south of the plaza. There are also buses (15hr) for the Paraguayan capital Asunción.

By micro/trufi Micros and trufis (1hr 30min) to and from Villamontes arrive and depart from outside the offices just off the plaza on the road to the bus terminal.

CROSSING THE ARGENTINE BORDER

By taxi The border crossing with Argentina is at Pocitos, 4km south of Yacuiba: to get there, take a collective taxi from the main plaza.

ACCOMMODATION

VILLAMONTES

Hotel El Rancho On Av Mendez opposite the train station ☎04 6722059. The mid-range *El Rancho* has cosy en-suite rooms with TVs, fridges and a/c, as well as a restaurant and a pool. Breakfast included. Bs350 ($50)

Residencial Raldes A block east of the plaza ☎04 6722088. A welcoming, family-run hotel with clean and good-value rooms set around a courtyard: choose from ones with a/c and private bathrooms or cheaper options with fans and shared bathrooms. Bs50

YACUIBA

Hotel Paris On Comercio ☎04 6822182, ⓦhotelparis. com.bo. The stylish *Hotel Paris* has comfortable modern rooms with a/c and TVs, plus a good restaurant. Bs240

Residencial Grand Victoria Near the bus station ☎04 6822320. If money is tighter, *Residencial Grand Victoria* offers basic rooms with aged a/c units and a choice of shared or en-suite bathrooms. Bs50

EATING

VILLAMONTES

Inexpensive meals can be found in the covered public market a few blocks north of the plaza on Av Mendez. On the road out of town towards Yacuiba a series of stalls serves delicious fried *surubí* fish from the nearby Río Pilcomayo, considered one of the finest fishing rivers in Bolivia.

YACUIBA

There are several good places to eat around the plaza, most of which serve tasty Argentine beef, as well as the usual mix of Bolivian standards, chicken, and pizza. Most restaurants open daily for lunch and dinner, though many close early on Sun.

DIRECTORY

VILLAMONTES

Telephones The ENTEL telephone office is just off the plaza to the west.

YACUIBA

Banks and exchange There are plenty of cambios along Comercio, that change cash but not traveller's cheques, plus a Banco de Credito ATM.

Internet The Cybernet Internet is on the plaza.

Telephones The ENTEL telephone office is on the plaza.

The Amazon

274 Rurrenabaque and
around
283 The Llanos de Moxos
286 Trinidad
293 The northern Amazon
298 Pando

OCELOT

The Amazon

Though the classic image of Bolivia seems forever tied to parched badlands, about a third of the country lies within the vast and often impenetrable wilderness of the Amazon basin, the same mind-bending expanse of swamp, savannah and tropical rainforest that first set Colonel Fawcett (see p.300) on his fatal quest to find El Dorado. Though deforestation has accelerated to a worrying degree in recent decades, it remains one of the most biodiverse regions in the world, with large areas virtually unexplored. Here, jaguars, tapirs and giant anteaters roam beneath the towering forest canopy; monstrous anacondas slither through the swamps; and the skies are filled by a kaleidoscopic variety of birds.

Often known as the **Beni**, after one of the rivers that are its dominant geographical feature, the Bolivian Amazon lies more than a thousand kilometres from the mighty Río Amazon as itself and contrary to what you might expect, not all of the region is covered by rainforest. Though the last foothills of the Andes are fringed with dense and humid **premontane forest**, the great watery plains that open up beyond are partially covered by a seemingly endless sea of savannah, dotted with islands of forest. Known as the **Llanos de Moxos**, these plains are flooded each year when the mighty rivers that meander slowly across them – the Beni, Mamoré, Guaporé and their tributaries – are swollen by innumerable Andean streams. Unsurprisingly, then, this entire region (similar in size to the whole of Great Britain) remains sparsely populated, apart from the great herds of semi-wild cattle that were first introduced by the Jesuit missionaries in the sixteenth century.

Sweltering quietly on the eastern edge of this area is **Trinidad**, the capital of the Beni and a bustling frontier outpost with few obvious attractions; for the adventurous, however, it's the starting point for slow boat journeys down the Río Mamoré to the Brazilian border. Of far more interest to most travellers is the ecotourist epicentre of **Rurrenabaque**, on the banks of the Río Beni. Given its proximity to the stunningly pristine forests of **Parque Nacional Madidi**, together with its commitment to sustainable. community-focused tourism, it's an obvious destination for anyone wanting to experience the Amazon's flora, fauna and indigenous peoples up close.

Further north, around the towns of Riberalta and Cobija towards the Brazilian border, the savannah gradually gives way to the high-canopied **Amazonian rainforest** (known as *selva*) more characteristic of the Amazon region as a whole, where logging and the collection of wild rubber and Brazil nuts are the only industries of any size. Roads in the whole region are poor in the best of conditions and in the rainy season between November and April are often completely impassable.

The real El Dorado? p.273.
Yossi Ginsberg and Rurre's tourist year zero p.276.
The threat to the forest p.281.
Ecotourism in Rurrenabaque p.283.
When San Ignacio ignites: The Fiesta Patronal p.284.
School of Baroque p.285.

Indigenous peoples of the Bolivian Amazon p.288.
Travelling down the Río Mamoré p.292.
The railway to nowhere p.296.
Nicolas Suárez: rubber baron p.297.
The Pando massacre p.298.
The mysterious Colonel Fawcett p.300

FIESTA PATRONAL, SAN IGNACIO DE MOXOS

Highlights

❶ Flying from La Paz to Rurrenabaque This short, low-altitude hop from Andes to Amazon has to be one of the best-value, dollar for dollar, in the world; feel your chin hit the floor as savage pinnacles and blinding icefields loom within touching distance, falling away to the infinite expanse of green that first shocked and awed the conquistadors. **See p.276**

❷ Chalalán Set deep in pristine Amazonian rainforest and owned by the local indigenous Tacana community, the Albergue Ecologico Chalalán is the ideal place to explore Parque Nacional Madidi, and a model of how ecotourism ought to be. **See p.277**

❸ San Ignacio de Moxos Quite possibly the friendliest village in all South America, with unique flute and drum music, a famous July fiesta and a historic, candle-lit Jesuit church. **See p.284**

❹ Río Mamoré Sling your hammock up and relax on a slow boat down this mighty wilderness river between Trinidad and the Brazilian frontier. **See p.292**

❺ Reserva Manuripi Get way off the beaten track in the Bolivian Amazon's northernmost reserve, a pristine stretch of rainforest that supplies the bulk of the world's Brazil nuts. **See p.301**

HIGHLIGHTS ARE MARKED ON THE MAP ON P.272

Brief history

Recent archeological evidence (see opposite), suggests that the pre-Columbian Bolivian Amazon supported a populous and sophisticated society of between five and six million people, 95% of whom were decimated through the sixteenth century by smallpox and flu introduced by Europeans.

The Jesuit missions

Failing to find the fabled El Dorado (see opposite), the Spanish turned the region over to the religious orders, above all the Jesuits, in the hope that they might have more success in subjugating the forest tribes and securing the northeastern border with Brazil. In the late seventeenth century a handful of **Jesuit missionaries** did just that, accomplishing in 25 years what the civil and military authorities had been unable to do in over a century. In a precursor of the theocratic society they were later to establish in Chiquitos (see box, p.252), the Jesuits founded a series of mission communities where the various indigenous tribes adopted Christianity and a settled, agricultural existence, raising cattle and growing crops. These missions flourished, and by the mid-eighteenth century were home to over 31,000 converts, supervised by just 45 European priests. But with the expulsion of the Jesuits from the **Spanish Empire** in 1767, the mission inhabitants were left at the mercy of Spanish landowners, with many being forced into slavery.

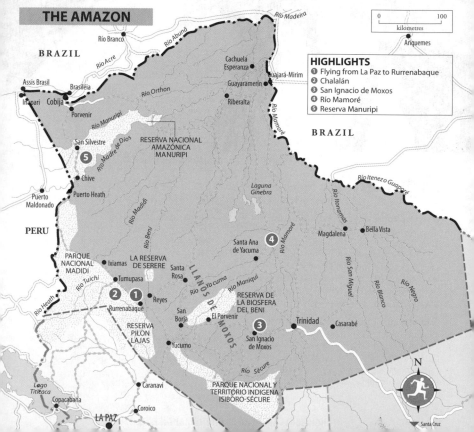

THE AMAZON

0   100
kilometres

BRAZIL

HIGHLIGHTS
❶ Flying from La Paz to Rurrenabaque
❷ Chalalán
❸ San Ignacio de Moxos
❹ Río Mamoré
❺ Reserva Manuripi

THE REAL EL DORADO?

Long before the Spaniards first arrived in the Americas, the Incas told stories of a mighty civilization in the watery plains to the east of the Andes. In the fifteenth century the Inca **Yupanqui** sent a great army down one of the rivers of the Upper Amazon in search of this kingdom. Ravaged by the exigencies of the jungle, the depleted army finally met its match in the warlike Musu, or Moxos peoples, among whom the surviving Incas settled. Hearing tales of this mythical realm, known, variously, as **El Dorado** and **Paitití**, Spanish conquistador Gonzalo Pizarro led a huge expedition down into the Amazon in 1541. Though the gold dust of their fevered imaginings was nowhere to be found and the expedition ended – like so many others after it – in despair and death, Dominican friar **Gaspar de Carvajal** chronicled sightings of roads, riverbanks thronged with people, exquisite ceramics and, famously, "cities that glistened in white". While his reports were initially shelved and later disparaged, recent archeological discoveries look, centuries later, to be finally proving him right.

6

THE ARCHEOLOGICAL EVIDENCE

Until about forty years ago archeologists doubted that any large, settled population could ever have survived in the Amazon Basin. The accepted wisdom was that the region's thin, **acidic soils** made intensive agriculture impossible, and that the area could support only small, scattered communities practising slash-and-burn agriculture along with hunting and gathering. But subsequent research has suggested that the forests and savannahs of the **Llanos de Moxos** were in fact once densely populated by well-organized societies who, sometime between 3000 BC and 1000 BC, modified the environment on a massive scale to allow intensive agriculture and large urban settlements. The region is dotted with hundreds of raised earth mounds, known as **lomas**, most of which are covered by forest. Seen from the ground, these mounds are hardly impressive, and were long thought to be merely the remnants of natural levees left by rivers as they meandered across the plain. But when archeologists looked at these mounds from the air, they realized they were far too extensive and regular to be natural.

Instead, they concluded that they were the remnants of a massive system of **earthworks** – including raised fields, canals, causeways, reservoirs, dykes and mounds stretching over hundreds of square kilometres – that could only have been built by a large and well-organized society. Excavations on some of the mounds revealed that they had been built up over many centuries. By cultivating these raised mounds, researchers believe the ancient inhabitants of the Moxos were able to overcome the problems of poor soil and seasonal flooding and drought, producing enough food to support a population density much greater than was previously believed possible in the Amazon. Moreover, further north in the Brazilian, once-Bolivian, territory of Acre, deforestation – together with the wonders of Google Earth – has revealed hundreds of **geoglyphs** of similar magnitude, while excavations of *terra preta*, or ultra-fertile soil cultivated by humans, seem to coincide with the locations of the riverside cities described by Carvajal.

These discoveries have enormous implications for both conservation and development in the Amazon. They suggest that, far from being a fragile natural environment, large areas of the Amazon are in fact **anthropogenic**, or man-made, ecosystems, modified by centuries of human activity and even now capable of supporting far larger populations than is currently the case.

The rubber boom

Worse was to come in the nineteenth century as a result of the growing international demand for rubber, a material derived from trees which were particularly abundant in the Bolivian Amazon. An unprecedented economic boom ensued, and the industry was quickly dominated by a small group of ruthless **rubber barons** who made overnight fortunes and subjected the indigenous population to a brutal regime of forced labour. The most famous of these was **Nicolás Suaréz** (see p.297), who ruled over a vast rainforest empire and remains a legendary figure in the Beni.

The richest rubber-producing area, the Acre, was largely settled by rubber collectors from Brazil. When the Bolivian government sought to tax rubber exports, these

Brazilians rebelled and declared independence. A short conflict – **the Acre War** – ensued, ending with Bolivian defeat, and in 1903 the Acre was annexed by Brazil. In the early twentieth century, the rubber boom collapsed after the English smuggled rubber seedlings out of the Amazon and established plantations in Asia, rendering wild rubber collection uncompetitive.

The twentieth century

By the middle of the twentieth century the economy began to recover as large landowners began exporting **cattle**, transporting them by river to the growing markets in Brazil and in military surplus aircraft to the Altiplano. Some landowners also made great fortunes during the **cocaine** boom of the 1980s and 1990s. Strategically positioned between the coca-growing Chapare and the markets to the north, the isolated ranches of the Beni provided the perfect location for clandestine drug laboratories, and their private airstrips were ideal bases for the light aircraft that used to smuggle the cocaine north, leapfrogging through the Amazon to Colombia.

Into the twenty first century

With ongoing road construction having opened up the Amazon's natural resources for exploitation to an unprecedented degree, and with attendant settlement from the highlands continuing apace, the consequences for the environment have become ever more obvious over the last decade or so: during the record-breaking **drought** of 2005, slash and burn fires flared out of control, with the resultant incineration of around five thousand square kilometres. The **floods** of 2011, meanwhile, were the worst for decades. A government schedule of new dams, roads and oil exploration, moreover, presents ever more challenges both for the environment and for an indigenous population already part of an ongoing struggle between conservationists, coca-growers, settlers and loggers.

Rurrenabaque and around

Set on the banks of the Río Beni some 430km by road north of La Paz, the small town of **RURRENABAQUE** has emerged in recent years as the most popular ecotourism destination in the Bolivian Amazon, and indeed one of the most popular tourist destinations in the whole country, with some thirty thousand visitors annually. If you've just arrived from the hassle and pollution of La Paz its appeal won't be long in beguiling you, as you're whisked from the timber-roofed airport on a motorbike with the wind in your hair, to be dropped off among some of the friendliest, most laidback people in the Beni. Picturesquely located on a broad sweep of the Río Beni, between the last forest-covered foothills of the Andes and the great lowland plains, Rurrenabaque – or "Rurre", as it's known to its residents – is close to some of the best-preserved and most accessible wilderness areas in the region, including the spectacular rainforests of **Parque Nacional Madidi** and the **Reserva de Biosfera y Territorio Indígena Pilon Lajas**, as well as the wildlife-rich pampas along the **Río Yacuma**. All of these are easily visited with one of Rurrenabaque's staggering number of tour agencies (see p.277). Though there's not a lot to see or do in the town itself – it's the kind of place you plan on visiting for a few days and end up spending a week, month or even longer.

Brief history

Rurrenabaque first came to prominence during the **rubber boom** in the late nineteenth century, serving as the gateway to the Amazon region from the highlands. Until fairly recently, the extraction and processing of **timber** from the surrounding

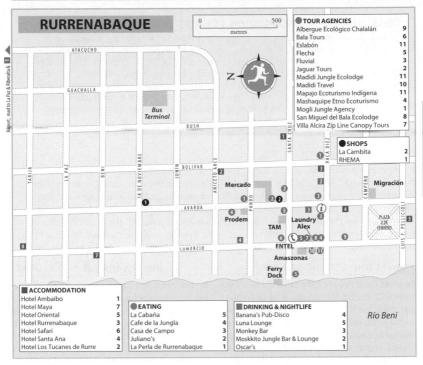

RURRENABAQUE

0 — 500
metres

N

● **TOUR AGENCIES**
Albergue Ecológico Chalalán	9
Bala Tours	6
Eslabón	11
Flecha	5
Fluvial	3
Jaguar Tours	2
Madidi Jungle Ecolodge	11
Madidi Travel	10
Mapajo Ecoturismo Indígena	11
Mashaquipe Etno Ecoturismo	4
Mogli Jungle Agency	1
San Miguel del Bala Ecolodge	8
Villa Alcira Zip Line Canopy Tours	7

● **SHOPS**
La Cambita	2
RHEMA	1

6

AYACUCHO

GUACHALLA

Bus Terminal

BUSH

Airport, road to La Paz & Rllberalta & 🡅

SANTA CRUZ

TARIJA

LA PAZ

BENI

18 DE NOVIEMBRE

JUNIN

BOLIVAR

ANICETO ARCE

Mercado

AVAROA

PANDO

Prodem

LUMERCIO

TAM

Laundry Alex

ENTEL

Amazonas

Ferry Dock

VACA DIEZ

CAMPERO

Migración

PLAZA 2 DE FEBRERO

LUIS F. PELLICCIOI

Río Beni

■ **ACCOMMODATION**
Hotel Ambaibo	1
Hotel Maya	7
Hotel Oriental	5
Hotel Rurrenabaque	3
Hotel Safari	6
Hotel Santa Ana	4
Hotel Los Tucanes de Rurre	2

● **EATING**
La Cabaña	5
Cafe de la Jungla	4
Casa de Campo	3
Juliano's	2
La Perla de Rurrenabaque	1

■ **DRINKING & NIGHTLIFE**
Banana's Pub-Disco	4
Luna Lounge	5
Monkey Bar	3
Mosskkito Jungle Bar & Lounge	2
Oscar's	1

rainforest was Rurrenabaque's main industry, but this has been curtailed somewhat by the exhaustion of valuable timber species and the establishment of Parque Nacional Madidi and other protected areas. The booming **ecotourism industry** has emerged as one of the few economic alternatives to this highly destructive and largely illegal activity.

Plaza 2 de Febrero

Though an increasing number of modern brick and concrete structures are springing up, Rurrenabaque's streets are still largely lined with traditional palm-thatched wooden houses. Official buildings are clustered around the pleasant **Plaza 2 de Febrero** at the south end of town, but most commercial activity is concentrated along the first few blocks of **calles Avaroa** and **Comercio**, which run north from the plaza parallel to the river, lined with ramshackle stores selling hammocks, rubber boots, machetes, chainsaws, tinned food and other supplies for people living in the surrounding area.

The riverside market

Sun early morning to early afternoon

The riverside is an interesting place to while away the time watching canoes arriving along the Beni and unloading cargoes of bananas or freshly caught fish. It's particularly lively during the small Sunday-morning **market**, when indigenous people from the hinterlands of the surrounding rainforest come to town to pick up supplies and sell fish, agricultural produce and (for tourists) handicrafts like woven baskets and wooden bows.

6

San Buenaventura

If you've got some time on your hands you can take the ferry (every 15min) across the river to the small village of **SAN BUENAVENTURA** on the opposite bank. Controversial plans for a proposed bridge are still rumbling on amid argument and counter argument over its potential impact on both the tourist trade and Parque Nacional Madidi, and complicated by the fact that San Buenaventura is actually within the political remit of La Paz Department. For that same reason, several public buildings are located here rather than in Rurrenabaque, including the park's SERNAP administration office (see p.73).

ARRIVAL AND GETTING AROUND

By plane Of all Bolivia's flight paths, the busy route between La Paz and Rurrenabaque is by far the most spectacular, and if you're going to splash out on any internal flights, this is the one to go for. The majority are operated by Amazonas (Comercio and Santa Cruz; ☎03 8922472, ⊛amazonas.com), whose nineteen-seat, twin-prop planes ensure a condor's-eye view of the Cordillera Real, swooping down through the scree and snow to the emerald hills of the Yungas and the endless, sweltering acres of jungle beyond, or vice versa if you're flying the other way. TAM on Santa Cruz and Avaroa (☎03 8922398) also operate a solitary flight to and from La Paz, on alternate days. Planes arrive at the recently paved airstrip a short distance north of the town, and are met by a shuttle bus that will take you to the respective airline office.
Destinations La Paz (5–8 daily; 40min); Trinidad (4 weekly; 30min).

RURRENABAQUE AND AROUND

By bus/micro Buses arrive at, and depart from, the Terminal Terrestre a few blocks away from the centre of town on the corner of Guachalla and 18 de Noviembre; you can get a motorbike taxi into the centre for about Bs3. At the time of writing, the road between Rurrenabaque and Yucumo was subject to major works and consequently in appalling condition; the times given below are for optimum dry season conditions – even a short cloudburst can extend them considerably.
Destinations La Paz (3 daily; 20hr); Riberalta (1 daily; 20–30hr); San Ignacio de Moxos (en route to Trinidad; 2 daily; 16hr); Trinidad (2 daily; 20hr); Yolosa (for connections to Coroico; 3 daily; 14hr).
By motorbike taxi Motorbikes pretty much rule the road in Rurre; standard local journeys cost Bs3.

INFORMATION

Tourist information Avaroa and Vaca Diez (daily 8am–7pm). The office offers a good map of the town, information about the national park and a list of authorized and certified tour agencies. Amiable manager Leo Janco is knowledgeable, incredibly helpful and will fill you in on the latest situation vis-à-vis the USAID-sponsored development of the various agencies. The most useful feature, however, is probably the pile of blue-bound volumes (titled "Ranking Bolivia") in the corner bookcase, full of detailed questionnaires filled in by tour-returning travellers.

TOURS

Rurrenabaque is the best place in the Bolivian Amazon to organize a trip into the wilderness (see p.283), either to the rainforests of **Parque Nacional Madidi** or the **Reserva de Biosfera y Territorio Indígena Pilon Lajas**, or into the **Pampas del Yacuma** along the Río Yacuma to the north. With the sheer, ever mushrooming number of tour agencies, however, **Calle Avaroa** is beginning to resemble La Paz's Calle Sagárnaga; the choice can be bewildering, and it's not always clear cut as to which companies are community-owned concerns and which are private. Note that prices do not normally include the Parque Nacional Madidi **entry fee** (Bs125). If you're going on a tour it's a good idea to book a room for your return (all places will store luggage when you're away).

PRIVATE TOUR OPERATORS

Generally cheaper than community-run operators and hence more popular with backpackers, private agencies offer trips to the rainforest and the pampas, generally lasting three nights, and with varying standards of rustic accommodation – this is long enough to see the pampas properly, though to really appreciate the rainforest it's worth taking a longer trip.

Bala Tours Santa Cruz and Comercio ☎03 8922527, ⊛balatours.com. Professional and highly regarded operator offering regular three-day pampas and *selva* tours, with jungle accommodation in their solar-powered, Río Tuichi-sited *albergue*, as well as a five-day combined option geared towards birdwatching.

Flecha Avaroa and Santa Cruz ☎03 8922723, ⊛flecha-tours.com. Super friendly, family-run agency long geared towards the backpacker market, with standard pampas and *selva* tours, as well as a boat tour to Guanay (and on to La Paz) if you're heading that way.

Fluvial Next to the Hotel Tuichi on Avaroa ☎03 8922351, ⊛fluvialtours@hotmail.com. The tour operator that started it all, with experienced guides and frequent departures to the pampas and *selva*, as well as longer jungle trips. The owner, Tico Tudela, "the original Bolivian Tarzan", apparently, was the man who helped find Yossi Ginsberg (see opposite).

Jaguar Tours Avaroa and Santa Cruz ☎7370 5600, ⊜jaguar.tours@hotmail.com. Owned by Germán, the amiable brother of the woman who runs Flecha, Jaguar is a more high-end operator staffed by long-serving guides and specializing in small-group tours.

Mogli Jungle Agency Avaroa and Pando ☎7251 9548, ⊛mogli-jungle.com. Run by the formidable Tereza Hodkova de Nava, with the motto "no chairs, no tables, no beds", Mogli offer ascetic three-day to three-week, well off-the-beaten-tourist-track expeditions with indigenous guides, no home comforts whatsoever and various levels of extremity, culminating in the three-day "hardcore survival" option; all you get is a machete, a mosquito net and a guide.

COMMUNITY TOUR OPERATORS

The alternative to a standard agency tour is to stay at one of the community-based projects established in the mould of the internationally renowned *Chalalán* lodge, the first such venture in the area. While you'll pay considerably more for a tour with most of the community projects (typically in the region of Bs1750–2100/$250–400 for an all-inclusive three-day/two-night trip), your money will help ensure that sustainable tourism continues to triumph over logging and hunting as a way of preserving community life.

★ **Albergue Ecologico Chalalán** Comercio ☎03 8922419, ⊛chalalan.com. A beautiful, multi-award-winning ecolodge in the heart of the park beside the Río Tuichi, four to five hours by boat from Rurrenabaque. The lodge overlooks a large lake, teeming with cayman and all manner of water birds, and the surrounding forest is covered by a 25km network of trails. Accommodation is in luxury thatched wooden cabins built in a traditional Tacana style, with mosquito netting, comfortable beds and solar-powered lighting and shared, or private, bathrooms. Pampas tours also available.

Eslabón Comercio ☎03 8922359, ⊛turismoeslabon.com. A new community operation, staffed by ex-Chalalán guides and covering the newly created Reserva Municipal de los Santos Reyes, on the frontier between the jungle and the pampas. Again accommodation is more basic, with shared rooms in a rustic *albergue*.

Madidi Jungle Ecolodge Avaroa ☎7128 2697, ⊛madidijungle.com. Another new project started by four families from San José de Uchupiamonas, the same community that founded Chalalán. With more basic, shared accommodation and capacity for fourteen people maximum, this is a relatively cheaper, more intimate alternative.

★ **Madidi Travel** Comercio ☎03 8922153, ⊛madidi-travel.com. This might not be a community-run project per se yet one hundred percent of the profits are ploughed back into the communities it works with. Accommodation at their private reserve, Serere, is in spartan yet stylish, two-storey *cabañas*, located by one of the area's four lakes, with a top deck for hammock lounging and serving food prepared from almost wholly organic ingredients sourced from local communities. A healthy population of big cats such as pumas, jaguars and ocelots attests to the health of the area's ecosystem, and with daily walks led by some of the best guides in Bolivia, as well as various viewing platforms, there's ample opportunity to experience it all. Volunteers are always welcome.

Mapajo Ecoturismo Indígena Avaroa ☎03 8922317, ⊜mapajo@mapajo.com. The *Albergue Ecologico Mapajo*, on the Río Quiquibey within the Reserva de Biosfera y Territorio Indígena Pilon Lajas, is three hours by motorized canoe from Rurrenabaque. A two- to four-day visit to the lodge offers excellent opportunities for exploring the rainforest and spotting wildlife, as well as the chance to visit the local indigenous communities. Benefitting from a beautiful setting on a high bluff overlooking the river, the lodge features six comfortable cabins built in traditional indigenous style, with the added luxury of mosquito-screening, balconies with hammocks and shared bathrooms and showers.

Mashaquipe Etno Ecoturismo Avaroa and Aniceto Arce ☎03 8922704, ⊛mashaquipe.com.bo. Run by indigenous Tacana, Tsimane and Mosetene families, this highly respected, community-oriented organization offer personalized deep-Madidi tours at very competitive prices, including a six-day, intriguing-sounding "Defying the jungle's spirits" jaunt.

6

San Miguel del Bala Ecolodge Comercio between Vaca Diez and Santa Cruz ☎03 8922394, ⓦsanmigueldelbala.com. Only half an hour down the river from Rurre, this is the perfect place to experience a taste of a traditional Tacana community, particularly if you're short on time. The project comprises two distinctive lodges, the handsome *San Miguel del Bala* with en-suite rooms, and the smaller, partly shared *Caquiahuara*. It goes without saying that the guides are all local, and full of forest folklore. Several trails fan out from the cabins, while a longer walk leads to a beautiful, winding canyon.

Villa Alcira Zip Line Canopy Tours Comercio, opposite Amazonas ☎03 8923875, ⓔziplinecanopy .bolivia@gmail.com. Run by the nearby Tacana community of Villa Alcira and offering two daily tours (8am and 2pm) on a series of zip lines, trips allow you to whizz through the upper canopy of the trees along 1500m of cable and across nine platforms. You can also stay overnight with the locals.

ACCOMMODATION

Hotel Ambaibo Santa Cruz and Bolívar, ☎03 8922017, ⓦhotelambaibo.com. An ample garden and the biggest pool in the centre of town is the main draw here, though the rooms – clean, spacious and inviting, with sloping, beamed ceilings and walls finished in sealed brick – are likewise almost worth the money; all are en suite. Breakfast included. Bs250

★ **Hotel Maya** Av Comercio and Beni ☎03 8922380, ⓔmayarurre@yahoo.com. Conveniently located midway between *Hotel Safari* (see opposite) and the centre, this is the only accommodation in Rurre that's right on the river, with divine views to match. Rooms – clean and fresh with chunky, rustic beds and striped cotton sheets – are grouped along the edge of an ample garden with pool, giving onto a communal balcony lined with altiplano-patterned deckchairs. All in all, probably the best deal in town, at least for non-a/c; if you want a/c you'll pay 100Bs more. Bs200

Hotel Oriental Plaza 2 de Febrero ☎03 8922401. This ever-reputable, family-run hotel remains one of Rurre's most appealing budget options, with cool, comfortable rooms (some of which are en suite) set around a peaceful courtyard garden with hammocks. Save for the occasional brass band parping away in the plaza of an evening, it's also one of the most ranquil; stern in-room notices make clear that neither alcohol nor noiseniks will be tolerated. Breakfast included. Bs150

Hotel Rurrenabaque Vaca Diez and Bolívar ☎03 8922481, ⓔhotelrurrenabaque@hotmail.com. As the oldest two-storey house in town, this is the place to stay if you want some character in your lodgings. Most of the floors and some of the walls still bear the original wooden boards, while the carved doors add a touch of class. The rooms themselves are clean and – owing to the thickness of the old walls – slightly cooler than you'll find elsewhere, and some are en suite. There's a communal balcony overlooking the street strung with a couple of hammocks, as well as a sizeable garden (camping available), restaurant, laundry service and free wi-fi. Breakfast included. Bs150

Hotel Safari Comerico and Tarija ☎03 8922210, ⓔhotel.safari@hotmail.com. A 10min walk from the town centre, with an estate-sized garden and a secluded, near-riverfront location, this friendly, Korean-run place is perfect if you really want to get away from the ubiquitous hum of cruising motorbikes. Its longhouse-like run of thatched, one and two storey cabins – with hardwood floors, pastel-blue walls and crisp, striped linen – is popular with older gringos and wealthy weekenders from La Paz. The swimming pool is as modest as the grounds are lavish, and there's also a restaurant overlooking the river. Breakfast included and credit cards accepted. Bs300

Hotel Santa Ana Corner of Avaroa and Vaca Diez ☎03 8922314. The best of the rock-bottom cheapies by far, and a veritable labyrinth of leafy courtyard rooms. Walls are partially tiled for at least the impression of some extra coolness, and there's a choice of shared or private bathroom. Staff are horizontally laidback, as is the atmosphere amid the *palalpa-roofed* patio's bevy of inviting hammocks. Bs60

Hotel Los Tucanes de Rurre Bolívar and Aniceto Arce ☎03 8922039, ⓦhotel-tucanes.com. Though the endearing, thatched-roof reception suggests the rooms may be slightly smarter than they are, this is nevertheless one of the nicer budget options, and even if the rooms deserve a lick of paint, they're clean and cool enough, come with private bath and are grouped around a small bar. The fact that breakfast is included, moreover, renders it a good-value cut above the bottom-end competition. Bs90

EATING

Note that time is conspicuously elastic when it comes to **restaurants**; don't be surprised to find somewhere closed when it should be open, or, occasionally in the middle of the afternoon for the whole town to be minus any eating options at all (if you're wise – and indeed, up in time – you'll eat a decent breakfast).

6

La Cabaña Bottom of Av Santa Cruz by the riverbank. Smack bang in the heart of the Sun market, this family-run, thatch-roofed institution is a great place to sample freshly caught river fish (in the Bs30 range), chance local speciality *Jochi Frito* (fried pork) or simply drink a cold beer and watch the sunset over the Río Beni. Mon–Sat 7am–11pm, Sun till 3pm.

★ **Cafe de la Jungla** Comercio and Vaca Diez. For breakfast at least, there's no beating this petite Argentine-owned café, with pavement-side seating to enjoy their nut-filled muesli. The house speciality is hot chocolate with red chilli, and they also do gourmet sandwiches filled with anything from teriyaki chicken to lentil burger. If you've carted along your laptop, they also provide free wi-fi. Mon–Sat 8am–8pm, Sun till noon.

★ **Casa de Campo** Vaca Diez and Avaroa ☎ 7921 5612. The best food in Rurre, served in a herbacious garden-side setting by a wonderfully warm couple, Adela and Luís. It's perfect if you're lusting after something more healthy and wholesome than standard backpacker fare, with a menu of natural fruit juices, quinoa and pumpkin soups, salads and the most delicious home-made croissants. There's also free wi-fi, as well as back copies of *The Economist* and Spanish-language versions of *The New York Times* to leaf through,

and don't miss the exquisitely patterned little bowls fashioned from orange peel (smell it to believe it); at only Bs25 each, they make for great value souvenirs. At the time of writing, a new branch was under construction down by the riverfront past the plaza, though the original Avaroa branch reviewed here will continue to operate alongside it. Daily 7am–9pm.

Juliano's Av Santa Cruz and Bolívar ☎ 7392 0088. The combination of experienced Bolivian *dueño* (proprietor) Juliano and Israeli manager Gili Agmon makes for one of Rurrenabaque's best restaurants, with a cosmopolitan menu and an easygoing atmosphere. As well as the usual fish, meat and pasta dishes (in the Bs30–40 range), they also do hummus and falafel, starters of fried cheese and other lesser-seen delicacies. The music isn't too shabby either, an often great if erratic selection jumping between Bob Dylan and asinine pop. Daily 6–10.30pm.

La Perla de Rurrenabaque Bolívar and Vaca Diez. A smattering of tables under two venerable mango trees, with a wailing soundtrack of *triste-tropique* boleros, has long made this place something of a local institution. A plethora of fish dishes – including house speciality *surubí* (river fish) in garlic – take up the bulk of the menu at around Bs40 a plate, and service is friendly and sweet. Daily 7am–9pm.

DRINKING AND NIGHTLIFE

Banana's Pub-Disco Comercio. Air-conditioned if sweaty nightclub – pretty much Rurre's only one – spinning *merengue*, salsa, *cumbia* and *reggaeton* as well as more gringo-centric rock and electronica. The crowd is usually a healthy mix of travellers and locals, and the entry fee a mere Bs5. Wed–Sun 9pm–3, 4 or even 5am.

Luna Lounge Comercio, opposite Amazonas ☎ 03 8922719. Open during the day for decent thin-crust pizza and a good variety of omelettes, this is more of a bar than a restaurant, with bamboo walls and shell drapes. Forget the cocktails and sample one of their heavenly papaya, strawberry, milk and yogurt concoctions instead. There's also a pool table and book exchange. Daily 10am–midnight.

★ **Monkey Bar** Avaroa, opposite Hotel Tuich ☎ 03 8922611. As unique in its own way as *Moskkito,* and with great bar staff and oven-baked pizzas to boot, this engaging Bolivian-owned bar has its own cache of outlandish cocktails (how about Dengue, Blow Job, or Hot Spiders in the Body...?). In line, perhaps, with their "Welcome to the jungle" motto, the music policy is slightly more rock-centric with classic Guns'n'Roses, Led Zeppelin,

The Doors and Creedence, and though the space is less intimate, the clientele is sometimes more evenly balanced between gringos and locals. Daily 9am till late.

★ **Moskkito Jungle Bar & Lounge** Vaca Diez ☎ 03 8922267, ⊕ moskkito.com. Something of a legend unto itself, this convivial bar continues to cater superbly to the adventured-out backpacker with cold beer, queasily named cocktails (Delirium Tremens, Jungle Wet Dreams or Anti-Yellow Fever anyone?) in the Bs20–30 range, pool, darts and an immense, 90s-centric CD collection (featuring the requisite Manu Chao and everything from Santana to The Cardigans) all set in a mellow jungle atmosphere. Daily 3am–3pm.

Oscar's In the hills to the north of town ☎ 03 8922710. Rurrenabaque's equivalent of a beach bar, this swimming pool eyrie is routinely packed out with people who've either returned from a tour, or are killing time till a tour leaves, and what a spot to do it in, with a glorious view back down over the Beni, not least at sundown when the heavens blush a roaring orange-red. Especially popular with Rurre's resident Israelis. Daily, hours vary.

SHOPPING

La Cambita Avaroa and Santa Cruz ☎ 7157 8493. This small yet perfectly formed *artesania* store is run by Natsumi Kawata, who buys jewellery and other craftwork from surrounding communities and sells

them in her professionally laid-out shop. Each piece of work is initialled with the name of the artist and a corresponding board provides a name and photograph. Daily 8am–9pm.

THE THREAT TO THE FOREST

Although the **forests** of the Beni can appear endless when you fly over them by plane or pass through by boat, in fact, they're disappearing at an alarming rate. In such a vast area no one can tell exactly how fast the forests are disappearing, even with satellite monitoring, but latest estimates suggest that Bolivia is losing about three thousand square kilometres of forest a year, one of the highest rates worldwide; much of it is in the Beni, with catastrophic consequences for the region's unique ecosystems.

The causes of this deforestation are various. The most obvious culprits are **timber companies**, ranging from small gangs with chainsaws to major commercial operations. Rather than clear-cutting the forest, they concentrate on valuable hardwood species such as mahogany and Spanish cedar. But for every tree they extract several others are damaged, and the trails they cut into even the most remote areas open the way for **colonists** who are responsible for even greater destruction.

Successive Bolivian governments have seen the comparatively empty lands of the Amazon as a solution to poverty and land shortage in the highlands, encouraging the migration of poor farmers from the Andes, who have moved down into the lowlands, clearing the forest to plant food and cash crops. Every year towards the end of the dry season the skies above Bolivia are obscured by thick smoke from thousands of fires set to clear the forest for **agriculture** and **cattle pasture**, a process known as *chaqueo*. Yet when the forest cover is slashed and burned on a wide scale, nutrients are quickly leached away by rain, and within a few years soil fertility declines so much that the land becomes useless for agriculture.

Having finally recognized the potential biological value of the country's rainforests, the government has now established extensive **national parks** and other protected areas in the Amazon, as well as recognizing large areas as indigenous territory (arguably the most effective way of protecting the rainforest) and introducing new laws to limit logging and forest clearance. Bolivia, moreover, is now the unlikely world leader in **forest certification**, with more than two million hectares of forest certified. Yet the immense scale and remoteness of the region makes enforcing legislation almost impossible, and many of the protected areas exist only on paper.

★ **RHEMA** Corner of Avaroa and 18 de Noviembre ☎03 8922173. Don't miss this fascinating artisans' collective, housed in a hulking palm-thatched building. The disarmingly warm families who live and work here (ask for Ivan) will be only too pleased to show you around the workshop area where they create all manner of traditionally worked bowls, vases, cooking implements, etc. from jacaranda, balsa and assorted hardwoods, modelled after the region's flora and fauna, and finished with natural, vegetable-based varnish. Much of the stuff ends up in the fairer trade outlets in La Paz. At present they use only off-cuts of wood, though they plan to purchase land, which they can re-forest for their own sustainable supply. If the front door is closed simply give a rap with the woodpecker and someone will let you in. Daily 11am–6pm.

DIRECTORY

Exchange Somewhat incredibly there are no banks in Rurrenabaque, so make sure you withdraw enough cash in La Paz before flying down. Failing that, you can obtain a cash advance on both Visa and Mastercard at Prodem on the corner of Pando and Avaroa (Mon–Fri 8.30am–12.30pm & 2.30–6pm, Sat 9am–noon); the commission is a hefty 5.3 percent. *Hostal Beni* on Comercio and Aniceto Arce, changes travellers' cheques and most currencies (the owner has a *cambio* in La Paz, apparently).

Internet There are numerous hole-in-the-wall internet cafés along Comercio, though prices are high (Bs8/hr) and speeds hardly the fastest.

Laundry The friendly Alex Laundry on Comercio and Santa Cruz charges a very competitive Bs8/kg for a same day wash-and-dry service and they'll even deliver the freshly laundered linen to your hotel free of charge.

Telephones There are Punto ENTEL offices all over Rurrenabaque, open all day every day.

Parque Nacional Madidi

SERNAP office Libertad, San Buenaventura • ☎03 8922540, ⓦ www.sernap.gob.bo • Bs125

On Rurrenabaque's doorstep, and covering nearly nineteen thousand square kilometres, **PARQUE NACIONAL MADIDI** is home to some of the most diverse plant and animal life in South America. In altitude it ranges from less than 300m to over 5500m above sea level, encompassing a variety of Andean and Amazonian ecosystems that range from dense tropical rainforests and seasonally flooded savannahs to pristine cloudforest and glacial mountain peaks. The park is home to an astonishing variety of wildlife: more than seven hundred species of animal have been recorded, along with some 860 species of bird, although the total may be more like one thousand – more than in the whole of North America. There are also more than five thousand species of flowering plant. Madidi was recognized as a national park in 1995 and, together with the neighbouring **Pilon Lajas** reserve and **Parque Nacional Tambopata-Candamo** across the border in Peru, forms a corridor of biodiversity that is generally considered to be one of the 25 most critical conservation areas in the world.

The real wonder of the park is its spectacular scenery and the bewildering complexity of the rainforest ecosystem, and you should treat viewing **wildlife** as a bonus rather than the main purpose of a visit to the park. Having said that, on a standard three- or four-day trip you should see a fair amount of wildlife, including several species of monkey, capybaras, caymans and a veritable cornucopia of birds, including brightly coloured toucans, macaws and parrots. If you're lucky you may also see larger animals like the mighty jaguar or the lumbering tapir. Be warned, though, that many species are rare, nocturnal and shy, and the areas of the park most easily accessible by river were logged and hunted until relatively recently.

If you want to get into the park's really pristine areas you'll need to go on a trip of about a week, travelling on foot or horseback into the more remote regions of the forest around the headwaters of the **Río Madidi**. The upper regions of the park can only be reached from the highlands north of La Paz, and even from there they are pretty much inaccessible unless you organize a serious expedition.

Pampas del Yacuma

Northeast of Rurrenabaque, the dense forests of the Andean foothills quickly give way to the **Pampas del Yacuma**: the vast, swampy grasslands that dominate much of the Beni. Though they have been grazed by cattle for hundreds of years, the pampas still support a great deal of wildlife, particularly along the forested banks of the great rivers that meander across them. The pampas themselves are not that impressive: a great expanse of swamp and tangled cattle pasture with the occasional lake. Tours with the agencies listed here (many of whom now have shared or private lodges in the pampas) are nevertheless worth it just for the amount of wildlife you'll see along the Río Yacuma. (p.277).

The Río Yacuma

In the rainy season (roughly Nov–April), the **Río Yacuma** river bursts its banks and floods great expanses of the surrounding grasslands, causing wildlife to become more dispersed and breeding ferocious mosquitoes. In the dry season, however, it's reduced to a narrow river that attracts an amazing abundance of fauna. Sinister black-and-white **caymans** – some over 2m long – lounge on the muddy banks, slipping quietly into the water as you pass; **turtles** queue up to sun themselves on logs protruding from the water; groups of **capybara**, the world's largest rodent, watch with apparent indifference as canoes pass right in front of their noses. Most spectacular of all, though, are the **pink freshwater dolphins**, known as *bufeos*, that fish and play in the wide bends of the river. In addition, all manner of **birds** live on the banks, including herons, three different species of kingfisher, elegant roseate spoonbills, massive storks and the clumsy hoatzin.

Reserva de Biosfera y Territorio Indígena Pilon Lajas

Just south of Rurrenabaque, some four thousand square kilometres of rainforest between the Río Beni and the road south to La Paz are now protected by the **Reserva**

ECOTOURISM IN RURRENABAQUE

The term **ecotourism** has, in the past, often been used in Rurre in connection with practices that are rather dubiously ecofriendly, and with tours where prices have been driven down to unhealthy and unsustainable levels. Yet things are changing: the local tour operators' association, ASOPTUR, has now established **minimum pricing** (currently Bs700 ($100) for a three-day pampas tour and Bs250 ($36)/day for the rainforest); as the signs displayed around town sternly warn, buy cheaper than this and you potentially expose yourself – and the environment – to all manner of danger. With support from both the German Development Service and USAID, moreover, **strict guidelines** have now been developed for standards in safety, environmental awareness, sustainable tourism and socio-cultural sensitivity which agencies must adhere to in order to be certified.

One of Rurre's great successes has been its community-run projects, with the internationally renowned **Chalalán** (see p.277) leading the way. Established with support from international conservation groups in a bid to demonstrate how rainforest conservation can provide sustainable livelihoods for local people who might otherwise turn to logging or other destructive activities, it's owned and managed by the 116 families that make up the Quechua-Tacana community of San José de Uchupiamonas, located 25km further up the Río Tuichi, and the only settlement of any real size inside Parque Nacional Madidi. Other respected community operators include **Mapajo Ecoturismo Indígena** (see p.277), whose *Albergue Ecologico Mapajo* is wholly owned by the indigenous communities of the Río Quiquibey, and was established at a fraction of the cost of Chalalán and with a greater degree of community autonomy; and **San Miguel del Bala** (see p.278), co-owned by 35 families and founded with help from both the United Nations Development Programme and USAID.

Parque Nacional Madidi itself wouldn't exist, however, without the efforts of the remarkable Rosa Maria Ruiz, manager of **Madidi Travel** (see p.277). The company emerged from Eco Bolivia, the foundation Ruiz created in the early 1990s and with which she convinced the government – with support from the World Bank and Conservation International – to create the national park. After a series of setbacks that could fill a book in their own right, she went on to create the Reserva de Serere, a pristine, privately owned, forty-square-kilometre protected area, which forms part of the Madidi Mosaic, a 150,000-square kilometre network of protected areas stretching to the Peruvian border.

6

de Biosfera y Territorio Indígena Pilon Lajas. Though threatened by loggers and migrant settlers along the road that marks its eastern boundary, the rainforests of Pilon Lajas, like those of Parque Nacional Madidi, are exceptionally biodiverse and survive in a largely pristine state. Declared a Biosphere Reserve by UNESCO in 1977, the reserve protects 642 species of flora, 499 species of bird and 170 species of fish. Pilon Lajas is also home to a small population of indigenous Mosetén, T'simane and Tacana communities, spread out along the length the Río Quiquibey, which runs through the centre of the reserve.

The Llanos de Moxos

Between Rurrenabaque and Trinidad stretch the vast, watery plains known as the **Llanos de Moxos** (or Mojos). Spanning the area between the ríos Mamoré and Beni, the region is largely covered by seasonally flooded savannah or natural grassland interspersed with swamp and patches of forest. During the November to April rainy season, the whole area is flooded for months at a time and the road between Rurrenabaque and Trinidad becomes impassable, while during the dry season between May and September the grasslands become very dry, resembling the savannahs of Africa much more than the lush greenery usually associated with the Amazon basin. This is **cowboy country**, and the economy of the plains is dominated by enormous ranches, stocked with the semi-wild descendants of the cattle first introduced by the

Jesuits in the seventeenth century. The Llanos are also home to semi-nomadic indigenous groups such as the T'simane (or Chimane), for whom hunting is still an important source of food, though shotguns have largely replaced bows and arrows as the weapon of choice.

Away from the former mission towns of **San Ignacio de Moxos** and San Borja, the Llanos remain a sparsely populated wilderness where most of the wild animal species of the Amazon still thrive, and because of the open vegetation they can be easier to spot than in the forest. Even from the road, the **birdlife** you'll see here is spectacular and abundant, with water species like storks and herons being particularly evident. Jaguars abound, and you may also spot species not found in the forest, like the maned wolf, a long-legged, solitary hunter that moves through the high grasses with a loping stride, or the rhea, a large flightless bird similar to the ostrich. A few hours west of San Ignacio de Moxos, a large area of this distinctive environment is protected by the **Reserva de la Biosfera del Beni**, Bolivia's longest-established protected area.

San Ignacio de Moxos

About 100km west of Trinidad lies the singular town of **SAN IGNACIO DE MOXOS**, the so-called "Spiritual Capital of the Jesuit Missions", originally founded by the Jesuits in 1689. It's a poor yet incredibly welcoming place with a unique and unforgettable atmosphere, where horse- or ox-drawn carts are as common as motor vehicles, and where the largely indigenous population retain more of the traditions of the Jesuit era than any other town in the Beni. While there's not much to do outside fiesta times, it's enough to simply marinate in San Ignacio's lost-in-time aura; don't be surprised if complete strangers stop you in the plaza simply to say "hello", ask where you're from and how long you'll be staying.

Plaza Principal 31 de Julio

Many of the village houses are simple, palm-thatched cane structures, but the **Plaza Principal 31 de Julio** is lined with stone houses whose tiled roofs extend over the pavement to provide shelter from the harsh tropical sun and frequent rain. In its centre stands a **statue** of an indigenous warrior in the same costume as that worn by the *Machetero* dancers during the July fiesta.

Iglesia de San Ignacio
Plaza Principal 31 de Julio • Daily 8am-8pm • Free

On the east side of the Plaza Principal is **Iglesia de San Ignacio**, the town's physical and spiritual centre. Built in the barn-like style favoured by the Jesuits, its interior is brightly painted in a beautiful naïve style with scenes from the life of Ignacio Loyola,

---

WHEN SAN IGNACIO IGNITES: THE FIESTA PATRONAL

For most of the year San Ignacio is a sleepy backwater, except in late July, when the **Fiesta Patronal** or Ichapekenepiesta rouses the town from its tropical torpor in celebration of its titular patron saint. Considered the greatest **folkloric festival** in the Bolivian Amazon, it reaches its zenith on the 31st in a riot of noise, colour, dancing and wonderful music, performed on flute, drums, violin and metre-long palm-leaf *bajones* – a kind of giant tropical equivalent to the highland quena (a type of traditional flute). The most iconic dance, the *Machetero*, is both a salutation to the sun and a thinly veiled portrayal of the struggles against Spanish rule, hypnotically performed by indigenous Moxeños dressed in brilliant feather headdresses and long cotton robes. The austere-looking *achus*, by contrast, represent the spirits of the ancestors, their dark suits topped off with carved wooden masks and raw-leather hats. Needless to say it's all accompanied by copious quantities of alcohol and the familiar whiff of cordite; just don't expect much sleep.

SCHOOL OF BAROQUE

In a kind of magic-realist reversal of the Manaus opera house bringing highbrow European culture to the Brazilian Amazon, the **San Ignacio de Moxos music school** on Ayacucho (☎03 4822347) is now taking their singular brand of indigenous Baroque from the Bolivian Amazon to Europe. Founded by a Navarrese nun and counting between two and three hundred students, the school has been teaching violin, cello and flute to the town's youth since the mid-1990s, creating a unique ensemble whose performances have brought acclaim from Buenos Aires to Barcelona. The school also has a concert hall; if you're in town it's worth checking to see if there are any upcoming recitals.

the mercenary soldier turned saint who founded the Jesuit order. The church is run by Spanish Jesuit priests, who are once again heavily involved in defending the rights of the indigenous population against logging companies and large landowners, and who continue to inspire a deep faith in their congregation. Hundreds of people attend Mass on Sundays, and it's even more atmospheric in the not so unlikely event of a power cut, when services are held by flickering candlelight.

El Centro Parroqueo Museo de Moxos

Ballivián, on Plaza Principal • Mon–Sat 8.30am–12.30pm & 2.30–6pm, Sun 9am–1pm • Music archive Mon–Fri only • Bs15

This small, church-run museum is housed around the Iglesia's peaceful cloisters and gardens, with illustrated displays on the history of both the Moxos people and the mission itself. The real reason to come here, though, is the famous archive of **Moxeña music**, containing over seven thousand antique pages. Many of its more recent acquisitions were retrieved from the scattered communities of the **Parque Nacional y Reserva Indígena Isiboro-Sécure**: polyphonic and antiphonic pieces, devotional songs and sacred operas of European origin, hybridized over time with indigenous music and dance, and, given the area's geographical isolation, all but immune from the tides of cultural change. Many of the scores have now been restored, catalogued and digitized, and the music revived in the performances of the local Baroque music school (see above).

Laguna Isirere

A fifteen-minute walk or five-minute motorbike taxi ride north of the plaza brings you to the attractive **Laguna Isirere**, where you can relax, swim and observe the abundant birdlife. Legend has it that anyone who drinks from the lagoon will never leave San Ignacio – not such a terrible fate. Lake transport is via either muscle-(Bs2) or motor (Bs5)-powered canoe.

ARRIVAL AND DEPARTURE   SAN IGNACIO DE MOXOS

By plane Though not for the faint hearted, the antiquated, two-passenger *avionetas* which fly between San Ignacio and Trinidad can make for a cheap and unforgettable way to experience the Llanos de Moxos. The standard fare is Bs400 ($57)/person but don't be surprised if you're offered a seat for as low as Bs100; locals in need of a fellow passenger sometimes search out people waiting

for buses. To hire one yourself, phone Captain Emilio Arios Diez (☎7114 9435), though be warned he doesn't suffer fools gladly.

By bus Buses and *autos* to and from Trinidad (4–5 daily; 4hr) and en-route from Trinidad to Rurrenabaque (2 daily; 16r) arrive and depart from the far end of Santiesteban, the road that heads out of town to the east.

ACCOMMODATION

Plaza Hotel On the main square ☎03 4822032. Basic, rudimentary rooms, leading off a sociable reception often bustling with locals. They also have their own generator so at least some of the rooms have power during blackouts. **Bs120**

Residencial San Joaquin On the main square ☎03 4822055. Delightfully antiquated, family-run clutch of spartan yet atmospheric, whitewashed rooms with ceiling fans, original beams and heavy furniture, all grouped around a courtyard garden with hammocks. **Bs100**

Laguna Isirere If you fancy staying the night on the lake, accommodation is available in basic palm-thatched huts (sleeping two) on the lagoon's far shore; ask in town for Mario. **Bs70**

EATING AND DRINKING

There are several basic restaurants on Calle Santiesteban, all of which open late and close early, and most of which offer good value **almuerzos**. If you're after an early breakfast, head for the small **covered market** on the same street.

Doña Anita Ballivián, just off the main square. A longstanding San Ignacio institution popular with locals and conveniently open right through the day; egg and cheese-garnished hamburgers are the house speciality though they also do sandwiches, fresh fruit juices and the like. Daily 7am–11pm.

★ **Restaurante Ecoturistico** Antonio de Orellana, three blocks from the plaza ☎03 4822709. An über-designer mirage of plate glass and hardwood columns, this NGO-funded restaurant is the unlikeliest edifice in San Ignacio, perhaps the whole Beni, designed and administered by multi-talented architect Yadıye Herrera; she even sings her own self-penned songs in the lovely upstairs bar. Service couldn't be friendlier and the great-value food (Bs20–30) is excellent, ranging from fried fish with yucca and plantain to a creamy macaroni cheese. Daily 6.30pm–11.30pm; bar: daily 8pm till late.

SHOPPING

Centro Artesanal Tiurina Alfonso Elorriaga ☎7688 3724. Just round the corner from the church, with a great selection of heavy, embroidered cotton hammocks, shirts, dresses and tablecloths, as well as musical instruments and palm-leaf *artesanía*.

Reserva de la Biosfera del Beni

Entry must be arranged in advance with the reserve office in San Borja, at the junction of Trinidad and 18 de Noviembre • ☎03 8953898 • Micros for San Borja (frequent; 3-4hr) depart throughout the day from the bus terminal in Rurrenabaque; the reserve office can advise on transport to and within the reserve itself

Covering some 1350 square kilometres of savannah and rainforest to the east of San Borja, the **Reserva de la Biosfera del Beni** (Beni Biosphere Reserve) was one of the first protected areas to be established in Bolivia. Standing at the intersection of two important biogeographical zones, the reserve is exceptionally biodiverse, hosting some five hundred species of birds and one hundred species of mammals – these include almost half the protected species in Bolivia, among them many that are in danger of extinction. Illegal hunting, unfortunately, still poses a major threat. While the reserve, did, at one time, offer very well-organized visitor facilities and ecotours, funds have now dried up, with barely enough money to support a skeleton staff of two rangers. You can still visit, though there's no accommodation and you'll have to bring in all your own food and water, as well as a tent or hammock. The funding crisis may change in future; check with SERNAP in La Paz (see p.73) for the current situation if you don't have time to visit the office in San Borja.

Trinidad

Close to the Río Mamoré, some 500km northwest of Santa Cruz, the city of **TRINIDAD** is the capital of the Beni and the commercial and administrative centre of a vast wilderness hinterland of swamp, forest and savannah where rivers remain the main means of transport and cattle-ranching is the biggest industry. Like most towns in the region, Trinidad was originally a Jesuit mission, but few signs of that past remain, and it's now a modern commercial city that's dominated by a vigorous cowboy culture and economy. Though you can organize excursions into the surrounding rainforest, Trinidad is a world removed from Rurrenabaque, with a distinct difference in atmosphere and much more conspicuous wealth. In addition, the streets are lined with open sewers which, while they may be necessary for drainage, emit a horrible stench (particularly at night), provide an ideal breeding ground for the mosquitoes that plague the town, and represent a dangerous obstacle for unwary pedestrians. The place is, however, the jumping-off point for an adventurous trip by cargo boat down the **Río Mamoré** to Guayaramerín on the Brazilian border.

Brief history

Trinidad was founded in 1686 by **Father Cipriano Barace**, a pioneering Jesuit missionary who introduced the first cattle herds to the region. The town prospered under the Jesuits, but fell into rapid decline after their expulsion in 1767, with many of its indigenous inhabitants – drawn from several different tribes from the surrounding area but known collectively as the **Mojeños** – being dragged off to work as virtual slaves on plantations near Santa Cruz. The Mojeños were still strong enough to play an important role in the Independence War, when an indigenous government led by Pedro Ignacio Muiba was briefly established in Trinidad in 1810, before being ruthlessly crushed by a royalist army, which also stripped the town of its last valuable Jesuit ornaments.

The rubber boom

With the advent of the **rubber boom** the town's population fell dramatically as thousands were forcibly recruited to work as rubber collectors in the forests to the north, while many others fled rather than face the same fate. In 1887, at the height of the rubber boom, the Mojeños launched their last uprising, a non-violent religious movement led by a messianic chief called Andrés Guayocho, who was said to be a great sorcerer and excellent ventriloquist. But the rebellion was swiftly and brutally put down

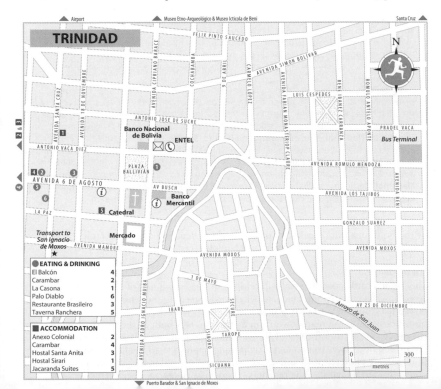

6

INDIGENOUS PEOPLES OF THE BOLIVIAN AMAZON

The Bolivian Amazon is home to twenty-nine indigenous peoples, each with their own distinct language and culture, ranging in size from the **Moxeños**, who number around 43,000, to groups like the **Araona**, now reduced to no more than about a hundred people. While the combined population of these indigenous peoples is in the region of one million, this is a mere fraction of the population that lived here before the arrival of European diseases and the near-genocidal impact of the rubber boom, when huge numbers were enslaved and forced to work in appalling conditions. After centuries of external contact – with conquistadors, missionaries, rubber barons, soldiers, drug traffickers, anthropologists and now tourists – many of the indigenous people of the Amazon now speak Spanish and have adopted a fairly conventional Bolivian lifestyle, engaging in the market economy as workers and consumers and preferring rubber boots and football shirts to their traditional handmade costumes. However, many others still survive by hunting, fishing and cultivating manioc and other crops in small clearings in the forest, much as they have done for thousands of years, and rely for medicine on the powers of traditional healers and their encyclopedic knowledge of thousands of different rainforest plants. The most traditional indigenous groups are the uncontacted tribes – known as the **Nahuas** and **Toromonas** – small nomadic bands thought to be living deep in the rainforest who eschew all contact with Bolivian society.

THE STRUGGLE FOR AUTONOMY

Largely dependent on the rainforest for their livelihoods, the indigenous peoples of the Bolivian Amazon were among the first to recognize the danger posed by the gathering pace of deforestation. In 1990 they staged the first of several "**Marches for Territory and Dignity**", walking 650km from Trinidad to La Paz to demand the recognition of their right to land and self-determination. This campaign drew international attention to their plight and led to new legislation and the recognition of large areas of the Beni as indigenous territorial reserves. While the 2005 election of Evo Morales brought further legislative successes, with the ratifying of indigenous rights to self-determination, self-government and financial management, the situation on the ground remains precarious, with Morales facing the uneasy contradictions of bolstering the rights of native people while developing the country's newly nationalized oil, gas and mineral reserves.

In May 2010, the region's indigenous groups declared themselves in a "state of emergency", demanding that the government protect them from oil, logging and mining companies, and speaking out against ongoing delays in the titling of indigenous lands. They also denounced corruption in governmental consultations with the Moxeño, Yuyucare and T'simane peoples of the **Parque Nacional y Reserva Indígena Isiboro-Sécure**, a beautiful wilderness region between the Ríos Isiboro and Sécure, through which the Morales administration has approved the construction of a major road. Yet, in addition to proposed dam projects, the government's approval in October 2010 of a Supreme Decree extending oil exploration into both **Parque Nacional Madidi** (see p.281) and the **Reserva de Biosfera y Territorio Indígena Pilón Lajas** (p.282), suggests the indigenous struggle isn't going to end any time soon.

by the Bolivian authorities, many of the survivors fled, and the town was left in the hands of non-indigenous merchants and landowners.

The modern era

The region's **cattle economy** really developed in the second half of the twentieth century, when enterprising ranchers began cross-breeding the semi-wild cattle descended from the herds brought in by the Jesuits with sleek Xebu cattle brought in from Brazil. Until the road down from Santa Cruz was built in the 1970s, Trinidad was effectively cut off from the rest of Bolivia, and it remains an isolated and somewhat inward-looking place, voluble in its right-wing opposition to the La Paz administration (the walls are plastered with anti-Evo Morales graffiti) and fiercely defensive of its *camba* (lowland) identity. The ranchers – known as *ganaderos* – see themselves as rugged, self-reliant pioneers who have tamed a wild region and created prosperity with almost no help from central government.

Plaza Ballivián

Though most of its buildings are modern, Trinidad maintains the classic layout of a Spanish colonial town, its streets set out in a neat grid pattern around a shady, well-maintained central square, the **Plaza Ballivián**, which the locals proudly insist is the biggest in Bolivia. On the south side of the plaza, the **Catedral** is an unexceptional modern structure built between 1916 and 1931 on the site of the earlier Jesuit church. The buildings around the plaza, meanwhile, are all built with eaves overhanging the raised pavements.

Museo Etno-Arqueológico del Beni "Kenneth Lee"

Universidad Autónoma del Beni, Av Ganadera • Mon–Fri 8am–noon, 2–6pm, Sat & Sun by appointment •Bs10 • ☎ 03 4624519

North along Avenida Cipriano Barace, some 1.5km from the centre of town, the beautiful grounds of the **Museo Etno-Arqueológico** are a fitting tribute to the research that suggests a mighty and sophisticated civilization existed in the Amazon basin between 3000 and 1000 BC (see p.273). The museum is dedicated to Kenneth Lee, a Texan engineer who was impassioned by the Moxos peoples and their apparently highly advanced hydro-agricultural systems of raised fields and earth mounds. Housed in a yellow, circular building, two rooms of ceramics, photos and storyboards outline the basic facts and findings, along with musical instruments and striking wooden masks: elegant, stylized human faces rather than the supernatural extravagances favoured in the highlands.

Museo Icticola del Beni

Universidad Autónoma del Beni, Av Ganadera • Mon–Fri 7.30am–3pm • Free • ☎ 03 4621705

Signposted on the right, past the entrance to the Museo Etno-Arqueológico on the same university's Dr Hernán Melgar Justiniano campus, the eerily atmospheric **Museo Icticola del Beni** is a large room of basic design that houses one of South America's most important collections of aquatic life, preserved in a series of tanks and jars. Well worth a visit, it contains over four hundred samples of the weird and wonderful fish and snakes captured in rivers in Beni and Pando. At the head of the collection is the imposing Piraiba – a huge specimen with numerous, sharp-looking teeth which was caught in Mamoré in 1998.

ARRIVAL AND DEPARTURE   TRINIDAD

By plane The airport, on the northwest outskirts of town, is served by Amaszonas, 18 de Noviembre 267 (☎03 4622426); Aerocon, Antonio Vaca Diez 26 (☎ 03 4624442) and TAM, Bolívar and Santa Cruz (☎ 03 4622363).
Destinations Cobija (2 daily; 1hr 40min); Guayaramerín (4–5 daily; 1hr); La Paz (11 daily; 1hr); Riberalta (4–5 daily; 1hr); Rurrenabaque (4 weekly; 30min); Santa Cruz (1–2 daily; 1hr).
By bus Buses arrive at, and depart from, the terminal on Av Mendoza on the corner with Viador Pinto Sucedo, eight blocks east from the centre of town.

Destinations Rurrenabaque (2 daily; 20hr); San Ignacio de Moxos (2 daily; 3–4hr); Santa Cruz (18–22 daily; 9–10hr).
By truck Trucks for San Ignacio de Moxos (2 daily; 3–4hr) arrive at, and depart from between Av Mamore and Nestor Suarez.
By boat Along the Río Mamoré arriving from, or departing for, Guayaramerín (2–3 weekly; 3–7 days) or Puerto Villaroel (2–3 weekly; 7 days), dock at Puerto Barador, Trinidad's river port, about 13km west of town (see box, p.292).

GETTING AROUND

By motorcycle taxi The easiest way to get around is by motorcycle taxi: they charge about Bs3 for journeys in the town centre, about Bs10 to or from the airport and Bs20 to the river port.

Motorbike rental Motorbikes are also available for rent on the plaza, where a basic moped will cost about Bs8/hr; a 125cc dirt bike about Bs12/hr or Bs140/24hr. You'll need to leave your passport as a deposit.

INFORMATION AND TOURS

TOURIST INFORMATION

The Prefectura building just south of the plaza on Av Ignacio Muiba (Mon–Fri 8am–12.30pm, 2.30–6 pm; ☎03 4624831). Though this is the main departmental tourist information office it's far more convenient to use the small, friendly and very helpful office on Av 6 de Agosto, next to *Hotel Campanario* (same hours; no phone), where you'll find a decent stack of brochures, maps and flyers on Trinidad and the surrounding area.

TOUR OPERATORS

Complejo Turístico Ecológico y Arcqueológico Chuchini 15km northwest of town ☎03 4657205. Though not a tour operator per se, this small reserve and animal rescue centre organizes various trips originating in Trinidad and taking in not only the reserve and its small ceramics museum but also Loma Suárez, a Moxos-built mound that was once the transport hub of the Suárez rubber empire (see p.297). The two and three-day options include cabaña accommodation at the reserve. Prices available on request. Volunteers welcome.

Fremen Av Cipriano Barace 332 ☎03 4622276, ⓦandes-amazonia.com. This La Paz-based agency specialize in 4-day/3-night cruises on the Mamoré aboard their luxury floating hotel the *Reina de Enin*. Prices are around Bs350–420 ($50–60)/person per day.

Paraiso Travel Av 6 de Agosto 138 ☎03 4620692 ⓦbolivien-beni.at. Trinidad's most professional operator, run by the inimitable Lyliam Gonzalez Melgar. Along with river trips, archeological tours and local festival jaunts they also offer dry season birdwatching based on a privately owned ranch where there's a possibility of seeing the extremely rare blue-throated macaw – a must for serious birders. Prices start at Bs1190 ($170)/person for birdwatching trips, falling to about half that price if you can round up eight people.

Turismo Moxos Av 6 de Agosto 114 ☎03 4621141,ⓔmoxosibc@hotmail.com. Various one- to three-day trips into the rainforest by motorized canoe along the Río Ibare, a tributary of the Mamoré, with plenty of opportunity for seeing wildlife (including pink dolphins) and visiting indigenous communities. They also offer shorter, two-night blue-throated macaw viewing trips, with prices starting at around Bs940 ($120)/person based on a group of four; river trip prices start at around Bs280 ($40)/person per day.

ACCOMMODATION

★**Anexo Colonial** Antonio Vaca Díez 344 ☎03 4634045. Arguably the best value accommodation in town, this is an annexe of the *Hotel Colonial* further up the street, run by the *dueña*'s friendly and welcoming son and located right next door to *Hostal Santa Anita* (see below). Rooms come in two classes: one airy with impossibly lofty ceilings and walls painted in café-crème neutrals, one more compact with beams: both have a lot of character. The breezy, mosaic-tiled courtyard is spanned by overhanging eaves and lit by faux-colonial lamps, and a bar and guests' kitchen are planned. **Bs120**

Carambar Av 6 de Agosto, between Santa Cruz and Villavicencio ☎03 4626097. This French-run *crèperie* (see p.292) also rents a quartet of clean, spacious, white-washed rooms off lush courtyard, itself overhung with beamed eaves, and all with private bathroom, a/c and – uniquely in Trinidad – an inclusive French breakfast. Wi-fi available. **Bs180**

★**Hostal Santa Anita** Antonio Vaca Díez 354 ☎03 4622257. Only a year old, this family-run hostel still smells as strikingly fragrant as it doubtless did the day it was opened, an olfactory surprise if you've suffered one too many stinking Amazonian bathrooms. The bright, capacious and spotlessly clean rooms come complete with private hammock, giving onto a slender, leafy patio, while masks and painted plant pots add some pizzazz. Free wi-fi and breakfast included. Rooms without a/c **Bs160**; rooms with a/c **Bs200**

Hostal Sirari Santa Cruz 538 ☎03 4624472, ⓔhsirari @hotmail.com. Though they could do with a little sprucing up, the *Sirari*'s ageing, beamed-ceiling rooms complement what has to be the most verdant courtyard in Trinidad, with a trio of gorgeous toucans pottering about amid the foliage. The lower rooms also come with lovely white-painted, glass-panelled doors, while the upper rooms are more modern. You'll pay double for a/c. Laundry service available. Rooms without a/c **Bs160**

Jacaranda Suites La Paz between Pedro de la Rocha and 18 de Noviembre ☎03 4622400, ⓔhoteljacaranda @yahoo.es. This place is unquestionably the most luxurious in Trinidad, and by some margin. Rooms are painted in cool coffee and burnt umber, with carved doors and bedsteads, original cornicing and cosy checked linen. Breakfast is inevitably included, and if you can't afford to stay here, you can at least pretend: public use of the modest pool is a mere Bs25. **Bs500 ($71)**

EATING AND DRINKING

Try the **market**, two blocks south of the plaza, for *masaco*, a deep-fried mixture of mashed plantain or yucca and dried meat. Another local speciality is *pacumutu*, great chunks of meat and chicken marinated and grilled on a skewer.

6

El Balcón Av 6 de Agosto and Traija ☎03 4641621. The newest, trendiest restaurant-bar in town with a roomy, vaguely colonial feel and an outside deck often filled to capacity as the night draws on. Alongside burgers, snacks and sandwiches, they also do *ceviche* and traditional standbys like *pique macho* (spicy beef, sausage and potatoes) and *sillpancho (breaded steak with rice and eggs)* for around Bs30–40. Daily 7.30pm–2am, with food served until 11.30pm.

★ **Carambar** Av 6 de Agosto, between Santa Cruz and Villavicencio ☎03 4626097. With its scattering of alfresco tables, reggae soundtrack and authentic crêpes cooked *en plein air*, this recently opened French-run place is a very welcome surprise amid Trinidad's somewhat staid eating scene. Savoury crepês will set you back Bs12, sweet ones a very reasonable Bs6. Wed–Sun 5–11pm.

La Casona Plaza Ballivián ☎03 4622437. As one of the few places on the plaza to offer outdoor seating (covered by a fancy awning no less), and to open right through the day, every day, this Trini institution is always busy, and a life-saver on Sun evenings when everyone else has shut up shop. Along with the obligatory almuerzos, they also serve up relatively pricey (Bs40–80) steak, fried river fish and *brochetas*. Daily 8am–midnight.

Palo Diablo Av Santa Cruz 385, between Av 6 de Agosto and La Paz ☎03 4627254. Atmospheric little hole-in-the-wall bar with a tiny stage for its pub-rock cover bands, playing anything from Pink Floyd to classic Chicano rock. It's worth stopping in just to admire the handmade table-tops, filled with various types of dried seeds. Daily Mon–Sat 5pm–4am.

Restaurante Brasileiro Av 18 de Noviembre, between Av 6 de Agosto and Antonio Vaca Diez ☎7096 2368. While the interior is strictly no-frills, this Brazilian-style *por kilo* place is a little oasis for hard-pressed vegetarians and a real bargain. At Bs45/kilo, you

TRAVELLING DOWN THE RÍO MAMORÉ

From Puertos Barador or Almacén, some 15km southwest of Trinidad (a motorbike taxi will take you for around Bs20), you can get a ride on the regular cargo boats that ply the waters of the **Río Mamoré**, either downstream to **Guayaramerín** on the Brazilian border or upstream as far as **Puerto Villarroel** in the Chapare (see p.225). In places more than 3km wide, the mighty Mamoré – its name means "Great Mother" in Moxeño – was once one of the great waterways of the Bolivian Amazon and still sees a good deal of traffic. Canoes, barges and double-decker river boats ply its silt-laden waters, carrying supplies to the isolated communities along the river bank, collecting cargoes of timber or bananas, and carrying cattle downstream to markets in Brazil.

Travelling this way is one of the classic Amazon experiences, and an excellent way to get a feel for the immense scale of the forest and the lifestyle of its inhabitants. The river boats glide through the forest at a languid pace, with plenty of opportunities for spotting **wildlife** along the way, particularly cayman, pink river dolphins and innumerable birds. Every so often the dense vegetation of the river bank breaks to reveal a riverside settlement, usually no more than a cluster of thatched houses on stilts. For the villagers, isolated in the midst of this immense wilderness, the arrival of a boat can be the main event of the day, and if yours stops to load or unload cargo it's likely to be besieged by locals selling bananas or fish, or simply seeking the latest news and gossip from upriver.

PRACTICALITIES

Boats depart up- and down-river two or three times a week, though when river levels fall in the **dry season** (May–Sept) the route south to Puerto Villarroel can be impassable. The trip downstream to Guayaramerín takes between three days and a week, depending on the level of the river, the size and power of the boat, whether it's equipped to travel by night, and how many stops it makes to load and unload cargo; upstream to Puerto Villarroel takes five to seven days. The trip downstream should cost around Bs175–280 ($25–40) including meals, but be prepared to bargain; the longer trip upstream will likely cost slightly more. The **food** served on board the boats is usually pretty bland, consisting mainly of rice, plantains and *charque*, so it's worth taking along fresh fruit and maybe some tinned food. It's also essential to take your own drinking **water** or at least some purifiers. **Accommodation** on board is fairly basic; you'll need your own hammock to string up on deck as well as a mosquito net if the boat is likely to moor at night.

To check departure dates and arrange passage, you really have to take a **motorcycle taxi** to either port and speak directly with the boat captains. You may have to wait around a few days before getting a ride; some captains will let you sleep on board while awaiting departure.

can heap your plate full of veggies, salad, grains, yucca and banana (though note that the rice and beans are both cooked with meat) and still pay much less than half of that, with a drink, soup and *postre* (dessert) thrown in. Daily 11.30am–3pm.

Taverna Ranchera Av 6 de Agosto, between Santa Cruz and Villavicencio ☎03 4628505. A brightly painted

if rather spartan little Mexican restaurant serving all the usual enchiladas, burritos and tacos for Bs15 a pop, though veggies should note that the beans are prepared with meat. They also serve some of Trinidad's best pizza. Be sure to sample their non-alcoholic, almost aniseed-like *chicha*, a strange but refreshing brew of maize, peanuts and sugar. Daily Tues–Sun 7–11pm.

DIRECTORY

Banks and exchange There are foreign-card compatible ATMs all over town, particularly around the plaza and Av 6 de Agosto. BR Cambios (Mon–Fri 8.30am–12.30pm & 2.30–6.30pm, Sat 8.30am–1pm) on Antonio Vaca Diez, opposite *Hostal Ibañez*, changes dollars, euros, soles and reis.

Internet Though there are internet cafés at every second

doorway, speeds can be harrowingly slow, the going rate is Bs3/hr.

Post office Just off the plaza on Av Ciprian Barace (Mon–Fri 8am–7.30pm, Sat till 6pm, Sun 9am–noon).

Telephones There are ENTEL cabins throughout the city, most of which open all day, every day.

The northern Amazon

Now a remote economic backwater, just over a hundred years ago Bolivia's **northern Amazon** frontier was one of the most commercially desirable stretches of territory on earth. The region supports some of the richest natural rubber forests in the whole of the Amazon, and in the late nineteenth century a surge in international demand for rubber generated an unprecedented economic boom. Great fortunes were made by the so-called "rubber barons" who controlled production, but for the indigenous peoples of the Amazon the **rubber boom** was an unmitigated disaster. They were recruited by force to work collecting wild rubber under conditions of appalling brutality, and their population declined catastrophically. Little of the money made was reinvested, and when the boom ended in the early twentieth century with the establishment of rubber plantations in Asia, the region – and its main towns, agreeable **Riberalta** and Brazilian flavoured **Guayaramerín** – slipped back into the economic torpor which characterizes it today, with collection of wild **Brazil nuts** (known as *castañas*) the main export industry. To the north of Guayaramerín, the small and sleepy town of **Cachuela Esperanza** provides an atmospheric insight into the days of the rubber boom.

Riberalta

Set on a bluff above a great sweep of the Río Madre de Dios, just after its silt-laden waters are joined by those of the Beni, **RIBERALTA** is the second-biggest town in the Amazon lowlands, with a population of about forty thousand, largely employed in the processing and export of Brazil nuts. Riberalta's economic fortunes never really recovered from the collapse of the rubber boom; while its valuable rubber exports once circumnavigated the globe it is now a net importer, and its roaring fleet of cheap Asian motorbikes now endlessly circumnavigate the central plaza. Though there's no great reason to stop here, there's an indolent charm about the place that makes it perhaps the most likeable of the Northern Amazon outposts.

Parque Costanera

While the optimistically named **Parque Costanera**, a couple of blocks north of the plaza, is really just a few square metres of weeds and broken rubble, it's worth sauntering down to its plank-less benches to witness the wholly surreal sight of a Scottish-built steamboat, the **Tahuamanu**, mounted in concrete; the first and last such craft to navigate the Bolivian Amazon. The park also offers a magnificent sunset view: a molten-glass ferment best accompanied by a cold beer, if you can find one. On weekends you might have some luck at the adjacent **Club Nautico**, a curiously dated, lido-esque pool ringed by thatched shades and a bar, where you can also take a dip (Bs20).

Tumi Chucua

20km south of town, towards the Cobija road junction • A taxi should cost Bs150 return

A taxi-ride south of town lies the lush, sinuous lake of **Tumi Chucua**, its centre filled by an oblong forested island and its shore lined with large, if increasingly dilapidated, timber houses once home to controversial US evangelist group the Summer Institute of Linguistics. There's a small jetty from which you can dive in, though the turbid waters are supposedly home to an anaconda; if you don't fancy swimming you may be able to rent canoes from the locals. Sadly, if typically, the area around the jetty is littered with rubbish, and the mouldering public toilets are best avoided completely.

Esmeralda Parque Ecológico

Roughly 20km along the road east to Guayaramerín • Bs25 • ☎ 7283 1099 (call for hours)

For a more salubrious jungle excursion, head to the manicured lawns of this Swiss-owned retreat, where tennis and volleyball courts, a huge swimming pool and a boating lake keep Riberalteños busy at weekends. There's also a restaurant and bar with a pleasant terrace. It's deliberately un-signposted, however, amid a labyrinth of forking tracks deep in the rainforest, so the only way to get here is with a taxi driver who knows the way (Bs120 return). There is also accommodation available (see below).

ARRIVAL AND DEPARTURE

By plane The airport is about 1km south of town (Bs3 on a motorbike taxi). Aerocon, at Plaza Principal (☎ 03 8523899); Amaszonas, at Chuquisaca and Sucre (☎ 03 8523933); and TAM (no office; ☎ 03 8522646) all operate from here. Maddeningly and hugely time consumingly, most flights are routed via Trinidad, with a change of plane and a long wait in the airport; for Cobija at least then, you're as well taking a bus and saving some money. Another alternative is one of the daily *avionetas* (light aircraft) that leave when they are full, which fly direct to Guayaramerín as well as Cobija; enquire at the airport. Destinations Note that most of these flights also include a lengthy stopover at Trinidad airport on top of the actual journey times given. Cobija (1 daily; 2hr 40min);

RIBERALTA

Guayaramerín (2 daily; 15–20min); La Paz (4 daily; 2hr 15min); Santa Cruz (2–3 daily; 2hr 10min); Trinidad (3 daily; 1hr).

By bus Buses arrive at, and depart from, the pot-holed terminal at the eastern edge of town (Bs3 on a motorbike taxi).

Destinations Cobija (2 daily; 12hr); Guayaramerín (6 daily; 2hr 30min); La Paz (2 daily; 30hr); Trinidad (1 daily; 28hr).

By boat You can still find occasional boats heading up the Madre de Dios to Puerto Maldonado in Peru: departures are posted on a notice board outside the Capitanía del Puerto office at Puerto El Pila 1km east of town. Boats also occasionally travel up the Beni to Rurrenabaque when the road is closed during the rainy season (Nov–March).

GETTING AROUND

By motorbike taxi The principal mode of transport here; standard journeys in town cost Bs3.

Motorbike rental Motorbikes are also available for rent a block south of the plaza on Av Nicolás Suárez (Bs15/hour, Bs120/24hr). You'll need to leave your passport as a deposit.

INFORMATION AND TOURS

Tourist information There's no tourist information office though the owners of *Hotel Jomali* (see opposite) are a good source of info, as is Riberalta Tours, Av Sucre 634 (☎ 03 8523475, ⊕ riberaltatours.com), which offers trips to local Brazil nut factories as well as Tumi Chucua (see above) and, further afield, the Reserva Manuripi (see p.301).

ACCOMMODATION

Esmeralda Parque Ecológico 15km south of centre ☎ 7283 1099 or 7112 2395. A cluster of freshly built brick chalets with heavy thatched roofs sit on the fringes of this Swiss-owned jungle park (see above). The interiors are cool and fresh, with tiled floors, small kitchens and sterling views from the upper floor balconies, and home-made Swiss yogurt is served at breakfast. All chalets (sleeping two) are solar-powered, though the guard dogs don't look too friendly, never mind ecofriendly. You'll need to give a couple of days' advance notice and take a taxi from town, as it's located down an un-signposted track deep in the forest. Bs400 ($57)

★ **Hotel Colonial** Plácido Méndez 145, just off the plaza ☎03 8523018, ✉hotelcolonial_rib@hotmail.com. One of the nicest surprises in the northern Amazon, this tranquil urban copse screens its whitewashed rooms behind a curtain of tropical fronds and a horde of heavy furniture, truly an olde worlde apart from the red-dust and fumes all around. An elegant common area maintains a library-calm hush, while the generous inclusive breakfast is served just off the central patio. A place to treat yourself for making it this far. Bs260

★ **Hotel Jomali** Av Nicolás Suárez, just off the plaza near Banco Ganadero ☎03 8522398, ✉jomali1717 @hotmail.com. Homely, newly opened hotel run by a hospitable brother and sister team, with freshly painted, sprucely furnished and immaculately tidy pastel rooms above a prepossessing courtyard scored with window boxes. There's a choice of ceiling fan or a/c, and breakfast and internet are gratis. Bs200; a/c Bs250

Hotel Shimose Nicolás Suárez with Santiestevan ☎03 8522326. Located a couple of blocks south of the plaza, this Japanese-owned place makes for a decent budget option, with clean, spacious upstairs rooms around a sun-baked yard. Decor is frilly with over-carved headboards, and there are several ample communal areas. Bs130; a/c Bs150

EATING

★ **Club Social Progreso** Plaza Principal ☎03 8523024. Of all Beni's Clubes Sociales, this one – 90 years old and counting – has by far the most ramshackle charm, as do its lovely proprietors, Dr Walter Pol and his wife Soraya. Under ancient ceiling fans, amid rickety chairs and huge window shutters, the couple serve cheap almuerzos, refreshing fruit juices and fantastic omelettes. Daily 9am–midnight.

Pizzeria Mia Pizza Av Dr Martinez, just off the plaza ☎03 8523061. Friendly, modern and efficient pizza joint with street-side seating (if you can stand the insects) and the usual variety of toppings, though the dough could do with a thin-crust makeover. Don't miss their aromatic, apple-like *cuyá* juice. Tues–Sun 4–11pm.

★ **Restaurante Tropical** Oruro 632, eight blocks south of the plaza ☎7688 3248. If you can get past the trophy skins and armadillo shells, this is one of the region's most enjoyable *jatata grande* joints, with a gregariously endearing owner and boa constrictor-sized servings of *pique macho*, chicken curry and fried river fish for Bs100 a whack. One portion more than feeds two. Mon–Sat noon–3pm & 7pm–midnight, Sun noon–3pm.

DIRECTORY

Banks and exchange Mercifully, the ATMs at Cooperativa Jesús Nazareno (Mon–Fri 8.30am–12.30pm & 2.30–6pm, Sat 9am–noon) and Banco Ganadero (Mon–Fri 9am–5pm, Sat till 1pm), both on the plaza, should accept foreign cards. Failing that, you can also change dollars at the latter, or obtain a cash advance on a credit card at five percent.

Internet A nameless café on the plaza charges Bs6/hr for a hopelessly slow connection.

Post office The post office (Mon–Fri 8am–noon & 3–6.30pm, Sat 9am–noon) is on the Plaza Principal.

Telephones The ENTEL office (Mon–Fri 9am–12.30pm & 3–6.30pm, Sat 9am–1pm) is next door to the post office.

Guayaramerín

Set on the banks of the Río Mamoré some 86km east of Riberalta, **GUAYARAMERÍN** is the main crossing point on Bolivia's northern border with Brazil, a modern and prosperous frontier town with a distinctly Brazilian flavour and a thriving economy based on duty-free sales. Many of the streets are lined with shops and boutiques selling perfume, electronic goods and designer clothes to the thousands of Brazilian bargain-hunters who flock over the border on shopping trips.

ARRIVAL AND DEPARTURE   GUAYARAMERÍN

By plane The primitive airport is just four blocks east of the plaza along 25 de Mayo. Flights are operated from here by Aerocon, 25 de Mayo and Beni (☎03 8555035) and TAM, Av 16 de Julio (☎03 8553924). Most flights are routed via Trinidad, though TAM fly direct to Riberalta. For Cobija, you're better off taking the bus, or an *avioneta* (light aircraft); enquire at the airport.

Destinations Cobija (1 daily; 2hr 40min); La Paz (4–5 daily; 2hr 15min); Riberalta (2 weekly; 20min); Santa Cruz (3 daily; 2hr 10min); Trinidad (3–5 daily; 1hr 10min).

By bus Buses arrive at, and depart from, the terminal about 3km from the centre of town along Beni.

Destinations Cobija (1–2 daily; 15–16hr); La Paz (2 daily; 32hr); Riberalta (6 daily; 2hr 30min); Trinidad (1–2 daily; 30hr).

THE RAILWAY TO NOWHERE

Guayaramerín is the last navigable point on the **Río Mamoré**, the most important waterway in the Bolivian Amazon. Downstream from Guayaramerín a series of nineteen cataracts and **rapids**, stretching for over 400km down the ríos Mamoré and Madeira, cuts off the Bolivian river network from Brazil and access to the Atlantic Ocean. During the rubber boom, Bolivians and foreign speculators dreamed of bypassing these rapids and opening up the Bolivian Amazon to trade with the world. In 1872 the US journalist and speculator **George Church** formed a company to build a railway circumventing the rapids. Yet the crews sent to begin the work met with immediate disaster: their boats sank, and ravaged by fever and Indian attacks the workforce abandoned their equipment and fled through the forest. Church's company went bankrupt and the contractors concluded that the region was "a welter of putrefaction where men die like flies. Even with all the money in the world and half its population it is impossible to finish this railway."

Church himself was undeterred, and by 1878 had raised enough financial support to launch another attempt, with equally disastrous consequences. By the time the project was abandoned three years later, five hundred workers had died but only 6km of track had been laid. But the dream of a railway around the rapids would not die. In 1903 **Brazil** promised to complete the project in compensation for the annexation of the Acre territory from Bolivia. Work began again in 1908, and three years later the Madeira–Mamoré Railway – or the **Devil's Railway**, as it had become known – was finally completed. More than six thousand workers are thought to have died in its construction, a sacrifice that was quickly shown to have been made in vain, since the railway opened for business just as the Amazon rubber boom collapsed. The Brazilian government kept it running until 1972, when it was finally abandoned, its rusting rails, swallowed by encroaching jungle, providing an eloquent testimony to a failed dream of progress in the Amazon.

By boat Trinidad (2–3 weekly; 5–8 days); enquire at the Capitanía del Puerto office opposite the *migración* office (see below) for forthcoming departures.

GETTING AROUND

By motorbike taxi The principal mode of transport; standard journeys in town cost Bs3; there's also a fleet of rickshaw taxis charging around Bs10.

Motorbike rental You can rent motorbikes on the southeast side of the plaza for Bs15/hr or Bs80/24hr, though you'll have to leave your passport as a deposit.

CROSSING THE BRAZILIAN BORDER

Via Guajará-Mirim From the port at the bottom of Av Federico Román, regular passenger boats (every 15min; Bs10) make the five-minute crossing to Guajará-Mirim in Brazil. The Bolivian *migración* (Mon–Fri 8am–8pm, Sat & Sun till noon) is to the right of the port as you face the river: you should get an exit stamp here if you're continuing into Brazil but it's not necessary if you're just making a day-trip across the river. From Guajará-Mirim there are frequent buses to Porto Velho, from where there are connections to other destinations in Brazil.

Visas and vaccinations If you need a visa, the Brazilian Consulate (Mon–Fri 9am–noon, 3–5pm) is on the corner of calles Beni and 24 de Septiembre, four blocks south of the port. Note that to enter Brazil here you need to have an international certificate of yellow fever vaccination; if you don't, there's a clinic beside the immigration office in Guajará-Mirim where you can get vaccinated.

INFORMATION AND TOURS

Tourist information There's no tourist office but Mary Tours, on the north side of the main plaza (✆ 03 8553883, ✉ mary-tours@hotmail.com) are a good source of info, and also run trips to Cachuela Esperanza (see opposite).

ACCOMMODATION

★ **Hotel Anexo Plaza** West side of main plaza ✆ 03 8553650. The oldest hotel in town, this friendly, low-key oasis boasts immaculate, crisp rooms along a mosaic-tiled courtyard far from the plaza's moped derby. Nor is there the logjam of Brazilian tourists you can get elsewhere in town. Great value. Bs140

Hotel Balneario San Carlos Av 6 de Agosto 347, a block north and east from the plaza ✆ 03 8553555,

@ sancarloshotel@hotmail.com. Accessed by a misplaced, nightclub-like awning yet minus a sign, this would-be top end boasts a/c, a decent swimming pool (guests only) and some pretty *azulejos*, though the stale pink and purple colour scheme may give you nightmares. **Bs 260**

Hotel Santa Ana Av 25 de Mayo ☎ 03 8553900. As the sole salubrious option on this street, *Hotel Santa Ana's* spotless, timber-ceilinged rooms are best booked in advance, thus avoiding the gaggle of hopefuls that routinely fill up reception after a flight. Relax in the cool courtyard garden instead, and look forward to some real granny-quality hospitality. **Bs100**

EATING

Antonella Northwest corner of the plaza. Fruity little *heladería* with a green and yellow colour scheme and a cluster of alfresco tin tables. Inside, antiquated display cases impart an old-fashioned ice cream parlour ambience. Don't miss their iced fruit salad, though they also do lasagne, empanadas and the like for around Bs20. Daily 8am–11.30pm.

★ **Los Cocos** Huacaraje and Oruro ☎ 03 8554150. Inside a lavish, brick-walled compound, under robust hardwood beams, *Los Cocos* serves up what most locals will tell you is the best food in town. The pricey (Bs75), double-portion dishes – *surubí*, *chicharrón*, etc – are nothing unusual but the bow-tied waiters will treat you like a real *rey* (king). There are even pepper grinders and Portuguese olive oil on the tables. Miss their flagons of peach juice at your peril. Daily 10.30am–3pm & 6.30–11pm.

DIRECTORY

Banks and exchange Cooperativa Jesús Nazareno, on the northeast corner of the main plaza, has an ATM that should accept foreign cards, and you can also obtain a cash advance on a credit card (five percent) and change both dollars and reis.

Internet A nameless café on 25 de Mayo, opposite *Hotel Rio Mar*, offers a snail-paced connection for Bs6/hr.

Post office The post office (Mon–Fri 8am–noon & 2.30–6pm) is on Oruro, two blocks south of the plaza.

Telephones The ENTEL office (daily 7.30am–11pm) is on Federico Román, three blocks north of the plaza.

Cachuela Esperanza

From Guayaramerín a rough dirt road runs 42km northwest to the small town of **CACHUELA ESPERANZA**. Founded in the heart of the wilderness in 1882, this was once the headquarters of **Nicolás Suárez** (see box below) and the most advanced town in the Bolivian Amazon, with modern offices and homes, state-of-the-art medical facilities, a theatre that attracted international stars and its own narrow-gauge railway. Though the long-decimated population has grown over the last decade, and a controversial $2.5 billion hydroelectric project has put it back in the media spotlight, Cachuela Esperanza remains a sleepy little backwater, for now at least. Its run-down yet sturdy Canadian pine and brick houses are nevertheless in remarkably good condition given their age and the ravages of heat and humidity. Some are now deserted, but others still

NICOLÁS SUÁREZ: RUBBER BARON

At the peak of his powers, **Nicolás Suárez** was the absolute ruler over more than six million hectares of rainforest where rubber was collected by a massive workforce of Caripuña Indians who were slaves in all but name. He also controlled the rapids that separated the Bolivian river system from the Amazon proper (charging huge tolls for the transport of cargo around them) and even raised a private army to fight the separatist rebellion of Brazilian settlers in the northern territory of Acre in 1899. With the annexation of Acre by Brazil, however, he lost many of his rubber holdings, and after the collapse of the rubber boom a few years later his empire gradually disintegrated. He died in Cachuela Esperanza in 1940, and though virtually forgotten elsewhere in Bolivia, in the Beni and Pando he is still revered by some as a heroic pioneer who brought progress and civilization to the wilderness. Ironically, decades later his great-nephew, **Roberto Suárez**, came to control a similarly powerful empire based on the export of another Amazonian product for which the industrialized world had developed an insatiable appetite – cocaine – amassing in the process a personal fortune so vast that in the 1980s he reputedly offered to pay off Bolivia's entire national debt.

serve as homes to the few people who continue to live here, imparting at least a flavour of the town's former grandeur, the faded shadow of which makes Cachuela such a fascinating place.

The wooden church and around
Coming into town along the road from Guayaramerín you pass a small **wooden church** built in 1909 that would look more at home in New England than here in the Amazon. Close by stands the modest stone **tomb of Suárez**, with an inscription praising him as a "heroic patriot and eminent industrial progressive". Just beyond the church on your left is the well-preserved **cinema-theatre**, built in the 1930s to entertain Suárez and his army of foreign technicians.

The riverfront
On the riverfront a **bust of Suárez** looks out over a fierce set of rapids known as Hell's Cauldron, the first in the series of riverine obstacles that effectively cuts Bolivia off from the Amazon mainstream; close by to the right a broken **monument** commemorates the men who died trying to negotiate these rapids, while along to the left stands a small **steam locomotive** that served the railway used to circumvent them (see p.296). Suárez's mansion, known as **Villa Luta** – the "House of Mourning" – occupies the highest point in town, a crumbling shell overgrown with vegetation.

ARRIVAL AND DEPARTURE

By truck/car Trucks and *autos* run between Guayaramerín and Cachuela Esperanza most of the day, leaving when full – ask a motorbike taxi to take you to the *paradero* (truck stop) on the edge of Guayaramerín.

By motorbike taxi Most motorbike taxis in Guayeramerín will charge around Bs150 for a full day-trip; try Victor Hugo on ☎ 03 8551030.

Pando

The northwestern-most tip of Bolivia is covered by the department of **Pando**, a remote and sparsely populated rainforest region where logging and the collection of wild rubber and Brazil nuts are the main economic activities. At one time Pando was accessible only by boat along the Madre de Dios, Tahuamanu and Orthon rivers, which flow into the region from Peru, but now a rough road cut through the rainforest runs from just south of Riberalta to **Cobija**, the departmental capital, on the Brazilian border. While the bus journey along this route is an adventure in itself, involving a short and somewhat surreal cruise along a tributary of the Madre de Dios, large swathes of land on both sides of the road have already been deforested, with blackened stumps of trees protruding like broken teeth from pale green pasture and scrubby secondary growth.

Though the southwest corner of Pando is covered by the **Reserva Nacional Amazónica Manuripi** (see p.301), the forests of much of this wild frontier region

---

THE PANDO MASSACRE
The events of September 11th 2008 proved just how dangerous standing up for your rights can be in the remote communities of Pando. In a now infamous incident near the settlement of Porvenir, described by UNASUR as a crime against humanity, nineteen indigenous protestors were shot dead – and many more injured – by right-wing paramilitaries organized by the authorities of Pando prefect, Leopoldo Fernández. While Fernández languishes in prison awaiting trial, many of his henchmen have yet to be brought to justice, with Amnesty International recently reporting claims that some of them are still walking around Cobija.

remain hotly disputed. The businessmen who control the collection of rubber and Brazil nuts, some of whom are descended from the nineteenth-century rubber barons, claim ownership rights over some thirty thousand square kilometres of forest – nearly half the department. But these claims are contested by the indigenous and *campesino* communities who collect the nuts and rubber – often working under a system of permanent debt so severe it amounts to a disguised form of slavery. While these communities are now using land-rights legislation to demand that the forest be recognized as theirs, with government plans to redistribute five hundred hectares per family, the political situation in the region remains volatile (see box opposite).

6

Cobija

Though its population of around 26,000 is expanding rapidly, **COBIJA** remains the smallest departmental capital in Bolivia, an isolated yet thriving border town with a distinctly Brazilian flavour. Founded in the early twentieth century as a rubber collection centre, the town's economic fortunes now depend more on **duty-free** sales to Brazil and central government investment in infrastructure, part of a Pando-wide policy aimed at attracting settlers and establishing a human frontier to prevent a repeat of what happened across the border in the Brazilian state of Acre (see p.312).

Most of the streets are well paved and the town boasts a modern airport out of all proportion to its needs, though with few obvious attractions and the highest rainfall in Bolivia, it's no surprise that few travellers make it here. Cobija does, however, offer an adventurous back route into Brazil and even Peru, and the chance to explore a rainforest region where organized tourism has yet to make an impact.

ARRIVAL AND DEPARTURE   COBIJA

By plane The modern airport was the scene of gun battles between right wing paramilitaries and the Bolivian army after the 2008 massacre (see opposite). It is on the outskirts of town, at the far end of Av 9 de Febrero; a motorbike taxi should cost around Bs10. Most flights are operated by Aerocon , Av 16 de Julio 37 (☏03 8424575) and TAM, Av 9 de Febrero 49 (☏03 8422267), and – at considerable inconvenience and expense to all – routed via Trinidad where you'll have to change plane, though TAM do run a much cheaper, direct daily flight to La Paz (1 hr), usually departing around 11.30am.
Destinations Guayaramerín (1 daily; 2hr 40min); La Paz (4–5 daily; 1hr–2hr 35min); Riberalta (2 daily; 2hr 40min); Santa Cruz (3–4 daily; 2hr 30min); Trinidad (2 daily; 1hr 30min).
By bus Buses from Riberalta and beyond arrive at offices strung out along 9 de Febrero.
Destinations La Paz (1 daily; 48hr); Riberalta (2 daily; 12hr).

GETTING AROUND

By motorbike taxi Though riders aren't as common in Cobija as elsewhere, they're still the cheapest and most convenient way to get around; most journeys cost Bs5.

CROSSING THE BRAZILIAN BORDER

Via Brasiléia The Bolivian immigration office (daily 8.30am–8.30pm) is on the main border crossing, the international bridge over the Río Acre at the end of Av Internacional. A taxi from the town centre across the bridge to the federal police office (where you'll need to clear immigration) in the Brazilian town of Brasiléia should cost about Bs30; otherwise it's a twenty-minute walk. You need an international yellow-fever vaccination certificate to enter Brazil here. If you need a visa, the Brazilian Consulate (Mon–Fri 9am–1pm & 3–6pm) is just off the plaza in Cobija. From Brasiléia there are regular buses to Río Branco, from where you can get onward connections.
Onward travel to Peru There's also an adventurous route into the Peruvian department of Madre de Dios from here. From Brasiléia you can get a bus to Asis Brazil, 95km west on the border with Peru, and cross over to the Peruvian settlement of Iñapari, from where a fully paved road (part of the new Carretera Interoceánica) heads south to Puerto Maldonado, a route plied by frequent colectivo cars. Puerto Maldonado is linked by road and regular flights to Cuzco.

6

THE MYSTERIOUS COLONEL FAWCETT

The forests of the Bolivian Amazon have long attracted adventurers, eccentrics and explorers, but few have matched the exploits of **Colonel Percy Harrison Fawcett**. An officer in the British Indian Army, Fawcett first came to Bolivia in 1906 to survey the unmarked and largely unexplored wilderness frontiers between Bolivia and Peru and Brazil. Over the next nineteen years, he travelled the length and breadth of the Beni, keeping a diary which his brother Brian would later use as the basis for the iconic **Exploration Fawcett** (see p.328). First published in 1953, the book painted a vivid if, as some have speculated, somewhat embellished picture of life in the Amazon at the peak of the rubber boom. This was a time when "slavery, vice and bloodshed ruled supreme on the rivers", and during which the indigenous inhabitants – considered "wild and hostile savages" – were "as a rule . . . either shot on sight like dangerous animals or ruthlessly hunted down to be sent as slaves to rubber estates". Fawcett's own adventures involved frequent close encounters with 20m-long anacondas, ferocious cannibal tribes, virulent tropical diseases and brutal and corrupt officials. On one occasion he and a small exploration party found their canoe marooned on a sandbar in the **Río Heath** and surrounded by heavily armed Guarayos warriors. Realizing that to fight would be hopeless, Fawcett says he ordered his companions to sing, accompanied by an accordion. After a few verses of "A Bicycle Made for Two", the previously hostile tribesmen were completely pacified.

FROM MAN TO MYTH

In other respects a typical product of the British Empire, the longer Fawcett spent in the Amazon, the more he came to love the wilderness and sympathize with its inhabitants. Over the years he became convinced that somewhere hidden deep in the forest stood a magnificent city inhabited by an ancient and highly advanced race of white Indians. Condemned by many of his contemporaries as a mystic and dreamer, in 1925 he set off to find this **mythical city** in the wilds of the Brazilian Amazon, and was never seen again. Since then, countless expeditions have gone in search of the colonel, while rumours concerning his possible end abound; according to David Grann's definitive *Lost City of Z* (see p.328), the most likely scenario is that Fawcett – along with his son Jack – was murdered by one of the warlike tribes in the **Xingu region** of Brazil. The truth behind his disappearance has never been established conclusively, however, and his own fate has now become the kind of mystery that so entranced him when he was alive. As the archeological evidence continues to mount up, moreover, his core theory of an advanced Amazonian civilisation looks more and more like the work of a visionary rather than a dreamer.

ACCOMMODATION

★**Hotel Asai** Km 3, Barrio Paz Zamora near the airport ☎03 8422478. While a little out of town, this tempting knot of palm-thatched cabañas – all handsome hardwood and white sheets – will at least serve to remind you're in the tropics, with an orange-dirt path running between hammock-strung balconies and palms swaying at every corner. Worth the money. **Bs350 ($50)**

Residencial Frontera Beni 55 ☎03 8422740. The town's most salubrious budget option, with clean if rather clinical rooms with part-tiled walls, ceiling and wall fans to cope with Cobija's heat and somewhat miserly windows giving onto a central corridor. **Bs120**

Villa Gloria Av Manuripi 95, 1.5km from the plaza ☎03 8422028, ✉hvgloria@hotmail.com. Whether you opt for one of a cluster of clean, self-contained *casitas* (sleeping two) with striped sheets and a/c, or the standard hotel rooms, all grouped around an ample swimming pool, this place isn't bad value at all. Tours to the Reserva Manuripi on request. *Casitas* **Bs315**; doubles **Bs210**

EATING

Churrasquería Paladar Av 16 de Julio ☎03 8422408. A packed, Brazilian-owned *por kilo* joint with a *baião* soundtrack, where a wedding-cake-high plate of yucca, beans, veggies, rice and meat or cheese fritters won't set you back much more than Bs40. Mon & Wed–Sat 11.45am–2pm & 7.30–11pm, Sun 11.45am–2pm.

Esquina de la Abuela Av Molina and Sucre ☎03 8422364. One of the most popular places in town, with friendly and professional service and a cluster of pavement tables sheltered by palm-thatched eaves. River fish, steaks, etc are in the Bs50 range, and don't miss the tropical-raspberry-esque taste sensation that is their *acerola* juice. Daily noon–3pm & 6.30–10pm.

Jalapeño Miguel Becerra ☏7114 3330. Choose between a herbaceous patio or a quasi-rustic interior to enjoy *Jalapeño's* decent range of Mexican classics in the Bs20–30 range, though veggies should note that pretty much all dishes are meat-based. Tues–Sun 6–11pm.

DIRECTORY

Banks and exchange Banco Unión on the plaza (Mon–Fri 9am–5pm & Sat till 1pm), has a foreign card-compatible ATM, will change dollars and reis, and you can also obtain a cash advance on a credit card.

Post office The post office (Mon–Fri 9am–8pm & Sat till 3pm) is on the plaza.

Telephones Punto Cotel (Mon–Fri 8.30am–10.30pm, Sat & Sun 8.30am–8pm) on Mariscal Santa Cruz. There's also pricey internet here but it's so prohibitively slow, it's hardly worth the effort.

6

Reserva Nacional de Vida Silvestre Amazónica Manuripi

South of Cobija between the ríos Tahuamanu and Madre de Dios, almost 7500 square kilometres of some of Bolivia's most pristine lowland Amazon rainforest are protected, at least on paper, as the **Reserva Nacional de Vida Silvestre Amazónica Manuripi**. With financial help from Germany, the park's SERNAP-administered staff have, for several years, been working with the reserve's scattered *campesino* communities to promote the sustainable extraction of rubber and Brazil nuts, while improving social and working conditions. While there are plans to develop ecotourism, there's no real infrastructure in the reserve as yet save for some very basic *cabañas* (Bs40); you'll need to take all your own food and bedding. There are plenty of trails used by the *castañeros* during the Brazil nut-collecting season (Nov–Feb), however, and at least one specific walking route, a two-hour-plus trek from the tiny community of Curichon to Lago Bay, from where you can continue to Arroyo Malecón, near the Peruvian border. Lago Bay is also accessible via the motorized canoes (Bs300) with which the guards patrol the river in search of illegal loggers. Before setting off you'll need to give advance notice – ideally a couple of days – to the park office in Cobija.

ARRIVAL AND DEPARTURE   RESERVA MANURIPI

By truck/boat Trucks depart for the small settlement (and main guard post) of San Silvestre (2 daily; 3–4hr) from the offices of Transbioceánica on Av 9 de Febrero in Cobija.

CROSSING THE PERUVIAN BORDER

Via Chivé From San Silvestre, irregular trucks continue south along the road through the reserve to Chivé on the Río Madre de Dios, where you may be able to catch a lift on a boat for an even more adventurous backdoor route upstream into Peru , or downstream to Riberalta. An exit stamp can usually be obtained from the Bolivian border post of Puerto Heath, though you'll probably have to go as far as Puerto Maldonado to sort out your entry into Peru.

INFORMATION

Park office Los Cedros 54, Barrio 11 de Octubre, Cobija ☏03 8423399. The staff will let the park guards know you're coming, and can arrange basic accommodation. Open Mon–Fri 8.30am–12.30pm & 2.30–6.30pm.

BOLIVIAN PRESIDENT EVO MORALES

Contexts

303 History

320 Wildlife and ecology

322 Music and dance

327 Books

329 Spanish

History

Bolivia's first inhabitants were descendants of the nomadic hunting groups that migrated into the Americas from Asia during the last Ice Age (20,000 to 40,000 years ago). Having crossed the Bering Strait between Siberia and Alaska, when a bridge of land and ice linked the two continents, successive generations gradually migrated throughout the Americas, reaching the Andes at least 20,000 years ago, where they lived in semi-nomadic tribes, hunting prehistoric animals like mastodons and giant sloths.

At the end of the Ice Age (around 10,000 years ago) these species became extinct. During the same period, humans began the long, slow transition to an **agricultural society**. By about 2500 BC, agriculture and herding had become the main form of subsistence in the highlands and along the Pacific coast, though in the forested lowlands a semi-nomadic lifestyle combining hunting and fishing with limited cultivation remained the norm. As population density increased and agricultural techniques developed, social organizations grew more complex and governments and ceremonial religious centres began to emerge. By about 1800 BC, **pottery** was in widespread use, and primitive metal smelting developed soon after.

Tiwanaku

The first major civilization to develop on the Bolivian Altiplano was the **Tiwanaku** (or Tiahuanaco) culture, centred on the city of the same name, which was located on the southern shores of Lago Titicaca. First founded around 1200 BC, by 100 BC Tiwanaku had become an important religious and urban centre with distinct classes of peasants, priests, warriors, artisans and aristocrats.

From around 700 AD Tiwanaku's influence dominated an area comprising much of modern Bolivia, southern Peru, northeast Argentina and northern Chile. At its height, Tiwanaku city was a sophisticated **urban ceremonial complex** with a population of over fifty thousand, lying at the centre of a vast empire of colonies and religious centres. Some time after 1000 AD, however, the Tiwanaku empire dramatically collapsed, its population dispersed and its great cities were abandoned. The reasons for this remain unclear: possible explanations include a cataclysmic earthquake or foreign invasion, though the most likely is **climate change** – from about 1000 AD, the region suffered a long-term decline in rainfall, suggesting that a prolonged drought may have wiped out the intensive agriculture on which Tiwanaku depended.

The Aymara

The Tiwanaku empire was succeeded by numerous much smaller regional states. The Altiplano around the shores of Lago Titicaca fell under the control of the **Aymara**, who

Around 18 000 BC	**1000 BC**	**1000 AD**
Bolivia's first inhabitants – descendants of Asian migrants who crossed the Bering Strait – appear.	The Tiwanaku culture becomes the first major civilisation to develop on the Bolivian Altiplano.	The Tiwanaku empire collapses, and is replaced by many regional states, including the Aymara kingdoms.

AYMARA SOCIETY

Aymara society was radically different from that of Tiwanaku: Aymaras lived in fortified settlements (**pucaras**), relied on large-scale llama and alpaca herding rather than intensive **cultivation**, and followed a much more localized religion, building few ceremonial sites other than the stone tombs (**chulpas**) where important individuals were buried. The basic unit of Aymara society was the **ayllu** – an extended kinship group – above which were powerful regional nobles, or **kurakas**, who held land independently from the *ayllus* over which they ruled; the *kurakas* were in turn subject to a warrior chief or king.

---

probably migrated to the region from the highlands to the east sometime after the empire's collapse. Aymara territory was subdivided into at least seven militaristic kingdoms, of which the **Lupaca** and **Colla** were probably the largest and most powerful. Though centred overwhelmingly on the Altiplano, the Aymara maintained colonies in different ecological regions to ensure access to a wide range of produce. As well as major livestock herders, the Aymara were also important producers of gold and silver, which were found in abundance on the Altiplano, making it one of the wealthiest Andean regions.

The Incas

By the mid-fifteenth century the Aymara kingdoms found themselves in growing competition with the **Incas**, an expansionist, Quechua-speaking people with their capital at Cusco in southern Peru. Despite their military power, the Aymara kingdoms proved incapable of uniting against this common threat and were gradually incorporated into the Inca empire. Initially, the Incas did little to alter Aymara society, contenting themselves with extracting tribute. In 1470, however, the main Aymara kingdoms around Lago Titicaca rose in revolt, prompting the Incas to dispatch a great army from Cusco to crush the rebellion.

Thereafter, the Incas reinforced their control of the Altiplano, building roads, storehouses and fortresses, and incorporating the region into their domains as the **Collasuyo**, one of the richest and most populous of the empire's four quarters, or **suyus**. The Aymara rulers were permitted to remain in place, though with limited autonomy; they were also required to send their young nobles to Cusco both to serve as hostages and be indoctrinated. A different system of government was used in the fertile inter-Andean valleys east of the Altiplano, where the Incas established military-agricultural colonies of loyal Quechua-speakers, known as **mitamaqs**. These guaranteed Inca control of this rich, temperate region and protected the southeastern frontier of the empire against raids by semi-nomadic peoples from the Eastern Lowlands.

With the conquest of the **Collasuyo** the Incas confirmed their status as the most powerful Andean empire since Tiwanaku, with which they consciously sought to associate themselves, claiming that their founding ancestor, Manco Capac, had been brought into being on the Isla del Sol in Lago Titicaca, the Andean world's sacred centre where it was believed the sun itself had been created. Within a century, the Incas had become masters of the greatest empire yet seen in the Americas – an empire stretching over five thousand kilometres from southern Colombia to northern Chile,

---

Mid-1400s	1470	1532	1533
The Aymara kingdoms are gradually incorporated into the expansionist Inca empire.	An Aymara revolt around Lago Titicaca is crushed. The Incas become the most powerful Andean empire.	A small band of Spanish conquistadors defeat Atahualpa's army at Cajamarca, Peru.	Atahualpa is killed. The Spanish install Manco Inca as a puppet emperor.

THEOCRATIC COMMUNISM: THE POWER OF INCA RULE

The Inca empire combined authoritarian government with rational and egalitarian social and economic organizations, a unique system that has been described as **theocratic communism**. Though the powerful Inca armies played a key role in the empire's expansion, many regional groups submitted voluntarily, such were the advantages of Inca rule (and the futility of resistance). Conquered peoples were required to accept the official state religion – which saw the Inca ruler as the direct representative of the sun god Inti – but beyond that they were also allowed to maintain their own religious and cultural practices. Local rulers who surrendered voluntarily were often allowed to remain in place, while the Andean peasantry was left to work the land in return for supplying tribute either in the form of produce or labour service (**mita**). The enormous food surplus created by this system was used to feed standing armies and the ruling Inca elite of priests, administrators and nobles, as well as providing insurance against crop failure and famine for the peasantry themselves. The labour service was used to construct a massive network of roads, the monumental palaces and temples that graced Cusco and other major Inca sites, and the sophisticated agricultural terracing and irrigation systems that greatly increased food production.

As well as this civil engineering, the genius of the Incas lay in their **administrative bureaucracy**, which succeeded in controlling the movements of goods and people to an astonishing degree, despite having no written language, creating a level of prosperity, wellbeing and security that the people of the Andes have probably never seen matched before or since.

boasting a population of perhaps twenty million, and which was ruled by a god-emperor who claimed direct descent from the sun.

Quite how this great empire would have developed, however, will never be known. Within eighty years of their conquest of the Altiplano, the Inca empire was brought to a catastrophic end by a small band of Spaniards led by **Francisco Pizarro**, who landed on the coast of northern Peru and set about a war of conquest that would change the Andean world forever.

The Spanish conquest

From the Incas' point of view, the arrival of the first conquistadors in 1532 could not have come at a worse time. Just five years before, the empire had been swept by a devastating epidemic – probably smallpox, introduced to the Americas from Europe by Spanish conquistadors. Almost a third of the population are thought to have died, including the ruling Inca, **Huayna Capac**. Huayna Capac left his empire divided between two of his sons: his favourite, **Atahualpa**, who had established himself at Quito in what is now Ecuador, and **Huascar**, the legitimate heir to the throne, who was based in Cusco. A bloody civil war broke out, from which Atahualpa emerged victorious.

Atahualpa retired to Cajamarca in northern Peru to savour his victory. It was here that he heard of the arrival of strange bearded foreigners on the coast nearby. At the first decisive encounter between the two, Pizarro and his 170 followers kidnapped Atahualpa and massacred thousands of his men, demonstrating their overwhelming military superiority: mounted on horseback (an animal never previously seen in South America), with **steel weapons and armour**, and backed by terrifying cannons, the Spanish

1537	1538–40	1545	1548
Inca rebellion is brutally put down as the Spanish conquer the whole of Alto Peru.	La Plata (now Sucre) is the first Spanish city founded in Alto Peru.	The world's largest silver deposits are discovered near Potosí.	The city of La Paz is founded.

THE RICHES OF ALTO PERU

With its dense **indigenous population** and rich **mineral wealth** – the two resources sixteenth-century conquistadors were keenest to exploit – Alto Peru offered a rich prize, though initial efforts to consolidate control of the region were delayed by an outbreak of fighting between rival Spanish factions, an episode in which more Spaniards were killed than in all the fighting with the Incas. The full extent of the region's potential became apparent in 1545, when South America's richest silver deposit was discovered southwest of La Plata at what became known as **Cerro Rico** (Rich Mountain). The mining city of **Potosí** that sprung up at the foot of this mountain shortly afterwards, quickly became the centre of the colonial economy and the source from which vast wealth flowed to the Spanish crown.

conquistadors were virtually invincible, and even small bands proved capable of defeating massive indigenous armies. Atahualpa was ransomed for a fabulous hoard of gold and silver and then treacherously killed, though not before sending orders for Huascar to be **executed**. Huascar's faction in Cusco initially welcomed the Spaniards, if not quite as liberators then at least as useful mercenaries who had defeated their enemy just as all seemed lost. With large areas of the Inca empire only recently conquered and not yet fully assimilated, the Spaniards also found indigenous allies among the subject tribes. They occupied Cusco without a fight and installed **Manco Inca** as a puppet emperor.

Manco Inca rebels

Following this military success, **Diego de Almagro** led the first Spanish expedition south into the Altiplano, reaching as far as present-day Chile. However, in 1537, Spanish abuses in Cusco and the realization that they were bent on permanent conquest prompted a massive Inca rebellion led by Manco Inca himself. After a series of bloody battles, the Spanish military conquest of the **Collasuyo** – which they referred to variously as Charcas, the Collao or, most commonly, **Alto Peru** – was swiftly completed.

Spanish settlement

The first Spanish city founded in Alto Peru was **La Plata** (or Chuquisaca, now Sucre), strategically located in a temperate valley southeast of the Altiplano. A second city, **La Paz**, was founded in 1548 just east of Lago Titicaca to reinforce control of the densely populated northern Altiplano and to secure the route between the Potosí mines and Lima, the centre of Spanish power on the Pacific coast of Peru. Further cities at **Cochabamba** and **Tarija** followed (both in 1574), strategically located in the well-populated, fertile and temperate inter-Andean valleys, where maize and crops introduced from Europe could be grown to supply food to Potosí. La Plata was confirmed as the **capital** of Alto Peru in 1558, when it was made the seat of an independent royal court and administration – the Audiencia de Charcas – with judicial and executive power over the entire region.

Like the Incas, the Spanish were initially only able to establish control over the highlands; the semi-nomadic peoples of the Amazon lowlands and eastern plains remained unconquered despite numerous military expeditions. In 1561 the city of **Santa Cruz de la Sierra** was founded in the midst of the Eastern Lowlands by a group of conquistadors who had marched across from Paraguay, the centre of Spanish power on

1558	1561	1570s
La Plata becomes the capital of Alto Peru.	The city of Santa Cruz de la Sierra is founded.	Viceroy Toledo launches a major reform programme of the empire's economic and social structures.

the Atlantic side of South America. Their aim was to reach the silver of the Andes and establish a strategic link across the continent, but the new settlement remained isolated, precarious and surrounded by hostile indigenous groups.

Colonial society

Initially, the Spanish sought to continue the Inca pattern of control through indirect rule. Colonial society was conceived of as consisting of two separate communities, the Spanish and the **Republica de Indios**. A class of indigenous nobles – **kurakas** or **caciques** – was left in place to act as intermediaries between the Spanish and the mass of Aymara and Quechua-speaking peasants, who were permitted to remain in control of their land in return for tribute in the form of produce and labour service. These peasants were administered through the exploitative **encomienda** system, whereby individual conquistadors were granted control of the tribute paid by large indigenous groups in return for taking charge of converting them to **Catholicism** and generally "civilizing" them – the standard moral justification for the Spanish conquest.

In the highlands, the strict boundaries the Spaniards had erected between themselves and the indigenous majority quickly broke down. The conquistadors were overwhelmingly men, and most took indigenous wives and concubines: soon they were surrounded by an ever-increasing number of mixed-race children – known as **mestizos** (or *cholos*). A complex system of class and caste developed, with Spanish-born *peninsulares* on top, followed by Spaniards born in the Americas – *criollos*. The middle

---

THE SPANISH SPIRITUAL CONQUEST

The need for a **spiritual conquest** to reinforce its successful military conquest of Alto Peru was taken seriously by the Spanish crown, which sponsored all the major religious orders to undertake the conversion of the Aymara and Quechua masses. Inca religious ceremonies, pilgrimages and public rituals were banned, and a great number of idols and ceremonial sites destroyed. Beneath the surface, however, their mystical and magical appeal endured and, while publicly accepting **Christianity**, the indigenous population preserved its own deep-rooted **pre-Inca cults**. In time, elements of Catholicism and traditional beliefs intermingled, as the Aymara and Quechua appropriated the symbolism of the Christian faith, turning it into a vehicle for their own religious expression.

The religious orders were also employed as a cheap means of pacifying the **tribes** of the Northern and Eastern Lowlands, who had resisted conquest. Small groups of missionaries had considerable success in drawing semi-nomadic groups into settled agricultural communities, where they were converted to Catholicism and enjoyed the mixed benefits of Spanish civilization – as well as, most importantly, being protected from the ravages of the conquistadors. However, the regime of forced labour and the constant epidemics that swept the settlements meant that many groups later abandoned or rebelled against the mission regimes, and many missionary priests met violent deaths. Missionary efforts reached their apogee in the seventeenth and eighteenth centuries in the **Jesuit missions** of Moxos and Chiquitos, where a handful of priests established a utopian, semi-autonomous society, using a kind of theocratic socialism, where thousands of indigenous people successfully adopted European agricultural techniques and built flourishing mission communities graced by some of the finest churches in all the Americas.

1572	1574	1780–82
The last ruling Inca, Túpac Amaru, is executed by the Spanish.	The cities of Cochabamba and Tarija are founded.	The Great Rebellion against Spanish rule takes place and is eventually crushed.

THE HUMAN TOLL OF TOLEDO'S REFORMS

During the 1570s the wide-ranging reforms of **Viceroy Francisco Toledo**, the Spanish king's representative in Peru, had a dramatic impact on what is now Bolivia. The **encomiendas** were gradually phased out, and the indigenous population moved into large communities (**reducciones**), where tribute payments could be more easily collected. To address the labour shortages in the Potosí mines, Toledo revived the Inca system of labour service, the **mita**. Under this regime, an area stretching from Cusco to northern Argentina was divided into sixteen districts, each of which had to send one-seventh of its male population to the mines each year. Among Toledo's other reforms was the establishment of a royal mint to ensure the Crown received its share of mining revenues. These reforms launched a century-long boom that turned Potosí into one of the world's biggest cities and the single most important source of wealth in the Spanish empire. For the indigenous population, however, the *mita* labour system was a catastrophe. Of the thousands of **mitayos** who went to the mines each year only a few ever returned to their home communities: under colonial rule, up to nine million indigenous workers and African slaves are thought to have died in the mines.

---

orders comprised several different mestizo classes, while at the bottom was the indigenous majority.

The initial colonial settlement was undermined by the catastrophic decline in the indigenous population caused by **European epidemics** and diseases, as well as by the harsh burden of the *encomienda* system. With the indigenous tribute base falling each year and the supply of labour for the mines in decline, and fearing that the *encomenderos* were becoming over-powerful, in the 1570s the representative of the Spanish king in Peru, the Viceroy **Francisco Toledo**, launched a major reform of the empire's social and economic structures (see above).

The Great Rebellion

Indigenous resistance to Spanish rule continued throughout the colonial period. Generally, these revolts tended to be local in nature, rather than wide-scale rebellions, and were usually easily crushed. In 1780–82, however, the Andes were swept by a massive indigenous rebellion that shook the Spanish colonial regime to its foundations. This so-called **Great Rebellion** encompassed the southern Peruvian highlands and Alto Peru. It was in part provoked by the **Bourbon reforms**, a tightening of the tribute system aimed at centralizing administration and boosting royal revenues, which had declined substantially during a long period of economic depression (caused by a decline in silver production) in the late seventeenth and early eighteenth centuries.

The revival of the Inca kings

Above all, though, the rebellion was inspired by the Andean belief that a **reincarnated Inca king** would return to drive out the Spanish. The uprising's leading figure was José Gabriel Condorcanqui, an indigenous *kuraka* who in November 1780 declared himself the direct descendant of the last ruling Inca (Túpac Amaru, who had been executed in 1572) and rightful Inca king of Peru, adopting the name **Túpac Amaru II**. Raising a large indigenous army and slaughtering a Spanish force, he seized control of most of

1808	**1809**	**1810**
After Napoleon's invasion, the Spanish government collapses, an event that inspires independence movements across the Spanish empire.	Open revolt by the criollos and mestizos. La Paz declares independence. The Spanish thwart revolts but still lose control of several rural areas.	Buenos Aires rebels against Spain, and repeatedly sends army to fight Spanish in Alto Peru.

the southern Peruvian highlands and laid siege to Cusco for several months. Though Túpac Amaru himself was subsequently captured and killed, his nephews – all of whom also took the name Túpac Amaru – continued the rebellion around Lago Titicaca. Here, they formed an uneasy alliance with Aymara forces led by the radical Julian Apaza, who adopted the name **Túpac Katari**.

Though they joined forces to lay siege to La Paz, however, the two movements were fatally divided by ideology and **factionalism**. While the moderate Túpac Amarus sought to form a broad-based, rebel coalition – including mestizos and even white criollos – Túpac Katari and his followers were extreme Aymara nationalists intent on killing all whites and completely erasing Spanish rule. Several powerful indigenous **kurakas** rejected the revolutionary message altogether and sided against the rebels, leading large indigenous forces to fight on the Spanish side. The war was characterized throughout by great brutality on both sides: in two years, about one hundred thousand people were killed.

In October 1781, La Paz was relieved by a royalist army from Argentina. The Túpac Amaru leaders surrendered in return for pardons or exile, while Túpac Katari was captured and executed. By early 1782, the rebellion had been comprehensively crushed, and the indigenous nobility destroyed. Thus ended the last major **indigenous uprising** against Spanish rule in the Andes. The next great rebellion was led by white criollos rather than would-be Inca kings.

The Independence War

By the early nineteenth century, growing discontent with **Spanish rule** had spread amongst the white criollo and mestizo population of Alto Peru, the result of severe economic depression, their exclusion from high-level administrative jobs (which were reserved for Spanish-born immigrants), and regulations preventing trade with any country other than Spain. At the same time the powerful ideas of the French Revolution and the Enlightenment, as well as the successful revolt in North America, made independence from Spain seem more realistic. However, the traumatic experience of the **Great Rebellion** had left the white criollo and mestizo population with an abiding fear of disorder and indigenous revolt, so it wasn't until the sudden collapse of the government in Spain, following Napoleon's invasion in 1808, that the impetus for revolutionary change arrived.

With Napoleon's brother **Joseph** crowned king of Spain, a radical "Junta Central" claiming to rule on in the name of the abdicated Fernando VII, and others supporting the claim to the throne of Fernando's sister Carlota, the elite classes throughout the **Spanish empire** were confronted with conflicting loyalties. Surprisingly, it was in Alto Peru that the first moves towards open revolt against Spanish rule took place. On May 25, 1809, the judges of the **Audiencia de Charcas** refused to recognize the authority of the Junta Central, arguing the colonies owed loyalty to the person of the king (now abdicated) rather than to Spain. In July, the citizens of **La Paz** declared an independent government – the first declaration of independence by a Spanish colony in America. These revolts were put down, but this only fuelled the growing criollo enthusiasm for independence. Though Spain controlled the main cities, pro-independence guerrilla forces quickly established control of six rural areas that became known as **Republiquetas**.

1825	**1829**	**1830**
Bolivia becomes the final South American country to win independence. General Sucre is made first president.	After surviving an assassination attempt and a coup, Sucre leaves office and goes into voluntary exile. He is replaced by General Andrés de Santa Cruz.	Sucre is killed in Ecuador by unknown assailants.

Argentina attacks

In May 1810, the citizens of Buenos Aires successfully rebelled against Spain, and the same year sent an army to drive the Spanish from Alto Peru. Supported by the Republiquetas and revolts in several cities, the **Argentine army** liberated the whole region before being routed by a Spanish force from Cusco. Over the next seven years three further Argentine armies were sent to Alto Peru, but each failed to permanently drive out the Spanish forces. Most major cities changed hands and were sacked several times, with the retreating Argentine armies showing the same contempt for local citizens as the Spanish. The forces unleashed by the independence struggle proved difficult to control, as both sides came to rely more and more on arming the **indigenous population** to provide troops, which led to growing violence and social conflict.

Though it was the first South American region to declare independence from Spain, Alto Peru was the last to achieve it. In 1817 the Argentine **General José de San Martín** liberated Chile, and by 1821 the great Venezuelan independence leader **Simón Bolívar – El Libertador** – was advancing south through Ecuador having finally freed Venezuela and Colombia. The two forces converged on Peru: Lima was occupied and, in 1824, Bolívar's general, **General Antonio José de Sucre**, destroyed the last Spanish army at Ayacucho in the southern Peruvian Andes, securing Alto Peru's freedom early the following year.

Despite its new freedom, **Alto Peru**'s fate remained uncertain. Bolívar himself initially opposed the creation of an independent state there, and handed control of the region over to General Sucre. In 1825, Sucre called a constituent assembly in the city that would later be renamed in his honour. The delegates unanimously rejected union with either Peru or Argentina, and on August 6 adopted a **declaration of independence**. Five days later they resolved to name the new republic **Bolivia**, rightly guessing that Bolívar would be less likely to obstruct the independence of a country named in his own honour.

The early republic

The new Republic of Bolivia faced enormous problems from the outset. Sixteen years of **war** had devastated the country's infrastructure and economy: the mining industry in particular was in sharp decline, thanks to scarcity of labour and the damage to the mines that had taken place during the war. Nor did independence change much for the vast majority of the population – the indigenous Aymara and Quechua campesinos of the highlands – who remained excluded from power, which was exercised by a narrow ruling elite of mostly white **criollos**. Though the **mita** system had been abolished by Bolívar, a head tax levied on indigenous community members was maintained, generating over half of all government income.

The country's first president, **General Sucre**, sought to organize the Bolivian state along classic liberal lines, but his efforts to introduce a modern tax system were frustrated by the lack of a trained bureaucracy, and he struggled to attract foreign capital to revitalize the mining industry. His one major success was confiscating most of the **Catholic Church's wealth** and property, a revolutionary act from which it never really recovered. After surviving a coup and assassination attempt, he left office in 1829 and went into voluntary exile (only to be killed a year later in Ecuador).

1835	1855	1870
Moves to form a confederation with Peru are thwarted by Chile.	The country's first civilian president, José María Linares, is elected.	Silver mining starts to grow phenomenally, creating a wealthy new elite.

Sucre's liberal and reformist policies were maintained by his successor, **General Andrés de Santa Cruz**. During his ten-year rule Santa Cruz created a relatively stable political and economic order, systemizing local administration and introducing modern law codes. Though he ruled as a dictator he kept bloodshed to a minimum by contemporary standards, but was also unable to revitalize the economy. His downfall followed his involvement in politics in neighbouring Peru, where he had served briefly as president in 1826–27. In 1835 he intervened decisively in Peru's civil war, defeating arch rival Peruvian **General Agustín Gamarra**. He then sought to join Bolivia and Peru together in a confederation, a move seen as a threat by Chile, which sent forces to Peru. In 1839, Santa Cruz was finally defeated by Chile, and the Peru–Bolivia confederation was dissolved.

The rise of the *caudillos*
For the next forty years Bolivia was characterized by political chaos, presided over by a series of military strongmen (*caudillos*). **General José Ballivián** (1841–47) defeated **General Gamarra** at the battle of Ingavi, ending the entanglement of Peru and Bolivia's affairs. He also reduced the size of the army and established the department of the Beni, sending military colonies to the Amazon lowlands where Cinchona bark – from which quinine is extracted – emerged as a major export. **General Manuel Isidoro Belzu** (1848–55), who took power a year after Ballivián was overthrown, was a populist demagogue. After surviving over forty coup attempts in just seven years, he handed over power peacefully in 1855 in Bolivia's **first legal elections** (although only 13,000 people were allowed to vote) and went into exile.

Bolivia's first civilian president was **José María Linares** (1857–61), though even he assumed dictatorial powers. Linares opened the country to free trade and foreign investment, but was unable to control the military and was ousted within four years and replaced by **General José María Achá** (1861–64). Achá's regime was the most violent of Bolivia's nineteenth-century governments but even his notoriety was exceeded by that of his successor, **General Mariano Melgarejo** (1864–71), the archetypal Bolivian *caudillo*, famous for his violence, drunkenness, womanizing and corruption – as well as for signing away a vast area of the Amazon lowlands and Pacific coast to Brazil and Chile. Though his hold on power proved resilient, he was overthrown in 1871 and killed a year later in Lima.

Surprisingly, the endless succession of military coups, plots and revolts that characterized the early decades of the republic caused relatively little social and economic disruption. During the middle of the century, the nation's economy actually began to improve, thanks to the silver-mining industry's revival. From 1870 the growth of Bolivian **silver production** was phenomenal, and an influential new class of mine owners emerged.

The War of the Pacific and the age of silver
As well as silver exports, economic growth in the second half of the nineteenth century was also spurred by the export of **guano** and **nitrates** (both used as fertilizer) found on Bolivia's coastal strip. In 1878, President Hilarión Daza, the latest military *caudillo*, increased export taxes, ignoring protests by Chilean and British companies – who controlled the nitrates industry – and offering Chile the excuse to pursue its longstanding expansionist aims. Early the next year Chilean forces began the **War of the**

1879	Late 1800s	1899
Bolivia loses its entire coastline to Chile in the War of the Pacific.	As silver prices plunge, a tin boom begins. Powerful tin barons emerge.	La Paz becomes capital city following the Federal Revolution.

THE RUBBER BOOM

The late nineteenth century saw the explosion of the **rubber boom** in Bolivia's Amazon lowlands. The massive increase in the international demand for rubber transformed the remote rainforests of northern Bolivia into some of the most valuable real estate in the world, and the region was quickly overrun by **rubber barons**, who made immense fortunes and forced the region's previously unconquered tribes to work as virtual slaves. The **indigenous population** declined catastrophically and was saved from total destruction only by the end of the Bolivian rubber boom in the early twentieth century, after rubber plantations had been successfully established by the British and Dutch in their **Asian colonies**, where production costs were much lower. One consequence of the rubber boom was the occupation of the richest rubber-producing area along the **Río Acre** by Brazilian rubber-tappers. When the Bolivian government sought to tax their production they rebelled, declaring the Acre an independent state in 1900. After three years of sporadic fighting – the **Acre War** – the region was annexed by Brazil, an act later recognized by Bolivia in return for compensation.

Pacific, occupying the entire Bolivian coastline and then invading Peru, which was allied to Bolivia. Bolivian forces sent to fight alongside the Peruvians were easily defeated, and Bolivia watched helplessly as its coastline was annexed and its ally Peru defeated and occupied. Though Bolivia officially ceded the territory to Chile in 1904, the loss of the coast was seen as a **national tragedy**. Ever since, Bolivian politicians have invoked this loss as a means of cementing national identity.

Having witnessed an incompetent military regime stumble into a conflict that disrupted their exports and damaged relations with Chilean investors, Bolivia's new silver-mining elite realized that a stable, financially sound government was vital to their interests. The mining entrepreneurs formed a new party, the **Partido Conservador**, which ruled Bolivia for the next nineteen years. They were opposed by the **Partido Liberal**, initially formed by those against an early settlement with Chile, but otherwise differing little in ideology. Between 1880 and 1936, the parliamentary system worked fairly well, despite the limited nature of the electorate (a tiny handful of men) and the fact that neither party was ever prepared to relinquish the presidency when voted out of office, ensuring that limited violence remained a feature of Bolivian political life.

The high point of conservative rule came during the presidency of **Aniceto Arce** (1888–92), a major silver-mine owner who completed the railway from La Paz to the Chilean port of Antofagasta, Bolivia's first rail link to the sea and a vital route for mining exports. The expansion of the mining industry and transport infrastructure had a strong impact on rural Bolivia. The growing demand for food in the mining centres of Potosí and Oruro stimulated the expansion of the **hacienda system**, with hacienda-owners acquiring indigenous land through purchase, fraud or outright force. Though some communities maintained their traditional social and political structure, many others broke down, and migration to the cities and mining centres increased.

The Federal Revolution and the rise of tin

Its dependence on mining exports made Bolivia increasingly subject to international economic forces, and towards the end of the nineteenth century the international price

1904	1922	1929
Bolivia officially cedes the coastline it lost during the War of the Pacific to Chile.	Trade unions launch a general strike as workers – especially miners – demand better conditions.	Tin production peaks, and then collapses as Bolivia's economy is hit by the Great Recession.

of silver collapsed, breaking the power of the silver-mining oligarchy. Fortunately for Bolivia, this collapse coincided with a growing global demand for **tin**, a formerly unimportant by-product of the country's silver mines. A tin boom ensued, centred on the Oruro mines and led by a new class of Bolivian entrepreneurs who replaced the traditional silver-mining barons.

The new tin-mining elite and the growing urban professional classes of La Paz (the main service centre for the tin mines) increasingly backed the **Partido Liberal**. Frustrated by the impossibility of taking power through peaceful means – election results were always rigged – they moved to overthrow the conservative regime. In 1898 a revolt broke out after the conservative government in Sucre rejected the demands of liberals in La Paz for local federalist rule, while a major Aymara uprising erupted simultaneously in the Altiplano. Breaking the traditional rules of elite politics, the liberal leader **José Manuel Pando** sought an alliance with the Aymara rebel leader **Pablo Zárate Willka**, promising to protect indigenous lands in exchange for support against the conservatives. With the help of thousands of Aymara, Pando defeated the conservatives in bloody fighting in 1899 and took power in what became known as the **Federal Revolution**. No sooner was this achieved, however, than Pando reneged on his promises and turned against his Aymara allies, crushing the uprising and executing or imprisoning its leaders. Nor did Pando's federalism last: once in power, the liberals simply made La Paz the seat of an equally centralized government (though Sucre remained the capital in name).

The Federal Revolution ensured the political supremacy of the new tin-mining elite, but rather than govern themselves they chose to rule indirectly through a class of professional politicians, a system that became known as **La Rosca** – "The Screw". Their dominance was such that, between 1899 and 1920, there was not a single coup attempt. In other respects, however, politics remained much the same: voting was restricted to a small elite, with the indigenous majority completely excluded; a liberal economic policy with low taxes was maintained for the benefit of the tin-mining entrepreneurs and major landowners; and the assault on indigenous landholdings continued.

Perhaps surprisingly, given that there were no restrictions on foreign investment in the mines, tin mining in the Altiplano during the late 1800s and early 1900s came to be dominated by home-grown capitalists, above all by three tin barons – **Simón I. Patiño**, **Mauricio Hochschild** and **Carlos Aramayo** – who between them owned most of Bolivia's mines. But when world demand for tin slumped in 1913–14, opposition within the Partido Liberal grew, leading to the formation of a splinter **Partido Republicano**. In 1920 the Republicans, led by **Daniel Salamanca** and **Bautista Saavedra**, seized power. Their new government quickly found itself under pressure, however: a major Aymara uprising erupted on the Altiplano, while the mostly indigenous miners had begun to organize trade unions to push for better conditions. The first **general strike** was staged in 1922, and a year later the army carried out the first of many massacres of striking miners at the Uncía mine near Oruro.

As the 1920s progressed, the increasingly factional Republicans faced economic decline and growing social unrest. The international price of tin fell, and the government found it difficult to make payments on its huge foreign loans. Tin production peaked in 1929, and then plummeted as the **Great Depression** struck Bolivia's economy with a vengeance. Massive job losses further fuelled labour unrest, while strikes and military intervention at the mines became ever more frequent.

1932–35	1935–1951	1952
Bolivia fights the disastrous Chaco War and loses to Paraguay, at the cost of some 65,000 soldiers.	New political parties – including the radical MNR – and a powerful mining union emerge.	The National Revolution ushers the MNR into power. A massive social and economic reform programme follows.

The Chaco War

By 1931 the government, led by Daniel Salamanca, was confronted by widespread opposition and deepening **economic crisis**; it responded by stepping up its oppression of trade unions and the opposition and increasing its military spending. At the same time, the Bolivian army began aggressively probing the disputed frontier with Paraguay in the Chaco: by July 1932, the **Chaco War** had broken out. Though many Bolivians afterwards came to believe the conflict had been provoked by foreign oil companies anxious to exploit deposits in the Chaco (they later turned out not to exist), in fact it's now clear Salamanca himself deliberately started the war, perhaps thinking that a quick victory would improve his political standing.

Over the next two years the Bolivian army was smashed and driven out of all the disputed territory with terrible loss of life. Late in 1934 the army forced Salamanca to resign; early the next year **Major Germán Busch** ended the Paraguayan advance, and both sides sued for peace. Some 65,000 Bolivian soldiers had died out of a population of around two million. Known as the "**Chaco Generation**", many Bolivians emerged from the war deeply critical of the traditional political system. The country became increasingly open to radical left-wing ideas, and the old political parties faded in importance.

These ideas also affected the army. In 1936 a group of young officers led by David Toro and Germán Busch, seized power, establishing a radical "**military socialist**" regime influenced by European fascism. In an unprecedented step, the next year the government nationalized without compensation the holdings of **US Standard Oil**, which had illegally sold Bolivian oil to Paraguay during the war while claiming it couldn't produce enough for Bolivia. In alliance with a range of left-wing parties, the military regime drew up a new constitution, but its radical initiatives ended in 1939 when Busch committed suicide. A more conservative military regime close to the tin barons followed, but the growth of radical ideas in the postwar period meant that any return to the prewar consensus was increasingly impossible.

The road to revolution

The most important of the many new political parties that emerged in the period following the Chaco War was the **Movimiento Nacionalista Revolucionario** (MNR), which had a pro-Nazi stance and advocated nationalization of the mines. Together with several left-wing groups, it quickly came to dominate the national congress. Meanwhile, the union movement was also growing more extreme, and began to stage frequent strikes – many of which were brutally put down.

In 1943, in alliance with a cabal of radical army officers, the MNR seized power. The new regime, with **Major Gualberto Villaroel** as president, supported the labour movement and sought to involve the indigenous masses in national politics. In 1944 mineworkers formed the **Federación Sindical de Trabajadores Mineros de Bolivia** (FSTMB; Federated Union of Mineworkers of Bolivia), which took over leadership of the labour movement and gave important support to the MNR – over the following decades it proved one of the most powerful political forces in the country. In 1945 the government sponsored the first **National Indigenous Congress** and banned the hated labour service obligation required of indigenous communities on hacienda lands (though this decree was never enforced). These populist measures, however,

1964	1967	1974
A coup ends civilian rule and results in successive repressive military governments.	Che Guevara is killed by US-trained Bolivian soldiers in La Higuera.	The army slaughters protesting peasants in the Cochabamba Valley, an event that becomes known as the "Massacre del Valle".

were accompanied by the vicious suppression of any opposition – when the Marxist **Partido de la Izquierda Revolucionaria** did well in elections in 1944, the government assassinated its leaders; the same happened to the traditional parties in 1945. The use of violence against politicians outraged public opinion, and in 1946 Villaroel was hanged by a civilian mob, while the army stood by.

For the next six years Bolivia was ruled by an **alliance** of the traditional parties, which struggled to cope with growing popular unrest and an economic downturn. During this period the MNR re-created itself as a radical populist party linked to the labour movement. In 1949, it launched a major civilian revolt; though crushed by the army, this revolt moved the MNR closer to the FSTMB, which had adopted communism and turned the mines into bastions of radical activism. Though its leaders remained in exile, in 1951 the MNR won the general elections outright, only for the army to intervene, making the party believe that a **popular armed uprising** was the only way it would return to power.

The National Revolution

The uprising that the MNR had been hoping for – the **National Revolution** – began in La Paz on April 9, 1952. MNR activists distributed arms to civilians, and miners marched on the city and stopped army reinforcements from reaching it. After three days of fighting in which over six hundred people died, the army surrendered, and the MNR's leader, **Víctor Paz Estenssoro**, took power. However, by arming the general population and involving the workers, the MNR effectively found itself committed to a massive social change far beyond its original programme. The first step was the introduction of **universal suffrage**, giving the indigenous majority the right to vote for the first time. This was followed by a drastic reduction in the size of the army. In addition, the government supported the organization of a powerful national workers' confederation, the **Central Obrera Boliviana** (COB), which was controlled by the influential miners' union. The COB, which represented the MNR's most important support base, immediately pressed for further revolutionary measures. In October, the government nationalized the holdings of the three big mining companies of Patiño, Aramayo and Hochschild, bringing two-thirds of the tin-mining industry under state control. The mines were managed by a new state mining company, **COMIBOL**, which, like the mines, was to be partly administered by the workers themselves. Despite these measures, the MNR was wary of offending the US by appearing communist, and so promised compensation to the tin barons and left medium-sized mines in private hands.

In the countryside, events quickly spiralled out of the new government's control. With no army or police to restrain them, the indigenous Aymara and Quechua campesinos began violently taking over haciendas. Though it had never been part of their policy, the MNR was forced to issue a radical **Reforma Agraria** (agrarian reform), under which hacienda lands were given back to indigenous peasants to be managed collectively through community organizations – the resulting indigenous federations emerged as a powerful force, and have played a major role in national politics ever since.

With the support of the newly enfranchised peasants and workers, the MNR easily won subsequent elections in 1956, with **Hernán Siles** taking over as president from **Paz Estenssoro**. But with the economy in crisis, the MNR leadership shied away from

1983	**1985**	**Mid-1980s**
Hernan Siles elected as president, marking a return to civilian rule.	The New Economic Plan, a series of neo-liberal shock policies, is introduced.	Cocaine trade helps to ease Bolivia out of recession, as well as creating massive corruption.

further revolutionary measures and turned to the US for financial aid; this was given, in return demanding open access for US oil corporations, an end to workers' control of the mines, a wage freeze, and limits on government expenditure and action.

These harsh measures stabilized the economy to a degree and helped attract foreign investment, while **US loans** were used to build an extensive road system, invest in health and education and drive development in the Santa Cruz region – all key aims of moderates within the MNR. Despite this, a bitter factional rift opened within the party, with Siles and the trade unions eventually driven into opposition. To counterbalance this, Paz Estenssoro began rebuilding and rearming the army in an attempt to shift the balance of military power away from the workers' militias. This quickly proved a terrible mistake. In 1964, Paz Estenssoro was elected for a third term with an army officer, **General René Barrientos**, as vice-president. Within a month, a military junta led by Barrientos had turned on Paz Estenssoro and ousted him from power.

Military rule

At first it was thought that the **coup** would be only a temporary break from civilian rule, but instead the army remained in government for the next eighteen years. Barrientos immediately moved against the left: the leaders of workers' organizations were sent into exile, wages were slashed and thousands of miners sacked; the army also occupied the mining camps to crush strike action, resulting in a major massacre at the Siglo XX-Catavi mine in 1967. A charismatic orator and fluent Quechua-speaker, Barrientos simultaneously maintained the support of the **peasant federations** (who, having secured their rights to land, had become relatively conservative) by promising not to reverse the Agrarian Reform in return for their continuing loyalty. This relationship underlay the failure of Argentine revolutionary **Che Guevara**'s attempt to launch a continent-wide guerrilla war in Bolivia, which was crushed in 1967 without gaining a single peasant recruit.

Barrientos remained in control until his death in a helicopter crash three years later. After a brief civilian interregnum he was replaced by **General Alfredo Ovando**, who was ousted just over a year later by **General Juan José Torres**. Torres sought to move military government to the left, but was ousted within a year by right-wing army colleagues backed by the US. This brought to power **Colonel Hugo Banzer**, whose regime lasted for the next seven years. Initially, Banzer ruled in coalition with the conservative Falange Socialista Boliviana and the rump of the MNR led by Paz Estenssoro, before seizing absolute power, after which he banned all political parties and established an entirely military regime. In this he was clearly influenced by similar events in neighbouring Chile and Brazil. Banzer employed ruthless violence to enforce his rule, including torture, mass detention without trial and the murder of hundreds of political opponents.

Banzer and the boom times

Banzer's regime coincided with unprecedented economic growth, fuelled by a long-term rise in mining production and mineral prices. Foreign investment poured into the privately owned mining sector and also into the **Santa Cruz region**, where vast areas of land remained concentrated in private hands. The region's subsequent

1993	1997	2000
Government starts broad wave of privatization of key industries, including oil and gas.	Coca eradication programme provokes resistance from campesino movements led by Evo Morales.	The sale of Cochabamba's water company into foreign ownership provokes a spontaneous non-violent popular uprising, the Guerra del Agua ("the Water War").

agricultural boom, plus the exploitation of local oil and gas deposits, produced massive economic growth in the Eastern Lowlands, transforming Santa Cruz itself into the country's second-biggest city.

Despite the economic success and the regime's brutality, Banzer was unable to prevent opposition to his rule. Although he maintained land grants under the Agrarian Reform, Banzer alienated the peasant federations by ignoring their demands for price controls, credit and government assistance. In 1974 the army machine-gunned protesting peasants in the Cochabamba Valley, an event that became known as the **Massacre del Valle**. Meanwhile the labour movement regained its strength and launched a series of strikes. Even Banzer's traditional middle-class nationalist support was eroded by his failure to negotiate a Bolivian outlet to the sea with his Chilean counterpart General Pinochet. Under pressure from the US, Banzer promised to hold democratic elections, but popular discontent with his regime was by now boiling over, and in 1977, amid widening protests and strikes, Banzer prepared to step down.

Coups and corruption

The next four years saw dramatic political turmoil. In 1978 elections were held then annulled after massive fraud by Banzer's chosen successor, **General Juan Pereda**, who was set to lose to a left–centre alliance led by Hernán Siles. Pereda seized power, but was then overthrown by younger officers who promised fresh elections with no military candidate. Two elections, two brief presidencies (including that of **Lidia Gueiler**, the first woman president) and a further bloody coup followed, as new political groupings formed and attempted to gain electoral majorities. Finally, in elections in 1980, the centre-left coalition led by Hernán Siles emerged victorious.

Before Siles could take office, however, hardline officers launched yet another military coup, bringing to power **General Luis Garcia Meza**. Backed by a fearsome conspiracy involving the Argentine military, the Italian fascist lodge P-2, drug barons and Nazi war criminals (including Klaus Barbie, the "Butcher of Lyon"), Garcia Meza presided over the most brutal and **corrupt** military regime in modern Bolivian history, enforced by paramilitary death squads and funded by his government's direct involvement in the emerging international cocaine trade. But, despite its repressive measures, the extent of popular hatred against the military government, together with growing economic chaos and international disapproval, was such that it could not survive long.

The return to democracy

Garcia Meza was deposed in an army revolt in 1981 and two years later the last military junta was forced to resign following massive protests. The recalled congress elected **Hernán Siles** as president, marking a return to **democratic rule** that has lasted ever since. Siles, however, was unable to control the economy, which had entered a sharp decline after years of mismanagement. With **hyperinflation** rampant, he stepped down in 1985. The largest share of the vote in the subsequent election was won by **Hugo Banzer**, standing as head of a new right-wing party, the ADN (Alianza Democratica Nacional). This wasn't enough to secure him the presidency, however: instead, 77-year-old **Víctor Paz Estenssoro**, the central figure of the National Revolution 33 years before, was elected for his fourth presidential term.

2002	2003	2005	2008
Evo Morales is narrowly defeated in the presidential elections by Gonzalo Sánchez de Lozada.	The country is paralyzed by public protests, forcing de Lozada to flee the country.	Morales is elected as South America's first indigenous president.	After winning two referendums, Morales continues his radical programme designed to benefit the indigenous majority.

THE COCAINE ECONOMY

Starting in the 1970s in response to rising demand for **cocaine** in the US, highland migrants in the Yungas and in the Chapare had begun growing **coca**, which was then processed in secret laboratories in the Beni and flown to Colombia and on to the US. By the 1980s, coca was a boom industry, generating good incomes for the peasant growers (whose numbers were swelled by thousands of laid-off miners after 1985) and huge fortunes for the traffickers. Much of the money made was reinvested in legitimate businesses in **Santa Cruz**, fuelling economic growth in the Eastern Lowlands – at the peak of the boom, cocaine exports were estimated to exceed all Bolivia's legal exports combined, and at one stage the leading Bolivian cocaine baron, **Roberto Suárez**, even offered to pay off the entire national debt in return for immunity from prosecution.

To great surprise, Paz Estenssoro turned his back on the traditional MNR approach and adopted the **New Economic Plan** – a raft of orthodox liberal shock policies designed to combat hyperinflation. The currency was devalued, price and wage controls scrapped, and government expenditure slashed, while steps were taken to dismantle the state mining corporation **COMIBOL**. Strikes and protests by the miners' union followed, until in 1985 the international price of tin crashed completely and the state-run industry effectively collapsed. The government sacked most of the miners and the power of their union was broken irrevocably.

The New Economic Policy was maintained by subsequent governments. Although it succeeded in ending hyperinflation, its immediate effect was to plunge Bolivia into a recession that was eased only by a growing trade in the production and export of **cocaine**. The huge wealth generated by the cocaine industry created enormous corruption at every level of Bolivian society, with all the major political parties forging links with drug traffickers.

Elections in 1989 saw the MNR win a majority of votes, but horse trading in the congress led to the third-placed candidate, MIR leader **Jaime Paz Zamora**, becoming president with the backing of the ADN. Dubbed the Patriotic Accord, this cynical alliance between two former enemies shocked many Bolivians, although it also highlighted the growing consensus between the main parties. In 1993 the MNR returned to power under **Gonzalo Sánchez de Lozada**, known popularly as Goni. He oversaw a programme of privatization, which saw oil, gas, mining, railways and utilities sold to foreign companies – a direct reversal of the MNR's revolution in the 1950s. Goni was followed as president in 1997 by **Hugo Banzer** – the former military dictator returning to power through electoral means – who pursued the same neo-liberal agenda. But while the leaders of Bolivia's main political parties were agreed on the direction of the country's development, new political forces were increasingly making themselves heard.

A New Revolution

Under pressure from the US, Banzer made the **eradication of coca production** a key policy – a particular irony given the known links of most of his government to drug traffickers. However, sending the army in to destroy coca crops in the Chapare provoked massive resistance from well-organized campesino syndicates, led by the radical indigenous activist **Evo Morales**. Meanwhile, on the Altiplano, a new generation

2009	**2010**	**2011**
Morales is re-elected for a second term as president.	Four major electricity companies are nationalized, giving the government control over eighty percent of Bolivia's power generation capacity.	Bolivia renounces a UN anti-drug convention because it classifies the coca leaf as an illegal drug.

of radical leaders was using the powerful national peasants union, the **CSUTCB**, to press for the complete transformation of Bolivian society to meet the needs of the indigenous majority. And in Cochabamba in 2000, the sale of the city water company into foreign ownership provoked a spontaneous non-violent popular uprising that became known as the **Guerra del Agua** – "the Water War".

Banzer responded to this rising tide of popular discontent by sending in the troops to clear the roads and crush the protests. Unrest continued to escalate when Goni returned as president in 2002, after a narrow election victory over Evo Morales. Peasants, miners and civic groups united around the demand for the re-nationalization of Bolivia's massive **natural gas** reserves, by now the mainstay of the economy. The widespread belief was that, as with silver and tin, Bolivia's richest natural resource was being exported unrefined with little benefit to the majority population. Tumultuous protests paralyzed the country, with the people of El Alto playing a key role in cutting off La Paz. After armed forces failed to quell the unrest, Goni fled into exile in 2003, leaving his vice-president, **Carlos Mesa**, to manage the crisis. Mesa held a referendum on the gas issue but refused to implement full nationalization and was himself forced to resign after mass demonstrations in 2005.

Bolivia's first indigenous president

In the 2005 elections Bolivia's indigenous population finally asserted its political weight at the polls. **Evo Morales** – head of the coca growers' union and leader of the Movement towards Socialism (MAS) – was elected president with an absolute majority, becoming the first indigenous head of state since the Spanish conquest five centuries before. Brought up in a humble adobe house by Aymara parents in Oruro province, Morales had worked as a llama herder and migrant sugar-cane cutter before moving to farm coca in the Chapare, where his career as a peasant activist began. As president, he immediately pursued what he called a **revolutionary agenda**, inspired both by traditional socialist ideals and indigenous dreams of a return to a more egalitarian society that existed before the Spanish conquest. The gas industry was nationalized, with troops occupying the foreign-owned wells, and a massive programme of agrarian reform was launched to redistribute land. **Indigenous languages** were taught at schools, and made obligatory for anyone working in the civil service. A new assembly was elected to rewrite Bolivia's constitution to reflect the needs and aspirations of the indigenous majority. Determined to end the influence of what he saw as US imperialism, Morales instead cultivated links with Fidel Castro in Cuba and the radical Venezuelan president, Hugo Chavez. But despite the excitement created by his election, Evo – as everyone calls him – still faced huge challenges in governing Bolivia. The powerful business elite in Santa Cruz bitterly opposed his **nationalization programme**, threatening to secede and using his own tactics of street protest and road blockades.

Despite this he retained widespread support among indigenous and working class Bolivians. In 2008 he won two **referendums** – one over whether he should stay in power, another over constitutional reform – and the following year was re-elected as president (with 64 percent of the vote). He later nationalized energy-generating firms and extended the state pension to millions of poor Bolivians, though was forced to back down when he attempted to end government fuel subsidies. Although his election marked a new dawn for Bolivia, old problems of poverty, underdevelopment and ungovernability are still to be resolved. Protests, demonstrations and blockades are likely to remain a regular occurrence for some time to come. However, Bolivia now appears a little more stable than in the past.

In recent years **coca** – and the crop's link to the international drug trade – has also remained a contentious issue. The Morales government scrapped legislation in 2010 that would have aimed to cut cocaine production after protests from coca growers. Then in July 2011 Bolivia renounced a UN anti-drug convention because it classified coca as an illegal drug, a decision criticised by the US and several other countries.

Wildlife and ecology

From the high peaks of the Andes to the tropical rainforests of the Amazon, the Pantanal wetlands and the arid scrub of the Gran Chaco, Bolivia's extraordinary range of geography and climates supports an astonishing array of plant and animal life. This is one of the most biodiverse countries on earth, home to more than 17,000 known plant species, around 1400 different birds, including many species found nowhere else, and around three hundred species of mammals. Moreover, large areas are still relatively undisturbed by human activity, and around twenty percent of the total land area is now covered by national parks and other protected areas.

The Andes

The Bolivian Andes are home to a huge range of ecological zones, from cactus-strewn semi-desert to swampy moorland and lush cloudforest. Much of the region has been settled for over two thousand years, and the original woodland has largely been replaced by eucalyptus imported from Australia. But patches of native Andean forest remain, including **qeñua (polylepis) woods** that survive at over 5000m – the highest forests in the world. The most visible animals in the Andes are domesticated, in particular the herds of **llama** and **alpaca** which graze the arid grasslands of the Altiplano, but in more remote regions their wild relative, the diminutive **vicuña**, can also be seen.

Large predators are rare, but the **puma** is still present at most altitudes. Its preferred prey includes Andean deer and **viscacha**, a rabbit-like animal. The more humid eastern slopes of the Andes are also home to the elusive **spectacled bear**, the only bear in South America. Though difficult to view close up, the revered **Andean condor** – with a 3m wingspan, the largest bird that can fly – can often be seen soaring at high altitudes (at the opposite end of the scale, there are 83 species of **hummingbird** in Bolivia). The margins of Lago Titicaca and other high-altitude lakes and marshes attract a great variety of swimming and wading birds, including ibis, grebes, geese, herons and – particularly in the far south of the Altiplano – three different species of **flamingo**, the Andean, the Chilean and the James's.

The Amazon

The greatest biodiversity in Bolivia – and indeed pretty much anywhere on earth – is found on the well-watered eastern slopes of the Andes, where the mountains plunge down into the Amazon basin through a succession of different ecological zones, from the high **cloudforest** or *ceja de selva* – whose gnarled trees are festooned with hundreds of different kinds of **orchid** – to the lowland tropical rainforest. With mighty trees soaring to create a canopy over 30m above the ground, the rich and luxuriant vegetation of the **Amazon rainforest** is in fact extremely fragile. The soils beneath forest are generally very poor, and the forest ecosystem flourishes only through a complex system of nutrient cycling involving plants, insects and fungi, so if the forest is cleared, the quality of the land disappears rapidly.

The rainforest ecosystem supports an incredible variety of plant and animal life: over six thousand species of plant have been recorded in one small tract of forest, and the Amazon's unidentified species of insect alone are thought to outnumber all earth's known animal species. Seeing wildlife in the Amazon is not easy, nevertheless on any rainforest trip you're likely to see innumerable **birds** including brightly coloured toucans, parrots, tanagers, kingfishers, trogons and macaws of various kinds. Several of Bolivia's more than thirty **monkey** species are also easy to spot, including long-limbed spider monkeys, howler monkeys, chattering squirrel monkeys and diminutive tamarinds and titis. Larger mammals include the **capybara**, the world's largest **rodent**, the tapir, a lumbering beast the size of a cow with an elephant-like nose, herds of **peccary**, a kind of wild boar, as well as **giant armadillos** and **sloths**. All of these are potential prey for a range of wild cats, the largest of which is the **jaguar**. The rivers of the Bolivian Amazon teem with fish, from giant catfish to the **piranha**. You'll also see **turtles** and **cayman crocodiles** of various kinds, as well as **giant anacondas** and **pink freshwater dolphins**.

Many of the larger animals are easier to see as you head east through the Bolivian Amazon, where the dense rainforest gives way to the more open vegetation of the **Llanos de Moxos**, where seasonally flooded grasslands are interspersed with islands of forest and patches of swamp. Here, you're more likely to spot creatures such as **giant anteaters** and **rheas** (large flightless birds similar to ostriches), or even **maned wolves**.

The Eastern Lowlands

To the south of the Bolivian Amazon the forest ecology gradually changes as it adapts to lower and more seasonally varied rainfall. The **Chiquitania** region east of Santa Cruz has some of the world's largest remaining tracts of **tropical dry forest**, which is home to many of the same animal species, plus a great variety of bird life. Heading further south, this forest gets drier still as it merges into the Gran Chaco. This vast, arid wilderness also supports abundant wildlife, including **jaguar**, **puma**, **deer**, at least ten different kinds of **armadillo**, and even an endemic species of wild boar, the **Chacoan peccary**.

The contrast between the Chaco and the far east of Bolivia could not be greater. Here, the plains and rainforests of Amazonia gradually give way to the immense watery wilderness of the **Pantanal**, the world's largest wetland ecosystem, which stretches far across the border with Brazil and is home to many Amazonian species. Though it does not match the overall biodiversity of the rainforest, the Pantanal is unique in terms of the sheer abundance of wildlife. Concentrations of fauna here are thought to be the highest in all the Americas, comparable to the densest wild animal populations in Africa – one estimate puts the number of **caymans** in the region at ten million. It's also one of the best places to see **jaguars** and the highly endangered **giant river otter**. Bird life too is extraordinarily abundant, including innumerable water birds such as **roseate spoonbills**, **herons**, **egrets** and the massive **jaburu stork**, the symbol of the Pantanal, and at least fifteen species of parrot, including the highly endangered **hyacinth macaw**.

Music and dance

Bolivia's music is vibrant and varied. Much of it has a similar flavour to that of neighbouring Andean countries, evidence of the continuity of musical traditions amongst the indigenous peoples of the Andes, and there's a wealth of popular music connected either with the various festivals that dot the year, or to key events in the agricultural calendar. Inevitably, much of this music is inextricably involved with dance: if you're lucky you might see the unforgettable sight of a full squad of young women *comparsas* swirling their *pollera* skirts, with *manta* shawls tied around their shoulders and bowler hats on their heads.

Andean instruments and traditions

The persistence of Bolivia's **agricultural traditions** means that musical life in most rural areas has enjoyed enormous continuity, and traditional music, bearing a direct relationship to that played in pre-Inca times, still thrives today at every kind of **celebration** and **ritual**. Because all the country's musical traditions are oral and bound to local events, music varies from one village to another – all over the Andes, villages have different ways of making and tuning instruments and composing tunes.

Many of Bolivia's distinctive **musical instruments** date back to pre-Hispanic times. Perhaps the most haunting and memorable are the breathy-sounding handmade sets of bamboo panpipes and quena flutes that are played across the Altiplano. In addition, other pre-conquest Andean instruments – conch shell trumpets, shakers (using nuts for rattles), ocarinas, wind instruments and drums – are still used by groups all over the country.

Panpipes and quenas

Panpipes (*siku* in Aymara, *antara* in Quechua, and *zampoña* in Spanish) are ancient instruments. While modern panpipes – played in the city or in groups with other instruments – may offer a complete scale, allowing solo performance, traditional models are played in pairs, as described by sixteenth-century Spanish chroniclers. The pipes share the melody, each playing alternate notes of the scale, so that two or more players are needed to pick out a single tune using a **hocket technique**. Usually one player leads and the other follows. Symbolically this demonstrates reciprocity and exchange within the community; in practice it enables players to play for a long time without getting too dizzy from over-breathing.

Played by blowing (or breathing out hard) across the top of a tube, panpipes come in various sizes. Several tubes made of **bamboo reed** of different lengths are bound together to produce a sound that can be jaunty, but also has a melancholic edge depending on tune and playing style. Many tunes have a minor, descending shape to them, and panpipe players traditionally favour dense overlapping textures and **syncopated rhythms**. Playing is often described as "breathy", as overblowing to produce harmonics is popular (modern city-based groups often evoke this breathiness using special microphone techniques).

Simple **notched-end flutes**, or **quenas** (which do not have a proper mouthpiece to blow through, just a cut in the open bamboo end), are another characteristic Andean instrument found in both rural and urban areas. The most important pre-Hispanic instrument, quenas were traditionally made of fragile bamboo and played in the dry season, with **tarkas** (stocky vertical flutes, like a shrill recorder made from the wood of a taco tree) taking over in the wet season. Another small Andean flute with a span of three octaves is called the **pinquillo**, also made of bamboo. The **moseño** is a long thin bamboo flute probably modelled on the European transverse flute and played from the side.

Charangos

The **charango** is another characteristic Andean instrument. This small, indigenous variant of the lute or mandolin was created in Bolivia in imitation of early string instruments brought by the Spanish colonizers, which indigenous musicians were taught to play in the churches. Its characteristically zingy sound was the result of the natural Andean preference for high pitches, and because its size was restricted by the fact that it was traditionally made from the shell of an **armadillo** (although modern charangos are now generally made of wood). There are many varieties of charango: from flat-backed instruments with strident metal strings to larger instruments with round backs that are capable of deeper and richer sounds. The charango usually has five pairs of strings, though tunings vary from place to place and from musician to musician. The charango may have acquired its name from the Quechua word *ch'ajranku*, from the verb *ch'ajray*, meaning to scratch, since in early colonial times indigenous Bolivians used to refer to the way Spanish musicians played their plucked instruments as *sumaj ch'ajranku*, meaning "rich scratch".

The charango is used to play a host of different types of music and dances. In many rural areas different instruments are played in different seasons: the charango is usually played during the **winter** months of June and July, when its shrill sound is thought to attract the frosts essential for freezing potatoes to make *chuño*; those in small towns and urban areas often play it all year round. In some areas, different tunings and melodies are used for different seasons.

Fiestas

Major fiestas and other significant social events call for musical performance on a more extended scale, including large **marching bands** of brass instruments, drums or panpipes. The drums are deep-sounding, double-headed instruments known as *bombos* or *wankaras*, originally made out of the hollowed-out trunk of a tree with the skins of a llama or goat. These marching bands exist for parades at fiestas, weddings and dances in the Altiplano and around Lago Titicaca. It is perfectly normal for a whole village to come together to play as an orchestra for important events and fiestas – music is an integral part of all communal celebrations and symbolically represents the sharing and interdependence of Andean rural life.

CHARANGOS, COURTSHIP AND MERMAIDS

In rural areas, particularly around Lago Titicaca, the charango is used by young, **single men** to woo the female of their choice. They are helped, at least according to local beliefs, by **mermaids** (*las sirenas*). The ethnomusicologist Tom Turino records that most towns and villages around Titicaca claim that a mermaid lives in a nearby spring, river, lake or waterfall, and notes that new charangos are often left overnight in such places to be tuned and played overnight by the mermaid. Some villagers even construct the **sound box** in the shape of a mermaid to invest their charango with supernatural power.

When young men go courting at the weekly markets in larger villages they not only dress in their finest clothes, but also decorate their charangos in elaborate **coloured ribbons** – these represent the number of women their charango has supposedly conquered. At times a group of young people will get together for the ancient **circle dance** called the *Punchay kashwa* where the men form a half circle playing their charangos, facing a half circle of young women. Both groups dance and sing in bantering fashion, participants using a set syllabic and rhyming pattern so that they can quickly improvise.

Andean fusion music

The political events of the 1950s and 1960s are crucial to an understanding of recent Bolivian folk music and the development of Andean fusion music. The **1952 Revolution** led to a period of social and economic reform that accorded more rights to Bolivia's indigenous inhabitants; such reforms conferred new respect on Andean traditions, and were enthusiastically supported by many Latin American intellectuals. At the same time, rural people migrated to urban areas, bringing their languages and traditions with them. The new Bolivian administration created a folklore division in the **Ministry of Education**, one of whose functions was the organization and sponsorship of traditional music festivals. Radio stations started to broadcast in **Aymara** and **Quechua** and play the music of these communities.

Los Jairas

Around 1965, an influential new form of Andean music emerged with **Los Jairas**, founded by Edgar "Yayo" Jofré. Jofré established the group to play at the Peña Naira in La Paz – one of a string of new urban venues where people could hear what became known as *música folklorica*. The idea was to form a **quartet** of charango, guitar, quena and *bombo*, instruments that had never been played together before. The quartet arranged the music to show off each of the instruments both individually and together, adapting Aymara and Quechua tunes and restructuring Andean melodies to suit an urban and European aesthetic. In addition, the group's quena player, the Swiss–French flautist **Gilbert Favre**, brought to his playing approaches learnt for the European flute, including the use of vibrato, dynamics and swooping glissandi, all of which were completely novel to the traditional Amerindian aesthetics. It was this style that became standard for urban folk music groups.

Numerous groups have followed the Los Jairas model. While some continue to deliver inspired arrangements of traditional tunes, others play **foreign music** on traditional instruments. There are also those who use both instruments and music as the basis for new compositions. As a result, the same tune can appear in different guises under different titles in various styles.

Los K'jarkas

Los K'jarkas, from Cochabamba, are one of the country's most influential and successful groups. In common with other Bolivian bands they retain a strong sense of national identity: the name "K'jarkas" refers to a pre-Spanish fortress, while the group's **logo** – a stylized anthropomorphic condor and carving from the archeological site of Tiwanaku – appeals to a pre-Columbian past and millenary culture at the heart of the Andes. Astute composition and arrangements, which take into account the multiple audiences within Bolivia itself, earned Los K'jarkas an enormous following in the late 1960s, which has carried through to the present day.

K'jarkas songs are largely sentimental, conjuring up a bucolic, rural vision of beautiful maidens, alongside evocations of **Pachamama** (Mother Earth). Where they score at home is in large part due to their incorporation of traditional urban dance forms. They mainly use the **huayño** dance, but also employ the hugely popular **sayas**, which originated with African slaves brought to Bolivia during the colonial period. *Sayas* are especially popular during fiestas, when they're usually played by the brass bands, as well as *música folklorica* groups.

Canto nuevo

The sound of Andean panpipes and quenas was also at the heart of early Chilean **nueva canción** through groups like Los Curacas, Inti Illimani and Quilapayún. Influenced by Los Jairas and the work of Chilean folklorist and composer Violeta Parra, they adopted Andean instruments and music in the 1960s and 1970s, adding extra Latin percussion, guitars and other instruments. The move neatly combined

DISCOGRAPHY

Awatiñas *Kullakita* (Awatiñas Records, France). Most tracks are new compositions in a traditional style, arranged with this band's characteristic taste and skill.

Emma Junaro *Canta a Matilde Casazola "Mi corazón en la ciudad"* (Riverboat, UK). Junaro's beautiful voice here brings to life the mestizo songs of the great poetess, singer, guitarist and painter Matilde Casazola.

Emma Junaro *Si De Amor Se Trata* (Tumi, UK). A passionate set of Latin American songs from Cuban to Bolivian composers, showing the full range of Junaro's political commitment.

K'jarkas *Canto a la mujer de mi pueblo* (Tumi, UK). This classic K'jarkas album is an idealistic tribute to Bolivian women. It contains the song Llorando se fue ("In tears, she left"), which later become the notorious Brazilian *lambada*.

K'jarkas *El Amor y La Libertad* (Tumi, UK). Another set of beautiful songs sung in the rich style of this group who epitomize modern folkloric styles. The passionate lyrics tell of the experiences and dreams of today's rural Bolivians.

Kallawaya *Shaman (Medicine Man)* (Tumi, UK). A magnificent album with superb ensemble performances of the group's own compositions, which draw on styles and traditions from the whole of the Americas.

Mallku de los Andes *On the Wings of the Condor* (Tumi, UK). One of the most popular Andean albums ever, but none the worse for that, with the engaging sound of its panpipes and charangos smoothly and beautifully arranged.

Rumillajta *Hoja de coca* (Tumi, UK). Beautifully produced and arranged album of Bolivian music displaying a full range of styles and delivered by a fine group of musicians, many of them playing instruments they've made themselves.

Various *Bolivia Calendar Music of the Central Valley* (Chant du Monde, France). Contemporary recordings of music dating back to pre-Columbian times, including music for panpipes, flutes and drums used for Quechua rituals and ceremonies. Excellent notes, with explanations of how different instruments are used with the seasons.

Various *Charangos et guitarillas du Norte Potosí* (VDE-Gallo/AIMP, Switzerland). Spirited local recordings from north Potosí department of songs in Quechua, often sung by a woman in high tones with a man contributing a lower second part, accompanied by charango, *vihuela*, guitar or *guitarilla*.

Various *Peru and Bolivia, The Sounds of Evolving Traditions: Central Andean Music and Festivals* (Multicultural Media, US). Lively and accessible introduction to today's sounds from both Peru and Bolivia, ranging from music performed in settings as various as private homes, clubs, fiestas and on the street, with harps, violins, drums, panpipes and many other instruments.

Various *The Rough Guide to the Music of the Andes* (World Music Network, UK). A vigorous and broad range of Andean music from contemporary urban-based groups – includes key 1960s musicians Los K'jarkas and Ernesto Cavou, and their 1980s European travelling brethren Awatiñas and Rumillajta; soloists Emma Junaro, Jenny Cardenas and Susana Baca; seminal Chilean group Inti Illimani and singer Victor Jara. Plus saxes and clarinets from Picaflor de los Andes.

music and politics: the Andean roots asserting collective values and an unmistakable ancient indigenous identity. Their styles fed back to Bolivia, where they were adapted into an even richer blend of harmonized singing, with alternating solo and chorus patterns. In Bolivia, *nueva canción* was subsequently reinterpreted as **canto nuevo**: top exponents include folk singer **Emma Junaro** and poetess and singer **Matilde Casazola**.

Modern music and dance

Salsa, **cumbia**, **merengue** and **reggaeton** have come down from Central America and the Caribbean to enjoy great popularity among young Bolivians, who are now making tropical hybrids with their own dance genres. Likewise, **samba** has come over from

Brazil. **Hip hop** is increasingly popular too, and a vibrant scene has sprung up in El Alto, with groups like Ukamau y Ké, Wayna Rap and Nueva Flavah rapping in a mix of Aymara, Spanish, Qucheua and English.

Many older dances still remain popular including the **huayño** which involves swirling partners and can be done processionally, like European country dances. Other dances include *taquiraris*, *tarqueada*, *sayas*, *chovena* and *machetero*, all of which come from ancient rituals influenced by Spanish tradition. Spanish and European folk and ballroom traditions spawned popular couple dances that still endure, including the **waltz** and the **cueca**, which imitates the amorous adventures and conquest of a farmyard cock and hen, with complex choreographic figures and footwork.

Jan Fairley

With thanks to Gilka Wara Céspedes in Bolivia and Henry Stobart in the UK

Books

There are few books published exclusively about Bolivia, and even fewer Bolivian writers ever make it into English. That said, the works listed below offer a good range of background material on Bolivian history, culture, society and the natural world. If you read Spanish, Bolivian novelists to look out for include Alcides Arguedas, Oscar Cerruto, Renato Prada Oropeza and Juan Recacochea. Titles marked ★ are especially recommended. In most of the following reviews, publishers in the UK and US are listed (where they differ) in the form "UK publisher/US publisher"; "o/p" signifies out of print.

HISTORY AND SOCIETY

★ **Jon Lee Anderson** *Che Guevara: a Revolutionary Life* (Bantam/Grove Press). Absorbing and exhaustively researched account of Latin America's most famous guerrilla, by the journalist whose investigations led to the discovery of Che's secret grave in Vallegrande.

Domitila Barrios de Chungara *Let Me Speak* (o/p). Harrowing autobiographical testimony of one of the miners' wives who took part in the hunger strikes that brought an end to the Banzer regime.

Brian S. Bauer and Charles Stanish *Ritual and Pilgrimage in the Ancient Andes: The Islands of the Sun and the Moon* (University of Texas Press). Richly detailed description of the archeology of Lago Titicaca's two sacred islands and their roles as major pilgrimage centres in the Inca and pre-Inca worlds.

John Crabtree *Patterns of Protest: Politics and Social Movements in Bolivia* (Latin America Bureau). A concise description of the tumultuous political movements that helped to bring Evo Morales to power.

James Dunkerley *Rebellion in the Veins: Political Struggle in Bolivia 1952–82* (Verso/Schocken Books). Dense but readable academic account of the 1952 National Revolution, and of the bitter cycles of dictatorship, repression and popular resistance that followed.

★ **Eduardo Galeano** *Open Veins of Latin America: Five Centuries of the Pillage of a Continent* (Latin America Bureau). A stunning history of the continent by the esteemed Uruguayan author, which offers, in particular, an excellent insight into the colonial exploitation of the Potosí mines.

Pete Good *Bolivia: Between a Rock and a Hard Place* (Plural Editores). Readable account of Bolivian history that is particularly good on the rise of Evo Morales and the impact of globalization.

Claire Hargreaves *Snowfields: The War on Cocaine in the Andes* (Zed/Holmes & Meier). Detailed journalistic account from the frontline of the war on drugs during the coca boom of the 1980s.

Olivia Harris *To Make the Earth Bear Fruit: Ethnographic Essays on Fertility, Work and Gender in Highland Bolivia* (ILAS). Collection of ethnographic essays exploring the culture and everyday lives of the deeply traditional *ayllus* of the northern Potosí department.

Kevin Healy *Llamas, Weavings and Organic Chocolate: Multicultural Grassroots Development in the Andes and Amazon of Bolivia* (Kellogg Institute). Intriguing portrait of nine different rural development projects – including one that led to the renaissance of traditional weaving techniques in Sucre – that have used imaginative and culturally appropriate approaches to tackle poverty in Bolivia.

John Hemming *The Conquest of the Incas* (Papermac/Harvest Books). The authoritative account of the Spanish conquest, combining academic attention to detail and excellent use of contemporary sources with a compelling narrative style.

★ **Herbert S. Klein** *Bolivia, the Evolution of a Multi-Ethnic Society* (Oxford). The best English-language history of Bolivia from the arrival of early man to the present day: concise, detailed and clearly written, if a little dry.

Alan Kolata *Valley of the Spirits: a Journey into the Lost Realm of the Aymara* (Wiley). Lively account of the rise and fall of Tiwanaku by the archeologist who has done most to reveal its secrets.

Anne Meadows *Digging Up Butch and Sundance* (Nebraska). Engaging tale of an adventurous quest to solve the mystery of what really happened to the infamous North American outlaws – were they really killed by police in Bolivia and buried in the bleak mining camp of San Vicente?

June Nash *We Eat the Mines and the Mines Eat Us* (Columbia). Fascinating and sensitive anthropological study of the daily lives of the miners of Potosí and the deeply rooted customs and beliefs that help them survive tremendous hardships.

Leo Spitzer *Hotel Bolivia: The Culture of Memory in a Refuge from Nazism* (Hill & Wang). Thoughtful account of the little-known history of the thousands of Jews who fled to Bolivia with the rise of the Nazis in Europe, forming a refugee community that never felt quite at home, and which has since largely migrated to Israel.

★ **Steve J. Stern (ed)** *Resistance, Rebellion, and Consciousness in the Andean Peasant World* (Wisconsin). Absorbing collection of richly detailed historical essays on Quechua and Aymara insurrections and uprisings, ranging from the Great Rebellion of the late eighteenth century to the radical peasant politics of today.

Chris Taylor *The Beautiful Game: A Journey through Latin American Football* (Victor Gollancz). Entertaining account of the history of the continent's sporting obsession. The chapter on Bolivia focuses on the country's struggle to defend its right to play international fixtures at high altitude, and a Santa Cruz football academy that turns street kids into major stars.

TRAVEL

Yossi Brain *Trekking in Bolivia: A Traveller's Guide* (Cordee). Specialist trekking guide covering a good range of routes throughout Bolivia, with clear descriptions, sketch maps and useful background information and advice.

Yossi Brain *Bolivia: A Climbing Guide* (Cordee). A must for all serious climbers visiting Bolivia, with expert route descriptions and excellent logistical advice and information by the man who was the leading climbing guide in the country.

Mark Cramer *Culture Shock! Bolivia* (Kuperard). Light-hearted and sometimes witty introduction to Bolivian culture, customs and etiquette from a US expatriate living in La Paz.

Percy Harrison Fawcett *Exploration Fawcett* (Weidenfeld and Nicolson). Rip-roaring account of the adventures of the eccentric British explorer who surveyed the borders of Bolivia at the height of the rubber boom in the early twentieth century. The book was published posthumously after the author disappeared looking for the mysterious civilization that he believed lay hidden somewhere deep in the Amazon.

Yossi Ginsberg *Jungle: A Harrowing True Story of Survival* (Boomerang New Media). First-hand account by the only survivor of a disastrous expedition by three young travellers who tried to reach Rurrenabaque overland through the forests of the Alto Madidi – this is the book that launched Rurrenabaque as a backpacker destination.

★ **Richard Gott** *Land Without Evil: Utopian Journeys in the South American Watershed* (Verso). Wonderful account of a journey through the former Jesuit mission towns of Brazil and eastern Bolivia, interspersed with finely researched histories of the many fruitless journeys and forgotten expeditions across the same region made by travellers through the centuries.

David Grann *The Lost City of Z: A Tale of Deadly Obsession in the Amazon* (Simon & Schuster). A fascinating account of gentleman explorer Percy Fawcett, who set off in the 1920s in search of the mythical kingdom of Z; although set mainly in Brazil, Bolivia also features.

Ernesto "Che" Guevara *Bolivian Diary* (Pimlico/Pathfinder Press). Published posthumously, the iconic Argentine revolutionary's description of his disastrous attempt to launch a continent-wide guerrilla war from the backwoods of Bolivia reads like the chronicle of a death foretold.

Ernesto "Che" Guevara *The Motorcycle Diaries* (Verso). Amusing account of Che's motorcycle trip through South America in the 1950s, providing an intimate portrait of a young beatnik traveller and romantic idealist undergoing some of the experiences – particularly in revolutionary Bolivia – that would later transform him into a ruthless guerrilla leader.

Michael Jacobs *Ghost Train through the Andes: On My Grandfather's trail in Chile and Bolivia* (John Murray). This book retraces the steps of the author's father as a British railway engineer in Bolivia in the nineteenth century, uncovering an extraordinary love story.

Rusty Young *Marching Powder* (Pan). Hilarious and terrifying account of a small-time English cocaine smuggler's experiences locked up in La Paz's notorious San Pedro prison.

WILDLIFE AND THE ENVIRONMENT

Michael Bright *Andes to Amazon: A Guide to Wild South America* (BBC). Good general introduction to the astonishing range of ecosystems and wildlife in South America, lavishly illustrated with colour photographs.

L. H. Emmons *Neotropical Rainforest Mammals: A Field Guide* (Chicago). Authoritative descriptions and beautiful illustrations of over two hundred species, ideal for identifying animals in the wild.

Susannah Hecht and Alexander Cockburn *The Fate of the Forest: Developers, Destroyers and Defenders of the Amazon* (Harper Collins). Comprehensive, highly readable account of the threat to the Amazon rainforest, with detailed description of the political and social conflicts that underlie the destruction of the rainforest.

John Kricher *A Neotropical Companion* (Princeton University Press). Enjoyable general introduction to the flora, fauna and ecology of the tropical lowlands of South and Central America, well written and packed with detail.

Norman Myers *The Primary Source: Tropical Forests and our Future* (Norton). Compelling account by a leading expert of the world's most diverse and complex ecosystem, the manifold ways in which humans benefit from it, and the dangers arising from its destruction.

Martin de la Pena *Illustrated Checklist: Birds of Southern South America and Antarctica* (Collins/Princeton University Press). Comprehensive field guide with over a thousand bird species the serious birdwatcher's best bet given the lack of a Bolivia-specific bird guide.

Spanish

Although Spanish is the main language of government and commerce, nearly sixty percent of Bolivians speak one or more of the country's thirty or so indigenous languages as their mother tongue, and over ten percent speak no Spanish at all. English and some other European languages are spoken in tourist centres and well-to-do hotels and agencies, but otherwise you'll need to know a bit of Spanish to get around and conduct day-to-day business.

The most widely spoken indigenous language is **Quechua**, the language of the Inca Empire, spoken above all in the highlands of Cochabamba, Potosí and Chuquisaca, followed by **Aymara**, which is spoken mainly in the Altiplano. Most of the country's other thirty languages are spoken by minority groups in the Amazon and the Eastern Lowlands, ranging in size from tens of thousands to just a few hundred speakers. As well as Spanish, Quechua, Aymara and **Guaraní** (the most commonly spoken lowland language) are all official languages, and since Evo Morales became Bolivia's first indigenous president in 2006, they are used much more frequently in the corridors of power, with all civil servants required to speak at least one indigenous language. Unless you're trekking in particularly remote regions, you're unlikely to come across communities where you can't get by with Spanish, although learning just a few phrases of Quechua or Aymara is a good way of making a favourable impression.

If you already speak Spanish you'll have little trouble adjusting to the way the language is spoken in Bolivia, which pretty much conforms to standard textbook **Castellano**, spoken without the lisped "c" and "z". That said, it does, of course, have its own idiomatic peculiarities, one of which is the tendency to add the ending *-ito* or *-cito* to words. Technically this is a diminutive, but in fact asking for a **cervezita** won't get you a smaller beer; it's more often used to express familiarity and affection, and failing to add it onto the ends of words can seem abrupt or impolite amongst the indigenous peoples of the highlands. Bolivian Spanish is also peppered with indigenous expressions, particularly **Quechua** and **Aymara** words such as *wawa* (baby), *pampa* (plain) and *soroche* (altitude sickness); the indigenous languages also influence the somewhat unorthodox grammar and sentence structure used by many highland Bolivians when speaking Spanish. Bolivian Spanish also readily borrows from **English**, resulting in a slew of words which are regarded with horror by the Spanish themselves, such as *chequear* (to check), *parquear* (to park), *rentar* (to rent), *mitín* (meeting) and *líder* (leader); this tendency is particularly evident in mining regions where a host of nineteenth-century English technical terms is still in use.

The fact that Spanish is a second language for most Bolivians means that they're generally patient with foreigners' attempts to speak the language and not too precious about the finer points of grammar. The slow, clear pronunciation of Bolivian Spanish (in the highlands, at least) also makes it a good place to learn Spanish, and a number of Spanish (and, Quechua and Aymara) language schools catering to foreign travellers have now opened in La Paz, Cochabamba and Sucre. In the Eastern Lowlands around Santa Cruz, Spanish is spoken with a much more relaxed, tropical drawl in which consonants often disappear at the end of words: thus "*arroz con pescado*", for example, becomes "*arro' con pe'ca'o*". Here, the diminutive *-ingo* is used instead of *-ito*.

On the following pages we've listed a few essential words and phrases, though if you're travelling for any length of time a dictionary or phrase book is obviously a worthwhile investment. If you're using a **dictionary**, bear in mind that in Spanish CH, LL, and Ñ count as separate letters and are listed after the Cs, Ls, and Ns respectively.

PRONUNCIATION

The rules of Spanish **pronunciation** are pretty straightforward and, once you get to know them, strictly observed. Unless there's an accent, words ending in d, l, r and z are **stressed** on the last syllable, all others on the second last. All **vowels** are pure and short.

a somewhere between the "a" sound of back and that of father

e as in get

i as in police

o as in hot

u as in rule

c is soft before E and I, hard otherwise: cerca is pronounced "serka".

g works the same way, a guttural "h" sound (like the ch in loch) before E or I, a hard G elsewhere: gigante becomes "higante".

h is always silent.

j is the same sound as a guttural G: jamón is pronounced "hamon".

ll sounds like an English Y: llama is pronounced "yama".

n is as in English unless it has a tilde over it, as with mañana, when it's pronounced like the "n" in onion or menu.

qu is pronounced like an English "K".

r is rolled, RR doubly so.

v sounds more like B, vino becoming "beano".

x is slightly softer than in English, sometimes almost SH except between vowels in place names where it has an "H" sound: for example México - (Meh-hee-ko).

z is the same as a soft "C", so cerveza becomes "servesa".

WORDS AND PHRASES

BASICS

Yes, No	Sí, No
Please, Thank you	Por favor, Gracias
Where, When	Dónde, Cuando
What, How much/many	Qué, Cuanto
Here, There	Aquí, Allí
This, That	Este, Eso
Now, Later	Ahora, Más tarde
Open, Closed	Abierto/a, Cerrado/a
With, Without	Con, Sin
Good, Bad	Buen o/a, Mal o/a
Big	Gran(de)
Small	Pequeño/a, Chico/a
More, Less	Más, Menos
Today, Tomorrow	Hoy, Mañana
Yesterday	Ayer

GREETINGS AND RESPONSES

Hello, Goodbye	Hola, Adiós
Good morning	Buenos dias
Good afternoon/night	Buenas tardes/noches
See you later	Hasta luego
Sorry	Lo siento/discúlpeme
Excuse me	Con permiso/perdón
How are you?	¿Como está (usted)?
I (don't) understand	(No) Entiendo
Not at all/You're welcome	De nada
Do you speak English?	¿Habla (usted) inglés?
I don't speak Spanish	(No) Hablo español
My name is ...	Me llamo ...
What's your name?	¿Como se llama usted?
I am English	Soy inglés/a
...American	...americano/a
...Australian	...australiano/a
...Canadian	...canadiense/a
...Irish	...irlandés/a
...Scottish	...escosés/a
...Welsh	...galés/a
...New Zealander	...neozelandés/a

HOTELS AND RESTAURANTS

Twin room	Una habitación doble
Room with double bed	Una habitación matrimonial
Single room	Una habitación sencilla/ simple
Private bathroom	Baño privado
Shared bathroom	Baño compartido
Hot water (all day)	Agua caliente (todo el día)
Cold water	Agua fría
Fan	Ventilador
Air-conditioned	Aire-acondicionado
Tax	Impuesto
Mosquito net	mosquitero
Key	Llave
Check-out time	Hora de salida
Do you know...?	¿Sabe...?
I don't know	No sé
There is (is there)?	(¿)Hay(?)
Give me...	Deme...
(one like that)	(uno así)
Do you have...?	¿Tiene ...?
...a room	...una habitación
...with two beds/ double bed	...con dos camas/cama matriomonial
It's for one person	es para una persona
(two people)	(dos personas)
...for one night	...para una noche
(one week)	(una semana)
It's fine, how much is it?	¿Está bien, cuánto es?
It's too expensive	Es demasiado caro

Don't you have anything cheaper?	¿No tiene algo más barato?
Can one…?	¿Se puede…?
camp (near) here?	¿…acampar aqui (cerca)? …
Is there a hotel nearby?	¿Hay un hotel aquí cerca?
I want	Quiero
I'd like	Querría
What is there to eat?	¿Qué hay para comer?
What's that?	¿Qué es eso?
What's this called in Spanish?	¿Como se llama este en español?

DIRECTIONS AND TRANSPORT

Bus terminal	Terminal terrestre, Terminal de buses
Bus	Bus, flota, movilidad
Ticket	Pasaje
Seat	Asiento
Aisle	Pasillo
Window	Ventana
Luggage	Equipaje
How do I get to…?	Como se llega a…?
Left, right, straight on	Izquierda, derecha, derecho
Where is…?	¿Dondé está…?
…the bus station	…el terminal de buses
…the train station	…la estación de ferrocarriles
…the nearest bank	…el banco más-cercano
…the post office	…el correo
…the toilet	…el baño
Where does the bus to …leave from?	¿De dónde sale el bus para…?
What time does the bus leave?	¿A qué hora sale el bus?
What time does the bus arrive?	¿A qué hora llega el bus?
How long does the journey take?	¿Cuánto tiempo demora el viaje?
Is this the train for …?	¿Es éste el tren para …?
I'd like a (return) ticket to…	Querría pasaje (de ida y vuelta) para…
What time does it leave (arrive at…)?	¿A qué hora sale (llega a…)?

NUMBERS AND DAYS

1	un/uno/una
2	dos
3	tres
4	cuatro
5	cinco
6	seis
7	siete
8	ocho
9	nueve
10	diez
11	once
12	doce
13	trece
14	catorce
15	quince
16	dieciséis
20	veinte
21	veitiuno
30	treinta
40	cuarenta
50	cincuenta
60	sesenta
70	setenta
80	ochenta
90	noventa
100	cien(to)
101	ciento uno
200	doscientos
201	doscientos uno
500	quinientos
1000	mil
2000	dos mil
first	primero/a
second	segundo/a
third	tercero/a
Monday	lunes
Tuesday	martes
Wednesday	miércoles
Thursday	jueves
Friday	viernes
Saturday	sábado
Sunday	domingo

FOOD AND DRINK

BASICS

Aceite	Oil	Comida típica	Traditional food
Ají	Chilli	Cuchara	Spoon
Ajo	Garlic	Cuchillo	Knife
Almuerzo	(Set) lunch	La cuenta	The bill
Arroz	Rice	Desayuno	Breakfast
Azúcar	Sugar	Ensalada	Salad
La carta	Menu	Galletas	Biscuits
Cena	(Set) dinner	Harina	Flour

Hielo	Ice
Huevos	Eggs
Llajua	Chilli sauce
Mantequilla	Butter
Mermelada	Jam
Miel de Abeja	Honey
Mostaza	Mustard
Pan (integral)	(Wholemeal) bread
Pimienta negra	Black pepper
Plato	Dish
Queso	Cheese
Sal	Salt
Salsa	Sauce
Tenedeor	Fork
Vegetariano	Vegetarian

COOKING TERMS

A la parilla	Barbecued
A la plancha	Griddled
Ahumado	Smoked
Al ajillo	In garlic
Al horno	Oven baked
Asado	Roast
Crudo	Raw
Duro	Hard boiled
Frío	Cold
Frito	Fried
Picante	Spicy
Relleno	Stuffed
Revuelto	Scrambled
Sancochado	Boiled

SOUP (*SOPA*), MEAT (*CARNE*), POULTRY (*AVES*) AND FISH (*PESCADO*)

Anticuchos	Skewered heart
Atún	Tuna (tinned)
Bistec	Beefsteak
Cangrejo	Crab
Carne de cerdo/chanco	Pork
Carne de res	Beef
Charque	Dried meat (usually llama)
Chicharron	Deep-fried pork
Chicharron de Pollo	Deep-fried chicken
Chuleta	T-bone steak
Chuleta de Cerdo	Pork chop
Churrasco	Minute steak
Conejo	Rabbit
Cordero	Mutton
Hamburguesa	Hamburger
Higado	Liver
Jamón	Ham
Lechón	Roast pork
Lomo	Filet steak

Milanesa	Breaded escalope
Parillada	Barbecued meat
Pato	Duck
Pavo	Turkey
Pejerrey	Kingfish
Pollo (a la brasa)	(Spit-roasted) chicken
Riñon	Kidney
Surubí	Catfish
Tocino	Bacon
Trucha	Trout

VEGETABLES (*VERDURAS*)

Arvejas	Peas
Camote	Sweet potato
Castaña	Brazil nut
Cebolla	Onion
Champiñon	Mushroom
Choclo	Corn on the cob
Espinaca	Spinach
Frijoles	Beans
Habas	Broad beans
Lechuga	Lettuce
Locoto	Chilli pepper
Maíz	Maize/corn
Maní	Peanut
Palmito	Palm heart
Palta	Avocado
Papa	Potato
Tomate	Tomato
Yuca	Manioc
Zanahoria	Carrot
Zapallo	Pumpkin

FRUIT (*FRUTAS*)

Banano/Guineo/ Plátano	Banana (the latter is also plantain)
Carambola	Star fruit
Chirimoya	Custard apple
Durazno	Peach
Frutilla	Strawberry
Limón	Lemon
Mandarina	Mandarin
Mango	Mango
Manzana	Apple
Maracuyá	Passionfruit
Naranja	Orange
Papaya	Papaya
Piña	Pineapple
Toronja	Grapefruit
Uvas	Grapes

SNACKS

Cuñapes	Yucca and cheese pastry
Empanada	Cheese or meat pasty

Humintas	Maize, cheese and raisin porridge wrapped in leaves
Papas fritas	Potato chips/French fries
Salteña	Juicy meat, chicken and vegetable pasty
Tostados	Toast
Tucumana	Fried meat and vegetable pasty

DESSERTS (*POSTRES*)

Arroz con leche	Rice pudding
Ensalada de frutas	Fruit salad
Flan	Crème caramel
Gelatina	Jelly
Helado	Ice cream
Torta	Cake

DRINKS (*BEBIDAS*)

| Agua | Water |

Agua hervida	Boiled water
Agua mineral (con gas/sin gas)	Mineral water (fizzy/still)
Api	Hot, thick, sweet maize drink
Café	Coffee
Café con leche	White coffee
Cerveza	Beer
Chicha	Fermented maize beer
Chocolate	Hot chocolate
Chopp	Draft beer
Chufflay	Singani and Sprite
Jugo (de naranja)	Orange juice
Limonada	(Real) lemonade
Leche	Milk
Mate	Herbal tea
Mate de coca	Coca tea
Mate de manzanilla	Camomile tea
Refresco	Soft drink
Té	Tea

GLOSSARY

Achachila/Apu Powerful mountain gods or spirits believed to inhabit high Andean peaks

Aguas termales Thermal baths, hot springs

Apacheta Stone cairn marking mountain passes, created by travellers carrying stones on the climb up as penance and as an offering to the mountain gods

Artesanía Traditional handicrafts

Ayllu Andean extended kinship group, roughly equivalent to a clan or tribe

Barrio Neighbourhood, quarter or suburb

Cabaña Cabin

Calle Street

Camba Old Inca term for lowland tribes, now used as slang term for people from the Eastern Lowlands

Camion Lorry

Camioneta Pick-up truck

Campesino Peasant: literally, from the countryside

Canoa Dugout canoe

Caudillo Chief, military strongman

Chaco Cultivated clearing in the forest, also the verb for creating such clearings through slash and burn

Challa Ritual offering of alcohol and sweets to the mountain spirits, often carried out as a blessing for a new house or car

Cholo Mixed race or urbanized indigenous person

Colla Ancient Aymara nation, now a slang term for people from the Altiplano

Cordillera Mountain range

Criollo "Creole": used historically to refer to a person of Spanish blood born in the American colonies

Curandero Healer

ENTEL Bolivia's national telephone company

Gringo Originally someone from the United States, now a non-derogatory term used for all white foreigners

Guardaparque Park guard

Hacienda Large private farm or estate

Huaca Sacred place or object

Indígena Used adjectivally to mean "indigenous", or as a noun to refer to an indigenous person

Junta A ruling council; usually used to describe small groups who've staged a coup d'état

Kuraka Indigenous nobleman in the colonial era

Lejía Alkaline reagent used when chewing coca

Mestizo Person of mixed Spanish and indigenous blood

Mirador Viewpoint

Nevado Snowcapped mountain

Pampa Plain

Peña Nightclub where live music is performed, often folk music

Plata Silver; slang for money

Puna High-altitude grassland, starting around 3000m

Quebrada Ravine, dried-out stream

Salar Saltpan or lake

Selva Jungle or tropical rainforest

S/n Used in addresses to indicate "sin número", or without a number

Soroche Altitude sickness

Tinku Andean ritual combat

Tranca Police roadblock

Wiphala Rainbow-chequered flag used as a symbol of indigenous Andean identity

Small print and index

335 Small print

336 About the authors

338 Index

344 Map symbols

A ROUGH GUIDE TO ROUGH GUIDES

Published in 1982, the first Rough Guide – to Greece – was a student scheme that became a publishing phenomenon. Mark Ellingham, a recent graduate in English from Bristol University, had been travelling in Greece the previous summer and couldn't find the right guidebook. With a small group of friends he wrote his own guide, combining a highly contemporary, journalistic style with a thoroughly practical approach to travellers' needs.

The immediate success of the book spawned a series that rapidly covered dozens of destinations. And, in addition to impecunious backpackers, Rough Guides soon acquired a much broader readership that relished the guides' wit and inquisitiveness as much as their enthusiastic, critical approach and value-for-money ethos.

These days, Rough Guides include recommendations from budget to luxury and cover more than 200 destinations around the globe, as well as producing an ever-growing range of eBooks and apps.

Visit **roughguides.com** to see our latest publications.

Rough Guide credits

Editor: Alison Roberts
Layout: Anita Singh
Cartography: Animesh Pathak
Picture editor: Rhiannon Furbear
Proofreader: Anita Sach
Managing editor: Mani Ramaswamy
Assistant editor: Prema Dutta
Production: Rebecca Short
Cover design: Nicole Newman, Anita Singh
Editorial assistant: Lorna North

Senior pre-press designer: Dan May
Design director: Scott Stickland
Travel publisher: Joanna Kirby
Digital travel publisher: Peter Buckley
Reference director: Andrew Lockett
Operations coordinator: Becky Doyle
Operations assistant: Johanna Wurm
Publishing director (Travel): Clare Currie
Commercial manager: Gino Magnotta
Managing director: John Duhigg

Publishing information

This third edition published February 2012 by
Rough Guides Ltd,
80 Strand, London WC2R 0RL
11, Community Centre, Panchsheel Park,
New Delhi 110017, India
Distributed by the Penguin Group
Penguin Books Ltd,
80 Strand, London WC2R 0RL
Penguin Group (USA)
375 Hudson Street, NY 10014, USA
Penguin Group (Australia)
250 Camberwell Road, Camberwell,
Victoria 3124, Australia
Penguin Group (NZ)
67 Apollo Drive, Mairangi Bay, Auckland 1310,
New Zealand
Rough Guides is represented in Canada by Tourmaline
Editions Inc. 662 King Street West, Suite 304, Toronto,
Ontario M5V 1M7
Printed in Singapore
© Brendon Griffin, Shafik Meghji, James Read 2012

Help us update

We've gone to a lot of effort to ensure that the third
edition of **The Rough Guide to Bolivia** is accurate
and up-to-date. However, things change – places get
"discovered", opening hours are notoriously fickle,
restaurants and rooms raise prices or lower standards. If
you feel we've got it wrong or left something out, we'd like
to know, and if you can remember the address, the price,
the hours, the phone number, so much the better.

Please send your comments with the subject line
"Rough Guide Bolivia Update" to ✉ mail@uk.roughguides
.com. We'll credit all contributions and send a copy of the
next edition (or any other Rough Guide if you prefer) for
the very best emails.

Find more travel information, connect with fellow
travellers and book your trip on ⓦ roughguides.com

ABOUT THE AUTHORS

Brendon Griffin has contributed to, and edited, various Rough Guides including West Africa, Central America, Spain, Portugal, Peru and New York, and has written numerous travel articles for the Rough Guide anthologies *Make The Most of Your Time on Earth* and *Make The Most of Your Time in Britain*. He has travelled widely in Bolivia and Latin America in general and also writes on African, Latin and Brazilian music.

Shafik Meghji A travel writer, journalist, editor and photographer, Shafik Meghji is based in South London but has travelled extensively throughout Bolivia since his first visit in 2004. He is also the co-author of the *Rough Guide to India* and has worked on Rough Guides to Chile, Central America on a Budget, Nepal, Egypt, Paris and the Baltic States.

James Read first travelled to Latin America in 1991. Expecting to be there for three months he stayed for three years, rebuilding Inca irrigation systems in the high Andes of Peru. Since then he's travelled throughout the region, writing sporadically. At home in England he's Latin American editor for the BBC World Service.

Acknowledgements

Brendon Griffin would like to thank Margarita Mujica, Eric Salinas and family for the generous use of their flat in La Paz; Jane, Marco-Antonio, Ida, Jorge and David for a wonderful time in Brazil; Vlady and Denise Salinas and family for their kindness and hospitality in Cobija; Freddy, Amanda and Andrew for a brief but memorable stay in Oruro; Joe for making the effort to come to the jungle; and all the Lavayen family in Cochabamba. Thanks also to Christian Menn in La Paz for his generous advice and time; to Stefan and Jeff at *Cafe Illampu*, also Mirko Vargas, Luc Cueppers, Juan Carlos Cárdenas and the hardworking chefs at *Restaurant El Consulado*; to the good people of San Ignacio de Moxos, especially Yadiye Herrera; to all the tour operators in Rurrenabaque for their time and advice, to all at *Monkey Bar* and to Ivan and family at RHEMA; to Mauricio Herrera for a Brazilian lunch in Trinidad; to Erika for coming along at the last minute; to my diligent editor Alison Roberts and last but not least, to Nick Griffin for holding (and completing) the fort in my absence.

Shafik Meghji Thanks to the many locals and travellers who helped out in big and small ways during the researching of this guide. A special *muchas gracias* must go to: Mani Ramaswamy for the initial commission; Alison Roberts for her editing skills and support; Brendon Griffin for his advice and suggestions; Fremen Tours staff throughout Bolivia for providing invaluable logistical support; VTB Tours in Tarija; Candelaria Tours in Sucre; Ariel for his insight into Villa Tunari, the Chapare and Cochabamba; Don Gilberto for his expert guiding along the Che trail, Pieter and Margarita in Samaipata for their hospitality and expertise; Jean, Nizar and Nina Meghji for all their love and support; and Sioned Jones for making even a grey and rainy day in Sorata seem magical.

Readers' letters

Thanks to all the readers who have taken the time to write in with comments and suggestions (and apologies if we've inadvertently omitted or misspelt anyone's name):

Sven Feghelm, Marian Feunekes, David and Priscille Francetti, Matthieu Fuzellier, Eddie Gerrard, Benzi Kahana, Eyal Keshet, Marko Lewis, Graham Macbryer, Deirdre O'Neill, Stephen Ollivier, Tatiana Robles, Joost Schouppe, Leo Schwartz, Chris Spencer.

Photo credits

All photos © Rough Guides except the following:
(Key/a-above; b-below/bottom; c-centre; f-far; l-left; r-right; t-top)

p.1 Getty Images/Sergio Ballivian
p.2 Robert Harding Picture Library/Pete Oxford
p.4 Getty Images/Art Wolfe
p.5 Corbis/Mariana Bazo/Reuters
p.9 Alamy/James Brunker (tr), Corbis/Carlos Cazalis (tl), Getty Images/Andy Kerry/Axiom (b)
p.11 Getty Images/Sergio Ballivian/Aurora (c), Jamie Marshall/Tribaleye Images (t), NHPA/Photoshot/Andre Baertschi (b)
p.12 Photolibrary/M&G Therin-Weise
p.13 Corbis/Ocean (b), Superstock/Photononstop (t)
p.14 Corbis/Nico Tondini/Robert Harding (c), Getty Images/Neil Emmerson/Robert Harding World Imagery (b), Hemis.fr (t)
p.15 Corbis/Theo Stroomer/Demotix (t), Photolibrary/imagebroker (b)
p.16 Corbis/Patrick Escudero/Hemis (t), Anders Ryman (b)
p.17 Alamy/James Brunker (br), Mike Greenslade (bl), Getty Images/Aurora Creative (t)
p.18 Alamy/Travelscape Images (c), Corbis/Patrick Escudero/Hemis (b), Getty Images/Gallo Images (t)
p.19 Axiom Photographic Agency/Greg Von Doersten (b), Superstock/Escudero Patrick (t)
p.20 Fotolia/Briseida - Fotolia.com (tl), NHPA/Photoshot/Nick Garbutt (tr)
p.22 Alamy/National Geographic Image Collection
p.51 Corbis/George Steinmetz
p.53 Corbis/Jorge Silva/Reuters
p.65 Corbis/Tim Clayton (b), Superstock/LatitudeStock (t)
p.83 Alamy/Bjorn Svensson (tl), Brent Winebrenner/Lonely Planet Images (tr), AWL Images/Peter Adams (b)
p.94 Getty Images/Andrew Geiger
p.97 Alamy/Luke Peters

p.105 Corbis/Paule Seux/Hemis (t), Getty Images/Steve Allen (b)
p.117 Alamy/Ville Palonen (bl), Getty Images/Carlos Sanchez Pereyra (br), Magical Andes photography/James Brunker (t)
p.136 Nicole Newman
p.139 Superstock/Lonely Planet
p.151 Corbis/Theo Allofs (t), FLPA/Pete Oxford (bl), Getty Images/Aizar Raldes/AFP (br)
p.163 Corbis/Eitan Simanor/Robert Harding World Imagery
p.175 4Corners/Massimo Borchi (t), Corbis/Theo Allofs (b)
p.190 Getty Images/Win Initiative
p.193 FLPA/Jurgen & Christine Sohns
p.199 Alamy/Michael Boyny (t), Getty Images/Neil Emmerson/Robert Harding World Imagery (b)
p.217 Corbis/Christophe Boisvieux/Hemis (br), Superstock/Sybil Sassoon (bl), SEUX Paule (t)
p.228 Corbis/Ira Block/National Geographic Society
p.231 4Corners/Massimo Borchi
p.253 4Corners/Massimo Borchi (br), AWL Images/DanitaDelimont (t), FLPA/ImageBroker (bl)
p.268 Photolibrary/P Oxford
p.271 Alamy/Leonid Plotkin
p.279 Alamy/Aivar Mikko (t), NHPA/Photoshot/Andre Baertschi (b)
p.291 NHPA/Photoshot/MARK BOWLER
p.302 Getty Images/AIZAR RALDES/AFP

Front cover Alamy/Paul Kennedy/Lonely Planet Images
Back cover Corbis Marco Simoni/Robert Harding World Imagery, Fotolia/S Duggan (br), Evgeny (bl)

Index

Maps are marked in grey

A

accommodation.........................28
  camping...............................30
  hostels................................29
  hotels.................................29
  prices..................................29
Acha, José María 311
Acre War........................297, 312
addresses...............................28
Afro-Bolivianos.......................134
Ahlfeld waterfall.....................263
airport tax..............................23
Akhamani..............................116
Albergue Ecologico Chalalán
....277, 283
Almagro, Diego de..................306
Altiplano, the southern..... 140
altitude sickness 38
Alto Peru................................306
Amazon, the 270–301
Amazon, the......................... 272
Amboró, Parque Nacional
.... 241–243
Aniceto Arce...........................312
Apa-Apa, Bosque Ecológico
....133
apus.......................................131
Arani......................................218
Arbol de Piedra 171
Arco Iris waterfall...................263
Area Natural de Manejo
  Integrado Nacional
  Apoplobamba........................113
Area Natural San Matías.........264
Argentine border...... 24,181,184,
  267
Arroyo Concepción..................265
Atahualpa...............................305
ATMs......................................47
Audiencia de Charcas 309
Avaroa....................................167
Avaroa, Reserva de Fauna
  Andina Eduardo 171
ayllu......................................304
Aymara 303, 329
Aymara New Year 89

B

Ballivián, José.........................311
Banzer, Hugo............316, 317, 318
Barrientos René......................316
Belzu, Manuel Isidoro.............311
Beni 270–298
bodegas, Tarija valley..............187
Bolívar, Simón.........................397
books.....................................327
border crossings 23

from Argentina 24, 181, 184, 267
from Brazil 24, 265, 296, 299
from Chile 24, 142, 167, 172
from Peru 23, 101, 299, 301
Bosque Ecológico Apa-Apa ...133
Brasiléia................................299
Brazilian border........24, 265, 296,
  299
Buena Vista............................240
Busch, Germán........................314
Butch Cassidy and the Sundance
  Kid 179

C

Cachuela Esperanza.................297
Cal Orko.................................207
Calama...................................167
Calderillas..............................188
Camino de Oro........................122
Camp Flor de Oro 263
Camp Los Fierros 262
Campamento Ahlfeld...............263
canoeing 35
canto nuevo............................324
Canyon del Inca 179
car rental.................................27
Caranavi.................................124
Carrasco, Parque Nacional 225
Cascadas las Cuevas................246
Castillo la Glorieta 207
Catedral de Concepción 255
Catedral de San Ignacio..........256
caudillos.................................311
Caverna de Umajallanta..........223
Cavernas del Repechón............226
Cementerio de Trenes..............166
Central Obrera Boliviana (COB)
....315
central valleys, the, Sucre &
  Cochabamba 194
Cerro Calvario 101
Cerro Cota 220
Cerro Khala Ciudad.................134
Cerro Rico..............................162
Cerro Tunari, Parque Nacional
....219
Cerro Uchumachi.....................128
Cerro Yunga Cruz....................134
Chacaltaya...............................88
Chaco, the..............................345
Chaco War..............................314
Chagas' disease 39
Chairo...................................129
Chalalán, Albergue Ecologico
....277, 283
Challa....................................108
Challapampa............................106
Challapampa (Choro Trail)......129

Challapata..............................149
Chapare, the 225–227
charangos...............................417
Charazani................................113
"Che" Guevara, Ernesto....250, 316
Che's mausoleum 249
chicha.....................................32
Chilean border.........24, 142, 167,
  172
Chipayas 149
Chiquitanos 254
Chiquitos 252–262
Chiquitos Missions Music
  Festival.................................255
Chivé.....................................301
Chochis..................................264
Chojila...................................130
Choquequta 130
Choro.....................................129
Choro Trail.............................128
Choro Trail 129
Chukura.................................129
Chulumani 131–133
Chulumani 132
Chuñavi..................................134
Chusaqueri..............................149
climate....................................46
climbing..........................35, 119
climbing guides.................. 34, 72
Cliza......................................218
Cobija....................................299
coca...............................318, 319
cocaine trade..........................318
Cochabamba 209–218
Cochabamba 212–213
Cochabamba, around........ 218
Cochabamba, Sucre & the
  central valleys................. 194
  accommodation.....................215
  arrival and departure 214
  cable car...............................214
  Colina San Sebastián 211
  Cristo de la Concordia..........214
  directory...............................216
  drinking and nightlife 216
  eating...................................215
  history..................................210
  information and tours...........215
  La Cancha 211
  La Catedral Metropolitana....211
  language classes...................216
  Mercado Inca Llajta..............212
  Museo Archeológico.............211
  nightlife................................216
  Palacio de los Portales 213
  Plaza 14 de Septiembre........210
  Water War 210
Colchani.................................170
Colla.....................................303
Collasuyo 304
Colonel Fawcett......................300

COMIBOL 315, 318
Complejo Turístico Ecológico y
    Arcqueológico Chuchuni
   290
Concepción..........................254
Concepción-Rugero bodega
   187
constitutional reform...............319
Copacabana..............................99
Copacabana 100
Cordillera Apolobamba
    ....113 118
Cordillera de Chichas... 178–180
Cordillera Kari Kari 164
Cordillera Real 118–123
    trekking and climbing in.............119
cordilleras, the, Lago Titicaca
    & the Yungas 98
Coripata 133
Coroico.......................... 123–128
Coroico.............................. 125
costs 43
Cotapata, Parque Nacional
   128
credit cards 47
crime 40
CSUTCB...................................319
currency...................................47
Curva....................................114
cycling 27

D

dance................................322–326
declaration of independence
   310
deforestation.............................281
Desaguadero..........................101
Devil's Railway 296
Diablada.................................143
dialling codes...........................48
diarrhoea 37
disabled travellers 43
discography.............................325
doctors 36
drink 32–32
dysentery....................................37

E

Eastern Lowlands, the, &
    Santa Cruz 232
eating..................................30–32
ecology......................................320
ecotourism in Rurrenabaque
   283
Eduardo Avaroa, Reserva de
    Fauna Andina......................171
El Dorado.................................273
El Encanto 262
El Fuerte 246
El Niño 111
El Ojo del Inca.........................164
El Sillar...................................179
El Tío.......................................164

electricity...................................43
embassies, Bolivian abroad 45
entry requirements....................43
Esmeralda Parque Ecológico
   294
Estancia Takesi......................130
exchange rate 47

F

far southwest, the.............. 169
Favre, Gilbert...........................324
Fawcett, Colonel Percy Harrison
   300
Federación Sindical de
    Trabajadores Mineros de
    Bolivia (FSTMB)..................314
Federal Revolution..................312
female travellers 43
Feria de Alasitas 66
festivals 33
fiestas 33
    Fiesta de la Virgen de Urkupiña... 220
    Fiesta del Gran Poder 58
    Fiesta Patronal...........................284
flights 23
    from Australia and new Zealand
       23
    from the UK and Ireland...........23
    from the USA and Canada...........23
    within Bolivia............................25
food 30
food poisoning...........................37
fossils, Tarija valley 186

G

Gamarra, Agustín......................311
Garcia Meza, Luis 317
Gas War...................................319
gay and lesbian travellers 43
general strike 313
Ginsberg, Yossi........................276
glossary..................................333
Great Depression......................313
Great Rebellion........................308
Gruta de San Pedro................122
Guajará-Mirim...........................296
Guaraní, the............................266
Guayaramerín 295
Guerra del Agua.......................319
Guevara, Ernesto "Che"....250, 316
guides......................................34, 72

H

hacienda system.......................312
health..36
history.........................303–319
Horca del Inca.........................104
Hospital Señor de Malta 249
hospitals 36
Huaca Huañusca 180
Huanchaca Plateau 262
Huarina..................................99
Huascar..................................305

Huatajata...........................99, 112
Huayna Capac.........................305
huayño 324, 326

I

Iglesia de San Javier 252
Iglesia de San Miguel...............257
Iglesia de San Rafael.................257
Iglesia de Santa Ana.................258
Illampu Circuit 122
Ilo-Ilo.......................................116
immunizations..........................37
Iñak Uyu 111
Incachani 116
Incallajta 220
Incarakay 219
Incas 304
Independence War, the..........309
indigenous peoples of the
    Bolivian Amazon...................288
insurance 44
internet 44
Intinkala 104
Irupana 133
Isla de la Luna 111
Isla de Pescado.........................171
Isla del Sol 106
Isla del Sol 106
Isla Kala Uta 112
Isla Pariti.................................112
Isla Suriqui...............................112
Ivirgarzama.............................226

J

Jatun Pampa...........................116
Jesuit missions of Chiquitos
    252–262
Jesuits 254

K

Kaa-Iya del Gran Chaco, Parque
    Nacional.............................266
Kakapi....................................130
Kallawayas..............................114
Kasani....................................101
Kasapata 107
kayaking 35
Kori Huayku Trail.....................128
kurakas 304
Kusijata..................................104

L

La Angostura 180
La Chincana 108
La Cumbre...............................124
La Higuera...............................250
La Muela del Diablo...................88
La Pajcha 246
La Paz...............................50–93
Central La Paz 57
La Paz & around 54
Sopocachi & Miraflores 67

accommodation..............74–78
airport................................70
altitude sickness.................55
antiques.............................86
arrival and departure..........70
artesanía............................85
books and maps..................86
buses.................................70
Calle Sagárnaga...................64
Catedral..............................56
Centro Cultural - Museo San
    Francisco.........................63
cholitas wrestling................70
crime.................................71
directory............................86
drinking and nightlife.........82
eating...........................78–82
Ekeko................................66
El Alto...............................69
El Prado.............................66
embassies and consulates.....86
entertainment....................84
Feria de El Alto...................69
getting around...................71
history..............................54
Iglesia de San Francisco......63
information and tours..........73
La Chola Paceña..................60
language schools.................87
Lucha libre de cholitas.........70
Mercado Buenos Aires.........64
Mercado de Hechicería.........64
micros...............................72
Museo Casa de Murillo.........61
Museo Costumbrista Juan de
    Vargas...........................60
Museo de Arte Contemporáneo
    Plaza.............................67
Museo de Etnografía y Folklore....59
Museo de Instrumentos Musicales
    de Bolivia.......................61
Museo de la Coca................64
Museo del Litoral Boliviano...61
Museo e Metales Preciosos....61
Museo Nacional de Arqueología
    Tiwanaku........................91
Museo Nacional de Arte........59
Museo Tambo Quirquincho....62
nightlife............................82
Palacio Legislativo..............58
Palacio Presidencial.............58
peñas................................85
Plaza Murillo......................56
Plaza San Francisco.............62
Plaza Sucre........................68
Río Choqueyapu..................54
San Pedro Prison.................68
scams................................71
shopping............................85
Sopocachi...........................66
soroche..............................55
street food..........................78
taxis.................................72
taxi drivers.........................71
textiles..............................60
tours from La Paz................72
trufis.................................72
Witches' Market..................64
wrestling............................70
Zona Sur............................69
Zoo Municipal Vesty Pakos....88
La Quiaca..........................181
La Rosca............................313

Lago Cáceres......................264
Lago Poopó........................149
Lago Titicaca..................98–112
Lago Titicaca, the cordilleras &
    the Yungas.................... 98
Lago Uru Uru......................149
Laguna Chaplín...................262
Laguna Colorada.................172
Laguna de San Idelfonso......164
Laguna Guapamó.................257
Laguna Isirere....................285
Laguna Polques...................172
Laguna San Sebastián..........164
Laguna Tajzara...................188
Laguna Verde.....................172
Lagunas Glacier and Chillata
    Trek.............................122
Lagunillas.........................115
language schools.................45
laundry..............................44
leishmaniasis......................39
lesbian and gay travellers......43
Linares, José María..............311
living in Bolivia...................44
Llama Chaqui......................224
Llanos de Moxos.................283
Loma Suárez......................290
lomas................................273
Los Jairas..........................324
Los K'jarkas.......................324
Los Pinos..........................188
Lowlands, the Eastern & Santa
    Cruz............................ 232
Lupaca..............................303

M

Macha................................165
Madidi, Parque Nacional
    373–375
Madidi Travel..............277, 283
mail...................................45
malaria...............................38
Mallasa...............................87
Manco Inca.........................306
Manuripi, Reserva Nacional
    de Visa Silvestre Amazónica
   301
Mapajo Ecoturismo Indígena
    ....277, 283
Mapiri Trail........................122
maps..................................46
marching bands...................323
markets...............................31
Massacre del Valle...............317
media..................................46
medical treatment................36
Melgarejo, Mariano..............311
Mesa, Carlos.......................319
mestizos............................307
Mennonites, the..................261
military dictatorship......316, 317
mita...................................305
mobile phones.....................48
money..................................47

Morales, Evo.... 55, 234, 288, 297,
    318, 319
mountain biking....................35
Movement Towards Socialism
    (MAS)............................319
Movimiento Nacionalista
    Revolucionario (MNR)..........314
Museo Comunal La Higuera...251
Museo Misional....................255
Museo Municipal Ruta del Che
    Guevara..........................248
music........................... 322–326

N

National Indigenous Congress
   314
national parks and reserves....36
National Revolution..............315
nationalization programme
   319
New Economic Plan...............318
newspapers..........................46
Noel Kempff Mercado, Parque
    Nacional..........................262

O

Ollagüe.............................171
opening hours......................47
Oruro...................... 142–148
Oruro...................... 144
    accommodation.................147
    arrival and departure.........147
    Carnaval.........................143
    Casa de Cultura Simón I. Patiño
       145
    directory.........................148
    eating and drinking...........148
    Faro de Conchupata...........145
    history............................143
    information......................147
    Museo Antropológico Eduardo
        López Rivas..................147
    Museo de Mineralogía.........147
    Museo Etnográfico Minero...146
    Santuario del Socavón........145
    Virgen del Socavón............146
Otuquis, Parque Nacional......264
outdoor activities..................34

P

Paitití...............................273
Pamapa Siloli......................171
Pampas del Yacuma..............282
Pando, José Manuel..............313
Pando..................... 298–301
Pando massacre...................298
panpipes............................322
Pantanal, the......................264
Paraguayan border...............346
Parque Nacional Amboró
    241–243
Parque Nacional Carrasco......225
Parque Nacional Cerro Tunari
   219

Parque Nacional Cotapata 128
Parque Nacional Kaa-Iya del
  Gran Chaco 266
Parque Nacional Madidi
  281–375
Parque Nacional Noel Kempff
  Mercado...............................262
Parque Nacional Sajama
  140–142
Parque Nacional Torotoro
  .... 222 224
Parque Nacional y Reserva
  Indígena Isiboro–Sécure.....288
Parque Machia.......................225
Partido Conservador.............312
Partido de la Izquierda
  Revolucionaria 315
Partido Liberal 312, 313
Partido Republicano..............313
Pasto Grande.........................133
Patiño, Simón.................. 146, 313
Paz Estenssoro, Víctor 315, 317
Paz Zamora, Jaime................318
peasant federations...............316
Pelechuco..............................115
personal safety........................ 40
Peruvian border 23, 101, 299,
  301
pharmacies.............................. 36
phones 48
photography 49
Pilko Kaina............................109
Pilon Lajas, Reserva de la
  Biosfera y Territorio Indígena
 282
police 41
Potosí 150–161
Potosí 153
  accommodation............................159
  Arco de Cobija.............................156
  arrival and departure 159
  Casa Real de la Moneda 154
  Catedral......................................152
  churches......................................156
  Convento-Museo Santa Teresa ...155
  directory.....................................161
  eating and drinking......................160
  fiestas...150
  getting around 159
  history...150
  Iglesia de Jerusalén.....................159
  Iglesia de la Merced.....................157
  Iglesia de San Agustín..................158
  Iglesia de San Bernardo................158
  Iglesia de San Lorenzo de Carangas
 158
  Iglesia de San Martín....................158
  Iglesia de Santo Domingo.............157
  Iglesia y Convento de San Francisco
 157
  information and tours...................159
  Ingenio San Marcos 157
  La Torre de la Compañia de Jesús
 155
  mines...152
  nightlife.......................................160
  Pérez de Holguín, Melchor...........155

Plaza 10 de Noviembre................152
  shopping.....................................161
  Virgen del Cerro 154
public holidays 33, 47
Pucará 251
Puente Español 149
Puente Mururata...................128
Puerto Almacén 292
Puerto Barrador.....................292
Puerta del Diablo...................179
Puerta del Sol..........................92
Puerto Heath.........................301
Puerto Maldonado.................301
Puerto Suárez.........................264
Puerto Villaroel......................226
Pujjlay...................................209
Punata 218
Putina....................................115

Q

Quebrada de Palala 178
Quebrada de Palmira.............179
Quebrada del Chura...............251
Quebrada Seca 180
Quechua.................................329
quenas...................................322
Quijarro.................................265
Quillacollo.............................219

R

rabies 39
radio....................................... 47
Reforma Agraria....................315
Republica de Indios...............307
Reserva Biológica Cordillera del
  Sama....................................188
Reserva de Fauna Andina
  Eduardo Avaroa....................171
Reserva de la Biosfera del Beni
 286
Reserva de la Biosfera y
  Territorio Indígena Pilon Lajas
 282
Reserva Nacional de Vida
  Silvestre Amazónica Manuripi
 301
  restaurants.................................. 30
Riberalta 293–295
Río Beni.................................274
Río Coroico.............................. 35
Río Heath...............................300
Río Ichilo...............................226
Río Iteñez...............................263
Río Madidi.............................282
Río Madre de Dios..................293
Río Mamoré 292, 296
Río Quiquibey.........................283
Río Tahuamanu 301
Río Torotoro...........................223
Río Tuichi 35, 276
Río Yacuma............................282
river trips...............................292
road distances 27

roadblocks 42
rubber boom...................297, 312
Rurrenabaque 274–281
Rurrenabaque 275

S

Sajama, Parque Nacional
  140–142
Sajama, Volcán.......................140
Sajama village........................141
Salamanca, Daniel...................313
Salar de Uyuni 169–171
  tours of..173
Sama, Reserva Biológica
  Cordillera del........................188
Samaipata 243–246
Samaipata 244
San Borja................................286
San Buenaventura...................276
San Ignacio de Moxos.............284
  music school...................................285
San Ignacio de Velasco............256
San Ignacio de Velasco 256
San Ignacio music archive......285
San Javier...............................252
San José de Chiquitos..............258
San José de Uchupiamonas
 283
San José mission complex 258
San Juancito...........................257
San Lorenzo............................187
San Martín, José de.................310
San Matías, Area Natural.........264
San Miguel.............................257
San Miguel del Bala 278, 283
San Pedro de Atacama 167,
  172
San Rafael..............................257
San Silvestre 301
San Vicente 180
Sánchez de Lozada, Gonzalo
 318
Sandillani...............................129
Santa Ana..............................257
Santa Cruz.................... 232–240
Santa Cruz 234
Santa Cruz & the Eastern
  Lowlands 232
  accommodation............................237
  arrival and departure 236
  Biocentro Güembé.......................236
  Catedral......................................235
  community-based tourism 240
  directory.....................................240
  drinking and nightlife 239
  eating..238
  information and tours...................237
  Mercado Los Pozos......................238
  Museo de Arte Contemporaneo
 235
  Museo de Arte Sacro 235
  Museo de Historia Natural Noel
    Kempff Mercado.........................235
  Museo Etnofolklórico 235
  Plaza 24 de Septiembre................235
Santa Cruz La Vieja.................258

Santa Cruz, Andrés de 311
Santiago de Okola..........106
Santuario 108
Santuario de Chochis..........264
sayas 324
scams 41
Sicuani 109
Siles, Hernán 315, 317
Sipe Sipe 220
snakebites 39
Sol de Mañana geyser 172
Sorata 118
Sorata **120**
   trekking from 122
soroche 38
Southwest, the far **169**
Spanish Conquest, the 307
Spanish language 329
Spanish phrases 330
studying Spanish 45
Suárez, Nicolás 297
Suárez, Roberto 297, 318
Sucre **195–206**
Sucre **196**
Sucre, Cochabamba & the
   central valleys **194**
   accommodation 204
   arrival and departure 203
   Casa de la Libertad 195
   Catedral 198
   Convento-Museo La Recoleta
     200
   directory 206
   eating and drinking 205
   fiestas 195
   history 195
   Iglesia de la Merced 198
   Iglesia de San Felipe Neri..........198
   Iglesia de San Francisco..........202
   Iglesia de San Miguel 202
   Iglesia de Santa Mónica..........202
   information and tours..........204
   language courses..........206
   Museo-Convento Santa Clara......200
   Museo de Arte Indigena 201
   Museo Eclesiastico 198
   Museo de Etnografía y Folklore
     202
   Museo Universitario Charcas 200
   nightlife 205
   Pérez de Holguín, Melchor..........200
   Plaza 25 de Mayo 197
   Universidad de San Francisco
      Xavier 203
Sucre, Antonio José de..........310
Sukakullos 90
Sunchuli Pass 116
sunstroke 38

T

Takesi Trail 130
Takesi Trail **130**
Tambo Quemado 142
Tarabuco 208
Tarapaya hot springs..........164
Tarija **181–186**
Tarija **182**

accommodation 185
arrival and departure 184
directory 186
eating and drinking 185
fiestas 181
getting around 184
information and tours..........185
Museo Paleontológico 184
teaching English 45
telephones 48
television 47
temperature 46
theft 40
time difference 49
Tinku 165
tin-mining 312, 318
Titicachi 109
Tiwanaku **89–93, 303**
Tocaña 128
Toledo, Francisco 308
Tomatitas 187
Torotoro, Parque Nacional
   ....**222–224**
Torotoro Canyon 223
Torotoro village 222
Torres, Juan José 316
Totora 220
tour operators 24, 28
   in La Paz 73
   in Rurrenabaque 277
tourist information 49
Trans-Apolobamba Trek..........116
transport 24
   boats 27
   buses 25
   cars 27
   lorries 26
   micros 26
   moto-taxis 26
   planes 25
   taxis 26
   trains 26
travel agents 24
travel insurance 44
travellers' cheques 47
trekking 34, 119
Trinidad **286–293**
Trinidad **287**
   accommodation 290
   arrival and departure 289
   directory 292
   eating and drinking 290
   getting around 289
   information and tours..........290
   Museo Etno-Arqeológico del Beni
      "Kenneth Lee"..........289
   Museo Icticola del Beni..........289
tropical disease 37
Tumi Chucua 294
Túpac Amaru II 308
Túpac Katari 309
Tupiza **174–178**
Tupiza **176**

U

Ulla Ulla plateau..........115
Ulla Ulla village..........115

Unduavi..........124
universal suffrage..........315
Urus 149
Uyuni **165–168**
Uyuni **166**

V

Valle Alto..........218
Valle de la Luna 87
Valle de Los Machos..........179
Vallegrande..........248
vegetarian food..........30
Ventilla..........130
Villa Tunari..........225
Villamontes..........266
Villaroel, Gualberto 314
Villazón..........180
vineyards, Tarija valley..........187
Virgen de Copacabana..........100, 101
visas..........43
Viscachani 116
Volcán Licancabur..........172
Volcán Parinacota..........141
Volcán Pomerata..........141
Volcán Sajama 140
volunteering..........45

W

War of the Pacific..........311
water 37
water purification..........37
Water War 319
weather 46
websites 49
whitewater rafting 35
wildlife 320
Wiñay Marka..........99, 112
wines, Tarija valley..........187
working in Bolivia..........45
world's most dangerous road,
   the 124

Y

Yacuiba 266
Yampupata..........109
Yanacachi 130
yellow fever 37
Yolosa 124
Yumani 109
Yunga Cruz Trail 134
Yunga Cruz Trail **130**
Yungas, the 123–135
Yungas, the, Lago Titicaca &
   the cordilleras **98**

Z

Zarate Willka, Pablo 313
Zoo Municipal Vesty Pakos......88

Maps

Map symbols

The symbols below are used on maps throughout the book

✈	Airport	♦	Place of interest	⚲	Campsite/ground	▢	Building
★	Bus/taxi	∴	Ruin	⌲	Mountain range	☐	Market
@	Internet café/access	∩	Arch	▲	Mountain peak	⇨	Church
✉	Post office	⊙	Statue	◢	Volcano	◯	Stadium
(i)	Information office	⛽	Petrol station	〰	Gorge	☐	Park
(C)	Telephone office	✖	Skiing	〰	Swamp	‖‖‖	Funicular
♣	Museum	⛾	Lighthouse	⌒	Bridge	⋯⋯	Paved road
⚶	Spring/spa	⛛	Viewpoint	⚓	Swimming pool/area	- - -	Unpaved road

Listings key

▪	Accommodation
●	Restaurant/café
▪	Bar/club
●	Shop
●	Tour agency
▪	Peña